The Translator and the Editor

WALTER ARNDT is Sherman Fairch manities, Emeritus, at Dartmouth College. He is the distinguished translator of Pushkin, Heine, Rilke, Anna Akhmatova, Christian Morgenstern, modern Russian women's poetry, and contemporary Polish prose writers, among others. His translation of Pushkin's *Eugene Onegin* was awarded a Bollingen Prize.

CYRUS HAMLIN is Professor of German and Comparative Literature at Yale University, where he has also served as Chairman of both those departments and as Director of the Special Programs in the Humanities. He is the General Editor of the Suhrkamp Edition of Goethe in English in twelve volumes (now published by Princeton University Press). With the late Frank Ryder he edited Goethe's plays and epics for that edition, translating *Götz von Berlichingen* and *Proserpina*. He has published widely in the field of European Romanticism and Hermeneutics, with particular emphasis on the poet Hölderlin. His collected essays on that subject appeared as a book, *Hermeneutics of Form: Romantic Poetics in Theory and Practice* (1998), with Henry R. Schwab. In 1990 he codirected, with Paul Hernadi and Jane K. Brown, the Summer Institute on Goethe's *Faust* at the University of California, Santa Barbara, supported by the National Endowment for the Humanities, and in 1992 he helped to organize the international conference *Interpreting Goethe's Faust Today*, proceedings of which were subsequently published through the sponsorship of the Goethe Society of North America.

FAUST
A Tragedy

AN AUTHORITATIVE TRANSLATION
INTERPRETIVE NOTES
CONTEXTS
MODERN CRITICISM

Second Edition

A NORTON CRITICAL EDITION

Johann Wolfgang von Goethe

FAUST

A Tragedy

INTERPRETIVE NOTES

CONTEXTS

MODERN CRITICISM

Second Edition

Translated by

WALTER ARNDT

DARTMOUTH COLLEGE

Edited by

CYRUS HAMLIN

YALE UNIVERSITY

W • W • NORTON & COMPANY • *New York* • *London*

Goethe's drawing for Faust's encounter with the Earth Spirit in the scene
"Night": Courtesy of Stiftung Weimarer Klassik, Weimar, Germany.
Giorgione, *Venus Sleeping in a Landscape*: Courtesy of
Staatliche Kunstsammlungen Dresden, Dresden, Germany.
Correggio, *Leda and the Swan*: Courtesy of Hänssler-Verlag, Holzgerlingen, Germany.

The text of this book is composed in Electra
with the display set in Bernhard Modern.
Composition by PennSet, Inc
Manufacturing by LSC Communications, Crawfordsville.
Book design by Antonina Krass.

Library of Congress Cataloging-in-Publication Data

Goethe, Johann Wolfgang von, 1749–1832.
  [Faust. English]
  Faust : a tragedy : interpretive notes, contexts, modern criticism / Johann Wolfgang
von Goethe ; translated by Walter Arndt ; edited by Cyrus Hamlin. — 2nd ed.
      p. cm. — (A Norton critical edition)
  Includes bibliographical references.

  ISBN 0-393-97282-8 (pbk.)

  I. Arndt, Walter W., 1916– II. Hamlin, Cyrus. III. Title.

PT2026.F2 F3313 2000
832'.6 — dc21   00-031052

W. W. Norton & Company, Inc., 500 Fifth Avenue, New York, N.Y. 10110
www.wwnorton.com

W. W. Norton & Company Ltd., 15 Carlisle Street,
London W1D 3BS

6 7 8 9 0

Contents

Modern Criticism   571

Preface

The Norton Critical Edition of Goethe's *Faust*, translated by Walter Arndt and edited by myself, first appeared in 1976. The opportunity to undertake this greatly revised and expanded edition after a full quarter century is most welcome. Much good work has been done on Goethe's drama during the past several decades, especially by scholars in the United States. *Faust's* importance for the study of literature at university level has been demonstrated in many ways, not least of these a continuing interest in this Critical Edition and Norton's decision to undertake the present revision. I have devoted considerable time and effort during the past year or so, which witnessed celebrations for the 250th anniversary of Goethe's birth on August 28, 1999, to preparing this new edition. A few words about this effort may be helpful to readers.

The verse translation by Walter Arndt remains unchanged from the earlier edition, apart from a few details that have been emended. The layout of the play, however, has been altered to correspond more closely to the arrangement of the German text in standard editions of the drama, which derives in large measure from Goethe's own published text. The beginning of each scene has been placed on a new page, and spaces have been introduced between units of the text, especially where the verse form changes. As much as possible, verses have been positioned so as to avoid breaking lines. In addition, line numbering has been corrected in a few scenes. Several illustrations have been added, including some of the most distinguished early illustrations by Peter Cornelius and Eugène Delacroix. Copies of paintings that inspired Goethe in the composition of several scenes — notably Giorgione's *Venus Sleeping in a Landscape*, Correggio's *Leda and the Swan*, and Raphael's *Triumph of Galatea* — are also included.

The critical apparatus has been changed considerably. The "Backgrounds and Sources" section of the first edition has been eliminated, since a serious study of the Faust legend and its tradition requires attention to complete texts, from the original Spiess chapbook of 1587 through Marlowe's *Dr. Faustus* (which was not included) to Goethe and beyond. (For readers interested in this tradition, the essay by Stuart Atkins newly included in the "Modern Criticism" section provides a valuable overview.) The selection of Goethe's comments on the drama has been expanded and given a more accurate chronological arrangement. The "Comments by Contemporaries" section has also been expanded, with the inclusion of initial responses by Wilhelm von Humboldt and Henrik Steffens; and *Faust's* reception in the English-speaking world is represented by Thomas Carlyle's anonymous essay from the *New Edinburgh Review* in 1822 and excerpts from essays by Margaret Fuller and Ralph Waldo Emerson published in *The Dial* in the early 1840s. "The Composition of *Faust*," an analytical table correlating the history of composition with the various verse forms used in the drama, remains unchanged. The essays by the translator and the editor included in the first edition, "Translating *Faust*" and "Reading *Faust*," have been omitted, since they largely reflected views defined by another era.

The selection of essays in "Modern Criticism" has been changed completely. This reflects the editor's conviction that critical approaches and viewpoints inevitably change and that many selections included in the first edition no longer provide the assistance for readers of *Faust* in English translation that was originally intended. The needs of students studying Goethe's drama in English, furthermore, are different from the issues addressed by the leading German scholars of *Faust*. Nor was the arrangement of critical essays under separate topics in the first edition entirely successful. The present selection represents in large measure work done on *Faust* by critics and teachers in the United States, where a distinctive approach to the drama has developed over the past several decades. Readers of the Norton *Faust* will thus have access to representative concerns and perspectives from current discussions of the drama in English.

The initial essay by Stuart Atkins, dean of American *Faust* scholars, surveys the tradition of the Faust legend in lucid and authoritative perspective. Two general position statements are then provided on the drama as a whole from recent studies with quite different concerns and approaches. Jaroslav Pelikan, in the opening chapter of his book *Faust the Theologian*, addresses the central challenge of the drama within the context of theological concerns, which are reflected through the central character's status as Doctor of Theology. Benjamin Bennett, in the opening chapter of his book *Goethe's Theory of Poetry: Faust and the Regeneration of Language*, traces the structural principle of "interrupted tragedy" as it is manifested through the entire work.

Two European scholars of literary history and literary theory, Franco Moretti and Friedrich A. Kittler, each writing from a radically different perspective, in books recently translated into English from the original Italian and German respectively, introduce central hypotheses for the study of *Faust* that are as creative as they are controversial. Moretti proposes a wide-ranging view of *Faust* as a model for "modern epic," where through fragmentation and discontinuity a world system is established that looks forward to such later works of modernity as Melville's *Moby-Dick* and Joyce's *Ulysses*. Kittler focuses on language as "discourse network," with regard to the question of writing and reading in *Faust* and the role of texts as indicative of Faust's dilemma as scholar.

Two essays by scholars of comparative literature whose work is not primarily associated with Goethe studies, Neil M. Flax and Marc Shell, focus on issues for interpreting the drama that have often been neglected. Flax traces the central semiotic challenge of *Faust* as tragedy, from the question of the sign in Faust's use of magic in the opening scene to related instances of symbolic images, above all in Part Two. Shell begins with a bold premise concerning the affinity of translation and economics in *Faust*, whereby the problem of origin and authenticity in the Gospel of John is related to the fiscal reform introduced to the empire by Mephistopheles in Act I of Part Two.

The last three essays, all from quite different sources and perspectives, focus on central aspects of Part Two and thus indicate how the complexities of this part command increasing critical attention, even for students of literature in translation. Jane K. Brown, whose book *Goethe's Faust: The German Tragedy* has established itself as the most important critical study of the drama as a whole by an American scholar, interprets Act II with particular emphasis on the symbolism of water in the "Classical Walpurgis Night," culminating in the Triumph of Galatea. Hans Rudolf Vaget, in an essay presented at the international Faust Conference at Santa Barbara in 1993, reads Act IV from a critical perspective on political issues subsequent to the fall of the German Democratic Republic in 1989. Finally, Marshall Berman comments on Faust as Developer from the wide-ranging perspective of his book *All That Is Solid Melts into Air: The Experience of Modernity*. Berman interprets Faust's land reclamation project in Act V with reference to issues of urban development in the late-twentieth century.

John Hollander's recent poem "What the Lovers in the Old Songs Thought" is not, strictly speaking, addressed to or about Goethe's *Faust*. The poem plays with the implications of Faust's famous conundrum concerning the translation of the opening statement from the Gospel of John. A concern for origins is central to Goethe's drama and to Faust's quest for the satisfaction of desire, as a number of the critical essays included in "Modern Criticism" emphasize. Hollander's poem affirms in its uniquely eloquent way the priority of metaphor for such origins, thus providing implicit support for Goethe's preoccupation in *Faust* with signs, symbols, myth, and theatrical show.

Some comments of a more personal nature may assist readers of the "Interpretive Notes." In the first edition, after negotiations with the publisher, the notes were included in truncated form and in very small print. Over the years, readers have frequently communicated their frustration with the format but their gratitude for the practical value of the notes. Reviewers and referees for this revision have also strongly supported the expansion of these notes, for which I am most grateful. No better measure can be imagined for the expanding awareness of the unique challenge that Goethe's *Faust* imposes upon readers than the often daunting and equally enticing range of comments the text elicits. No other literary work since Dante's *Divine Comedy* provides such a comprehensive and authoritative image for the challenge of individual existence in modern Western culture. Goethe's *Faust* serves as a gateway to the full complexity of life in the modern world. No other literary work offers an equal challenge to readers or such powerful and diverse insight after sustained and sympathetic inquiry. Yet *Faust* yields its riches only reluctantly. The greatly expanded interpretive notes bear witness to the problems and issues for understanding at every stage of the work that have become apparent to me

over many years of teaching and studying. Goethe's *Faust* should be regarded as a companion along life's way, continually challenging productive
thought in the ironic and often perverse manner of the devil who accompanies Faust on his ill-fated quest-journey. For readers of this edition, most
of them presumably encountering Goethe's masterpiece for the first time
in a language other than its own, the interpretive notes should serve to
stimulate critical inquiry. If they elicit responses in opposition to my views,
that too will be appropriate to the experience of reading *Faust*.

Finally, I wish to express my sincere gratitude for the various kinds of
support and assistance received from students and friends over all these
years in my continuing struggle to achieve a confident understanding of
Goethe's drama. I have taught *Faust* at virtually every level, from beginning survey courses in English to advanced graduate seminars in German.
Students at all these levels have provided genuine insights, for which I
remain grateful, even if I no longer remember the particular sources. I
have also been invited to lecture and provide guidance to teachers of *Faust*
at a number of colleges and universities, settings that always provided stimulating and challenging discussion. At various times I have also had the
opportunity to lecture on *Faust* to undergraduates in Directed Studies at
Yale and in Literary Studies at the University of Toronto. Soon after the
initial publication of the Norton *Faust*, a sabbatical from the University
of Toronto, combined with a research grant from the Canada Council,
provided the opportunity to do intensive research on the drama at Oxford's
Taylor Institute, with its unusual resources in German literature.

A particularly powerful stimulus was provided in 1990 by a Summer
Institute on Goethe's *Faust* at the Interdisciplinary Humanities Center of
the University of California, Santa Barbara, sponsored by the National
Endowment for the Humanities. I remain most grateful for that event to
my fellow directors—Paul Hernadi, then Director of the Center, and my
former student Jane K. Brown—as also to all the teachers and scholars
who participated. Two years later we organized, with generous funding
from the Goethe Institute, an international conference at the same university, proceedings of which were published through the Goethe Society
of North America in a volume of essays, *Interpreting Goethe's* Faust *Today*,
edited by Jane K. Brown, Meredith Lee, and Thomas P. Saine (Columbia,
SC: Camden House, 1994). Most recently, during a year as Visiting Professor at the Free University in Berlin, I had the opportunity to study recent
commentaries published with German editions of *Faust*—those by Albrecht Schöne in the *Bibliothek Deutscher Klassiker* and by Dorothea
Hölscher-Lohmeyer for *Faust*, Part Two, in the Hanser Goethe edition.
An invitation to lecture on Faust and the Earth Spirit at the University of
Heidelberg and at the Free University, Berlin, provided occasions for lively
critical exchanges. During my stay in Berlin in 1998 I began to prepare
the revised and expanded interpretive notes for *Faust*, subsequently completed at Yale the following winter.

My friend and colleague Howard Stern read the "Interpretive Notes"
with care and made a number of suggestions for improving both my argument and my prose, for which I am most grateful. I do not expect to
attempt yet another revision of my notes to *Faust*—for that, alas!, life is

too short, as both Wagner and Mephistopheles knew—but I hope on the basis of what is now nearly four decades of work on Goethe's drama to continue indefinitely my exploration into the riches of this unique and inexhaustible masterpiece of our culture.

January, 2000   CYRUS HAMLIN
                                                     Jonathan Edwards College
                                                     Yale University

The Text of
FAUST
A Tragedy

Dedication[1]†

Once more you near me, wavering apparitions
That early showed before the turbid gaze.
Will now I seek to grant you definition,
My heart essay again the former daze?
You press me! Well, I yield to your petition,   5
As all around, you rise from mist and haze;
What wafts about your train with magic glamor
Is quickening my breast to youthful tremor.

You conjure up delightful days and places,
And there ascends so many a cherished shade;   10
Like an old legend's half-forgotten graces,
First love's and friendship's echoes are replayed;
Old grief revives, a mournful plaint retraces
Life's labyrinthine and erratic gait,
And names the dear ones who, by fortune cheated   15
Of blissful hours, before me have retreated.

They do not listen to the later cantos,
The souls to whom I once intoned the first;
Long waned those early echoes and mementos,
The friendly multitude, alas, dispersed   20
Indifferent ears my song of sorrow[2] enters,
Their very praises weigh upon my heart,
And those my lyre might still have pleased and flattered,
If living yet, are swept abroad and scattered.

And I am seized by long-unwonted yearning   25
For that domain of spirits calm and grave,
To tenuous notes my lisping song is turning,
Like Aeol's harp[3] it fitfully would wave,
A shudder grips me, tear on tear is burning,
With softening balm the somber heart they lave;   30
What I possess I see as from a distance,
And what has passed, to me becomes existence.

---

1. As he resumes work on his drama after an interruption of several decades, the poet addresses the half-formed figures and ideas out of his past that crave full embodiment.
† Each dagger indicates a corresponding interpretive note (see pp. 345–491).
2. The first edition of Part One contained a misprint here (*Leid*, "Sorrow," for *Lied*, "Song"), which Goethe subsequently retained. Arndt's phrase retains the ambiguity.
3. The wind harp, which produces musical tones in response to the play of the wind, was often associated during the Romantic era with poetry generally.

Prelude in the Theater[1]†

DIRECTOR, DRAMATIC POET, MERRY PERSON.

DIRECTOR. Let's hear, you two, who have so long
  Here by my side endured and suffered,
  What might be hoped for from this effort   35
  In countries of the German tongue?
  I would prepare the crowd a special revel,
  For they believe in living, letting live.
  The posts are raised, the boards laid down and level,
  All are in hopes we have a feast to give.   40
  With eyebrows raised they sit in the enclosure
  And long to be amazed, with due composure.
  I know how people's taste may be caressed;
  And yet I am in direr straits than ever;
  While they are not accustomed to the best,   45
  Still they are frightfully well-read and clever.
  How can we see that all is fresh and new
  And, with significance, engaging too?
  Of course I find a crowd of people pleasing,
  Delight in throngs at our pavilion queued,   50
  In pulsing pangs of mighty labor squeezing
  Through the tight portals of beatitude,
  When in bright daylight, well before it's four,[2]
  They fight their way up to the cashier's slot
  And, as in time of famine by the baker's door,   55
  For tickets break their necks, as like as not.
  Upon such diverse folk can work this wondrous sway
  None but the poet; friend, do it today!
POET. Invoke me not the motley crowd unsteady,
  Whose very aspect puts the mind to flight!   60
  Oh, shroud from me the swirling human eddy
  That draws us downward, struggle as we might.
  Find me that nook of heaven's stillness, heady
  With blossom of the poet's pure delight,
  Where for the heart both love and friendship flourish,   65
  With godly hands create its bliss and nourish.
  Ah, what broke forth where deeply it lay buried,
  What lip has shyly lisped in private hours,
  Accomplished now, at other times miscarried,

1. The three figures here belong to a troupe of itinerant players, preparing a production of the *Faust* that follows for an unspecified German theater. Such ironic juxtaposition of opposing attitudes toward the theater is derived from traditional prologues in Renaissance drama and techniques of improvisation in popular comedy. A specific source is found in *Śakuntalā* by the fourth-century Indian poet Kālidāsa, which attracted Goethe's interest, in a German translation by Georg Forster (published 1791).
2. The normal starting time for theater performances in Goethe's Weimar was 5:30 or 6:00 in the evening.

The savage moment's vehemence devours.   70
It often is through years of waiting ferried
Before it issues in its ripened powers.
What shines is for the moment born, must perish;
The genuine, posterity will cherish.
MERRY PERSON.   That talk about posterity won't sell me;   75
If I talked of posterity, just tell me
Who would supply the fun for now?
Now claims its time and wants it pleasant.
I find an honest fellow's present
Is always something, anyhow.   80
Him who with comfort can convey his sense,
The people's mood will not embitter, surely;
He wants a broader audience
To grip their hearts the more securely.
So do be good and act in model fashion,   85
Show Fancy in her fullest panoply:
Sense, understanding, sentiment, and passion,
And mind you, last not least, some foolery.
DIRECTOR.   Above all, let there be sufficient plot!
They like to look, so let them see a lot.   90
You give the audience a solid eyeful,
So they can gape and marvel all the time,
You'll grip them by sheer quantity of trifle,
Your popularity will climb.
Mass calls for mass in order to be won,   95
Each ends up choosing something for his own;
Who brings a lot, brings bits for everyone,
And they will all be happy going home.
You stage a piece—serve it in pieces, do!
Why, it's a snap to make this kind of stew;   100
It's served as fast as cooked up in your head.
What use is it to bring your whole instead,
The public shreds it anyway for you.
POET.   You do not sense how cheap this is, how tawdry,
How shamefully true art is thus maligned!   105
The charlatan's ragout of tricks and bawdry,
I see, is now an axiom in your mind.
DIRECTOR.   Such reprobation leaves me cool:
To do a proper job you choose the tool
That is adapted to your timber.   110
The wood you are to split is soft, remember,
Just look for whom you will have striven!
This one may be by boredom driven,
That one is comatose from overfeeding,
And what is most reluctantly forgiven,   115
A lot arrive here fresh from journal-reading.
Mere curiosity will spur their paces,
They come with scattered wits as for a masquerade,

The ladies show their get-ups and their faces,
Each plays an extra, though unpaid.   120
Why daydream on your poet's eminence?
Why should a full house gladden you?
Look closely at your patrons, do!
One half is cold, the other dense.
One, when the show ends, looks to cards and booze,   125
Another to a wild night with a trollop;
Would you spur Pegasus to gallop
For this, poor fools, and plague the Muse?
I tell you, just give more, and ever, ever more,
And you will never stray off-target.   130
Endeavor to confuse your human market,
To sate it truly is a chore—
What's come upon you? Ecstasy or ache?
POET.   Begone and find yourself another minion!
The poet should forgo, in your opinion,   135
The loftiest human right of which he may partake
By nature's gift, profane it grossly for your sake?
How does he kindle every heart?
How conquer every elemental part?
Not by the chords that from his bosom waft   140
And snare the universe back by his craft?
The while indifferent nature helter-skelter
Twists the eternal thread upon her spindle,
When all created things' discordant welter
Would coalesce into a graceless brindle,   145
Who parts the sequence, changeless and perpetual,
Enliveningly into rhythmic ease,
Who calls the single to the common ritual,
Where it resounds in glorious harmonies?
Who lets the tempest's passions rage their maddest,   150
Imparts grave meaning to the sunset glow?
Who strews the bloom of springtime at its gladdest
Where the beloved is wont to go?
Who braids the insignificant green laurels
To every merit's honorific wreaths?   155
Who firms Olympus? unifies Immortals?
The might of man, which in the poet breathes.
MERRY PERSON.   So draw on them, those fine perfections,
And ply your lyrical transactions
As one conducts an amorous intrigue.   160
One happens in, feels, lingers, is in league
And more and more drawn in and interested;
Enchantment grows, and then it is contested,
As you rejoice, now pain receives its chance,
Before you know it, presto! there is your romance.   165
Such is the spectacle we should be giving!
Just reach into the wealth of human living!

Each lives it, those who know it are but few,
And grip it where you will, it's gripping too.
In colorful show less light than dark,   170
Much error, and of truth a spark,
Thus is the headiest mixture brewed
To slake and edify the multitude.
Then flocks to you the finest youthful splendor
And listens as to revelation holy,   175
To every soul of sentiment you tender
The suck and sustenance of melancholy.
There is stirred up now this, now that soft part,
Each sees what is sequestered in his heart.
Their gift for laughter, tears, is undiminished,   180
Illusion yet delights, élan still ranks;
There is no pleasing someone who is finished;
He who still grows will ever render thanks.
POET.   Then to me, too, return those times
When I myself was growing still,   185
When a clear fount surcharged with rhymes
Sprang self-renewing from the well,
The time the world was swathed in veils,
When yet the bud held wondrous bowers,
When I would pluck the thousand flowers   190
That richly covered all the dales.
Nothing I had, and yet enough for youth,
Delight in fictions, and the thirst for truth.
Return untamed to me those surges,
That agonizing blissful ruth,   195
The strength of hate, love's mighty urges,
Alas, return to me my youth!
MERRY PERSON.   Your youth, good friend, you need at best
When enemies in battle press you,
When, falling on your neck with zest,   200
A throng of lovely girls caress you,
When, racing hard, you stole a glance
Where goal and distant laurels beckoned,
When after reckless whirling dance
You drink the night through, time unreckoned.   205
But on the long-familiar lyre
To sound a chord with pluck and grace,
To self-appointed goal aspire
At charmingly erratic pace—
Old fellows, that's your proper game,   210
And we shall not revere you less for it.
Old age does not make childish, as they claim,
It merely finds us genuine children yet.
DIRECTOR.   Sufficient speeches have been bandied,
Now let me see some deeds at last;   215
While mutual compliments are candied,

The time might usefully be passed.
What use to prate of inspiration?
The laggard it will ever flee.
Call yourselves poets by vocation?   220
Then order up your poetry.[3]
What we require is known to you,
We want to sip a potent brew;
Start brewing it without delay!
Tomorrow's late for what's not done today.   225
There's not a day to lose, and so,
Whatever's possible, resolve robust
Should take it by the forelock fast,[4]
Then it is loath to let it go
And labors on because it must.   230
You know, upon our German stages
Each man puts on just what he may;
So spare me not upon this day
Machinery and cartonnages.
The great and little light of heaven[5] employ,   235
The stars you may as freely squander;
Cliff-drops and water, fire and thunder,
Birds, animals, are in supply.
So in this narrow house of boarded space
Creation's fullest circle[6] go to pace,   240
And walk with leisured speed your spell
From Heaven through the World to Hell.[7]

---

3. See Goethe's use of these lines in his letter to Wilheim von Humboldt of December 1, 1831, below.
4. In an adaptation of a popular adage, "resolve" (personified) is urged to seize opportunity ("whatever's possible") by the forelock.
5. The sun and the moon, traditionally represented on the canopy above the platform stage.
6. A traditional metaphor of the theater as the world, *theatrum mundi* (see Shakespeare's "wooden O" in the Chorus of *Henry* V, Prologue, line 13).
7. Applied to *Faust*, this progression extends from the "Prologue in Heaven" to the hell-mouth of the scene following Faust's death (see stage direction preceding line 11644).

Prologue in Heaven†

THE LORD. THE HEAVENLY HOST. *Later* MEPHISTOPHELES.

[*The* THREE ARCHANGELS *step forward.*]
RAPHAEL.†   The sun contends in age-old fashion
With brother spheres in hymnic sound,
And in far-thundering progression   245
Discharges his appointed round.[1]
His aspect lends the angels power,
While none may gauge his secret way;
Sublime past understanding tower
Those works as on the primal day.   250
GABRIEL.   The earth's resplendence spins and ranges
Past understanding swift in flight,
And paradisiac lucence changes
With awe-inspiring depths of night;
The ocean's foaming seas run shoreward,   255
On rocky depths rebound and rear,
And rock and ocean hurtle forward,
Sped by the ever-hurrying sphere.
MICHAEL.   And tempest roars, with tempest vying,
From sea to land, from land to sea,   260
In their alternate[2] furies tying,
A chain of deepest potency.
A flash of fiery disaster
Precedes the thunder on its way;
Thy envoys,[3] though, revere, o Master,   265
The gentle progress of Thy day.
THE THREE.   [*in unison*] This aspect lends the angels power,
As none may gauge Thy secret way,
And all Thy sovereign works still tower
Sublime as on the primal day.   270

MEPHISTOPHELES.[4]   Since once again, o Lord, I find you deigning
To walk amongst us, asking how we do,
And in the past you thought me entertaining,
You see me too here with your retinue.
Fine speeches are, beg pardon, not my forte,   275
Though all this round may mock me; but I know,
My rhetoric, you'd laugh it out of court,

---

1. The sun's path is associated with the musical harmony of the heavenly spheres. See also Job 38.7, "When the morning stars sang together, and all the sons of God shouted for joy."
2. Note the adjectival stress: *altérnate*.
3. A translation of the Greek for "messengers" (*angeloi*), from which the word *angels* is derived.
4. The origin of the name is uncertain (*Mephostophiles* in the chapbook of 1587; *Mephostophilis* in Marlowe's *Dr. Faustus*), though possibly derived from the Hebrew *Mephistoph*, "destroyer of the good." Here in the court of the Lord, as later in the court of the Emperor (Part Two, Act I), Mephistopheles plays the role of jester, "rogue" (line 339).

Had you not cast off laughter long ago.
On suns and worlds I can shed little light,
I see but humans, and their piteous plight. 280
Earth's little god runs true to his old way
And is as weird as on the primal day.[5]
He might be living somewhat better
Had you not given him of Heaven's light a glitter;
He calls it reason and, ordained its priest, 285
Becomes more bestial than any beast.
He seems to me, begging your Honor's pardon,
Like one of those grasshoppers in the garden
That leg it skip-a-skimming all day long
And in the grass chirp out the same old song. 290
If only he'd just lie in the grass at that!
But no, he sticks his nose in every pat.

THE LORD.   And do you have no other news?
Do you come always only to accuse?
Does nothing please you ever on the earth? 295

MEPHISTOPHELES.   No, Lord! I find it still of precious little worth.
I feel for mankind in their wretchedness,
It almost makes me want to plague them less.

THE LORD.   Do you know Faust?

MEPHISTOPHELES.   The doctor?

THE LORD.   Yes, my serf![6]

MEPHISTOPHELES.   Forsooth! He serves you in a curious fashion. 300
Not of this earth the madman's drink or ration,
He's driven far afield by some strange leaven,
He's half aware of his demented quest,
He claims the most resplendent stars from heaven,
And from the earth each pleasure's highest zest, 305
Yet near or far, he finds no haven
Of solace for his deeply troubled breast.

THE LORD.   Though now he serve me but in clouded ways,
Soon I shall guide him so his spirit clears.
The gardener knows by the young tree's green haze 310
That bloom and fruit will grace it down the years.

MEPHISTOPHELES.   You'll lose him yet! I offer bet and tally,
Provided that your Honor gives
Me leave to lead him gently up my alley!

THE LORD.   As long as on the earth he lives, 315
So long it shall not be forbidden.
Man ever errs the while he strives.[7]

MEPHISTOPHELES.   My thanks to you; I've never hidden
An old distaste for dealing with the dead.
Give me a full-cheeked, fresh-faced lad! 320

5. A parody of the refrain in the Archangels' song (lines 269–70).
6. See the Lord's question to Satan concerning Job, 1.8.
7. This wager between the Lord and Mephistopheles concerning the salvation of Faust should be compared to the wager between Faust and Mephistopheles in the pact scene (lines 1692–706).

A corpse with me is just no dice,
In this way I am like a cat with mice.
THE LORD.   So be it; I shall not forbid it!
Estrange this spirit from its primal source,
Have licence, if you can but win it,   325
To lead it down your path by shrewd resource;
And stand ashamed when you must own perforce:
A worthy soul through the dark urge within it
Is well aware of the appointed course.
MEPHISTOPHELES.   May be—but it has never lasted yet;   330
I am by no means worried for my bet.
And if I do achieve my stated perpent,
You grant me the full triumph that I covet.
Dust shall he swallow, aye, and love it,
Like my old cousin, the illustrious serpent.[8]   335
THE LORD.   Then, too, enjoy free visitation;
I never did abominate your kind.
Of all the spirits of negation
The rogue has been least onerous to my mind.
Man all too easily grows lax and mellow,   340
He soon elects repose at any price;
And so I like to pair him with a fellow
To play the deuce, to stir, and to entice.
But you, true scions of the godly race,[9]†
Rejoice you in the font of living grace!   345
By ever active, ever live creation
In love's enchanting fetters be you caught,
And that which sways in wavering revelation,
May you compact it with enduring thought.
        [*Heaven closes; the* ARCHANGELS *disperse.*]
MEPHISTOPHELES.   [*alone*][1]
At times I don't mind seeing the old gent,   350
And try to keep relations smooth and level.
Say what you like, it's quite a compliment:
A swell like him so man-to-man with the Devil!

---

8. See God's judgment on the serpent after the Fall from paradise in Genesis 3.14, "Upon thy belly
   shalt thou go, and dust shalt thou eat all the days of thy life."
9. The sons of God, the angels, represented in this scene by the Archangels of the opening hymn.
1. Following the tradition of the comic actor in popular theater, Mephistopheles often addresses
   himself directly to the audience.

The Tragedy's First Part

Night[1]†

In a narrow, high-vaulted Gothic chamber, FAUST, *restless in his armchair by the desk.*

FAUST. I have pursued, alas, philosophy,
  Jurisprudence, and medicine,   355
  And, help me God, theology,[2]
  With fervent zeal through thick and thin.
  ·And here, poor fool, I stand once more,
  No wiser than I was before.
  They call me Magister, Doctor,[3] no less,   360
  And for some ten years, I would guess,
  Through ups and downs and tos and fros
  I have led my pupils by the nose—
  And see there is nothing we can know!
  It fair sears my heart to find it so.   365
  True, I know more than those imposters,
  Those parsons and scribes, doctors and masters;
  No doubt can plague me or conscience cavil,
  I stand not in fear of hell or devil—
  But then, all delight for me is shattered;   370
  I do not pretend to worthwhile knowledge,
  Don't flatter myself I can teach in college
  How men might be converted or bettered.
  Nor have I estate or moneyed worth,
  Nor honor or splendor of this earth;   375
  No dog would live out such wretched part!
  So I resorted to Magic's art,
  To see if by spirit mouth and might
  Many a secret may come to light;
  So I need toil no longer so,   380
  Propounding what I do not know;
  So I perceive the inmost force
  That bonds the very universe,

---

1. The first half of this scene (to line 605, excluding 598–601) was one of the earliest sections composed by Goethe. The opening part of the monologue, in archaic popular meter (*Knittelvers*), adopts the satirical tone of the puppet plays, which began—following Marlowe's *Dr. Faustus*— with Faust alone in his study.
2. Faust mentions the four traditional faculties of the medieval university.
3. The two advanced degrees beyond the baccalaureate.

12

View all enactment's seed and spring,
And quit my verbiage-mongering.   385

Oh full moon radiant, would that you,
Who many a midnight vigil through
Have found me wakeful in this chair,
Might look your last on my despair!
As over books I used to bend,   390
You would appear to me, sad friend;[4]
Ah, would that on high mountain ways
I wandered by your lovely rays,
Might haunt with sprites a cavern rift,
On meadows in your twilight drift,   395
And rid of learning's fetid fume,
Bathe whole my spirit in your spume!

Woe! stuck within this dungeon yet?
Curse this dank frowsty cabinet,
Where even Heaven's dear ray can pass   400
But murkily through tinted glass!
Entombed within this book-lined tower,
Which dust envelops, worms devour,
By fumigated charts unrolled
As high up as this vault can hold;   405
In instruments all choked and furled,
Hemmed in by flagon, jar, and trunk,
Stuffed tightly with ancestral junk—
This is your world! Call this a world!

And still you wonder what constrained   410
Your thwarted spirit's anxious surge,
Still ask what torment unexplained
Will cramp your every vital urge?
Shut out from Nature's teeming throng,
Which God made man to dwell among,   415
You skulk in reek and mold alone
'Mid ribs of beast and human bone.

Flee! Up! Escape to open fields!
Full-armed with that mysterious script
Which Nostradamus'[5] wisdom yields,   420
Why ask for more companionship?
In Nature's proper school enrolled,

4. In the following lines, Goethe employs the language of the sentimental sublime from eighteenth-century nature poetry, popular especially from the *Songs of Ossian* in the 1760s and also used by Goethe in his novel *The Sorrows of Young Werther* (1774).
5. Michael Notredame (1503–1566), known for a collection of prophecies concerning future events. The interaction of spirits and heavenly bodies described in the lines following is thought to derive from Emmanuel von Swedenborg (1688–1772), especially his theosophical treatise *Arcana Coelestia* (1749).

You learn the course of stars and moons,
Then will your power of soul unfold
How spirit with its like communes.   425
In vain to hope reflection dry
Could make the sacred tokens clear—
You spirits, you who float nearby,
Give me an answer, if you hear!
    [*He opens the book and perceives the sign of the Macrocosm.*]
Ah—what enchantment at the sight of this   430
Suffuses every sense, what lovely verve!
I feel new-burgeoning life, with sacred bliss
Reincandescent, course through vein and nerve.
Was it a god that fashioned this design
Which calms the tumult in my breast,   435
Floods my poor heart with happiness,
And with a secret thrust divine
Makes Nature's powers about me manifest?
Am I a god? I feel such light in me!
Within these tracings pure and whole   440
There lies creative Nature open to my soul.
At last I comprehend the sage's plea:
"The world of spirits is not barred,
Your sense is shut, your heart is dead!
Go, bathe, disciple, undeterred   445
Your mortal breast in sunrise red!"
    [*He scrutinizes the sign.*]
How all one common weft contrives,
Each in the other works and thrives!
How heavenly forces rising and descending
Pass golden ewers in exchange unending,   450
On wings with blessing fragrant
From Heaven the earth pervading,
Fill all the world with harmonies vagrant!

What glorious show! Yet but a show, alas!
How, boundless Nature, seize you in my clasp?   455
You breasts where, all life's sources twain,
Both heaven and earth are pressed,
Where thrusts itself my shriveled breast,
You brim, you quench, yet I must thirst in vain?
    [*Moodily he turns up another page and perceives the sign of the*
EARTH SPIRIT.[6]]
Not so this sign affects my soul, not so!   460
You, Spirit of the Earth, are nigher,
I sense my powers rising higher,
Already as with new wine I am aglow,
I feel emboldened now to venture forth,

---

6. Primarily Goethe's own conception, despite esoteric sources in the *archeus terrae* of Paracelsus or *anima terrae* of Giordano Bruno, sixteenth-century natural philosophers.

To bear the bliss, the sorrow of this earth,   465
Do battle with its tempests breaking,
Brave crunching shipwreck without quaking.
Above me vapors swirl—
The moon conceals her rays—
The lamplight wanes!   470
It steams, and scarlet lightning plays
About my head—there wafts
A tremor down the vaulting
And seizes me!
I feel you float about me, spirit I adjured.   475
Reveal yourself! Ah—how it wrenches at my soul!
All senses reeling
And rooting darkly toward new feeling!
I feel my very soul is yours to take!
You must! You must! And were my life at stake!   480
[*He seizes the book and mysteriously pronounces the sign of the*
SPIRIT. *A reddish flame flashes; the* SPIRIT *appears in the flame.*[7]]
SPIRIT.   Who calls for me?
FAUST.   [*face averted*] Appalling vision!
SPIRIT.   Long have you drawn me here,
With potent summons sucking at my sphere,
And now—
FAUST.   I cannot bear you! Woe!   485
SPIRIT.   With bated breath you yearn to meet me,
To hear my voice, to gaze upon my face;
Swayed as your mighty soul-pleadings entreat me,
I yield, am here! What horrors base
Now seize you superman! Where's the soul's call you hurled?   490
Where is the breast that wrought in it a world,
That bore and nursed it, that with joyous tremble
Swelled up to soar, us spirits to resemble?
Where is the Faust whose voice rang out to me,
Who urged himself on me with utmost energy?   495
Could you be he, who at my wafting breath
Is shaken even unto death,
Shrinking aside, a fearful writhing worm?
FAUST.   Am I to yield to you, semblance of flame?
No, I am Faust, your match, I am the same!   500
SPIRIT.   In tides of living, in doing's storm,
Up, down, I wave,
Waft to and fro,
Birth and grave,
An endless flow,   505
A changeful plaiting,

7. A drawing by Goethe survives, showing the Earth Spirit as a gigantic head hovering over the stage
(see p. 494). In a letter of June 2, 1819, to Count Brühl, theater director in Berlin, Goethe stated
that he envisioned the projection of a transparency that would show a head resembling the Zeus
of Otricoli in the Vatican Museum, Rome.

Fiery begetting,
Thus at Time's scurrying loom I weave and warp
And broider at the Godhead's living garb.
FAUST.   You who bestride the world from end to end,   510
Spirit of deeds, how close I feel to thee!
SPIRIT.   Close to the wraith you comprehend,
Not me!
        [*Vanishes.*]
FAUST.   [*collapsing*] Not thee?
Whom, then? What, I,   515
Made in God's likeness,
Yet like—not even thee?
        [*A knock at the door.*]
Death! It's my famulus[8]—I know that knock;
My fairest hour of luck is spoiled.
Oh, must this wealth of visions then be foiled   520
By that dry sneaking cluck?
        [WAGNER *in dressing-gown and night-cap, a lamp in his hand.* FAUST
        turns around with distaste.]
WAGNER.   Your leave! I heard declaiming—in this art[9]
I stand to profit from your kind directive.
You read, I think, a Greek dramatic part?
Such nowadays is most effective.   525
I've often heard the claim at least
That a comedian could instruct a priest.
FAUST.   Yes, if the priest is a comedian, I suggest;
As I am told from time to time befalls.
WAGNER.   Ah me, thus pent within one's study walls,   530
Seeing the world on holidays at best,
By spyglass from afar, on rare occasion,
How can one influence it by persuasion?
FAUST.   What you don't feel, you won't hunt down by art,
Unless it wells from your own inward source,   535
And with contentment's elemental force
Takes sway of every hearer's heart.
Just sit there, pasting joints to members,
Concoct from others' feasts your hash,
And blow a puny glow of embers   540
Up from your little heap of ash!
From minds of babes and apes you may be coining
Tribute of awe, if this be what you seek;
But never heart to heart will you be joining
Unless you let your own heart speak.   545
WAGNER.   Delivery, though, commends a speaker's mind;

---

8. Faust's academic assistant. The name "Wagner" derives from the chapbooks, and in the puppet
plays Faust's assistant provided a comic foil to the magus. In the "*Faust* Plan of 1800" (see below),
Goethe referred to Wagner as "bright, clear scientific striving."
9. An allusion to rhetoric, one of the three disciplines in the medieval trivium, part of the liberal
arts.

I feel it well, I still am far behind.
FAUST.   Seek you but honest recompense!
Be not a fool with jangling bells!
For solid reason and good sense   550
With little art commend themselves.
If you're in earnest to be heard,
Should there be need to chase the word?
That edge of rhetoric that glints and cleaves
By which you curl the shavings of mankind   555
Is idle as the fog-wind to my mind
That rustles through the dry autumnal leaves!
WAGNER.   Dear me! how long is art!
And short is our life![1]
I often know amid the scholar's strife   560
A sinking feeling in my mind and heart.
How difficult the means are to be found
By which the primal sources may be breached;
And long before the halfway point is reached,
They bury a poor devil in the ground.   565
FAUST.   Of parchment then is made the sacred spring,
A draught of which forever slakes all thirst?
From naught can you refreshment wring
Unless from your own inmost soul it burst.
WAGNER.   Your pardon! yet the joy is unsurpassed   570
Of insight into eras long ago,
To see how wise men then thought thus and so,
And how we reached our splendid heights at last.
FAUST.   Oh, starry heights, indeed!
To us the times of yore, it is decreed,   575
Are like a book by seven seals protected;[2]
The so-called spirit of the age, you'll find,
In truth is but the gentlemen's own mind
In which the ages are reflected.
And there you're apt to face a scene of gloom!   580
One glance is quite enough to make you stagger:
A refuse barrel or a lumber-room,
At best a stiff bombastic masque aswagger
With such sagaciously pragmatic saws
As might come fitly from a puppet's jaws.   585
WAGNER.   But take the world of man—his heart and mind!
We all seek some perception of the same,
FAUST.   Ah, yes—perception of a kind . . .
Who dares to call the child by its right name?
Those few who were vouchsafed of it one whit,   590
And rashly failed to curb their full heart's throb,

---

1. An adaptation of the familiar Latin aphorism derived from the ancient Greek doctor Hippocrates, *Ars longa, vita brevis.*
2. Revelation 5.1, "And I saw in the right hand of him who was seated on the throne a scroll written within and on the back, sealed with seven seals."

Bared what they felt and witnessed to the mob,
Were ever burnt and crucified for it.
I beg you, friend, the night is halfway gone,
For now we must break off discussion.   595
WAGNER.   I should have willingly stayed on and on,
  Disputing with you in this learned fashion.
  Tomorrow, though, it being Easter Day,[3]
  Indulge me for some further questioning.
  I've studied with a will and worked away;   600
  Though I know much, I would know everything.
      [*Exit.*]
FAUST.   [*alone*]
  How does the mind sustain some hope and pleasure
  That's stuck forever to the same old terms,
  With greedy fingers grubbing after treasure,
  And gratified to dig up worms![4]   605

  May such a human accent here resound,
  Where all about was spirit wealth and worth?
  Alas, this once, though, I am bound
  To thank you, poorest of the sons of earth.
  You banished the despair that held me fast,   610
  That was about to overthrow my mind.
  Alas! the apparition was so vast,
  It showed me all too well my dwarfish kind.

  I, godhead's likeness, who had soared in mind
  Close to the mirror of eternal verity,   615
  Self-relishing in heaven's radiant clarity,
  The son of earth quite left behind;
  I, more than cherub, whose free energy
  Foreboding dared through Nature's veins to flow,
  And, through creation, joyously to know   620
  Godlike estate—must I now rue it so!
  A thunder word rang out and withered me.

  No, I may not presume to be your equal:
  While I had strength to draw you here, the sequel,
  The strength to hold you, was denied to me.   625
  That fleeting moment of high bliss,
  I felt myself so small, so great;
  Until you thrust me, merciless,
  Back to uncertain human fate.
  Who teaches me? What should I shun?   630
  That urge I feel—should I obey?

3. This reference to Easter, added around 1800, provides the first indication of the time of year in
   which this scene takes place.
4. The so-called great lacuna in *Faust*, which Goethe filled c. 1800–01, begins here and extends to
   line 1770.

Both what we do and what we suffer to be done,
Alas, impedes us on life's way.

The greatest glory ever mind received,
By alien stuff becloyed, is choked and flawed,   635
When what this earth calls good has been achieved,
The better is accounted dream or fraud.
Those feelings, which were glorious rebirth,
Congeal amidst the welter of this earth.

Where fancy in audacious flight expanded   640
To the Eternal once its buoyant hope,
Now it contents itself with little scope,
As ship on ship in whirls of time is stranded.
Deep in the heart, gray Care[5] anon will settle,
In secret plant her stinging nettle,   645
With restless rocking spoil repose and joy,
Ever new masks for her disguise employ;
And be it wife and child or land and corn,
Be it knife, poison, fire or water,
At blows that never fall you falter,   650
And what you never lose, you must forever mourn.

Not like the gods am I—profoundly it is rued!
I'm of the earthworm's dust-engendered brood,
Which, blindly burrowing, by dust is fed,
And crushed and buried by the wanderer's tread.   655

These hundred shelves, is it not dust that bent
Their lofty wall into a cell which stifles,
A universe of moths where I am pent
Into a dustbin with a thousand trifles?
Here would I find the thing I lack?   660
Am I to plow a thousand books to read
Of man at all times stretched upon a rack,
And, here and there, one happy one, indeed?—
Ho, grinning hollow skull,[6] well you may leer,
To think that once your brain, like this one here,   665
In murky bondage sought the easeful day,
And parched with thirst for truth went grievously astray,
You instruments, you mock me, I can see,
With wheel and pulley, cylinder and cords:[7]
I faced the gate, you were to be the key,   670

---

5. See the aged crone of Part Two, Act V (lines 11384 ff.). The scene called "Midnight," in which
  she appears, was drafted c. 1800, about the same time as the passage here.
6. The skull indicates the ancient theme of *momento mori*, "remember (you must) die," for which
  see Hamlet with the skull of Yorick in Act 5 of Shakespeare's play.
7. The instrument described here is probably an electrostatic machine containing a rotating disk and
  comblike collectors (invented in the mid-seventeenth century).

But cannot lift the bolts, however shrewd your wards.[8]
Mysterious in bright daylight, never
Will Nature be defrauded of her veil,
What to your spirit she reveal not, that you fail
To torture out of her with screw or lever.   675
You ancient gear I never used, you loom
About here just because my father worked you.
You ancient scroll, you have been cured with fume
While at this desk the feeble lamp bemurked you.
Far better to have squandered free of care   680
My pittance than to sweat withal and scoff it!
What you received but as your father's heir,
Make it your own to gain possession of it!
What is unused is ballast hard to bear:
Alone what moment has begot can yield it profit.   685

Why is that spot there riveting my glances?
Is that small flask a magnet to my sight?
A sudden lovely gleam my soul entrances
Like moonlight wafting through the woods at night!

I bid you greeting, vial unique!   690
Which now with veneration I fetch down,
In you I reverence of human wit the peak,
Of gracious slumber saps the inmost flower,
Quintessence of all subtly lethal power,
Prove to your lord your favor and renown!   695
I see you, and the agony decreases,
I grasp you, and the striving half-releases
Its hold, the spirit's floodtide ebbs betimes.
Out to the open sea am I directed,
Its mirror flood bright at my feet reflected,   700
And day new-dawning lures me to new climes.

A fiery chariot wings on pinions light,
Approaches![9] I am ready, I feel free
To cleave the ether on a novel flight,
To novel spheres of pure activity.   705
Such lofty life, such godly benison!
You, but a worm as yet, deserve it, you?
With firm resolve, then, turn your back upon
This lovely sun of earth, the sun you knew.
Embold yourself to fling apart the gate   710
Past which all other men would crawl weak-kneed!

---

8. Metaphorical reference to the instrument as if it were the key to a lock where "wards" and "bolts"
   do not fit.
9. Faust may refer here to the sun as it rises (which has clearly happened by line 736). The image
   of the fiery chariot is both biblical (see Elijah's ascent to heaven, 2 Kings 2.11) and classical (the
   chariot of Apollo, god of the sun).

That manhood does not yield to gods' high state,
Now is the moment to affirm by deed.
To tremble not before the somber hollow
Wherein our fancy on itself but preys,   715
And gird oneself that passageway to follow
About whose narrow mouth all Hell's ablaze;
Resolve serenely to essay no less—
Be it on pain of ebbing into nothingness.

Now then, o flawless crystal shell,[1] descend!   720
Forth from your ancient casing, friend,
Of whom I have not thought in many a year!
You gleamed at fathers' festival of spring,
Helped turn their gravity to cheer,
When to their mutual pledges you would ring.   725
Your many splendid pictures' opulent craft,
The drinker's task to rhyme upon their truth,
To drain your hollow in a single draught,
Puts me in mind of many a night of youth.
I shall not pass you to a neighbor now,   730
I shall not hone my wits against your graven brow;
Here is a juice whose punch is swift and thorough!
With flood of brown it fills your hollow bowl.
I brewed it, and I choose it, so
With this for my last drink, from all my soul,   735
With festive high salute, I hail Tomorrow!
[*He raises the bowl to his lips.*]

[Sound of bells and choral song.[2]†]

CHORUS OF ANGELS   Christ is arisen!
                        Joy to the mortal,
                        Him whom invidious,
                        Subtle, insidious   740
                        Blemishes prisoned.

FAUST.   What solemn droning, what melodious fluting
    Perforce arrests the goblet in mid-way?
    Are you already, deep-toned bells, saluting
    The festive breaking hour of Easter Day?   745
    You choirs, do you the solace-hymn resume
    That angels lips intoned in the Sepulchre's gloom,
    New covenant's sure warranty?

1. A ceremonial drinking chalice with carved scenes on the outside. Such a chalice used at a banquet
   may be associated with the cup of Christ's Last Supper, symbolized in the Eucharist of Holy
   Communion, about to be celebrated in the Easter Mass.
2. According to traditions of medieval liturgy, the Easter Mass is celebrated by a dramatic representation of the discovery of Christ's empty tomb (see Matthew 28, Mark 16, Luke 24, John 20).
   Three choruses are heard singing from a nearby cathedral in an antiphonal cantata adapted from
   the style of medieval Latin plainsong.

CHORUS OF WOMEN.[3]   We stayed to tend Him.
                       With spices rare,   750
                       Last to befriend Him,
                       We laid Him there,
                       His body binding
                       In wrappings sheer;
                       Lo, now we find Him   755
                       No longer here.

CHORUS OF ANGELS.   Christ is arisen!
                       Blest the love spirit
                       Whose suffering merit
                       Earned grace from flesh's prison   760
                       For us to inherit.

FAUST.   Why, o celestial music, strong and gentle,
    Pursue me here where in the dust I grieve?
    Ring out your notes where men are sentimental:
    I hear the message, but I can't believe;   765
    Belief's beloved child is Miracle.
    To yonder spheres I venture not to strive
    Whence issues the enchanting spell;
    And yet, inured from childhood to this knell,
    Now also to its summons I revive.   770
    Time was, the kiss of heavenly love
    Sank down on me in earnest sabbath calm,
    So bodefully the bell-notes throbbed above,
    And praying was voluptuous balm;
    A lovely longing no one understands   775
    Drove me to roam in woods and meadowlands,
    Of scalding tears I paid a generous toll
    As a new world unfolded in my soul.
    The merry games of youth this song is pealing,
    The spring rite's happy grace;   780
    And now remembrance rouses childlike feeling
    To bar the path that none retrace.
    Resound, sound on, o sweet celestial chord!
    The tear wells up, to Earth I am restored!

CHORUS OF DISCIPLES.   While the Envaulted   785
                       From the tomb's prison,
                       Revives exalted,
                       In splendor risen,
                       In rapt gestation
                       Nears joyous creation: 790
                       Woe! in earth's furrow

---

3. Mary Magdalene and Mary the mother of James and Salome (see Mark 16.1), who have brought
spices with which to anoint the body of Christ.

We know but sorrow.
Who once were his,
He left to languish;
We mourn in anguish,   795
Master, Thy bliss!

CHORUS OF ANGELS.   Risen is Christ
Out of corruption's trough:
You too arise,
Your bonds cast off!   800
Who praise him in action
Practice affection,
Nourishing brothers,
Preaching to others
Glad resurrection—   805
For you, the Lord is near,
For you, is here!

Outside the City Gate†

People of all sorts coming out for walks.

SOME APPRENTICES.   Why there? Where are you bound?
OTHERS.   We're heading for the Stag-and-Hound.
THE FORMER.   We meant to strike out for the Mill.   810
ONE APPRENTICE.   Let's make it Lakeside Hostel if you will.
ANOTHER.   The road down there is not the best.
THE OTHERS.   What will you do?
A THIRD.   I'm going with the rest.
A FOURTH.   Come up to Burgdorf, there you'll find it true
    They have the prettiest girls, the finest brew.   815
    And there'll be first-rate hassles for us.
A FIFTH.   An over-lusty lad, I swear!
    You're itching to be tanned a third time there?
    No, not for me, that place gives me the horrors.
SERVANT GIRL.   No, no! I'm going back to town, just see.   820
ANOTHER.   I'm sure he's waiting by the poplars there.
THE FIRST.   That's precious little fun for me;
    You'll have a lark, two make a pair;
    Sure, arm in arm with you he'll go
    And dance with no one else, I know.   825
THE OTHER.   But there'll be two today, you're wrong:
    He said that curlyhead would be along.
STUDENT.   Gad, how those sturdy wenches sail!
    My word, we mustn't let them go to waste.
    A pungent smoke, a hearty mug of ale,   830
    A dolled-up maid—such, brother, is my taste.
GIRL OF THE BURGHER CLASS.
    Look, will you, at those handsome lads!
    That really seems a shame to me;
    Here they could have the choicest company,
    And who do they run after? Maids!   835
SECOND STUDENT.   [*to the first*]
    No, wait—here comes a turnout to explore,
    Both very pretty and well-dressed;
    One is a girl who lives next door
    In whom I take warm interest.
    They trip along there, all demure,   840
    Yet would not mind our company, I'm sure.
FIRST STUDENT.   No, friend! No parlor tricks for me, I say.
    Be quick, or we may lose that other game.
    The hand that plies the broom on Saturday
    Will best caress you Sunday, all the same.   845
CITIZEN.   No, I don't like him, the new burgomaster!
    Now that he's in, he just gets bolder faster.

And for the town what is he doing, pray?
Are we not worse off every day?
It's Do-what-you-are-told as never,   850
And fork out taxes more than ever.

BEGGAR.   [*singing*][1]
    Fair ladies, kindly sirs, for pity,
    So red of cheek and fine of dress,
    Be pleased to heed my poor entreaty,
    And see and lighten my distress!   855
    Let me not vainly grind my barrel:
    He who can give, alone is gay.
    A day on which all men make merry,
    Be it for me a harvest day!

ANOTHER CITIZEN.
    On holidays I know of nothing cozier, neighbor,   860
    Than a good chat of war and war's alarms,
    When far away, in Turkey,[2] tribes in arms
    Whack one another and belabor;
    While you stand by the window, down your glass,
    Watch the bright-colored ships glide down the breeze,   865
    And in the evening amble home at last
    With blessings upon peace and peacetime ease.
A THIRD CITIZEN.   Well spoken, friend, just what I always say!
    Let them crack noggins freely, sir,
    Let things go every which-a-way,   870
    If just at home they stay as they were.
OLD WOMAN.   [*to the burgher girls*]
    What stately finery, my! What pretty faces!
    Who would not fall for such a dainty dish?
    Never you mind those airs and graces!
    I might just find a way to what you wish.   875
FIRST YOUNG GIRL.   Quick, Agatha, it really wouldn't do
    To walk in public with a witch like her;
    Though on St. Andrew's Eve[3] she let me view
    My future love in person, I prefer . . .
THE OTHER.   She showed me mine, too, in the crystal's face,   880
    A soldier, like, with others bold and trim;
    I've looked about, been searching every place,
    But cannot seem to meet with him.

SOLDIERS.   Castles with frowning
        Battlements rude,   885

1. Presumably onstage from the outset, the beggar accompanies his song with a barrel organ.
2. No specific historical allusion is intended. Wars with the Turks were often fought during the
   sixteenth and seventeenth centuries.
3. According to popular tradition, on the eve of this saint (November 29) young girls by incanting
   magical verses could see their future husbands in their dreams.

Maidens in haughty
Mettlesome mood,
These I would savor,
Keen is the labor,
Splendid the prize.   890

Trumpets blaring
Do our wooing,
For love's delight,
For foe's undoing.
Boisterous onslaught   895
Cruel or tender,
Maidens and castles,
Both must surrender!
Keen is the labor
Sweet the reward!   900
After the contest,
Soldiers depart.

[*Enter* FAUST *and* WAGNER.]
FAUST.   Freed from the ice are brooks and rivers
   By spring's enchanting, enlivening gaze;
   The valley is blithe with hope's green haze;   905
   Hoary winter with senile shivers
   Back to his mountain lair withdrew.
   Thence he flings, shorn of his powers,
   Granules of ice in spiteful showers
   Streaking over the verdant site;   910
   The sun, however, allows no white,
   All is astir with shaping and striving,
   All he would dower with hues and enliven;
   The flower season still lies ahead:
   Folk in their finery do instead.   915
   Turn around with me, look down
   From these lofty hillsides back toward town,
   See how the gate's dark cave exudes
   Teeming colorful multitudes.
   All seek the sun with glad accord,   920
   They exult in the rising of the Lord;
   For they are resurrected themselves,
   Freed from the shackles of shops and crafts,
   From stuffy dwellings like narrow shelves,
   From smothering roofs and gable lofts,   925
   From the city streets with their smothering press,
   From out the churches' reverend night,
   They have all been raised to light.
   Look, look, how nimbly the human crest
   Breaks and surges through field and park,   930
   How the length and width of the river's breast

Cradles many a pleasure bark;
Yonder, laden full to sinking,
The last of the fragile craft unties;
From the very hilltops far off winking   935
Bright-colored dresses strike our eyes.
I hear the village buzz already,
True people's heaven, crowded, heady;
And young and old exult in glee:
"Here I am Man, am free to be!"   940
WAGNER.   To stroll with you, Sir Doctor, never
But profits and exalts the mind;
But on my own I would not stray here ever,
Because I shun all that is unrefined.
How I abominate these vulgar revels,†   945
The fiddling, roaring, clash of the bowling-run!
They rave as if pursued by a thousand devils,
And call it singing, call it fun.

PEASANTS.   [*under the linden tree*]

   [*Dance and song.*][4]

      The shepherd dressed him for the jig,
      With ribbon and wreath, a colorful rig,   950
      He made a handsome show.
      The throng around the linden pressed
      And whirled about as if possessed.
      Heigh-ho! Heigh-ho!
      Heigh nonny nonny ho!   955
      Went fiddle and flying bow.

      In clumsy haste he crowded hard,
      And straightway with his elbow jarred
      A maiden dancing near.
      The pert young wench, she turned about   960
      And said: "Be off, you stupid lout!"
      Heigh-ho! Heigh-ho!
      Heigh nonny nonny ho!
      "You mind your manners here!"

      But round and round in whisking flight,   965
      In circles left, in circles right,
      Spun skirts and furbelow.
      They grew so flushed, they grew so warm,
      Encircled breathless arm in arm,
      Heigh-ho! Heigh-ho!   970

4. This folk song (mentioned in the first draft of Goethe's novel *Wilheim Meister*, Book 4, chapter
   13) was probably composed by Goethe in the early 1780s, not intended for *Faust* at all.

Heigh nonny nonny ho!
His hand, her waist, just so.

Don't you make up to me, my lad!
I know of many a maiden sad,
Forsaken and betrayed!   975
Aside he coaxed her anyhow,
And far off from the linden now,
Heigh-ho! Heigh-ho!
Heigh nonny nonny ho!
Rose shouts and fiddles played.   980

OLD PEASANT.   Sir Doctor, it is kind of you
  On this our day to be not proud,
  But, full of learning though you are,
  To mingle with the jostling crowd.
  So I present the finest jug,   985
  Which we have freshly filled with beer,
  And pledging you, pronounce the wish
  That it not just refresh you here,
  But that your span of days have gained
  One for each drop that it contained.   990
FAUST.   I take the cooling potion here
  And bid you all a grateful cheer

     [*The people gather in a circle.*]

OLD PEASANT.   It is well done, and fit indeed,
  That this glad day you pay us call,
  Who formerly in days of need   995
  Have done so kindly by us all.
  For many a man here drawing breath,
  Caught in the fever's parching grasp,
  Was by your father snatched from death,
  The time he stemmed the plague at last.[5]   1000
  You also did, a young man then,
  Attend each sick-bed without fail,
  And many a corpse was carried hence,
  But you did issue safe and hale.
  You passed through many a hard ordeal;   1005
  The Healer helped his helpmeet heal.
ALL.   May health attend this man of worth,
  Long to help others on this earth!
FAUST.   Obeisance make to Him on high,
  Who teaches help, whose help is nigh!   1010

---

5. The story that Faust's father had been a doctor of medicine who treated peasants during an
   epidemic of the plague is Goethe's own invention.

[*He walks on with* WAGNER.]

WAGNER.   What sentiments, great man, must swell your breast
Upon the homage of this multitude!
Ah, he who can derive such good
From his own gifts indeed is blessed!
Fathers lift boys up as you go,   1015
All push and run and ask the cause,
The fiddle rests, the dancers pause.
You pass, they stand there, row on row,
And all the caps go flying high:
They all but genuflect and bend down low   1020
As if the Sacrament came by.[6]

FAUST.   A few steps further up yet to that stone—
Here we may rest us from our expedition.
Here I sat often, thoughtful and alone,
And plagued myself with prayer and inanition.   1025
Steadfast in faith and rich in confidence,
I wrung my hands with many a tear and sigh
To wrest the lifting of that pestilence
From the Almighty Lord on high.
Now people's cheers to me ring jeering fun.   1030
Could you but read within my soul the story
How little father and son
Were truly worthy of such glory!
My father, man of honor though unsung,
Brooded on Nature with a crotchety passion,   1035
And—in all probity yet in his fashion—
Upon her sacred circles raptly hung;
By secret recipes unending,
Locked up in the Black Kitchen[7] with retorts,
He brewed away with adepts, blending   1040
Contrariness of every sort.
There was a Scarlet Lion, intrepid wooer,
Wed to the Lily in a tepid ewer,
And then by open flames the two were vexed
From one new bridal chamber to the next.   1045
And when at last, with rainbow colors vying,
The Young Queen glistened in the yield,
There was your dose, the patients went on dying,
And nobody enquired: who was healed?
And thus with our infernal tonic   1050
Upon these hills, these dales we visited

---

6. An allusion to the custom of kneeling before the Host as it passed in religious processions.
7. Faust refers to the alchemical laboratory and experiments in black magic. He describes the creation of an elixir used as a medicine against the plague. With imagery of a marriage, a union occurs between the masculine "Scarlet Lion" (reddish mercuric oxide) and the feminine "Lily" (hydrochloric acid), which are heated over a flame to yield as offspring the "Young Queen," the sublimate that served as the specific.

A plague far worse than the bubonic.
Why, with this poison I myself defrauded
Men by the thousands, leaving them for dead;
Now I must hear the brazen killers lauded.   1055
WAGNER.   Why feel so bitterly disgusted?
Come, does an honest man do ill
Pursuing with good faith and will
The art with which he was entrusted?
If you revere your father as a youth,   1060
You will accept from him with pleasure;
If as a man you swell the store of truth,
Your son may grow to yet more lofty measure.
FAUST.†   Oh! Lucky who can still aspire
To surface from this sea of aberration!   1065
What we know not, of that our need is dire,
And what we know lacks application.
However, this bright hour's fair benison
Let such low spirits not embitter!
Observe how in the flaming evening sun   1070
Those green-embowered cabins glitter.
He yields and sinks, the day is lived and done,
He hastes beyond, new life to breed and nourish.
Oh, that I have no buoyant wings to flourish,
To strive and follow, on and on!   1075
I'd see in endless vesper rays
The silent world beneath me glowing,
The valleys all appeased, each hill ablaze,
The silver brooks to golden rivers flowing.
No more would then this rugged bluff deny   1080
With cliff and precipice the godlike motion;
Already with its sun-warmed bays the ocean
Reveals itself to the astonished eye.
At last, it seems, the god is downward sinking;
Yet to new urge awakes the mind,   1085
I hasten on, his ceaseless radiance drinking,
The day ahead of me, night left behind,
The waves below, and overhead the sky.
A happy fancy—meanwhile he must pass.
To spirit wings will scarce be joined, alas,   1090
Corporeal wings wherewith to fly.
Yet it is innate in us all
That feeling ever upward, forward presses
When, lost above in heaven's azure spaces,
The skylark trills his jubilant call,   1095
When over craggy fir-clad highlands
On outspread wings the eagle rides,
And striving over plains and islands,
The crane toward his homeland glides.
WAGNER.   I too have been to moody crotchets given,   1100

By such an urge, though, I was never driven.
The charm in watching woods and fields is brief,
I never shall begrudge the bird its soaring.
Compare the mind's delights which wing us poring
From book to book, from leaf to leaf!   1105
Then nights of winter bloom with grace and zest,
Your limbs glow with a blissful warming leaven,
And, ah! should you unroll a worthy palimpsest,
Then there descends on you the whole of heaven.
FAUST.† You are by just a single urge possessed;   1110
Oh may you never know the other!
Two souls, alas, are dwelling in my breast,
And either would be severed from its brother;
The one holds fast with joyous earthy lust
Onto the world of man with organs clinging;   1115
The other soars impassioned from the dust,
To realms of lofty forebears winging.
Oh, be there spirits in the air
Who 'twixt the earth and heaven reigning hover,
Descend ye from the golden fragrance there,   1120
To new and changeful living lead me over!
Why, if a magic cape were only mine
And were to bear me over alien borders,
I'd trade it not for choicest robes and orders,
Not for the royal cloak incarnadine!   1125
WAGNER. Forbear to call on the notorious clan
Which, all abroad in misty concourse faring,
In thousandfold disguise imperils man,
Hazards from every side preparing.
From North with arrow-tapered tongues that threaten   1130
The ghostly razor fang is thrust at you;
From Orient with withering breath they drew
Upon your parching lungs to batten;
While Noon sends those who from the desert burst
And glow on searing glow amass around you,   1135
West brings the swarm who will, refreshing first,
Pour floods on fields and pasturelands and drown you.
They gladly listen, being glad to grieve,
To cheat us keen, hence eagerly complying,
As if from Heaven sent, they make believe   1140
With angel lisps as they are lying.[8]
But let us go; the world about has paled,
The air grown chill, in vapors veiled.
At dusk the home we doubly prize.
Why do you stand and peer in moot surmise?   1145
What can engage you so here in the gloaming?

---

8. In the preceding lines, Wagner has described spirits of the weather associated in popular belief
with the four directions of the compass.

FAUST. See that black dog through seed and fallow roaming?[9]
WAGNER. I saw it long before and paid it little heed.
FAUST. Look at it well! What would you call its breed?
WAGNER. A poodle, I should say, with canine snooping   1150
  At pains upon its master's trail.
FAUST. Do you observe him near and nearer, looping
  A narrowing spiral like the convolute snail?
  Unless I err, there rises in his track
  A swirling fiery effusion.   1155
WAGNER. I see a poodle, and I see it's black;
  Yours must have been some optical illusion.
FAUST. He seems to snare our feet with magic, weaving
  Some future bondage, thread by stealthy thread.
WAGNER. He's circling us in wonder or misgiving   1160
  To see two strangers in his master's stead.
FAUST. The ring grows tight, already he is near!
WAGNER. You see? A dog—there is no specter here.
  He gives a growl, he wonders, lies down flat,
  He wags his tail—all canine conduct, that.   1165
FAUST. Come here and join us! Come to me!
WAGNER. A skittish fool of a poodle, see?
  You stop, he sits and begs;
  You speak to him, he rears on his hind legs;
  Lose something and he will retrieve it,   1170
  Swim out for sticks you throw, believe it.
FAUST. You must be right; for watch him as I will,
  I find no trace of spirit; all is drill.
WAGNER. A dog, if ably trained and clever,
  Will even gain a wise man's favor.   1175
  Yes, he deserves your good will without scruple,
  The undergraduate's accomplished pupil.
      [*They pass under the city gate.*]

---

9. There is no precedent in the popular legend of Faust for the appearance of Mephistopheles in the guise of a dog. In one of the chapbooks that Goethe knew, Faustus was said to have owned a black dog named Praestigiar, which had demonic powers.

Study†

FAUST. [*entering with the poodle*]
    I have forsaken field and meadow,
    Now sunken deep in darkness, when
    To boding sacred awe night's shadow   1180
    Awakes the better self in men.
    Now lie aslumber savage urges
    With every vehemence of deed;
    Now love of man for man resurges,
    The love of God is stirred and freed.   1185
Where are you running, poodle? Cease your riot!
Why snuffle at the threshold for outdoors?[1]
Go lie behind the stove in quiet,
My finest cushion shall be yours.
As you amused us on our hillside ramble,   1190
Running and jumping without rest,
Accept my care in here with never a gambol,
Be welcome as a silent guest.
        Ah, when in our restricted cell
        The lamp resumes its kindly blaze,   1195
        It lights the inner self as well,
        The heart aware of its own ways.
        Then reason reasserts its forces,
        New hope begins to stir and flow;
        One yearns again to trace life's courses,   1200
        Alas—life's springs one yearns to know.
Stop growling, poodle! Poorly suited
To the sacred tones that gently clasp
My soul entire, is that animal rasp.
We know that men have always hooted   1205
At what they cannot grasp,
And that the beautiful and good
Is often hissed as irksome to boor and varlet;
For dogs, then, too, is it fit to snarl at?

But oh! though my resolve grows even stronger,†   1210
I feel contentment welling from my soul no longer.
Yet why must the flood so soon run dry,
And we be left again in thirst to lie?
I have had proof of it in such full measure.
Still, for this lack there's compensation: 1215
The supernatural we learn to treasure,
We come to long for revelation,

---

1. The poodle, in trying to leave the study, discovers that the "Druid's claw" prevents him from going (see lines 1259 and 1395).

Which nowhere burns so finely, so unflawed,
As in the Gospel of our Lord.
I feel an urge to reach   1220
For the original, the sacred text, appealing
To simple honesty of feeling
To render it in my dear German speech.

[*He opens a tome and sets forth.*]

"In the beginning was the Word"[2]—thus runs the text.
Who helps me on? Already I'm perplexed!   1225
I cannot grant the word such sovereign merit,
I must translate it in a different way
If I'm indeed illumined by the Spirit.
"In the beginning was the Sense." But stay!
Reflect on this first sentence well and truly   1230
Lest the light pen be hurrying unduly!
Is sense in fact all action's spur and source?
It should read: "In the beginning was the Force!"
Yet as I write it down, some warning sense
Alerts me that it, too, will give offense.   1235
The spirit speaks! And lo, the way is freed,
I calmly write: "In the beginning was the Deed!"

Poodle, stop your barking,
If you wish to go on sharing
This room with me, not a growl or yap!   1240
Such a noisy larking chap
Near my person I find past bearing.
One of us, I can tell,
Must quit this cell.
It pains me to cancel the guest right—still: 1245
The door is open, run where you will.
But what is this, I say?
Could this occur in the natural way?
Is it real or some shadow-fraud?
How my poodle grows long and broad!   1250
See him hugely swell and rise—
This is not canine shape or size!
What have I brought to the house, an incubus?
By now it's like a hippopotamus,
With fiery eyes and fearsome tooth.   1255
Ah, I'll make sure of you, forsooth!
For such half-hellish brood
Solomon's key is good.[3]

---

2. The opening line of the Gospel of John.
3. Faust turns to a book of magic well known in the sixteenth century, *Clavicula Salomonis*, falsely
   attributed to Solomon, which contained chants and spells for controlling spirits.

SPIRITS. [*in the hallway*][4]
> One is caught in there, you hear?
> No one follow, all keep clear!   1260
> Like a trapped fox there shrinks
> Some wily old hell's lynx.
> But pay heed!
> Upward soar, downward flow,
> To and fro,   1265
> Soon he'll be freed.
> There's tricks to show him,
> Aid to be tendered,
> We all here owe him
> For favors rendered.   1270

FAUST. First the brute I score
With the Spell of the Four:[5]
> Let Salamander flare,
> Undine coil,
> Sylph thin to air,   1275
> Hobgoblin toil.

Who knows not the lore
Of the elements four,
Each one's merits
And dower,   1280
Has no power
Over spirits.
> Shrink in fiery flashing,
> Salamander!
> Curb thy waters rushing,   1285
> Undine!
> Glow with meteor sheen,
> Sylph!
> Bring domestic help,
> Incubus! Incubus!   1290
> Be the last, step forth for us.

None of these four
Is the brute's core.
He lounges there with a careless grin;
As yet I've left no mark on him.   1295
I'll be at your shell
With a stronger spell
> Might you be, tell,
> A truant from Hell?
> Then see this sign![6]   1300

4. Of uncertain origin and without explanation, these spirits, who appear subject to Mephistopheles' command, try to come to his aid.
5. The following spells, read from the book, are addressed to the spirits of the four elements: Salamander for fire, Undine for water, Sylph for air, Incubus (or Hobgoblin) for earth.
6. Surmising that the spirit is a demon from hell, Faust confronts it with the sign of Christ, the title inscribed on the Cross at the Crucifixion (see John 19.19): *INRI, Jesus Nazareneus Rex Judaeorum* ("Jesus of Nazareth, King of the Jews").

Before whose power
The black hosts cower.
There, it swells up with bristling spine.
Monster degraded,
Dare you see him,   1305
The never-created
Ineffable being,
Through all the heavens poured,
Heinously gored?
In the stove-nook's gloom   1310
Swelled to elephant size,
It fair crowds the room,
Into vapor would blur;
To the ceiling do not rise!
Down, to your master's heel, cur!   1315
You see, mine are no idle threats.
I sear you with sacred fire jets!
Dare not bide
The thrice-glowing light![7]
Dare not bide   1320
The strongest art within my sway!

[MEPHISTOPHELES, *clothed like a medieval traveling student, steps
forth from behind the stove as the vapor clears.*]

MEPHISTOPHELES.
Why all the fuss? What's milord's pleasure, pray?
FAUST.   So this was at the poodle's core!
A traveling scholar? Most amusing case!
MEPHISTOPHELES.   Allow me to salute you, learned sir!   1325
You really had me sweating for a space.
FAUST.   What are you called?
MEPHISTOPHELES.   For one so down on the word,
Who, so remote from everything external,
Past all appearance seeks the inmost kernel,
This question seems a bit absurd.   1330
FAUST.   With gentry such as you, their nature
Is aptly gathered from the nomenclature,
Whence all too clearly it transpires
When you are labeled Lord of Flies,[8] corrupters, liars.
All right—who are you, then?
MEPHISTOPHELES.   Part of that force which would   1335
Do ever evil, and does ever good.[9]
FAUST.   And that conundrum of a phrase implies?

7. Faust holds up the sign of the Trinity, a triangle with the eye of God in the center.
8. A literal translation of the Hebrew *Baal-zebub* (see 2 Kings 1.2).
9. See Milton, *Paradise Lost*: "His providence / Out of our evil seek[s] to bring forth good" (1.162–
63, Satan speaking of God) and "all his malice served but to bring forth / Infinite goodness, grace,
and mercy" (1.217–18, the poet speaking of Satan).

MEPHISTOPHELES.   The spirit which eternally denies![1]
And justly so; for all that which is wrought
Deserves that it should come to naught;   1340
Hence it were best if nothing were engendered.
Which is why all things you have rendered
By terms like sin, destruction—evil, in brief
Are my true element-in-chief.
FAUST.   You call yourself a part, yet whole you stand in view?   1345
MEPHISTOPHELES.   I speak a modest truth for you.
Whereas your Man, that microcosmic fool,
Regards himself an integer as a rule,
I am but part of the part that was the whole at first,
Part of the dark which bore itself the light,   1350
That supercilious light which lately durst
Dispute her ancient rank and realm to Mother Night;
And yet to no avail, for strive as it may,
It cleaves in bondage to corporeal clay.
It streams from bodies, bodies it lends sheen,   1355
A body can impede its thrust,
And so it should not be too long, I trust,
Before with bodies it departs the scene.[2]
FAUST.   Now I perceive your worthy role!
Unable to destroy on the scale of the whole,   1360
You now attempt it in the little way.
MEPHISTOPHELES.   It does not come to much, I'm bound to say.
What bids defiance to the Naught,
The clumsy lumber of the Aught,
Endeavor what I would against it,   1365
I never have discountenanced it
By waves or tempests, quake or firebrand—
Sedately rest at last both sea and land!
As for that scum of beast- and humanhood,
There's just no curbing it, no quelling,   1370
I've buried them in droves past telling,
Yet ever newly circulates fresh blood.
And so it goes, it drives one to distraction!
From air, from water, as from soil
A thousand germinating seeds uncoil,   1375
In warm or cold, in moist or dry-as-bone!
Had I not fire for my preserve of action,
I should not have a place to call my own.
FAUST.   And so against the ever sanely,
Benignantly creative might   1380
You clench your devil's fist, inanely
Upraising it in frigid spite!

---

1. This is a paraphrase of the meaning of the name Satan (literally, "adversary"). See also line 338.
2. Mephistopheles applies the distinction of darkness and light to the doctrine that light derives from physical bodies and can manifest itself only against physical bodies.

Come, seek another occupation,
Hoar Chaos's fantastic son!
MEPHISTOPHELES.   It merits earnest contemplation;   1385
We shall talk more of this anon!
For now, though, would you let me quit you?
FAUST.   Can I forbid you or permit you?
Now we have met, feel free to pay
Your further calls in any way.   1390
Here is the window, there the door,
The chimney, too, may be conceded.
MEPHISTOPHELES.   I might as well own up! I am impeded
Of egress by a minor flaw,
That Druid's claw[3] at the threshold's center—   1395
FAUST.   The pentagram can make you wince?
Confide to me, Gehenna's[4] prince,
If that confines you, how then did you enter?
How was a mind like yours betrayed?
MEPHISTOPHELES.   Look at it closely: it is not well made;   1400
One of the corners of it, as you see,
That faces outward, is a little split.
FAUST.   Then I have chance to thank for it!
So you are now a prisoner to me?
That was a windfall, quite unearned!   1405
MEPHISTOPHELES.   The poodle scampered in quite unconcerned;
Now we are on a different tack,
The Devil can't get back.
FAUST.   Why not out through the window, then?
MEPHISTOPHELES.   Devils and ghosts obey a regimen;   1410
They must slip in and out by the same track.
Entry is of our choice, for exit we're enslaved.
FAUST.   Is even Hell with statutes paved?
I am intrigued—then with you gentlemen
A compact could, and safely too, be entered?   1415
MEPHISTOPHELES.
That which is promised shall be neatly rendered,
And nothing stinted or subtracted.
But this cannot be hastily transacted,
We may consider it when next we meet.
But now I urge you and entreat   1420
That for the nonce I might be gone.
FAUST.   A moment more let me insist upon,
Perhaps you have glad tidings to present.
MEPHISTOPHELES.   Now let me go! I shall be back anon.
Then you may question to your heart's content.   1425
FAUST.   I used no trap or stratagem,

---

3. The "Druid's claw," or pentagram, is a sign like a five-pointed star, one point of which is here
   split open (line 1402).
4. Another name for hell.

All on your own you walked into my pen.
Who holds Old Nick had best hang on to him!
He will not capture him so soon again.
MEPHISTOPHELES. I am quite willing, if such be your pleasure,   1430
To stay in company with a man of parts;
Provided I may while away your leisure
In some rewarding fashion by my arts.
FAUST. By all means do, you may feel free,
But mind the art appeals to me.   1435
MEPHISTOPHELES. In this one hour, my friend, your senses
Will garner in more recompenses
Than in the year's monotony.
What songs the delicate spirits sing you,
The pleasing pictures they will bring you,   1440
They are no idle magic game.
Smell will be set to rapt enjoyment,
The palate to superb employment,
Your touch not least be set aflame.
No preparation needs our art;   1445
We are forgathered, let us start!
SPIRITS.†   Melt, ye confining
             Vaults up yonder!
             Yield to the shining
             Ether's fonder   1450
             Cerulean gaze!
             Cloudbanks darkling
             Dwindle for sparkling
             Starlets winking,
             Milder sun-rays   1455
             Drinking the haze!
             Heavenly offspring's
             Graces uplifting,
             Swaying and turning,
             Drifting they wander,   1460
             Lovelorn yearning
             Follows them yonder.
             And their garments'
             Fluttering garlands
             Cover the far lands,   1465
             Cover the arbor
             Where thought-rapt lover
             Lifelong trusting
             Pledges to lover.
             Arbor on arbor!   1470
             Tendrils thrusting!
             Plump grape clusters
             Plunging in masses
             To groaning presses,
             With froth and rumble   1475

Wine floods tumble
Down craggy tunnels,
Crystalline runnels
Through pure gem funnels
Downward heading,   1480
To lakes outspreading,
Embedding, embanking,
Calm hills' green flanking.
And winged creation
Imbibes elation   1485
Sunward streaming
Soars on to dreaming
Islands skimming
On wavelets gleaming,
Sinking and lifting;   1490
Where we hear choiring
In jubilant chorus,
See dancers gyring
On meadows before us,
Dispersing at pleasure   1495
In airy leisure.
Some go scaling
The mountain quarters,
Others trailing
The lake's slow waters,   1500
Others sailing
The air; all to living,
All to afars
Of stars love-giving,
Of blessed requital.   1505
MEPHISTOPHELES.   Asleep! Well done, my airy cherubim!
You found the proper lullaby for him!
I am obliged to you for this recital.
You are not yet the man to hold on to the Devil!
In welters of sweet fancy make him revel,   1510
Plunge him into an ocean of deceit;
Meanwhile, the spell cast at this threshold level
Demands a rat's tooth to defeat.
No need to conjure—one is near me,
Close-by he rustles, and will forthwith hear me.[5]   1515

The lord of rats and mice,
Of flies, frogs, bedbugs, lice,
Hither bids you dare!
Gnaw the threshold there,
Where the oil I rub—   1520

---

5. Mephistopheles calls forth a rat to nibble a hole in the pentagram big enough for him to squeeze through.

There you come scampering up!
To work, fall to! The gap that needs enlarging,
You'll find it at the outmost margin.
Another bite, and it is done.—
Now, Faust, until we meet again, dream on!   1525
FAUST.   [*awakening*] Am I then once again deluded?
Thus fades for me the spirits' rich array,
That in a cheating dream the Devil had intruded,
And that a poodle slipped away!

Study†

FAUST. MEPHISTOPHELES.

FAUST.   A knock? Come in! Who now will try my patience?   1530
MEPHISTOPHELES.   It's me.
FAUST.   Come in!
MEPHISTOPHELES.   It takes three invitations.
FAUST.   Come in, then!
MEPHISTOPHELES.   Now you know the cue.
  We two, I trust, will have no altercations!
  For to chase off your lucubrations,
  I'm here as a young nobleman for you,   1535
  In scarlet suit with golden braiding,
  A mantlet stiff with silk brocading,
  Cock-feather perched on beret brim,
  A rapier, long and pointed nicely:[1]
  And I advise you now, concisely,   1540
  To throw yourself in similar trim,
  So that, emancipated, free,
  You may explore what life can be.
FAUST.   I greatly fear, regardless of attire,
  I'll walk in pain the narrow earthly way.[2]   1545
  I am too old to be content with play,
  Too young to be without desire.
  What does the world hold out by way of gain?
  Abstain! it calls, You shall abstain!
  Thus goes the sempiternal song   1550
  That every mortal creature hears,
  That our entire existence long
  Each hour comes rasping to our ears.
  Each morning I awake in desperation,
  Sick unto tears to see begun   1555
  Yet one more day that in its ambulation
  Will grant me not a single wish, not one,
  That with its stubborn carping tempers
  Each mere presentiment of joy,
  With thousand shams of living hampers   1560
  My live creative mind's employ.
  When night descends and I would seek for slumber,
  Then, too, I am not granted rest;
  I dread to bed me down—wild visions cumber
  My dreams and make repose unblessed.   1565

---

1. Mephistopheles wears the conventional theatrical costume of a Spanish cavalier.
2. Faust's drastic change of mood to pessimism and despair is unmotivated as the drama now stands. Goethe intended to write a disputation scene between the study scenes that would have explained the change. (See interpretive notes.)

The lord within my bosom bowered
Can stir me to the inmost kernel;
The one past all my powers empowered,
He cannot alter anything external.
Existence seems a burden to detest, 1570
Death to be wished for, life a hateful jest.
MEPHISTOPHELES.
And yet death never is a wholly welcome guest.
FAUST. O, blessèd he about whose brow he winds
The bloodstained laurels of victorious war,
Or whom, spun breathless off the ballroom floor, 1575
Locked in a maiden's arms he finds!
Oh, had I sunken lifeless, wasted
Of bliss before the lofty Spirit's might!³
MEPHISTOPHELES. And yet a certain person left untasted
A certain brownish elixir that night.⁴ 1580
FAUST. In spying, it would seem, you have a special touch.
MEPHISTOPHELES. All-knowing I am not; albeit aware of much.
FAUST. What if a sweet familiar pealing
Recalled me from that fearsome maze,
Lured what remained of childlike feeling 1585
With echoings of happier days?⁵
My curse† I hurl on all that spangles
The mind with dazzling make-belief,
With lures and blandishments entangles
The soul within this cave of grief! 1590
Accursed, to start, the smug delusion
Whereby the mind itself ensnares!
Cursed, brash phenomenal intrusion
That blinds the senses unawares!
Cursed, what in lying dreams assures us 1595
Of name and glory past the grave!
Cursed, pride of ownership that lures us
Through wife and children, plow and slave!
Accursed be Mammon, when his treasure
To deeds of daring eggs us on, 1600
For idle self-indulgent leisure
Spreads a luxurious divan!
Cursed be the balsam of the grape!
Cursed, highest prize of lovers' thrall!
A curse on faith! A curse on hope! 1605
A curse on patience, above all!

CHORUS OF SPIRITS. [invisible] Woe! Woe!
You have destroyed it,

3. An allusion to the Earth Spirit (see lines 482–513).
4. An allusion to Faust's temptation to suicide (see lines 720–36).
5. An allusion to Faust's recovery in response to the Easter Chorus (see lines 762–84).

The beautiful world,
With mighty fist;[6]   1610
It crumbles scattered,
By a demigod shattered.
Forlorn,
We bear the ruins into the void,
And mourn   1615
For beauty destroyed.
Mighty one
Of the earth's sons,
In splendor perfected
See it rewon,   1620
In your own breast re-erect it!
Set forth
Upon rebirth
With freshened sense;
And new-sung mirth   1625
Re-echo thence!

MEPHISTOPHELES.   Hear the smallest of all
Who are at my call,
Precociously suing
For joyous doing!   1630
To the world entire,
From this lonesome plot
Where thought and juices clot,
They bid you aspire.

Be done with nursing your despair,   1635
Which, like a vulture, feeds upon your mind;
The very meanest company bids fair
To let you feel a man among mankind.
It's not that we propose
To toss you in among the rabble.   1640
I am no ranking devil;
But let us say you chose
To fall in step with me for life's adventure,
I'd gladly, forthwith, go into indenture,
Be yours, as well as I know how.   1645
I'm your companion now,
And if this meets with your desire,
Will be your servitor, your squire!

FAUST.   And for my part—what is it you require?

MEPHISTOPHELES.   Never you mind, it's much too soon to worry.   1650

FAUST.   No, no! Old Nick's an egoist—it's hard
To picture him in any special hurry
To be of service for the love of God.[7]

6. In German, the term *Faust* introduces an intentional pun on the protagonist's name.
7. This colloquial phrase means "without payment."

Spell out just what the bargain turns upon;
Not safely is such servant taken on.   1655
MEPHISTOPHELES.   I shall be at your service by this bond
Without relief or respite here on earth;
And if or when we meet again beyond,
You are to give me equal worth.
FAUST.   Beyond to me makes little matter;   1660
If once this earthly world you shatter,
The next may rise when this has passed.
It is from out this earth my pleasures spring,
It is this sun shines on my suffering;
If once from these I draw asunder,   1665
Then come to pass what will and must.
I do not further choose to wonder
If hate may then be felt or love,
Or whether in those regions yonder
They still know nether or above.   1670
MEPHISTOPHELES.   So minded, you may dare with fitness.
Engage yourself; these days you are to witness
Examples of my pleasing arts galore.
I'll give you what no man has seen before.
FAUST.   What is, poor devil, in your giving?   1675
Has even human mind in its high striving
Been comprehended by the likes of you?
What's yours but food unsating, the red hue
Of gold which, shifting and untrue,
Quicksilverlike will through the fingers run,   1680
A game which always stays unwon,
A girl who at my very breast
Trades winks already with another's eyes,
But honor's fair and godly zest
Which like a meteor flares and dies?   1685
Show me the fruit which, still unplucked, will rot,
Trees freshly green with every day's renewal!
MEPHISTOPHELES.   Such a commission daunts me not,
I can provide that sort of jewel.
But nonetheless, there comes a time, my friend,   1690
When good things savored at our ease give pleasure.
FAUST.   Should ever I take ease upon a bed of leisure,
May that same moment mark my end!
When first by flattery you lull me
Into a smug complacency,   1695
When with indulgence you can gull me,
Let that day be the last for me!
This is my wager![8]

8. In addition to the traditional pact, Faust offers a wager (lines 1699–706), which Mephistopheles accepts. Compare the earlier wager between Mephistopheles and the Lord in the "Prologue in Heaven" (lines 312–7).

MEPHISTOPHELES.   Done!

FAUST.   And beat for beat!
If the swift moment† I entreat:
Tarry a while! You are so fair!   1700
Then forge the shackles to my feet,
Then I will gladly perish there!
Then let them toll the passing-bell,
Then of your servitude be free,
The clock may stop, its hands fall still,   1705
And time be over then for me!

MEPHISTOPHELES.   Reflect upon this—we shall not forget it.

FAUST.   That is your right, by no means to be waived!
My stake was in no wanton spirit betted.
Once come to rest, I am enslaved—   1710
To you, whomever—why regret it?

MEPHISTOPHELES.   This very evening, at the doctoral feast,
Watch me my servant's duty plying.
Just one more thing—for living or for dying,
I'd like a line or two at least.   1715

FAUST.   Cannot you pedant do without a screed?
Have you not met a man, not found his word his deed?
What, is it not enough my spoken word should force
My days into eternal peonage?
Does not the world rush on with brimming course,   1720
And I am to be prisoned by a pledge?
Yet this conceit is lodged within our breast,
And who would gladly see it leave him?
Who bears good faith in his pure soul is blessed,
No sacrifice will ever grieve him!   1725
A square of parchment, though, all writ and stamped,
Becomes a specter that repels all men.
Still in the pen, the word is cramped,
And wax and leather lord it then.
What, evil spirit, say your rules?   1730
Parchment or paper? Marble? Brass? What tools,
The stylus, chisel, pen? How shall I write it?
You are at liberty to choose.

MEPHISTOPHELES.   How can you with so puny a fuse
Get such hot rhetoric ignited?   1735
Just any slip will do, it's all the same.
You draw a drop of blood and sign your name.

FAUST.   On with the hocus-pocus—I am game,
If this is all you need to be requited.

MEPHISTOPHELES.   Blood is a very special juice.   1740

FAUST.   Oh, never fear my promise might be broken!
My utmost striving's fullest use
Is just the part I have bespoken.
I sought to puff myself too high,
Your rank is all I may attain.   1745

The lofty Spirit spurned me, and I pry
At Nature's bolted doors in vain.[9]
The web of thought is all in slashes,
All knowledge long turned dust and ashes.
Let in the depths of sensual life   1750
The blaze of passions be abated!
May magic shrouds unpenetrated
With every miracle be rife!
Let's hurl ourselves in time's on-rushing tide,
Occurrence's on-rolling stride!   1755
So may then pleasure and distress,
Failure and success,
Follow each other as they please;
Man's active only when he's never at ease.
MEPHISTOPHELES.   No bars or bounds are set for you.   1760
If anywhere you feel like snatching
Chance relish, sweets of passage catching,
May what delights prove wholesome too.
Just help yourself and don't be coy.
FAUST.   You heard me, there can be no thought of joy.   1765
Frenzy I choose, most agonizing lust,
Enamored enmity, restorative disgust.
Henceforth my soul, for knowledge sick no more,
Against no kind of suffering shall be cautioned,
And[1]† what to all of mankind is apportioned   1770
I mean to savor in my own self's core,
Grasp with my mind both highest and most low,
Weigh down my spirit with their weal and woe,
And thus my selfhood to their own distend,
And be, as they are, shattered in the end.   1775
MEPHISTOPHELES.   Oh, take my word, who for millennia past
Has had this rocky fare to chomp,
That from his first breath to his last
No man digests that ancient sourdough lump!
Believe the likes of us: the whole   1780
Is made but for a god's delight!
He dwells in an eternal aureole,
Us he committed to the depth of night,
And you make do with dark and light.
FAUST.   And yet I choose it!
MEPHISTOPHELES.   Worthily decided!   1785
I fear just one thing, for my part:
Short is the time, and long is art.[2]

9. Faust here recalls his meeting with the Earth Spirit in the opening scene. Goethe may have
   intended, in composing this c. 1800–01, to make a transition to the text of the *Fragment* published
   in 1790, which recommences at line 1770.
1. Lines 1770–867 were published in the *Fragment* of 1790. Since line 1770 begins in mid-sentence
   and lines 1770–1 rhyme with the two lines preceding, it may be that some of what immediately
   precedes had already been written before 1790.
2. Adapted from the aphorism of Hippocrates earlier cited by Wagner (lines 558–9).

In this, I trust, you will be guided.
Associate yourself with a poetaster,
And let that sportsman brood and roam   1790
And all the noble virtues cluster
Upon your venerable dome.
The lion's audacity,
The stag's swift surge,
The Italian's fiery urge,   1795
The North's tenacity;
Let him reveal the arcane style
Of joining generosity and guile,
Whereby, youth's ardor freshly fanning,
One falls in love with proper planning.   1800
I should myself be glad to meet him,
"Sir Microcosm" I would greet him.
FAUST.   What am I, if it is past human power
To conquer mankind's loftiest plane,
The crown toward which all senses strain?   1805
MEPHISTOPHELES.   You are, all told—just what you are.
Put wigs on of a million powdered rolls,
Increase your height with ell-high actors' soles,
You still remain just what you are.
FAUST.   In vain all treasures of the human mind,   1810
I feel it, have I raked to me; at length,
When I sit down to marshal them, I find
There wells within no fresh resource of strength;
Not by a hairsbreadth am I grown,
No nearer to the limitless unknown.   1815
MEPHISTOPHELES.   Dear Sir, you look on things as crudely
As men are apt to do; instead,
We must conduct ourselves more shrewdly,
Before the joys of life have fled.
Bah! Hands and feet belong to you,   1820
And head and arse too, if you please,
But what I freely taste and view,
Is that less mine than these?
If I can pay for half-a-dozen horse,
Have I not bought their sixfold thew?   1825
I run and show off with the force
Of four-and-twenty legs, not two.
Cheer up! Throw over all reflection,
And off into the world post-haste!
Take it from me; the slave of introspection   1830
Is like a beast on arid waste
By some foul fiend led round and round,
While, all about, green meadowlands abound.
FAUST.   How do we set about it?
MEPHISTOPHELES.   We set off, that's all.
What is this place, a penitents' hive?   1835

What sort of life is this, to drive
Both self and students up the wall?
Let that be neighbor Potbelly's concern!
Why thresh that straw in the sweat of your brow?
The best you can expect to learn   1840
You cannot tell the youngsters anyhow.
There—I can hear one now outside.
FAUST.   I cannot bring myself to face him.
MEPHISTOPHELES.   The poor boy, he has long been pacing,
He must not go unsatisfied.   1845
Come, let me have your cap and gown;
A priceless mask they should provide
    [*He changes into* FAUST's *garb.*]
No fear, my wits won't let me down!
I only need a quarter-hour's delay;
Meanwhile prepare to start upon our merry way!   1850
    [*Exit* FAUST.]

MEPHISTOPHELES.†   [*in Faust's long robe*]
Go, spurn intelligence and science,
Man's lodestar and supreme reliance,
Be furthered by the liar-in-chief
In works of fraud and make-believe,
And I shall have you dead to rights.   1855
Fate has endowed him with a forward-driving
Impetuousness that reaches past all sights,
And which, precipitately striving,
Would overleap the earth's delights.
Through dissipation I will drag him,   1860
Through shallow insignificance,
I'll have him sticking, writhing, flagging,
And for his parched incontinence
Have food and drink suspended at lip level;
In vain will he be yearning for relief,   1865
And had he not surrendered to the devil,
He still must needs have come to grief!

    [*Enter a* STUDENT.][3]
STUDENT.†   I have been here but a short span,
And come with reverent emotion
To wait upon and know a man   1870
Whom all regard with deep devotion.
MEPHISTOPHELES.   I am much pleased by your polite address!
You see a man like others, more or less.
Have you had time to look about elsewhere?

---

3. The Student scene (to line 2050) derives with some revisions from the *Urfaust* and was published
in its present form in the *Fragment*. Goethe omitted discussion of the Student's living quarters
from the original version and expanded the satirical attack on the university faculties, with lines
1964–2000 added. See Goethe's comment on the Student in the *"Faust* Plan of 1800," below.

STUDENT.   I beg of you, receive me in your care!   1875
   With every good intention I am here,
   In tolerable funds and best of cheer,
   My mother would scarce hear about my going,
   I'd truly like to learn a thing worth knowing.
MEPHISTOPHELES.   You've found the very place, forsooth.   1880
STUDENT.   I feel like pushing on, to tell the truth:
   These vaults, this maze of brick and wall
   Will not agree with me at all.
   It's such a close, constricted place,
   No tree, no green thing—when I face   1885
   These halls, these benches, tier on tier,
   I cannot think or see or hear.
MEPHISTOPHELES.   It all depends on what you're used to.
   Thus many a child has first refused to
   Take nourishment at mother's breast,   1890
   And soon begun to nurse with zest.
   So you will suck the breasts of learning
   With rising appetite and yearning.
STUDENT.   I will hang on with joyful clasp;
   But tell me how to bring them within grasp!   1895
MEPHISTOPHELES.   Tell me, before we come to that,
   What Faculty are you aiming at?
STUDENT.   I want to get a power of learning,
   Fill up with everything concerning
   The earth and heaven you could mention,   1900
   Science and nature, at the source.
MEPHISTOPHELES.   Then you are on the proper course;
   But do not spare your full attention.
STUDENT.   I will go to it with a will;
   Of course, time-off and relaxation   1905
   Might sometimes take my fancy still,
   Like when it's summer and vacation.
MEPHISTOPHELES.   Husband your time, it flies so swiftly past;
   Yet order teaches you to make time last.
   So first, dear friend, you should make room   1910
   For the Collegium Logicum.
   This leaves the mind all trained and dressed,
   In Spanish trusses[4] tightly pressed,
   So that it, slow and undistraught,
   Will potter down the train of thought,   1915
   Not like a will o' the wisp cavort
   Hither and yon, aside, athwart.
   They teach you for a year or so
   That what you did all at one go,
   Like eating and drinking, fancy-free,   1920
   Needs stages one, and two, and three.

---

4. An instrument of torture that was fastened to the victim's legs and screwed on like iron boots.

What though the thought-assembly shop
Is like a master-weaver's job,
Where one tread stirs a thousand points,
The shuttles back and forward fly,   1925
Threads flow too swiftly for the eye,
One downbeat strikes a thousand joints:
Enter: Philosopher, and lo!
He proves to you it must be so;
The first being thus, the second thus,   1930
The third and fourth must needs be thus,
And were it not for one and two,
The three and four could not be true.
His pupils laud him, busy as beavers,
And somehow never turn into weavers.   1935
Who would know and describe a living thing,
Seeks first to expel the spirit within,
Then he stands there, the parts held in his grasp,
Lost just the spiritual bond, alas!
Encheiresin naturae,[5] chemistry declares,   1940
Mocking itself all unawares.
STUDENT.   I don't quite follow you, I fear.
MEPHISTOPHELES.   It soon will grow more nearly clear,
When you learn how to analyze,
And properly categorize.   1945
STUDENT.   All this leaves me as limp and dull
As it millstones were grinding in my skull.
MEPHISTOPHELES.   Next, Metaphysics I should mention
As the foremost study for your attention!
There make your deepest insight strain   1950
For things out of scale with the human brain;
For whatever fits into it and what doesn't
Some wondrous word is always present.
This first semester, though, have patience,
Minutely observe the regulations,   1955
Five lecture hours is your daily spell,
Be there at the very stroke of the bell,
Having prepared yourself well before,
Cramming *paragraphos,* what's more,
To make quite sure with no further look   1960
The man says nothing that's not in the book.[6]
Yet by all means take it down in writing,
As though it were the Holy Ghost reciting.
STUDENT.   You shall not have to tell me twice!
I sense that it is good advice.   1965

5. This phrase, a mixture of Greek and Latin meaning "handholds of nature," derives from a book
by a professor of chemistry at the University of Strassburg whom Goethe heard lecture when he
was a student there (J. R. Spielmann, *Institutiones chemiae,* 1763).
6. Mephistopheles refers to the practice at German universities in the eighteenth century of lecturing
from a textbook, where the subject matter was defined by numbered paragraphs (*paragraphos,* a
Greek term) to be studied ahead of time by the students.

What one has black on white recorded
May safely be borne home and hoarded.
MEPHISTOPHELES.   Select a Faculty, however.
STUDENT.   For Jurisprudence I feel no special bent.
MEPHISTOPHELES.   I scarcely blame you for the sentiment.   1970
I know about the state of this endeavor,
We drag prerogatives and laws
From place to place by slow degrees,
Age handing age ancestral flaws
Like an inherited disease.   1975
Sense turns to nonsense, boon to plague,
Woe to the grandson that you are!
Our human birthright prior to the bar,
On that, alas! the gentlemen are vague.
STUDENT.   You make my own revulsion rise.   1980
Lucky the man whom you advise!
Theology looks more like my profession.
MEPHISTOPHELES.   I would not give the wrong impression
As it concerns this discipline.
It's all too easy to get sidetracked in,   1985
So much of poison lies concealed within
That's scarce distinguishable from the medicine.
Here too the risk is least when just one voice is heard;
Swear only by the master's word.
In sum—have words to lean upon,   1990
And through that trusty gateway, lexicon,
You pass into the shrine of certainty.[7]
STUDENT.   Yet with each word there must a concept be.
MEPHISTOPHELES.   Oh, quite—no need, though, to be racking
One's brain, for just where concept's lacking   1995
A word in time supplies the remedy.
Words are good things to be debated,
With words are systems generated,
In words belief is safely vested,
From words no jot or tittle can be wrested.†   2000
STUDENT.   I dare not waste your time with many questions,
But there is one more discipline;
I wonder if concerning Medicine
You might not have some down-to-earth suggestions?
Three years are very quickly past,   2005
And Lord! the field is far too vast.[8]
With just a hint on what is right or wrong
It's easier to feel one's way along.
MEPHISTOPHELES.   [aside] I've had enough of the didactic vein,

---

7. Preference for the word over the sense or spirit agrees with Wagner's trust of rhetoric (lines 546–
7) and opposes Faust's rejection of "Word" as a translation of *Logos* (lines 1224–37).
8. An unintentional allusion by the Student to the aphorism of Hippocrates earlier cited by Wagner
(lines 558–9) and Mephistopheles (line 1787).

I must go back and play the Deuce again.   2010
[*aloud*] The gist of Medicine is grasped with ease.
You study up on macro-, microcosm, just so
That in the end you let things go
As God may please.
It's vain to roam afield the scientific way,   2015
For everyone learns only what he can;
He who will seize the moment when he may,
He is the proper man.
You're fairly well-built, to my mind,
I'd say there is some spunk in you;   2020
If you just trust yourself, you'll find
The other folk will trust you too.
Especially the women learn to guide;
Their everlasting ahs and ohs,
Their myriad woes,   2025
Can all be cured at one divide.
If you adopt a halfway decent air,
You'll lure them all into your lair.
First win their trust, by some well-chosen title,
That your art puts all other arts to shame;   2030
Then for a start you grope for portions vital
That cost another many a year's campaign;
You squeeze her pulse a little harder,
Then lay with cunning looks of ardor
Your arm about the slender waist   2035
To see how tightly she is laced.
STUDENT.
Now that sounds better! Much less guesswork or surmising.
MEPHISTOPHELES.   Gray, dear young fellow, is all theorizing,
And green, life's golden tree.
STUDENT.   I swear, this all seems like a dream to me.   2040
Might I another time entreat your leisure
To draw more fully on your deep sagacity?
MEPHISTOPHELES.   What I can do I'll do with pleasure.
STUDENT.   I find I cannot bear to see
My way to go until I have bespoken   2045
Into my album of your grace some token[9]
MEPHISTOPHELES.   Oh yes, indeed.
    [*He writes, and returns the book.*]
STUDENT.   [*reads*] Eritis sicut Deus, scientes bonum et malum.[1]
    [*Closes the album reverently and takes his leave.*]

---

9. University students in Goethe's time often collected signatures in an album from friends and teachers, with words or verses of advice.
1. "You will be like God, knowing good and evil" (Genesis 3.5), the words with which the serpent tempts Eve to eat the forbidden fruit.

MEPHISTOPHELES.
Go on, heed the old saying, and my cousin, the Snake;
There'll come a time your godlike state will make you quake!   2050

[*Enter* FAUST.]
FAUST.   Where are we off to now?
MEPHISTOPHELES.   Wherever you choose.
The small world, then the great we shall peruse.
Ah, with what profit, with what glee
You'll take this seminar for free!
FAUST.   My long gray beard, though, spoils my chance,   2055
It cramps the proper nonchalance.
This venture won't be a success;
I never had a vein for worldliness.
In company I feel so small;
I'll never be at ease at all.   2060
MEPHISTOPHELES.
Acquiring confidence, good friend, the more you try,
You'll get the hang of living by and by.
FAUST.   But tell me, how are we to ride?
Where are your groom and coach and horses?
MEPHISTOPHELES.   We simply spread my mantle wide,   2065
It shall convey us on our airy courses.
Embarking on this daring flight,
You will do best to travel light.
Some fiery air which I shall fashion here
Will buoy us up from earth quick as you please.   2070
Light as we'll be, we should soar up with ease.
Congratulations on your new career!

Auerbach's Tavern in Leipzig†

JOLLY FELLOWS *carousing.*

FROSCH.   Nobody drinking? No guffaws, grimaces?
I'll teach you not to make long faces!
Like crackers you used to fizz and pop,   2075
And now you're gay as a sodden mop.
BRANDER.   It's all your fault; you brought no pig in your poke,
No bit of nonsense, not a dirty joke.
FROSCH.   [*pours a glass of wine over his head*]
There's both in one!
BRANDER.   You double pig! Nitwit!
FROSCH.   That's what you wanted, wasn't it?   2080
SIEBEL.   Who starts a quarrel here, goes out!
A rollicking round-song, come now, swill and shout!
Hey! Holler! Ho!
ALTMAYER.   That does for me, my God!
Bring cotton, or he'll burst my ears, the sod.
SIEBEL.   When hall and vault reverberate,   2085
That's when you feel the bass's might and weight.
FROSCH.   That's right, out with the boob that takes offense!
A, tralala, trala!
ALTMAYER.   A, tralala, trala!
FROSCH.   Our throats are tuned, I sense.
   [*Sings.*]
                   Oh Holy Roman Empire dear,   2090
                   What holds you still together?[1]
BRANDER.   A nasty song! Phew! a political song,
A wretched song. Praise God for each day's bliss
That the old Empire's not your business!
For I at least account it ample profit   2095
That I'm not emperor or chancellor of it.
Still, we shan't lack a chief, I hope:
Let us elect a tippling pope.
You know what qualities avail
To mark the man and turn the scale.   2100
FROSCH.   [*sings*]
                   Miss Nightingale, o soar above,
                   Take ten thousand greetings to my love.
SIEBEL.   No love to females! I'll have none of this!
FROSCH.   Don't interfere—I still say love and a kiss!
   [*Sings.*]
                   Unbolt the door, in dark of night;   2105
                   Unbolt the door, the lover cries;

1. The political satire of Frosch's song reflects an eighteenth-century attitude toward the Empire, at
that time little more than a medieval remnant.

Bolt up the door, at dawn's first light.
SIEBEL.   Oh yes, go on and yodel, praise her to the skies![2]
I'll have the last laugh, time will tell.
She's pulled my leg, and she'll pull yours as well.   2110
She'd haunt the crossroads if she had her merit,
To bill and coo there with some evil spirit;
A rank old buck, from Hallowe'en returning,
Should bleat goodnights to her with tender yearning,
A regular lad of flesh and blood   2115
Is thrown away upon that slut.
For compliments that really mattered
I'd like to see her windows shattered!
BRANDER.   [*slamming his fist on the table*]
Look here! Attention! Listen, you!
Confess, I know a thing or two;   2120
I see some swains among us sitting,
To them I offer, as is fitting,
A piece that should be right on cue.
Attend! A song in latest vein!
Chime in with vigorous refrain!   2125

[*He sings.*]
In a cellar nest there lived a rat,
Had butter and lard to suit her,
She wore a belly-bag of fat,
A pouch like Dr. Luther.[3]
The cook had poison scattered out;   2130
That drove her hither and about,
As if the love-bug bit her.
CHORUS.   [*cheering*]
As if the love-bug bit her.

BRANDER.   She hurried, scurried, pawed and clawed,
And swilled from every puddle,   2135
The house was all scratched up and gnawed,
To soothe her frantic muddle;
Tried many a leap in fear and pain,
But all she tried was tried in vain,
As if the love-bug bit her.   2140
CHORUS.   As if the love-bug bit her.

BRANDER.   In fright she sought the light of day,
Came running in the kitchen,
Fell at the stove and there she lay,
With piteous gasp and twitching.   2145

2. Frosch has stolen a girl away from Siebel, and from spite the latter abuses her as a witch haunting
a crossroads or joining in the "Hallowe'en" orgies of the Walpurgis Night.
3. Martin Luther, a contemporary of the historical Faustus, visited Leipzig in 1525, the year following
the supposed visit by the magus.

The poisoner only laughed, she knew
She'd bit off more than she could chew,
As if the love-bug bit her.
CHORUS.   As if the love-bug bit her.

SIEBEL.   Guffaws! That shows these dolts' horizon!   2150
A worthy pastime, it would seem,
To prey on helpless rats with poison!
BRANDER.   They must stand high in your esteem?
ALTMAYER.   That greasepot with his shining pate!
He takes the ballad much to heart;   2155
He honors in the swollen rat
His natural kin and counterpart.

[*Enter* FAUST *and* MEPHISTOPHELES.]
MEPHISTOPHELES.   My foremost duty is, you see,
To show you merry company,
How one may idle best and worry least;   2160
The people here make every day a feast.
With comfort ample, humor stale,
Each spins in his constricted round,
Like kittens chasing their own tail.
Provided that their heads are sound,   2165
And while the landlord's credit holds,
They are right merry and carefree souls.
BRANDER.   I bet these two have come wayfaring,
You look at their outlandish bearing;
They haven't been an hour in town.   2170
FROSCH.   I think you're right! That's Leipzig's new renown!
A lesser Paris, and it polishes its people.[4]
SIEBEL.   Who are these strangers, would you guess?
FROSCH.   Let us accost them—over a toast, forsooth,
I'll pull their secret like a baby tooth;   2175
Trust me to pump them with finesse
They seem to be of notable descent,
They both look arrogant and ill-content.
BRANDER.   They're quacks, I bet, that on the market holler.
ALTMAYER.   Perhaps.
FROSCH.   I'll squeeze 'em—watch them twist!   2180
MEPHISTOPHELES.   [*to* FAUST] They never recognize the devil's fist
Though he may have them by the collar!
FAUST.   Our greetings, gentlemen!
SIEBEL.   Our thanks for quit-salute.
[*under his breath, looking sideways at* MEPHISTOPHELES]
I say, the fellow limps upon one foot![5]

4. In the eighteenth century, Leipzig prided itself on being "a lesser Paris," Paris being regarded as the center of European taste and culture.
5. A reference to the devil's traditional cloven hoof, also attributed to Mephistopheles in lines 2490, 4065, and 6335–9.

MEPHISTOPHELES.   May we sit down here and in lieu   2185
Of decent drink one cannot find,
Enjoy good company with you?
ALTMAYER.   You seem a most fastidious kind.
FROSCH.   You must have left your Cattlebury late—
Did you have supper with Sir Bumpkin first?[6]   2190
MEPHISTOPHELES.   This trip, we bypassed his estate;
We saw him last time, though; he was immersed
In memories of many a country cousin,
And charged us greetings by the dozen.
[*He bows in* FROSCH'S *direction.*]
ALTMAYER.   [*under his breath*] My word! No flies on him!
SIEBEL   He got you, mate!   2195
FROSCH.   I'll have him squirming yet, you wait!
MEPHISTOPHELES.   Just now, did we not hear the sound
Of voices trained in part-song pealing?
For sure, good singing must resound
Right smartly from this vaulted ceiling!   2200
FROSCH.   Why—might you be a professional?
MEPHISTOPHELES.
Oh no! My talent's small, though there is much good will.
ALTMAYER.   Give us a song!
MEPHISTOPHELES.   As many as you choose.
SIEBEL.   But only of most recent date!
MEPHISTOPHELES.   We're back from sunny Spain of late,   2205
The land of wine and of the tuneful Muse.
[*Sings.*]
There ruled a king among us,
Who had a mighty big flea—[7]
FROSCH.   Hark! Had a flea! A flea, you catch the jest?
A flea must be a savory guest.   2210
MEPHISTOPHELES.   [*sings*]
There ruled a king among us,
Who had a mighty big flea,
He paid him princely honors,
So fond of him was he.
He called his tailor mincing,   2215
Who bowed and scraped and rose:
A doublet for the princeling,
Here, measure him for hose!
BRANDER.   Be sure now to impress upon the tailor
To ply the tape with bated breath,   2220
So that no wrinkle shows, for failure
Will bring about his instant death!

6. A local joke in Leipzig concerning a village named Rippach ("Cattlebury"), where a certain Hans
Arse resided.
7. The source of the song of the flea, a satire against court dandies, is thought to be a fable, "The
Rooster and the Eagle," by C. F. D. Schubart (1739–91), first published in 1774. Thus Goethe
would have written the final version of this scene in the *Urfaust* after that time.

MEPHISTOPHELES. In silk with velvet lining
He now was dressed,
Wore atlas sashes shining,   2225
A ribbon and a crest,
At once he was a minister
And had a glittering star;
His kin at court, oh sinister,
Advanced almost as far.   2230

The lords and maids-in-waiting
At court were sorely plagued,
And titled fleas were baiting
The Queen and her chambermaid.
Nor could they like us others,   2235
Rub, itch and scratch what ails,
We pinch and crunch what bothers
With pouncing fingernails.

CHORUS. [*cheering*]
We pinch and crunch what bothers
With pouncing fingernails.   2240

FROSCH. Bravo! Bravo! That was good fun!
SIEBEL. Thus shall to every flea be done!
BRANDER. Stalk 'em, snip 'em with fingertips fine!
ALTMAYER. And long live freedom! Long live wine!
MEPHISTOPHELES.
I'd gladly raise my glass to freedom, let it clink,   2245
If just your wines were halfway fit to drink.
SIEBEL. You've said this once too much, I think.
MEPHISTOPHELES. I only fear the landlord might protest,
Or I'd provide each honored guest
From my own cellar a fine drop.[8]   2250
SIEBEL. I'll square the landlord—let it pop!
FROSCH. Bring us good drink, you'll hear our praise ring out.
But see you make the portions ample,
For if I am to judge a sample,
I do it on a well-filled snout.   2255
ALTMAYER. [*under his breath*]
They're from the Rhineland, doubt it not.
MEPHISTOPHELES. Find me a drill!
BRANDER.   What for? Why do you ask it?
You have your barrels just outdoors, or what?
ALTMAYER. Back there, the landlord keeps some tools in a basket.
MEPHISTOPHELES. [*takes the drill; to* FROSCH]
Now say what wine you wish from me.   2260
FROSCH. How do you mean? You've many a vintage then?

---

8. The wine trick, part of the popular Faust legend, derives from the original chapbook of 1587 (chapter 55).

MEPHISTOPHELES.   To each his chosen specimen.
ALTMAYER.   [to FROSCH]
   Aha! One here already licks his chops, I see.
FROSCH.
   Good! If I am to choose, I choose the Rhine wine's flower.
   One's native land bestows the finest dower.   2265
MEPHISTOPHELES.
   [drilling a hole in the table's edge at FROSCH'S place]
   Find us some wax to make the stoppers from!
ALTMAYER.   Oh, these are parlor tricks, come on!
MEPHISTOPHELES.   [to BRANDER] And you?
BRANDER.   I want to drink champagne,
   And it should foam with might and main!
       [MEPHISTOPHELES drills; someone has by now made the wax stoppers
       and does the plugging.]
BRANDER.   One can't become one country's henchman,   2270
   Much good hails from a distant spot;
   Your proper German can't abide a Frenchman,
   But likes French vintages a lot.
SIEBEL.   [while MEPHISTOPHELES is approaching his place]
   I own I do not like the sour stuff,
   Tap me the true, the honeyed juice!   2275
MEPHISTOPHELES.   [drilling]
   You'll have Tokay[9] to sample soon enough.
ALTMAYER.   Oh come, own up, Sirs, what's the use?
   I know full well you lead us up the garden.
MEPHISTOPHELES.   With guests of rank, I beg your pardon,
   I would be bold indeed to try.   2280
   Quick, place your order, don't be shy!
   What kind of vintage may I serve you?
ALTMAYER.   Stop asking—anything will satisfy.
       [when the holes have all been drilled and plugged]
MEPHISTOPHELES.   [with weird gestures][1]
                   Grapes on the vinestock,
                   Horns on the goat-buck;   2285
                   Juice is the wine, wood is the vine,
                   A wooden table can flow with wine.
                   A singular gaze up Nature's sleeve—
                   Here is a miracle—believe!
   Now draw the plug, hold out your cup!   2290
ALL.   [as they draw the stoppers and each has the chosen wine run
       into his glass]
   Oh joyous fountain bubbling up!
MEPHISTOPHELES.   Be careful, though, let no on one spill a drop!
   [They drink repeatedly.]

---

9. A sweet wine from Hungary, grown near the town for which it is named.
1. The following incantation begins with lines from a children's rhyme and degenerates into
nonsense.

ALL. [*singing*]   Carouse like aborigines,
    Five hundred wallowing swine!
MEPHISTOPHELES. Free men, you see, at play in nature's state!   2295
FAUST. I'd like to quit their playing-field.
MEPHISTOPHELES. You wait a while—their bestial estate
    Will soon be splendidly revealed.
SIEBEL. [*drinks carelessly, spilling some wine on the floor, where it
    turns to flame*]
    Help! Hell's a fire! Help, a curse!
MEPHISTOPHELES. [*adjuring the flame*]
    Down, friendly element, be quiet   2300
    [*to the fellow*] A purgatory drop—as yet no worse.
SIEBEL. Next time think twice before you try it,
    Or else get measured for a hearse!
FROSCH. You do not know us yet, I fear!
ALTMAYER. I think we ought to lead him gently hence.   2305
SIEBEL. I say, Sir! Damn your impudence,
    To work your hocus-pocus here!
MEPHISTOPHELES. Dry up, old wine tub!
SIEBEL.   Broomstick you!
    What next? He would insult us, too!
BRANDER. Just wait, we'll tan your hide for you!   2310
ALTMAYER. [*draws a plug from the table; fire leaps out at him*]
    I'm burning!
SIEBEL.   Sorcery, I vow!
    Stab home, the cad's an outlaw now!
    [*They draw their knives and lunge at* MEPHISTOPHELES.]
MEPHISTOPHELES. [*with a solemn gesture*]
    Double-face, pretense,
    Alter place and sense!
    Be here and hence![2]   2315
    [*They stand in amazement, looking at each other.*]
ALTMAYER. Where am I? What a lovely land!
FROSCH. They're vineyards, are they not?
SIEBEL.   And grapes, right close at hand!
BRANDER. In this green arbor, what a cluster
    Of swelling grapes! What size! What luster!
    [*He seizes* SIEBEL *by the nose; the others do the same in pairs and
    raise their knives.*]
MEPHISTOPHELES. [*as above*]
    Now mark the devil's pranking! Error,   2320
    Release their vision from thy throes!
    [*He vanishes with* FAUST; *the fellows leap apart.*]
SIEBEL. What happened?
ALTMAYER.   How?

---

2. The hypnotizing of the four drunkards, so that they imagine themselves transported to a beautiful
vineyard, is derived from the popular Faust legend (in the historical account by Philipp Came-
rarius, 1591).

FROSCH.   Was that your nose?
BRANDER.   [*to* SIEBEL] And I am clutching yours!
ALTMAYER.   Oh terror!
  I felt a shock go through me like a dagger!
  Get me a chair, someone, I stagger!   2325
FROSCH.   No, fellows, say, what was all this?
SIEBEL.   One sniff of where the bastard's hiding,
  And he won't leave here in one piece!
ALTMAYER.   He's gone, I saw him, he was riding
  Outdoor upon a keg . . . I couldn't miss . . .   2330
  I've leaden weights in legs and toes.
  [*turning toward the table*]
  My! Is the wine still running, you suppose?
SIEBEL.   It was all lies and fraud, a juggler's game.
FROSCH.   I tasted wine, I tell you, all the same.
BRANDER.   What of those grapes, those sights that stunned us?   2335
ALTMAYER.   And then they tell you, don't believe in wonders!

Witch's Kitchen†

*On a low stove a large caldron stands over the fire. In the steam rising up
from it appear various figures. A* FEMALE MARMOSET *is sitting by the caldron,
skimming it and keeping it from running over. The* MARMOSET TOM *with
the young ones are sitting nearby, warming themselves.*[1] *Walls and ceiling
are decorated with the quaintest witches' furnishings.*

FAUST, MEPHISTOPHELES.

FAUST.   I find this magic-mongery abhorrent;
  And I am to be cured, you warrant,
  In this hotchpotch of lunacy?
  Do I seek counsel from some skirted quack?   2340
  Will this absurd swill-cookery
  Charm thirty winters off my back?
  If that's your best, then woe is me!
  My hopes already seem confounded.
  Might there not be some balm, some remedy   2345
  By nature or a noble mind compounded?
MEPHISTOPHELES.   The know-it-all, as always! Look—
  True, nature's way to youth is apter;
  However, that comes in a different book,
  And it's a curious chapter.   2350
FAUST.   I want to know it.
MEPHISTOPHELES.   Very well; it comes your way
  Without physician, gold, or magic-rigging:
  Go out into the fields, today,
  Fall to a hoeing, digging,
  Contain yourself, your mind and mood,   2355
  Within the narrowest of spheres,
  Subsist on uncommingled food,
  Live as a beast with beasts and spurn not chores unsung,
  In person spread your crop-fields with manure;
  This is the best resource, you may be sure,   2360
  Through eighty years to stay forever young!
FAUST.   I am not used to that, it goes against my marrow
  To put my hand to hoe or harrow.
  A narrow life would suit me not at all.
MEPHISTOPHELES.   So back to witching after all.   2365
FAUST.[2]   What need have we of that old bat?
  Why cannot you yourself concoct it?
MEPHISTOPHELES.   I can just see myself at that!

---

1. The Marmosets were apparently a gift to the Witch by Mephistopheles, and their main duty is to
  tend the brew cooking in the Witch's cauldron.
2. Lines 2366–77 were added to the text of Part One (1808) to explain why Mephistopheles could
  not himself transform Faust into a young man.

A thousand bridges I could have constructed
Meanwhile; not merely craft and art,   2370
Patience is needed for the part.
This takes a quiet sprite a year or longer;
It's time that makes the subtle ferment stronger.
And what all goes into the brew!
A power of wondrous things, you take it   2375
From me; the Devil taught it, true,
And yet the Devil cannot make it.
[*catching sight of the animals*] Look—is it not a graceful clan?
This is the maid! That is the serving man!
[*to the animals*] It seems the lady's not about?   2380
ANIMALS.   Gone out,
              To gad about,
              Up the chimney spout!
MEPHISTOPHELES.   Does she stay out long when she gads?
ANIMALS.   Long as it takes to warm our pads.   2385
MEPHISTOPHELES.   The dainty darlings—aren't they striking?
FAUST.   In quite the worst of taste, I find.
MEPHISTOPHELES.   Why, chat like this is just the kind
That is most truly to my liking!
[*to the animals*] Tell me, confounded puppet troupe,   2390
What do you stir that porridge for?
ANIMALS.   We're cooking a broad beggar's soup.
MEPHISTOPHELES.   You'll have a crowd to forage for.
MARMOSET TOM.   [*sidles up and fawns on* MEPHISTOPHELES]
                  Come sir, be nice
                  And throw the dice,   2395
                  Things have been vile, sir,
                  Win me a pile, sir,
                  And rich in pence
                  Is rich in sense.
MEPHISTOPHELES.   How happy would the monkey be   2400
Could he, too, play the lottery![3]
[*Meanwhile, the* YOUNG MARMOSETS *have been playing with a large
sphere, which they now roll forward.*]
MARMOSET TOM.   The world's a ball,
                  Will rise and fall,
                  Roll far and wide;
                  Like glass its tune,   2405
                  Can break as soon!
                  It's hollow inside.
                  Here it gleams fair,
                  More brightly there,
                  I am alive!   2410
                  Son, use your wit,

---

3. The lottery, popular in the eighteenth century (especially in Italy), would provide even a monkey
with the means of getting rich.

                    Stay clear of it,
                    Death's in the matter,
                    It's clay from the pit,
                    It may shatter.   2415
MEPHISTOPHELES.   Why the sieve?
MARMOSET TOM.   [taking it down]
                    Were you a thief,
                    I'd know it and proclaim[4]
        [He runs to the female and has her look through it.]
                    Look through the sieve,
                    You see the thief,   2420
                    Yet may not tell his name?
MEPHISTOPHELES.   [approaching the fire]
                    And this pot?
BOTH MARMOSETS.   The silly sot!
                    Knows not the pot,
                    Knows not the kettle!   2425
MEPHISTOPHELES.   Ill-mannered clod!
MARMOSET TOM.   Here, take this rod
                    And sit in the settle![5]
        [He makes MEPHISTOPHELES sit down.]

FAUST.   [who during this time has stood before a mirror, now
         approaching it, now standing off]
    What do I see? A form from heaven above
    Appears to me within this magic mirror[6]   2430
    Lend me the swiftest of your wings, o love,
    And lead me nearer to her, nearer!
    Alas! but when I fail to keep my distance,
    And venture closer up to gaze,
    I see her image dimmed as through a haze!   2435
    The loveliest woman in existence!
    Can earthly beauty so amaze?
    What lies there in recumbent grace and glistens
    Must be quintessence of all heaven's rays!
    Or could its like on earth be found?   2440
MEPHISTOPHELES.
    You know, a god can't strain six days, my friend,
    And vote himself a bravo at the end,
    Unless the job was pretty sound.
    This once, keep gazing at your leisure;
    I may just sniff you out a peach like this,   2445
    And lucky he whom fate allots the pleasure
    To lodge her at his hearth in wedded bliss.

4. According to popular superstition, a thief could be recognized if observed through a sieve.
5. Mephistopheles now presides over the scene, holding the feather duster as a scepter and seated
   upon the settle as a throne, a Lord of Misrule.
6. The magic mirror is presumably there from the start. What causes the image of the Feminine
   (presumably resembling Italian Renaissance paintings of the nude Venus) to appear is not stated.

[FAUST *keeps looking into the mirror.* MEPHISTOPHELES, *lounging in the armchair and playing with the feather duster, goes on speaking.*]
Here is my scepter, this my royal seat,
Now for a crown, and I'll be all complete.
ANIMALS. [*who up to now have been going through various weird movements and evolutions, bring* MEPHISTOPHELES *a crown, with much shouting*]
            Please be so good   2450
            With sweat and blood
            The crown to glue!
[*They handle the crown clumsily and break it into two pieces, with which they scamper about.*]
            There, that's done it!
            We rhyme and pun it,
            We hark and view;   2455
FAUST. [*facing the mirror*] Alas! My mind becomes disjoint.
MEPHISTOPHELES. [*pointing at the animals*]
By now this fairly has my own head spinning.
ANIMALS.   If haply point
            Is joined to point
            With luck it's meaning!   2460

FAUST. [*as above*] A blaze is kindled in my bosom!
Let us escape from here and flee!

MEPHISTOPHELES. [*in previous posture*]
At least we've seen in microcosm
The workings of true poesy.

[*The caldron, neglected by the* FEMALE MARMOSET *in the interim, starts running over; a great flame arises and flares up the chimney. The* WITCH *comes down through the flames with horrendous screaming.*]
WITCH.   Ouch! Ow! Ow! Ouch!   2465
Infernal sow! Confounded slouch!
Forget the kettle and singe my pouch!
A curse on you!
[*catching sight of* FAUST *and* MEPHISTOPHELES]
            And who is new?
            Who are you two?   2470
            Strangers rude?
            Come to intrude?
            A fiery splash
            At you trash!
[*She plunges the skimming ladle into the caldron and splashes flames at* FAUST, MEPHISTOPHELES, *and the* ANIMALS. *The* ANIMALS *whimper.*]
MEPHISTOPHELES. [*turning around the duster in his hand and striking at the pots and glassware with it*]

In two! In two!   2475
There goes the stew!
There goes the glass!
Just fun, my lass,
To your tune, foul shrew,
A gay tattoo.   2480
[*while the witch recoils in wrath and terror*]
You recognize me? Bag of bones! Vile trash!
You know me now, your lord and master?
What odds I lay about and smash
Hellcat and cattery with joint disaster?
When did the scarlet doublet fall from grace?   2485
Is the cock-feather hard to recognize?
Did I perhaps conceal my face?
You need my name to know my guise?
WITCH.   My rudeness, Sir, deserves reproof!
I missed, for one, the cloven hoof,   2490
And your two ravens, for another![7]
MEPHISTOPHELES.   For this time I will let you off:
It's been some little time now, true enough,
Since last we ran into each other.
Civilization, glossing all we knew,   2495
Has rubbed off on the Devil, too.
That Nordic spook has nowadays been banished;
Those talons, horns, and tail—all vanished!
As for the foot I cannot be without,
It would impair my social chances;   2500
So for some years now I have eked it out,
Like many young men, with false appurtenances.[8]
WITCH.   [*dancing*] My senses reel with joy and fear
To see young Esquire Satan here!
MEPHISTOPHELES.   That name's forbidden, hag, you hear? 2505
WITCH.   Why of a sudden is it bad?
MEPHISTOPHELES.
It's been consigned to storybooks for youngsters;
Mind you, men are no better off for that.
The Fiend is gone, the fiends are still amongst us.
Call me Sir Knight, the rest we can forgo;   2510
I am a gentleman like other gentry.
My noble blood is not in doubt, I know;
Look, here's the coat of arms that gives me entry!
[*He makes an indecent gesture.[9]*]

---

7. The cloven hoof (see line 2184) and the ravens (thought to derive from the companions of the pagan war god Wotan; see lines 10664 ff.) are traditional attributes of the devil.
8. An allusion to the eighteenth-century practice among men of padding their stockings to make their calves appear more muscular.
9. Goethe later instructed an actor to represent this "indecent gesture" by turning his back on the audience, raising one leg, and slapping his thigh.

WITCH. [*laughing immoderately*]
    Ha, ha! That's in your former vogue!
    You are as you have ever been, a rogue.   2515
MEPHISTOPHELES. [*to* FAUST]
    Friend, mark it well for your own sake:
    With witches that's the tone to take.
WITCH. Now tell me, Sirs, what brought you here.
MEPHISTOPHELES. A good glass of the well-known elixir,
    But I would have the oldest vintage;   2520
    It's strength increases year by year.
WITCH. A pleasure! Here's a flagon from my shelf
    From which I like to steal a nip myself;
    What's more, it has completely lost its stink;
    I'll let you have a sample of its power.   2525
    [*drops her voice*] But if this man, unprimed, should take a drink,
    You know it well, he won't live out the hour.
MEPHISTOPHELES.
    He's a good friend of mine, he'll come out whole;
    He's welcome to the finest of your kitchen.
    Now draw your circle, do your witching.   2530
    And let him have a bowl.
        [*The* WITCH *with strange gestures draws a circle and places peculiar
        objects in it; meanwhile the glassware begins to ring, the caldrons to
        drone, making music. Finally she brings a great tome and within
        the circle arranges the* MARMOSETS, *who must serve her for a pulpit
        and hold the torch. She beckons* FAUST *to join her.*]
FAUST. [*to* MEPHISTOPHELES] No, tell me what is here intended?
    This mummery, this gesturing demented,
    I've seen preposterous low-grade mime
    Enough to gag on in my time.   2535
MEPHISTOPHELES. Oh, stuff! You don't know what a joke is.
    Come, don't be such a solemn stick!
    She must work up some doctor's hocus-pocus
    Or else the juice might make you sick.
        [*He makes* FAUST *step into the circle.*]
WITCH. [*beginning to recite from the book with great emphasis*]

                Now mind me, son,   2540
                Make ten of one,
                With two have done,
                Make even three,
                And rich you'll be.
                Let four go free!   2545
                The five and six
                Contrive and hex
                To seven and eight,
                That does the trick;
                And nine is one,   2550

And ten is none,
And there's your witch arithmetic[1]

FAUST. I think the crone speaks in a fever fit.
MEPHISTOPHELES. You haven't heard the half of it;
I know the tenor of that kind of fiction,   2555
I've lost much time exploring it for rules;
You see, a perfect contradiction
Is equally occult to sages as to fools.
My friend, this art is new and old.
It has at all times been the custom   2560
By Three in One and One threefold[2]
To propagate not truth but fustian.
That's how they teach and prattle undisturbed;
Who wants to argue color with the blinded?
For people by and large, just given a word,   2565
Believe there needs must be some sense behind it.
WITCH. [continuing]
                    The potent core
                    Of nature lore
                    From all that seek it shrinking!
                    Who's never thought   2570
                    Finds it unsought,
                    Possesses it unthinking.

FAUST. What babble does she mouth before us?
I am about to lose my mind.
She sounds to me just like a chorus   2575
Of hundred thousand fools combined.
MEPHISTOPHELES. Enough, oh excellent sybil, say no more,
Bring up your elixir and quickly pour
The bowl brimful, he'll drain it to the lees;
My friend here will withstand it well enough: 2580
He is a man of multiple degrees,
Who's downed some strong libations in his puff.
      [With much ceremony, the WITCH pours the potion into a bowl; as
      FAUST raises it to his lips, a faint flame forms.]
MEPHISTOPHELES. Well, down with it, and no excuse!
Soon you will have your heart's desire.
As thick as you are with the deuce,   2585
Why fuss about a lick of fire?
      [The WITCH dissolves the circle. FAUST steps forth.]
MEPHISTOPHELES. Out, with a will! No time to lose.
WITCH. I hope my draught will soothe your vitals!

---

1. All speculation concerning the possible significance of this number sequence, despite ingenious
   attempts by many scholars, seems fruitless.
2. An allusion to the Christian doctrine of the Trinity.

MEPHISTOPHELES.   As for a favor in return, just choose,
And on Walpurgis night we'll have requitals.[3]   2590
WITCH.   Here is a song to sing, and when you do,
You will perceive an added virtue.[4]
MEPHISTOPHELES.   Quick, for a walk now, let me urge you,
You must work up a sweat to purge you,
So that the power may permeate through and through.   2595
Later I'll teach you noble sloth's employment,
And soon you'll feel with exquisite enjoyment
Young Cupid[5] stir and skip about in you.
FAUST.   Just one more glance before into that mirror!
That beauty was so fair, so fresh!   2600
MEPHISTOPHELES.   No, no! That paragon of women, sirrah,
Shall soon confront you in the flesh.
[aside] No fear—with this behind your shirt
You'll soon see Helen of Troy in every skirt!†

3. At the witches' Sabbath on Walpurgis Night (see the later scene of that title) the devil was supposed
to render his thanks to the witches who had served him.
4. The Witch gives Faust a lewd song printed on a broadsheet, intended to arouse his sexual desires.
5. The god of love, here associated by Mephistopheles with sexual desire.

Street

FAUST. MARGARETE *walking past.*[1]†

FAUST.   My fair young lady, may I make free   2605
To offer you my arm and company?
MARGARETE.   I'm neither fair nor lady, pray,
Can unescorted find my way.
  [*She frees herself and exits.*]
FAUST.   God, what a lovely child! I swear
I've never seen the like of her.   2610
She is so dutiful and pure,
Yet not without a pert allure.
Her rosy lip, her cheek aglow
I never shall forget, I know!
Her glance's timid downward dart   2615
Is graven deeply in my heart!
But how she was so short with me—
That was consummate ecstasy!
  [MEPHISTOPHELES *enters.*]
FAUST.   Here, get me that young wench—for certain!
MEPHISTOPHELES.   Which one?
FAUST.   The one that just walked past.   2620
MEPHISTOPHELES.   Her? I just happened by the curtain
At her confession; she's just been
Pronounced absolved of any sin;
She's a right innocent young lass
Who brought mere nothings to confess;   2625
On her I have no hold at all!
FAUST.   She's over fourteen, after all.
MEPHISTOPHELES.   You're like a loose Lothario
Who thinks that all dear blossoms blow
For him, can see no honest name   2630
Nor favor that is not fair game;
It does not always work, I fear.
FAUST.   Your pious Worship, spare my ear
Your wise proprieties and charters!
Let me be plain, and hear me right,   2635
Unless I have that sweet delight
Nestling in my embrace, tonight,
The selfsame midnight hour will part us.
MEPHISTOPHELES.   Come, think what can be and what can't!
A fortnight even will be scant   2640
To spy out chances, scheme ahead.

---

1. As indicated in a draft, Goethe originally intended Gretchen to appear at the end of a procession coming from the cathedral. Mephistopheles later acknowledges (lines 2621–6) that the girl has just received confession.

FAUST.   If I were granted seven hours,
I should not need the devil's powers
To lure a fledgling to my bed.
MEPHISTOPHELES.   That sounded like a Frenchman's boast.   2645
Don't wolf your pleasures like a glutton,
Who would gulp down a quail like mutton!
This thing is half the treat at most
Unless you knead, by guile and art
And flummery of every sort,   2650
Your sweetmeat to the proper turn,
As from the Gallic tales we learn.
FAUST.   My appetite is keen enough.
MEPHISTOPHELES.   Once and for all, a laugh's a laugh,
But you just cannot have your way   2655
With that young cherub in a day.
Assault head-on will net us bruises.
We must bethink ourselves of ruses.
FAUST.   Get me some thing of hers for keeps!
Lead me to where my angel sleeps!   2660
Bring me a bosom-cloth, a garter!
Some token for my love to barter!
MEPHISTOPHELES.   To show you how I strive and strain
To serve and soothe your amorous pain,
I will not waste another minute: 2665
I know her room—tonight you shall be in it.
FAUST.   And shall I see her, have her?
MEPHISTOPHELES.   No.
She will be at a neighbor's, though,
Meanwhile you'd be alone, and so
Sensing delight to come you may at will   2670
Of her ethereal aura breathe your fill.
FAUST.   Can we go now?
MEPHISTOPHELES.   No, it is early yet.
FAUST.   I need a gift for her—you see to that.
    [*Exit.*]
MEPHISTOPHELES.   Well! He'll go far. A gift right off, no loitering!
I know no end of likely spots,   2675
Sequestered treasure-burying plots;
I'll do a little reconnoitering.
    [*Exit.*]

Evening[1]
A Clean Little Room

MARGARETE.   [*braiding her hair and putting it up*]
I'd give a deal if I could say
Who was that gentleman today.
I liked his looks and how he spoke;   2680
He must be born of noble folk,
That I could tell from brow and eyes—
Would he have been so forward otherwise?
[*Exit.*]

MEPHISTOPHELES *and* FAUST.
MEPHISTOPHELES.   Go on, come in, on silent feet!
FAUST.   [*after a brief silence*] Leave me alone now, I entreat.   2685
MEPHISTOPHELES.   [*snooping around*]
Not every maiden is so neat.
[*Exit.*]

FAUST.   [*gazing up and about*] Ah, welcome, blessèd twilight haze
That hovers in this sanctuary's scope!
Ignite my heart, love's sweet and searing blaze,
Soothed but to languish by the dew of hope!   2690
How all here breathes a sense of stillness,
Of order and of calm content!
Within this penury, what fullness!
What bliss in this imprisonment!
[*He throws himself into the leather armchair by the bed.*]
Receive me, who for generations flown,   2695
Have welcomed many a glad or mournful pilgrim!
To think, about this patriarchal throne
Time and again has swarmed a throng of children!
I seem to see my little darling stand
As she, round-cheeked, with joys of Christmas thrilling,   2700
Devoutly kissed her grandsire's withered hand.
I sense, dear girl, your very spirit
Of plenitude and order all about,
Benignly counseling domestic merit,
Seeing the tablecloth all tidily spread out,   2705
Even the sanded floor in patterns fine.
Oh dearest hand! so near divine!
Through you this cabin turns into a shrine.
And here!
[*He lifts a bed-curtain.*]

1. This scene invites comparison with Shakespeare's *Cymbeline* 2.3, in which Jachimo observes the sleeping Imogen in her bed.

What thrill of ecstasy! Forlorn,
Here I would linger many hours.   2710
Here, Nature, did you nurse, with gentle showers
Of dreams, this angel native-born;
Here came, its bosom gently heaving
With tender life, the child in bloom,
And here in chaste and sacred weaving   2715
God's image ripened in the bloom!

And you? Do you recall your quest?
How deeply all my soul's astir!
What do you want? Why is your heart oppressed?
Ah, wretched Faust—no longer what you were!   2720

Am I in thrall to fairy fragrance here?
Impelled to dally at my ease,
In dream of love I melt and disappear;
Are we but sport to any passing breeze?

If she this very instant were to come,   2725
How you would expiate your desecration!
Big Thomas, woe, would shrink into Tom Thumb,
Swept to her feet in adoration.
            [MEPHISTOPHELES enters.]
MEPHISTOPHELES.   Quick! I can see her by the gate.
FAUST.   Off, never to return! I'm gone.   2730
MEPHISTOPHELES.   Here is a box of middling weight
    That somewhere else I came upon.
    Just leave it in this cabinet,
    I warrant it will drive her silly;
    I've baited it with this and that,   2735
    Enough for quite another filly.
    A child's a child, a toy's a toy.
FAUST.   I wonder—should I?
MEPHISTOPHELES.   Why so coy?
    You mean perhaps to keep the hoard?
    Then I advise my greedy Lord   2740
    To save the precious time of day
    And spare me further trouble. Say,
    I trust you're not the grasping sort!
    I scratch my head, I fret and scurry—
        [He places the box in the cabinet and presses the lock back in.]
    Away now, hurry!   2745
    Take all this trouble just to bend
    That sweet young thing to your heart's wish and end;
    And you look glum,
    As if you faced an auditorium
    And looming in it, in the flesh, all gray,   2750

Physics and Metaphysica!²
Away!
  [*Exeunt.*]

MARGARETE. [*holding a lamp*]
  It is so sultry here, so hot—
    [*Opens the window.*]
  And yet outdoors it's not uncommon warm
  There's something here, I don't know what—   2755
  If only my mother were coming home.
  I'm all of a shudder, I declare—
  What a timid little goose, for fair!

        [*She starts singing as she undresses.*]
            There was a king in Thule,³†
            Right faithful unto death,   2760
            Whom she who loved him truly
            Gave a cup with her dying breath.

            Naught dearer in his keeping,
            He drained it at every sup;
            And never could help weeping   2765
            Each time he raised the cup.

            And when it came to dying,
            His cities all he told,
            Naught to his heir denying
            Save for the cup of gold.   2770

            He held a banquet royal
            In his sea-girt castle tall,
            Filled with his vassals loyal
            The high ancestral hall.

            There stood the hoary drinker   2775
            And sipped of life's last glow,
            Then flung the holy trinket
            Into the brine below.

            He saw it plunging, winking
            And sinking deep at sea,   2780
            His lids grew heavy, sinking,
            No other drop drank he.

2. Allusion to academic disciplines and Faust's former life as a scholar. For the contrast of gray learning and the "green of life's golden tree," see lines 2038 f.
3. *Ultima Thule* was the mythological name given by ancient geographers to the northernmost habitable region of the world.

[*She opens the cabinet to put away her clothes and notices the jewel-box.*]
How did this handsome casket get in there?
I surely locked the closet, I could swear.
What might be in it? What a strange affair!   2785
Did someone bring it here to pawn,
And Mother took it for security?
A little key is fastened on,
I think I'll open it and see!
What is this? Look at it! God bless—   2790
I never saw such jewels! What rich array—
Why, such a set a noble baroness
Could wear on a high holiday.
How would this necklace look on me?
Who calls this gorgeousness her own?   2795
[*She tricks herself out with it and steps before the mirror.*]
Were these fine ear-bobs mine alone!
They give one quite another air.
What use are simple looks and youth?
Oh, they are well and good in truth;
That's all folk mean, though—pretty fair.   2800
The praise you get is half good-natured fuss.
For gold contend,
On gold depend
All things and men. . . . Poor us!

On a Walk[1]

FAUST, *walking to and fro in thought.* MEPHISTOPHELES *joins him.*

MEPHISTOPHELES.
By love disdained and spurned! By hellfire infinite!   2805
I wish I knew of something worse so I could swear by it!
FAUST.   What irks you? You're all out of level!
I never saw quite such a phiz!
MEPHISTOPHELES.   I swear I'd send myself straight to the devil
If I were not a devil as it is!   2810
FAUST.   Have you been struck in the upper story?
You really look the part, all grim and gory!
MEPHISTOPHELES.   Just think, the hoard for Gretchen fetched
A meddling priest has gone and snatched.
Her mother had scarce laid eyes on it   2815
And straightway threw a shivering fit:
That woman's nose is mighty clever,
It's stuck in the prayer-book forever,
And with each mortal thing can tell
Profane from sacred by the smell;   2820
This finery had, she never doubted,
No odor of sanctity about it.
My child, she cried, ill-gotten wealth
Ensnares the soul, beshrews one's health,
Let's give it into the Virgin's keeping,   2825
Manna from Heaven to be reaping![2]
Little Meg made a long face, of course,
Thought: after all, it's a gift horse,
He surely did not lack God's fear
Who had so cleverly brought it here.   2830
The mother, though, had a priest come in
Who, the moment the trick was explained to him,
Cast a well-pleased eye upon the lot
And called it a truly pious thought:
He who abstains is he who gains!   2835
The Church has a superb digestion,
Has swallowed whole countries without question
And never suffered from stomach pains;
She, ladies, can alone digest
Ill-gotten goods along with the rest.   2840
FAUST.   I'd say the trick was trite enough,
Both Jews and princes bring it off.
MEPHISTOPHELES.   With this he slipped into his pocket

---

1. *Allee,* "avenue" (as the scene is titled in the *Urfaust*), a public pathway outside the city walls.
2. See Revelation 2.17, "To him that overcometh will I give to eat of the hidden manna." Manna was the food sent by God to nourish Israel in the wilderness (Exodus 16).

Ring, clasp, and bracelet, chain and locket,
With no more thanks or ifs and buts   2845
Than if he were given a bag of nuts,
Promised them heavenly wage beside,
And they were greatly edified.
FAUST.   And Gretchen?
MEPHISTOPHELES.   Sits there all distraught
And knows not what she would or ought,   2850
Thinks day and night of that display,
Still more of him by whom it came her way.
FAUST.   I hate to have the darling fret.
Get her at once another set!
The first was really no great hoard.   2855
MEPHISTOPHELES.   Oh yes, it's all just child's play to Milord!
FAUST.   Come on, arrange things as I say,
Involve her neighbor in some way!
You're like cold porridge, Devil, stir your bones
And bring a new array of stones!   2860
MEPHISTOPHELES.   I'm proud to serve you, gracious Sir.
      [*Exit* FAUST.]
Your lovestruck fool thinks nothing of
Puffing sun, moon, and stars into the air
Like fireworks to please his lady love.
      [*Exit.*]

The Neighbor's House

MARTHE.[1] [*alone*] God pardon my husband if He can,   2865
He has done ill by me, dear man.
Left for the wide world, just like that,
And me a grass widow on the mat.
Yet never did I grieve him or oppose
But loved him tenderly, God knows.   2870
          [*She cries.*]
For all I know he's dead—oh grief!—
Had I at least a Coroner's brief![2]
          [MARGARETE *enters.*]
MARGARETE.   Frau Marthe!
MARTHE   Gretchen! What, my pet?
MARGARETE.   My knees are shaking, I declare!
I've found another casket there,   2875
Of ebony, in my cabinet,
And full of jewels, star on star,
More precious than the first by far.
MARTHE.   You must keep mum about it to your mother;
She'd take it to confession, like the other.   2880
MARGARETE.   Just look and see! Oh, just look here!
MARTHE.   [*does her up with the jewelry*]
Aren't you the luckiest girl! My dear!
MARGARETE.   Just that I dare not wear it in the street,
Nor yet at church be seen in it.
MARTHE.   Come over oftener, don't look sour,   2885
And give the things a secret try,
Parade before the mirror for an hour,
And we'll enjoy them on the sly.
On some occasion then, a feast or such,
We'll show them one by one, so folk won't notice much.   2890
The chain will keep a while, we'll try an ear-bob first;
Your Ma may never see; we'll hoodwink her at worst.
MARGARETE.   Whoever left these chests for me to find?
Here's something quite uncanny, to my mind.
          [*A knock at the door.*]
Could this be Mother? Oh my sin!   2895
MARTHE.   [*peering through the little curtain*]
It's a strange gentleman. Come in.
          [*Enter* MEPHISTOPHELES.]
MEPHISTOPHELES.   I step straight in—my forthright venture
I hope the ladies will not censure.

---

1. The traditional role, in domestic drama, of the gossip or matchmaker (see the Nurse in *Romeo and Juliet*).
2. The Coroner's brief would prove Marthe to be a widow and free her to look for a new husband.

[*Respectfully steps back before* MARGARETE.]
It's for Frau Marthe Schwerdtlein I inquire!
MARTHE.   I'm she, Sir—what is your desire?   2900
MEPHISTOPHELES.   [*under his breath to her*]
I know you now; that is enough for me;
I see you have distinguished company.
I took a liberty, excuse me, pray.
I'll wait till later in the day.
MARTHE.   [*aloud*] God help us, child, by all that's human!   2905
He takes you for a gentlewoman.
MARGARETE.   I'm nothing but a poor young maid.
My lord's too kind, I am afraid.
These gems and chains are not my own.
MEPHISTOPHELES.   Oh, it is not the gems alone;   2910
You have a way, a look so *distinguée*.
How glad I am that I may stay!
MARTHE.   You bring . . . ? I'm eager, you'll excuse . . .
MEPHISTOPHELES.   I wish I had more cheerful news!
Please not to blame it on your guest: 2915
Your husband's dead and sends his best.
MARTHE.   He's dead? The faithful heart! Oh no!
My husband dead! I won't survive the blow!
MARGARETE.   My poor dear Madam, don't despair!
MEPHISTOPHELES.   Let me relate the sad affair.   2920
MARGARETE.   God spare me loving and its cost!
I could not bear it if I lost.
MEPHISTOPHELES.
Joy must with grief, and grief with joy be stirred.
MARTHE.   Recount me how his passing came!
MEPHISTOPHELES.   He lies at Padua interred,   2925
Of Saint Antonius' fame,[3]
Upon a grave-site duly blessed,
Bedded for cool eternal rest.
MARTHE.   And have you nothing more along from him?
MEPHISTOPHELES.   Oh yes, a large and grave request: 2930
Be sure to have three hundred masses sung for him!
My pocket's empty, for the rest.
MARTHE.   What! Not a gift, a prize to cheer the heart with,
What any journeyman saves in his satchel's deeps,
To carry home for keeps,   2935
Would sooner beg or starve than part with?
MEPHISTOPHELES.   Madam, your troubles truly grieve me;
He did not waste his substance, though, he swore.
He rued his errors much, believe me,
Oh yes, and his ill fortune even more.   2940
MARGARETE.   Alas, that people are so sorely tried!

---

3. The basilica of St. Anthony in Padua was sacred to the patron saint of women in love, brides,
and wives.

Sure, many a requiem for him I'll pray.
MEPHISTOPHELES.   You're worthy to be married any day:
You are an amiable child.
MARGARETE.   Oh no, that won't be soon, for sure.   2945
MEPHISTOPHELES.   Well, if not husband, then a paramour.
It's bliss of Heaven's highest grace
To cradle such in one's embrace.
MARGARETE.   That's not the custom with us, Sir.
MEPHISTOPHELES.   Custom or no, it will occur.   2950
MARTHE.   Do tell!
MEPHISTOPHELES.   I stood beside his bed at his last breath,
It was of something better than manure,
Half-rotten straw; and yet, he died a Christian death,
And mourned his dying more in debt than merely poor.
"Alas," he cried, "with what self-hate it fills me,   2955
Thus to forsake my calling, thus my wife!
Ah, it's this consciousness that kills me.
Had I but her forgiveness in this life!"
MARTHE.   [crying] The poor dear man! I've long forgiven him.
MEPHISTOPHELES.
"But she, God knows, was more to blame than I."   2960
MARTHE.   He lied! With one foot in the grave, to lie!
MEPHISTOPHELES.   He doubtless raved in a delirious dream,
Or I'm no judge at all—a dying trance.
"There was," he said, "no idling for a second,
To get first children and then bread for her; bread reckoned   2965
In the most all-inclusive sense;
And I could never eat my share in peace, what's more."
MARTHE.   Oh! could he so forget all love, all vows he swore,
The drudgery by day and night?
MEPHISTOPHELES.   No—he was warmly mindful of your plight;   2970
Said: "As I sailed from Malta on my trip,
I prayed for wife and child with fervor rare;
And Heaven duly heard my prayer,
In that our vessel caught a Turkish ship
Which bore a cargo of the Sultan's treasure.   2975
Then valor reaped its just reward,
And I received my well-earned measure
Out of the Ottoman hoard."
MARTHE.   Oh yes? Oh where? Perhaps he buried it?
MEPHISTOPHELES.
Who knows where the four winds have carried it?   2980
A fine young Neapolitan took pity
On him, a stray in a strange city;
She proved to him a dear and faithful friend,
Of which he felt the blessings to the end.[4]

---

4. These blessings from the Neapolitan lady, presumably a prostitute, would be the *mal de Naples*, euphemism for syphilis.

MARTHE.   The thief! Defrauder of his child and wife!   2985
  That neither grief nor misery
  Could wean him from his shameful life!
MEPHISTOPHELES.   Well, now he's dead for it, you see.
  If I were in your place,
  I'd mourn him for a decorous year   2990
  Meanwhile discreetly look for some new face.
MARTHE.   The kind my first one was, oh dear!
  I'd not find easily another such.
  There never was more winsome scamp than mine!
  He only liked the roving life too much,   2995
  And foreign women, and foreign wine
  And those confounded dice.
MEPHISTOPHELES.   Well, tit for tat, and give and take,
  If he made light of, for your sake,
  An equal pinch of harmless vice.   3000
  I swear, were this proviso true,
  I might myself change rings with you!
MARTHE.   Oh now, my Lord is pleased to jest.
MEPHISTOPHELES.   [aside] I'd best be off before this gets absurd!
  She'd hold the very devil to his word.   3005
  [to GRETCHEN] Where lies your own heart's interest?
MARGARETE.   What is your meaning, Sir?
MEPHISTOPHELES.   [aside]   Dear artless innocence you!
  [aloud] Good ladies, my farewell!
MARGARETE.   Farewell!
MARTHE.   Before you go!
  I should be thankful for a witness,
  Where, how, and when my spouse found rest eternal.   3010
  I've always liked propriety and fitness,
  Would want to read his passing in the journal.
MEPHISTOPHELES.   Yes, Ma'am—by what two witnesses attest
  Truth's always rendered manifest.[5]
  I have a mate, a quite superior sort,   3015
  That I can call upon before your court,
  I'll bring him here.
MARTHE.   Be sure you do!
MEPHISTOPHELES.   And will our Miss be present too?
  A gallant lad, been everywhere,
  Speaks all young ladies passing fair.   3020
MARGARETE.   I'd have to blush for my low birth.
MEPHISTOPHELES.   Before no sovereign on earth!
MARTHE.   Behind the house there, in my garden, then,
  Tonight we shall await the gentlemen.

---

5. Testimony by two witnesses would qualify as legal proof of an undocumented event.

Street

FAUST. MEPHISTOPHELES.

FAUST.   How now? Soon ready? Are things nearly right?   3025
MEPHISTOPHELES.   Bravo! Stoked up and going strong!
You'll have your Gretchen before long.
You'll see her at Frau Marthe's house tonight.
Oh, there's a woman needs no jogging
For pander's work and pettifogging!   3030
FAUST.   Good work!
MEPHISTOPHELES.   But first we're asked—no bother—
FAUST.   Done—one good turn deserves another.
MEPHISTOPHELES.   We merely testify, just for the docket,
That her late husband kicked the bucket
And rests at Padua in hallowed ground.   3035
FAUST.   So we must make the trip first! That was smart!
MEPHISTOPHELES.   Sancta Simplicitas![1] You are not bound
To know much, you just speak your part.
FAUST.   If that's the best you know, the deal is off.
MEPHISTOPHELES.   A saint! Just hear him huff and puff!   3040
Is it unheard of, a new start,
For you to deal in perjured witness?
Of God, the world, its every moving part,
Of Man, the stirrings in his head and heart,
Have you not judged with utmost force and glibness?   3045
With bold assertion, fluent breath?
And yet, confess it, if you searched your soul,
You knew of all this, on the whole,
About as much as of Herr Schwerdtlein's death!
FAUST.   You are a liar, a sophist, and were ever so.   3050
MEPHISTOPHELES.   Yes—if one weren't more deeply in the know!
Tomorrow won't you try, in honorable guise,
To pull the wool about poor Gretchen's eyes,
And pledge her soul-love as you go?
FAUST.   Yes—and sincerely!
MEPHISTOPHELES.   I can tell!   3055
Then deathless faith and love, a generous surge
About that single, all-o'erpowering urge . . .
Will that be so sincere as well?
FAUST.   Have done! It will! For when I feel, all blinded,
And for that well, that teeming wealth   3060
Search for a name and cannot find it,
Then through the world send all my senses casting,
For most sublime expression grasping,

_____
1. Sacred Simplicity (Latin).

And call this blaze that leaves me breathless
Eternal, infinite—yes! deathless! 3065
Is that a trick of devilish stealth?
MEPHISTOPHELES.   Still I am right!
FAUST.   Here, take this in,
I beg of you, and spare my lung:
Who wants the last word, using but his tongue,
Is sure to win. 3070
Let's go, I'm weary of your voice,
You're right, the more so since I have no choice.

Garden

MARGARETE *on* FAUST'S *arm,* MARTHE *with* MEPHISTOPHELES, *strolling to and fro.*

MARGARETE. I feel quite well Your Honor deigns to spare
And shame me with the kind intention.
A voyager is used to common fare   3075
And takes pot-luck with condescension.
I know too well, a traveled man of parts
Can't be diverted by my homely arts.
FAUST. One glance from you, one word holds more dear mirth
Than all the wisdom of this earth.   3080
   [*He kisses her hand.*]
MARGARETE.
   Oh, don't—how can you kiss my hand? You shouldn't!
   It is so coarse, so rough to touch!
   The work I have been set to, would or wouldn't!
   My mother asks so much.
   [*They pass on.*]
MARTHE. And you, dear Sir, are always on the road?   3085
MEPHISTOPHELES.
   Would bounden duty were not always stronger!
   How hard to leave is many a dear abode,
   Yet one just cannot tarry longer!
MARTHE. It's fine to roam one's flighty years,
   Enjoy the wide world to the fullest,   3090
   But when that ill time nears,
   To drag oneself unto the grave unsolaced
   Brings but regrets and tears.
MEPHISTOPHELES. I see it from afar and dread it.
MARTHE.
   Take thought in time, dear Sir, mind where you're headed.   3095
   [*They pass on.*]
MARGARETE. You have such ready courtesy—
   But out of sight is out of mind!
   You must have friends of every kind,
   All folk much cleverer than me.
FAUST. Dear heart—believe me, what most men call clever   3100
   Is oftener vain and shallow.
MARGARETE.   How on earth?
FAUST. That artlessness, that innocence should never
   Respect itself and know its holy worth!
   That meekness, modesty, the gifts most true
   Of fondly lavish Nature can—   3105
MARGARETE. If you but think of me a little span,
   I shall have time enough to think of you.

FAUST. You must be much alone?
MARGARETE. Oh yes; our household is a modest one,
  Yet it's no little thing to run.   3110
  We have no maid; I cook and sweep and knit
  And launder, late abed, early to rise,
  And Mother has on all of it
  Such watchful eyes!
  Not that we are so pressed to keep expenses down,   3115
  We could spread out far more than many another:
  There's quite a tidy sum left us by Father,
  A little house and garden out of town.
  But now my days go by more calmly rather;
  My brother's soldiering,   3120
  My little sister's dead.
  I had a deal of trouble with the little thing,
  But I would have it all again, twice more instead,
  She was so dear to me.
FAUST.   An angel, if like you.
MARGARETE. I brought her up, and how she loved me too!   3125
  She wasn't born yet when we lost our father.
  We'd all but given up my mother,
  So weakly did she lie.
  And she got well but slowly by and by.
  She could not dream, such was her plight,   3130
  Herself to nurse the little mite,
  And so I reared it all alone
  With milk and water; thus it grew my own,
  And in my arms and on my lap
  It kicked its legs, turned cheerful, and grew up.   3135
FAUST. That must have been the purest bliss for you.
MARGARETE. But with it came long hours of hardship, too.
  At night the little one would sleep
  Beside my bed; it uttered hardly a peep
  And I was up;   3140
  I'd lay it down beside me, get it fed,
  Or if it didn't stop, get out of bed
  And jog it on my shoulder, on and off,
  Then at first light stand by the laundering-trough,
  Then mind the stove, then do the marketing,   3145
  And so day in, day out, the same old thing.
  It's hard at times to keep in cheerful mood;
  But rest tastes sweeter then, and so does food.
      [*They pass on.*]
MARTHE. Ah, women's lot is wretched—to subdue
  A crusty bachelor is vain exertion.   3150
MEPHISTOPHELES. It's surely up to ladies such as you
  To give me reason for conversion.
MARTHE. You have not found it yet? Speak frankly, Sir,
  Your heart has not yet chosen anywhere?

MEPHISTOPHELES.   An honest wife, a home and hearth,   3155
   They say, is more than gold and jewels worth.[2]
MARTHE.   I meant to say, you've never really wooed?
MEPHISTOPHELES.   I've always met with kind solicitude.
MARTHE.   I mean, was it in earnest ever, on your part?
MEPHISTOPHELES.   A knave who trifles with a lady's heart.   3160
MARTHE.   Oh, you mistake my words!
MEPHISTOPHELES.   I'm pained to be remiss!
   But this I know—you are all kindliness.
     [*They pass on.*]
FAUST.   You knew me then, dear little elf,
   Right as I came into the garden?
MARGARETE.   I dropped my eyes, you must have seen yourself.   3165
FAUST.   And did my liberty then win your pardon?
   What impudence presumed to do and say,
   By the cathedral steps the other day?
MARGARETE.   I was dismayed, I'd never known this pass,
   Could think of no good reason to be slandered.   3170
   Has he in my deportment seen, I wondered,
   Something unseemly, forward, crass?
   Here is a wench, he seemed impelled to say,
   You'd come to business with right away.
   Yet to be frank—something, I hardly knew,   3175
   Stirred in my heart at once to plead for you;
   I know I felt quite angry that I could
   Not get as angry with you as I should.
FAUST.   Sweet love!
MARGARETE.   No, wait a bit!
     [*She breaks a star-flower and plucks the petals off, one by one.*]
FAUST.   What is this, a nosegay?
MARGARETE.   No, just a game.
FAUST.   What game?
MARGARETE.   You'll laugh, just stay away.   3180
FAUST.   What are you whispering?
MARGARETE.   [*under her breath*] He loves me—loves me not.
FAUST.   Oh, bless your innocent heart!
MARGARETE.   [*continuing*] He loves me—not—he loves me—not—
     [*plucking off the last petal, in a touching tone of exultation*]
   He loves me!
FAUST.   Yes, my child! Yes, let this flower-word
   Be godly oracle to you. He loves you!   3185
   Ah, know you what this means? He loves you!
     [*He takes both her hands.*]
MARGARETE.   I'm shuddering!
FAUST.   Oh do not shudder! Let this gaze,
   This pressure of my hands express to you

---

2. A combination of a folk saying, "One's own hearth is gold's worth," and Proverbs 31.10, "Who can find a virtuous woman? for her price is far above rubies."

What is ineffable: 3190
To give one's whole self, and to feel
An ecstasy that must endure forever!
Forever!—For its end would be despair,
No, without end! No end!

> [MARGARETE *presses his hands, frees herself and runs away. He stands there, pensive, for a while, then follows her.*]

MARTHE. [*entering*] It is near night.

MEPHISTOPHELES. Yes, and we would be gone. 3195

MARTHE. I should have gladly asked you to stay on,
But this is such a wicked neighborhood.
You'd say no one had anything he should
Or wants to think upon,
But snoop upon his neighbor, fuss and buzz, 3200
And gossip sticks to one, no matter what one does.
And our young pair?

MEPHISTOPHELES. Flown down the alley there.
Frolicking butterflies!

MARTHE. I'd say he's fond of her.

MEPHISTOPHELES. And she of him. That's how it ever was.

A Garden Pavilion[1]

MARGARETE *slips inside, hides behind the door, fingertip to her lips, and peeks through the crack.*

MARGARETE.   He's coming!
FAUST.   [*enters*]   Scamp, you're teasing me!   3205
Now you'll see!
[*He kisses her.*]
MARGARETE.   [*seizing him and returning the kiss*]
Dearest man, I love you with all my heart.
[MEPHISTOPHELES *knocks.*]
FAUST.   [*stamping his foot*] Who's there?
MEPHISTOPHELES.   A friend!
FAUST.   A brute!
MEPHISTOPHELES.   It must
be time to part.
MARTHE.   [*entering*] Yes, it is late, good sir.
FAUST.   Might I escort . . . ?
MARGARETE.   My mother would—Farewell!
FAUST.   Must I leave then?
Farewell!
MARTHE.   Adieu!
MARGARETE.   To see you soon again!   3210
[*Exeunt* FAUST *and* MEPHISTOPHELES.]
MARGARETE.   The things and things a man like he
Can think of in his mind—dear me!
I stand and gape in shy distress,
And all I find to say is Yes.
I'm such a poor young goose, and he—   3215
The Lord knows what he sees in me.
[*Exit.*]

---

1. This brief scene immediately follows the preceding one.

Forest and Cave†

FAUST, *alone.*

FAUST.   You gave me, lofty spirit,[1] gave me all
I pleaded for. Not vainly did you turn
Your countenance to me amid the fire.
You gave me splendored Nature for my kingdom,   3220
And strength to feel her, relish her. Not merely
A coldly wondering visit did you grant,
But suffered me into her inner depth
To gaze as in the bosom of a friend.
You led the varied muster of the living   3225
Before me, teaching me to know my brothers
In leafy stillness, in the air and water.
When in the wood the tempest roars and crunches,
The giant fir shears down its neighbor boughs,
Its brother columns in its bruising fall,   3230
The hill reechoing its thunderous thud,
You lead me to the cavern refuge, show
My own self to me, and of my own breast
The secret deep-laid miracles unfold.[2]
And when before my gaze the limpid moon   3235
Ascends and, soothing, wafts across, there rise
From rocky cliffs, from out the moisty foliage
The silver shapes of some anterior age
And milden contemplation's joy austere.

Ah, nothing perfect is vouchsafed to man,   3240
I sense it now. Unto this ecstasy
That takes me near and nearer to the gods,
You joined me that companion,[3] whom already
I cannot miss, though, chill and insolent,
He does debase me to myself, makes naught   3245
Your gifts with but the vapor of a word.
He fans within my breast a raging fire
For that fair image with his busy spite.
Thus reel I from desire to fulfillment,
And in fulfillment languish for desire.   3250

[*Enter* MEPHISTOPHELES.]

MEPHISTOPHELES.   Well, had your fill yet, living in the rough?
It may be pleasant for some innings;
But come, a single sampling is enough,

---

1. An allusion to the Earth Spirit.
2. Recall the Ossianic vision of landscape in the opening monologue (lines 762–84).
3. Mephistopheles.

Then it is time for new beginnings!
FAUST. I wish you'd find yourself some other use   3255
Than spoil a good day with your riot.
MEPHISTOPHELES. Well, well! Stew on in your own juice,
I'm glad to let you rest in quiet.
One has a precious lot to lose
In one like you, all quirks and quills and dudgeon!   3260
One wears out patience, wears out shoes,
But what to shun for him and what to choose,
You try to tell it by my Lord Curmudgeon!
FAUST. That was a speech in proper vein!
He pesters me and wants a thank-you too.   3265
MEPHISTOPHELES. Without my help, how would you fain
Have led your life, poor earthling you?
I've cured you from the crochety throng
Of vague imaginings for years;
But for my coming you would long   3270
Have tiptoed from this vale of tears.
Why make your perch in caverns foul
And rock-cracks like a moulting owl?
Why slurp from dripping cliff and oozing root
Your slimy diet like a newt?   3275
A pretty path to health and wisdom!
There's still the doctor in your system.
FAUST. You know with what new zest I am imbued
By every ramble in this solitude?
Yes—could you share this revelation,   3280
You would be fiend enough to grudge me my elation.
MEPHISTOPHELES. A truly transcendental binge!
By night and dew lie on a mountain range,
Of earth and sky essay ecstatic capture,
Swell up to girth divine with mystic rapture,   3285
Root up earth's core with urgent divination,
Feel in one's breast six day's worth of creation,
In pride of potency I don't know what bestowing,
Soon maudlin-lovingly all borders overflowing,
Those earthly coils completely rend—   3290
Then the transcendent act of knowing
[*with a gesture*] I won't say how to end.
FAUST. Fie, fie on you!
MEPHISTOPHELES.   You find this hard to swallow;
Outraged decorum's fie rings sadly hollow!
One mustn't to the modest ear blurt out   3295
What modest heart yet cannot do without.
There, there, I will not grudge you on occasion
The luxuries of innocent evasion.
But soon you'll tire of dissembling;
You are already all at sea,   3300
And, driven farther, you will be

Worn out in madness, fear and trembling.
Enough of this! Your lovebird sits and feels
Downcast in spirit and confined,
She is in love head over heels   3305
And cannot drive you from her mind.[4]
First your love-craze brimmed over in a torrent,
Just as a freshet floods its banks when swelled by thaw;
You poured into her heart the raging current,
And now your brook is shallow as before.   3310
Instead of haunting forests, on reflection
It would behoove his lordship to requite
The poor young monkey with a mite
Of your reciprocal affection.
She has been waiting pitifully long;   3315
Stands by the window, sees the clouds, so free
Across the city ramparts flee,
Were I a little bird, thus goes her song,[5]
Day after day, and half the night.
Now she will be serene, more often blue,   3320
Sometimes shed tear on tear,
Then be in fair good cheer,
And always loving you.
FAUST.   Ah, serpent! Venomous wretch you![6]
MEPHISTOPHELES.   [aside] I thought that this might fetch you!   3325
FAUST.   Vile profligate, betake thee hence![7]
Name not her sweetness that enslaves me!
Make not my lust for her who craves me,
Enflame again the exacerbated sense!
MEPHISTOPHELES.   No need to fret! She thinks you flown afar;   3330
And in a way, I think you are.
FAUST.   However far, I'm near to her and crave her,
She never is forgotten, never spent,
I grudge the very body of the Savior
Her lips that touch it at the Sacrament.   3335
MEPHISTOPHELES.   Well said! I've often envied you, my friend,
That pair of twins beneath the roses pent.[8]
FAUST.   Off, pimp!
MEPHISTOPHELES.   You tickle me, all bark and fizz!
The god who lads and lassies made
Discerned at once the noblest trade: 3340
Himself to see to opportunities.
Cheer up, o effigy of dread!
You're going to your lady's bed,

---

4. See "Gretchen's Chamber," immediately following.
5. An allusion to a popular folk song: "If I were a little bird / and also had two wings, / I would fly
   to you."
6. An allusion to the biblical myth of the Fall, identifying Mephistopheles with the serpent.
7. An allusion to Christ's rejection of Satan's temptation in the wilderness (Matthew 4.10).
8. An allusion to the Song of Songs 4.5, "Your two breasts are like two fawns, twins of a gazelle,
   that feed among the lilies." (Luther's German Bible substitutes "roses" for "lilies.")

Not to the tomb!

FAUST.   What use her love's celestial graces?   3345
As I grow warm in her embraces
Do I not always sense her doom?
Am I not fugitive, the homeless rover,
The man-beast void of goal or bliss,
Who roars in cataracts from cliff to boulder   3350
In avid frenzy for the precipice?
And to one side, she, still in childhood's shadow.
All in domestic cares enfurled,
In a small cabin on an alpine meadow,
Encompassed by the little world?   3355
And I, the God-forsaken,
Was not content
With cliffsides shaken
And granite crushed and rent,
No, she, her sweet composure, must be shattered too!   3360
This victim, Hell, must needs be proffered you!
Make shorter, fiend, my time of dread contrition!
Let it be now, what needs must be!
May then her destiny collapse on me
And she be joined in my perdition.   3365

MEPHISTOPHELES.   Aboil again, all hiss and spout!
Go in and comfort her, you dunce!
Where such a birdbrain finds no quick way out
He sees the end of things at once.
He prospers who stands undeterred!   3370
You're surely well traduced to our affairs;
To me there's nothing more insipid in the world
Than a devil who despairs.

Gretchen's Chamber[1]†

GRETCHEN *by the spinning-wheel, alone.*

GRETCHEN. My peace is gone,
My heart is sore;   3375
Can find it never
And never more.

When he is fled,
My soul is dead,
My world is all   3380
As bitter gall.

My wretched head
Is all askew,
My bit of sense
All come in two.   3385

My peace is gone,
My heart is sore;
Can find it never
And never more.

Just him I spy   3390
At the window for,
Just him I fly
To meet outdoor.

His noble frame,
Tall gait and stand,   3395
The smile of his lips,
His eye's command,

And then his speech
Of magic bliss,
His hand on mine,   3400
And oh, his kiss!

My peace is gone,
My heart is sore;
Can find it never
And never more.   3405

1. Despite frequent musical settings for Gretchen's monologue at the spinning wheel (notably by Schubert), she apparently speaks the lines of this scene, the short, rhymed lines of which intensify and formalize her emotions.

My bosom strains
Unto his clasp,
Ah, could I gather
And hold him fast,

And kiss him, oh,   3410
The way I felt,
Under his kisses
Would swoon and melt!

Marthe's Garden[1]

MARGARETE, FAUST.

MARGARETE. Oh, Heinrich,[2] promise!
FAUST.   Anything I can.
MARGARETE. What is your way about religion, pray?   3415
    You are a dear and kindly man,
    And yet you pay it little heed, I'd say.
FAUST. No matter, dear! I'm fond of you, you feel,
    And this my love with my life's blood would seal;
    Nobody's church and creed would I presume to slight.   3420
MARGARETE. One must have faith, though, it just isn't right.
FAUST. Must one?
MARGARETE.   O that I could prevail on you!
    You pay the Sacraments scant honor, too.
FAUST. I honor them.
MARGARETE.   But from no inner need.
    How long since you were shriven, been to Mass, indeed?   3425
    Do you believe in God?
FAUST.   My dear one, who may say:
    I believe in God?
    Ask all your sages, clerical or lay,
    And their reply appears but sport
    Made of the questioner.
MARGARETE.   So you don't believe?   3430
FAUST.† Do not mishear me, dear my heart,
    For who may name Him
    And go proclaiming:
    Yes, I believe in him?
    Who search his heart   3435
    And dare say for his part:
    No, I believe him not?
    The All-comprising,
    The All-sustaining,
    Does he comprise, sustain not   3440
    You, me, himself?
    Are not the vaulted heavens hung on high?
    Is earth not anchored here below?
    And do with kindly gaze
    Eternal stars not rise aloft?   3445

---

1. An uncertain length of time passes between each scene in the latter half of the Gretchen tragedy.
   This scene prepares for the consummation of Faust's love through the administering of a sleeping
   potion to Gretchen's mother.
2. In the traditional legend, Faust is named "Johann." Goethe may have chosen this name because
   it occurs side by side with "Margareta" in the Catholic calendar (July 12 and 13). It is also possible
   that Faust has not revealed his correct name to Gretchen.

Join I not eye to eye with thee,
Does all not surge
Into thy head and heart,
And in perpetual mystery
Unseenly visible weave beside thee?   3450
Fill full your heart, all it will hold, with this,
And when you're all suffused and lost in bliss,
Then call it what you will,
Call it fulfillment! Heart! Love! God!
I have no name for it!   3455
Feeling is all;
Name is but sound and fume
Befogging heaven's blaze.
MARGARETE.   All well and good; the turn of phrase
Is something different, but I presume   3460
What Parson says means much the same.
FAUST.   It's what all hearts proclaim,
All places in the light of heaven's day,
Each in its language;
Why not I in my own?   3465
MARGARETE.   Put in this way, it has a likely tone.
And yet it's all askew to me;
For you have no Christianity.
FAUST.   Dear child!
MARGARETE.   It's long been grieving me
To see you in that company.   3470
FAUST.   How so?
MARGARETE.   That man from whom you never part
Is hateful to me in my inmost heart;
Nothing in all my life
Has stabbed me to my soul as with a knife,
Like that man's horrid leer.   3475
FAUST.   Dear baby, have no fear!
MARGARETE.   His presence rouses up my blood.
I find most every person good;
But, as I long to see you night and morning,
He makes my hackles rise in secret warning.   3480
What's more, I take him for a knave, as well!
God pardon me if I should judge him ill!
FAUST.   It takes all kinds of folk, you'll find.
MARGARETE.   I would not mingle with his kind!
He's hardly through the door to me,   3485
And he puts on that face, half mockery,
And half grim;
One knows there's nothing rouses sympathy in him;
You read on his brow as on a scroll
That he cannot love a single soul.   3490
I come to feel so blissful in your arm,

So warmly yielding, free and calm,
But his presence chills my heart with loathing.
FAUST.   Ah, tender angel of foreboding!
MARGARETE.   I am so overcome,   3495
Let him just enter and survey us,
I fancy all my love for you grows numb,
Nor could I in his presence say my prayers,
And that just cuts my heart in two;
O, Heinrich, you must feel it too!   3500
FAUST.   You simply have this prejudice.
MARGARETE.   I must be gone.
FAUST.   Must I forgo the bliss
Of knowing at your bosom an hour's rest,
Thrusting together soul to soul and breast to breast?
MARGARETE.   Oh, if I only slept alone!   3505
I'd gladly leave my door unlocked tonight;
But any little thing will wake my mother,
And if she found us with each other
I would just perish at her sight!
FAUST.   You angel, this is no sore plight.   3510
Here is a flask—three drops to take,
Mixed with her drink, will steep
Her nature in profoundest sleep.
MARGARETE.   What would I not do for your sake?
And she will take no harm from it?   3515
FAUST.   Would I advise it, darling, if she did?
MARGARETE.   Just looking at you, dearest man,
What drives me to your will—I wish I knew;
With all I have already done,
I've precious little left to do for you.   3520
         [Exit.]

MEPHISTOPHELES.   [enters] The mama-doll Gone yet?
FAUST.   What, spying still?
MEPHISTOPHELES.   Well, I took in a pretty earful;
Herr Doctor went through catechism drill;
I hope it left you fairly cheerful.
Girls long to know if one will follow still   3525
The plain old ways and pieties; they know
If he's in go-strings there, they'll keep him on the go.
FAUST.   You monster, cannot you conceive
How this pure faithful dear,
Bred to implicit trust   3530
In faith, and to believe
It sole salvation, writhes in holy fear
To see him she holds dearest damned and lost?
MEPHISTOPHELES.   Oh you transsensually sensuous squire!
A lassie has you by the nose!   3535
FAUST.   You miscreant of filth and fire!

MEPHISTOPHELES.   And Physiognomy[3] she truly knows,
 Behind my mask divines some hidden truth,
 In my poor presence feels I don't know how;
 I am some sort of genie, she would vow,   3540
 Perhaps the Devil himself, forsooth.
 Well, and tonight—?
FAUST.   What's it to you?
MEPHISTOPHELES.   I take my pleasure in it too!

---

3. The eighteenth-century pseudoscience of deducing character from the features of the face and head.

At the Well[1]†

GRETCHEN *and* LIESCHEN *with jars.*

LIESCHEN.   You heard about dear Barbara?
GRETCHEN.   Not a word. I don't see much of people.   3445
LIESCHEN.   It's so, I just heard it from Sybill
   She has at long last gone too far.
   That comes from stuck-up airs!
GRETCHEN.   What does?
LIESCHEN.   It stinks!
   She's feeding two now when she eats and drinks.
GRETCHEN.   Oh!   3550
LIESCHEN.   At last she's getting her comeuppance.
   How long she's hung upon the fellow's neck!
   I would like tuppence
   For each stroll, each tryst on common and dancing-deck,
   Everywhere had to be first in line,   3555
   He making up to her, pastries and wine,
   Always flaunting her so-called beauty,
   And yet so lost to honor and duty
   As to take gifts from him. Oh, fine!
   The billing and cooing that went on;   3560
   So now the wee cherry-blossom is gone!
GRETCHEN.   The poor thing!
LIESCHEN.   What, you pity her still?
   When our sort sat at the spinning-wheel,
   And our mothers wouldn't let us go out,
   She'd be with her sweetheart, mooning about   3565
   On the door-bench, in a dark alleyway,
   Not a dull moment they had, I'd say.
   Now she might as well keep her stiff neck bowed,
   Doing penitence in the sinner's shroud![2]
GRETCHEN.   He'll take her for his wife, I'm sure.   3570
LIESCHEN.   He'd be a fool! His kind of night-flier
   Has more than one iron in the fire.
   Besides, he's gone.
GRETCHEN.   That is not fair!
LIESCHEN.   If she gets him, we'll make it hot for her.
   The lads will tear off her wreath, and we,   3575

---

1. A public well where girls in the small town fetch water. Gretchen apparently already knows she is pregnant by Faust.
2. It had been customary in the eighteenth century for an unwed mother, wearing a sinner's smock, to appear in church, where she was subject to the abuse of both the preacher and her neighbors.

We'll scatter chaff at her door, you'll see!³
[*Exit.*]

GRETCHEN.   [*on her way home.*] How readily I used to blame
Some poor young soul that came to shame!
Never found sharp enough words like pins
To stick into other people's sins!   3580
Black as it seemed, I tarred it to boot,
And still never black enough to suit,
Would cross myself, exclaim and preen—
Now I myself am bared to sin!
Yet all of it that drove me here,   3585
God! was so innocent, was so dear!

---

3. A woman who had borne an illegitimate child was forbidden to wear a bridal wreath if she married.
If she did so, her neighbors were free to grab it and tear it apart. Chaff or sawdust was scattered
instead of the traditional flowers before the door of such a woman on her wedding day.

By the City Wall†

A niche in the masonry contains a shrine depicting the Sorrowing Mother of Christ, with flower jars before it.

GRETCHEN.   [*putting fresh flowers into the jars*]
          Incline,
          Thou rich in grief, oh shine
          Thy grace upon my wretchedness!

          Pierced to the heart   3590
          With thousandfold dart,
          Thou gazest up to thy dead son's face.

          To Him in the highest
          Thou gazest, sighest
          For thine and thy son's distress.   3595

          Who gauges
          How rages
          Pain in my marrow and bone?
          My poor heart's reaching,
          Quaking, beseeching,   3600
          Thou knowest, thou alone!

          Wherever I go,
          Woe, woe, oh woe
          Rends my bosom apart!
          Scarce left alone,   3605
          I moan, moan, moan,
          And weep to break my heart.

          At morn I plucked thee flowers,
          My bitter tears did rain,
          Bedewed the shards with showers   3610
          Outside my window pane.

          When in my room at dawning
          The sun its brightness shed,
          I sat in wakeful mourning
          Already up in bed.   3615

          Mercy! Save me from shame and death!
          Incline,
          Thou rich in grief, oh shine
          Thy grace upon my wretchedness!

Night
Street in Front of Gretchen's Door

VALENTINE, *a soldier,* GRETCHEN'S *brother.*[1]

VALENTINE. When I would sit at a drinking bout,   3620
  Where many a lad might brag and shout,
  Commending the flower of maidenhood
  To my face as loudly as they could,
  Bloating their praise with a flowing cup,
  I'd sit there with my head propped up,   3625
  Secure and snugly as you please,
  Let all the bombast roll at ease,
  I'd chuckle, pass my beard through my hand,
  Reach for my well-filled mug and say:
  All this is fair enough in its way!   3630
  But is there one in all the land
  Who with my Gretel can compare?
  One that can hold a candle to her?
  Hear! Hear! Clink, clank! rang cup to cup,
  And some would shout with flashing eyes: 3635
  He's right! She is the maidens' prize!
  That shut the noisy champions up.
  And now? I feel like tearing my hair,
  Running up walls from sheer despair!
  With needling speeches, sly mockery,   3640
  Any scoundrel may wipe his mouth on me!
  I sit like a sponger long in debt,
  Whom any chance remark can sweat!
  And if I mangled the whole damned crew,
  I never could call them liars, too!   3645

  What's coming there? What sneaks along?
  There's two of them, unless I'm wrong.
  If it is he I'll have his fleece,
  He shall not leave here in one piece!

          [*Enter* FAUST, MEPHISTOPHELES.]
FAUST. How from the vestry's narrow window-cleft   3650
  The everlasting flame does upward glimmer
  And filter sideways, dim and dimmer,
  And darkness throngs it right and left!
  So night does in my bosom writhe.
MEPHISTOPHELES. I feel more like a tomcat, slim and lithe   3655

---

1. Valentine has learned of Gretchen's affair with Faust, though it has not yet become public knowledge. He apparently has come to confront her lover.

About the fire ladders[2] sneaking,
Past masonry and gutters streaking;
I feel quite virtuous and blithe,
A dram of thievery, a pinch of buck in heat.
My blood runs hot already for the treat   3660
Of great Walpurgis Night ahead—
Two nights to go. Ah, on that beat
One knows why one is not in bed.
FAUST.   Will these two nights avail to raise the treasure
Which I see shimmer thereabout?[3]   3665
MEPHISTOPHELES.   Yes, you may soon enjoy the pleasure
Of lifting the container out.
I took a squint from out-of-bounds,
It's full of splendid lion crowns.[4]
FAUST.   But not a gem set, not a ring   3670
Wherewith I might adorn my lover?
MEPHISTOPHELES.   I think I saw beneath the cover
A string of pearl or some such thing.
FAUST.   I'm glad of that. It pains me so
To go to her with nothing to show.   3675
MEPHISTOPHELES.   For once it should not be unpleasant
To have the prize without the present.
Now that the sky is all with stars aglitter,
Here is a *tour de force*—surprise!
I'll sing a moral song, the better   3680
To throw the stardust in her eyes.

        [*Sings to the zither.*][5]
            Why do you wait,
            Sweet Kate,
            At lover's gate
            At early light of day?   3685
            Do not begin!

---

2. Reference to the ladders kept by the sides of houses, especially those with thatched roofs, to
   facilitate swift extinguishing of fires.
3. Faust apparently has agreed to accompany Mephistopheles to the Walpurgis Night to secure
   additional buried treasure (see lines 2675 ff.). According to popular superstition, such treasure
   would shine by night (see lines 3916 ff.).
4. Lion crowns were silver coins of considerable value used for trade in the Levant and in Bohemia.
5. As Goethe later acknowledged to Eckermann (January 18, 1825; see below), this song derives
   from Shakespeare's *Hamlet*, where it is sung by the deranged Ophelia for St. Valentine's day:

                   To-morrow is Saint Valentine's day,
                       All in the morning betime,
                   And I a maid at your window
                       To be your Valentine.
                   Then up he rose and donned his clothes,
                       And dupped the chamber door;
                   Let in the maid, that out a maid
                       Never departed more.

   Goethe's use of the name "Kate" (line 3683), which is not in Shakespeare, indicates that the
   translation by A. W. Schlegel (published 1797), where the name appears, was Goethe's source.
   The second stanza of the song, its ironic "moral," has no parallel in the Shakespearian source.

He'll let you in,
A maiden in,
A maiden not away.

Take heed, take flight!　　　　　　　3690
Once out of sight,
It is good night.
Good night, poor piteous thing!
For your own sake
Have with a rake　　　　　　　3695
No give and take,
But with a wedding ring.

VALENTINE.　[*steps forward*] Whom would you lure here? Ah, the pox!
　Ratcatcher,[6] damn you to perdition!
　To hell first with the music-box!　　　　　　　3700
　To hell then with the foul musician!
MEPHISTOPHELES.
　The zither's done for—nothing left worth hitting.
VALENTINE.　Now for a merry noggin-splitting!
MEPHISTOPHELES.　[*to* FAUST]
　No yielding, doctor, there's no need!
　Keep close to me, quick, do not tarry!　　　　　　　3705
　Out with your duster! Mark my lead,
　You do the lunging! I will parry.
VALENTINE.　Here, parry this then!
MEPHISTOPHELES.　　　　　　　Dead to rights.
VALENTINE.　And this.
MEPHISTOPHELES.　　　Of course.
VALENTINE.　　　　　　　Methinks the devil fights!
　What can this be? My arm's already lame.　　　　　　　3710
MEPHISTOPHELES.　[*to* FAUST] Now lunge!
VALENTINE.　[*falling*]　　　　　　　O Jesus!
MEPHISTOPHELES.　　　　　　　There, the lout
　　is tame.
　Now off post-haste, though! Things are getting ugly,
　The hue and cry is up, and not in vain.
　I cope with the police extremely snugly,
　Not quite so smoothly with the murder bane.[7]　　　　　　　3715
MARTHE.　[*at her window*] Out, people, out!
GRETCHEN.　[*at her window*] A light, bring light!
MARTHE.　[*as above*] They swear and scuffle, shout and fight.
PEOPLE.　One lies already dead!

---

6. An allusion to the Pied Piper of Hamelin, who was the subject of a ballad by Goethe entitled
　"Ratcatcher" (published 1803). Also an echo of Shakespeare's *Romeo and Juliet* 3.1.70, where
　Mercutio draws his sword to fight with Tybalt, who subsequently kills him: "Tybalt, you ratcatcher,
　come, will you walk?"
7. The court of law concerned with matters of life and death pronounced sentence in God's name,
　which explains why Mephistopheles could not control such judgments.

MARTHE. [*stepping out*]   The murderers—where did they run?
GRETCHEN. [*stepping out*] Who's lying there?
PEOPLE.   Your mother's son.   3720
GRETCHEN. What grief, oh God! upon my head!
VALENTINE. I'm dying. It is simply said,
  More simply brought about.
  Why stand there, cry and moan? Instead
  Come up and hear me out!   3725
    [*All surround him.*]
  Dear Gretchen—you are young, my pet,
  And not half wise enough as yet,
  You're in a sorry way.
  I tell you, just for you and me,
  You are a whore, what's there to say?   3730
  It can't be helped, you see.
GRETCHEN. My brother! God! What cruel shame!
VALENTINE. Call not on the Almighty's name.
  What's done is done, alas, and past,
  Now it will go the way it must.   3735
  With one in stealth it was begun,
  Soon there'll be some in place of one,
  And when a dozen's been with you,
  Then all the town has had you too.

  Where once Disgrace[8] has made its entry,   3740
  It is in deep concealment born,
  And veils of night are diligently
  About its head and shoulders drawn.
  Aye, they would smother it and murther;
  But as it grows, it breaks away,   3745
  Walks naked in the light of day,
  And grows no fairer as it goes further.
  The keener light shines on disgrace,
  The more repulsive grows its face.

  Indeed, I see the time upon you   3750
  When, harlot, all good folk will shun you
  And step around you, lifting their feet,
  As at infected carrion-meat.
  When people look into your eyes,
  The very heart in you shall quail,   3755
  You shall no more wear chain or prize,
  Step up no more to the altar rail,
  In handsome collars of lace no more
  Make merry on the dancing floor!
  No, you shall hide, a wretched mourner,   3760

---

8. The allegorical personification of Disgrace may derive from Milton's *Paradise Lost*, Book 2, in
which Satan meets Death and Sin outside the gates of hell.

Midst cripples and beggars in a dark corner,
And if God at last your sin forgive—
On earth be cursed as long as you live!
MARTHE.   Seek for your soul God's merciful ease!
Why burden it more with blasphemies?   3765
VALENTINE.   If I could fly at your shriveled throat,
You shameless, pandering nanny-goat,
Forgiveness I might hope to win
In heaping measure for every sin.
GRETCHEN.   My brother! Brother! What agony!   3770
VALENTINE.   I tell you, don't waste tears on me.
When you renounced your honor first,
Then was my heart most sorely pierced.
I pass through death's brief slumber-span
To God, a soldier and an honest man.   3775
   [Dies.]

Cathedral †
Mass, Organ and Singing

GRETCHEN, *among many people,* EVIL SPIRIT *behind* GRETCHEN.

EVIL SPIRIT.   How changed, Gretchen, you feel
  Since full of innocence
  You would approach this altar,
  From the well-thumbed booklet
  Prattling prayers,   3780
  Half childish games,
  Half God in your heart!
  Gretchen!
  Where now your mind?
  Within your heart   3785
  What misdeed?
  Do you pray for your mother's soul, through you
  Sent in her sleep to long, long agony?
  Whose blood upon your threshold?
  And here beneath your heart   3790
  Is it not swellingly astir already,
  Alarming you, itself,
  With its foreboding presence?
GRETCHEN.   Oh! Oh!
  Would I were rid of thoughts   3795
  That course my mind along, athwart,
  To spite me!
CHOIR.   *Dies irae, dies illa*
  Solvet saeclum in favilla.[1]
  [*Organ chords.*]
EVIL SPIRIT.   Wrath clutches you!   3800
  The trumpet sounds!
  The graves are quaking!
  And your heart,
  From ashen stillness
  To flaming torment   3805
  Raised again,
  Starts with quailing![2]
GRETCHEN.   Would I were far!
  I feel as though the organ here
  Stifled my breath,   3810
  The singing severed

1. "Day of wrath, that day / will dissolve the world into cinders." The Choir sings from the medieval Latin sequence concerning the Last Judgment traditionally used as part of the Requiem Mass for the dead.
2. The Evil Spirit paraphrases several stanzas in the Latin from the Requiem and applies them directly to Gretchen. The biblical source for this passage is St. Paul, 1 Corinthians 15.52, "For the trumpet will sound, and the dead will be raised imperishable, and we shall be changed."

My very soul.

CHOIR. *Iudex ergo cum sedebit,*
quidquid latet adparebit,
Nil inultum remanebit.[3]

GRETCHEN. I feel pent in!
The stony pillars
Confine me!
The vaulted heights
Press in on me! Air!

EVIL SPIRIT. Go hide! Yet sin and shame
Will not stay hidden.
Air? Light?
Woe unto you!

CHOIR. *Quid sum miser tunc dicturus?*
Quem patronem rogaturus?
Cum vix iustus sit securus.[4]

EVIL SPIRIT. Transfigured spirits
Avert their countenance,
Shrinking, the pure ones,
From your hand's touch.
Woe!

CHOIR. *Quid sum miser tunc dicturus?*

GRETCHEN. Neighbor! Your salts![5]
  [*She faints.*]

---

3. "Thus when the judge holds court, / whatever is hidden will appear, / nothing will remain unavenged."
4. "What am I, wretched one, then to say? / whom for patron to implore? / when scarcely the just man is secure."
5. As Gretchen falls unconscious, she asks her neighbor in the pew for her smelling salts, the small flask often carried by women in the eighteenth and nineteenth centuries to sniff if they felt faint.

Walpurgis Night†
The Harz Mountains; the Country Around
Schierke and Elend[1]

FAUST. MEPHISTOPHELES.

MEPHISTOPHELES. Would you not have a broomstick rather?   3835
    I wish I rode a buck, however tough.
    Our route will take us yet a good way farther.
FAUST. While I'm still fresh upon my legs and gay,
    I find this knotted stick enough.
    What good is shortening one's way?   3840
    To trudge along the winding valley's shoulder,
    Then to climb up this rugged boulder,
    Whence ever plunging torrent hurls its spray,
    This is what lends such paths their zest and charm!
    Spring is already weaving in the birches,   3845
    The fir begins to sense its balm;
    Shall not our limbs, too, feel its livening purchase?
MEPHISTOPHELES. Forsooth, it leaves me numb and calm.
    I'm in the proper tune for winter,
    I wish my path were still in frost and snow.   3850
    How drearily the moon-disk's ragged cinder
    Swims up with its belated reddish glow,
    And shines so poorly that one risks collision
    At every step with crag or rooted snare!
    I'll call a will-o'-the-wisp,[2] with your permission! 3855
    I see one yonder that's in merry flare.
    Hey you, my friend, may we enlist your service?
    Why blaze away there to no purpose?
    Please be so kind and light us up that way!
WILL-O'-THE-WISP. My reverence for you, I hope, will force   3860
    My flighty temper to your course;
    Our usual path is zigzag and astray.
MEPHISTOPHELES. Well, well! He looks to men and does the same.
    Just you go straight, in devil's name!
    Or with one puff I'll end your flickering spell.   3865
WILL-O'-THE-WISP. You are the master here, that I can tell,
    I'll gladly straighten for your vision.
    Tonight the mountain's mad with magic, though,
    And if a will-o'-the-wisp shall show you where to go
    You mustn't ask too much precision.   3870

---

1. The names of two villages along the road that leads to the Brocken.
2. Ignis fatuus, associated in folklore with the devil, a spirit that leads travelers astray into marshes
   and bogs.

FAUST. MEPHISTOPHELES. WILL-O'-THE-WISP. [*chanting by turns*]
Here, it seems, we pass the gateway
Into magic dreams and mazes.
Guide us well and earn our praises,
Speed us on our courses straightway
Through the vast deserted spaces.   3875

See how tree with tree enlaces,
Past each other swiftly scudding,
And the cliffsides squatly nodding,
And the rocky noses goring,
Roaring in the gale and snoring![3]   3880

Down through sward and pebbles pouring,
Rill and rivulet are springing.
Are they bubbling? Are they singing?
Lament sweet of lovelorn maidens,
Voices of celestial cadence?   3885
Hope and love anew imagined!
And the echo like a legend
Conjures bygone ages back.

Oo-hoo! Shoo-hoo! hear them call,
Screech-owl, plover, jaybird all,   3890
Did they all remain awake?
Newts among the rootwork crouching,
Lanky legs and bellies pouching,
Serpent roots, their reptile creepers
Up through rock and bracken wending,   3895
Weirdly writhing loops extending,
Bent to scare us, snare us, keep us,
From their sturdy tendrils sloping
Sending mollusk fringes groping
For the wanderer. Mice are teeming,   3900
Thousand-hued battalions streaming
Through the moss and heath in millions.
Fireflies in squadrons gather,
Add their mind-bedazzling brilliance
To the turmoil high and nether.   3905

Tell me, someone, are we halting
Or advancing? All is vaulting,
All revolves and swirls and races,
Crags and trees' distorted faces,

---

3. An intentional transformation of the natural landscape into the animated forces of a fairy realm. The "snoring cliffs" are two large rocks that actually exist on the road between Schierke and Elend.

And the jack-o'-lanterns floating, 3910
Breeding as they spin and bloating.[4]

MEPHISTOPHELES. Hold my coat-tail, clutch it tight!
Here we reach a middling height
Whence you glimpse a sight astounding,
Mammon glistening through the mountain.[5] 3915
FAUST. How strangely in the vales it glimmers,
As of a lurid sunrise sheen,
And probes with summer-lightning shimmers
The deepest clefts of the ravine!
There vapor wells, in billows sweeping, 3920
There mist and haze with embers glow,
Now like the finest webwork seeping,
Now breaking forth in bubbling flow.
Here it will thread in disalignment
Downhill, a hundred veins of light, 3925
And cornered there in close confinement,
All of a sudden reunite.
Close by us, points of fire are sparkling
Like golden sand-grains scattered low,
But watch! The entire rock-face darkling 3930
Is kindled now from top to toe.
MEPHISTOPHELES. How splendidly Lord Mammon is contriving
To light his palace for the feast!
I'm glad you caught a glimpse at least;
I sense the boisterous company arriving. 3935
FAUST. Ah, how the stormwind roars and hisses!
What blows it rains upon my neck![6]
MEPHISTOPHELES. Cleave to the ribwork of the ancient rock,
Or it will hurl you down these deadly precipices.
Fog thickens the nocturnal dark; 3940
Hark, all the forests clatter,
Owls flutter up and scatter,
Hear it shatter the stanchions
Of evergreen mansions,
Boughs whirring and snapping, 3945
Trunks thunderclapping,
Roots creaking and gaping,
Fearfully tangled all
Crashes in smashing fall,
And over the trammeled vales 3950

4. Intentional confusion of all spatial relations results from the chant, as the Will-o'-the-Wisp also
disappears among the other "jack-o'-lanterns."
5. An open pit reveals buried treasure glowing within the mountain (see lines 3664–5). Mammon
is a personification of these metals (see Matthew 6.24, "You cannot serve God and Mammon";
also, Milton's *Paradise Lost*, Book 1, in which Mammon takes charge of building the infernal city
of Pandemonium).
6. The procession of witches riding upwards on the air is described as a stormwind. Mephistopheles'
description of it in the speech following conjures up the wild troop from Germanic folklore, the
spirit army of Wotan, which manifested itself as a storm roaring through the forest.

Whistle and howl the gales.
Hear the voices on high,
Far off and nigh?
Yes, all the mountain long
Surges maniacal magical song!   3955

WITCHES IN CHORUS.   The witches to the Brocken fare
                      By acres green and stubble bare,
                      There to assemble, host on host,
                      Sir Urian[7] sitting uppermost,
                      By sticks and stones that flash and wink,   3960
                      The witches fart, the billies stink.
VOICE.   Here comes old Baubo[8] riding now
   Alone astride a mother sow.
CHORUS.   Give honor then to whom it's due![9]
                           Frau Baubo forward! Lead the crew!   3965
                           A proper pig and mother too,
                           The witches' train will follow you.
VOICE.   Which way did you come?
VOICE.   By the Ilsenstone, dearie,
   Took a peep into the cliff-owl's eyrie,
   Oh, how she stared!
VOICE.   O, hell and blast!   3970
   You're riding too fast!
VOICE.   She skins you and scores,
   Look at these sores!
WITCHES IN CHORUS.   The road is wide, the road is long,[1]
                      Ah, what an antic, frantic throng!   3975
                      The pitchfork pokes, the broomstick thrusts,
                      The infant chokes, the mother busts.[2]
WARLOCKS.[3]   FIRST HALF-CHORUS.
                           Like snails in shells we crawl and poke,
                           Outrun by all the womenfolk;
                           For in the Devil's Handicaps   3980
                           Girls lead us by a thousand steps.
SECOND HALF-CHORUS.
                      We do not take it much to heart;
                      Girls have a thousand paces' start,
                      But as she pants and swings her rump,

---

7. Not a traditional name for the devil, but rather a title for anyone of uncertain name who appears
   unexpectedly.
8. Originally the name of a lewd nurse in classical mythology who tries to console Demeter after
   her daughter Persephone is carried off by Hades. Here it suggests any fantastic female creature.
   The idea of a witch riding a pig is of uncertain origin.
9. A parody of Romans 13.7, "honor to whom honor is due."
1. A parody of Matthew 7.13–4, "Enter by the narrow gate; for the gate is wide and the way is easy,
   that leads to destruction, and those who enter by it are many. For the gate is narrow and the way
   is hard, that leads to life, and those who find it are few."
2. An allusion to the cutting open of a pregnant woman's womb by the force of a witch's broomstick,
   so that both infant and mother die.
3. The distinction of sexes between witches and warlocks was originally intended to anticipate the
   sexual orgies to take place at the summit of the Brocken.

     Man leaps it in a single jump.   3985
VOICE. [*above*] You there, join up, the Rock Lane crew!
VOICES. [*below*][4] We'd gladly fly aloft with you.
 We're washed all clean and scrubbed all sore,
 But barren too, for evermore.
BOTH CHORUSES.   The wind is mute, the star is fled, 3990
      The hazy moon would hide its head
      In rushing flight the magic choir
      Spurts forth a myriad sparks of fire.
VOICE. [*from below*] Halt! Halt!
VOICES. [*from above*] Who calls there from the craggy fault? 3995
VOICE. [*below*] Wait for me! Wait for me!
 Three hundred years I climb and sweat,
 And haven't reached the summit yet.
 I want my kin and company!
BOTH CHORUSES.   The stick, the broom buoy up and float, 4000
      So does the fork, so does the goat;
      Who cannot rise aloft tonight
      Must be forever lost from sight.
HALF-WITCH. [*below*] I'm sadly lagging in the race;
 The others are so far ahead!   4005
 I cannot rest content in bed,
 Nor yet attain the witches' pace.
CHORUS OF THE WITCHES.
      The ointment[5] makes the witches hale,
      A patch of rag will do for sail,
      Each trough a schooner under weigh; 4010
      He'll never fly, who won't today.

BOTH CHORUSES.   And as above the peak we flow,
      You others trail along below
      And all the heather overflood
      With your array of hexenhood! 4015
  [*They glide down.*[6]]

MEPHISTOPHELES. It throngs and rustles, thrusts and clatters,
 It swirls and hisses, sucks and chatters,
 It glows and sputters, burns and stinks,
 A sea of hexendom, methinks!
 Hold tight! or we'll be parted in two winks. 4020
 Where are you?
FAUST. [*in the distance*] Here!
MEPHISTOPHELES.   So far adrift already?
 I must assert my birthright. Steady!

---

4. No adequate explanation for the voices from below has been given. Clearly some satirical allusion
 is intended, perhaps to the Reformation.
5. Witches were said to smear their broomsticks with the fat of unborn babies to make them fly (see
 lines 3976–7).
6. The swarm of witches settles down on an open plateau like a flock of birds landing.

Make room! It's Nick, Squire Nick, sweet mob, give ground!
Here, doctor, take my hand, and in one bound
Let us escape the crush and flee.   4025
This is too wild for even the likes of me.
Close by there shines a most peculiar glow;
There's something draws me to that undergrowth.
Come, come! We'll slip in from below.
FAUST.   You Prince of Paradox! Lead on, I am not loath.   4030
It does appear a queer proceeding, though.
We go to taste Walpurgis with the elves,
And promptly start to isolate ourselves.
MEPHISTOPHELES.   Look at that flame of varying hue!
There sits a merry clique for you.   4035
No feeling lonesome at a small affair.
FAUST.   I'd rather be up over there!
I spy a glow and fumes awhirl.
There flocks the crowd to Evil-kind;[7]
There many a riddle should unfurl.   4040
MEPHISTOPHELES.   And many a one be newly twined.
You let the great world spin and riot,
We'll nest contented in our quiet.
You know, an old tradition runs
That the great world produces little ones.   4045
Here bare young witchlets prance and hover,
There old ones wisely under cover.
Be sociable, just for my sake;
It's lots of fun and little ache.
There, listen, instruments start blaring!   4050
A hellish screech! But soon one gets past caring.
Come on, step up, it cannot be refused,
I'll introduce you, you will be amused,
And change of company will keep you so.
What say you, friend? We are not tightly penned.   4055
Let your eyes rove, you hardly see the end.
A hundred fires are burning in a row;
There's dancing, chatter, brewing, drinking, wooing—
Now name me anything that's more worth doing!
FAUST.   Do you intend to gain us recognition   4060
By showing off as devil or magician?
MEPHISTOPHELES.   My custom is to go incognito,
A state occasion calls for medals, though.
While not by star and garter decked,
I find the cloven hoof here held in high respect.   4065
You see the snail there crawling up?[8] It glides about,
It can but snoop and slide,
Yet with no other guide has smelled me out.

---

7. Possibly an allusion to Satan, at the summit of the Brocken.
8. The snail may be associated with the aged, indolent group encountered shortly.

I could not hide myself here if I tried.
Come now from fire to fire with me as tutor;   4070
I am the broker here and you the suitor.
  [*to some figures sitting about dying embers*]
Well now, old gentlemen, why sit apart and fiddle?
You'd please me better in the very middle,
Amid the youngsters' swirl and foam;
One surely is alone enough at home.   4075
A GENERAL.   My trust in nations is but feeble!
One may have served them ever so well;
Just as on women, so upon the people
Youth always works the strongest spell.
A CABINET MINISTER.
  They've strayed so far away from law and creed,   4080
  That's why I like the old and pious;
  The time when we were rated highest,
  That was the golden age indeed!
SOCIAL CLIMBER.   We none of us have played the dunce,
  And often acted as we oughtn't;   4085
  Now we've attained what was important,
  It's unimportant all at once.
AUTHOR.   How many living now amongst us
  Can read a piece that's halfway clever!
  And as for our delightful youngsters,   4090
  They are more impudent than ever.
MEPHISTOPHELES.   [*who suddenly appears very old*[9]]
  On this my last ascent of the witching mountain
  I find the masses ripe for the Last Accounting,
  For since my keg is running dregs,
  The world must be on its last legs.   4095

PEDDLING WITCH.[1]   Good sirs, do not pass by like that,
  Or you might miss a pretty chance!
  Spare me a more attentive glance,
  My stock is well worth looking at.
  There's nothing here to which an armful   4100
  Of earthly merchandise compares,
  No single thing but has been harmful
  To mortal man and his affairs.
  There is no sword here has not tasted gore,
  No cup from which into a healthy frame   4105
  Some searing venom did not pour,
  No trinket here but that has brought to shame
  Some lovely woman, nor a dagger but designed
  To pierce a trusting ally from behind.

---

9. Mephistopheles, by appearing old, parodies the inactivity of the old men.
1. As at any village fair, the peddler's booth is set up with wares for sale.

MEPHISTOPHELES.   You are behind the times, dear cousin;   4110
   What's done is done, what's past is trite;
   Your stuff is fifteen to the dozen,
   For only novelties excite.
FAUST.   This entertainment gives me pause—
   The strangest fair that ever was!   4115
MEPHISTOPHELES.   Uphill now, all the surging crew;
   You think you're pushing, but they're pushing you.
FAUST.   Who is this?
MEPHISTOPHELES.   Take a good look at her!
   It's Lilith.[2]
FAUST.   Who?
MEPHISTOPHELES.   Adam's first wife. Beware,
   Yield not to the allure of those fair tresses!   4120
   Her sole adornment is her lovely hair;
   Once a young man is captured in that snare,
   He is not soon released from her caresses.
FAUST.   Those two there, the old crone and the young thing,
   Already had a merry old fling!   4125
MEPHISTOPHELES.   There's none tonight would seek repose.
   Here's a new dance; come on, it's time we chose!
FAUST.   [*dancing with the* YOUNG ONE]
            In a fair dream that once I dreamed,
            An apple-tree appeared to me,
            On it two pretty apples gleamed,   4130
            They beckoned me; I climbed the tree.[3]
THE FAIR ONE.   You've thought such apples[4] very nice
            Since Adam's fall in Paradise.
            I'm happy to report to you,
            My little orchard bears them too.   4135
MEPHISTOPHELES.   [*with* THE OLD ONE[5]]
            In a wild dream that once I dreamed
            I saw a cloven tree, it seemed,
            It had a black almighty hole;
            Black as it was, it pleased my soul.

THE OLD ONE.   I welcome to my leafy roof   4140
            The baron with the cloven hoof!
            I hope he's brought a piston tall
            To plug the mighty hole withal.

2. Adam's first wife, according to rabbinical tradition (see interpretive notes).
3. An echo of the Song of Songs 7.8–9, "I say I will climb the palm tree and lay hold of its branches.
   Oh, may your breasts be like clusters of the vine, and the scent of your breath like apples, and
   your kisses like the best wine that goes down smoothly, gliding over lips and teeth."
4. The Witch applies the metaphor of her breasts as applies to the myth of the Fall, when Eve,
   tempted by the serpent, gave the apple to Adam.
5. Critics have surmised that this may be the Witch from the scene "Witch's Kitchen."

PROCTOPHANTASMIAC.[6]   How dare you, you abandoned crew?
  It's long been proved and well propounded   4145
  That ghosts are utterly unfounded!
  And here you even dance as humans do!
THE FAIR ONE.   [*dancing*] What is he doing at our spree?
FAUST.   [*dancing*] Oh, he goes everywhere, you see.
  What others dance, he must appraise.   4150
  Unless he prattles over every phase,
  There simply wasn't any dancing.
  What most annoys him is when we're advancing,
  We could just go in circles, if you will,
  As he does in his creaking mill,   4155
  And we might win his qualified assent;
  The more so if we pay him due acknowledgment.
PROCTOPHANTASMIAC.   Still here? This is unheard of, I declare!
  Clear out! We have enlightened! Much they care.
  That devil's brood, they squirm through and finagle;   4160
  We're so advanced, and still it spooks in Tegel.
  How hard I swat at ghosts and sweep away,
  It's never clean; unheard of, I must say!
THE FAIR ONE.   Be off and stop annoying us, you hear?
PROCTOPHANTASMIAC.   Ghosts, to your faces I declare   4165
  That spirit tyranny I will not bear;
  My intellect can't banish it, I fear.
    [*The dancing continues.*]
  This hasn't been my lucky day, I know it;
  But I don't grudge the trip for it,
  And still have hopes before I quit   4170
  To conquer both the devil and the poet.
MEPHISTOPHELES.   He'll squat into a puddle soon, you'll find,
  That's what he does by way of purges,
  And when the leeches feast on his behind,
  He's cured of spirits and spiritual urges.   4175
    [*to* FAUST, *who has left the dancing*]
  Why did you let that pretty damsel go,
  Who sang so sweetly as you romped?
FAUST.   Imagine—in mid-song there jumped
  A red mouse from her mouth.
MEPHISTOPHELES.   Oh yes?
  Well, what of that! who cares at such a feast,   4180
  While he is dallying with a shepherdess?
  It wasn't a gray mouse at least.
FAUST.   And then I saw—
MEPHISTOPHELES.   What?
FAUST.   Look, Mephisto, yonder,
  Lone and apart, the maiden pale and sweet?

6. This figure is a parody of Friedrich Nicolai (1733–1811), a representative of Enlightenment rationalism in Berlin and a critic of Goethe (see interpretive notes).

But haltingly she seems to wander,   4185
As if advancing with unparted feet.
There would appear to me, I swear,
A likeness to dear Gretchen there.
MEPHISTOPHELES.   Leave that alone; no good can come of it.
It is a wraith,[7] a lifeless counterfeit,   4190
A changeling perilously met.
She clots a man's blood with her staring threat,
And he may turn into a monolith;
You've heard, of course, of the Medusa myth.[8]
FAUST.   Not so—a dead girl's eyes I see   4195
That no dear hand closed for her as she died.
This is the breast that Gretchen proffered me,
This the enchanting body I enjoyed.
MEPHISTOPHELES.   You gullible fool, it's all a magic spell!
Each sees in her the one he loves too well.   4200
FAUST.   What torment, yet how sweetly relished!
That gaze—I cannot seek escape.
How strangely is the graceful neck embellished
By a red strand from throat to nape,
A scarlet knife-edge, as it were!   4205
MEPHISTOPHELES.   Quite so! I too see it on her.
You're apt to find her walking head in hand;
Perseus cut off her head, you understand.
You're always off upon some fancy!
Come up that little hillock there—   4210
Here's quite a merry Prater fair![9]
Unless I'm fooled by necromancy,
It is indeed a stage I see.
What's playing here?
SERVIBILIS.[1]   You're just in time to see
The last of seven courses on the play-bill;   4215
Here that's the usual evening's repast.
An amateur writes up the fable,
And amateurs make up the cast.
I make a callow exit now, excuse me!
I am the immature who lifts the curtain.   4220
MEPHISTOPHELES.   To see you on the Blocksberg will amuse me;
That's one place where you all belong for certain.

7. *Idol* in the German (see interpretive notes).
8. Mephistopheles associates the cut through the neck of the wraith with the myth of the beheading by Perseus (see line 4208) of the Medusa, one of the Gorgons, whose face turned men to stone.
9. A transition to the "Intermezzo." The Prater is a famous amusement park in Vienna, first opened to the public by the Emperor Joseph II in 1766. The anachronism is clearly intentional.
1. It has been argued that this curtain-raiser may represent satirically the rector of the school in Welmar, Karl August Böttiger (1760–1835), a fawning courtier who took an active interest in the Weimar Theater.

Walpurgis Night's Dream†
or
the Golden Wedding of Oberon and Titania

Intermezzo

STAGEMASTER.   Well, tonight we rest a spell,
                Mieding's valiant breed;[1]
                Ancient mountains, moisty dell,   4225
                Are all the props we need.

HERALD.   Weddings, to be golden praised,
                Should fifty years pass muster;
                To me, contention's sieges raised
                Is gold of finer luster.   4230

OBERON.   At my side if spirits be,
                Show forth these hours, invited;
                King and Royal Consort, see,
                Troth have freshly plighted,

PUCK.[2]   Enter Puck and turns athwart   4235
                And shifts his feet at dancing;
                Hundreds follow to cavort
                And share his joyous prancing.

ARIEL.[3]   Ariel strikes his lyre pure
                To strains of heavenly cadence;   4240
                Masks bizarre his song will lure,
                But also lures fair maidens.

OBERON.   Where spouses strive for concord fair,
                On our example start them;
                To foster fondness in a pair   4245
                You only need to part them.

TITANIA.   Husband sulking, wife in moods?
                Then swiftly up and grip her;
                Lead her to southern latitudes,
                Him to the northern Dipper.   4250

---

1. Johann Martin Mieding (d. 1782), a Weimar carpenter, was stagemaster for the amateur theater of the court, in which Goethe also participated.
2. The elf from Shakespeare's *Midsummer Night's Dream*, who here leads the dancing chorus of spirits.
3. A spirit of the air, from Shakespeare's *Tempest*.

ORCHESTRA TUTTI. [*fortissimo*]
Jack-a-fly and Tim-a-bug
With kindred and relation,
Grassy cricket, leafy frog
Provide the orchestration!

SOLO.[4]   Here's the bagpipe's tootle-sack,   4255
A soap-bubble its belly;
Hear it leak and squeak and quack
Up through its crooked sally.

SPIRIT AS YET IN GESTATION.[5]
Spider claw and hoptoad paunch
And winglets to the gnome!   4260
No true beastie will you launch,
Albeit a little poem.

PAIR OF PARTNERS.
Tiny step and springy skip
Through honey dew and fragrance;
Bravely tripped, though scarce a trip   4265
Aloft to airy regions.

CURIOUS TRAVELER.[6]
Is this not mummery for fun?
Should I believe my eyes?
Fair immortal Oberon
Here too tonight? Surprise!   4270

ORTHODOX.[7]   Neither tail nor talons, true,
And yet past doubt or cavil:
As with the gods of Greece, here too
We're up against a devil.

NORTHERN ARTIST.[8]
My catch today remains for fair   4275
On sketch and fragment levels,
I'm well in train though to prepare
For my Italian Travels.

PURIST.   Alas! an evil day for me:
Lewd speech, and diction clouded;   4280

4. A soap bubble speaks with the sound of a bagpipe.
5. A grotesque mixture of insects, like a creature from a painting by Bosch or Breughel.
6. An allusion to Nicolai (see lines 4144 ff. and note). In 1783–96 he had published his *Description of a Journey through Germany and Switzerland* in twelve large volumes.
7. Count Friedrich Leopold zu Stolberg (1750–1819), poet of the Sturm und Drang and translator of Homer, who came to oppose the poets of Weimar from the standpoint of pious Christianity.
8. Goethe, associating himself with northern European artists' preoccupation with subjects from the classical realm. Goethe was planning an Italian journey when he wrote this scene in 1797, though ultimately he did not go.

In all the witch-host here, I see
No more than two are powdered.

YOUNG WITCH. A powdered head and covering frock
Are good for gray old hexen;[9]
So I sit naked on my buck   4285
And show up firm and buxom.

MATRON. We have too much of *savoir-faire*
To bandy words with witches;
But you may rot, for all I care,
As young and tender bitches.   2490

BANDMASTER. Jack-a-fly and Tim-a-bug,
Don't swarm about the naked!
Grassy cricket, leafy frog,
You *can* keep time, I take it?

WEATHERVANE.[1] [*pointing one way*]
The best of company, in truth,   4295
All hopeful brides amongst us!
And bachelors to a man; forsooth,
Most eligible youngsters!

WEATHERVANE. [*pointing other way*]
And if the ground won't split apart
To swallow lads and ladies,   4300
I'm off to take a flying start
And leap straight into Hades.

XENIEN.[2] Insect-shaped we flutter up,
Sharp little scissors flitting,
To offer unto Beelzebub,   4305
Our father, worship fitting.

HENNINGS.[3] Look at them milling here in strength,
Ingenuously joking!
They'll have the crust to claim at length
That they are kindly-spoken.   4310

MUSAGETE. How I should love to lose myself
Amid this witches' pageant,

9. Witches.
1. The same figure speaks the following two stanzas, a flatterer who totally changes the direction of his opinion according to the audience he addresses.
2. A reference to the collection of satirical epigrams published in 1796 by Goethe and Schiller.
3. August Friedrich Hennings (1746–1826), a minor writer and editor who in 1798–99 published a collection of poems entitled *Musagete* in two volumes (see lines 4311 ff.; the title is an epithet of Apollo, "one who leads the Muses"). He also was editor of a literary journal first entitled *Spirit of the Age*, then (after 1800) *Spirit of the Nineteenth Century* (Goethe acknowledges this change of title with his French term *ci-devant*, "erstwhile").

I'm better with this kind of elf
Than as the Muses' agent.

CI-DEVANT SPIRIT-OF-THE-TIMES.
　　　　Here, grab my coat-tail! Any flop   4315
　　　　Thus soars above the masses;
　　　　The Blocksberg has a spacious top
　　　　Like Germany's Parnassus.

CURIOUS TRAVELER.[4]
　　　　What do they call this haughty man,
　　　　So poker-stiffly walking?   4320
　　　　He snoops and sniffs as hard as he can.
　　　　"It's Jesuits he's stalking."

CRANE.[5]
　　　　I take my pleasure both in clear
　　　　And muddy waters angling;
　　　　Thus you may see the pious here   4325
　　　　Amongst the devils dangling.

THIS WORLD'S CHILD.[6]
　　　　Believe me, to the pious all
　　　　Is grist to prayer mills;
　　　　Upon the Blocksberg here they call
　　　　Lots of conventicles.   4330

DANCER.
　　　　Another chorus coming in?
　　　　I hear a distant drumming.
　　　　Be easy! It's the unison
　　　　Of moorland bittern thrumming.

DANCEMASTER.[7]
　　　　How all the dancers lift their feet   4335
　　　　And manage hook-or-crook-like!
　　　　The hunched turn limber, awkward fleet,
　　　　Not caring what they look like.

FIDDLER.
　　　　This mob is all at daggers drawn,
　　　　At odds like ice and fire;   4340
　　　　Just on the tootlebag they fawn
　　　　Like beasts on Orpheus' lyre.

---

4. Nicolai, as above (lines 4267 ff.), whose hatred for Catholics was well known.
5. From Goethe's comment to Eckermann on February 17, 1829, we know that he here alludes to Johann Caspar Lavater (1741–1801), the Swiss physiognomist, with whom he came into contact as a young man.
6. A third allusion to Goethe himself, in accord with his earlier poem "Dinner in Coblentz" (1774), in which he speaks of himself as sitting between Lavater and Basedow: "prophet to the right, prophet to the left, the world's child in the middle."
7. This and the stanza following were written much later than the rest of the "Dream"—apparently early in 1826—in response to an English translation of the scene by John Heavyside.

DOGMATIC.[8]   I shan't be flustered by critique,
                    For all their doubts and cavils;
                    There must be something to Old Nick   4345
                    Or how could there be devils?

IDEALIST.[9]   This once by fantasy, my bliss,
                    I feel too harshly saddled;
                    Forsooth, if I am all of this,
                    Today I must be addled.   4350

REALIST.[1]   I find their doings hard to stand,
                    I never was a squirmer;
                    For once I have two feet on sand
                    Instead of *terra firma*.

SUPERNATURALIST.[2]
                    With these carousers I concur,   4355
                    And do enjoy the ball so!
                    For from the devils I infer
                    Benignant spirits also.

SCEPTIC.[3]   Each trails and trusts his will o'wisp
                    To lead him to the treasure;   4360
                    The devil-cavil rhyme is crisp,
                    For me it's made to measure.

BANDMASTER.   You frog and cricket make us sound
                    Like amateur auditions;
                    You fly and beetle, I'll be bound,   4365
                    I thought you were musicians!

NIMBLE ONES.[4]   They call us sports the *Sans-souci*,
                    Our feet are sore from slogging;
                    We carry on right merrily,
                    Each walking on his noggin.   4370

AWKWARD ONES.[5]
                    We've sponged and toadied all we knew,
                    But now have shot our wadding;
                    Our dancing shoes are worn right through,
                    Barefooted we are plodding.

8. Pre-Kantian dogmatists, specifically in Christian doctrine.
9. Post-Kantian idealism, especially the philosophy of Fichte and Schelling.
1. A general allusion to empiricists, who would base their judgment of reality on observation.
2. An allusion to belief in a transcendent realm, of which the enthusiast Friedrich Heinrich Jacobi
   (1743–1819) served as a conspicuous example.
3. Presumably an allusion to such a philosopher as the Scotsman David Hume (1711–1776).
4. Opportunists who merely changed their political leanings after the French Revolution "without a
   care" (i.e., *sans-souci* in French).
5. Aristocratic emigrés from France after the Revolution, who frequently became parasites at the
   various courts of Europe.

WILL O' THE WISPS.[6]

    We came directly from the swamp.   4375
    Where we originated;
    But here we shine in serried pomp,
    As glittering gallants rated.

SHOOTING STAR.[7]

    Wreathed in fire I plunged from high
    In sparks of starry glitter;   4380
    Now prostrate in the grass I lie,
    Who'll help me to a litter?

MASSIVE ONES.[8]

    Room! More room here! Let us through!
    Down tender herbs are trodden.
    Spirits coming, spirits too   4385
    Come uncouth and plodding.

PUCK.

    One needn't lumber so and sway
    Like elephant babies, must one!
    Let loudest thumping come today
    From Puck himself, robust one!   4390

ARIEL.

    Whether Nature bountiful
    Or spirit gave you pinions,
    Track me lightly up the hill
    To the rose dominions!

ORCHESTRA.   [pianissimo]

    Cloudy drift and vapor's edge   4395
    Are lighted from above.
    Leafy sough and breezy sedge,
    And all is wafted off.

6. Figures who emerged from nowhere through the Revolution to shine in the public arena. (See
   the Will-o'-the-Wisp in the preceding scene, lines 3855 ff.)
7. Radical revolutionaries whose political day was over.
8. The "masses" released by the Revolution.

Dreary Day[1]†
A Field

FAUST. MEPHISTOPHELES.

FAUST.   In misery! Despairing! Long roaming the earth, a wretched waif, and now imprisoned! Locked up in the dungeon as an evildoer to suffer appalling torture, the lovely luckless creature! To this! To this pass!— Faithless, degraded spirit—and this you concealed from me? Yes, stand there, stand! Roll those demon eyes in your head in speechless spite! Stand there and defy me with your unbearable presence! Imprisoned! In unredeemable ruin! Abandoned to evil spirits and to judging, un- feeling mankind! And through it all you lull me with insipid distractions, hide from me her deepening wretchedness, and let her helplessly perish!

MEPHISTOHELES.   She is not the first.[2]

FAUST.   Cur! Abominable monster!—Transform him, thou infinite spirit,[3] change the viper back into its dog shape, as it was pleased to lope before me of a night, tumbling at the harmless wanderer's feet and dragging him down by the shoulders as he fell. Return him to his favorite guise, that he may crawl on his belly in the sand before me, and I may spurn him with my foot, the offal!—Not the first!—Piteous grief! Too piteous for human soul to grasp, that more than one being should have sunk to this depth of misery, that the first did not atone enough for the guilt of all the rest, writhing in deathly agony before the eyes of the eternally Forgiving! I am rent to the living core by this single one's suffering: you pass with a carefree grin over the fate of thousands!

MEPHISTOPHELES.   There we are, back once more at our wits' end, where your human minds snap. Why make common cause with us if you cannot see it through? You would fly, yet are not proof against vertigo? Did we obtrude ourselves on you, or you on us?

FAUST.   Do not flash your voracious teeth at me so! I am sickened!— Glorious lofty Spirit, who didst deign to appear before me, who knowest my heart and my soul, why forge me to this profligate who relishes injury and gloats over perdition?[4]

MEPHISTOPHELES.   Are you finished?

FAUST.   Save her! Or woe unto you! The most hideous curse upon you for millennia!

MEPHISTOPHELES.   I cannot loose the avenger's bonds, nor undo his bolts. "Save her!" Who was it that plunged her to her ruin? I or you?

[FAUST *gazes about him savagely.*]

---

1. From the earliest stage of composition on *Faust*, the only scene in the published text that is prose. Faust's rage indicates that he has just learned of Gretchen's fate, though the later text of the "Walpurgis Night" (despite the appearance of the wraith) does not fully clarify how this has happened. (See interpretive note on the Gretchen tragedy.)
2. This statement occurs in the literature on infanticide, which was known to Goethe, and also in the court documents from actual trials for the same crime.
3. An invocation of the Earth Spirit from "Night," lines 482 ff.
4. This speech may be the germ of Faust's monologue (written in 1788) in "Forest and Cavern," lines 3240–50.

MEPHISTOPHELES.   Are you groping for thunder? It is well that it was not given you wretched mortals! To shatter the innocent reasoner—there's true tyrant fashion when seeking relief from any straits.

FAUST.   Take me there! She shall be free!

MEPHISTOPHELES.   And the danger you court? Know, there still weighs upon the town blood-guilt from your hand. Over the site of the slain hover avenging spirits in wait for the slaver's return.

FAUST.   That, too, from you? Murder and death of a world upon your head, monster! Lead me there, I say, and free her!

MEPHISTOPHELES.   I will lead you, and what I can perform, hear it! Do I have all the power on earth and in heaven? The gaoler's senses I will befog, you possess yourself of the keys and lead her out by human hand. I will stand guard! The magic steeds are ready, I will carry you off. Thus far my power.

FAUST.   Up and away!

Night†
Open Field

FAUST, MEPHISTOPHELES, *charging along on black steeds.*

FAUST.   Why do they hover there, by the raven-stone?[1]

MEPHISTOPHELES.

Who knows what they are brewing and wreaking.   4400

FAUST.   Weaving and wavering, bowing and crouching . . .

MEPHISTOPHELES.   A witches' guild.[2]

FAUST.   Strewing and conjuring . . .

MEPHISTOPHELES.   Away! Away!

---

1. The block on which Gretchen will be beheaded.
2. Possibly influenced by the Witches in Shakespeare's *Macbeth* or similar figures in the famous ballad "Lenore" by Gottfried August Bürger (1747–1794). The purpose of these witches is uncertain, though they may be consecrating the place for death according to some occult rite.

Dungeon†

FAUST, *holding a bunch of keys and a lamp, in front of a small iron door.*

FAUST. I shudder with a long-unwonted spell;   4405
  The woe of all mankind rends me apart.
  Behind this sodden wall here does she dwell,
  And her transgression was a trusting heart!
  You shrink from being here!
  You are afraid of seeing her!   4410
  Forward! Your tarrying tardies forth her death.
       [*He seizes the lock. Singing is heard from inside.*[1]]
MARGARETE. My mother, the whore
         Who smothered me,
         My father, the knave
         Who made broth of me!   4415
         Wee sister shy
         The bones laid by
         In a cool dale;
         Of a sudden I was a fair nightingale;
         Fly, pretty bird, fly!   4420
FAUST. [*unlocking the door*]
  She little knows, her lover at the door
  Can hear the clanking chains, the rustling straw.
       [*He enters.*]
MARGARETE. [*trying to hide on her pallet*]
  Woe! They are coming. Bitter death is here!
FAUST. [*softly*] Hush! Hush! I've come to set you free.
MARGARETE. [*writhing up to him*]
  If you be human, pity my despair!   4425
FAUST. No, hush! You'll have the guards on me.
       [*He seizes the chains to unlock them.*]
MARGARETE. [*on her knees*] Say, who has given you this power,
  Headsman, over me?
  You come already at the midnight hour,
  Oh feel for me and let me be!   4430
  I'm due at dawn—is that too long?
       [*She rises to her feet.*]
  I am so young, oh God, so young
  And am to die!
  And I was pretty too, that was my ruin.
  Far is my friend, who once was nigh;   4435
  Torn lies the wreath, the petals strewn.
  Do not so roughly wrench my arm!
  Be gentle—have I done you any harm?

1. The source for Gretchen's song is discussed in the interpretive notes.

Oh, let me not in vain implore—
Have I so much as looked on you before?   4440
FAUST.   Oh pity! I can bear no more.
MARGARETE.   Now I am wholly in your might.
Just let me nurse the child before.
I hugged it to me all last night;
They've taken it away to make me cry,   4445
And now they say I made it die,
And I shall never again be glad.
They sing songs about me. People are horrid!
An ancient folk tale ends like that,
Why blame me for it?[2]   4450
FAUST.   [*throwing himself down*] See at your feet a lover kneeling,
Your grievous bonds to be unsealing!
MARGARETE.   [*throwing herself down beside him*]
Yes—let us beg the saints for intercession!
This threshold beneath,
Under these steps,   4455
Hell's depths seethe,
The Devil, gnashing
In wrath appalling,
Crashing and brawling!
FAUST.   [*loudly*] Gretchen! Gretchen!   4460
MARGARETE.   [*attentively*] That was my dear one calling!
            [*She jumps up. The chains fall off.[3]*]
Where is he? I heard him well, he called me.
I am free! There's nobody shall hold me.
To his arms I shall fly,
At his bosom lie!   4465
He called Gretchen! On the threshold he stood,
Through the clangor and howl of the Devil's brood,
Through the sneers, the infernal infuriate drone,
I knew it, the sweet, the enchanting tone.
FAUST.   It is I!
MARGARETE.   It's you! Oh, say it again!   4470
[*seizing him*] It's he! It is he! Where is all my pain?
The chains, the dungeon where I languish?
You, come to end my anguish!
I am saved![4]
Already I see the street anew,   4475
Where first you came upon my sight,
And the dear garden bright,
Where I and Marthe were awaiting you.
FAUST.   [*straining away*] Come with me, come!

2. Gretchen confuses the song she has just sung with the songs peddled by ballad-mongers, who
   presumably will commemorate her own death in such a way.
3. Apparently a miraculous liberation from her bonds.
4. Not in the *Urfaust*, this line anticipates the voice from above at the end of the scene (see line
   4611).

MARGARETE.   Oh do not hurry!
   I love to tarry where you tarry! [*caressing him*]   4480
FAUST.   Hurry!
   For if you tarry
   We shall have much to rue it for.
MARGARETE.   What? You can kiss no more?
   My friend, so lately gone amiss,   4485
   And has forgotten how to kiss?
   Why am I fearful now in your embrace?
   When from your speeches, from your face
   A wave of very heaven overbroke me,
   And you would kiss as if you were to choke me?   4490
   Kiss me!
   Or I'll kiss you!
      [*She embraces him.*]
   Oh no—your lips are cold,
   Are clay.
   Where is your love abiding,   4495
   In hiding?
   Who took it away?
      [*She turns away from him.*]
FAUST.   Take heart, dear love, come, let us go,
   I will caress you with a thousandfold glow;
   Just follow—that is all I beg of you!   4500
MARGARETE.   [*turning toward him*]
   And it is really you? Is it all true?
FAUST.   It is! Come on!
MARGARETE.   And you cast off this strap,
   Take me again into your lap.
   How is it that you do not shrink from me?
   Why, do you know, my friend, whom you set free?   4505
FAUST.   Come, while the night is deep and stilled.
MARGARETE.   My mother I killed,
   My child I drowned.
   Was it not given us both, and bound
   Thee too? Thee! No—I can't believe it yet.   4510
   Give me that hand! No, it's no dream!
   My dearest hand! But it feels wet!
   Oh! Wipe it off! It would seem
   There's blood on it.[5]
   Oh God! Whom did it hit?   4515
   Put up that sword,
   I beg of thee!
FAUST.   Let what is past be past—oh Lord,
   You're killing me.
MARGARETE.   No, no, you must outlive us!   4520

---

5. An allusion to Faust's murder of Valentine. The theme of guilt is derived from the sleepwalking
   scene in Shakespeare's *Macbeth*, in which Lady Macbeth tries to wash out the spot of blood.

Here is what manner of graves to give us,
I charge you, go to it,
Tomorrow do it.
The best place give to my mother,
Right next her put my brother,   4525
And me at a distance, pray,
But not too far away!
And the little one at my right breast.
There's no one else will lie by me![6]—
To nestle against your side was rest,   4530
Was purest, sweetest happiness!
But now it seems I lost the feel of you,
As if I had to brace myself, as if you too
Repulsed me, spurning my caress;
Yet it is you, as ever kind and dear.   4535
FAUST.   Then if you feel it's I, come out from here!
MARGARETE.   Out where?
FAUST.   To freedom.
MARGARETE.   Is the grave out there?
Death ambushed? Then I go with you!
From here to the eternal resting-place,   4540
Else not one pace—
You're leaving now? Oh Heinrich, if I could too!
FAUST.   You can! Just want to! See, the door is open.
MARGARETE.   It must not be; for me there is no hoping.
What use is fleeing? Still they lie in wait for you.   4545
I dread the beggar's staff and purse,
And a sinner's conscience makes it worse!
It's so wretched to err in far-off lands,
And still at last I'll fall into their hands!
FAUST.   I'll stay with you.   4550
MARGARETE.   Quick, run![7]
Save your little one.
Quick, follow the trail
Up the river dale,
Cross on the trunk   4555
Into the copse,
Left, where the planking stops
Into the lake.
Snatch it, for God's sake,
It hasn't sunk,   4560
Is kicking still!
Save it, save!
FAUST.   Oh love—you rave!
One step—and you can leave at will!

6. As an executed infanticide, Gretchen would not be allowed burial in hallowed ground.
7. Gretchen imagines herself with Faust as a fugitive beggar, reenacting the drowning of her infant
son.

MARGARETE.   If only we were past that hill!   4565
  There sits my mother upon a stone,
  It sets my flesh ashiver,
  There sits my mother upon a stone,
  Her heavy head aquiver;
  She won't beckon or nod, her head is too sore,   4570
  She has slept so long, she'll awake no more.
  She slept so that we might kiss.
  Those were the days of our bliss!
FAUST.   No pleading avails, no talking sense.
  I must lift you up and carry you hence.   4575
MARGARETE.   Let go! I'll suffer no violence!
  Don't seize me with such murderous grasp!
  Haven't I done all else you asked?
FAUST.   The dawn shines gray! Oh love, my love!
MARGARETE.   Day! Yes, day is here, it dawns so gray;   4580
  This was to be my wedding-day![8]
  Tell no one that Gretchen was yours already.
  My poor wreath's shredding!
  What's done is done!
  We shall be one,   4585
  But not at a wedding.
  The crowd is thronging, no word, no laugh;
  The square is milling,
  The streets o'erfilling.
  There tolls the bell, they break the staff.[9]   4490
  How they pounce on me, bind me!
  Already I am on the scaffold laid,
  All necks shrink back from the winking blade
  That will glint and find me.
  Mute lies the world like the grave!   4595
FAUST.   This day is my undoing!
MEPHISTOPHELES.   [appearing outside] Up! Or you risk your ruin!
  Unmanly mutter! Vain chatter and putter!
  My stallions shudder,
  The night is ending.[1]   4600
MARGARETE.   What rises there, from the pit ascending?
  He! He! send him away!
  What does he want on this solemn day?
  He wants me![2]
FAUST.   You shall be whole!
MARGARETE.   Judgment of God! To thee I give my soul!   4605

---

8. The association of execution day and wedding day, with the bell tolling and the townspeople gathering, is thematic to Gretchen's derangement, since Faust presumably never intended to marry her.
9. Traditionally, the "sinner's bell" was tolled as the condemned was led to execution, and a staff was broken over the head of the condemned at the gallows as a symbol of the death penalty.
1. The magic stallions must disappear at daybreak.
2. Sensing that Mephistopheles is the devil, Gretchen imagines that he has come to carry her off to hell.

MEPHISTOPHELES. [*to* FAUST]
Come, come! Or I'll forsake both her and thee.
MARGARETE.   Thine I am, Father! Rescue me!
Ye heavenly host of angels, sally
To be my refuge, about me rally![3]
Heinrich! I shrink from thee!   4610
MEPHISTOPHELES. She is condemned!
VOICE.   [*from above*]   Redeemed![4]
MEPHISTOPHELES. [*to* FAUST]   Hither! To me!
[*Disappears with* FAUST.]
VOICE.   [*from within, dying away*] Heinrich! Heinrich![5]

---

3. See Psalms 34.7, "The angel of the Lord encamps around those who fear him, and delivers them."
4. Not in the *Urfaust*, which contained no hint of Gretchen's salvation.
5. This concluding line of Part One echoes the traditional ending of the Faust legend, where eternal damnation is pronounced against Faust: "Fauste! Accusatus es!" "Fauste! Iudicatus es!" "Fauste! Fauste! In aeternum damnatus es!" In contrast to the assurance of Gretchen's salvation, Mephistopheles may thus seem to drag Faust off to damnation.

The Tragedy's Second Part in Five Acts

ACT I

Charming Landscape†

FAUST, *bedded on a flowery mead, weary, restless, seeking sleep.*
Twilight. A ring of SPIRITS, *graceful little shapes, floating and weaving.*

ARIEL.[1] [*singing, to the accompaniment of Aeolian harps*[2]]
    When the vernal blossom showers
    Wafting sink on all the earth,
    And the fields their verdant dowers   4615
    Shine to all of mortal birth,
    Elfin power of fairies dainty
    Hies to help where help it can,
    Be he wicked, be he saintly,
    Pitying the luckless man.   4620
Ye who surround this head with aerial wheeling,
Here prove the noble elfin way of healing,
Soothe now the wearied heart's contention dire,
Withdraw the searing arrows of remorse,
Of horrors suffered cleanse his soul entire.   4625
Four are the vigils of the night's dim course,[3]
With kindly care to plenish them conspire.
First rest his head upon the cooling pillow,
Then bathe him in the dew of Lethe's bourn:[4]
And soon the cramp-enrigored limbs grow willow,   4630
As strengthened he will rest against the morn;
Do fairest duty of the sprite—
Return him to the sacred light.

---

1. The same spirit of the air from Shakespeare's *Tempest* who concluded the "Walpurgis Night's Dream" (lines 4391 ff.). We may assume that he has come directly to this "charming landscape" with his companion spirits from the "Intermezzo."
2. See "Dedication," line 28 and note.
3. An allusion to the traditional watches of the night, extending in three-hour periods from six in the evening to six in the morning.
4. Drinking the waters of the river Lethe, according to classical mythology, caused the mind to forget its earthly existence.

CHORUS. [*in alternating solos, duos, groups, and unison*]
    When an aerial mildness vagrant
    Green-embowered lowland rings,   4635
    Swathing mists and ambience fragrant
    Dusk in its descending brings,
    Languor dulcet, lisping lowly,
    Lulls the heart to child's repose,
    On the weary sufferer slowly   4640
    These diurnal portals close.

    Night has sunk already, darkling,
    Ranking star on holy star,
    Lambent lantern, tiny sparkling,
    Shimmer near and glimmer far;   4645
    There in cloudless night aglimmer,
    Mirrored here in watery planes,
    Sealing blissful rest, the shimmer
    Of the moon in splendor reigns.

    Rueful hours are fading, ending,   4650
    Ache and bliss are washed away;
    Bode it now! Already mending,
    Trust the newly pledging day.
    Vales are greening, hillocks swelling,
    Bushes shady rest afford,   4655
    And in pliant silver welling,
    Crops are swaying harvestward.

    Send your gaze to yonder brightness,
    Wish on wish at will to reap,
    You are cradled but in lightness,   4660
    Cast it off, the shell of sleep!
    Scruple not to be audacious
    As the doubting rabble gasp;
    All is open to the gracious
    Who perceive and swiftly grasp.   4665

    [A *stupendous clangor proclaims the approach of the sun.*]
ARIEL.   Hark the storm of hours rounding,
    Clear to spirit ear rebounding,
    Knell of day's renewal sounding!
    Granite portals groan and clatter,
    Wheels of Phoebus roll and spatter,   4670
    What great din the dawning brings!
    Trumpet-blaring and fanfaring,
    Ears bedazing, eyes beglaring,
    Fear to hear unheard-of things.
    Blossom clusters seek to hide in,   4675
    Deep in sheltered hush abiding,

Down the crags, beneath the leaf;
If it strikes you, you are deaf.

FAUST.   Revived, life's pulse is throbbing fresh and heady,
  Gently to greet the dawn's ethereal wreathing;   4680
  This night, too, earth, you have persisted steady
  And, newly quickened, at my feet are breathing;
  Fresh joy to grant you have already striven.
  Already set resolve astir and seething
  Toward peaks of being to be ever driven.—   4685
  In luminous haze the world would pierce its cover,
  The woods resound to myriad notes of living,
  Down clefts and vales where drifts of vapor hover,
  Cerulean clarity is downward seeping,
  And twigs and branches, freshly laved, recover   4690
  From fragrant depths of their enchanted sleeping;
  Where leaf and petal drip from dewy shower,
  Now hue on hue from somber ground are leaping,
  And all about me turns to Eden's bower.

  Raise up your gaze!—The mountain titans waken,   4695
  Swift to proclaim the consecrated hour,
  Of deathless lucence they have first partaken,
  Before the day to lowlands here inclined it.
  But now the alp's green slants have also shaken
  The dusk, for gleam and contour newly minded,   4700
  And light descends triumphant, stepwise darting;—
  He clears the rim!—Alas, already blinded,
  I turn aside, my mortal vision smarting.

  Thus also, as we yearningly aspire
  And find at last fulfillment's portals parting,   4705
  Wrung within tender reach our prime desire,
  There will erupt from those eternal porches,
  Dumbfounding us, exorbitance of fire;
  We only meant to kindle up life's torches,
  And flame engulfs us, seas of torrid blazes!   4710
  Love? Hatred? Which? envelops us and scorches,
  Sends pain and joy in vast alternate phases,
  Till we gaze back upon our homely planet
  And shelter in most young of youthful hazes.

  So, sun in back, my eye too weak to scan it,   4715
  I rather follow, with entrancement growing,
  The cataract that cleaves the jagged granite,
  From fall to fall, in thousand leaps, outthrowing
  A score of thousand streams in its revolving,
  From upflung foam a soaring lacework blowing.   4720
  But in what splendor from this storm evolving,

Vaults up the shimmering arc, in variance lasting,
Now purely limned and now in air dissolving,
A cooling fragrance all about it casting.
This mirrors all aspiring human action.   4725
On this your mind for clearer insight fasten:
That life is ours by colorful refraction.

Imperial Residence[1]†
Throne Room

COUNCIL OF STATE *awaiting the* EMPEROR.
Trumpets.
[COURT ATTENDANTS *of every sort, splendidly attired, step forward.*]
[*The* EMPEROR *reaches his throne, on his right the* ASTROLOGER.]

EMPEROR.   My trusty well-beloved, well met,
  Assembled here from far and near;—
  The Magus is beside me here,   4730
  The Fool, though—he is missing yet.
SQUIRE.   Why, hard behind your train of state
  He seemed to drop of his own weight;
  They bore his Lardship off from here,
  If dead or drunken was not clear.[2]   4735
SECOND SQUIRE.   At once, with wondrous speed of pace
  Intrudes another in his place,
  In costly garb, but such a fop
  That people stare at him and stop;
  The sentries fling before his face   4740
  Their halberds crossed, his zeal to cool—
  Yet here he is, the daring fool!
MEPHISTOPHELES.   [*kneeling near the throne*]
  What is desired and yet rejected?
  What is upbraided, and yet nursed?
  What is unceasingly protected?   4745
  What bitterly denounced and cursed?
  Whom must we shun by common warning?
  Whom are we glad to call by name?
  What would approach your royal awning?
  What is self-banished from the same?   4750
EMPEROR.   Save us your riddles for the nonce!
  Conundrums are *de trop* for once;
  These gentlemen will pose a few.—
  I'd gladly hear them solved by you.
  My former Fool, I fear, went far and wide;   4755
  Assume his place and step up to my side.
    [MEPHISTOPHELES *ascends and takes his stand at left.*]
CROWD MUTTERING.[3]
    Another fool—For new dismay—

---

1. Faust's visit to the court of the Holy Roman Emperor is already included in Goethe's "Outline of the Contents for Part Two" (see below).
2. Goethe acknowledged (in a conversation with Eckermann, October 1, 1827; see below) that the true jester had been removed by Mephistopheles.
3. Each half line in the following four lines (as in similar instances four times more in this scene—lines 4885–8, 4951–4, 4973–6, 4993–8) is spoken by an individual in the crowd of assembled courtiers.

    Whence did he come—How find his way—
    The old one fell—He shot his wad—
    There was a keg—Here is a rod—   4760
EMPEROR. Well, then, Our trusty ones who love Us,
    Be welcome both from near and far,
    You meet beneath a favoring star,
    For hail and bliss are writ on high above us.
    But why, with Carnival so near,   4765
    The time we banish care and fear,
    In bearded masquerade appear,
    Serenely bent on pure enjoyment,
    Should we consult in toilsome state employment?
    Still, since you feel there is no other way,   4770
    We are convened—each have his say.
CHANCELLOR. The highest Good has like a halo shone
    About the Emperor's head, and he alone
    May validly accord it from above:
    The equity of Law!—What all men love,   4775
    What all demand, desire, can't do without,
    His office must dispense it all about.
    But oh! what good is reason to man's mind,
    To hands good will, to hearts intention kind,
    When Commonwealth's in feverish upheaval,   4780
    And evil rankly overhatches evil?
    Who from this lofty hall could train his sight
    Onto the realm, would view a nightmare fright,
    Where failing plies misshapen failing,
    A lawful lawlessness prevailing,   4785
    A world of errors in its courses trailing.
    This one a flock, that one a wife will seize,
    From altars, cross and candle, jewelled host,
    Of their possessions many years may boast
    Unscathed of body, in untroubled ease.   4790
    Now plaintiffs crowd the justice-dwelling,
    The judge on lofty pillow lolls,
    While just outside it, fiercely swelling,
    The floodtide of rebellion rolls.
    He robs and rapes without repentance   4795
    Whom base accomplices support,
    And Guilty! sounds the lying sentence,
    Where innocence is sole resort.
    The world is rent by mutual maiming,
    Destroys what should be held in awe;   4800
    The sense of right seems past reclaiming
    Which solely leads us to the Law!
    A man of pure intention bends
    To bribes and flattery in time,
    A judge who cannot punish ends   4805
    By throwing in his lot with crime.

Would that my picture, somber as it was,
Could have been veiled in darker gauze.
    [*Pause.*]
Remedial counsels must be offered:
Privation dealt, privation suffered,   4810
Leave very Majesty bereft.
QUARTERMASTER.   What wild unrest, these savage days!
A man is either slain or slays,
To all command remaining deaf.
Within their walls the burgomasters,   4815
Upon his rocky perch the knight,
They have conspired to outlast us
And hold their forces gathered tight.
The mercenary soldier rages,
Impatiently demands his pay,   4820
And if we did not owe him wages,
He would long since have run away.
If one denies what all expected,
One has stirred up a hornet's nest;
The realm they were to have protected   4825
Lies ravaged now and sore distressed.
Forfeit is half the earth's dominion,
They prey and loot without redress,
And though there still are kings, in their opinion
This hardly could concern them less.   4830
TREASURER.   Who trusts in allies now or clients?
The subsidies in which we placed reliance
Run dry like water in a spout.
Oh Lord, in your dominions vast
To whom have all the titles passed?   4835
Look where you will, incumbents new stand out,
And each would lord it all unheeding;
All we can do is just look on;
So many rights we have been ceding,
No right remains for us to lean upon.   4840
As for the parties, as they're called,
You cannot trust them nowadays;
You may be scolded or extolled,
Indifferent are abuse and praise.
The Ghibellines and Guelfs at war[4]   4845
Have gone in hiding to regroup;
Who helps his neighbor any more?
Each wants to cook his private soup.
The ports of gold are tightly jammed,
Each one has scraped and raked and crammed,   4850
But our exchequer is to let.

---

4. An allusion to two warring factions in the empire during the twelfth and thirteenth centuries, totally anachronistic here; presumably indicating any such warring factions.

MARSHAL.   To me, too, fate such ills dispenses:
  Each day is to curtail expenses,
  Each puts us deeper into debt,
  And growing anguish will extort.   4855
  The cooks and scullions need not fear;
  Of boar and stag, of hare and deer,
  Of ducks and geese and Gallic hens,
  Allowances in kind, fixed rents,
  There's still an inflow of a sort.   4860
  But wine at last is running short.
  Where cask on cask the vaults would stow us,
  Prime vintages of premier growers,
  My lords' relentless swillings show us
  The final barrel's final drop.   4865
  The City Council has to draw its pegs,
  We're down to jugs and bowls from kegs,
  Beneath the table lies the sop.
  I am to settle all accounts,
  The Jew will not rebate an ounce,   4870
  Liens and attachments will pronounce
  Which swallow up the next year's crop.
  The swine are short of fattening forage,
  We sleep on pillows under mortgage,
  At table serve premasticated bread.   4875
EMPEROR.   [after some reflection, to MEPHISTOPHELES]
  And you, fool, have no tale of woe to add?
MEPHISTOPHELES.   Not I. To see the radiance effused
  By you and yours! Could confidence be bruised
  Where sovereignty brooks no insolence,
  Where instant force stands ready for defense,   4880
  Where goodwill acts, braced by intelligence,
  And bounteous energy, instructed by good sense?
  What could toward misadventure be combining,
  Or gloom, where galaxies like these are shining?
PEOPLE MUTTERING.
      There is a rogue—Knows how to cast—   4885
      He plays his fish—Both loose and fast—
      What's up his sleeve—We know these jokes—
      Some plan, what else—Another hoax—
MEPHISTOPHELES.   Who in this world has not some lack or need?
  One this, one that—here it is cash. Indeed,   4890
  There is no gathering it off the pavement;
  Yet wisdom taps its most profound encavement
  In lodes and masonwork, where gold unstinted
  Waits underground, both minted and unminted;
  And who can raise it to the light of day?   4895
  Man's gifts of Nature and of Mind, I say.
CHANCELLOR.   Nature and Mind—un-Christianlike address,
  Your atheist burns at the stake for less,

Because such talk is dangerous and wild.
Nature is sin, the Mind is Satan,   4900
Doubt they engender in their mating,
Their epicene misshapen child.
Not for this Empire! Only two professions
Have graced of old His Majesty's possessions
And worthily support his throne: 4905
Divines and knights—they quell upheaval,
And as twin shields against all evil
Call justly church and state their own.
The vulgar spirits of sedition
With aid and comfort, though, are plied;   4910
By whom? The heretic! The black magician!
Corrupting town and countryside.
Their kind it is you would be smuggling
Into this Court with jests and juggling;
A noisome changeling you are suckling,   4915
The wizard and the fool live hide in hide.
MEPHISTOPHELES.   I recognize the learned scholar's speech!
What is not there to touch is out of reach,
What is impalpable is wholly missed,
What is not countable does not exist,   4920
What you can't weigh is air upon your scale,
What you don't coin you think does not avail.
EMPEROR.   All this will hardly whisk our woes away;
What is your Lenten sermon good for, pray?
I'm sick of the perennial how and when;   4925
We're short of money—well, procure it then.
MEPHISTOPHELES.   I can perform as much, more than you say;
It's easy—easy in a difficult way;
The stuff lies there all ready, yet to reach it—
There is the subtle art, and who can teach it?   4930
Just think: on those calamitous occasions
When land and folk were swept by armed invasions,
How this or that man, deep in terror's meshes,
Would rush to hide all that he held most precious.
This was in ancient Roman times the way,   4935
And ever since, till yesterday, today.
These hoards lie buried in the ground, and it—
The soil's the Emperor's, his the benefit.
TREASURER.   This, from a fool, is not devoid of wit;
Indeed, thus runs an old Imperial writ.[5]   4940
CHANCELLOR.   Gold bait—it smacks of Satan, not Messias;
That scheme sounds neither sound to me nor pious.
MARSHAL.   For means to make our style at Court more regal
I should be glad to be a shade illegal.

---

5. According to ancient law, any buried treasure lying below the cut of a plow would belong to the Emperor.

QUARTERMASTER. The fool is clever, pledges each his share;   4945
 You pay the soldier—how? he does not care.
MEPHISTOPHELES. Lest you suspect yourselves by me defrauded,
 Here is a man to ask! Astrologer much-lauded,
 Of every orbit knows the house, the hours;
 You tell us then: What say the heavenly powers?[6]   4950
MUTTERING.
  They're hand in glove—Two rogues as one—
  A royal fool—A charlatan—
  An ancient tune—And played to death—
  The Magus speaks—The Fool lends breath—
ASTROLOGER. [speaking while MEPHISTOPHELES prompts]
 The Sun himself is gold of pure assay,   4955
 Mercurius the Envoy serves for pay,
 Dame Venus charmed you all with her sweet grace;
 Early and late shows you her lovely face;
 Chaste Luna, all caprices, minces,
 Mars, though he miss you, yet his threat convinces;   4960
 Jupiter shines the brightest even so,
 Saturn is great, though distance dims his glow,
 As metal we do not respect him much,
 In value low, yet heavy to the touch.
 Yes! Sol and Luna in conjunction seen,   4965
 To silver gold, turns all the world serene.
 With this you may engarner all the rest,
 Palace and garden, rosy cheek and breast,
 All this provides the deeply learned man,[7]
 Who may accomplish what no other can.   4970
EMPEROR. I hear twice-echoed his address,
 And yet I hardly doubt it less.
MUTTERING.
  Oh, let us off—All warmed-up stuff—
  It's number mystic—Alchymistic—
  I heard it oft—False hope it puffed—   4975
  You probe the joke—It's up in smoke—
MEPHISTOPHELES. There they all stand amazed and snivel,
 Trust not the riches to be found,
 The one of mandrake root will drivel,
 The other of the coal-black hound.[8]   4980
 What use is it for one to giggle,
 The other of Black Art to wail,

---

6. The speech by the Astrologer that follows is spoken to promptings by Mephistopheles, indicating
  that the skepticism expressed by the crowd is well founded. The entire speech, however faithful
  to traditional astrological lore, is willfully mystifying and whimsical. Sun and moon, "Sol and
  Luna" (line 4965), representing the metals gold and silver, are said to be in conjunction, signifying
  happy times when all things may be accomplished.
7. An allusion to Faust.
8. The mandrake root, said to grow in human form beneath a gallows when the sperm of a hanged
  man falls to the earth, could be pulled out only by a "coal-black" dog according to an elaborate
  ritual. The root was thought to provide its owner with miraculous powers.

When all the time his soles will tickle,
And his accustomed footstep fail?

You all can feel the secret virtue   4985
Of Nature constantly at work,
As rising effluents alert you
To powers that deep within her lurk.[9]
When every limb will twitch and tweak,
Uncanny signs disturb the mind,   4990
There resolutely delve and seek,
There lies the fiddler, lures the find!
MUTTERING.
            I drag my foot like weight of lead—
            I feel the gout—My arm is dead—
            My big toe itches—   4995
            My back's in stitches—
            By all such signs, here should be found
            The very richest treasure-ground.
EMPEROR.   To work! I fear you are adepter
   At pledge than proof; go test your lather   5000
   Of lies at once, let us foregather
   In those fine halls. Downed sword and scepter,
   With these imperial hands I shall,
   If you speak truth, dig deep and well,
   Or if you lie, send you to Hell.   5005
MEPHISTOPHELES.   I'd find the way myself, came worst to worst . . .
   Let me impress upon you first
   What unclaimed riches many a place would yield.
   A peasant ploughing in the field
   Will lift a treasure from the furrow's fold,   5010
   Or, as he scrapes a nitre-crusted wall,
   Recoil, rejoice to see a roll of gold,
   Pure gold, into his frugal fingers fall.
   What vaulting must await exploding,
   What shafts and passageways well worth unloading   5015
   Be thrust at by the treasure-boding
   New neighbors of the underground!
   In long-sealed cellars to the seekers
   Plump golden salvers, bowls, and beakers
   In rich refulgent rows abound.   5020
   Here goblets glow with ruby glare,
   And, to employ them then and there,
   An ancient vintage waits the taste;
   But—as by experts truly told—
   Its staves long sunk away in mold,   5025

---

9. An allusion to the notion that certain persons are sensitive to the magnetic force of buried metals.
   As he describes this, to support the plan to uncover such treasures, Mephistopheles casts a spell
   on the crowd that causes them to respond sympathetically.

In keg of tartar now encased.[1]
Such rare intoxicating essence,
As well as jeweled incandescence,
In dread nocturnal darkness hide.
The sage will search it readily enough;   5030
To see in light of day is trivial stuff,
It is in gloom that mysteries abide.
EMPEROR.   Those you may keep! I like the noonday's lustre.
If something is of worth, it should pass muster.
Who can tell friend from villain in the night,   5035
When all the cows are black, all catseyes bright?
Those hoards of gold below ground, coin and cup,
Go pull your plough and pry them up.
MEPHISTOPHELES.   Seize pick and spade yourself and battle,
Your peasant labor reaps great spoil,   5040
You'll see a flock of golden cattle
Be wrested from the harrowed soil.
Joyful, unstinting, from the treasure trove
Then deck yourself, adorn your lady love;
A rainbow shower of gems will freshly arm   5045
Both majesty and feminine charm.
EMPEROR.   Get on, get on! How long shall we be bored?
ASTROLOGER.   [MEPHISTOPHELES *prompting him as before*]
Such urgent craving deign to quell, my Lord,
Let first the motley pageantry unroll;
A scattered purpose will not win the goal.   5050
In calm atonement let us shrive desire,
Seek to deserve the lower through the higher.
Who wants the good should be it first;
Who would sip joy should tame his thirst;
Let him tread ripened grapes who asks for wine;   5055
Who hopes for wonders, tread the path divine.
EMPEROR.   So let the time in merriment be passed!
Then we shall welcome the Ash Wednesday Fast.
Meanwhile we celebrate in any case
Gay Carnival at all the wilder pace.   5060
         [*Trumpets. Exeunt.*]
MEPHISTOPHELES.   How luck and merit blend in men's affairs,
That never dawns upon this foolish lot;
If the philosopher's stone were theirs,
Stone would seek sage and find him not.

---

1. According to popular belief, the tartar that forms as a deposit from old wine on the inside of casks
can be hard enough to contain the wine even after the wooden staves rot away.

Spacious Hall
With Adjacent Apartments, Decorated and Festively Adorned for the Carnival†

HERALD.[1] Place not in Germany this revel,   5065
With dance of fool and death and devil,
Expect a feast of joy, not grief.[2]
Our Lord, in his Italian questing,
His profit in your pleasure vesting,
The lofty Alpine bulwark breasting,   5070
Has won himself a happy fief.
First to the sacred soles he bent,
For the Imperial rule to sue,
And when to fetch the crown he went,
He carried back the fool's cap too.[3]   5075
Now we are all reborn to fit;
Every sophisticated man
Will snugly wrap his head and ears in it;
It makes of him some sort of addle-wit,
He hides therein such wisdom as he can.   5080
I see the throng already starting,
With cozy pairing, veering, parting,
An eager concourse, group on group.
Surge in, flow out, my busy jollies;
Why, all the world, not just your troupe,   5085
With all its hundred thousand follies
Is but a vast collective dupe.

FLOWER GIRLS.[4] [*singing, to mandolin accompaniment*]
Finery, to earn your favor,
We have donned for this night's sport,
Maids of Florence, come to savor   5090
Splendors of the German court;

Chestnut locks we twined with tippets
Of the gayest floral art;
Silken flosses, silken snippets,
Playing their appointed part.   5095

1. The first part of the Masque (to line 5456) is introduced and staged by the Herald, who serves as a master of ceremonies.
2. The Herald alludes by contrast to German carnival practice (the *Fastnacht*) and perhaps to the medieval "Dance of Death."
3. These lines suggest that the Emperor brought back the Italian masque when he visited Rome for his coronation by the pope (whose slippers he kissed, line 5072).
4. These are apparently natives of Florence dressed in a traditional costume of the Italian masque.

For we count it gift of reason,
Altogether worth your praise,
That our flowers outbloom each season
In their artificial glaze.⁵

Colored scraps and slips assorted   5100
Found in symmetry their due;
Any bit you're free to snort at,
But the whole will dazzle you.

Flower girls appeal, admit it,
Charmingly to eyes and hearts;   5105
For a bond of nature fitted
Female temper for the arts.
HERALD.   Show us on your head the precious
    Burden carried in each basket,
From your hampers what is freshest,   5110
What each fancies, let him ask it.
Quick, let lanes in leafy shrouding
Into garden paths be made us,
Worthy of our eager crowding
Are both merchandise and traders.   5115
FLOWER GIRLS.   Strike your bargains, gaily playing,
    But tonight no bargain binds!
By an apt and pithy saying
May each know the thing he finds.⁶
OLIVE BRANCH BEARING FRUIT.
    Bursts of bloom I envy none,   5120
All contrarity I shun—
Blight on all for which I stand.
Am I not the country's marrow,
Warrant sure to plow and harrow,
Sign of peace to every land?   5125
Here I hope to—happy duty—
Grace a head of worth and beauty.
WREATH OF GOLDEN CORN-EARS.
    Wreaths to charm and to embellish
Ceres'⁷ gifts will make on you:
What is welfare's foremost relish   5130
Be to you adornment too.
FANCY WREATH.   Hollyhock and mallow aping,
    Wondrous blossom from the moss!
This is none of Nature's shaping,
Fashion, though, may breed it thus.   5135

---

5. The flowers are artificial, imported in Goethe's day from Italy.
6. The Flower Girls here introduce figures dressed to represent the kind of flowers they are selling.
7. Ceres was the Roman goddess of the grain.

FANCY BOUQUET.
> It would stump botanic masters
> All the way to Theophrastus[8]
> To define me, yet I rather
> Hope to please the one or other,
> One to whom I would consign me   5140
> If into her hairs she'd twine me,
> If she should decide to bear me
> Off and at her bosom wear me.

ROSEBUDS.   [*challenge*]
> Let the motley fancies flower
> For the fashion of the hour,   5145
> Wondrously and subtly molded,
> Nature never thus unfolded:
> Golden bells on verdant stalks
> Peep from out luxurious locks!—
> But we—stay concealed, reminders   5150
> Of delight for lucky finders.
> Summer come, itself proclaiming
> Season of the rosebud's flaming,
> Who but finds it bliss enchanting?
> Charms of pledging, charms of granting   5155
> In the realm of Flora[9] strike
> Gaze and sense and heart alike.

[*Under the greenery of leafy lanes the* FLOWER GIRLS *daintily arrange their wares.*]

GARDENERS.   [*singing to the accompaniment of lutes*][1]
> Let the blossoms' meretricious
> Compliments adorn your tresses,
> Fruits attract without caresses,   5160
> In the tasting prove delicious.

> Fruit in tawny-purple flushes
> Buy! Your palate, tongue, and budget,
> Not the eye, are fit to judge it—
> Peach and plum and cherry luscious.   5165

> Fruits for joy and taste to sample
> At their ripest and most ample!
> For the rose are poems written,
> But the apple should be bitten.

> Suffer us to build a neighbor   5170
> To your youthful floral spray,

---

8. Theophrastus of Lesbos (b. 390 B.C.), a Greek philosopher, student of Aristotle, who wrote several works on plants.
9. The Roman goddess of flowers.
1. The Gardeners, accompanied by archaic bass lutes (in contrast to the mandolins that accompanied the Flower Girls), offer ripe fruit for sale in competition with the flowers.

Heaping bounty ripe, we labor
To erect a twin display.

Gay with bunting, booth and arbor,
Gaily vine-beribboned bower,   5175
Everything together harbor,
Bud and foliage, fruit and flower.
[*Alternating in song, accompanied by mandolins and lutes, the two
choruses continue to dress and heap their wares up by stages and to
invite customers.*]

[*Enter* MOTHER *and* DAUGHTER.[2]]

MOTHER.   When you were my tiny girl
                 I primped you in your carriage,
                 Sweet of face and fine of curl,   5180
                 Fairest in the parish;
                 Thought of you—so high—allied
                 To the richest man for bride,
                 Saw my girl in marriage.

                 Many years have since, alas,   5185
                 Uselessly been squandered,
                 Spooners, suitors, used to pass,
                 Stopped and swiftly wandered.
                 One to whirling reel you begged,
                 One your elbow subtly egged   5190
                 To endearments pondered.

                 Feasts we would on purpose plan
                 Every time fell short there,
                 Games of forfeit and third-man[3]
                 Didn't what they ought there.   5195
                 But tonight, love, bait your trap,
                 Fools are loose, so spread your lap,
                 One may well be caught there.
[PLAYMATES, *young and beautiful, join the scene; unconstrained
chattering is heard.* FISHERMEN *and* BIRDCATCHERS, *equipped with
nets, rods, lime-twigs, and other gear, mingle with the pretty girls.
Efforts on both sides to attract, captivate, evade, and detain occasion
most agreeable dialogues.*]

WOODCUTTERS.   [*entering, boisterous and uncouth*][4]
                 Give room! Untrammeled!
                 We must be limber,   5200
                 We fell the timber,

---

2. In association with the playful juxtaposition of the sale of flowers and sensuous pleasure, this
   anxious mother uses the opportunity to put her daughter on display, as if she also were for sale.
3. Parlor games familiar in Goethe's time.
4. In contrast to the dancelike pantomime of Flower Girls and Gardeners, the Masque now shifts
   to clumsier groups representing various fringes of human society.

Crunch, crash! We're rugged,
And where we lug it
Someone is pommeled.

If praise is needed,   5205
Weigh this and heed it:
Unless the crude ones
Performed their own,
How would the shrewd ones
Get on alone,   5210
For all they're petted?
You hark to reason!
You'd die a-freezing
Unless we sweated.

PULCINELLI.[5] [awkward to the point of farce]
You are the zanies,   5215
For drudging sent.
We are the brainies
Who never bent;
For our caps,
Jackets, and flaps   5220
Are feather-light wraps.
We take our pleasure
As market trippers,
In constant leisure
And floppy slippers,   5225
On saunters bent
Or standing and gaping,
Each other japing;
Upon such calls
Through crowded stalls   5230
With eel-like slipping
We join for skipping,
Wild merriment.
You may commend us
Or reprehend us,   5235
We are content.

PARASITES.[6] [suggestively fawning]
You trusty porters
With your good takers,
The charcoal-makers,
Are who support us.   5240
For all that bowing,
Nodding, allowing,
Involute phrases'

---

5. Maskers wearing the traditional clown costume of Italian popular comedy, including dunce caps
   and colorful, baggy suits.
6. Stock figures from ancient comedy, possibly representing political opportunists.

Dubious praises,
Blow hot and cold,   5245
As one may hold,
What could it profit?
Take heaven's fire,
Say lightning dire
Were splintered off it—   5250
If wood were missing
Or kindling sawed of it,
Would hearth be hissing
The long and broad of it?
Such broiling and frizzling,   5255
Such boiling and sizzling!
Smack-lips are stirred,
Plate-lickers spurred
By roasts delicious,
By whiff of fishes,   5260
To feats of fable
At patron's table.

TOPER.   [under the influence][7]
Just so nothing is contrary!
Ah, I feel so fine and free;
Lusty mood and chanties merry,   5265
All myself procured for me.
So I'm drinking, drink-a-drink!
Click your glasses, clink-a-clink!
Hallo, back there, you come up!
Clink with me and down your cup,   5270

How my missus railed and butted,
Bridling at these motley drapes,
And, however much I strutted,
Scolded me a jackanapes.
But I'm drinking! Drink-a-drink!   5275
Glasses tinkling, clink-a-clink!
Toast you, all you masks-on-sticks!
Let it tinkle as it clicks.

I'm all right here, do not shake me,
For the place is fine for thirst.   5280
If the landlord will not stake me,
Wife or maid will, worst to worst.
Still I'm drinking! Drink-a-drink!
Up, you others! Clink-a-clink!
Everyone, to everyone!   5285
Seems to me the thing's well done.

---

7. The costume of the drunkard was traditional to the carnival. He invites all whom he meets to
drink along with him.

Let my pleasures overtake me;
If they get a little strong,
Let me lie and do not wake me,
I've been on my feet too long.   5290

CHORUS.   Every brother drink, oh drink!
Toast each other, tink-a-tink!
Firmly sit your bench, each one,
That one down there is all done.

[*The* HERALD *announces various* POETS, *poets of nature, bards of
Court and Chivalry, lyricists as well as rhapsodists. In the throng of
competitors of every sort no one allows the other to recite. One shuf-
fles by with a few words.*][8]

SATIRIST.   As a poet-pamphleteer,   5295
What would be my delight?
If they let me sing and cite
What no one wants to hear.

[*The* POETS *nocturnal and sepulchral beg to be excused because they
are just then engaged in most interesting conversation with a freshly-
formed vampire, which might possibly give rise to a new mode of
literature;*][9] *the* HERALD *must admit the force of this, and meanwhile
calls upon Greek mythology, which even in modern guise loses nothing of its character or charm.*]

[*The* GRACES.][1]
AGLAIA.
It is grace we bring to living;
Equal grace impart to giving.   5300
HEGEMONE.
Equal grace be in receiving,
Graceful is a wish's achieving.
EUPHROSYNE.
And in bounds of tranquil living,
Highest grace be in thanksgiving.

[*The* PARCAE.][2]
ATROPOS.
Me, the eldest, they selected   5305
To be spinning here this once;

8. Goethe intended to write verses satirizing various contemporary schools of poetry but did not
complete the scene. Poets of nature were writers of ballads and folk songs; bards of Court and
Chivalry were pseudomedieval poets who imitated the romances and the *Minnesang*.
9. An allusion to supernatural and Gothic tendencies in later Romantic fiction (such as E. T. A.
Hoffmann's *Night Pieces* of 1817 and Polidori's *Vampire* of 1819).
1. The Graces were goddesses of social intercourse in general. The name "Hegemone" ("the one
who leads the way") is substituted for the more traditional "Thalia." "Aglaia" ("the resplendent
one") and "Euphrosyne" ("the merry one") are the other two traditional names.
2. The three Parcae (Fates) were traditionally associated with spinning the thread of human life
(Clotho), measuring its length (Lachesis), and cutting it at death (Atropos). Their roles are playfully
confused for this festival occasion.

Much is mused on, much reflected,
As the tender life-thread runs.

Finest flax I sought for sleaving,
Screened you soft and limber strands;   5310
How to smooth it slim and even
Cunning finger understands.

Lest of revelry and dancing
You too lavishly partake,
Mark this tenuous thread's advancing   5315
And beware! For it might break!

CLOTHO.

I have latterly been handed,
You must know, the shears of fate;
For our Elder's[3] ways were branded
Unacceptable of late.   5320

Rankly useless strands she nurses
Over-long in air and light,
Hopes of utmost worth she curses,
Snapping, to sepulchral night.

Yet I too have erred already   5325
Scores of times, in youthful way;
To contain myself and steady,
See, my shears are sheathed today.

So I gladly curb my powers,
Look with kindness on this fair;   5330
You, exempt these festive hours,
Revel on with never a care.

LACHESIS.

I, who am alone discerning,
Kept the sorting of the thread,
And my reel, though ever turning,   5335
Never yet has oversped.

Fibers sliding, fibers spooling,
Each upon its track I guide,
Every outflow overruling,
Bend it to a rounded glide.   5340

If I once forgot or slumbered,
I would fear for mankind bane,

---

3. The Elder is Atropos.

Hours are counted, years are numbered,
And the weaver takes the skein.

HERALD. Who now approach, you will not recognize,   5345
However steeped in ancient screeds you be;
You would esteem them welcome company,
To look at them, who so much ill devise.

They are the Furies,[4] no one will believe us,
Are pretty, young in years, well-shapen, kind;   5350
But try to mingle with them, you will find
How serpentinely sore such doves may grieve us.

They're vicious—but today, 'mid all and sundry,
When every fool will advertise his faults,
They too forgo dissembling their assaults,   5355
And own themselves a plague on town and country.

[*The* FURIES.]
ALECTO.
No good to warn you, you will trust us still,
We are a pretty, young, insinuating coven;
If one among you has a loving-doving,
We'll stroke him under chin and ears until—   5360

Till eye to eye with him we may confide:
For this one, that one she is also primping,
Is hollow-headed, pigeon-chested, limping,
And good for nothing, if his promised bride.

His bride will next be molded in our fingers: 5365
Her friend has, not so many weeks ago,
Disparaged her before Miss So-and-so!—
They make it up, but yet a something lingers.

MEGAERA.
All these are harmless games! for, once they marry,
The task is mine; I know how to embroil   5370
The fairest happiness in whim and bile;
The hours are variable, men will vary.

None firmly clasps the wished within his arm
Without for yet more wished inanely lusting,

---

4. The Furies were traditionally associated with anger (Alecto), envy (Megaera), and vengeance
(Tisiphone). Here they perform social roles as the cause of, respectively, lovers' quarrels, infidelity
in marriage, and the jilted lover's revenge.

From highest bliss of which he has the custom;   5375
He flees the sun and goes the frost to warm.

All this I am most expert at pursuing,
By sending Asmodeus,[5] faithful devil,
At proper time to sow out what is evil,
And thus by pairs the human race undoing.   5380

TISIPHONE.

    Not barbed tongues, but poison, dagger
    Do I sharpen for the traitor,
    Change your love and sooner, later,
    Under vengeance you will stagger.

    What of sweetness may perfuse it   5385
    Must be turned to gall and tartar;
    There's no bargaining, no barter
    Over circumstance—he rues it.

    No one urge me to forgive!
    At the cliffs my cause I monish,   5390
    Echo, listen! answers 'punish!';
    He who changes shall not live.

HERALD.   Be pleased to step aside, if you don't mind,
What now approaches is not of your kind.[6]
A cumbrous mountain lumbering up one sees,   5395
Its flanks ornate with colored tapestries;
A snaking trunk, a head with tusks immense,
A mystery—but I reveal its sense.
A lady rides his neck, shaped slimly-nicely,
With slender wand she guides his course precisely.   5400
The other, upright, glorious to see,
Blinds me with luster of high majesty.
Below, two noble ladies shackles carry,
The one of anxious mien, the other merry,
One wishing, one perceiving herself free.   5405
Let each announce who she might be.

FEAR.   Smouldering torches, candles, lanterns
    Glint through this disordered train,
    Oh, amid these lying phantoms
    I am prisoned by this chain.   5410

    Off, you tittering detractors!
    Suspect are your grins to see;

---

5. An evil spirit from Jewish demonology who causes discord between husband and wife.
6. The pageant of Victory, climax of the allegorical sequence, is discussed in the interpretive notes.

All my foes and malefactors
On this night beleaguer me.

Ha! a friend has turned to foe   5415
His disguise I know unasked;
That one sought my death, I know,
There he creeps away, unmasked.

Anywhere I'd gladly wander
To the outside world in flight;   5420
But the threat of ruin yonder
Holds me here 'twixt fog and fright.

HOPE.   Dearest sisters, friendly greetings.
Though two nights of festive meetings
Saw you mummed by mask and curtain,   5425
Still I know of you for certain
You will stand unveiled tomorrow.
And if by the torches' blaze
We were ill at ease and drooping,
Surely then, in smiling days,   5430
We shall roam sweet pastures, musing,
As may please us, free of sorrow,
Now alone, now gaily grouping,
Still or active, by our choosing,
Free of care's incessant driving,   5435
Never lacking, ever striving;
Like an ever-welcome guest
We feel certain of our ground:
We are confident the best
Must be somewhere to be found.   5440

INTELLIGENCE.
Two worst foes of man's existence,
Fear and Hope, in chains enslaved,
I retain at prudent distance;
All step back there! you are saved.

See this live colossus, cumbrous,   5445
Turret-laden, in my sway,
How untiringly he lumbers
Step by step his arduous way.

Lastly, though, enthroned on high,
See the goddess with her spacious   5450
Wing-spread, ever poised to fly
For the prize of the audacious.

Rays of gloria proclaim her,
Shining far and wide wherever;

And Victoria we name her,   5455
Patroness of all endeavor.

ZOILO-THERSITES.[7]   Bah! Pooh! I enter right on cue
To scold the worthless lot of you!
But what I choose for target fair
Is Lady Victory up there,   5460
No doubt she thinks her snowy wings
Make her an eagle, of all things,
And that whichever way she stirs
All folk and property are hers;
But when a feat has earned its prize,   5465
It promptly makes my hackles rise.
For high laid low, and low made high,
The crooked straight, the straight awry,
Just that keeps me in health and mirth,
That's how I relish things on earth.   5470
HERALD.   Then feel, you wretched mongrel-birth,
The pious mace's master-blow,
There, writhe and curl you ever so![8]—
But how the dwarfish double stump
So swiftly forms a nauseous clump!—   5475
The clump becomes an egg—o wonder!
And now balloons and bursts asunder.
A double issue, hatched from that,
Falls out, an adder and a bat;
In dust the one is wriggling off,   5480
The other blackly darts aloft,
To reunite their stratagem;
I would not make a third with them.[9]
MUTTERING.
Quick! there's dancing, bands at play—
No! I wish I were away—   5485
Don't you feel all snarled and clewed
By that godless phantom brood?
Something swooped and touched my hair—
At my foot I was aware—
None of us is injured here—   5490
Still we all are put in fear—
What the monsters counted on
They have done—the fun is gone.
HERALD.   Ever since I first accepted
Herald's duty at the pageants,   5495
I have watched the gate and kept it

---

7. Mephistopheles, still in his role of court jester, enters as the traditional antimasque, in the guise of the classical debunkers: Zoilos, a scathing critic of Homer, and Thersites, the ugly and dissident rogue from the *Iliad* 2.
8. The Herald strikes him with his staff, as Odysseus struck Thersites (*Iliad* 2.265).
9. Mephistopheles, employing his devilish magic, transforms himself into a gigantic egg that hatches an adder and a bat.

Closed to any baneful agents
Apt to mar the festive flavor;
And I neither wink nor waver.
Yet I fear that ghostly raiders   5500
Through the windows might invade us,
And from spooks and spells that bait you
I could never liberate you.
If the dwarf was suspect-seeming,
Yonder, look! a mighty streaming.   5505
Of the figures there, my station
Calls for due interpretation.
But what passes comprehension,
Explanation also passes,
Help you all my good intention!—   5510
See it sweeping through the masses?[1]—
Splendid chariot, with four horses,
All the crowd with ease percourses;
Yet it crosses never parting,
I see no one sideways darting.   5515
Colorful, it glitters yonder—
Errant sparkles gleam and wander,
Magic lantern, one might ponder?—
Storms up with tempestuous snort.
All make way! I shudder!
BOY CHARIOTEER.   Halt!   5520
Steeds of mine, your pinions idle,
Honor the accustomed bridle,
As I curb you, curb your fire,
Rush along when I inspire—
To these rooms let us add luster!   5525
Look about you, how they cluster,
Our admirers, round on round.
Herald, up, as you are bound,
And before afar we flee,
Name us here, describe and show us;   5530
We are allegories, see,
And as such you ought to know us.
HERALD.   I could not tell your name by sight;
But to describe you—that I might.
BOY CHARIOTEER.   Why don't you try!
HERALD.   One may aver: 5535
For one thing, you are young and fair.
A half-grown boy; the ladies, though, might own
That they would gladly see you fully grown.
You seem to me a ladies' man *in spe*,
A native-born seducer, I should say.   5540

---

1. This new float, prepared by Mephistopheles and Faust, is unexpected and beyond the Herald's
ability to interpret. Upon a splendid carriage hitched to dragons (cf. lines 5677 ff.) rides Plutus,
the god of wealth (Faust in disguise), pulled by the Boy Charioteer.

BOY CHARIOTEER.   Not bad at all! Go on, let's see
    You earn yourself the riddle's merry key.
HERALD.   The eye's black lightning, ringlets dusky,
    Cheered by a jewelled band for crown!
    And what a captivating gown   5545
    Flows from your shoulders to the buskin
    With purple hem and glittery down!
    You could be slanged a girl with ease,
    But as you are, for weal or woe,
    The girls would eye you even so.   5550
    They'd help you learn your ABC's.
BOY CHARIOTEER.   And this one, who, a form of splendor,
    Enthroned upon the chariot glows?
HERALD.   He seems a monarch, rich and tender,
    He prospers whom his favor chose!   5555
    There's nothing left for his endeavor,
    For any hardship spies his gaze,
    His pure delight in giving ever
    Both bliss and luxury outweighs.
BOY CHARIOTEER.   You must not rest content with these—   5560
    Supply more details if you please.
HERALD.   How can one capture worth and grace?
    We saw the healthful, rounded face,
    The swelling lips, the cheeks full-blown
    That by the splendid turban shone;   5565
    The robe's luxurious caress!
    And what of his august address?
    Renown and reign is what I sense.
BOY CHARIOTEER.   Plutus, the god of opulence,[2]
    Comes driving up in pomp and state,   5570
    His Majesty can hardly wait.
HERALD.   Now tell us who, and how, yourself may be?
BOY CHARIOTEER.   I am profusion, I am poetry;[3]
    The poet who fulfills himself
    By squandering his inmost wealth.   5575
    I, too, am rich beyond all measure,
    Count myself Plutus-like in treasure,
    I quicken and adorn his feast,
    By lavishing what he has least.
HERALD.   This boasting suits you all too well,   5580
    Now for a sample of your spell.
BOY CHARIOTEER.   I snap my fingers, see! it gleams
    About the wheels in sparkles, beams.
    A string of pearls goes skimming there;
        [*Keeps snapping his fingers all about.*]

2. The Greek word *ploutos* means "wealth." There is an ancient connection with the Greek and
    Roman god of the underworld, Pluto (cf. Plato, *Cratylus*, 403A), "so called because riches arise
    from the earth."
3. See interpretive notes.

There, golden clasps for neck and ear;   5585
Now precious combs and diadems,
Now, set in rings, the choicest gems;
Sometimes a flick of flame I throw,
To see what it might set aglow.
HERALD.   Look, grasping, snatching, my fine host!   5590
The giver comes to grief almost.
Bright gems, his snapping fingers pour them,
And right and left, they're snapping for them.
But now the scheme is twisted meanly:
What one has grasped, however keenly,   5595
Affords but wretched ownership,
The keepsake flutters from his grip,
Like dream dissolves the pearly band,
And beetles scamper in his hand,
When he, poor fellow, throws them out,   5600
Around his head they buzz about,
The others, for more solid prize,
Are left with wanton butterflies.
The scamp, for rich rewards foretold
He offers but the gleam of gold!   5605
BOY CHARIOTEER.
How to announce the masks, you know, I gather,
Their inwardness to fathom, though, is rather
Beyond the herald's courtly sphere;
Acuter sight is needed here.
But any acrimony I eschew;   5610
With speech and question, Sire, I turn to you.
[to PLUTUS] Did you not to my hands entrust
The chariot's fourfold rushing gust?
Did I not steer it as you led me?
Am I not where your finger sped me?   5615
Did I not fly on pinions eager
To win the palm for your quadriga?
For you, as often as I fought
I came triumphant from the quarrel;
If now your brow is decked with laurel,   5620
By this my mind and hand was it not wrought?
PLUTUS.   If testimony's due for all to hear it,
I gladly say: You're spirit of my spirit.
Your deeds enact my mind alone,
Your wealth is greater than my own.   5625
This twig of green, your service to redeem,
Above all crowns and circlets I esteem;
Hear all this truthful eulogy:
My cherished son, I take delight in thee.[4]

---

4. A playful paraphrase of the Father's words at the baptism of Christ, Matthew 3.17, "This is my
beloved Son, with whom I am well pleased."

BOY CHARIOTEER.   The greatest gifts at my command,   5630
   See! I have spread with lavish hand.[5]
   On this or that one's head there flare
   The flamelets that I scattered there,
   From one onto the next it skips,
   On this one rests, from that one slips,   5635
   But seldom glares in upward rush
   To glow in sudden transient flush;
   On many, unaware of it,
   It sadly guts as soon as lit.
FEMALE GOSSIP.
      The one up on the chariot there,   5640
      He is a charlatan, I swear;
      Hunched up in back, an owlish clown,
      By thirst and hunger shriveled down,
      As no one ever saw him yet;
      He cannot feel a pinch, I bet.[6]   5645
THE STARVELING.   Shoo, sickening females, let me go,
   You I can never suit, I know.
   When yet the wifely virtues shone,
   As *Avaritia* I was known;
   Domestic rules were sound and stout: 5650
   They meant much in, and nothing out!
   I scrounged for chest and cabinet;
   Now they would make a vice of it.
   Since women, though, have not been craving
   Of late to learn the art of saving,   5655
   And like your true delinquent shopper
   Have three desires for every copper,
   The hapless husband sorely frets,
   Whichever way he looks are debts;
   And what her distaff may recover   5660
   Goes for the body of her lover;
   Or dining better, drinking more
   With the philanderers' plaguey corps;
   This makes my love of gold more tender:
   My name is Greed, and male my gender!   5665
LEADER OF THE WOMEN.
   Share, dragon, dragon's hoarding honors!
   It's all just make-believe and bluff:
   He's come to sic our husbands on us,
   Who are quite troublesome enough.
WOMEN EN MASSE.
      That scarecrow! Slap him off his wagon!   5670
      Scare us, that dried-up gallow-log?

---

5. Possibly an allusion to the spirit at Pentecost, which seized the apostles, appearing as a flame
   above their heads and causing them to speak in tongues (Acts 2.1–4).
6. This "starveling" whom they describe is Mephistopheles in yet another disguise, who first calls
   himself *Avaritia* (line 5649), then Greed (line 5665).

We, shy before his shriveled mug?
Who minds a wood-and-paper dragon?
Let's up and at him, kick and slug!

HERALD.   To order! Order, by my mace!—   5675
But hardly needed is my calling,
See how the grisly monsters, crawling
Within the quickly-yielded space,
Their double pairs of wings unspread.[7]
The dragons undulate in ire   5680
Their scaly gorges, spewing fire;
The place is clear, the crowd has fled.
     [PLUTUS *descends from the chariot.*]

HERALD.   Now he descends, how like a king!
He makes a sign, the dragons swing
The heavy coffer down the chariot   5685
Whereon both gold and Greed were carried,
And set it down before his feet;
A marvel, was the way of it.

PLUTUS.   [*to* CHARIOTEER]
Now you are rid of weights that overwhelm,
Are free and fresh; now briskly to your realm![8]   5690
Here it is not! Here we are hemmed, surrounded
By weird contortions, checkered, wild, confounded.
Lift clear your gaze to clear and lovely regions,
But in yourself your trust and sole allegiance,
Where only please the beautiful, the good,   5695
There go create your world—to solitude!

BOY CHARIOTEER.   As I will be your cherished envoy, then,
So I shall love you as my next of kin.
Where you reside is plenty; where I rest
All feel themselves most gloriously blessed.   5700
They often veer in life's perplexity:
Should they devote themselves to you? to me?
While idleness rewards your devotees,
My followers can never rest at ease.
Nor are my actions furtive or concealed,   5705
I only have to breathe to stand revealed.
Farewell! You grudge me not my bliss, I know,
But your first lisp will fetch me, even so.
     [*Exits, as he came.*]

PLUTUS.   Time now to loose the hoard of gems and metal!
To strike the locks I use the Herald's rod.   5710
It opens! Watch! In brazen bowl and kettle
It starts uncoiling, wells with golden blood,
Upmost the wealth of chain and ring and crown;

---

7. These allegorical dragons are attached to the float (see note to line 5511) as guardians of the
   treasure, presumably controlled by the Boy Charioteer.
8. This recalls Prospero's farewell speech to Ariel in Shakespeare's *Tempest* (5.1.317 ff.): "Then to
   the elements / Be free, and fare thou well."

It seethes and would, engulfing, melt it down.
CRIES OF THE CROWD, ALTERNATING.
     Look here! and there! just see it brim,   5715
     It fills the coffer to the rim;
     Great vessels, gold ones, swallowing,
     Great rolls of coinage wallowing.—
     The ducats flip like newly struck,
     My heart goes skipping with such luck—   5720
     To look on all I hankered for!
     There they go rolling on the floor.—
     It's offered you, just don't delay,
     You stoop and get up rich that way.—
     And we fall to and lightning-swift   5725
     Pounce on the chest and make short shrift.
HERALD.   Why do you scramble, fools? What for?
   This is all mummery, no more;
   All that is asked tonight is mirth;
   You think they'd give you gold or worth?   5730
   Why, in this game to entertain
   Tin tokens would be excess gain.
   You dolts! a graceful trick, forsooth,
   Must promptly count for clumsy truth.
   What's truth to you—when all you've pawed   5735
   By random grabs was musty fraud?
   Mummed Plutus, hero of the masque,
   Drive me this rabble off, I ask.
PLUTUS.   What could be fitter than your mace?
   Lend it to me for a short space.—   5740
   I dip it, quick, in seething heat.—
   Now, masques! be nimble on your feet.
   Bright flash, sparks spurting to and fro!
   The end already is aglow.
   Whoever has too rashly neared   5745
   At once is mercilessly seared—
   With this I start upon my round.
TUMULT AND SHOUTS.
     Help! it's all up with us! Give ground,
     Escape who can escape from here!—
     Stand back, make room there, in the rear!   5750
     Hot sparks are flying in my face.—
     I feel the heavy glowing mace—
     We're lost and done for, one and all.—
     Give way, you masquers' serried wall!
     Fall back, fall back, insane array!   5755
     Oh, had I wings, I'd fly away.—
PLUTUS.   The circle is already cleared,
   And no one, I believe, is seared.
   The rabble shrinks,
   Scared off, methinks.—   5760

For pledge of order now restored
I draw, invisibly, a cord.
HERALD.   You worked a brilliant feat of force,
How much I owe your shrewd resource!
PLUTUS.   Be patient yet, my noble friend: 5765
Not all the tumult's at an end.
GREED.   At least now anyone who wishes
Can get a pleasant ringside view;
For idle gaping, or forbidden dishes,
You'll find that women always head the queue.   5770
No, I am not yet altogether brittle!
A handsome woman's handsome yet;
And since today it costs me little,
Let me go boldly courting for a bit.
But since in crowded spots as here   5775
Not every word will reach to every ear,
I'll try the trick, and hope I shall not miss it,
By being pantomimically explicit.[9]
Hand, foot, and gesture will not do, I see,
I'll have to reach for some burlesquerie.   5780
Like pliant clay I will work up the gold,
That stuff complies with any shape you mold.
HERALD.   What's he about, the antic stick?
A starveling with a parlor trick?
To dough he's kneading all the gold,   5785
It softens for him, fit to mold,
But squeeze and lump it as he will,
Its form remains misshapen still.
He now turns to the women's side,
They all cry out and try to hide,   5790
With bearing mightily disgusted;
The rogue, I see, could not be trusted.
I greatly fear he seeks his glee
By injuring morality.
I must not stand for such offense.   5795
Pass me my staff, to drive him hence.
PLUTUS.   It's foolery, let him proceed;
He little knows the menace in the offing,
There soon will not be scope for him to scoff in;
The law is mighty, mightier is need.   5800

TURMOIL AND SONG.
              The savage host stride up in strength,
              Down mountain height and valley's length,
              And irresistible their gait:
              Great Pan is whom they celebrate.

9. True to the devil's traditional sexual role, Mephistopheles molds the magic gold into a gigantic phallus with which he threatens and shocks the ladies present.

What no one knows, they've known it long,   5805
  Into the vacant space they throng.[1]
PLUTUS.   I know you well and the Great Pan you lead!
  Together you have ventured daring deed.
  Full well I know what only few can know,
  And open this tight circle, as I owe.   5810
  May a propitious fate attend them!
  Most wondrous things might come to be;
  They know not where their strides may send them,
  They are proceeding carelessly.
DISCORDANT SONG.[2]
    You dolled-up show of tinsel fun!   5815
    They come up crude, they come up rough,
    By soaring leap, at flying run,
    Robust their nature is, and tough.
FAUNS.[3]   In dancing flocks
  The faunic folk,   5820
  With wreath of oak
  On twisting locks,
  An ear, drawn finely to a point,
  Onto the curly head is joint,
  Snub nose in a blunted face asprawl   5825
  With women does you no harm at all.
  Where faun for the dance plump hand should proffer,
  The fairest hardly would decline the offer.
SATYR.[4]   Here skips the satyr, next in rank,
  With foot of goat and skinny shank,   5830
  He needs them sinewy and lank,
  For chamois-like on mountain heights
  He gladly scans the lofty sights.
  Refreshed in freedom's aura then,
  He jeers at the families of men,   5835
  Who deep in lowland's reek and stew
  So blandly think they are living, too,
  Whereas he knows he holds secure

---

1. The appearance of this group of wild men—a traditional costume in baroque allegorical masques—presumably follows the plan of events the Herald had been announcing. As indicated (line 5805), only his followers, along with the Herald and Plutus-Faust (Mephistopheles as Greed speaks no lines after 5782 and perhaps has left the stage), know that the figure of Pan is the Emperor himself. The name "Pan" is associated through a false etymology with the Greek neuter adjective *pan*, "all" (cf. line 5873), which is appropriate to the Emperor's status as absolute monarch; but the goat-god Pan, as lord of woods and protector of shepherds, is in fact identified mythologically with excess, wildness, lechery, and debauch.
2. The followers of Pan (here and above, lines 5801 ff.) usurp the Herald's role as announcer, referring to themselves in the third person as "the savage host" (line 5801) and addressing the assembled crowd as "You dolled-up show of tinsel fun!"
3. Named for Faunus, a nature god often confused with Pan, fauns were minor Roman deities, later represented as sexually active hybrids of goat and youth, with short horns, pointed ears, and (as they say) oak wreaths in their hair.
4. Satyrs, the Greek counterpart of fauns, were usually followers of the god Dionysus and were familiar (by represensation at least) from the satyr plays of the Greek tragic festivals, where they indulged in ribald and lewd acts as a kind of slapstick comedy.

That upper world, untouched and pure.[5]
GNOMES.[6]   The little men come tripping there.   5840
They'd rather not go pair and pair;
With lantern bright and smock of moss,
They dance in swarms, and intercross,
Each for its own self laboring so,
A teeming mass of ants that glow,   5845
And hurry, scurry to and fro
And back and forth their errands go.

To worthy brownie-folk allied,
As mountain-surgeons certified:
We bleed the lofty mountain chains,   5850
And tap their brimming fountain-veins;
The metals all aheap we throw
With miner's hail: Luck-ho! Luck-ho![7]
And quite sincerely thus we hail:
We wish the kindly people well.   5855

And yet the gold that we unseal
Is what they use to pimp and steal,
Our iron arms the haughty man,
Though wholesale murder be his plan.
Who these commandments[8] takes in vain   5860
Holds all the others in disdain.
All this is not our fault, you see,
So bear with it, for so do we.
GIANTS.[9]   The Wild Men named, and so renowned,
The heights of Harz is where they're found,   5865
Like Nature naked in their might,
And all of giant girth and height.
A trunk of fir in each right hand,
About the waist a bushy band
Of leaves and branches rudely twined;   5870
Such bodyguard no pope could find.
NYMPHS IN CHORUS.   [*surrounding* GREAT PAN]
He too draws near!—
The whole world here

---

5. Here Goethe alludes also to the literary mode of satire (lines 5834 ff.), which derives from a Latin tradition (*saturna*) unrelated to the Greek satyrs.
6. "The little men" (the term *gnomes* was invented by Paracelsus in the sixteenth century, synonymous with "pygmies") are hobgoblins or dwarfs of Germanic folklore who live within the Earth and guard its treasures. They are represented here as miners, carrying their lanterns and wearing smocks of moss (line 5842).
7. The theme of mining precious metals is purposefully associated with Mephistopheles' plan to dig up the buried treasures of the realm. "Luck-ho!" (*Glück auf!*) is the traditional miner's greeting.
8. An allusion to the biblical Ten Commandments, specifically the three concerning murder, theft, and adultery (as suggested by lines 5857 ff.).
9. "Wild men" from the Harz mountains, figures from Germanic mythology. Here they also support the coat of arms of the eighteenth-century kingdom of Prussia and thus seem plausible (though anachronistic) bodyguards for the Emperor as Pan.

Now meets our eyes
In Great Pan's guise.   5875
Surround, you gayest, his advance,
About him weave in graceful dance,
For, being grave, in kindly way,
He'd have the company be gay.
Beneath the vaulted roof of blue   5880
He stayed intently wakeful too,
But brooklets lisp to him and seep,
Small breezes gently rock him to sleep.
And when he takes his midday ease,
No leaf will stir upon the trees;   5885
But wholesome herbs with fragrant balm
Perfume the ether's tranquil calm;
Nor may the nymph stay on her toes
But falls aslumber where she goes.
When of a sudden unawares   5890
His mighty voice resounds and blares,
Like ocean roar and lightning crash,
All wits are scattered in a flash,
Brave armies break and run astray,
And heroes tremble in the fray.[1]   5895
So praise him to whom praise is due,
Hail him who led us here to you![2]

DEPUTATION OF GNOMES.   [to GREAT PAN][3]
When the heart-lode rich and shining
Threads its streaks from cleft to cleft,
Only to astute divining   5900
Shows its labyrinthine weft,

We, where cryptic tunnels darkle,
Vault our troglodytic lair,
But where day's pure breezes sparkle
You vouchsafe us treasures fair.   5905

Here we now discover bubbling
Wondrous fountain ready-breached,
Promising to yield, untroubling,
What before could scarce be reached.

Its full gain is in your giving.   5910
Take it in safekeeping, Lord:

1. An allusion to the terror caused by the shout of Pan, described here in association with the sublime forces in nature, lightning and the roar of the sea.
2. An ironic paraphrase of St. Paul's epistle to the Romans 13.7, "Render . . . honor to whom honor is due."
3. The ballad that follows is filled with the technical terminology of mining. (See note to line 6070.)

Benefice for all the living
In your hands is any hoard.

PLUTUS. [*to* HERALD]
We must compose ourselves in high assurance,
And let occur what will with stout endurance.   5915
Your pluck is of the highest, after all.
There soon will come to pass most gruesome riot,
Age after age will stubbornly deny it:
Inscribe it truly in your protocol.
HERALD. [*touching the mace still held by* PLUTUS][4]
The gnomes conduct Great Pan, their Sire,   5920
Sedately to the source of fire,
It surges up from depths profound,
Then sinks and settles to the ground,
And dark the gaping mouth is found;
Wells up once more to seethe and sear,   5925
Great Pan observes it in good cheer,
Rejoicing in the wondrous sight,
And pearly foam spurts left and right.
In portents dark like these should he confide?
He stoops and gazes deep inside.—   5930
But now we see his beard fall in!—
Whose could it be, that shaven chin?
His hand conceals it from our view.—
A great mischance might now ensue,
The beard caught fire, back upward flew,   5935
Sets hair and chest and wreath aglow,
Serenity is turned to woe.—
To quench the fire in throngs they came,
But none escape a share of flame,
And as they thrash and as they slap,   5940
New brands are stirred for new mishap;
Entangled in the fiery haze,
The whole masked huddle stands ablaze.

But what report is passed, I hear,
From mouth to mouth, from ear to ear?   5945
O memorably ill-starred night,
That brought on us such grievous plight!
Tomorrow will proclaim it true,
What nobody will wish he knew;
Yet everywhere their outcries go: 5950
"The Emperor" is stricken so.
On fire are—were it but untrue!—
The Emperor and his retinue.

4. The historical source for the fire is discussed in the interpretive notes.

So cursed be they who tempted him,
Enlaced themselves in resinous trim,   5955
Stampeded here, a raucous host,
For universal holocaust.
O youthful spirit, will you ever
Exuberance with judgment season?
O sovereignty, will you never   5960
Compound supremacy with reason?

The glade⁵ already stands on fire,
With pointed tongues it flicks still higher,
The cross-beamed ceiling soon it dooms,
A wholesale conflagration looms.   5965
Ah, brimful is our cup of grief,
I know not who can bring relief.
The splendor of Imperial might
Will be the ash-heap of one night.
PLUTUS.⁶   Fright enough has now been spread,   5970
Now relief be wrought instead!—
Hallowed staff let smite the ground,
Make it quiver and resound!
Spacious ether, it is willed,
Let with fragrant cool be filled.   5975
Waft, you foggy wisps and wander,
Sated vapors, here and yonder,
Damp the twisted whorls of flame;
Trickling, purling, cloudlets curling,
Seeping, steeping, gently drenching,   5980
Dousing every place and quenching,
You, the soothing, smoothing, slightening,
Milden into summer lightning
Rank incendiary game.⁷—
For where spirits seek to harm us,   5985
Magic art shall shield and arm us.

---

5. A reference to the hall (or stage), decorated to resemble a woodland scene.
6. Perhaps abandoning his mask (as Mephistopheles will later do at the end of Act III), Faust here speaks both as master of ceremonies, having usurped the Herald's staff, and as demonic magician, presumably relying on Mephistopheles' assistance.
7. Faust's incantatory lines describe a process of quenching the fire with water that implies some prearranged sprinkler system, unless (as is also likely) both the fire and the water are to be understood as products of Mephistopheles' magic.

Pleasance†
Morning Sun

The EMPEROR, COURTIERS; FAUST, MEPHISTOPHELES, *dressed decently and*
inconspicuously in current fashion, both kneeling.

FAUST. You pardon, Sire, the pyromantic sport?
EMPEROR. [*beckoning them to rise*]
    I would have more amusement of this sort.—
    I all at once stood in a fiery sphere,
    I almost fancied I was Pluto here.   5990
    Of night and coal there yawned a rocky gorge
    Aglow with lights. From this or that hot forge
    A myriad raging flames whirled ever higher
    And flared into a wall, a vault of fire.
    Into the loftiest sky-dome it was raised,   5995
    Which ever faded as it ever blazed.
    Far off through twisted fiery trunks and steeples
    I saw the endless moving files of peoples
    In serried concourse press to where I stood,
    And render homage as they always would.   6000
    I recognized a courtier now and then—
    Of thousand salamanders seemed my reign!
MEPHISTOPHELES. You rule them, Sire—for every element
    Owes Majesty unquestioning assent.
    You sampled now the fire's obedient ravage:[1]   6005
    Next plunge into the sea at its most savage,
    And scarcely do you tread its pearly ground,
    When all about you forms a glorious round;
    For undulating nile-green swells, upwelling
    With coral edges, mold a splendored dwelling   6010
    With you for center. Every step you do,
    The glassy palaces advance with you,
    Alive the very confines of your shelter
    With darting swarms, a glistening, cross-laced welter.
    The mild new gleam draws portents of the ocean,   6015
    They bound and lunge—the walls arrest their motion.
    Gold dragons sport, prismatic scales and claws,
    There gapes a shark, you laugh into his jaws.
    How much your Court may teem with fond dependents,
    You've never had such thronging of attendants.   6020
    Yet they will not impede the loveliest view:
    Inquisitive young nereids press too
    Against the crystal carapace's limit.

---

1. In what follows, Mephistopheles envisions an underwater domain, including the Nereids, in particular Thetis (line 6025), wife of Peleus and mother of Achilles, anticipating the role of these sea nymphs in the "Classical Walpurgis Night."

The youngest fish-like, curious and timid,
The elder wise. Soon Thetis learns of this,   6025
Grants the new Peleus her salute and kiss.—
Forthwith a seat on Mount Olympus fair—
EMPEROR.   I'll let you off the regions of the air,
One reaches all too soon that lofty berth.
MEPHISTOPHELES.   And you, great Sire, already have the Earth.   6030
EMPEROR.   What pleasing turn of fate has brought you here,
Straight from Arabian Nights, it would appear?
If you have Shehrazade's rich invention,
I pledge you my most generous attention.[2]
Stand ever ready when the world of day,   6035
As oft it does, seems made of loathly clay.
MARSHAL.   [entering in haste]
Exalted Sire, in all my days to this
I never hoped to tell of higher bliss
Than what, most seasonably gay,
Sends me before your throne today.   6040
Account upon account is squared,
The usurers' talons have been pared,
I'm rid of such infernal care,
That Heaven could not seem more fair.
QUARTERMASTER.   [following in haste]
Paid in advance the soldier's due,   6045
The Army's all been pledged anew;
The man-at-arms feels born all over,
Mine Host and wenches are in clover.
EMPEROR.   How does your breath come deep and free!
The furrowed face, all wreathed in glee!   6050
How briskly now you cross the hall!
TREASURER.   [joining] Enquire of these, to whom we owe it all.
FAUST.   The full report's the Chancellor's to render.
CHANCELLOR.   [approaching slowly]
Whose waning years are gilded with new splendor.
See then and hear ye the momentous screed   6055
Which turned all woe to happiness indeed.
        [He reads.]
"To All it may Concern upon Our Earth:
This paper is a thousand guilders worth.
There lies, sure warrant of it and full measure,
Beneath Our earth a wealth of buried treasure.   6060
As for this wealth, the means are now in train
To raise it and redeem the scrip again."[3]
EMPEROR.   I sense gross fraud here, blasphemous counterfeit!

---

2. The anonymous collection of Arabian tales, *The Thousand and One Nights*, told each night by Scheherazade to her tyrannical husband, the emperor of the Indies, to prevent him from putting her to death, as he had threatened.
3. The use of paper money (called *assignats* in France) developed in Europe during the eighteenth century; it resulted in fraud and inflation during the old regime and the French Revolution.

Who dared to forge the Emperor's name and writ?
Has no one thought to punish such a crime?   6065
TREASURER.   Recall—Your own self signed it at the time,
Only last night. You stood in Great Pan's mask,
And with the Chancellor we approached to ask:
"Allow yourself high festive joy and nourish
The common weal with but a pen's brief flourish."[4]   6070
You signed; that night by men of thousand arts
The thing was multiplied a thousand parts;
So that like blessing should to all accrue,
We stamped up all the lower series too,
Tens, Thirties, Fifties, Hundreds did we edit,   6075
The good it did folk, you would hardly credit.
Your city, else half molded in stagnation,
Now teems revived in prosperous elation!
Although your name has long been widely blessed,
It's not been spelt with such fond interest.   6080
The alphabet has now been proved redundant:
In this sign everyone finds grace abundant.
EMPEROR.   It circulates like gold of true assay?
The Court, the Army take it in full pay?
I scarce believe it, though you say I ought.   6085
MARSHAL.   The fugitives could never now be caught;
The stuff was scattered broadside in a wink.
The money-changers' benches groan and clink,
Each single sheet is honored in their court
In gold and silver, though a trifle short.   6090
To butcher, baker, inn it next flits down;
Just feasting seems to busy half the town,
The other half show off their fine new clothes.
The draper cuts the bolt, the tailor sews,
Here cellars toast the Emperor, barrels plashing,   6095
There waiters jostle, steaming platters clashing.
MEPHISTOPHELES.   You roam the terraces alone, it happens,
And meet a beauty decked in costly trappings,
One eye by haughty peacock feathers hidden:
The other winks, by such a voucher bidden;   6100
More swiftly than by turn of speech or wit
The rich rewards of love are lured by it.
One is no longer plagued by purse or package,
A note borne next the heart is easy baggage,
It aptly couples there with love epistles.   6105
In priestly breviaries it chastely nestles,
The soldier, too, for ease of hips and loins
May now discard the ponderous belt of coins.
Your Highness pardon if this stately matter

---

4. The Chancellor and Treasurer must have constituted the Deputation of Gnomes in the Carnival
Masque (lines 5898–913). (See interpretive notes.)

I seem to slander by such lowly chatter.   6110
FAUST.   The plethora of treasure which, congealed,
The depths of Your dominions hold concealed
Lies unexploited. Concept most immense
Is to such wealth a negligible fence,
Imagination in its loftiest flight   6115
Will not encompass it, strain as it might.
Yet spirits gifted with profoundest sense
Place in the boundless boundless confidence.
MEPHISTOPHELES.   Such currency, in gold and jewels' place,
Is neat, it bears its value on its face,   6120
One may without much bargaining or barter
Enflame onself with Bacchus', Venus' ardor;
If metal's wanted, there's the banker's pile,
If he falls short, one digs a little while.
Gold dish and jewelry are auctioned off,   6125
The paper, validated soon enough,
Disarms the wag who with his darts would stab it.
They ask for nothing else now, it's a habit.
Henceforth the crown lands guard an ample store
Of specie, gems, and scrip, as not before.   6130
EMPEROR.   The Empire owes you signal benefit;
May the reward be of a kind with it.
Receive the Empire's inner soil in fief,
Its treasures' fit custodians-in-chief.
You know the hoards, far-flung and well-protected,   6135
When digging's to be done, you shall direct it.
Unite, chiefs of my surface and sub-surface,
Rejoice to clothe with dignity your office,
As upper now and nether world, elate
In close-bound harmony, collaborate.   6140
TREASURER.   There shall not be the faintest breath of trouble:
I cherish a magician for my double.
      [*Exit with* FAUST.]
EMPEROR.   I'll grant a gift to everyone at Court;
What will they use it for? Let each report.
PAGE.   [*receiving*] I'll live as gaily as in paradise.   6145
ANOTHER.   [*likewise*] I'm off to buy my love a chain and locket.
CHAMBERLAIN.   [*accepting*]
From now on I drink wine at twice the price.
ANOTHER.   [*likewise*] My word, the dice are itching in my pocket.
BARON.   [*with deliberation*]
I'll clear of debt my manor house and field.
ANOTHER.   [*likewise*] I'll lay it by, more interest to yield.   6150
EMPEROR.   I hoped for pluck and zest for ventures new;
I should have known you, and what each would do.
For all new bloom of wealth, it's plain to see
That each remains just what he used to be.

FOOL.[5] [*approaching*] You deal out favors—let me have a few.   6155
EMPEROR.   So you revived in time to waste these too!
FOOL.   Those magic leaves! I cannot grasp them quite.
EMPEROR.   No wonder, for you do not use them right.
FOOL.   Some more come fluttering down—what should I do?
EMPEROR.   They fell your way, so let them fall to you.   6160
        [*Exit.*]
FOOL.   Five thousand guilders—wondrously collected!
MEPHISTOPHELES.   Wineskin on legs! Have you been resurrected?
FOOL.   Been often raised, but never to such profit.
MEPHISTOPHELES.   You're in a sweat with the excitement of it.
FOOL.   Look—does this really work in money's stead?   6165
MEPHISTOPHELES.   Enough to keep you drunk and overfed.
FOOL.   Can house and land and ox be bought for it?
MEPHISTOPHELES.   Why not? Just make your bid and seal a writ.
FOOL.   A hunt, a trout-stream, park and lodge?
MEPHISTOPHELES.   Yes, all!
        I'd love to see you in your manor-hall!   6170
FOOL.   This night I dote on deeds of property!
        [*Exit.*]
MEPHISTOPHELES.   [*solus*] Not every jester is a fool, you see!

---

5. The true court jester, who had been removed by Mephistopheles at the outset of his sojourn at the court (lines 4731 ff.).

Dark Gallery†

FAUST. MEPHISTOPHELES.

MEPHISTOPHELES.
Why do you draw me down these somber hallways?
Is there not sport enough within,
There in the motley court-throng, always   6175
Good for a swindle and a grin?
FAUST.   Don't tell me that, it is a threadbare ruse,
You've rubbed it thin like worn-out shoes.
These to's and fro's are just your way
To keep from being brought to bay.   6180
But I am pestered, courtiers fret me,
The Marshall and the Chamberlain beset me;
The Emperor bids, there must be no delay,
Helen and Paris he must see straightway;
Ideals female and male, ideally mated,   6185
He would inspect distinctly corporated.
To work! I must not be forsworn or feckless.
MEPHISTOPHELES.   The promise was nonsensically reckless;
FAUST.   You failed, my friend, to see the hitch
In all the hoaxes you were using.   6190
First we arranged to make him rich,
Now we're expected to amuse him.
MEPHISTOPHELES.   You think it's just a sleight-of-hand;
But here the climbing looms more steeply,
You stray on deeply alien land,   6195
Perhaps incur new guilt at random;
You'd magic Helen up as cheaply
As now the guilders' paper phantom.
With witches' switches, troll-spawn, polter-poultice
I'm always at your service at short notice,   6200
But devil's trulls, though not as cheap as beans,
Can hardly stand for Grecian heroines.
FAUST.   Again that barrel-organ litany!
With you one always flounders past reliance;
A veritable fount of non-compliance,   6205
For every trick you ask an added fee.
I know it can be done with but a mutter,
Two winks, and you can have her on the spot.
MEPHISTOPHELES.   I have no commerce with that pagan clutter,
They have their segregated plot.   6210
There is a way, though,
FAUST.   Speak, and do not fiddle!
MEPHISTOPHELES.   I loathe to touch on more exalted riddle.—
Goddesses sit enthroned in reverend loneliness,

Space is as naught about them, time is less;
The very mention of them is distress.   6215
They are—the Mothers.

FAUST.   *[starting]*   Mothers!

MEPHISTOPHELES.   Are you awed?

FAUST.   The Mothers! Why, it strikes a singular chord.

MEPHISTOPHELES.   And so it ought. Goddesses undivined
By mortals, named with shrinking by our kind.
Go delve the downmost for their habitat;   6220
Blame but yourself that it has come to that.

FAUST.   Where is the road?

MEPHISTOPHELES.   No road! Into the unacceded,
The inaccessible; toward the never-pleaded,
The never-pleadable. How is your mood?
There are no locks to probe, no bolts to shift;   6225
By desolations harrowed you will drift.
Can you conceive of wastes of solitude?

FAUST.   I'd hope you'd spare me verbal witching;
This reeks of the old sorcery kitchen,[1]
Of times long buried and unrued;   6230
Did I not move in worldly company?
Not study, and not lecture, vacancy?—
I spoke, with reason, as I thought, endowed,
And contradiction sounded doubly loud.
I even had to seek from rank affliction   6235
Escape in wilderness and dereliction;
And, not to be quite outcast and alone,
At last enlist myself the devil's own.

MEPHISTOPHELES.   And had you even swum the trackless ocean,
Lost in its utter boundlessness,   6240
You still saw wave on wave in constant motion,
Though for your life in terror and distress.
Still there were sights. You would have seen a shift
Of dolphins cleave the emerald calm, the drift
Of clouds, sun, moon and stars revolve in harness;   6245
There you see Nothing—vacant gaping farness,
Mark not your own step as you stride,
Nor point of rest where you abide.

FAUST.   You speak your part of mystagogue in chief
That ever played on neophyte's belief,   6250
With just the sign reversed—send me to limbo
As if to make my strength and craft more nimble;
You use me, like the tomcat one remembers,
To scrabble out your chestnut from the embers.[2]
But I am game! Let me explore that scope,   6255

---

1. The Witch's Kitchen in Part One.
2. In a fable of La Fontaine (Book 9, number 17), the cat Raton is persuaded by the monkey Bertrand
to pull chestnuts out of the fire for him.

Within your Naught to find the All, I hope.
MEPHISTOPHELES.   A compliment before our ways must part:
   You are no stranger to the devil's art;
   Here, take this key.
FAUST.   This little bit?
MEPHISTOPHELES.   First grasp it well and then belittle it.   6260
FAUST.   It grows within my hand! It glitters, glows!
MEPHISTOPHELES.   Ah—do you sense the virtue it bestows?
   This key will scent the true site from the others;
   Follow it down—it leads you to the Mothers.
FAUST.   [with a shudder]
   The Mothers! Still it strikes a shock of fear.   6265
   What is this word that I am loath to hear?
MEPHISTOPHELES.   Are you in blinkers, rear at a new word?
   Would only hear what you already heard?
   Shy at no further sound, weird as it be,
   Long since no more at odds with oddity.   6270
FAUST.   Yet not in torpor would I comfort find;
   Awe is the finest portion of mankind;
   However scarce the world may make this sense—
   In awe one feels profoundly the immense.
MEPHISTOPHELES.   Well then, sink down! Or I might call it: soar!   6275
   It's all one and the same. Escape the norming
   Of what has formed, to forms' unbounded swarming!
   Delight in what long since has been no more;
   Like cloud-drifts whirl the shades of past existence;
   You wield the key and make them keep their distance.   6280
FAUST.   [enraptured]
   Yes! clutching it, I feel my strength redoubled,
   My stride braced for the goal, my heart untroubled.
MEPHISTOPHELES.   A glowing tripod will at last give sign
   That you have reached the deepest, nethermost shrine;[3]
   And by its light you will behold the Mothers;   6285
   Some may be seated, upright, walking others,
   As it may chance. Formation, transformation,
   The eternal mind's eternal recreation,
   Enswathed in likenesses of manifold entity;
   They see you not, for only wraiths they see.   6290
   Then arm your heart, for peril here is great,
   Sight on the tripod and approach it straight
   And touch it with the key!
        [FAUST strikes an attitude of peremptory command with the key.]
MEPHISTOPHELES.   [inspecting him] That is the pose to take!
   Then it will trail, true servant, in your wake;
   You calmly rise, on fortune's buoyant air,   6295
   Return with it before they are aware.

---

3. The tripod, glowing with some burning substance, suggests the traditional accoutrements of the
   ancient oracles, as at Delphi, associated with the ecstatic trance of the priestess.

Once you have brought it here, you have retrieved it,
May summon hero, heroine from night's retreat,
The very first to have essayed that feat;
It will be done, and you will have achieved it.   6300
Its incense fumes, by magical arranging,
Henceforth to godly figures must be changing.
FAUST.   How do I start?
MEPHISTOPHELES.   Your essence downward prise;
   Sink down by stamping, stamping you will rise.
      [FAUST *stamps and sinks out of sight.*]
MEPHISTOPHELES.   Let's hope the key still has the former knack!   6305
   I wonder if we'll ever see him back.

Brightly Lit Ballrooms

The EMPEROR *and* PRINCES, *the* COURT *in movement.*

CHAMBERLAIN. [*to* MEPHISTOPHELES]
　　You owe us still the spirit scene, you know;
　　The master is impatient—start the show.
MARSHAL.　His Grace was pleased this moment to enquire;
　　You! Don't dishonor Majesty's desire.　　　　　　　　　6310
MEPHISTOPHELES.　Why, for this very thing my mate went out,
　　He knows quite well what he's about,
　　He labors, shut from human eyes,
　　In quiet strains with all his heart;
　　For who would raise that treasure, beauty's prize,　　6315
　　Needs wisdom of the Magi, highest art.
MARSHAL.　It does not matter by what kind of skill—
　　Let all be ready, is the Emperor's will.
BLONDE.　[*to* MEPHISTOPHELES]
　　A word, dear Sir! You see an unflawed face,
　　But in the summertime, it's a disgrace!　　　　　　　6320
　　Then in their hundreds reddish spots and brownish
　　Make my complexion look so coarse and clownish.
　　Some salve!
MEPHISTOPHELES.　A pity! Luscious little thing,
　　And spotted like a leopard cub, come spring.
　　Take frog-spawn, tongue of hoptoad, cohobated,[1]　　6325
　　By the full moon's light duly distillated,
　　And as the moon wanes, spread it neatly on:
　　When May arrives, the freckles will be gone.
BRUNETTE.　On favors bent, the fawning crowd advances.
　　I beg a remedy! A frozen foot　　　　　　　　　　　6330
　　Inhibits me at walking and at dances,
　　To drop a curtsey even I'm hard put.
MEPHISTOPHELES.　If you would let me kick you with my foot . . .
BRUNETTE.　Well—I am told that courting couples love it.
MEPHISTOPHELES.　My kick, child, has a meaning far above it;　6335
　　Hair of the dog, whatever ill you pick.
　　Foot for a foot, all parts are cured like that.
　　Come close! Here goes! Mind, there's no tit for tat.
BRUNETTE.　[*screaming*]
　　Ow! Oh! that hurts! that was a dreadful kick,
　　As from a hoof.
MEPHISTOPHELES.　But it has done the trick.　　　　　6340
　　You'll dance now as you please, all light and level,
　　Play footsie, too, at table as you revel.

---

1. Technical term in alchemy meaning "purified by distillation."

LADY. [*pressing forward*] Oh, let me pass! Too painfully I smart,
  The seething rancor sears my inmost heart;
  Till yesterday he sought my eye with glee,   6345
  Now chats with *her* and turns his back on me.
MEPHISTOPHELES.   The thing's precarious, to be sure, but hark.
  Steal up to him in close proximity;
  Here, take this coal and make a stealthy mark
  On shoulder, sleeve, or coat, whatever part;   6350
  Remorse will sweetly stab him to the heart.
  But you must promptly swallow down this ember
  And take no water and no wine, remember;
  He'll languish at your door before it's dark.
LADY.   It is not poison?
MEPHISTOPHELES.   [*indignantly*] What a slur to cast!   6355
  To find its like you'd walk a pretty stretch;
  The stake to which I went this coal to fetch²—
  We used to stoke it harder in the past.
PAGE.   I am in love—she thinks it puppy stuff.
MEPHISTOPHELES.   [*aside*]
  Where listen first? This thing is getting tough.   6360
  [*to the* PAGE] Don't try the very youngest ones just yet;
  Those longer in the tooth are your best bet.³
  [*others crowd up*] More yet! They're coming at me hard and fast.
  I'll be reduced to telling truth at last.
  The worst resort! The plight is pressing, though.—   6365
  O, Mothers! Mothers! Won't you let Faust go?
  [*looking about*] In the great hall I see the lights' dim blur,
  The entire court is all at once astir.
  I see them move in decorous array
  Through distant gallery, long passageway.   6370
  There—they assemble in the spacious Hall
  Of Chivalry, it hardly holds them all.
  With costly carpeting wide walls ornate,
  The nooks and niches decked with armor plate:
  This surely needs no magic spells or elves;   6375
  Here spirits find their way all by themselves.

---

2. Coal from the ashes of a fire used to burn a witch or a heretic; according to superstition, it
   possessed rare magical powers.
3. Recalls the final advice offered to the Student about his studies by Mephistopheles in Part One
   (lines 2011 ff.).

Hall of Chivalry†
Dim Illumination

[EMPEROR *and* COURT *have made their entrance.*]

HERALD. Announcement of the play, my wonted office,
   The spirits' secretive employment ruins;
   One vainly dares by proper reasoned preface
   To fathom the inexplicable doings.   6380
   All readied are the chairs and settles all;
   The Emperor they seat to face the wall,
   There he may view in peace the warlike rages—
   On tapestry—of our heroic ages.
   Now all are seated, Lord and courtiers' bustle,   6385
   Deep in the background crowded benches jostle;
   And love with love, this somber ghostly hour,
   Most lovingly beside each other cower.
   And so, all being in their proper places,
   We're ready; let the spirits show their paces!   6390
     [*Trumpets.*]
ASTROLOGER. Begin the play, the stage assume its shape,
   The lord commands it, let the firm walls gape!
   Here magic is at hand, all hindrance banish,
   As if rolled up by surf, the carpets vanish,
   The wall splits up, it turns about,   6395
   A deep-spaced theater seems fitted out,
   All lighted for us by a mystic glare,
   And I to the proscenium repair.[1]
MEPHISTOPHELES. [*from the prompter's box*]
   From here I hope to gain the crowd's support,
   For prompting is Old Nick's persuasive forte.   6400
   [*to the* ASTROLOGER]
   You know the pulse of stars and their direction,
   You should pick up my whispers to perfection.
ASTROLOGER. Here is revealed to view by wondrous might,
   Quite massive, too, an ancient temple site.
   Like unto Atlas holding up the skies,   6405
   In rows aligned, sufficient columns rise;
   For all the mass they bear, they won't fall short,
   Just two would lend an edifice support.
ARCHITECT. So this is Classic! It deserves no prize,
   It's clumsy, over-heavy to my eyes.   6410
   The coarse is counted noble, bulk sublime.

---

1. The walls open inward to establish a deeper space on the stage, with an indefinite openness ("mystic glare") subsequently to be filled with the façade of a Doric temple (lines 6403–8). Both the Astrologer and Mephistopheles (concealed from the audience within the prompter's box) are placed on the proscenium at the edge of the stage looking into the set.

I like slim pillars, striving up in endless climb;
The pointed apex elevates the mind;
That style uplifts us most of all, I find.

ASTROLOGER.   Receive with awe the hour by stars conferred;   6415
Let reason be restrained by magic word;
Instead, from farthest space let wander free
Magnificent audacious fantasy.
Lay eyes upon your bold desire-in-chief,
It is impossible, and hence deserves belief.[2]   6420

[FAUST *mounts the proscenium from the other side.*]

ASTROLOGER.   In priestly garb and wreath, a wondrous man,
Who now completes what boldly he began.
From hollow crypt a tripod climbs with him,
I sense already incense fragrance dim.
Now he prepares the lofty work to bless,   6425
Naught henceforth can befall but happiness.

FAUST.   [*with magnificent pathos*]
You I invoke, great Mothers, you whose throne
Is boundless space, who dwell forever lone
And yet in company. Encircling you,
Life's images are floating, live, yet lifeless too,   6430
What was, in all its gleam and effigy,
There is astir; eternal it would be.
You, sovereign powers, assign it to diurnal
Bright tabernacle and to vault nocturnal.
The ones, the lovely course of life embraces,   6435
The others but the bold magician[3] traces;
He confidently shows, a lavish host,
To each the wondrous, what he craves the most.

ASTROLOGER.   The glowing key has barely touched the rim,
And foggy vapor makes the spaces dim,   6440
It steals within, with cloudy billow glides,
It stretches, clusters, twines to pairs, divides.
And now—the master stroke of spirits know:
Their wafting drifts make music as they go.
Of aerial notes who knows what eerie croon,   6445
As they proceed, all changes into tune.[4]
The columns ranked, the very triglyphs[5] ring,
Now the entire temple seems to sing.
The mist descends; from out the gauzy space
A comely youth steps forth with rhythmic pace.   6450
My office rests—who needs to be apprised?

2. Tertullian, a Carthaginian theologian (160?–230?), asserted about Christ's resurrection, in his treatise *On the Body of Christ*, chapter 5, "It is certain, because it is impossible."
3. Goethe's manuscript for this line first read "the bold poet." The word *Dichter* was later crossed out and *Magier* written above it.
4. A reference to the shapes that form out of the cloud from the tripod and subsequently assume the forms of Paris and Helena.
5. A figure in the frieze of a Doric temple consisting of a protruding block with two parallel vertical channels on its face.

By all sweet Paris will be recognized!
    [PARIS *steps forth.*]
LADY.   Oh, what a glow of freshly blossomed youth!
SECOND LADY. As fresh and juicy as a peach, in truth!
THIRD LADY. That finely sculptured, sweetly swelling lip!   6455
FOURTH LADY. A cup from which you would be pleased to sip?
FIFTH LADY. He's very handsome, yes, though underbred.
SIXTH LADY. Some more finesse would stand him in good stead.
KNIGHT. I sense an aura of the shepherd lad,[6]
  No prince in him, no courtliness—too bad.   6460
ANOTHER. Well, yes—half naked he's a likely whelp;
  To see him wearing armor, though, would help.
LADY. Now he sits down, so sinuously sweet.
KNIGHT. You think his lap would make a cozy seat?
OTHERS. How gracefully his head sinks on his arm!   6465
CHAMBERLAIN. The lout! This might pass muster on a farm!
LADY. You men must always carp and be unpleasant.
THE FORMER. To loll and wallow when the Emperor's present!
LADY. It's just a play—he thinks that no one sees.
THE FORMER. The stage itself here owes proprieties.   6470
LADY. Soft slumber now overcome the fair!
THE FORMER. Soon he will snore! Most natural, I swear!
YOUNG LADY. [*rapturously*]
  What fragrance mingles with the incense fume?
  So fresh—deep in my heart it seems to bloom.
OLDER LADY. It's true! A breath of soul-pervading essence,   6475
  It comes from him!
OLDEST LADY.   The bloom of adolescence,
  Ambrosia,[7] by the youth exuded here
  And wafted outward on the atmosphere.
    [HELENA *steps forth.*]
MEPHISTOPHELES. So this is she! She'd steal no sleep from me.
  She's pretty, yes, but not my cup of tea.   6480
ASTROLOGER. This once for me there's nothing left to do,
  As man of honor I confess it true.
  Beauty made flesh, and had I tongues of fire![8]
  Of beauty they have sung to many a lyre;
  Who glimpses her is reft of every sense,   6485
  Who calls her his—too rich his recompense.
FAUST. Have I yet eyes? Is deep within my breast
  All beauty's fount incontinently lavished?
  Most blessèd gain has brought me my dread quest;
  How was the world inane to me, bleak, ravished!   6490

---

6. Paris had herded sheep for his father, King Priam of Troy, on Mount Ida, where the three
  goddesses appeared to him with the golden apple of Eris. We may surmise that the event here
  represented occurs just after Paris has made his judgment in favor of Aphrodite.
7. A traditional food of the gods, bestowing immortality.
8. An allusion to Acts 2.3–4, "And there appeared to them tongues as of fire, distributed and resting
  on each one of them."

What is it now, since my new priesthood's term?
As never yet, desired, enduring, firm!
Ah, may I lose life's very breath and germ
If I am ever rehabituated!—
The pleasing shape of which I was enamored,   6495
By magic mirroring beglamored,
Was to this form a wraith, of froth created!—
To thee I vow the stirring of all force,
All passion's sum and source,
Desire, love, worship, adoration, frenzy!   6500
MEPHISTOPHELES.   [*from prompter's box*]
  Don't blow your part, man! Will you curb your fancy!
OLDER LADY.   Good height, good figure—just the head too small.
YOUNGER LADY.   What clumsy ankles, look! They spoil it all.
DIPLOMAT.   I have seen princesses with less appeal,
  She seems to me a beauty, head to heel.   6505
COURTIER.   She nears the sleeper now with gentle stealth.
LADY.   How coarse, beside that purest youth and health!
POET.   He shines with her reflected beauty's glow.
LADY.   Endymion and Luna! A tableau![9]
THE FORMER.   Quite so. It seems the goddess, downward sinking,   6510
  Leans over, of his aura to be drinking.
  Ah, enviable!—A kiss!—The crowning touch.
CHAPERONE.   Right here in public! This is just too much!
FAUST.   Dread favor to the stripling!—
MEPHISTOPHELES.   Hush! Be still!
  Let the poor ghost disport itself at will.   6515
COURTIER.   She lightly tiptoes off; he's waking, though.
LADY.   She's looking back! I could have told you so.
COURTIER.   He marvels! Well, a wonder *did* occur.
LADY.   What she can see is no surprise to *her*.
COURTIER.   She turns to him with wellbred elegance.   6520
LADY.   I see she's planning to become his teacher;
  In such a matter all you males are dense,
  He fancies too he is the first to reach her.
KNIGHT.   You let her be! Majestic and refined!
LADY.   The strumpet! She's a downright vulgar kind!   6525
PAGE.   To be where he is now—I wouldn't mind.
COURTIER.   There's few, I think, would find these meshes cruel!
LADY.   It's passed through many a hand before, that jewel,
  What's more, the gilt on it is rather worn.
OTHERS.   She was no good ten years since she was born.[1]   6530
KNIGHT.   Each takes the best in season he can get;
  I think these fair remains would do me yet.
SAVANT.   I must say, though I see her from close in,

---

9. In response to Endymion's surpassing beauty, the goddess of the moon, Luna, fell in love with him. When Jupiter discovered this, he offered Endymion a choice between death or eternal sleep. He chose the latter and continued to be watched over by the moon.
1. Helena was abducted by Theseus when she was ten years old (see lines 7415–26 and 8848 ff.).

I have my doubts that she is genuine.
The present tends to court exaggeration,   6535
That's why I rather trust documentation.
There I do read she was the special joy
Of every grizzlebearded man in Troy.[2]
The situation fits here to a tee:
I am not young, and yet she pleases me.   6540
ASTROLOGER.   No longer boy! Bold man of hero race,
He sweeps her helpless into his embrace.
With newly strengthened arm he lifts her up,
What—not abducting her?
FAUST.   Audacious pup!
You dare! Halt, hear me? Let her go at once!   6545
MEPHISTOPHELES.
It's your own work, this ghostly mask, you dunce!
ASTROLOGER.   One final word! Now things have gone so far,
I call the play The Rape of Helena.
FAUST.   What rape! Is it for nothing here I stand?
Does this key count for nothing in my hand?   6550
It led through wave and swell and awesome strand
Of desolation back here to firm land.
Here I stand firm, here it's realities,
The mind may battle spirits, based on these,
The greater double realm prepare at ease.   6555
Far as she was, how can she be more near!
She will be doubly mine if rescued here.
Dare! Mothers! Mothers! it is yours to give!
Who knew her once, without her cannot live.
ASTROLOGER.
What would you? Faustus! Faust! With violence loud   6560
He seizes her, the shape begins to cloud.
He wields the key, turns it to touch upon
The youth!—Woe to us, woe! All vanished! Gone!
      [Explosion;[3] FAUST lies on the ground. The spirits dissolve into mist.]
MEPHISTOPHELES.   [taking FAUST upon his shoulder]
There now! You take aboard damned fools, don't wonder
At last the very Devil is dragged under.   6565
      [Darkness, tumult.]

---

2. An allusion to Homer's Iliad 3.156 ff., where the old men of Troy, watching the battle from the
walls of the city, observe Helen as she passes them: "Surely there is no blame on Trojans and
strong-greaved Achaians if for a long time they suffer hardship for a woman like this one. Terrible
is the likeness of her face to immortal goddesses."
3. Two sources have been suggested for the explosion. First, a poem by Hans Sachs, "Story of the
Emperor Maximilian," in which Maximilian attempts to embrace the conjured spirit of his dead
wife, who vanishes "amid noise and smoke and loud tumult." Second, a story by Anthony Hamilton (1646–1720), "Faustus, the Enchanter," in which Queen Elizabeth seeks to embrace the
shade of the Fair Rosamund, conjured up by Faustus, causing thunderclaps to shake the palace
and a thick smoke to fill the gallery. After the tumult has subsided, Faust is found lying on his
back.

ACT II

Narrow, High-vaulted Gothic Chamber†
Erstwhile Faust's, Unchanged

MEPHISTOPHELES. [*stepping out from behind a curtain. As he lifts it and looks back,* FAUST *is disclosed stretched on an antique bed.*]

Lie on here, luckless dreamer, bound
By gyves of love not soon unpried!
Whom Helena has stupefied,
He will not easily come round,
[*looking about*] As I look up, and here, and there, I find it   6570
All quite intact here and unmodified;
The colored panes, I think, are further blinded,[1]
The spiders' webs have multiplied;
The paper's yellowed, ink dried up, but still
All is in order, stacked and level;[2]   6575
Here even lies the very quill
With which Faust signed himself unto the Devil.
Yes! Here is stuck within the rim
A droplet of the blood I lured from him.[3]
A single item of this sort   6580
Would grace the foremost antiquarian's hoard.
Here, too, on the same hook the same old gowning;[4]
Reminds me of that bit of clowning
When I dispensed instructions to that youth,
Whereon perhaps he browses still. Forsooth!   6585
I swear I feel a little yen,
Old fur-warm shroud, in your disguise
To swagger as a lecturer again,
In consciousness of being wholly wise;
A trick that scholars seem to know,   6590
The Devil dropped it long ago.
     [*He takes down the fur and shakes it; cicadas, beetles, and farfarellas fly from it.*[5]]

CHORUS OF INSECTS.   Well met! We are hailing
                       Our patron of yore,
                       We're buzzing and sailing,

---

1. See Faust's mention of the stained-glass windows in his opening monologue, line 401.
2. See the renewal of the monologue in "Night," lines 656–85.
3. See the pact scene, lines 1714–41.
4. See the Student scene, in which Mephistopheles wears the same robe (lines 1868–2048).
5. These insects may recall Faust's reference to "a universe of moths" in his earlier monologue in "Night," lines 658–59. "Farfarella," a variant of the Italian *farfalletta*, a diminutive of "moth," may derive from Dante's *Inferno*, 21.123, where "Farfarello" is one of the demons guarding the pit of the barrators.

Have known you before.   6595
Each singly, dear Father,
You planted us once,
In thousands now rather
We issue to dance.
The rogue will not surface,   6600
He hides himself so,
The lice in the fur-piece
Are quicker to show.

MEPHISTOPHELES.   How they surprise and cheer me, the young fry!
Just sow, and you will harvest by and by.   6605
I shake once more the venerable vair,
Still more come fluttering forth now here and there.—
Soar up! About! In myriad nooks aside
Bestir yourselves, my little dears, to hide.
There, where old reticules are found,   6610
Here, in the ancient parchments browned,
Where in the dust old potsherds wallow,
In yonder deathshead's staring hollow.
This den of antiquated evils
Must ever shelter whims and weevils.   6615
        [*He slips into the fur.*]
Once more enfold my shoulders, pray,
I am the Dean again today.
But what's the use adopting just the name,
Let's get some folk who recognize the claim!
        [*He pulls at the bell, which resounds with a piercing clangor;
        whereof the halls tremble and the doors burst open.*]

FAMULUS.   [*tottering up the long dark passage*]
What a booming! What a shaking!   6620
Staircase trembles, wall is quaking;
Through the colored panes ashiver
Summer lightning flashes quiver.
Ceiling cracks, and from its shifting
Plaster clatters, chalk is sifting.   6625
And the door, securely bolted,
Wonder! from its haspings jolted.—
What! Oh dread! A giant hulking
There in Faust's old furpiece skulking!
As he gazes, as he beckons,   6630
I'll be on my knees in seconds.
Shall I linger, shall I flee?
Oh, what will become of me!

MEPHISTOPHELES.   [*beckoning*]
Come here, my friend!—Your name is Nicodemus.[6]

FAMULUS.   Most Reverend Sir! That is my name—*Oremus.*[7]   6635

---

6. A Pharisee who visited Jesus by night (John 3.1).
7. Latin for "let us pray," indicating a pious gesture to ward off evil spirits.

MEPHISTOPHELES.   Not that!

FAMULUS.   I'm glad! You know me, it appears.

MEPHISTOPHELES.   I do; a student still, though up in years,
    An ivied mossback! Even a learned man
    Will study on because that's all he can.
    And so a middling house of cards one piles,   6640
    No genius ever laid the final tiles.
    But your professor is no slouch, at all:
    The noble Doctor Wagner, known to all!
    The arbiter of learned circles now,
    Authority to whom they all kowtow,   6645
    Wisdom's continual augmentor.
    Of students, auditors, about this center
    A great assembly daily flocks.
    Sole luminary of the Faculty,
    He like St. Peter wields the key,[8]   6650
    The lower and the higher he unlocks.
    And as he shines supreme and sparkles,
    No fame, no name can hold its own,
    Faust's reputation even darkles,
    For his researches stand alone.   6655

FAMULUS.   Permit, Your Worship, if I say to you,
    If you will pardon my gainsaying you,
    That what you have surmised is far from true:
    For modesty is his alloted part.
    The great man's enigmatic disappearance   6660
    He never could accept—his reappearance
    Is source of hope and solace to his heart.
    The Doctor's rooms are in the same repair
    As he abandoned them, untouched to date
    Their former master they await.   6665
    I hardly dare to venture there.
    What could it be, this hour's strange star?—
    The masonry, methinks, is riven,
    Doorposts were shaken, bolts undriven,
    Or you had never come this far.   6670

MEPHISTOPHELES.   What is the man engaged upon?
    Lead me to him, or bring him on.

FAMULUS.   Oh, his decree was too severe,
    I doubt that I dare ask him here.
    For months, to guard the great work from intrusion,   6675
    He's lived in most secluded of seclusion.
    This frailest of the erudite
    Looks like a charcoal-burner quite,
    In soot from ear to nose entire,
    Eyes red from blowing on the fire,   6680

---

8. In founding his church upon the rock of Simon Peter, Christ gave him "the keys of the kingdom of heaven" (Matthew 16.19).

Each panting moment now he longs;
His tune the ringing of the tongs.
MEPHISTOPHELES.   Would he prohibit me admission?
I am the man to further his ambition.
> [*Exit* FAMULUS. MEPHISTOPHELES *seats himself with mock*
> *gravity.*]
I barely settle in this chair,   6685
And lo! a guest—no stranger—stirs back there.
But now he holds the freshest Bachelor's brief;
He will be fresh beyond belief.
BACCALAUREUS.[9] [*storming up the passage*]
      Gate and door, I see, are open,
      At long last, then, there is hoping   6690
      They can't cure the living carcass
      Any more in mold and darkness,
      Trussing, stunting, till they've killed you,
      Dead of life as if of mildew.

      Sagging, tilting edifices,   6695
      All about to fall to pieces—
      We must quit them on the double
      Or they'll smother us in rubble.
      Though I'm daring like no other,
      No wild horses drag me farther.   6700

      What, I wonder, will befall me?
      This is just where I recall me
      Heart in mouth, all in a pother
      Years ago and fresh from Mother,
      When those greybeards used to awe me,   6705
      And their guff was gospel for me.

      From these musty tomes they drew it,
      Pickled wisdom as they knew it,
      Knew it, aye, and knew it worthless,
      Made their lives and others' mirthless,   6710

      Wait a while!—That far-off cloister
      Still contains some dim old oyster!
      There he perches—well, I never!
      In his old brown fur as ever,
      Still the same museum piece,   6715
      Huddled in its shaggy fleece.
      Wise he seemed before I knew him,
      When I hadn't yet seen through him,
      Him or any bearded bogey—
      Let me have at the old fogey!   6720

---

9. This is the Student of Part One (see interpretive notes).

Unless that hairless noggin lists with mud
Washed up, old man, by Lethe's turbid flood,
You will acknowledge here a former pupil,
Released from academic drill and scruple.
I find you still just as I left you then;   6725
I, though, am quite a different specimen.
MEPHISTOPHELES.   I'm glad you answered to my ringing.
I held you then in high esteem;
The chrysalis, the caterpillar clinging,
Presage the butterfly's resplendent gleam.   6730
You took as much delight as little girls
In your lace collar and your head of curls.
You never wore a queue that I recall?
And now you sport a Swedish poll.[1]
You look so resolute and trim to boot,   6735
Just don't go home quite in the absolute.
BACCALAUREUS.   Old man—we took our former stations,
But note the time is not the same,
And spare us your equivocations;
We're smarter now than when we came.   6740
You led this good young fellow by the nose,
It did not take much doing, I suppose,
What no one now would dare to do.
MEPHISTOPHELES.   If one tells youngsters what is really true,
But is not up the greenhorns' avenue,   6745
And then, quite painfully, years hence,
They come to know it at their own expense,
They think they cut it all off their own loaf;
Then they opine their master was an oaf.
BACCALAUREUS.   A fraud, more like. Where is the teacher who   6750
Would tell us to our faces what is true?
They all know how to brew it strong or mild,
Now grave, now smiling, for the docile child.
MEPHISTOPHELES.   A time for learning, true, is set for each;
You, I can see, are quite prepared to teach.   6755
In many a moon, why, in a sun or more,
You must have gained experience galore.
BACCALAUREUS.   Experience hogwash! Froth and grit!
In no way equal to the spirit.
What has been always known, admit,   6760
Is worthless and devoid of merit . . .
MEPHISTOPHELES.   [after a pause]
Methought so long ago. I was a dunce,
I feel quite stale and silly all at once.
BACCALAUREUS.   I am so glad! You may see reason yet;

---

1. The Baccalaureus, butterflylike, wears the latest student fashions, including the close-cropped
hairdo (which replaced the powdered wigs of the eighteenth century) called "Swedish poll" because it was thought to have been introduced by Swedes.

The first old man of insight I have met!   6765
MEPHISTOPHELES.   At hidden hoards of treasure I would nibble,
And horrifying slag I took for it.
BACCALAUREUS.
Your balding dome amounts, then, not to quibble,
Just to those hollow ones there, you admit?[2]
MEPHISTOPHELES.   [*good-naturedly*]
You know how rude you're being, I surmise?   6770
BACCALAUREUS.   In German, if one is polite, one lies.[3]
MEPHISTOPHELES.   [*who has been inching closer to the proscenium
          in his roller chair, to the stalls*]
Up here I'm running out of light and air,
Might I find refuge with you over there?
BACCALAUREUS.   I find conceit untimely in a man
Who wants to count where he no longer can.   6775
Man's life is in his blood, and where, in truth,
Is blood as lively ever as in youth?
There is fresh blood that briskly circulates
And out of very life new life creates.
All is in motion, all astir with deeds,   6780
The weak succumbs, the vigorous succeeds.
While we won half the world, what were you doing?
Deliberating, contemplating, stewing,
Daydreaming, where each plan another breeds.
I swear, old age is like a frigid fever,   6785
Of aches and shakes and crotchets bred.
One who is thirty years or over
Already is as good as dead.
It would be best if you were put away.
MEPHISTOPHELES.   This leaves the Devil nothing much to say.   6790
BACCALAUREUS.   He can't exist without my will, I claim.
MEPHISTOPHELES.   [*aside*]
Old Nick will shortly trip you, all the same.
BACCALAUREUS.   Ah—this is youth's most noble destiny!
The world was not, until I made it be;[4]
I guided up the sun from out the sea;   6795
The moon began her changing course with me;
And lo! the day adorned itself to meet me,
The earth turned green and blossomed forth to greet me.
I beckoned, and upon that earliest night.
The firmament made all its splendors bright.   6800
Who, tell me, if not I, freed all you thinkers
From narrow philistines' confining blinkers?
But I, true to my spirit's dictates, free,
In joy pursue the flame that burns in me,

---

2. An allusion to the skull that was already here in "Night," line 664.
3. A commonplace about the German language as blunt and rude.
4. See Goethe's conversation with Eckermann on this scene (December 6, 1829), below.

And pace along, entranced with my own kind,   6805
The light before me, darkness left behind.
   [*Exit.*]
MEPHISTOPHELES.   Godspeed, Original, in all your glory!—
How stung you'd be to realize:
Who can think anything, obtuse or wise,
That ages back was not an ancient story,—   6810
But there's no threat in even such romantics,
A few years hence this will have passed;
Young must, for all its most outlandish antics,
Still makes some sort of wine at last.
   [*to the younger public in the stalls who fail to applaud*]
I see my discourse leaves you cold;   6815
Dear kids, I do not take offense;
Recall: the Devil, he is old,
Grow old yourselves, and he'll make sense!

Laboratory†
In the Medieval Manner,
Extensive Cumbrous Sets of Apparatus
for Fantastic Purposes

WAGNER.   [at the furnace]
  There booms the bell,[1] from sooty wall
  Thrills shuddering reverberation.   6820
  No longer can the doubt endure
  Of most momentous expectation.
  There, there the veils of darkness fall;
  In the alembic's inmost member
  A glow is lit like living ember,   6825
  Yes—like a glorious jewel's spark
  It shoots its flashes through the dark!
  A glare of dazzling white is sent!
  This once, let me not lose the battle!—
  Oh God, the door! What is this rattle?   6830
MEPHISTOPHELES.   [entering] My welcome! It is kindly meant.
WAGNER.   [apprehensively] Ah, welcome to the hour's good star.
  [under his breath] But word and breath from egress firmly bar.
  A glorious work will shortly be displayed.
MEPHISTOPHELES.   [more softly]   What's going on?
WAGNER.   [more softly]   A man is being made.   6835
MEPHISTOPHELES.   A man? And what young pair in passion
  Did you imprison in the flue?
WAGNER.   Oh, God forbid! Begetting in the former fashion
  We laugh to scorn beside the new.
  The tender point from which new life would surge,   6840
  The potent grace that from within would urge,
  And taking, giving, was to limn itself,
  Absorb first kindred, then remote for self,
  Has now been ousted from its age-old sway;
  If brutes delight still in the former way,   6845
  Then man with his superior resource
  Must henceforth have a higher, higher source.
  [turning to the furnace]
  It shines! Now one may properly start hoping
  That if, 'mid hundreds of ingredients groping,
  By mixing—for on mixture things depend—   6850
  The stuff of humankind we keep composing,
  In a retort enclosing,
  And cohobating well the blend,
  The quiet toil will prosper in the end.

---

1. Wagner refers to the bell rung by Mephistopheles (before line 6620), as if no scene had intervened.

[*turning to the furnace*]
It's coming now! The swirl is clearing duly,   6855
Conviction, too, more truly, truly:
What we extolled as Nature's deep conundrum,
We venture now to penetrate by reason,
And what she did organically at random,
We crystallize in proper season.   6860
MEPHISTOPHELES.   He who has lived has learned a lot,
    To him the world can offer nothing new;
    Upon my wanderings from spot to spot
    I've come across synthetic people too.
WAGNER.   [*still continuing to watch the alembic attentively*]
    It swells, it gleams, piles up and on,   6865
    In just a moment it is done.
    A great design appears at first insane;
    But chance will soon seem quaint and blind,
    And such an exemplary thinking brain
    Will soon by thinkers be designed.   6870
[*watching the alembic in rapture*]
    The glass grows tuneful with its lovely power,
    It's clouding, clearing, nearly done within!
    I see in shapely harmony cower
    A dainty little mannikin.
    What more do we desire, what more the world?   6875
    For now the secret is in reach.
    Let this vibration but be heard,
    And it will turn to voice, to speech.[2]
HOMUNCULUS.   [*in the alembic, to* WAGNER]
    Well, there, Papa! How now? It was no jest.
    Clutch me affectionately to your breast,   6880
    But not too roughly, or the glass might shatter.
    Such is, you see, a property of matter:
    Things natural find all the world scant space,
    While things synthetic want a sheltered place.
[*to* MEPHISTOPHELES]
    What ho, the rogue! Sir Cousin, you here, too?   6885
    You're right on cue, I am obliged to you.
    A thoughtful fate has timed it well enough;
    Since I exist, I must be ever active,
    I feel like getting down to work right off.
    Where I need shortcuts, you should be effective.   6890
WAGNER.   A word before! I have been much embarrassed,
    By old and young with ceaseless problems harassed.
    No one has fathomed—naming one at random—
    How body and soul form such a jointless tandem,
    A timeless-seeming bond, like brother and brother,   6895

2. See Goethe's conversation with Eckermann of December 20, 1829, below.

And yet make life so wretched for each other.
Secundo—
MEPHISTOPHELES.   Stop! I would consult him rather
Why man and wife fall out with one another?
A poser, friend, a quest that never ends.
Here's work to do—just what the imp intends.   6900
HOMUNCULUS.   What's there to work on?
MEPHISTOPHELES.   [*pointing to a side door*]
                                        Here your gifts employ!
WAGNER.   [*still gazing into the alembic*]
    My word, you are a captivating boy!
        [*The side door opens, revealing* FAUST *stretched on the couch.*]
HOMUNCULUS.   [*astonished*] Momentous!
        [*The alembic slips from* WAGNER'S *hands, to float over* FAUST *and illuminate him.*][3]
                                Fair-environed!—Limpid waters
    In a dense grove, young nymphs their garments shedding;
    Sweet sight! Now sweeter still. Yet 'mid these daughters   6905
    One who outglistens all her lustrous setting,
    Of hero kin, perchance of godly name.
    She dips a foot into that lucidness;
    The flawless body's graceful living flame
    Is cooled in pliant crystalline caress.   6910
    But there, what whirring rush of pinions flashing,
    What churns that lambent glass with stir and splashing?
    The timid maidens scatter, and at once
    The queen remains alone; but calm her glance,
    With woman's proud complacency she sees   6915
    The splendid swan prince nestling to her knees,
    Intrusive-tame. He grows inured, serene . . .
    But of a sudden, mist, a vaporous gauze,
    Arises and a close-meshed curtain draws
    About the most enchanting scene.   6920
MEPHISTOPHELES.   How aptly you have improvised it all!
    You are as tiny as your tales are tall.
    I cannot see a thing.
HOMUNCULUS.   No wonder. From the North,
    In foggy centuries spawned forth,
    Knighthood-befuddled, cleric-ridden,   6925
    How could your eye be free to roam?
    In murk alone you feel at home.
    [*gazing about him*] Stonework begrimed and moldy-green,
    Weird-curlicued, arch-pointed, mean!—
    If he awakes, we face a sorer plight,   6930
    He'll catch his death upon the sight.
    Wood-pools and swans and naked sirens,
    Of such was his foreboding dream;

---

3. Homunculus describes what Faust sees in his dream (see interpretive notes).

How could he take to these environs!
I hardly stand them, easy as I seem.   6935
Away with him!
MEPHISTOPHELES.   I shouldn't be the sorrier.
HOMUNCULUS.   Why, into battle bid the warrior,
    The maiden summon to the reel,
    And you have answered their appeal.
    Just now, if I recall aright,[4]   6940
    Is classical Walpurgis Night;
    Occasion truly heaven-sent—
    Transport him to his element.
MEPHISTOPHELES.   The like has never come my way.
HOMUNCULUS.   How would it come to your attention, pray?   6945
    Romantic ghosts alone are known to you,
    A genuine ghost must do the Classic too.[5]
MEPHISTOPHELES.   Where is it then, the place where we convene?
    Antiquish colleagues roil me sight unseen.
HOMUNCULUS.   Northwestward, Satan, lies your pleasure-ground,   6950
    Southeastward, though, for this time we are bound.
    A spacious plain, Peneios flowing through
    Enshrubbed and treed, with bights and meadows still,
    The lowland spreads from hill to cloven hill,
    Above it lies Pharsalus, old and new.[6]   6955
MEPHISTOPHELES.   Oh no! Away! let's have no mention
    Of slavery and tyrant in contention
    It bores me; they are hardly through,
    And then it all begins anew;
    And no one realizes they're in thrall   6960
    To Asmodeus,[7] who has staged it all.
    They fight for "liberties"—to the observant
    In actual fact it's servant against servant.
HOMUNCULUS.   Leave men's obstreperous nature its free field,
    For each of them must fend as best he can   6965
    From boyhood up; at length, there is a man.
    Our problem is how this one may be healed.
    Here try it if you have a remedy,
    If you can't manage it, leave it to me.
MEPHISTOPHELES.
    Well, many a Brocken trick might be rehearsed,   6970

4. On the plan for the "Classical Walpurgis Night," see Goethe's "Second Sketch for the Announce-
    ment of the *Helena*," below.
5. See Goethe's conversation with Eckermann on this scene (December 16, 1829), below.
6. Along the traditional geographical-historical axis of cultural orientation in the West, Homunculus
    describes the setting for the coming "Classical Walpurgis Night." The river Peneios in Thessaly
    runs from the slopes of the Pindus Mountains through the Vale of Tempe, between Mt. Olympus
    and Mt. Ossa, flowing thence into the Aegean Sea on the northeast coast of Greece. Pharsalus
    (Latin form of the name of the Greek city of Pharsalos) was located on the river Apidanos in
    Thessaly. On the plains outside the city, the epochal battle took place on August 9, 48 B.C.,
    between Caesar and Pompey that marked the transition from the ancient to the modern world
    and the death of mythological creatures from the former, who assemble once a year on the
    anniversary of the event to commemorate their own demise.
7. See line 5378 and note.

But pagan bolts would have to open first.
This Grecian tribe was never up to much!
They lure you with free sensuous play and such,
And tempt men to a cheerful kind of sinning;
While ours seems glum and never half as winning.   6975
What now?
HOMUNCULUS.   Why, you're not shy about your itches;
If I make mention of Thessalian witches,[8]
Perhaps I do not have to shout.
MEPHISTOPHELES.   [*lecherously*]
Hmm! They are persons, those Thessalian witches
That I have often asked about.   6980
With them night after night to hang one's britches
Would be discomforting, no doubt;
But just a spot . . . ? Why not!
HOMUNCULUS.   Let's have your wrap,
Fling it about our knightly brother!
As it has done before, that scrap   6985
Will do to lift one and the other;
I light the way.
WAGNER.   [*timidly*]   And I?
HOMUNCULUS.   Why, you—
You'll find at home important things to do.
There are old parchments there to be inspected,
Life elements by rule to be collected   6990
And circumspectly fitted edge to edge.
The How needs even more thought than the What.
While I go on a little pilgrimage
I may discover to your i the dot.
Thus to the lofty goal you may advance;   6995
These will be the rewards for having striven:
Gold, honor, fame, long span of healthy living,
And scholarship and virtue—too, perchance.
Farewell!
WAGNER.   [*distressed*] Farewell! my heart is sore, alack!
I fear I may not ever see you back.   7000
MEPHISTOPHELES.   Peneius-ho, then! My young friend
Should not be underestimated.
[*ad spectatores*] At last we after all depend
Upon dependents we created.

---

8. The Thessalian witches, devotees of the moon who also transform men into beasts, are derived
from Lucan, *Pharsalia* 6; they are mentioned also in Plato, *Gorgias* 38, and Aristophanes, *Clouds*
7897. They appear in the "Classical Walpurgis Night" as Lamiae to confront Mephistopheles
(lines 7676–790).

Classical Walpurgis Night†
The Pharsalian Fields
Darkness

ERICHTHO.   For dread observance of this night, as oft before,   7005
I here proceed, Erichtho,[1] I, the somber one;
Not as repulsive as the poets in their excess
Have rudely slandered me . . . immoderate as they are
In praise or blame . . . Already bleached appears to me
From the gray tide of tents the vale from end to end,   7010
The afterview of that most dire and awestruck night.
How often has it not recurred! And will recur
Eternally . . . Not one but grudges sovereign rule
To others, most to him who seized it by his strength
And strongly reigns.[2] For he who has not learnt to rule   7015
His inner self, is only too intent to rule
His neighbor's will to suit his own imperious mind.
But here a famous precedent was battled out
How might arrays itself against still greater might,
And Freedom's lovely thousand-blossomed wreath is rent,   7020
Stiff laurel coiled about the ruler's brow instead.
Here Pompey dreamt of early glory's flowering day,
There wakeful Caesar harked the balance-tongues of fate!
These will be matched; and who prevailed, the world knows
        well.

Watch-fires are glowing, lending crimson flames,   7025
The earth exhales again the reck of blood spilt then,
Lured by the wondrous rare effulgence of the night,
The legion of Hellenic legend gather here.
About each fire there waver mootly, or recline
At ease, the fable-woven shapes of ancient days . . .   7030
There rises, not at full, yet gleaming fair,
The moon and sheds a gentle radiance all about;
The mirage of the tents dissolves, the fires burn blue.

But overhead, unlooked for, what a meteor?[3]
It radiates, and lights some sphere corporeal.   7035
I scent the breath of life. It ill befits me, then,

---

1. The witch Erichtho is mentioned for her ugliness in both Ovid, *Heroides* 15.139, and Lucan, *Pharsalia* 4.507. Pompey had consulted her on the night before the original battle to learn who the victor would be.
2. Here and in the following lines, allusion is made to the political struggle between Pompey and Julius Caesar that caused the battle of Pharsalus.
3. What Erichtho takes to be a meteor is in fact Faust and Mephistopheles riding through the air on the magic cloak, accompanied by Homunculus in his phial, which casts a dazzling light on all of them.

To close with things alive to which I am of harm.[4]
This yields me ill-renown, and nothing gained.
Already it descends. I prudently withdraw!
    [*Departs.*]

    [*The* AERONAUTS *above.*][5]

HOMUNCULUS.	Sail with us another round	7040
	Over flame and terrors dread;	
	For such ghostly sights abound	
	In the dale and valley-bed.	
MEPHISTOPHELES.	When, as in the northland's horrors	
	Through some window-arch, I see	7045
	These most noisome ghosts before us,	
	Either place is home to me.	
HOMUNCULUS.	Look! a bony female striding,	
	Vast of step, before us here.	
MEPHISTOPHELES.	Through the air she saw us gliding,	7050
	Likely she is struck with fear.	
HOMUNCULUS.	Let her stride away! and stand	
	On his feet your knight; at once	
	He'll revive, and not by chance:	
	He seeks life in fable-land	7055

FAUST.   [*touching the soil*] Where is she?
HOMUNCULUS.   Hard to tell; but ask about,
And you can probably find out.
Explore, before the dawn is here,
From one flame hasten on to others:
He who has dared amongst the Mothers   7060
Has precious little left to fear.
MEPHISTOPHELES.   I too feel in my element;
But deem it best for our content
That each should range the fires alone,
To seek adventure on his own.   7065
And then, in order to unite us,
You, midget, flash your ringing flare and light us.
HOMUNCULUS.   Here's how it flashes, how it rings.
    [*The glass gives off a powerful drone and glare.*]
Now off to fresh unheard-of things!
    [*Exit.*]

FAUST.   [*alone*] Where is she!—Do not question now for long . . .   7070
For even were it not the soil that bore,
The surf that rose against her at this shore,
It is the air which spoke her native tongue.

---

4. Lucan, *Pharsalia* 6.510 ff., states that Erichtho shunned human company and inhabited the tombs of the dead.
5. The following exchange corresponds to the chant with the Will-o'-the-Wisp in the "Walpurgis Night" of Part One, lines 3871–912.

Here! By some magic, here, in Grecian land!
I sensed at once the earth whereon I stand;   7075
As, in my sleep, fresh spirit fired my heart,
Awake, I stand here in Antaeus'[6] part.
Though strangest blend of most unlike and same,
I'll earnestly explore this maze of flame.
    [*Departs.*]

6. A giant with whom Hercules wrestled. Son of the Earth, he renewed his strength whenever his
feet touched the ground.

[On the Upper Peneios¹]

MEPHISTOPHELES.† [prying about]
    And as I roam about these spots of flame,   7080
    I do feel quite estranged and disconcerted;
    Stark naked all, just here and yonder shirted:
    The sphinxes brazen, griffins bare of shame,²
    So all the crowd that, curly-fleeced or feathered,
    From front and rear display themselves untethered.   7085
    We too, of course, are heartily indecent,
    But this antique lot feels too live and recent;
    Quite à la mode these moot points should be mastered
    And fashionably-triply overplastered . . .
    A nasty lot! Yet a new guest, to meet them,   7090
    Must take the trouble decently to greet them . . .
    Salute to you, fair ladies, grizzling sages.
GRIFFIN. [rasping] Not grizzling! Griffin! No one likes to be
    Addressed as grizzled. Words still bear within
    Echoing traces of their origin: 7095
    Grey, grumbling, gruesome, graveyard, grimly, grunted,
    Alike etymologically fronted,
    Affront us.³
MEPHISTOPHELES.   Take this point: while "grizzled" teases,
    The "grip" in the proud name of griffin pleases.
GRIFFIN. [as above, and continuing henceforth]
    Of course! the association is well-tried,   7100
    And widely lauded, if at times decried.
    One's grip be laid on maidens, gold, or crowns,
    On graspers Lady Fortune seldom frowns.
ANTS. [of the colossal sort]
    You speak of gold, we had collected masses,
    Secreted deep in rock and cave crevasses;   7105
    The Arimaspians nosed it out and bagged it,
    They're giggling there at how far off they've dragged it.⁴
GRIFFINS.   Don't worry, we shall force them to confess.
ARIMASPIANS.   Not this free night of merriment.

---

1. Goethe neglected to indicate changes of geographical setting within the "Classical Walpurgis Night" in a consistent way. This stage direction (in brackets, as before line 7249) was added by editors.
2. The Sphinxes—traditionally represented with the head and upper body of a woman, the lower body of a lion—appear with naked breasts; the Griffins—with the head and wings of an eagle and the body of a lion—are "shameless" in the greed with which (according to Herodotus, *History* 4.13) they traditionally stood guard over buried treasure.
3. On the etymological theory of the Griffins, see interpretive notes.
4. According to ancient legend (as in Herodotus, *History* 4.27, or Pliny, *Natural History* 11.31), gigantic ants dug up particles of gold from beneath the earth in order to build their underground homes. *Arimaspians*: also mentioned in Herodotus; one-eyed monsters from Northern Scythia who were the traditional enemies of the Griffins, often attempting to steal their treasure.

For by the morning it's all spent,   7110
This time we'll bring it off, we guess.
MEPHISTOPHELES.   [*who has seated himself among the* SPHINXES]
How I got settled here in moments!
I understand them, one and all.
SPHINX.   We emanate our spectral comments,
And you make them corporeal.⁵   7115
Now, pending more acquaintance, state your name.
MEPHISTOPHELES.   By many names they name me—so they claim;
Are any Britons here? They're always traveling,⁶
To track down sites of battles, tumbling brooks,
Long-tumbled ruins, musty classic nooks;   7120
For them this place would be the very thing.
They'd bear me out that in a bygone age
As *Old Iniquity*⁷ I held their stage.
SPHINX.   Why so?
MEPHISTOPHELES.   I do not know myself what for.
SPHINX.   So be it. Are you versed in stellar lore?   7125
About the present hour, what do you say?
MEPHISTOPHELES.   [*looking up*]
Star shoots on star, a clipped moon shines fair ray,
And I feel good in this congenial spot,
What with your lion skin to keep me hot,
To climb about up yonder is no feast,   7130
Let's have some riddles, or charades at least.
SPHINX.   To make a riddle, just enounce yourself.
Try and resolve your inmost self and action:
"To good and bad alike in satisfaction,
To one, a corslet for ascetic lunging,   7135
The other, vice-companion for mad plunging,
And either, just for Father Zeus' distraction."⁸
FIRST GRIFFIN.   [*rasping*] I'm sick of him!
SECOND GRIFFIN.   [*rasping harder*]   Who's he to interfere?
BOTH.   The ugly fright, who needs him here?
MEPHISTOPHELES.   [*brutally*]
You think perhaps the guest's claws rip, on balance,   7140
Not quite as well as do your own sharp talons?
SPHINX.   [*mildly*] Do stay as long as you've a mind;
You'll volunteer to leave us, you will find;
At home your self-importance may be strong,

---

5. Here and in what follows, the Sphinx performs its traditional role of setting riddles of identity, as in the legend of Oedipus at Thebes.
6. An anachronistic allusion to the reputation of the British as world travelers in the late-eighteenth and early-nineteenth centuries.
7. The name "Old Iniquity" (so used in English by Goethe) derives from late-medieval morality plays. The same name is used by Shakespeare in *Richard III* 3.1.82 and by Ben Jonson in *The Devil Is an Ass*, Prologue, 49.
8. The answer to this riddle, which Mephistopheles does not bother to acknowledge, is apparently himself.

Here you feel out of place, unless I'm wrong.   7145
MEPHISTOPHELES.
  You look quite appetizing, Sphinx, your top at least,
  But gruesome farther down, the part that's beast.
SPHINX.   You counterfeit find in us sharp reproof,
  In that our claws and paws are sound;
  You, with your shrunken horse's hoof,   7150
  Are ill at ease amid our round.
         [SIRENS *tuning up for song above.*[9]]
MEPHISTOPHELES.   Who are those birds who settled, swaying,
  That poplar grove in crown and bough?
SPHINX.   Beware! Their sing-song has been slaying
  The very finest before now.   7155
SIRENS.   Ah, why be habituated
               To the hideously wondrous!
               Hark, we're coming in our hundreds,
               And with notes well-modulated;
               Thus for Sirens it is fated.   7160
SPHINXES.   [*mocking them to the same tune*]
               Try to make them leave their branches!
               Deep in foliage to their haunches,
               They conceal their claws of raptors,
               They will turn pernicious captors
               If you listen to their tune.   7165

SIRENS.   Down with hate! Down envy! Rather,
               Purest pleasures let us gather,
               Here beneath the heavens strewn!
               On the earth, upon the ocean,
               None but the serenest motion   7170
               To the welcome guest be shown.
MEPHISTOPHELES.   Here is the newest and the choicest
  Which pours from strings or human voices,
  All interbraided part with part.
  This sing-song's lost on me, I fear,   7175
  It makes a tingling in my ear,
  But never filters to the heart.
SPHINX.   Speak not of heart! I doubt but whether
  To claim a shrunken pouch of leather
  Would not be apter on your part.   7180
FAUST.   [*approaching close*]
  How wondrous, just the aspect of these creatures!
  In the repellent, great and valiant features.

---

9. According to legend, the Sirens were nymphs transformed to birds (or at least with the wings of
  birds) who were banished to an island in the sea, where they sang sweet songs that enticed passing
  mariners to their death by shipwreck on the rocks. In Homer's *Odyssey*, they are encountered by
  Odysseus in his wanderings (12.39–54 and 154–200). Here the Sirens have apparently come inland
  for the "Classical Walpurgis Night" (cf. the "Second Sketch for the Announcement of the *Helena*," below), and they depart precipitously in immediate response to the earthquake later on,
  apparently swimming downstream in the river Peneios to the Aegean Sea (cf. lines 7503 ff.).

They seem to augur me a happy chance;
Where does it take me back, this earnest glance?
[*referring to the* SPHINXES]
In front of such did Oedipus stand once;[1]   7185
[*referring to the* SIRENS]
For these, Ulysses writhed in hempen bonds;[2]
[*referring to the* ANTS]
By such as these was highest treasure stored;
[*referring to the* GRIFFINS]
By these most vigilantly watched the hoard.[3]
By a fresh spirit's breath I feel affected,
Grand are the forms, and grandly recollected.   7190
MEPHISTOPHELES.   You used to blast it with abuse
What now you willingly abide;
No doubt the lover who pursues
His love takes monsters in his stride.
FAUST.   [*to the* SPHINXES]
Abide my question, dames of high estate: 7195
Has one of you seen Helena of late?
SPHINXES.   She is above our ken, her days are newer,
The last of us met Hercules,[4] who slew her.
Through Chiron,[5] though, you might perchance pursue her;
This night of ghosts, he's always roved and pranced,   7200
If he responds, you will be much advanced.
SIRENS.   Sad your loss if you repel us! . . .
When Ulysses came sojourning
With us, did not pass us spurning,
He had many tales to tell us;[6]   7205
To all these we pledge to make you
Privy if you will betake you
To our ocean realms of jade.
SPHINX.   Noble youth, be not betrayed.
Than bound Ulysses in your turn,   7210
Be rather by good counsel bound.
If highborn Chiron can be found,
What I foretold, you stand to learn.
        [FAUST *withdraws.*]
MEPHISTOPHELES.   [*peevishly*]
What whistles croaking, flapping past,
That is too quick for eye to seize,   7215
Each followed by the next so fast?

1. See note to line 7115.
2. See note preceding line 7152.
3. See note to line 7107.
4. The story that Hercules killed the last of the Sphinxes appears to be Goethe's invention.
5. Chiron the centaur, who appears in the next scene (lines 7330 ff.), was the tutor of many heroes, including Achilles and the twin half-brothers of Helena, Castor and Pollux.
6. The Sirens here distort the truth as Homer tells it. Ulysses was forewarned of the Sirens and had his men fill their ears with wax and himself tied to the mast of his ship in order to guard against the irresistible lure of their song.

They'd wear out any huntsman, these.
SPHINX.　Like winter tempest storming fiercely,
　To arrows of Alcides[7] scarcely
　In range—the swift Stymphalides,[8]　　　　　　　　　7220
　With web of goose and vulture's bill
　Their croaking hail intends no ill.
　All they desire is to join in
　And prove themselves our next of *kin*.
MEPHISTOPHELES.　[*as if intimidated*]
　There's more goes hissing in between.　　　　　　7225
SPHINX.　These surely need not make you quake,
　They are the heads of the Lernaean Snake,[9]
　Cut from the trunk, but still convinced of being.
　But say, what will you turn to next?
　What gestures, restless or perplexed?　　　　　　7230
　Where would you go? Begone and further fare! . . .
　I see, the chorus over there
　Has made you swivel-necked. Don't stand on graces,
　Make your way over, greet some charming faces.
　These are the Lamiae,[1] wenches lewdly tender.　　7235
　Of swelling lips and scruples slender,
　Just such as suit the Satyr pack;[2]
　With them, a goatfoot has the inner track.
MEPHISTOPHELES.　You're staying? So I find you here again?
SPHINX.　Yes. Go and mingle with the airy clan.　　7240
　We, by our Old Egyptian past affected,[3]
　Are long accustomed to millennial stays.
　And if our site be but respected,
　We tell the lunar and the solar days:[4]
　　　　　　　Crouched before the pyramids—　　　　7245
　　　　　　　Nations pass the judgment bar,
　　　　　　　Inundation, peace and war—
　　　　　　　And we never blink our lids.

7. Another name for Hercules, grandson of Alcaeus.
8. Monstrous birds with iron beaks and claws, from the valley of Stymphalus. Hercules killed them as one of his twelve labors.
9. The Lernaean Hydra had nine heads, one of which was immortal. As one of his labors, Hercules was assigned to kill it. Whenever he cut off a head, two new heads grew in its place. Finally, he burned them all off and buried the immortal head.
1. Ghosts who thirst for human flesh and blood and who assume different shapes, especially those of young women, in order to attract their victims (See lines 7676 ff. and 6977.)
2. See note to line 5829.
3. The association of the Sphinxes with ancient Egypt enhances their primeval mystery. Correspondingly, they later remain unmoved by the earthquake and the appearance of Seismos (which they describe, lines 7523–49).
4. The great statue of the Sphinx at Giza in Egypt was placed so as to measure time astronomically.

[On the Lower Peneios¹]

PENEIOS *surrounded by waters and* NYMPHS.

PENEIOS.²†   Sough of sedges, stir your whispers,
 Softly breathe, my reedy sisters,   7250
 Waft, you airy willows, wispy
 Poplar feathers, lull with lisping,
 Mending interrupted dream! . . .
 For a fearsome shiver wakes me,
 Deep all-moving quiver shakes me,   7255
 From the restful rolling stream.
FAUST.   [*stepping toward the riverbank*]
 Surely, if I trust my senses,
 Through these laced arboreal fences,
 Tangled boskets, from the beaches
 Issue notes like human speeches.   7260
 Ripples chatter as they rollick,
 Breezes titter like . . . a frolic.
NYMPHS.   [*to* FAUST]
  'Twere best of all for thee
  Here to be bedding,
  Cool would restore thee,   7265
  Weariness shedding,
  Savor the heart's rest
  That everywhere flees thee;
  Our wafting and purling
  And whispering ease thee.   7270

FAUST.   No slumber now! Oh let me ponder
 Those peerless apparitions yonder
 My eye envisions. To the core
 How wondrously I am affected!
 Why, do I dream this? Recollect it?   7275
 This blissful sight was mine before.
 Still waters stealing through the luscious
 Array of softly swaying rushes,
 They do not splash, scarce seep their path;
 From every side, a hundred sources   7280
 Unite their flawless crystal courses
 To form a limpid shelving bath.
 Young female forms, their healthy fitness
 Redoubled by the mirror's witness
 For the enchanted eye's delight!   7285

---

1. See note to line 6955 and note before line 7080.
2. The river speaks as a person. Parallels for this may be found in classical literature and art (the Skamander in *Iliad* 21 and the Tiber in *Aeneid* 8).

Then playful fellowship of bathing,
Emboldened swimming, timid wading,
Gay shouts at last and water fight.
On these my eye should rest contented,
Yet, though a feast be here presented,   7290
On more my striving mind is keen.
Beyond the probing gaze will hover,
Where emerald folds of leafy cover
Must harbor the exalted queen.[3]

Marvels! From the bays emerging,   7295
Swans come drifting down, converging,
Poised at motion's purest peak.
Grouped in graceful ease, unhastened,
Haughty, though, and self-complacent
As they cradle crown and beak . . .   7300
One, more boldly than the others[4]
Breasting, bridling, leaves his brothers,
Forging swiftly through their flight;
Bulging plumage proudly swelling,
Wave himself, on wavelets welling,   7305
He invades the sacred site . . .
The rest are cruising here and thither
In calmly gleaming shells of feather,
At times with splendid truculence
The timid maidens' minds deflecting,   7310
So that, their guardianship neglecting,
They think but of their own defense.
NYMPHS.   Sisters, come and hold your ear
                To the bankment's verdant scallop:
                For I fancy what I hear   7315
                Is the sound of horse's gallop.
                How I wish to learn who might
                Bear swift tidings here this night.
FAUST.   Do I hear the earth resounding
    To a charger's rapid pounding?   7320
                Thither glance!
                Happy chance,
                Is it already lent me?
                O peerless wonder sent me!
A horseman cantering ahead   7325
He seems highminded, spirited,
And of a dazzling white his mount . . .
No doubt! I know him from afar,

---

3. Leda is queen of the nymphs and mother of Helen of Troy. The event described is identical to
   that seen by Faust in his dream (lines 6903–20), though differences of style, focus, and emphasis
   are important.
4. Zeus in the form of a swan.

The famous son of Philyra!⁵
Halt, Chiron! Halt! I would request account . . .   7330
CHIRON.   What is it? What about?
FAUST.   Your paces ease!
CHIRON.   I do not rest.
FAUST.   Then take me with you, please!
CHIRON.   Mount! I may freely ask then and respond.
　　Where are you bound? You stand here by the banks,
　　I am prepared to carry you beyond.   7335
FAUST.   [mounting] Whither you wish. Take my eternal thanks . . .
　　The famous man, the noble pedagogue
　　Who, to his honor, reared a hero folk,
　　The circle of the noble Argonauts,⁶
　　And all who have enriched the poet's thoughts.   7340
CHIRON.   We'd better let it go at that!
　　As mentor, Pallas even had small credit;⁷
　　You give instruction—then, off their own bat,
　　They act as though they'd never had it.
FAUST.   The leech to whom no plant is strange,   7345
　　Who knows the roots to deepest range,
　　Can heal the sick, the wounded ease and bind,
　　I here embrace in body as in mind!
CHIRON.   For heroes stricken where I was
　　I knew relief and cure to find!   7350
　　But in the end bequeathed my cause
　　To quacks—diviner and divined.
FAUST.   You show the truly great man's ways,
　　Who cannot stomach words of praise;
　　His modesty will squirm and parry,   7355
　　Pretending to be ordinary.
CHIRON.   You have a sycophantic flair
　　For flattering prince or commoner.
FAUST.   But this you will concede me yet:
　　The greatest of your era you have met,   7360
　　To emulate the noblest deeds have striven,
　　In earnest demigodly wise been living.
　　Now, of your hero friends, whom have you deemed
　　The doughtiest, whom have you most esteemed?
CHIRON.   Within the Argonauts' high round   7365
　　Each had a virtue all his own, I found,
　　And by the strength with which he was endowed
　　He would excel where others bowed.
　　The Dioscuri,⁸ now, could ever boast

---

5. Chiron was the son of Chronos and Philyra (see note to line 7199).
6. A group of fifty heroes organized and led by Jason in his quest for the Golden Fleece. Their ship
　was called the Argo.
7. In Homer's Odyssey 2 and 3, Pallas Athena appears to Telemachus in the guise of Mentor, a
　family friend, to lead him on his journey to find his father.
8. Castor and Pollux, twin half-brothers of Helena, sons of Leda.

Success where youth and beauty count for most.   7370
Resolve and rapid deed to others' profit—
The Boreads[9] had the pleasant favor of it.
Thoughtful and strong, of ready counsel, clever,
Thus Jason ruled, to women pleasing ever.
Frail Orpheus,[1] musing quietly, withal   7375
Would strike the mightiest lyre among them all.
Sharp-eyed Lynceus[2] was, by night and day
He steered the sacred bark past cliff and spray . . .
Concerted toil on perilous quest I laud:
When one achieves, the others all applaud.   7380
FAUST.   Of Hercules shall I be learning?
CHIRON.   Alas! Do not excite my yearning . . .
Phoebus[3] I never gazed upon,
Of Ares, Hermes saw no sign,
Then stood before my eyes the one   7385
Whom men would worship as divine.

Born to be king above all others,
In youth most splendorous to view;
Meek servant of his elder brother's
And of the loveliest women too.   7390
No like of his will Earth engender,
Nor Hebe[4] lift to Heaven's throne;
Here must the laboring lyre surrender,
In vain do they torment the stone.
FAUST.   Though sculptors vaunted each his token,   7395
So grand he never came to view.
Of fairest hero you have spoken,
Now speak of fairest women too!
CHIRON.   Bosh! . . . Beauty's often lifeless; not in feature
True loveliness is found expressed.   7400
I keep my praises for the nature
That overbrims with joy and zest.
Beauty but blesses her own face,
But irresistible is grace,
Like Helen's when she rode on me.   7405
FAUST.   You carried her?
CHIRON.   I did; this back she used.
FAUST.   Am I not quite enough confused
Without such seat entrancing me?
CHIRON.   Into my hair she sank her fingers, just
As you do now.

---

9. Zetes and Calais, sons of Boreas (the North Wind).
1. A legendary poet who accompanied Jason on the *Argo*.
2. An Argonaut renowned for his keenness of sight. The watchman in Act III, lines 9218 ff., and
   Act V, lines 11143 ff., is given the name "Lynceus," presumably with this figure in mind.
3. Apollo, god of the sun.
4. The goddess Hebe became Hercules' wife after his deification.

FAUST.   Oh, I am lost,   7410
  Lost altogether! Tell of her!
  She is my prime, my sole desire!
  Whence did you bear her? Oh, and where?
CHIRON.   I grant with ease what you enquire.
  The Dioscuri had redeemed just then   7415
  Their little sister, prey to highwaymen,[5]
  But these, unused to being foiled of loot,
  Took courage and came storming in pursuit.
  The marshes near Eleusis[6] bade to slow
  The threesome's rapid flight, and so   7420
  The brothers waded through, I splashed and swam across.
  Then she dismounted and began caressing
  My dripping mane, and, self-possessed, addressing,
  Endearingly astute, sweet thanks to me.
  So charming—young, an old man's joy—was she!   7425
FAUST.   Aged only ten . . . !
CHIRON.   Philologists,[7] I see,
  Have swathed your mind, like theirs, in pedantry.
  A myth-born female is a thing apart,
  Steps forth as needed by the poet's art,
  Never of age nor over age,   7430
  At ever appetizing stage,
  Abducted young, wooed in senescence yet,
  Unbound by chronometric etiquette.
FAUST.   Thus Helen too—no lapse of time shall bind her!
  Did not at Pherae[8] great Achilles find her,   7435
  Beyond all time? What bliss more rare or great:
  Love wrested from the tyranny of fate!
  And could I not by fierce desire contrive
  To will the incomparable back alive,
  Peer of the gods, imperishable treasure,   7440
  August and loveable in equal measure?
  I saw her here and now, as you did there,
  So fair as lovely, as desired, so fair.
  The harshest bonds my mind and soul confine,
  I will not live if she can not be mine.   7445
CHIRON.   Dear stranger, as a man you are enthused,
  To spirits, though, your mind appears confused.
  Yet here you are in luck, for it so chances
  That yearly I exchange brief words and glances
  With Manto,[9] who in silent imprecation   7450
  Entreats her father—she's Asclepios' daughter—

---

5. See notes to lines 6530 and 7369. Chiron's participation in the rescue is Goethe's invention.
6. A town in Attica ten miles east of Athens, site of the Eleusinian mysteries.
7. Goethe's original manuscript read "Mythologists" (*Mythologen*).
8. After her death, Helena reportedly married Achilles, who was released from death to live with her
   on the island of Leuce. Goethe substituted Pherae, a town in Thessaly near the home of Achilles.
9. The daughter of Tiresias; to substantiate her medical skills, Goethe introduces her as the daughter
   of Asclepios, Greek god of medicine and healing.

That for his own endangered reputation
He shed in doctors' minds illumination
And wean them from the wont of brazen slaughter . . .
Of Sybils[1] she's to me the most attractive,   7455
Not all contortions, charitably active;
She shortly may contrive, I dare assure you,
With power of roots most thoroughly to cure you.
FAUST.   I ask not to be cured, my mind is sound,
Else it would drag, like others', on the ground.   7460
CHIRON.   Spurn not the bounty of the noble fount!
Here, we have reached it. Quick, dismount!
FAUST.   Say, whither have you, of a fearsome night,
Through gravelled waters borne me to alight?
CHIRON.   Here Rome and Greece were locked in stubborn fight,[2]   7465
Olympus left, Peneios on their right,
The greatest empire sinking in the sand;
The king in flight, the burgher in command.
Look up! Majestic, close before you loom
The eternal temple[3] walls in moonlit gloom.   7470
MANTO.   [*within, dreaming*]
                     With hooves' pounding
                     The sacred stair resounding,
                     Demigods are nigh.
CHIRON.   Quite so!
                     Just open an eye!   7475
MANTO.   [*wakening*] Welcome! I see you're not remiss.
CHIRON.   As steadfast as your temple edifice!
MANTO.   Still roving ever, unabating?
CHIRON.   You ever dwell in sheltered stillness pure,
While I delight in circulating.   7480
MANTO.   Time circles me, while I endure.
And this one?
CHIRON.   Ill-famed night of late
Has whirled him hither in its spate.
For Helen do his addled senses yearn,
It's Helen he would woo and earn,   7485
And knows not how, or where to turn;
Needs more than most the Aesculapian leech.
MANTO.   I hold him dear who craves beyond his reach.
          [CHIRON *is far off by now.*]
MANTO.   Rejoice, bold youth, come follow me;
This gloomy shaft leads to Persephone.[4]   7490

---

1. Soothsayers prominent in Roman historical legend and literature.
2. Allusion to the battle of Pydna (168 B.C.), in which the Romans under Aemilius Paullus defeated Perseus, king of Macedonia.
3. The temple of Apollo, presided over by Manto.
4. Persephone, queen of Hades. (See the "Second Sketch for the Announcement of the Helena," below.)

Within Olympus' hollow root
She hears in stealth prohibited salute.
Here in his time I smuggled Orpheus through,[5]
Make better use of it; take courage, in with you!
    [*They descend.*]

<hr>

5. See note to line 7375. Faust follows the example of Orpheus, who pleaded before Persephone to
  bring the dead Eurydice back to life.

On the Upper Peneios, as Before[1]†

SIRENS.	Plunge into Peneios' flood!	7495
	There we should be splashing, ranging,	
	Tuneful part-song interchanging,	
	For the wretched people's good.	
	Far from water nothing thrives!	
	If we hastened all our host	7500
	Down to the Aegean coast,	
	Every bliss would grace our lives.[2]	

[*Earthquake.*]

Backward rush the waves with foaming,
Down their bed no longer roaming;
Earth is shaken, water staunched,   7505
Smoking banks are upward launched.
We must flee! Come, every one!
Such a portent profits none.

Noble merry guests are fleeing
To the feast of the Aegean,   7510
Where the glinting ripples' welling
Wets the beach with gentle swelling;
There, where Luna doubly glistens,[3]
Dews us with her sacred essence.
There, a careless animation,   7515
Here, dread jolts of earth's foundation;
Hurry, all who know their good!
Haunted is this neighborhood.

SEISMOS.[4] [*in the depths, grumbling and rumbling*]
One more shove, but stronger, bolder,
One more heave with mighty shoulder!   7520
Thus we rise through earth and boulder
Up where all must give us way.

SPHINXES.   What a mind-revolting tremor,
Noisomely uncanny clamor!
What a swerving, lurching, jolting,   7525

---

1. After Faust departs with Manto, the scene shifts back to the place where Mephistopheles earlier met the mythological beasts.
2. The Sirens here look ahead to the festival at the Aegean Sea and its celebration of the creative power of water.
3. The double glistening of Luna is presumably caused by the reflection on the surface of the sea.
4. The name is Greek for "earthquake" and was used as an attribute of Poseidon, god of the sea (cf. Herodotus, *History* 7.29). According to legend, Poseidon caused the island Delos to rise up in the midst of the Aegean to provide a suitable birthplace for Apollo and Artemis. Goethe owned a copy of Raphael's painting of the liberation of Paul from prison, which showed such a giant breaking free from below the earth.

Dizzy back and forward bolting!
What unbearable dismay!
Yet we shall not change our roost,
Not if all of hell were loosed.

Now the ground is vaulting, surges,   7530
Wondrous! He of yore emerges,
Hoary ancient, grizzle-pated,
Delos' Island he created,
At a laboring mother's plea
Drove it up from out the sea.[5]   7535
He, with striving, thrusting, prying,
Tautened arms and back applying,
Atlas-like[6] in straining toil,
Lifts the ground with sward and soil,
Gravel, pebble, sand, the bed   7540
Of our tranquil riverstead.
So he tears a gash with gloating
Through the valley's quiet coating.
With untiring labor tense,
Caryatid[7] of bulk immense;   7545
Heaves a fearful rocky prison,
From the ground but halfway risen;
But no more must be permitted,
Note it, here are Sphinxes seated.

SEISMOS.   This is of my unaided making,   7550
As should be granted everywhere;
Had I not buffeted and shaken,
How would the world have been so fair?
How could your lofty peaks be drifting
Proud in the pure ethereal blue,   7555
Had I not done the strenuous lifting
For picturesquely ravished view?
When in the sight of highest ancestry,
Of Chaos, Night,[8] I proved myself robust,
And with the Titans for my company   7560
Ossa and Pelion[9] for playballs tossed.
We frolicked on there, youth in seething sap,

5. See note preceding line 7519. The mother of Apollo and Artemis, Leto, was being pursued by
   Hera, angry at the infidelity of her husband, Zeus, in begetting the twins, and Poseidon created
   Delos to provide a refuge for her.
6. An allusion to the Titan who was thought to support the vault of heaven upon his shoulders.
7. In classical Greek architecture, the name for a supporting column carved in the form of a woman,
   derived from the maidens of Caryae (Karyai) in Laconia, who wore a ring upon their heads for
   carrying baskets.
8. Seismos claims that his parents are Chaos and Night, in Hesiod's Theogony the primal powers
   who created the Earth.
9. Mountains in northeastern Greece. The Titans were said to have tried to scale heaven by piling
   Ossa on Mt. Olympus and Pelion on Ossa.

Till, wearying, right at the last,
On Mt. Parnassus wantonly we cast
Both of the others like a double cap . . .[1]   7565
Now merry concourse rallies yonder
Apollo and his Muses fair,
For Jove himself, with all his thunder,
I raised aloft his easy-chair.[2]
Now likewise, with stupendous heaving,   7570
I from the deeps thrust up and out
And loudly challenge to new living
Gay dwellers for me hereabout.

SPHINXES.   Ancient is, one would surmise,
What here castled up is found,   7575
Had it not before our eyes
Wrung itself from out the ground.
There bush-lined woods are spreading up the side,
While rock on rock surge up with thrust and slide;[3]
A sphinx this cannot incommode   7580
Or trouble in her sanctified abode.

GRIFFINS.   Gold in slices, gold in slivers
In the cracks and crannies quivers.
Such a hoard, let no one snatch it;
Up, you emmets, pick and catch it!   7585

CHORUS OF ANTS.
        As giant thew
        Labored to lift it,
        Scrabble-feet you,
        Scurry to sift it!
        In and out, nimbly!   7590
        In every cleaving
        There is a crumblet
        Worth the retrieving.
        However little,
        Be nothing left,   7595
        Take pains and scuttle
        To every cleft.
        Scan every fold,
        You teeming flock,
        Hurry in the gold,   7600
        Let go the rock.

GRIFFINS.   Come up! Come up! bring gold in heaps,
We lay our claws on it for keeps;
They serve for bolts of surest kind,
The greatest hoard is well enshrined.   7605

---

1. Mt. Parnassus has twin peaks that are not otherwise associated with Pelion and Ossa.
2. Seismos here claims to have built the halls of the Olympians, the "easy-chair" of Jove (Zeus) and the place where Apollo and the Muses sing.
3. The newly formed mountain immediately becomes overgrown with plants and trees, a swift recapitulation of geological history.

PYGMIES.[4]

Truly, we have found our spot here,
Little knowing how or where.
Do not ask us how we got here,
For the fact is, we are there!
To support high spirits, fitting   7610
We consider any land;
Anywhere a rock is splitting,
Promptly there's a dwarf on hand.
Dwarf and dwarvess, quick and steady,
Exemplary couples all,   7615
Hard to say if things already
Worked like this before the Fall.
But we find this of the best,
Thank our star for pleasant setting;
For in East as well as West   7620
Mother Earth enjoys begetting.

DACTYLS.[5]

If overnights
She bore little wights,
She'll bear least ones to boot,
Who'll find partners to suit.   7625

PYGMY ELDEST.   Hurry, make haste
To be properly placed!
To work, and bustle;
Speed is our muscle!
While peace is yet,   7630
Your forge be set,
Weapon and shield
The host to yield.
You emmets all,
Surge you and sprawl,   7635
Ore for us haul!
And Dactyls canny,
Tiny but many,
Yours to secure
Timber, be sure   7640
To nurse sly flame
In well-stacked frame
Coal to procure.

GENERALISSIMO.[6]   With arrow and bow
A-hunting, ho!   7645

---

4. According to Greek legend (Homer, *Iliad* 3.6 ff.), the Pygmies who dwelt on the shore of Oceanus fought an annual war with migrating cranes. These figures have been made by Goethe to resemble the gnomes (or "dwarfs") of the carnival in Act I (lines 5840 ff.).
5. These little creatures, named for the Greek *dactylos* ("fingers"), are used by the Pygmies as slave labor to mine and forge the gold (along with the Ants, or Emmets, below, lines 7634 ff.).
6. This pompous military leader of the Pygmies apparently wants to kill the egrets (or herons) in order to use their feathers for decorating his helmet.

That tarn is teaming
With egrets gleaming,
Countlessly nesting ones,
Haughtily breasting ones,
Shoot all together!   7650
Shoot the whole host;
That we may boast
Helmet and feather.

EMMETS AND DACTYLS.
Who saves our lives!
We bring the ore,   7655
They forge but gyves.
To rise defiant
Is premature,
We must be pliant.

THE CRANES OF IBYCUS.[7]
Cries of murder, deathly anguish!   7660
Flailing pinions falter, languish!
What a wailing, what a moan
Sends aloft its plaintive tone!
Ah, already all are dead,
With their blood the lake is red;   7665
Avarice misshapen, gory,
Rapes the egret's noble glory.
On the helmets, there! it waves
Of those bowleg fat-paunch knaves.
Flight companions of the seaways,   7670
Comrades of our serried relays,
You to vengeance here we call
In a cause akin to all;
No one spare his strength or blood,
Feud eternal to this brood![8]   7675
[*They disperse in the air with hoarse cries.*]

MEPHISTOPHELES.   [*on the plain*][9]
With northern witches my control was sounder,
But with these foreign sprites I seem to flounder.
The Blocksberg[1] makes so snug a rendezvous,
Wherever one may be, there's others too.
Frau *Ilse* on her *Stone* maintains her stand,   7680
Upon his *Peak* Herr *Heinrich* is on hand,

---

7. On the Cranes of Ibycus, derived from a ballad by Schiller, see the interpretive notes.
8. The call to arms of the Cranes may be modeled on the opening chorus in Aristophanes' *Birds*, where the bird chorus prepares to attack the intruders from Athens.
9. We are here to assume a cinematic shift of scene from the surface of the newly formed mountain down to the plain, where we pick up Mephistopheles in his pursuit of the Lamiae (which began at the end of the scene on the Upper Peneios, line 7248).
1. An allusion to the setting of the "Walpurgis Night."

The *Snorers* snarl at *Misery*,[2] no doubt,
But all of this will last millennia out.
But here, you take a step, and there's no telling
When earth blows up at you like bladders swelling! . . .   7685
I roam a level valley, all serene,
Abruptly rearing at my back is seen
A mountain—small indeed to earn the name,
To part me from my sphinxes, all the same,
Quite high enough—here many a flame is bounding   7690
All down the vale, the prodigy surrounding . . .
That wanton company of roguish flirts[3]
Still skips and skims before me, tempts and skirts.
Step softly now! Too much inured to snatching,
One takes in dubious dainties for the catching.   7695

LAMIAE.[4]   [*drawing* MEPHISTOPHELES *after them*]

Faster and faster!
And on and on!
Then lag and chatter
With rapid patter.
It is such fun   7700
So to be easing
The old whoremaster
To heavy penance.
With rigid tendons
He dogs us, humping   7705
Along and stumping,
Dragging his leg;
Wherever we tease him,
Clatters his peg![5]

MEPHISTOPHELES.   [*stopping*]

Accursed are menfolk! Dupes and rubes   7710
Since Adam's fall, befuddled boobs!
Who ends up wise, though old and hoar?
Were you not fool enough before?

One knows they're rotten to the core, their faces
All paint and rouge, the rest held up by laces.   7715
There's nothing sound there, nothing answers, lives,
Wherever you may touch them, something gives.

---

2. Mephistopheles is here punning on the names of some of the places in the Harz Mountains in the vicinity of the Brocken, where the "Walpurgis Night" of Part One took place (see note preceding line 3835). They were there left in their German forms: *Ilsenstein* ("Stone of Frau Ilse"), *Heinrichshöhe* ("Peak of Herr Heinrich"), *Schnarcher* ("Snorers"), and *Elend* ("Misery")—see line 3880.
3. Mephistopheles refers to the Lamiae, whom he is pursuing.
4. See note to line 7235. In contrast to the primal complacency of the Sphinxes, the Lamiae are constantly moving, constantly changing, constantly deceiving. In their coarse sexual temptation of Mephistopheles, the Lamiae are also analogous to the witches of the "Walpurgis Night" in Part One.
5. An allusion to the devil's cloven hoof.

You see it, touch it, know it in advance,
And yet, just let the baggage pipe, you dance!

LAMIAE.   [*pausing*] He's wondering, hesitating; stay!   7720
  Turn back again, don't let him get away.

MEPHISTOPHELES.   [*striding ahead*]
  Don't be a fool! avoid the stitches
  That mark the web of doubt and cavil;
  If there were not any witches,
  Who the deuce would play the devil!   7725

LAMIAE.   [*most captivatingly*] Ring this hero round and urge him,
  Surely, in his heart emerging,
  Love for one of us will burgeon.

MEPHISTOPHELES.   Twilight, I confess it freely,
  Shows you quite attractive really,   7730
  I give credit where it's due.

EMPUSA.[6]   [*intruding*] Due to me, no less than you!
  Take me in your circle too.

LAMIAE.   She's out of place, the pushy one,
  She always comes and spoils our fun.   7735

EMPUSA.   [*to* MEPHISTOPHELES] Your little cousin greet, I beg,
  Empusa with the donkey-leg;
  Yours is a horse-foot, I regret,
  Sir Cousin—still, a warm well-met!

MEPHISTOPHELES.   Here was I, braced for new sensations,   7740
  And all I find is near relations;
  The world, there's well-thumbed tomes to tell us,
  Is thick with kin, from Harz to Hellas!

EMPUSA.   My habit is direct and bold;
  The shapes I choose are manifold,   7745
  But in your honor, I was led
  To don this little ass's head.

MEPHISTOPHELES.   I notice that these people's sense
  Of family is most intense;
  But come what may, and all the same,   7750
  The ass I'd just as soon disclaim.

LAMIAE.   Let go this nasty fright, she'll scare
  What has a fair and lovely air;
  What fair and lovely was before,
  When she comes up, is so no more!   7755

MEPHISTOPHELES.   These dainty slinky cousins here
  Will all bear watching too, I fear;
  The roses on their cheeks may please,
  But warn of metamorphoses.

LAMIAE.   There's lots of us, just show some pluck!   7760
  Fall to! and if you are in luck,
  The winning ticket you may snatch.

---

6. This horrifying ghost was able to change its shape at will. Usually appearing to travelers, it could
  be chased away with shouts and curses. Goethe chose to have it appear with the head of an ass
  in satirical association with Mephistopheles' hoof. The "donkey-leg" (line 7737) was traditional.

Why all this drooling gibberish?
Is this your wooing, you poor fish?
You strut about like some prize catch!—   7765
Now he's amongst us as we ask;
Give way now, each let down her mask
And lay her inner nature bare.

MEPHISTOPHELES.   I choose the fairest of the fair . . .
  [embracing her] A scrawny broomstick! Oh despair!   7770
  [seizing another] And this one? . . . What a hideous fright!

LAMIAE.   You think it doesn't serve you right?

MEPHISTOPHELES.   This charmer I should like to nip . . .
  A lizard slithering from my grip!
  Her braid feels like a snake, all slick,   7775
  I'll grab that lanky one instead . . .
  Now I embrace a thyrsus stick!⁷
  And with a pine-cone for a head.
  Where will it end? . . . That chubby one
  May yet provide a bit of fun;   7780
  Here goes—the last one that I woo!
  All lush and mushy, as is sold
  To pashas for its weight in gold . . .
  Oh, phew! the puffball bursts in two!

LAMIAE.   Now dart asunder, veer and hover,   7785
  Now lightning lunges blackly cover
  The interloping witch's spawn!
  From eery random circles drawn
  Swoop down on noiseless wings of bat!
  He's getting off too easily at that.   7790

MEPHISTOPHELES.   [shaking himself]
  Not much new wisdom do I carry forth;
  Absurdness here, absurdity up north,
  Ghosts, here as yonder, problematic,
  Poets and public, both pathetic.
  It was all mummery, no more,   7795
  Phantasmagoria, as before.
  At luring masquers I would run,
  And what I touched left me aghast . . .
  I find to be deceived quite fun—
  If only it were made to last.   7800
  [losing his way among the rocks]⁸
  Where am I now? Where should I stumble?
  This was a path, now it's a jumble.
  The way was level, free of trouble,
  Now I am up against all rubble.

---

7. A staff, tipped with a pinecone and twined with ivy, carried by the Maenads, followers of the god Dionysus, at feasts and celebrations in his honor.
8. Mephistopheles has apparently wandered to the limits of the plain and now begins to climb about the rocks and cliffs of the Pindus Mountains (see line 7814), a range running north to south in the west of Thessaly, in northwest Greece.

I clamber up and down in vain,   7805
Where will I find my Sphinx again?
I never dreamt so wild a sight,
Such mountains in a single night!
A pretty lusty witches' trot!
They bring their Blocksberg to the spot.   7810
OREAS.[9]   [*from the living rock*] Up here to me! Old is my height,
     Kept its primeval shape and site.
     Revere the dizzying rocky brinks,
     The Pindus chain's most forward links.
     Just as unshaken stood my head   7815
     When over me Great Pompey fled.[1]
     Whereas the shapes of fancy born
     Fade on the cock's crow at the dawn.[2]
     I watch such figments rise up now and then
     And of a sudden sink again.   7820
MEPHISTOPHELES.   Be honored, venerable head!
     By noble oak engarlanded;
     Not Luna's very clearest light
     Can penetrate your somber night.—
     But by those bushes makes its way   7825
     A light that sheds a modest ray.
     How paths do cross in this affair!
     Homunculus! I do declare.
     Where do you come from, Sparkleface?
HOMUNCULUS.   I float like this from place to place,   7830
     Keen on the finest manner of becoming;
     I cannot wait to smash my glass and flare;
     But judging by the morning's slumming,
     To venture into this I hardly dare.
     In confidence, I'm tracking down a pair   7835
     Of sages[3] whom I want to question next;
     I listened: Nature! Nature! went the text.
     These I should like to fasten on as teachers;
     They're bound to know the way of earthly creatures;
     I think I see a chance at last to learn   7840
     Which is the wisest way for me to turn.
MEPHISTOPHELES.   You'd better try by your own lights.
     For anywhere that spook holds sway
     Philosopher has right of way.
     And to ingratiate his art he makes   7845
     A dozen new ones in two shakes.

---

9. This is the term for a mountain nymph, identified with the spirit of this "living rock" (i.e., a primal rock such as granite).
1. See note to line 6955. After his defeat at Pharsalus, according to Plutarch, Pompey fled past Larissa and Tempe (towns in Thessaly) to the sea.
2. An allusion to the mountain Seismos, which has suddenly appeared in the midst of the "Classical Walpurgis Night" and will apparently disappear again with the following dawn.
3. A reference to the philosophers Anaxagoras and Thales, who appear at line 7851. (See interpretive notes.)

By going wrong alone you come to rights!
If you would be, become by your own lights.
HOMUNCULUS.   Good counsel, though, is not a gift to flout.
MEPHISTOPHELES.   Away then! We shall see how it turns out.   7850
    [*They separate.*]
ANAXAGORAS.   [*to* THALES]
    Your stubborn mind will not be moved?
    You want still more than this to stand disproved?
THALES.   The wave will bend to any wind and tide,
    But from the jagged cliff it holds aside.
ANAXAGORAS.   That cliff exists by dint of swathes of flame.   7855
THALES.   It is in moisture, though, that life became.
HOMUNCULUS.   [*between the two*]
                        Admit me to your company,
                        I too aspire to come to be!
ANAXAGORAS.   Have you, oh Thales, in but one night's flood
    Raised such a mountain from a mass of mud?   7860
THALES.   Never was Nature and her fluid power
    Indentured yet to day and night and hour.
    She shapes each form to her controlling course
    And be the scale immense, eschews all force.
ANAXAGORAS.   But not so here! Here fierce Plutonian plasmas,   7865
    Explosive rage of vast Aeolic miasmas,[4]
    Broke through the level bottom's ancient crust,
    That a new mountain could arise, and must.
THALES.   What is the sequel, now that this is past?
    It is in place, and that is good at last.   7870
    This sort of quarrel fritters time away
    And only leads the credulous astray.
ANAXAGORAS.   With Myrmidons the mountain teems,
    Who occupy all chinks and seams,
    With pygmies, emmets, gnomes, Tom Thumbs,   7875
    And their minute but active chums.[5]
    [*to* HOMUNCULUS]. You never have set high your sight,
    Lived sparsely like an anchorite;
    If you can take to governing,
    I plan to have you crowned as king.   7880
HOMUNCULUS.   What says my Thales?
THALES.   He objects;
    With little men go little acts,
    Among the great a small one grows.
    See there![6] the cranes' black thundercloud,

---

4. The winds and fires of volcanic explosion are described in mythological allusions to Pluto, god
    of the underworld, and Aeolus, god of the winds.
5. Anaxagoras reintroduces a perspective on the figures moving about the mountain of Seismos, both
    the Ants (Emmets) digging the gold and the Pygmies and Dactyls at war with the Cranes, all
    observed apparently from a separate vantage point. "Myrmidons" (line 7873) were the warriors
    who fought under Achilles at Troy, originally created by Zeus out of ants (*myrmēkes*) to repeople
    plague-stricken Aegina, the island kingdom of Achilles' pious grandsire, Aeacus.
6. Thales describes the action of the battle between the Pygmies and the Cranes.

It threatens the excited crowd,   7885
And you with them, if you were king.
With raking claws and beaks like talons
They dive upon the pygmy columns,
Pale doom like lightning flickering.
An outrage felled the egret ranks,   7890
Encircling their pacific banks.
Those very missiles' murderous rain
Draws cruel blood-revenge in train,
Brings nearest kin in fury red
For tainted pygmy-blood to shed.   7895
Shield, helmet, spear, what use are these?
What good to dwarves the egret feather?[7]
How dactyls, emmets cringe together!
Now breaks the host, now melts, now flees.

ANAXAGORAS. [*after a pause, solemnly*]
While hitherto I praised those underground,   7900
In this case my appeal is upward bound . . .
To Thee on high, unagingly the same,
Of threefold form and threefold name,
Out of my people's woe I cry to thee,
Diana, Luna, Hecate![8]   7905
Thou inmost-sensing, soul-enlarging,
Thou placid seeming, fiercely charging,
Unclose Thy shadows' fearful maw to sight,
Without a spell reveal the ancient might.
        [*Pause.*]
                Has prayer brought curse?   7910
                Has my cry uncurbed
                Those heights, disturbed
                The order of the universe?
Already ever greater, closer, nears
Her seat of majesty, inscribed in spheres,   7915
Appalling, monstrous to the sight!
A dusky red its darkling light . . .
No! Orb of threatening might, halt your pursuing!
Or we and land and sea are swept to ruin.

So those Thessalian women—could it be?—   7920
Trusting their lawless tuneful sorcery,
Did sing you down, and from you wrested
What is with direst peril vested? . . .
The glowing shield is swathed in dark—
Now rent with lighting flash and spark!   7925
What rushing hiss! what rattling spatter!

---

7. A reference to the helmet feathers extracted from the egrets slaughtered by the Pygmies (see note
   preceding line 7644).
8. Anaxagoras invokes the moon as a triple-name goddess.

Now thunders, monstrous stormwinds scatter!—
Fall at the throne in humble suing!
Forgiveness! For it was my doing.
    [*He prostrates himself on the ground.*]
THALES.   The things this man contrived to see and hear!   7930
As to what happened I am less than clear;
In what he witnessed I shared even less.
These hours are out of joint, we must confess,
And Luna rocks her slanted face
Quite cozily in her old place.   7935
HOMUNCULUS.   The mound, look, where the pygmies sat,
It's pointed now where it was flat.
I felt a shock of force appalling,
Out of the moon a rock had fallen,
And instantly, without ado,   7940
Both friend and foe it crushed and slew.
Yet praise is due to arts, you know,
By which in one night, one creative throw,
Both from above and from below,
This mountain edifice was wrought.   7945
THALES.   Rest easy! It was all in thought.
Let them go hang, the nasty brood!
That you were not their king is good.
Now to the happy sea-feast we repair,
For wondrous guests they hope to honor there.   7950
    [*They depart.*]
MEPHISTOPHELES.†   [*climbing on the opposite side*]
Here I must toil up stairs of slanting rocks,
Across unyielding roots of ancient oaks!
Upon my homely Harz, the whiff of resin
Is redolent of pitch, which I find pleasant;
Second to sulphur . . . Here, among these Greeks,   7955
You hardly sense a trace of suchlike reeks;
I feel an itch to nose out, all the same,
With what they stoke hell's agony and flame.
DRYAD.⁹   In your own land apply your native wit,
Abroad, you haven't the resource for it.   7960
Toward the homeland you should leave off peering,
The grandeur of these sacred oaks revering.
MEPHISTOPHELES.   One thinks of that which one forsook;
The wonted stands for Eden in one's book.
But tell me, what in yonder lair   7965
By murky light is triply huddling?
DRYAD.   The Phorcyads!¹ To their cavern dare,
Address them, if you can for shudd'ring.

---

9. A tree nymph.
1. Three of Phorcyas's daughters, also called the Graiae, were gray-haired, ancient witches who
    shared one eye and one tooth. They were said to live in a place where neither the sun nor the
    moon shone.

MEPHISTOPHELES.   Why not? I gape at what I see within it.
 Proud as I am, I must admit   7970
 I never saw the like of it,
 The hideous mandrake is not in it! . . .[2]
 Can the transgressions loathed of yore
 At all seem ugly any more
 Upon this triple ogre's sight?   7975
 I think these monsters would offend us
 Where Hell yawns at its most horrendous.
 And here they roost in beauty's land of fable
 That bears the honorable classic label . . .
 They stir, have sensed me now, I'd say,   7980
 With whistling twitter, vampire bats at bay.
PHORCYAD.   Sisters, pass me the eye, that it make query
 Who dares approach our sanctuary so nearly.
MEPHISTOPHELES.   Oh most revered! May I solicit leave
 To venture near and threefold grace receive?   7985
 Unknown indeed, without recommendation
 I come, yet by all signs a far relation.
 I have laid eyes on gods of ancient awe,
 To Ops and Rhea[3] deeply bowed of yore.
 The Parcae,[4] yours and Chaos' sisters hoar,   7990
 I saw them yesterday—or day before;
 But none to match you did I ever see,
 And I fall silent now in ecstasy.
PHORCYADS.   He seems a spirit of judicious mind.
MEPHISTOPHELES.   How comes it that no poet lauds your kind? 7995
 Say! What accounts for this, how could it be
 You worthiest I never saw in effigy?
 Let chisel strain your splendor to describe,
 Not Juno, Pallas, Venus[5] and their tribe.
PHORCYADS.   In stillest night and solitude confined,   8000
 The thought of it has never crossed our mind!
MEPHISTOPHELES.   How could it, seeing that the world you shun,
 See no one here and are beheld by none.
 For that, you would have to inhabit places
 Where pomp divides a throne with art's high graces, 8005
 Where nimbly every day at double speed
 A hero from a marble slab is freed.
 Where . . .
PHORCYADS.   Give us peace from the temptation of it!
 If we knew better even, would we profit?
 Sprung forth from Night, to the nocturnal prone,   8010

---

2. See note to line 4980.
3. Ops, the Roman goddess of sowing and harvest, and Rhea, the wife of Saturn, were often identified with one another.
4. The three Fates (see note preceding line 5305).
5. Juno (Hera), Minerva (Pallas Athena), and Venus (Aphrodite) here represent the Olympian goddesses.

Wholly to all, half to ourselves unknown.
MEPHISTOPHELES.   In such a case this is no special bother,
  One may transmit one's self unto another.
  Your threesome finds one eye, one tooth enough,
  Then for mythology it could not be too tough   8015
  To lodge in two the essence of the three
  And leave the likeness of the third to me,
  For a brief time.
ONE.   How does it seem to you?
THE OTHERS.   Excepting eye and tooth—yes, it would do!
MEPHISTOPHELES.   With that you have excluded just the best;   8020
  How could the form's full rigor be expressed?
ONE.   Just close one eye, 'twill do it even so,
  Let forthwith but a single eye-tooth show,
  In profile then you will attain the semblance
  Of a perfected sisterly resemblance.   8025
MEPHISTOPHELES.   Too kind! So be it!
PHORCYADS.   Be it!
MEPHISTOPHELES.   [as PHORCYAS, in profile] There, it's done,
  I stand as Chaos's beloved son!
PHORCYADS.   We stem from Chaos by undoubted right.
MEPHISTOPHELES.   Oh pain! they'll call me an hermaphrodite.
PHORCYADS.   In our new triad, what adornment new!   8030
  Of eyes as well as teeth, we now have two.[6]
MEPHISTOPHELES.   But I must hide from everybody's sight,
  To give the devils of the Pit a fright.
     [Exit.]

---

6. Mephistopheles, in assuming the guise of Phorcyas, has lent the Phorcyads one of his eyes and
  one tooth.

Rocky Inlets of the Aegean Sea†
The Moon at Rest at the Zenith[1]

SIRENS.   [*reclining here and there on the cliffs, piping and singing*][2]
    While Thessalian witching women
    Once in spectral lunar dimming   8035
    Impiously drew you down,
    Now gaze calmly from your sweeping
    Vault of night on tremulous leaping,
    Quivering wavelets mildly gleaming,
    And illuminate the teeming   8040
    Forms now rising from the waves.
    Eager for your service know us,
    Grace, oh fairest Luna, show us!

NEREIDS AND TRITONS.   [*in the shape of sea prodigies*][3]
    Make a louder, sharper sounding,
    Through the ocean sea resounding,   8045
    Dwellers of the deep call here!
    At the tempest's fearsome riot
    We withdrew to depths of quiet,
    Tuneful singing draws us near.

    See, we take most joyous pleasure   8050
    Donning chains of golden treasure,
    Into precious crown-gems shining
    Clasps and jeweled girdles joining,
    All of it your hoard and prey.
    Barks that bore them, men and master,   8055
    You have sung them to disaster,
    You, the demons of our bay.

SIRENS.   Well we know, in cool of ocean
    Fish rejoice in gliding motion,
    Veering void of grief or wish;   8060
    But—you swarms in festive moving,
    Now we hope to find you proving
    That you can be more than fish.

NEREIDS AND TRITONS.
    Ere we came, and unreminded,

---

1. The entire festival takes place at a moment of suspended time, the climax of the mythical process that unfolds throughout the "Classical Walpurgis Night."
2. The Sirens play a central role throughout this scene, providing the musical continuity of the celebration.
3. Presumably, mermaids and mermen with fish tails who emerge from the depths in response to the song of the Sirens. The Nereids are daughters of Nereus, one of the two old men of the sea who appear shortly. The Tritons are offspring of Poseidon, god of the sea; they carry conch shells, which they blow like trumpets at Poseidon's command to soothe the restless waves.

We ourselves had long designed it,   8065
Sisters, brothers, be not late!
On a voyage, not the longest,
Gathering witness of the strongest
That we top the fish's estate.

[*They depart.*]

SIRENS.   Off, and vanished straight!†   8070
Toward Samothrace⁴
With favoring wind they race.
What sends them speeding, so keen,
To the lofty Cabiri's⁵ demesne?
Gods they, deep wonderment waking,   8075
Themselves ever newly remaking,
And never knowing their own state,

On your heights, we pray,
Gracious Luna, stay;
Let moon-dusk be dense,   8080
Lest day drive us hence.

THALES. [*on the shore, to* HOMUNCULUS]
I'd gladly lead you to old Nereus⁶ too;
His cavern is not far from here, it's true,
His head, though, is as hard as rock,
Cantankerous old vinegar-crock.   8085
Not the entire human race
Can ever please him, sour-face.
He sees the future, though—a lore
Which everyone respects him for,
And pays him honor for its sake;   8090
He's granted many a kindness, too.
HOMUNCULUS.   Knock at the door, let's try him, do!
There'll scarce be glass and flame at stake.
NEREUS.   Are these men's voices that my ears impart!
What instant wrath they stir deep in my heart!   8095
Those artifacts, to godly likeness prone,
Yet sentenced to be ever but their own.
Gray years I could have savored godlike rest,
But was impelled to benefit their best;

---

4. An island in the northeast Aegean Sea famous for its ancient mystery rites and the cult of the so-called great gods.
5. The generic name for the deities celebrated in the mysteries of Samothrace, *Kabeiroi*, non-Greek, possibly Phoenician, in origin. Goethe was attracted to these obscure deities by contemporary speculation concerning their significance, particularly by Friedrich Creuzer, *Symbolism and Mythology of the Ancient Peoples* (1810–12, Vol. 2, pp. 302 ff.), and by the philosopher Schelling's monograph *On the Gods of Samothrace* (1815). Both Creuzer and Schelling were convinced that the Cabiri represent the earliest, most primitive deities of Greek mythology, from which all subsequent Hellenic religion and culture developed.
6. This ancient and prophetic sea god is provided with uniquely Goethean features as an aged father and sage, "cantankerous" and pessimistic about humankind, who subsequently enjoys and comprehends the moment of epiphany with a fullness unsurpassed by any of the other participants (see lines 8134–5, 8150, and 8424).

And when at last account of deeds was rendered,   8100
My counsel might as well have not been tendered.
THALES.   Yet you, Sea Elder, hold their confidence;
You are the wise one, do not drive us hence!
This flame here, quasi-human though it be,
Puts all its trust in your advice, you see.   8105
NEREUS.   Advice! Do men respect it? It is fated
That sapient word congeal in hardened ears.
How grimly have not deeds themselves berated,
And still the tribe in self-will perseveres.
How I gave Paris fatherly advice   8110
Lest his quick lust an alien wife entice![7]
There stood he boldly on the Grecian shore,
And I foretold him what I saw in store:
Smoke-stifled air, infused with crimson glow,
Roof-trees ablaze, assault and death below: 8115
Troy's day of doom, in epic rhythms cast,
As dread as well-known to millennia past.
That pup, he counted sport what old men tell,
He took his lust for guide, and Ilion fell—
Titanic corpse, stiff after long ordeal,   8120
To Pindus' eagles a most welcome meal.[8]
Ulysses,[9] too! Why, did I not foretell
The cyclops' savagery, and Circe's spell?
His own delays, his comrades' reckless whim,
Who knows what else! And did that profit him?   8125
Till late enough, and soundly tossed before,
By grace of waves he reached a friendly shore.
THALES.   True, such misconduct gives the wise man pain;
The good man, though, will try it once again.
A dram of thanks in pleasure will outweigh   8130
Some hundredweights of thanklessness, I say.
No less a thing than this one is our plea:
This boy would know how best to come to be.
NEREUS.   No, chase me not this rarest mood away!
Quite other things await me yet today.[1]   8135
For I have summoned hither all my daughters,
The comely Dorids, Graces of the waters.
Not your earth's soil and not Olympus bears
A lovely being of such graceful airs.
They fling themselves, most captivating motion,   8140
From sea-dragons to Neptune's steeds of ocean,

---

7. Paris supposedly sought the advice of Nereus before he abducted Helena.
8. The fallen city is personified as a corpse being fed upon by the eagles of the Pindus Mountains.
9. Ulysses' consulting Nereus about his wanderings after the fall of Troy appears to be Goethe's
   invention.
1. Nereus offers a detailed description of the festival procession that is to come, thus serving as herald
   or stage manager.

Most gently wedded to the brine their will,
So that the very spume would raise them still.

In opal flush of Venus' shell-coach gliding,
Now comes the fairest, Galatea,² riding,   8145
Who, since the Cyprian's face was turned elsewhere,
Won Paphos' awe and reigns as goddess there.
Thus ever after she has owned, the fairest,
Both temple-town and chariot-throne as heiress.

Be off! In father's hour of joy depart   8150
Harsh words from lips, and hatred from the heart.
Be off to Proteus now! Ask how one can
Take shape and vary, of that wonder-man.
    [*Departs toward the sea.*]
THALES.   There's nothing gained for us by this foray,
Proteus, if met, at once dissolves away;   8155
Even at bay at last, what he propounds
Is what discountenances and astounds.
Still, counsel is what you depend upon,
Let us attempt it then, and wander on!
    [*They depart.*]

SIRENS.   [*above, on the cliffs*]
    What from afar comes gliding   8160
    The realm of billows riding?
    As if by Aeol's choosing
    Some snowy sails were cruising,
    So bright they are with radiance,
    Transfigured ocean-maidens.   8165
    Down, let us seek the beaches,
    Already voices reach us.
NEREIDS AND TRITONS.
    What we bear you, will call
    For rejoicing by all.
    Chelone's³ huge shell here   8170
    Gleams forth with shape austere:
    They're deities we bring;
    High anthems you must sing.
SIRENS.   Little in height,
    Awsome in might,   8175
    Saviors at sea,⁴
    Revered from gray antiquity.

2. Galatea has inherited the place of the Cyprian Venus, or Aphrodite, goddess of love, and will ride in the shell that first carried the goddess when she was born from the foam of the sea.
3. A nymph transformed by Hermes into a sea tortoise. The creatures of the sea carry the Cabiri upon a gigantic tortoise shell.
4. The Cabiri were traditionally regarded as beneficial to sailors, rescuing them from shipwrecks.

NEREIDS AND TRITONS.

Cabiri here we bear
To hold a peaceful fair;
Where they hold sacred honors,   8180
Neptune will smile upon us.

SIRENS.   We yield you the prize,
Should vessel capsize,
Invincible, you
Will salvage the crew.   8185

NEREIDS AND TRITONS.

Three we took off beside us,
The fourth of them denied us,
He told us he had the call,
And thought for one and all.[5]

SIRENS.   One god may be brought   8190
By another to naught.
All powers revere ye,
All injury fear ye.

NEREIDS AND TRITONS.

Seven we know them to be.

SIRENS.   Where are the other three?   8195

NEREIDS AND TRITONS.

That's asking more than we know,
Enquire on Olympus, though;
That's where the eighth, too, must be sought
Whom no one yet has given thought!
Aware of us in grace,   8200
But none as yet in place.

Far horizons they beseech,
Peerless, distance-cherishers,
Ever-famished perishers
For the out-of-reach.   8205

SIRENS.   It is our way,
Wherever its sway,
In sun or moon, to pray,
It's bound to pay.

NEREIDS AND TRITONS.

How matchless our renown, behold,   8210
To usher in this pageant!

SIRENS.   The heroes of legend,
Of theirs we grow weary,
Wherever, however extolled,
They carried off the fleece of gold,   8215
You, the Cabiri.[6]

---

5. See note to line 8074. Goethe here follows Schelling's argument on the hierarchy of the Cabiri.
6. For their achievement in bringing the Cabiri, the Nereids and Tritons are praised as superior to the ancient heroes, even to the Argonauts, who carried off the golden fleece.

[*repeated in unison*]
   They carried off the fleece of gold,
   We! ⎱
   You! ⎰ the Cabiri.
[NEREIDS *and* TRITONS *pass by.*]

HOMUNCULUS.   These freakish shapes, I judge them pots
   Of clayware, frail and battered;   8220
   Now sages clash with them, and lots
   Of hardened heads are shattered.
THALES.   That's just what's in demand on earth,
   It's rust that gives the coin its worth.
PROTEUS.[7]   [*unnoticed*]
   This warms my fabler's heart, for the more striking,   8225
   The more I find things to my liking.
THALES.   Where are you, Proteus?
PROTEUS.   [*as if ventriloquizing, now near, now far*]
                    Here! and here!
THALES.   Come, I forgive the tired jest;
   But spare a friend vain prattle, I suggest!
   I know you're not where you appear.   8230
PROTEUS.   [*as if from afar*] Farewell!
THALES.   [*under his breath to* HOMUNCULUS]
                  He is quite near. Now flash your flare,
   He is as nosy as a bear;
   However shaped, wherever moored,
   By flames of fire he will be lured.
HOMUNCULUS.   A flood of light, then, watch me pass;   8235
   Yet modestly, or I might burst the glass.
PROTEUS.   [*in the shape of a giant turtle*]
   What shines so exquisitely fair?
THALES.   [*covering up* HOMUNCULUS]
   Good! Look at it more closely if you care.
   Just do not grudge the little trouble
   To show yourself on feet humanly double.   8240
   By our indulgence be it, with our will,
   If someone wants to view what we conceal.
PROTEUS.   [*nobly shaped*] You still excel in worldly cleverness.
THALES.   In changing shapes you take delight no less.
   [*having revealed* HOMUNCULUS]
PROTEUS.   [*astonished*] A shining little dwarf! Never did see!   8245
THALES.   He begs advice, would gladly come to be.
   He has, so I have heard him say,
   Been born but half in some prodigious way.
   Of intellectual traits he has no dearth,

---

7. The old man of the sea is famous for his power of self-transformation even in Homer, where
   Menelaus describes his confrontation with Proteus in the *Odyssey* 4. Proteus here represents the
   power of nature in constant change and variety.

But sorely lacks the solid clay of earth.   8250
So far the glass is all that keeps him weighted,
But he would gladly soon be corporated.
PROTEUS.   A genuine spinster's progeny,
You are before you ought to be!
THALES.   [*under his breath*]
In other ways, too, things are critical.   8255
I think he is—hermaphroditical.[8]
PROTEUS.   The more assuredly then it thrives,
He'll suit, whichever form arrives.
No need to ponder this a minute,
In the broad sea you must begin it!   8260
There first the tiny way you try,
The tiniest life contently chewing,
Thus you grow larger by and by
And shape yourself for higher doing.
HOMUNCULUS.   Here a most gentle ether breezes,   8265
It smells so fresh, and the aroma pleases!
PROTEUS.   That, my dear boy, I understand!
Out there the cozy aura gets much denser,
Upon that narrow tongue of strand
The nimb ineffably intenser;   8270
A little further we espy
That floating train from closer by.
Come there with me!
THALES.   I'm joining you.
HOMUNCULUS.   Thrice-odd spiritual retinue!

[TELCHINES *of* Rhodes[9] *on sea-horses and sea-dragons,*[1] *wielding*
Neptune's trident.]
CHORUS.   'Tis we who have fashioned Poseidon's great trident,   8275
The billows to soothe in their turmoil most strident.
When clouds are split wide by the Thund'rer's unfolding,
Poseidon replies to the terrible rolling;
What glare from on high may be jaggedly flashed,
There's wave upon wave from below for it splashed;   8280
And what in between may have quakingly wallowed,
Long tossed, by the nethermost depth it is swallowed;
Wherefore he has lent us the scepter today—
And carefree we float now, all festive and gay.
SIRENS.   You, to Helios consecrated,   8285
For this feast-day's blessing fated,

---

8. As pure spirit, Homunculus precedes all sexual division and contains an ambivalent potential to
become either male or female.
9. A primitive, diminutive people, representative of a chthonic (Earth) cult associated with the Cabiritic mysteries. Rhodes, the island on which they lived, was sacred to Apollo. (See interpretive
notes.)
1. The Telchines ride upon fantastic mythological creatures (called Hippocampi) with the bodies of
horses and the tails of dolphins.

      Greetings, at this hour which pays
      Luna highest awe and praise!
TELCHINES.   All-loveliest Queen of yon canopy vaulted!
  You hear with enchantment your brother exalted.   8290
  To Rhodes, blessed island, kind hearing you lend,
  Whence paeans[2] of praise to him ever ascend.
  At onset and closure on each of his days
  He sends us his fiery radiant gaze.
  The mountains, the cities, the shoreline, the bight,   8295
  The god finds them pleasing, so lovely and bright.
  No fog wafts about us, and should it creep in,
  A beam and a breeze, and the island is clean.
  His shape finds the god there in hundredfold guise,
  As youth, as colossus, yet gentle and wise.   8300
  We wrought this, we first ones, who nobly began
  To cast godly might in choice likeness of man.
PROTEUS.
      You let them swagger, let them praise!
      The sun-god's sacred living rays
      Make sport of works in rigid style.   8305
      There they will smelt and mold undaunted,
      And once it's cast in bronze, they vaunt it,
      Imagining it is worth while.
      How does it end, this proud renown?
      The godly images stood tall—   8310
      A jolt of earth destroyed them all;
      Long since they have been melted down.[3]
      Terrestrial life, whatever sort,
      Is and remains an irksome sport;
      To ocean, life is better married;   8315
      To timeless floods you shall be carried
      By Proteus-Dolphin.
      [*He transforms himself.*]
               Done, you see!
  And there most prosperously fare you,
  Upon this arching back I bear you
  And wed you to the ocean sea.   8320
THALES.   Espouse the recommended part,
  Begin creation from the start.
  For swift enactment gird your will!
  You move there by eternal norms,
  Through thousand, countless thousand forms,   8325
  There's time enough for manship still.[4]
    [HOMUNCULUS *mounts* PROTEUS-DOLPHIN.]

---

2. Formal odes of celebration dedicated to Apollo.
3. The Colossus of Rhodes is reported to have been destroyed by an earthquake in 223 B.C. and the metal from it melted down and sold.
4. Thales describes a process of organic evolution through stages of metamorphosis, with which Goethe as poet and scientist essentially agreed.

PROTEUS.
>   Come with me into moisty distance,
>   To lead a long and broad existence,
>   And cruise at will the wide and nether;
>   But higher orders do not covet,   8330
>   Once you are human and above it,
>   You will be done for altogether.

THALES.   It all depends, each to his fad;
>   A fine man of his time is not so bad.

PROTEUS.   [to THALES] You mean perhaps a type like yours!   8335
>   That for some little time endures;
>   Indeed, amid a wan and ghostly cast
>   I've seen you now for many ages past.

SIRENS. [on the cliff]
>   Who about the moon has planted
>   Cloudlets in a ring so bright?   8340
>   Doves they are, by love enchanted
>   Wings as dazzling-white as light.[5]
>   It is Paphos that released them,
>   Sent her love-enraptured swarm;
>   All perfected is our feast then,   8345
>   Fully clear our joy and calm.

NEREUS.   [approaching THALES] True, a wanderer might rather
>   Call this halo "emanation;"
>   We, the spirits, have another
>   And the proper explanation.   8350
>   Doves they are, my daughter's pages,
>   Which her roving shell escort,
>   Flight of rare and wondrous sort,
>   Learnt from immemorial ages.

THALES. No good man would prize it lowly,   8355
>   Nor can I but call it best,
>   When one nurtures something holy
>   In the warm and tranquil nest.

PSYLLI AND MARSI.[6] [on bulls, calves, and rams of the sea]
>   In Cyprus' rugged cave recesses,
>   By Poseidon unburied,   8360
>   By Seismos unharried,[7]
>   Fanned ever by breezy caresses,
>   As of old, and time without end,
>   Bliss-aware leisure we spend,

5. The doves of Aphrodite from the seat of her cult at Paphos had originally served to pull the carriage in which she rode. Here, since Galatea rides in the scallop shell that had conveyed the goddess across the water after her sea birth, the doves function as the attendants of her train, flying ahead of the others.
6. Obscure, primeval inhabitants of Cyprus, the island of Aphrodite, who here declare that they have tended the shell of the goddess since she first came ashore there. They represent the earliest stage of human culture, cave dwellers like the Cyclopes of Homer's Odyssey 9.
7. Just as the sea is momentarily blessed and becalmed for the festival, so also the caves of the Psylli and Marsi are said to be free of the destructive forces of either Poseidon, the sea god, or Seismos, the earthquake.

Cytheria's[8] chariot we tend,   8365
And lead, at the whisper of night,
Through the waves' cross-broidered delight,
To the tribe of the day, out of sight,
Forward the loveliest maid.
On our still courses defying   8370
Both eagle and winged lion,
Crescent and cross as well;[9]
However aloft it may reign and dwell,
Changeably stir and mill,
Harry each other and kill,   8375
Crops and towns wreak ill,
Forth, as ever begun,
We usher the loveliest lady on.

SIRENS.   Softly gliding, gently pacing,
         Round the chariot, ring on ring,   8380
         File on file now interlacing,
         Serpentine meandering,
         Buxom Nereids, come near,
         Pleasing-wild unto the sight,
         Bring, sweet Dorids, Galatea,   8385
         Her high mother's image quite.[1]
         Grave she seems like godly faces,
         Shares immortals' earnest worth,
         Yet with all the luring graces
         Of the loveliest maid of earth.   8390

DORIDS.   [in chorus, as they glide past NEREUS, all on dolphins]
         Luna, light and shade, to render
         Youth's bloom clearer, we desire;
         Cherished bridegrooms now we tender
         Suppliantly to our sire.[2]

  [to NEREUS.]
         These are lads we rescued, headed   8395
         For the breakers' grim-toothed face,
         Warmed to light of living, bedded
         Soft on moss and reedy lace,
         Who with fervent kisses tender
         Now their faithful thanks must render;   8400
         Show the charming ones your grace!

NEREUS.   It must pay off in double measure
To blend, as you do, charity and pleasure.

---

8. A title of Aphrodite associated with her cult on the island of Cythera.
9. These four heraldic signs—the eagle, the winged lion, the cross, and the crescent moon—are identified with the historical sequence of powers that have held Cyprus: Rome, Venice, the Christian crusaders, and Turkey.
1. The Nereids, who earlier appeared with the Tritons to fetch the Cabiri (lines 8044 ff.), and the Dorids are sisters, named respectively for their father (Nereus) and their mother (the sea nymph Doris).
2. The Dorids, traditionally fifty in number, ride upon dolphins (similar to Homunculus on Proteus), accompanied by young sailors whom they have rescued from shipwrecks.

DORIDS.   Father, if you don't dislike us
                 For the joy from ocean wrung,   8405
                 Be they clasped, immortal like us,
                 To our breast forever young.
NEREUS.   Do let the handsome catch enchant you,
     Each mold her own from youth to man;
     I am unable, though, to grant you   8410
     What only the Olympian can.
     The wave, your changeful fellow-rover,
     Grants love continuance no more,
     And once the tender charm is over,
     You set them gently back ashore.   8415

DORIDS.   Sweet youths, we sadly part, it seems,
                 Though warmly fond, we vow it;
                 Enduring faith was in our dreams,
                 The gods will not allow it.

YOUTHS.   Just pour us out such further bliss,   8420
                 Brave sailor-lads implore,
                 We've never known a life like this,
                 And look for nothing more.

          [GALATEA *approaches in her shell chariot.*][3][†]
NEREUS.   It's you, oh my dearest!
GALATEA.   Dear Father, well met!
     What bliss! Oh my dolphins, do tarry just yet![4]   8425
NEREUS.   Past it glides, the hurrying throng,
     In plunging circular motion;
     What do they care for fervent heart's devotion!
     Ah—would they only carry me along!
     Yet a single loving gaze   8430
     All the empty year outweighs.
THALES.   Hail! Hail again, glad sight!
     New burgeons my delight,
     With truth and beauty I feel rife . . .
     From the water has sprung all life!   8435
     All is sustained by its endeavor!
     Vouchsafe us, Ocean, your rule forever.
     But for you, rain-clouds sending,
     Freshets richly spending,
     Streams now here now yonder bending,   8440
     Noble rivers ending,
     Where would the earth be, where lowland and mountain?
     Of life's renewal, you are the fountain.

---

3. The iconographic high point of the festival is here achieved with the epiphany of Galatea.
4. Galatea's call echoes the terms used by Faust in his wager with Mephistopheles (line 1699).

ECHO.   [*chorus of all the circles*]
Of life's renewal you are the fount.
NEREUS.   They turn and roll in far-off haze,   8445
No longer render gaze for gaze;
In drawn-out curving chain,
To prove their festive vein,
The thronging circles swirl and veer.
Galatea's throne, though, shell-bedecked,   8450
Now and then I do detect.
It gleams like a star
Through the crowd between;
Through teeming masses love's light is seen,
Were it ever so far,   8455
It shines bright and clear,
Ever true and near.

HOMUNCULUS.   In this lovely damp,
Whatever lights my lamp
Is sweetly tender.   8460

PROTEUS.   In this live damp alone
Has your bright lamp shone
With sound of splendor.[5]

NEREUS.   Amid the attendants, what secret untested
Would now be to wondering eyes manifested?   8465
What glares at the shell, by Galatea's feet,
Now mightily glowing, now gracious, now sweet,
As though by the pulses of love it were stirred?
THALES.   Homunculus is it, by Proteus ensnared . . .
These symptoms betoken imperious craving,   8470
The clamorous drone of an agonized raving;
He'll crash at her glittering throne and be shattered;
It's flaming, now flashes, already is scattered.[6]
SIRENS.   What lights us the billows, what fiery wonder
Sets blazing their clashes and sparkling asunder?   8475
It lightens and wavers and brightens the height:
The bodies, they glow on the courses of night,
And ringed is the whole by the luminous wall;[7]

---

5. In these final speeches of Proteus and Homunculus, now far out at sea, the lyrical-musical quality of the festival achieves its highest fulfillment.
6. The final speeches of Nereus and Thales constitute a question and an answer, in which the mythical father-figure, the old man of the sea, must learn the meaning of what is happening from the human philosopher.
7. The Sirens conclude the festival by offering their response to the mystery of Homunculus's self-sacrifice in exalted, hymnic tones. What they perceive and describe is the blending and fusion of opposites—of fire and water, of spirit and substance, of the masculine and the feminine—through which life is created in the sea.

May Eros[8] then reign who engendered it all!

> Hail the sea, the ocean swelling!   8480
> Wreathed in sacred fiery torrents:
> Hail the fire, the waters welling!
> Hail the singular occurrence!

ALL IN UNISON.[9]

> Hail the gentle airs benignant!
> Hail the deeps with secrets pregnant!   8485
> Solemnly here be ye sung,
> All four elements as one!

---

8. Not the playful Cupid of later mythology, nor even exclusively the daimon celebrated in Plato's *Symposium*, but a much more ancient, even primal, concept, the original creative force that produces life and light out of chaos. By implication, Homunculus is here the embodiment of Eros, spirit motivated by love (line 8468).
9. Not merely all the participants in the festival but the entire cosmos of ancient Hellas here assumes a single choric voice.

ACT III†

Before the Palace of Menelaus at Sparta[1]

[*Enter* HELENA *and* CHORUS OF CAPTIVE TROJAN WOMEN.[2] PAN-
THALIS,[3] *leader of the chorus.*]

HELENA. Exalted much and much disparaged,[4] Helena,
I leave behind the strand where first we came ashore,
Still in a stupor from the nimble tilt and pitch   8490
Of rolling seas that brought us from the Phrygian[5] plain
Astride high-bristling backs, thanks to Poseidon's[6] grace
And Euros'[7] strength, to inlets of the native land.[8]
King Menelaus is rejoicing down below
In his return amidst the bravest of his host.   8495
But you, bid welcome to me now, oh lofty house,[9]
Which Tyndareos,[1] my father, back from Pallas' hill,[2]
Erected for himself along the nearby slope
And raised in splendor over any Spartan house,
As I with sister Clytemnestra[3] here grew up,   8500
With Castor, too, and Pollux, playing happy games.[4]
Be greeted, then, the bronzen gate's twin portals you!
It was your hospitably wide-flung openness
By which that time to me, elected out of many,
Shone forth bright Menelaus in a suitor's garb.[5]   8505

1. The first of the three sections of the *Helena* (lines 8488–9126) consists of an elaborate imitation
   of the form and structure of Greek tragedy, specifically the drama of Euripides. The meter of the
   dialogue (with some exceptions in the final scene, for which see note to line 8909) is iambic
   trimeter, a six stress iambic line used in Greek drama, which Goethe—in his initial draft of the
   Helena, in 1800—was the first to imitate in German. The stage is also set in imitation of the
   ancient Greek theater, with the façade of a palace as the backdrop and a main entrance through
   the central palace doors.
2. A similar chorus of captive Trojan women is used by Euripides in *The Trojan Women* and *Hecuba*.
3. The name derives from Pausanias's description of the painting by Polygnotos (fifth century B.C.)
   of the fall of Troy, which was to be found in the hall of the Cnidians at Delphi, where Panthalis
   is one of Helen's attendants.
4. Helena refers to her reputation in literature, the history of her praise and abuse at the hands of
   poets.
5. Inaccurately used for the region about Troy (Troas).
6. The god of the sea.
7. The east wind.
8. Helena's stupor, caused by the motion of the sea, which the rhythm of the lines seeks to imitate,
   must also allude to the journey from the underworld that she has just completed (though
   she does not remember it).
9. Helena's address to the palace may be an imitation of similar speeches by the Herald in Aeschylus's
   Agamemnon, lines 518–9, or by Menelaus in Euripides' *Orestes*, lines 356 ff., where both characters are also returning from Troy.
1. King of Sparta and, according to variant genealogical accounts, the father of Helena, Clytemnestra,
   Castor, and Pollux. According to the alternative myth of Leda and the swan (see lines 6904 ff.
   and 7277 ff.), Helena's father was the god Zeus.
2. The Acropolis of Athens, sacred to Pallas Athena.
3. Clytemnestra married Agamemnon, and Helena married his brother Menelaus.
4. See note to line 7369.
5. Helena alludes to her marriage with Menelaus, who won her hand in competition with many
   other princely suitors.

Now open them to me once more that I fulfill
In faith a pressing royal charge, as behooves a wife.
Allow me entry! and let all be left behind
That stormed about me hitherto so fatefully.
For since the time I left this threshold free of care   8510
For Cytherea's temple, mindful of sacred troth,
But then a pirate seized me, the Phrygian, on that quest,[6]
Full many things have passed which people far and wide
Are fond of telling, yet which grate on the ear of one
Of whom reports spun out have grown to a fairy-tale.   8515
CHORUS.[7]   Do not disdain, oh wondrous Queen,
          The proud possession of the highest good!
          For on you alone was bestowed the greatest bliss,
          The fame of beauty, surpassing all the rest.
          The hero's name rings out before him,   8520
          Lends pride to his gait,
          Yet straight away the most stiffnecked man
          To all-conquering beauty bends his mind.
HELENA.   Enough! together with my lord I voyaged here
And to his city now am sent ahead by him;   8525
Yet what there may be in his heart I cannot guess.
Is it as wife I come here? Is it as a queen?
Is it as victim for the Prince's bitter smart
And for the Greeks' so long sustained calamities?
A conquest am I—whether captive too, who knows!   8530
For fate and repute did the immortals allot me indeed
Equivocally, of beautiful form the hazardous
Concomitants, who even at this threshold here
Attend my side with presence of portentous gloom.[8]
Still in the hollow ship my lord would look at me   8535
But seldom, nor let fall a single word of cheer.
Like one who harbors ill did he sit facing me.
But presently, as sailing up the bay-shore deep
Of the Eurotas,[9] the leading vessels' beaks were just
Saluting the land, he spoke, as though by a god impelled: 8540
Here shall my warriors disembark, in order due,
I shall review their lines, drawn up along the beach,
But you move onward, keep ascending up the bank,

---

6. According to one version of the myth, Paris (the Phrygian "pirate") met Helena at the temple of Aphrodite on the island of Cythera. Paris had awarded the golden apple of Eris, the prize of beauty, to Aphrodite in response to her promise to unite him, as a reward, with the world's most beautiful woman (see note to line 6459). This allusion also recalls the spirit show of Paris and Helena in "Hall of Chivalry" (lines 6421–565).
7. The three choral insertions to the prologue (lines 8516–23, 8560–7, 8591–603) are metrically identical to constitute a choral ode, as strophe, antistrophe, and epode respectively. Goethe's imitation in the *Helena* of the Greek choral ode is without precedent in German drama.
8. The description of Helena's supposed homecoming and her relation to Menelaus derives from Euripides' *Orestes*, where upon his arrival at Argos, Menalaus sends Helena ahead to the palace to pour libations on Clytemnestra's grave, and from *The Trojan Women* (lines 860–1059), where Menelaus indicates to Hecuba that he will sacrifice Helena after he returns with her to Sparta.
9. The main river of Laconia, on the banks of which the city of Sparta was located, about twenty miles inland from its mouth.

Endowed with fruit, of sacred Eurotas, on and up,
And guide the steeds onto the moisty meadow's sheen   8545
Until you shall have made your way to the lovely plain
Where Lacedaemon,[1] once a spacious fertile field,
By somber mountains closely neighbored, holds its site.
Then, entering the lofty-towered princely house,
Hold muster for me of the serving-maids whom I   8550
Relinquished there, with the astute old stewardess.[2]
Let her display to you the treasure's rich array,
As by your father handed down, and by myself
In war and peace, by steady increment, amassed.
There you will find it all maintained in order: for,   8555
Such his prerogative, the prince on his return
Finds all within his house in faithful keeping still,
Each thing in its own place, just as he left it there.
For in the serf no power resides to make a change.

CHORUS.   Let now feast on the glorious hoard,   8560
           The ever increased, your eyes and heart;
           For the neck-chain's shimmer, the diadem's glow,
           They loll in pride there, vaunting themselves;
           But enter boldly and challenge them,
           They will marshall their strength,   8565
           I rejoice to look on as beauty contends
           Against gold and pearls and the pride of gems.

HELENA.   Then there ensued the Master's further imperious word:
Once you are done surveying all in order due,
Then take as many tripods as you deem of need,   8570
And sundry vessels such as one at sacrifice
Wants close at hand as he performs the sacred rite,
The caldrons and the bowls, the shallow salver too,
Set purest water from the holy fountain by
In its tall pitchers, and the well-dried kindling too,   8575
Swift to accept the flame, keep there in readiness,
A well-honed knife should not be lacking, for the last.
All the remainder, though, I leave unto your care.
Thus spoke he, urging my departure; but no thing
That draws life's breath did he in his ordaining mark   8580
For slaughter worshipful of the Olympian gods.
This gives me pause, yet I, dismissing undue care,
Commit it all into the hands of gods on high,
Who bring to pass what they may harbor in their thought,
And whether it by human minds be judged benign   8585
Or else of evil, we, the mortals, suffer it.[3]
At times, one sacrificing has raised the heavy axe
In consecration to the earth-bowed victim's neck,

---

1. Another name for Sparta.
2. Phorcyas-Mephisto.
3. Helena's puzzlement concerning the lack of an animal to be slaughtered suggests an allusion to
   the story of Abraham and Isaac (Genesis 22.7), where Isaac also asks about the missing victim.

And could not consummate it, being hindered by
The foe's approach, or intervention by a god.   8590
CHORUS.   What may come to pass you will not divine;
                Therefore, oh Queen, stride on
                Stout of heart.
                Blessing or ill on man
                Unexpectedly falls;   8595
                Even forewarned we believe it not.
                Did not Troy burn, did we not see
                Death before us, infamous death?
                And are we not here,
                Joined to you, joyful in service,   8600
                Seeing the dazzling sun of the heavens,
                And of earth what is fairest,
                You, whose favor has blessed us?
HELENA.   Be that as might be! It behooves me, come what may,
        To mount without delay into the royal house,   8605
        Which, almost forfeited, long missed, and longed-for much,
        Stands once again before my eyes, I know not how.
        My feet no longer take me up so pluckily
        Those lofty stairs I used to skip up as a child.
                [Exit.]

CHORUS.   Cast any suffering   8610
                Far away, sisters, you
                Dolefully captive ones;
                Share in our lady's bliss,
                Helena's happiness,
                Who joyously, on feet   8615
                Returning belatedly, to be sure,
                But all the firmer for that,
                Nears her paternal hearth.

                Honor the holy
                Gods who restore us,   8620
                Homeward to joy conduct us!
                One unbound, after all,
                Floats as on pinions
                Over the roughest ground, while in vain
                The prisoner eats out his heart,   8625
                Over the dungeon's pinnacles
                Arms spread wide in yearning.

                But her an immortal seized
                In the distance,
                Out of Ilion's dust   8630
                Bore her back here
                Into the old, the newly adorned
                House of her father,

After ineffable
Joys and torments   8635
To be mindful afresh
Of earliest times of youth.

PANTHALIS.   [*as leader of the chorus*]
Abandon now the joy-embowered path of song
And to the portals of the door apply your gaze.
What do I see, oh sisters? Is it not the Queen   8640
Returning, vehement emotion in her steps?
What is it? What, exalted Queen, could you have met
Within the halls of your own house in welcome's stead
To shatter your composure? You conceal it not;
It is abhorrence that I read upon your brow,   8645
A noble indignation struggling with surprise.
HELENA.   [*who has left the portals open, in accents of emotion*][4]
Ignoble panic ill becomes the child of Zeus,[5]
The fleeting brush of terror's fingers touch her not;
But the stark horror which, since time's first origin
Uncoiled from hoar Night's womb, of many shapes as yet   8650
Like glowing clouds from out the mountain's fiery maw,
Comes rolling up, will shake a very hero's heart.
Thus awe-inspiringly the Stygian[6] gods have marked
The entrance to my house today that I as soon
Let the oft-trodden, sorely longed-for threshold go   8655
And seek my distance from it, like a guest dismissed.
Yet no! I have withdrawn here to the light, nor shall
You drive me farther, powers, whoever you may be.
On consecration will I set my mind, then, cleansed,
Let the hearth's embers greet the lady like the lord.   8660
CHORUS LEADER.   Reveal, oh noble Lady, to your serving maids,
Who reverently stand by you, what has occurred.
HELENA.   What I have seen, you shall lay eyes upon yourselves,
Unless it be that ancient Night at once engulfed
Her form back in her womb's portentous depth.   8665
But I will put it into words so you may know:
When mindful of the task at hand, I gravely stepped
Into the somber mid-space of the royal house,
The hush of vacant passageways astonished me.
No sound of purposefully passing traffic met   8670
The ear, nor swiftly bustling busyness the gaze,
And not a maid appeared to me, no stewardess,
Who used to welcome any stranger graciously.

---

4. Helena's return from the palace recalls a similar incident in Aeschylus's *Eumenides*, where the Pythian priestess enters the temple at Delphi only to emerge again immediately in panic at the sight of the Furies asleep around the altar.
5. Helena alludes to the alternative myth of her birth, whereas she earlier called Tyndareus her father (see line 8497).
6. The gods of the underworld, named for the river Styx.

But when I neared the shelter of the fireplace,
I saw, by barely smoldering embers' tepid glow,   8675
A rangy shrouded female sitting on the ground,
Recalling not a sleeper, more a musing shape.
In accents of command I summon her to work,
Supposing her the stewardess installed perchance
At his departure by my husband's providence;   8680
But all enfolded she continues motionless;
At length, upon my threat, she raises her right arm
As if to banish me away from hearth and hall.
I turn away from her, incensed, and hasten straight
Toward the steps that reach the ornate thalamus   8685
Upon its dais, and close to it, the treasure-room.
The portent, though, springs up abruptly from the ground,
Imperiously bars my way, and shows itself
Of stature gaunt, and hollow, bloody-blear of eye,
And weird of shape as to confound the eye and mind.   8690
However, I address the breeze; for quite in vain
The word will strain creatively to build up shapes.
Look—there she is! She even ventures forth to light!
Here we are masters till the King our lord arrives.
Night's dread abortions are by Phoebus, beauty's friend,   8695
Thrust off and banished into caverns, or subdued.

    [PHORCYAS *appears on the threshold between the doorposts.*]

CHORUS.   Much have I lived through, although the tresses
           Youthfully cluster about my temples!
           Many the terrors that I witnessed,
           War's desolation, Ilion's night   8700
           When it fell.[7]

           Through the beclouded, dust-swirling tumult of
           Warriors raging, I heard the awesome
           Hail of the gods, hearkened discord's
           Brazen-voiced clangor clash downfield   8705
           Toward the wall.[8]

           Still they were standing, ah,
           Ilion's walls, but the flaming blaze
           Coursed already from neighbor to neighbor,
           Spreading farther from here to there   8710
           By its own tempest's blast
           Through the night-shrouded city.

7. The description of the fall of Troy may derive in part from the conclusion of Euripides' *Trojan Women*, where the burning city is described. More likely, however, Goethe is following the longer and more vivid description in Book 2 of Virgil's *Aeneid*, where Aeneas describes to Dido the fall of the city.
8. The association of violent destruction in battle with the shout of a god is Homeric, as when Ares or Poseidon shouts with the voice of ten thousand men (*Iliad* 5.859 ff. and 14.147–48). Eris, "discord" (whose "clangor" is mentioned here, line 8705), also shouts in this way (*Iliad* 11.2–12).

Fleeing, I saw through reek and glow
And the blaze of the flickering flame
Frightful wrath of approaching gods,   8715
Striding portents,
Titan shapes, through dusky
Flame-reddened smoky writhing.[9]

Yet, did I see it or did
Fear-smothered spirit shape   8720
So tangled a skein? This I
Never could tell, but that I stand
Eye to eye with this horror here,
That I can tell for certain;
Could I not grasp it with my hand,   8725
Were it not for the peril of it
Staying my will with panic?

Which might you be, then,
Of Phorcys' daughters?
For to his kindred   8730
I must compare you.
Perchance as one of the gray-born—
Of but one eye and one tooth
Turn by turn partaking—
Graiae are you not come?[1]   8735

Dare you then, monster,
Thus beside beauty
Stand before Phoebus'
Arbiter's gazes?
Fear not to venture forth, however,   8740
For the ugly his sight omits,
As his holy eye has not
Ever perceived the shadows.

But us mortals, alas, condemns
All too grievous misfortune   8745
To the ineffable anguish of eye
Which what is luckless, forever deplorable,
Stirs in lovers of beauty.

Aye then, listen, you, as you dare
Meet us brazenly, hear a ban,   8750
Hear all menace of scolding speech,

---

9. The Chorus begins to confuse in its memory the fall of Troy with the supernatural powers of the underworld.
1. The Chorus correctly associates Mephistopheles' guise with the Phorcyads, or Graiae (see note to line 7967).

Hear execration from lips of the fortunate
Who are fashioned by gods above.

PHORCYAS.   Old is the saying, yet enduring its high truth,
That Modesty and Beauty never hand in hand   8755
Pursue their way along the verdant road of earth.[2]
So deeply rooted dwells in both an ancient hate
That wheresoever it might happen that their paths
Should meet, each on the other turns a hostile back.
Then both again, more vehemently, rush apart,   8760
Modesty sad of heart, but Beauty brazenly,
Till Orcus'[3] hollow night wraps her about at last,
Unless it be old age has chastened her before.
Now you I find, bold hussies, wantonly poured forth
This way from alien parts, enclamored like the hoarse   8765
And raucous-sounding flight of cranes that overhead
In clongated cloud its croaking riot sends
Below, and lures the quiet wayfarer to raise
His gaze aloft; yet they go drifting on their way
While he goes his; just so it will turn out with us.   8770

Who are you, pray, to take upon yourselves to rave
Like Maenads[4] wild, or drunk, about the King's great house?
Yes, who are you, to meet the royal stewardess
With such a howl as does a pack of hounds the moon?
You think it is concealed from me what kith you are,   8775
Young brood, begot of war, reared up in battle-clash?
Man-mad, as readily seducing as seduced,
Who sap the strength of citizen and warrior both.
I watch your throng, and seem to see a locust-swarm
Swoop down and cover up the fields' green crops.   8780
Devourers of the thrift of others! Sneaking thieves
Destroying young prosperity just up from seed,
Cheap booty goods, knocked down at sale, at barter, you!
HELENA.   Who scolds a lady's waiting maids before her face
Presumptuously encroaches on her household right;   8785
For it is hers alone to praise the laudable
And lay reproof upon what is to blame.
Moreover, I am well content with the services
They rendered me when Ilion's mighty eminence
Beleaguered stood, and fell, and prostrate lay; no less   8790
When we endured the griefs and dire vicissitudes
Of errant voyage, where each but regards himself.

2. Phorcyas begins with a familiar saying, which derives from a Roman idea (as in Juvenal, *Satire*
   10.297, "Rare indeed is the friendly union of beauty of form and chaste modesty," or Ovid, *Epistles*
   16.288, "There is strife between exalted form and shame"). What follows is an extended double
   epic simile in the Homeric or Virgilian manner.
3. The classical underworld.
4. Drunken or ecstatic followers of Dionysus.

Here I expect like service from the lively band.
Not what the serf be, asks the lord, but how he serves.
You hold your peace, therefore, and sneer at them no more.   8795
If hitherto you tended well the royal house
In absence of the mistress, this speaks well of you;
But now she comes herself, you in your turn withdraw,
Lest there be punishment in place of earned reward.

PHORCYAS.   To raise domestic threats remains a weighty right   8800
Well-earned by a god-favored ruler's noble spouse
In view of prudent governance of many years.
But since, acknowledged now! you occupy anew
The former place of Queen and Lady of the House,
Seize hold of the long-slackened reins and govern now,   8805
Take charge again of treasure and us all to boot.
Above all else, protect me, elder that I am,
Against this gaggle who, beside your beauty's swan,
Are but a swarm of cacklesome, ill-feathered geese.

CHORUS LEADER.[5]   How ugly is, seen next to beauty, ugliness.   8810

PHORCYAS.   How foolish is, seen next to wisdom, foolishness.

[*From here on, single* CHORETIDS *step out of the* CHORUS *to make retorts.*]

CHORETID I.   Of father Erebus[6] report, report of mother night.

PHORCYAS.   Speak you of Scylla,[7] then, your very kith and kin.

CHORETID II.

There's many a monster clambering up your pedigree.

PHORCYAS.   To Orcus off with you! There seek your kinfolk out.   8815

CHORETID III.

The ones who dwell there are all much too young for you.

PHORCYAS.   Tiresias[8] the Ancient try your lewdness on.

CHORETID IV.

Orion's[9] wet-nurse was great-great-grandchild to you.

PHORCYAS.   By harpies[1] you were reared on offal, I should judge.

CHORETID V.

Say, what do you sustain such well-groomed leanness with?   8820

PHORCYAS.   Not with the blood that you are all too avid for.

CHORETID VI.   It's carcases you lust for, loathsome corpse yourself.

PHORCYAS.   It's vampire teeth that glitter in your shameless jowls.

---

5. Goethe here employs stychomythia, the form of one-line exchange used in Greek tragedy for
   scenes of rapid pace and emotional intensity. Six separate lines are assigned to six Choretids (solo
   speakers). These six presumably constitute one half of the Chorus, grouped with the Chorus
   Leader on one side of Phorcyas. The other half stands with Helena and catches her when she
   faints (following line 8881).
6. The lowest level of the underworld. In Hesiod, *Theogony*, lines 123 ff., Erebus and Night are the
   offspring of Chaos, and together they beget the Day and the Aether.
7. A monster with six heads, serpent-shaped and baying with the bark of dogs (see Homer's *Odyssey*
   12.211–59). Scylla was a daughter of Phorcyas and thus a sister of the Phorcyads.
8. The blind prophet of Thebes who appears in Sophocles' *Antigone* and *Oedipus the King* as an
   old man.
9. The hunter, son of Poseidon, who was killed by Artemis and then transformed by Zeus into a
   heavenly constellation.
1. Mythical creatures with the heads and breasts of women and the bodies of birds, who pollute
   whatever they touch.

CHORUS LEADER.
　Yours I could stop, were I to say just who you are.
PHORCYAS.
　Name first yourself, then, and the riddle will be solved.   8825
HELENA.   In sorrow, not in anger, do I intervene
　Between you and forbid such rash and fierce exchange!
　For nothing more of harm can face the ruling lord
　Than loyal servants' secret festering enmity.
　No longer does the echo of his orders then   8830
　Return to him in swift fulfillment's tuneful chord,
　No, then a willful tumult all about him roars,
　Who is himself distracted, chiding all in vain.
　Nor is this all. In your unconscionable wrath
　You conjured up unhallowed pictures' frightful shapes,   8835
　Which throng about me so that I myself feel snatched
　To Orcus, in defiance of the sights of home.
　Is this remembrance? or delusion seizing me?
　Was I all that? Or am I now? Or shall I be
　The nightmare image of that ravager of towns?[2]   8840
　The maidens shudder, but as you, the eldest one,
　Stand with composure, speak to me a word of sense.
PHORCYAS.   To him who recollects long years of varied bliss,
　The highest godly boon at last will seem a dream.
　But you, by fortune favored past all bounds and goal,   8845
　Saw only those by love enardored line your life,
　Those swiftly kindled to all manner of bold deed.
　Why, Theseus early snatched you up with quickened lust,
　Like Heracles in strength, of glorious manly form.
HELENA.   Abducted me, ten-year-old slender doe I was,   8850
　And then Aphidnus' castle closed on me in Attica.[3]
PHORCYAS.   But soon set free at Castor's and at Pollux' hands,[4]
　You stood, by an array of choicest heroes wooed.
HELENA.   But secret favor over all, I freely own,
　Patroclus[5] won, who was Pelides' second self.   8855
PHORCYAS.   To Menelaus did a father's will betrothe you, though,
　Bold rover of the seas, but home-preserver too.
HELENA.   He gave his daughter, gave the kingdom's governance.

---

2. The confusion of past, present, and future time in these questions is important for the sense of
　timelessness in the *Helena*, in which the heroine participates (though it confuses her). The phrase
　"ravager of towns," which imitates the type of epithet used by Homer, probably derives from
　Euripides' *Trojan Women* (lines 892–3), where Hecuba speaks of Helen to Menelaus as follows:
　"She looks enchantment, and where she looks homes are set on fire; / she captures cities as she
　captures the eyes of men."
3. Theseus (here compared with Heracles; see lines 7381 ff.) and his companion Pirithous abducted
　the ten-year-old Helen from a temple of Artemis where they saw her dancing. Theseus then
　entrusted her to his friend Aphidnus to keep her in his castle, since Helena was still too young
　for love. Attica is the region of Greece where Athens, the city Theseus ruled, is located.
4. Helena was freed from Theseus by her twin half-brothers (see lines 7369 and 7415 f.).
5. It is uncertain why Helena mentions Patroclus, who was the close friend of Achilles in Homer's
　Iliad, as the favorite among her suitors (Achilles, son of Peleus, is here styled Pelides).

From wedded concourse then sprang forth Hermione.[6]
PHORCYAS.   But when afar he boldly seized the prize of Crete,   8860
Into your loneliness came all too fair a guest.[7]
HELENA.   Why do you bring to mind that all-but-widowhood,
And what appalling doom emerged from it to me?
PHORCYAS.   To me, a free-born Cretan woman, that same quest
Brought in its train enslavement, long captivity.[8]   8865
HELENA.   He forthwith then installed you here as stewardess,
Entrusting much, both keep and treasure boldly seized.
PHORCYAS.   Which you relinquished, bound for tower-ringed Ilion
And ever inexhaustible delights of love.
HELENA.   Do not recall the joys! For all too bitter grief's   8870
Infinitude was poured me over breast and head.
PHORCYAS.   And yet they say that you appeared in double shape,
Observed in Ilion as well as Egypt too.[9]
HELENA.   Do not confound a turbid mind's confusion quite.
Why, even now I know not which of these I am.   8875
PHORCYAS.   And more they say: from out of the realm of shades
Achilles rose at last and joined you too, enflamed!
Who loved you once against all settled rule of fate.[1]
HELENA.   I as a myth allied myself to him as myth.
It was a dream, the words themselves proclaim it so.   8880
I fade away, becoming to myself a myth.[2]
     [*Swooning, she sinks into the* SEMI-CHORUS' *arms.*]

CHORUS.   Silence, silence![3]
Ill-gazing, ill-speaking as you are!
Past so hideous one-toothed lips
What would indeed waft forth   8885
From such gruesome horrors' maw!

For the wicked in the guise of benevolence,
Wolfish-fierce under woolly sheep's fleece,
Far more terrible seems to me than the three-
Headed Hell-hound's jaws.[4]   8890

6. Hermione, daughter of Helena and Menelaus, appears as a character in Euripides' *Andromache* and *Orestes*.
7. Menelaus went to Crete after the death of his maternal grandfather, Creteus, to receive his share of the estate, during which time Paris seduced Helena.
8. Possibly derived from the false stories Odysseus tells of himself as a fugitive from Crete after his return to Ithaca in Homer's *Odyssey* (13.256 ff., 14.192 ff., 17.415 ff., 19.165 ff.).
9. An allusion to the later legend, which Euripides used satirically in his *Helen*, that Helena was actually carried off by Hermes to Egypt, while a false figure of her (idol) was taken to Ilion (Troy).
1. The spirits of Achilles and Helena were united on the island of Leuce at the request of Achilles and there produced a son, Euphorion (mentioned earlier, line 7435, where Goethe erroneously refers to the city of Pherae).
2. *Idol* in the German, from the Greek *eidolon*, "a phantom or ghost." Helena recognizes that in her marriage with Achilles she was such an "idol," as also in the legend that she never went to Troy; and that here in this place, as a spirit released from the underworld, she is the same. (See line 4190.)
3. The plea by the Chorus for silence because of Helena's swoon follows the example of Euripides' *Orestes* (lines 140 ff.), where both Electra and the Chorus move on tiptoe so as not to wake the sleeping Orestes.
4. A reference to Cerberus, the dog that guards the entrance to Hades.

Anxious listeners here we stand:
When? how? where might it break forth,
Of such malice
The deeply lurking monster?

Thus you—for kindly-meant, solace-rich discourse,   8895
Lethe-outpouring, most loving-kind speech—
Stir up instead in all that is bygone
Evilest more than good,
Sombering all at once
Not the present's glow alone,   8900
But the future's
Soft glint of hope as it glimmers forth.

Silence, silence!
That the soul of the Queen,
Poised on the brink of flight,   8905
Might yet hold on, hold fast
To that form of all forms
Ever touched by the light of the sun.

[HELENA *has recovered and resumed her place at center.*]
PHORCYAS.[5]
Issue forth from fleeting vapors, sun exalted of this day,
Which, while shrouded yet, delightful, now in dazzling splendor
    reigns.   8910
As the world unfolds, you answer with a lovely gaze yourself.
Let them scold me ugly; still I know true beauty well enough.
HELENA.
As I, swaying, quit the void that lay about me in my swoon,
I would gladly rest me further, for so weary are my limbs:
It behooves a queen, however, as I think it does all men,   8915
To encounter with composure any dire and sudden turn.
PHORCYAS.
Now you face us in your grandeur, in your beauty once again,
This your gaze bespeaks commandment; speak then, what is
    your command?
HELENA.
Be in readiness to render what your brazen strife withheld;
Quick, prepare a sacrifice as by the King's behest to me.   8920
PHORCYAS.
All is ready in the palace, basin, tripod, sharpened axe,
For the sprinkling, incense-burning; indicate the victim now!
HELENA.   This he left undesignated.
PHORCYAS.   Left unsaid? O, grievous word!

---

5. Goethe here—as in several parts of this episode (lines 8909–29, 8957–61, 8966–70, 9067–70,
9122–6)—employs trochaic tetrameter, favored by Euripides at moments of emotional intensity
in his later plays.

HELENA.   What distress has overcome you?

PHORCYAS.   It is you he meant, o Queen!

HELENA.   I?

PHORCYAS.   And these.

CHORUS.   O woe, o pity!

PHORCYAS.   You shall fall beneath the axe.   8925

HELENA.   Dreadful! yet divined; ah me!

PHORCYAS.   And ineluctable it seems.

CHORUS.   Oh! And we? What will befall us?

PHORCYAS.   She will die a noble death;
As for you: among the rafters on the rooftree's lofty beam
Shall you twitch and dangle, thrushes which the fowler strung
     in line.[6]

> [HELENA *and* CHORUS *stand in amazement and terror, forming an
> expressive, well-arranged tableau.*]

PHORCYAS.   Bewraithed!—As if congealed to effigies you stand,   8930
Scared to be parting from the day that is not yours.
The spectral breed of man, wherever, just like you
Renounce unwillingly the lofty sunshine glow;
Yet no one begs them off or saves them from the end;
They're all aware of it, yet only few approve.   8935
Enough, you are undone! To work then, with a will.

> [*She claps her hands, whereupon at the portals appear muffled dwarf-
> ish figures,*[7] *which promptly and deftly carry out the orders pro-
> nounced.*]

Come here, you saturnine misbrood, round as a ball!
Come rolling up, you'll find your fill of mischief here.
The hand-borne altar, golden-horned, make room for that,
The axe should lie and glint across the silver rim,   8940
Fill up the ewers, there will be work in rinsing off
The hideous polluting stain of blackening blood.
Spread exquisitely here the rug across the dust,
So the victim might kneel down in royal wise,
And duly swathed, head promptly severed, to be sure,   8945
Yet all decorum satisfied, be laid to rest.

CHORUS LEADER.   The Queen is standing to one side here,
          wrapped in thought,
Whereas her maidens wilt like meadow-grass mown down;
But I, the eldest, feel impelled by sacred trust
To seek a word with you, the Great-great-eldest one.   8950
You are experienced, wise, not ill-disposed to us,
I think, though, brainless lot, we judged and used you ill.
Speak, therefore, of such rescue as there might still be.

PHORCYAS.   Soon spoken: it depends upon the Queen alone

---

6. Phorcyas-Mephisto describes the death that will be imposed on the Chorus in terms borrowed
   from Homer's *Odyssey* 22.462–73, where the faithless servant girls are put to death after the
   slaughter of the suitors.
7. The "dwarfish figures" that here appear at Phorcyas-Mephisto's call are presumably infernal spirits
   who serve him in his capacity as stage manager of this show.

To save herself, and you, as bonus lives, with her.[8]   8955
Resolve is needed, and of the nimblest sort, what's more.
CHORUS.   Oh most reverend of Parcae, wisest of the Sibyls you,[9]
   Keep the golden shears from closing, then proclaim us day and
      life;
   For we sense already lifted, swinging, dangling, most uncouthly,
   These sweet limbs, which would much rather first take pleasure
      in the dancing,   8960
   Then repose at lover's breast.
HELENA.   Leave these to quaver! What I feel is pain, not fear;
   But should you know reprieve, you shall be thanked for it.
   One shrewd and far-seeing is apt indeed to discern
   Within the hopeless the barely possible. Do speak.   8965
CHORUS.   Speak and tell us, tell us quickly: how do we escape the
      gruesome
   Nasty noose which ominously, like the meanest sort of
      necklace,
   Twines about the neck? Poor wretches, we can sense it all
      beforehand,
   To unbreathing point, to choking, if you, Rhea,[1] noble mother
   Of all gods, do not relent.   8970
PHORCYAS.   And have you patience, then, in silence to hear out
   The long-drawn-out recital? Many a tale it holds.
CHORUS.   Patience sufficient! Listening, we at least live on.[2]
PHORCYAS.   He who remains at home, preserving choice estate,
   At pains as much to caulk the tall apartments' walls   8975
   As to secure the roof before the thrust of rain,
   Will surely prosper all the long days of his life;
   But he who frivolously crosses, on flighty soles,
   The hallowed straight-rule of his threshold, lawless of mind,
   He will, returning, find the old place, to be sure,   8980
   But altogether changed, if not destroyed outright.
HELENA.   Why treat us to this kind of long-familiar saw?
   You have a tale; touch not on what must give offense.
PHORCYAS.   It is historical, by no means a reproach.[3]
   From bay to bay, freebooting, Menelaus rowed,   8985
   Islands and littoral all felt his stabbing raids,
   And he returned with spoils, as now abound in there.
   At Ilion he lingered all of ten long years;
   How long he took for his returning I know not.
   What is the state right here, though, of the noble house   8990
   Of Tyndareos? What of the kingdom all about?

---

8. We perhaps are to assume here that one of the conditions for releasing Helena from the underworld to meet with Faust is that she must herself request it.
9. Phorcyas is addressed as one of the Parcae, or Fates (see lines 5305 ff.), and as a Sibyl, or
   prophetess.
1. The wife of Chronos or Saturn and mother of the Olympian gods (see line 7989).
2. Possibly a playful allusion to the tales of Scheherazade in *The Thousand and One Nights*. (See
   lines 6031–3 and note.)
3. In the German, "historical" (*Geschichtlich*) echoes "stories," "tales" (*Geschichten*), in line 8972.

HELENA. Why, can you be so bodily perfused with blame
That you can move your lips no more but to reprove?
PHORCYAS. Deserted stood so many years the rim of hills
Which to the rear of Sparta northward rises high,   8995
Taygetos[4] left behind—where as a playful brook
Eurotas scampers down and then, by reeds spread out,
Flows broadly through our valley, nourishing your swans.
Back in the glen there, quietly a daring clan
Have settled, thrusting up from out Cimmerian[5] night,   9000
And raised themselves a towering keep, unscalable,
From where they harass land and people as they please.[6]
HELENA. They could contrive this? Quite impossible it seems.
PHORCYAS. They had the time; it has been twenty years, or near.
HELENA. Is there one lord? A numerous brigand host in league?   9005
PHORCYAS. They are not brigands; one, however, is their lord.
I do not scold him, though he did descend on me.
He could have taken all, yet chose to be content
With some—not tribute—voluntary gifts, he said.[7]
HELENA. How are his looks?
PHORCYAS.   Not bad! I like him well.   9010
He is high-spirited, bold-tempered, nobly made,
Judicious, too, like few among the Greeks.
They call his kind barbarians, yet I suspect
Their likes might not be cruel as, besieging Troy,
More than one hero ravened like a cannibal.[8]   9015
I note his breadth of soul, to him I'd trust myself.
And there's his castle, too! You should lay eyes on that!
Far different indeed from clumsy mounds of stone
Such as your fathers helter-skelter jumbled up,
Like Cyclopes, walls Cyclopean, crashing down   9020
Raw stone on stone unhewn;[9] there, on the other hand,
All's perpendicular and level, by the rule.[1]
Look at it from the outside; heavenward it sweeps,
So rigid, truly jointed, mirror-smooth as steel.
To try to scale it—why, the very thought slides off.   9025
Within—the spaciousness of courtyards wide, enclosed
By edifice galore, of every kind and end.

4. A mountain range to the west of Sparta in the Peloponnesus.
5. According to Homer's *Odyssey* 11.14 ff., the Cimmerians are a people dwelling in a land hidden in fog and cloud where the sun never shines.
6. Presumably an allusion to medieval crusader castles, such as that built in the mid-thirteenth century at Mistra in the Peloponnesus by "Frankish" (i.e., West European) knights of the Fourth Crusade.
7. Such gifts would be owed by feudal law to the liege lord.
8. Presumably an allusion to Achilles' statement to the dying Hector in Homer's *Iliad* 22.346 ff., "I wish only that my spirit and fury would drive me to hack your meat away and eat it raw for the things that you have done to me."
9. A reference to the rough walls and huge stones of Mycenaean fortresses. In Greek drama these fortresses were described as having been built by the Cyclopes (one-eyed giants, familiar from Homer's *Odyssey* 9), as in Euripides' *Iphigenie at Aulis*, line 265. Rough-hewn Sparta was traditionally contrasted with the splendor of Troy (see *The Trojan Women*, lines 992 ff.).
1. A feature of the Gothic style of architecture, which Goethe and his contemporaries regarded as characteristically Germanic.

There's columns large and small, vaults, arches, arculets,
Arcades and galleries for looking out and in,
Escutcheons, too.

CHORUS.   What are escutcheons?[2]

PHORCYAS.   You have seen   9030
Ajax display upon his shield a serpent coiled.[3]
The Seven against Thebes all bore depicted shapes,
Each on his shield, replete with rich significance.[4]
Here moon and stars on the nocturnal firmament,
There goddess, champion, ladder, swords and torches, too,   9035
And what aggression grimly threatens goodly towns.
It is such figurements our band of heroes too
Display in gleaming hues from dim ancestral times.
There you see lion, eagle, also beak and claw,
The horns of buffalo, wings, roses, peacock-tail,   9040
As well as bars—gold, sable, argent, azure, gules.
The like is hung in great apartments, row on row,
In state-rooms limitless, as wide as all the world;
There's room for you to dance!

CHORUS.   Say, are there partners, too?

PHORCYAS.

The best! A golden-curled, boyishly fresh-skinned band,   9045
Fragrant with youth! No one but Paris had this scent,
When he approached too near the Queen.

HELENA.   You quite forget
Your proper part; come now to your concluding word.

PHORCYAS.   The final word is yours—an earnest, audible yes!
And forthwith I surround you with that castle.[5]

CHORUS.   Speak,   9050
Oh speak that short word, save yourself and us as well!

HELENA.   What! should I stand in fear King Menelaus might
Commit such fierce transgression as to do me harm?

PHORCYAS.   Have you forgotten the unheard-of way he maimed
Your Deiphobos, the brother of Paris battle-slain,   9055
Who stubbornly besieged and won your widowed bed
And freely relished it? His nose and ears he lopped
And mutilated more—a horror to behold.[6]

HELENA.   The thing he did to him, it was on my account.

PHORCYAS.   On his account he now will do the like to you.   9060
Beauty is indivisible: who held it whole,

---

2. The medieval heraldic arms associated with tournaments and festivals of the chivalric courts.
3. In Homer's *Iliad*, Ajax is often described as carrying a great shield with seven layers of leather.
4. In Aeschylus's *Seven Against Thebes* (lines 378–650), the Messenger describes the shield of each of the seven chieftains who have joined with Polyneices to attack the city of Thebes.
5. Phorcyas-Mephisto here indicates the conditions that must be met in order for Faust to meet Helena. His statement also hints at the theatrical nature of the transformation of scene that he proposes.
6. Menelaus's mutilation of Deiphobus (who married Helena after the death of Paris; see Euripides' *Trojan Women*, lines 959–60) is described in Virgil's *Aeneid* 6.494–7.

Destroys it rather, execrating partial hold.
  [*Trumpets in the distance; the* CHORUS *gives a violent start.*][7]
As blaring trumpets sharply lay on ear and bowels
A rending grip, thus jealousy will sink its claws
Into the bosom of the man who can't forget   9065
What once he owned, and now has lost, to own no more.
CHORUS.
  Don't you hear the horns resounding? see the glint of weaponry?
PHORCYAS.
  Welcome to the King and Master, gladly shall I lay account.
CHORUS.   *What of us?*
PHORCYAS.   You know it well: you bear close witness to her
    death,
  Minding well your own within there; no, there is no help for you.   9070
    [*Pause.*]

HELENA.   I have reflected on the step I next may dare.
  You are a froward demon,[8] this I sense full well,
  And feel misgiving lest you bend benign to ill.
  Yet I will follow you into that castle first;
  The rest is mine to know; whatever more the Queen   9075
  Sequesters deep within her breast in this regard,
  Be inaccessible to all. Crone, lead the way!

CHORUS.[9]   'Oh how gladly speed we thither
        Hurrying footsteps;
        Death at our backs,   9080
        Before us once more
        A looming stronghold's
        Impregnable bastion.
        May it shelter as well
        As Ilion's citadel did,   9085
        Which succumbed at length
        But to treacherous stratagem.[1]
  [*Fog spreads about, shrouding the background, and the foreground
  as well, at will.*]

        What? what is this?
        Sisters, look about!
        Was it not smiling day?   9090
        Mists arise in wavering streaks
        From Eurotas' sacred flood;[2]

---

7. The sound of trumpets, arranged by Phorcyas-Mephisto, causes the Chorus and Helena to believe
   that the army of Menelaus is really approaching.
8. Helena appears to sense that Phorcyas is indeed a devil, though she would presumably associate
   him with the classical underworld.
9. This ode concludes the classical section of the *Helena*.
1. An allusion to the Trojan Horse.
2. See note to line 8539.

Lost to sight already the lovely
Reed-engarlanded bank;[3]
No more, alas, do I see   9095
The soft on-glide of the swans,
Allies in floating joy,
Free in its pride and grace.

Yet, after all,
I hear their call,   9100
Their far-off husky note!
Death-heralding note, they say;[4]
Ah, would that when all is done,
It may not have augured us too
Ruin in promised rescue's stead;   9105
To us, who are swanlike, long,
Fair, and white of neck; nor, oh,
To her, our swan-begotten.[5]
Woe to us, woe!

All is covered by now;   9110
Shrouded in mist all round.
Are we not losing sight of each other?
What is it? Are we walking?
Or merely floating
Trippingly over the hidden ground?   9115
Can you see? Is it not perchance
Hermes[6] floating ahead? Not his golden staff
Flashing, bidding us back again
To ill-favored, gray-dawning Hades,
Full of impalpable figments,   9120
Overthronged, eternally void?

Yes, it darkens of a sudden, lifting mists unveil not brightness,
Gloomy gray and dun of stonework. Masonry confronts the
    vision,
Rigidly defies its ranging. Are we in a court? a dungeon?
Either case is horrifying! Sisters, oh, we are imprisoned,   9125
Captive if we ever were.[7]

---

3. Analogous to the scene at the edge of the Peneios in the "Classical Walpurgis Night" (see lines
   7249 ff.).
4. Apparently some kind of music is heard (as a demonic entr'acte? as an accompaniment to their
   song?), which the Chorus associates with the legend of the swan's song at the moment of death.
5. Helena is "swan-begotten," recalling the legend of Leda and the swan (see lines 6903 ff. and
   7277 ff.).
6. Traditionally, as Psychopompos, Hermes led dead spirits into the underworld. Here the Chorus
   may see the shape of Phorcyas-Mephisto. They are quite aware that a descent to Hades would be
   a return to the place from which they came.
7. In their guise as captured Trojan girls, the Chorus associates the medieval fortress with the palace
   of Sparta as a prison.

Inner Courtyard of a Castle†
Surrounded by Opulent and Fanciful
Medieval Architecture

CHORUS LEADER.[1]
Forward and foolish, chips off the block of womankind!
Fluff driven by the weather, playthings of the hour,
Of fortune or misfortune, neither have you learnt
To take with calm. Does each not contradict the rest   9130
With passion always, and in turn the others her?
In joy and grief, it's howl or laugh in unison.
Now hush! and listening bide whatever our lady may
Highmindedly resolve here for herself and us.

HELENA. Where are you, Pythonissa?[2] whatsoever called;   9135
Step from beneath these vaultings of the somber keep.
Should you have hastened to announce me to the lord,
This wondrous champion here, for worthy welcome's sake,
Accept my thanks and quickly lead me in to him.
I crave an end to roaming; crave repose alone.   9140

CHORUS LEADER.
In vain you gaze about, my Queen, to every side;
The odious form is vanished, has remained perhaps
Back in the fog from out the swathes of which we came,
I know not how, with speed, and yet unpacingly.
Or else she errs astray within this citadel's   9145
Moot labyrinth which fuses muchness into one,[3]
To seek the lord anent a princely high salute.
But look, up there, already swarming into sight
In galleries, at windows, crossing double doors,
A throng of serving-folk,[4] all bustling back and forth;   9150
This heralds grateful rites of lordly welcoming.

CHORUS.[5] My heart sings! oh, just see, over there
          How decorously, with leisurely tread,
          Pages in flower of youth move down
          The orderly train. How? and on whose behest   9155
          Could there emerge, so early trained to the ranks,
          Of boyish youth such splendorous throng?

1. A loose trimeter continues until the appearance of Faust (line 9192), who speaks in blank verse.
2. A medieval Latin form of the title used by the priestess of Apollo at Delphi (after the sacred serpent Pytho, slain there by Apollo). It came to refer to any prophetess or seer and here refers to Phorcyas-Mephisto, who has disappeared from the scene (returning only at line 9419) to make way for Faust.
3. This description of Gothic architecture corresponds to the Romantic view of that style, which Goethe shared.
4. Spirits conjured up by Mephistopheles to assist Faust in the encounter with Helena. They function as supernumeraries in the show, remaining silent throughout.
5. The meter of the following speech approximates the traditional anapestic march-measure often used in Greek drama for the first entrance of the Chorus. Here the Chorus chants in time to the procession of page boys, describing them as they enter the stage.

What to admire the most? Is it elegant gait,
Curly locks, perhaps, that cluster the dazzling brow,
Cheeks, perhaps, that bear twin flush of the peach,   9160
And just as downy a fleece?
I long for a bite, yet I shudder and shrink;
For in similar instance, the mouth only filled,
Repulsive to mention! with ashes.[6]

Here come the fairest   9165
Stepping toward us;
What is it they bear?
Steps to a throne,
Carpet and dais,
Canopy, tent-like   9170
Drapery rich;
Billowing over,
Cloud-garlands forming
Over our Lady's head;
For now she has mounted,   9175
Duly bidden, the sumptuous bolster.[7]
Draw you near,
Stair by stair,
Form a solemn file.
Worthy, oh worthy, threefold worthy   9180
Be such a welcome's answering grace!
[*All that is proclaimed by the* CHORUS *is enacted in due order.*]

[FAUST. PAGES *and* SQUIRES *having descended in a long procession,
he appears at the top of the staircase in the knightly court garb of
the Middle Ages and descends with slow, dignified steps.*]

CHORUS LEADER.   [*inspecting him attentively*]
This man—unless immortals, as they often do,
Have lent him admirable parts, superb address,
And amiable presence for a transient span
Of tenure only,—must be certain of success   9185
In all he undertakes, be it in clash of arms,
Be it in minor skirmish with the fairest maids.
He is in truth to be preferred to many a man
Whom my own eyes in high esteem have seen.
At grave and measured pace of reverent restraint   9190
I see the prince advancing; turn about, oh Queen!

6. The idea of cheeks that resemble peaches, enticing the Chorus to take a bite, and the apprehension that they will bite only ashes, presumably derives from the apples of Sodom, described by
Milton in *Paradise Lost* 10.564 ff., when the devils in hell are transformed into serpents. The
Chorus apparently recalls a similar experience from the underworld, here surmising (correctly)
that the page boys are only spirits like themselves.
7. The page boys construct an elaborate throne with a canopy above it where Helena is to be seated
as queen of this court.

FAUST.   [*approaching, a* BOUND MAN *at his side*][8]
    In lieu of ceremonial salute,
    In lieu of reverent welcome, as were fitting,
    I bring you, harshly chained, a servant, who
    Failing his duty, wrested mine from me.   9195
    Down on thy knees! and to this royal lady
    Confession render of thy heavy guilt.
    This is, exalted sovereign, the man
    Installed, by virtue of his eye's rare blaze,
    Keen look-out on the tower's great height, to scan   9200
    The scope of heaven and the breadth of earth,
    Whatever here or there might come in view,
    Might stir down circling hills into the vale
    To this firm keep, be it the swell of herds,
    Perchance a marching host; we shelter those,   9205
    Bid check to these. Today, what dereliction!
    As you approach he gives no sign, we fail
    Of most distinguished honors plainly due
    To such exalted guest. For which outrage
    His life is forfeit, and his blood were spilt   9210
    Long since by his deserts; but you alone
    May punish or may pardon, as you please.
HELENA.[9]   Such lofty dignity as you award,
    Of source of justice, ruler, be it but
    By way of trial, as I may surmise—   9215
    So I fulfill the judge's premier charge,
    To grant defendants hearing. Speak you, then.

LYNCEUS, WARDEN OF THE TOWER.[1]
                Keep me kneeling, keep me gazing,
                Whether dying, whether living,
                All my soul is freely given   9220
                Her, by Heaven sent, amazing.

                As the glory of the morning
                In the east I would espy,
                Wondrously, without a warning,
                From the south it dazed my eye.   9225

                So it cast my sight in harness
                That in peak and gorge's stead,
                Mid the earth's and heaven's farness
                On this star alone it fed.

8. With his first speech to Helena, Faust introduces blank verse, the form used in Shakespearian and German classical drama.
9. Helena replies to Faust in blank verse, indicating her willingness to accommodate her form of speech to his.
1. The lyrical form of Lynceus' defense is totally alien to classical literature, a form of rhymed ballad stanza from medieval Germanic love poetry, the so-called *Minnesang.*

Like the lynx on treetop perching   9230
I am dowed with sharpest sight;
Now I blink as though emerging
From a murky dream of night.

Could I tell, my senses drifting,
Moat and gateway, south from north?   9235
Vapors shifting, vapors lifting,
Such a goddess gleaming forth!

Facing her and lost in gazing,
I imbibed her balmy light,
By her fairness, all bedazing,   9240
This poor wretch was dazzled quite.

I forgot the warden's duty,
Quite the horn I hold by oath;
Forfeit is my life—yet beauty
Conquers guilt and anger both.   9245

HELENA.   The evil that I brought on him myself
I must not punish. Woe! What stern decree
Pursues me, to be fated everywhere
So to enthrall men's hearts they will not spare
Themselves nor aught of worth! Abducting now,   9250
Seducing, battling, snatching there and thither,
Heroes and demigods, immortals, aye, and demons
Have carried me at random here and yon.
Come once, I stirred the world, redoubled—more,
Now threefold, fourfold I bring woe on woe.   9255
Release this worthy one, let him go free;
No shame befall him whom the gods bewitched.
FAUST.   In wonderment, o Queen, I see at once
Unerring markswoman, and here her prey;
I see the bow from which the arrow sped   9260
And this one drooping.[2] Arrow follows arrow,
Striking myself. All over and athwart
I sense their wingèd whir in space and keep.
What am I now? You render all at once
Rebellious my most faithful, insecure   9265
My battlements. I come to fear my army
Obeys already her who wins unarmed.
What choice have I but to consign myself,
And all I owned in fancy, unto thee?

---

2. A poetic commonplace from medieval love poetry, even more from conventions of Petrarchan
(i.e., Renaissance) love poetry.

Let me in chosen fealty at your feet   9270
Acknowledge you as mistress unto whom
By her mere advent fell estate and throne.

[LYNCEUS *with a casket, and men carrying more after him.*]
LYNCEUS.[3]   You witness, lady, my return!
   One gaze the man of wealth would earn;
   He looks at you and feels at once   9275
   Enriched and beggared by the glance.

   What was I once? What now would claim?
   What to desire? At what to aim?
   Alas, the eye's acutest ray
   Against your throne is dashed to spray.   9280

   From out the teeming East we pressed,
   Wrought swift disaster on the West;
   A sea of peoples broad and vast,
   The first knew nothing of the last.

   The first might fall, the second held,   9285
   The third one's halberd flashed and felled;
   Each one enforced a hundredfold,
   A thousand slain could go untold.

   We thrust ahead, we stormed apace,
   As masters entered place on place,   9290
   And where one day I harshly vexed,
   Another robbed and stole the next.

   We looked, no sooner looked than seized;
   One snatched a girl his fancy pleased,
   The next a steer of stolid gait,   9295
   And all the horses shared its fate.

   But I was fond of seeking out
   The rarest ever seen about,
   And if another matched my prize,
   It turned to sawdust in my eyes.   9300

   On treasure traces I would tread
   And send my searching gaze ahead,
   For me no pocket was too dark,
   Transparent every cask and ark.

---

3. The second song of devotion by Lynceus develops further the thematic and historical implications
 of the encounter between Helena and Faust, as between the classical and Germanic cultures.

And mounds of gold became my own,   9305
More splendid still, much precious stone:
But now the emerald counts alone
If green upon your breast it shone.

Let quiver now twixt ear and lips
The oval drop from ocean deeps;   9310
The ruby, though, is put to flight,
The blooming cheek will bleach it quite.

And so the most prodigious hoard,
Here at your footstool be it stored,
In homage at your feet be laid   9315
The spoils with blood of battles paid.

So many chests I dragged before.
As many I could add, and more,
If but my presence you indulge,
The strongrooms shall with treasure bulge.   9320

For you did scarce ascend the throne.
And to the godly form alone
All wisdom, opulence, and power
Already bow, already cower.

All this I tightly clutched as mine,   9325
Now it is loose and turned to thine,
I thought it valid, worthy, fair,
But now I hold it cheap and bare.

All wilted what I held with pride,
As meadow grasses mowed and dried: 9330
Deign to return with one gay glance
Its former worth to it at once!

FAUST.   Forthwith remove the burden boldly seized
   And unrewarded go, though unreproved.
   All that the castle harbors in its depth   9335
   Is hers already. Proffering her particulars
   Is useless. Go and posit hoard on hoard
   In ordered piles. Create the unseen splendor's
   Exalted likeness! Make the vaultings gleam
   Like the fresh skies, prepare her paradises   9340
   Of simulated life devoid of life.
   Outrun her progress with the ready bloom
   Of rug on rug unwound; her tread be met
   By dainty ground, her gaze by that supreme
   Lucence which dazzles all but the divine.   9345
LYNCEUS.   Master's bidding needs small wit,
   Servant makes light work of it:

Does not flesh and treasure all
Own this sovereign beauty's thrall?
All the host has long been tame,   9350
Broadswords all are dull and lame,
Sun himself but wan and cold
By the splendor of her mold,
By the riches of her face
All is empty, all is base.   9355
   [*Exit.*]

HELENA.   [*to* FAUST] I wish to speak with you, but first ascend
  To join me at my side. The vacant place
  Calls for the master and ensures my own.
FAUST.   Be pleased, exalted Queen, to entertain
  My faithful kneeling homage first; this hand   9360
  Which to your side would raise me, let me kiss it.
  Confirm me as co-regent of your realm
  Uncognizant of borders, and procure yourself
  Adorer, server, warder, all in one!
HELENA.   Manifold wonders do I see and hear,   9365
  Amazement strikes me, I have much to ask.
  Yet I desire instruction why that man's
  Converse rang strange to me, both strange and pleasing.
  Each sound seems to accommodate the other,
  And as one word repairs unto the ear,   9370
  There comes another to caress the first.[4]
FAUST.   Already pleased, then, with our nation's parlance,
  You will be surely ravished by their song,
  Which satisfies the ear and sense profoundly.
  But we had safest practice it at once;   9375
  Exchange of speech allures it, calls it forth.
HELENA.   Tell, then, how can I speak with such fair art?
FAUST.   It's easy, it must well up from the heart,
  And when the breast with longing overbuoys,
  One looks about and asks—
HELENA.   who shares our joys.   9380
FAUST.   Now seeks the mind no forth or back from this,
  Alone the present moment—
HELENA.   is our bliss.
FAUST.   Is hoard, high prize, possession, earnest, and
  Whence comes its confirmation?
HELENA.   From my hand.

CHORUS.   Who would reprehend our princess   9385
  If she grants the castle's lord
  Kind accommodation?
  For confess, all of us are

---

4. Goethe alludes to the historical origin of rhyme in Western poetry.

Prisoners, not for the first time
Since the lamentable downfall   9390
Of Ilion, and the fearsome
Labyrinthine voyage of grief.

Ladies to men's love accustomed
Are not hesitant choosers,
Rather expert judges.   9395
Be it shepherds,[5] gold of ringlet,
Be it fauns of swarthy bristle,
As occasion may afford,
To their limbs' luxuriance
Equal claim they grant in full.   9400

Near and nearer they are seated,
One to the other inclining,
Shoulder to shoulder, knee to knee,
Hand in hand they sway
Over the throne's   9405
High-upholstered opulence.
Nor does majesty forbear
Before the people's eyes
Private affections'
Exuberant displaying.   9410

HELENA.[6]   I feel so far away and yet so near,
   And all too gladly say: Here am I! Here!
FAUST.   Breathless I seem, my tongue is faltering, chained;
   This is a dream, and place and day have waned.
HELENA.   I feel of life bereft, and yet so new,   9415
   Warp to your weft, unto the stranger true,
FAUST.   Probe not in thought the choicest lot, I ask!
   Were it but short, existence still is task.

PHORCYAS.   [making a violent entrance][7]
            Spelling-books of love construing,
            Playfully bemused in wooing,   9420
            Vainly cooing, idly suing,
            But there is no time, I say.
            Blind to distant lightning's flaring.
            Listen to the trumpet blaring,
            Ruin is not far away.   9425
            Menelaus is descending

---

5. The theme of pastoral poetry anticipates the final section of the *Helena*.
6. This sequence of couplets constitutes the consummation of the love between Faust and Helena
   and also a moment of fulfillment for Faust that would appear to satisfy the terms of his wager
   with Mephistopheles.
7. Through a parody of their rhyming, Phorcyas-Mephisto intentionally disrupts the illusion of fulfillment that Helena and Faust have achieved. Thematically, this intrusion corresponds to a similar
   occasion in the affair with Gretchen in the "Garden Pavillion" of Part One, lines 3207 ff.

On your camp with swarms unending,
Arm yourselves for bitter fray!
By victorious throngs encumbered,
Like Deiphobus dismembered,   9430
You will rue your courting play.
Trash will dangle by a halter,
Then in this one at the altar
Fresh-honed axe will find its prey.

FAUST.   Uncouth disturbance! Insolently it intrudes;   9435
In hazards even I dislike insensate vehemence.
No messenger so fair but that ill tidings foul him;
You, ugliest of all, delight but in ill news.
But this time you shall not prevail; with empty breath
You agitate the air. There is no danger here,   9440
And even danger would appear an idle threat.
     [*Signals, explosions from the towers, trumpets and coronets, military
     music, powerful forces marching through.*][8]

FAUST.[9]   No—heroes' muster you shall savor,
Ringed in assembly here at length:
For none deserves the ladies' favor
But who can guard them with most strength.   9445
     [*to the commanders, who separate from the columns and approach*]
Incessant in your silent raging,
Sure warrant of the foeman's doom,
You, blossom of the North unaging,
And you, the Orient's pith and bloom.

In steel encased, aglare with flashes,   9450
The band that shattered realms and states,
They tread the earth, it quakes with crashes
And in their wake reverberates.

At Pylos we secured our landing,
Hoary Nestor is no more,   9455
All petty royal troops disbanding,
The boundless host sweep all before.

---

8. A theatrical illusion suggesting that the forces of the castle are rallying to the defense against the approaching army of Menelaus. Critics have argued a historical allusion here to the invasion of the Peloponnesus by Guillaume de Villehardouin early in the thirteenth century, when the principalities of Morea and Achaia were established on the model of the French feudal order, where Norman, French, and German chieftains received fiefdoms (see lines 9466–73).

9. Three separate historical periods are intentionally blended here: 1) the Dorian invasion of Mycenaean Greece in the era shortly after the Trojan War, when all the centers of the heroic age fell and Greece entered an era of darkness and barbarism; 2) the migrations of the Germanic tribes across Europe from the north and east (lines 9448 ff.), gradually overrunning the ancient world during the early centuries of the Christian era; and 3) the invasion of the Peloponnesus by the armies of the crusades in the thirteenth century. An allusion may also be intended to the intervention of European interests in the Greek War of Independence from the Turks in the early 1820s, the war in which Lord Byron was fighting when he died of fever in 1824 (which event is commemorated in connection with the death of Euphorion; see notes preceding lines 9903 and 9907).

And forthwith from the fastness yonder
Thrust Menelaus back to sea;
There let the vagrant lurk and plunder,   9460
Such was his bend and destiny.

As dukes I am to hail you captains,
Thus Lacedaemon's queen ordains;
Bring hills and dales for her acceptance,
And yours shall be the Empire's gains.   9465

Corinthus' bays, Teutonic warrior,
You shall defend with shield and wall!
You, Goth, shall guard by trusty barrier
Achaia with her gorges all.

To Elis set the Frank in motion,   9470
The Saxon be Messene's bane,
The Norman go to sweep the ocean
And found great Argolis again.

Then each will hold domestic charter,
Let might and fury outward rage;   9475
But over all enthroned be Sparta,
The Queen's redoubt from age to age.

While you she sees enjoy securely
Domains untouched by want or blight,
You at her feet will seek as surely   9480
Legitimation, law, and light.
[FAUST *descends; the* PRINCES *form a circle about him to hear more
closely his orders and directions.*]

CHORUS.   He who craves for himself the prize of beauty,
          Valiant above all,
          Wisely let him look to weapons;
          Blandishing, he won indeed   9485
          What is highest on earth;
          Yet calmly he owns it not:
          Shrewdly stealthy ones unblandish,
          Boldly brigands snatch her from him;
          Let him take thought to prevent it.   9490

          Hence our Prince I praise,
          Esteem him high before others,
          For so allying himself, brave and astute,
          That the stalwart stand obedient,
          Biding his every beck.   9495
          Loyal, they do his bidding,
          Each for his own good as much

As rendering thanks to the ruler,
Winning loftiest fame for either besides.

For who will snatch her now   9500
From the potent possessor?
His she is, and ungrudged to him let her be,
Doubly ungrudged by us, whom alike with her,
With surest wall he encompassed within,
With mightiest host without.   9505

FAUST.† The patrimony here awarded—
To each an opulent domain—
Is grand; let them depart to guard it,
We hold the center for our reign.

And they will vie to shelter, reckless   9510
Of leaping waves on every side,
Un-island, thee, by slender hilly necklace
To Europe's last redoubt of mountains tied.

Before all others by the raptured
Of every tribe accounted blest,   9515
Thou sun-land, for my queen recaptured,
That gazed at her the earliest.

When to Eurotas'[1] reedy whispers
She broke in radiance from the shell,
Her noble mother's, twin-born sister's   9520
Eyesight outstabbing by her spell.

This land, all else for you forsaking,
Presents the finest of its worth;
Than all the globe—yours for the taking—
Prefer, o choose the native earth.   9525

Though on its ridge the jagged peak must suffer
The solar arrow with a frigid glare,
The boulders have a blush of green to offer,
The goat collects a toothsome frugal share.

The torrent tumbles, fed by countless rillets,   9530
Already gorges, rises, alps are green.
On meadows stippled with a hundred hillocks
Sedately spreading woolly flocks are seen.

One at a time, with measured caution striding,
The hornèd beasts approach the sheer ascent,   9535

---

1. The river that flows south from Arcadia to Sparta, in which Leda was seduced by Zeus in the form of a swan.

But, shelter for the whole of them providing,
The rocky wall with scores of caves is rent.

There Pan[2] protects them, nymphs of life inhabit
The dewy shade that bushy cliffsides lend,
And serried trees, for higher regions avid,   9540
Their laced array of branches skyward send.

Hoar forests these! The oaktree looms defiant,
And limb on willful limb enjagging jut;
Rising in purity, the maple pliant
Sports with its load, with syrup juice aglut.   9545

And tepid milk in shady rounds of quiet
Wells up maternally for child and lamb;
Not far is fruit, the lowland's ripened diet,
And honey trickles from the hollowed stem.

Their miens, their gazes are serener,   9550
Bliss is inherited like wealth,
Each is immortal in his own demesne here,
They live contented and in health.

One watches the enchanting child[3] attaining,
Down flawless days, to father's vigor then,   9555
And stands amazed—the question still remaining
If these are gods or mortal men?

So was Apollo shaped to shepherd likeness
That of their fairest, one resembled him;
Where Nature works within her own pure cycle,   9560
All worlds link up without an interim.
[*sitting next to her*]
     Thus things for me, for you, have blithely ended,
Let all the past be put behind and gone;
O feel from the all-highest god descended,
To that first world you appertain alone.   9565

No cramping fortress would be rightful
Abode for you; in wiltless verdure set,
To make our residence delightful,
Arcadia encircles Sparta yet.

For refuge lured to smiling harbors,   9570
You fled to fortune's blithest kiss!

---

2. The goat-god who traditionally dwells as lord within the woods and groves of the pastoral landscape.
3. An allusion to Euphorion, whether or not Faust himself explicitly refers to the as yet unborn offspring of his union with Helena.

These thrones are changing into arbors,
Arcadian-free shall be our bliss!
[*The scene changes completely.*]

[*Closed arbors leaning against a number of rock caverns. A shady
grove extends up to the steep cliffsides surrounding all.* FAUST *and*
HELENA *are not in evidence. The* CHORUS *lies bedded here and there,
asleep.*][4]

PHORCYAS.

Who knows how long the maidens have been slumbering,
Nor can I tell if what with perfect clarity   9575
My eyes beheld, they even dared perchance to dream.
So I will wake them. Let the youngsters be amazed;
You bearded ones no less, who sit and hide below
To find the key at last to wonders worth belief.
Arise! Arise forthwith and swiftly shake your locks;   9580
Have done with sleep, stop blinking, and attend to me![5]

CHORUS.[6]

Speak, say on, and let us hear it, what of marvels has befallen,
We are eager, and the harder to believe your tale, the better,
For we find it poor amusement to be staring at these boulders.

PHORCYAS.   Hardly rubbed your eyes, you children, and already
    time is slow?   9885
Listen, then: within these caverns, in these grottos, in these
    arbors,
Screen and shelter have been granted, as to lovers in an idyll,
To our liege lord and our lady.

CHORUS.   What, within there?

PHORCYAS.   Yes—secluded
From the world, but me alone they summoned for discreet
    attendance.
Thus distinguished, I stood by, but as befits a trusted servant,   9590
I took care to find employment some way off, turned here and
    thither
Seeking mosses, worts, and tree-bark, privy to their divers
    virtues;
Thus the two remained alone.

CHORUS.   One might think that these enclosures harbored worlds
    of space within them,

4. Goethe here employs a deep stage that distinguishes between a proscenium and a perspective set
   with receding areas that represent caves (in one of which Faust, Helena, and Euphorion are later
   discovered). Such a theatrical structure was first developed in Italy in the late-sixteenth century,
   especially in conjunction with the musical drama imitating Greek tragedy that subsequently
   emerged as opera. The most famous example of this new theater was the Teatro Olympico in
   Vicenza, designed by Andrea Palladio (1518–80), which Goethe visited at the start of his Italian
   journey in the fall of 1786. The visual style of this pastoral stage set may be modeled also on the
   landscapes of the French painter Nicolas Poussin (1594–1665).
5. The sleeping Chorus is borrowed from Aeschylus's *Eumenides*, where the Furies are discovered
   asleep around the altar of Apollo at Delphi, having been put under a spell by the god.
6. Goethe imitates (using again trochaic tetrameter) the parabasis of ancient Greek comedy, where
   the Chorus interrupts the dramatic continuity of the play in order to address the audience directly
   in sharp, satirical terms.

Wood and meadow, lakes and freshets; truly, fairy yarns you
    spin![7]   9595
PHORCYAS.†   So they do, you callow children! Those are recesses
    unfathomed,
Hall on hall, and court on courtyard, these I pensively explored.
All at once, a peal of laughter echoes through the hollow
    spaces;
As I watch, a boy is tumbling from our lady's lap to master's,
From the father to the mother, tender frolic, fond caresses,   9600
Teasing love's inane endearments, playful shouts and gay
    exulting
Variously strike my ear.[8]
Naked genius unfledged, a faun exempt of faunic coarseness,
He will leap on solid ground, which like a springboard
    countervailing
Flings him upward high and higher, till by second, third
    rebounding   9605
He has touched the lofty vault.

Anxiously his mother calls him: leap and spring as fancy takes
    thee,
But forbear to fly, untrammeled flight is not vouchsafed to thee.
Thus the honest father warns him: in the earth inheres
    resilience
Which will buoy thee up, if only thou adhere to it on tiptoe,   9610
Like the son of earth, Antaeus, it will strengthen thee at once.
Then he skips upon this rocky mass of cliff, and from its edges
To another, keeps rebounding as a driven ball will bounce.

All at once, though, he has vanished in a jagged gorge's crevice,
Lost, it seems to us, already. Mother moans and father comforts, 9615
I attend with frightened shrugging. Then, what startling
    reappearance!
Were there treasures hidden yonder? Drapings striped as if with
    flowers
Worthily adorn him now.[9]
Tassels swinging from his forearms, ribbons fluttering at his
    bosom,
In his hand the golden lyre, exactly like a little Phoebus,   9620
Quite serenely he approaches the projecting edge; we marvel.
And his parents from enchantment each fall in the other's arms.

---

7. The sense of a fairy tale expressed here by the Chorus is crucial for the entire last section of the
    Helena.
8. Euphorion was the name of the son born to Helena and Achilles from their posthumous marriage
    on the blessed island of Leuce (see also lines 7435 and 8876 ff.). As we know from his conversation
    with Eckermann of December 20, 1829 (see below), Goethe intended Euphorion to personify
    the spirit of poesy; such is also indicated by the Chorus when they address him as "poesy pure"
    (line 9863).
9. The transformation of Euphorion is associated by Phorcyas-Mephisto with the theme of buried
    treasure, so central to *Faust.* Euphorion emerges from the depths like a youthful Phoebus Apollo,
    the god of poetry and song.

For what fulgence at his head, a gleam not easily determined,
Whether glittering gold or blaze of high prepotency of mind.
Thus he is proclaimed already by his boyish look and bearing   9625
Heir apparent to all beauty, sentient members agitated
By imperishable music; and as such you are to hear him,
And as such you will behold him in unique astonishment.

CHORUS.   Is this a marvel to you,
           Offspring of Crete?   9630
           Have you not hearkened then
           To lessons from poets' lips,
           Never have heard of Hellas',
           Nor of Ionia's
           Hoary ancestral hoard   9635
           Of goldly and kingly lays?

           All that can ever befall
           These late days of our own
           Apes but with dolorous sound
           Glories of yore.   9640
           Paler is what you relate
           Than the delightful lies—
           More worthy of faith than is truth—
           Fabled of Maia's son.

           He, of finely wrought strength,   9645
           Whom, as a babe scarce born,
           Gossiping gaggle of nurses,
           Sluggish of wit,
           Swaddled in purest down
           Strapped into exquisite wraps;   9650
           Nimble and strong, though, the scamp
           Smoothly withdrew his lissom
           Supple elastic limbs,
           Leaving behind in his stead
           The sedulous purple encumbrance,   9655
           Calmly, a vacant shell;
           As when a butterfly, rid
           Of worn-out chrysalid armor,
           Thrills the unfolded wings
           And boldly its wayward course   9660
           Tumbles through sun-drenched air.

           So does he, the adroitest,
           Patron spirit to be
           Ever to thieves and rogues,
           And all intent upon vantage.   9665
           This he forthwith enacts
           By most dexterous arts.

Nimbly the Lord of the Sea
He robs of the trident, slily in Ares' sight
Steals from its sheath the sword,   9670
Bow, too, and arrow from Phoebus,
And from Hephaistos his tongs;
All but snatches the lightning of Zeus, his father,
But for awe of its fire;
Albeit Eros he bests   9675
At foot-tripping wrestling game,
And from Cytherea's breast
Trims, as she hugs him, the belt.[1]

[*String music, charming and melodiously pure, resounds from the
cavern.*[2] *All take notice and soon appear deeply moved. From here
on until the noted pause, the action is accompanied throughout by
full-toned music.*][3]†

PHORCYAS.   Listen, strings, in sweet collusion!
                 Quick, be rid of fable play,   9680
                 Ancient deities' confusion
                 Put to rest, it had its day.

                 Rest, old tales, for none will miss you,
                 We demand a higher art:
                 From the living heart must issue   9685
                 What would work upon the heart.
          [*She withdraws toward the cliffs.*]
CHORUS.   Dreaded one, if you are giving
                 To these graceful notes your ear,
                 We, so lately saved for living,
                 Melt away in joyous tears.   9690

                 Let the sun withdraw its lustre,
                 Once the dawn within unfolds,
                 From our hearts we amply muster
                 What the whole wide world witholds.

---

1. The young Hermes' most famous theft is not mentioned here. On the day of his birth, he stole
   the cattle of Apollo, and then, to appease the older god, presented him with the gift of the lyre,
   which he had invented from the shell of a tortoise. From this lyre, Apollo fashioned music and,
   because of it, subsequently became the god of poetry. Euphorion emerges from the crevice into
   which he disappeared carrying a golden lyre (line 9620), "like a little Phoebus."
2. To sound—at least at first—as if played by Euphorion on his golden lyre.
3. From this point to the death of Euphorion, the drama is transformed into opera, and the text
   becomes no more than a libretto for music that Goethe hoped would be written but that never
   has been. This libretto was influenced in significant ways by a fragmentary sequel to Mozart's
   Magic Flute that Goethe wrote in the late 1790s. Goethe envisioned music for *Euphorion*—as he
   stated to Eckermann (February 12, 1829; see below)—in the manner of Mozart's *Don Giovanni*.
   Yet the style of the opera is not tragic but burlesque. The heroic grandeur of Euphorion is
   transformed into a kind of puppet play that elicits only a sense of resignation and irony from Faust
   and Helena and from Phorcyas-Mephisto and the Chorus. Goethe's opera-ballet, like a grandiose
   shadow game, finally dissolves into thin air.

[HELENA, FAUST, *and* EUPHORION, *costumed as described above.*]

EUPHORION. Hearken childish songs a-singing,   9695
            Take at once your proper parts;
            As you watch my rhythmic springing,
            Skip parentally your hearts.

HELENA.   Love, to lavish human blessing,
            Links a noble pair-to-be;   9700
            Godly joy to be expressing,
            He creates a peerless Three.

FAUST.   All is then enacted rightly;
            I am yours and you are mine;
            See us interwoven tightly   9705
            As we must by love divine.

CHORUS.   Joy of many ages' reaping
            In their offspring's gentle glow
            On this pair descended heaping.
            Oh, their union moves me so!   9710

EUPHORION. Now let me leap
            Skyward and higher,
            Now let me skip,
            Buoyant desire
            Takes me already   9715
            Into its grip.

FAUST.   But steady, steady!
            Not danger courting,
            Lest heedless sporting
            Bring fall and ruin,   9720
            Our dearest son
            Be our undoing.

EUPHORION. I will not linger
            In earthbound clinging,
            Let go my finger,   9725
            My locks let go,
            Let go my garments,
            For they are mine!

HELENA.   Oh, think, believe us,
            Here you belong!   9730
            How you would grieve us,
            How sorely wrong
            The fair and hard-won
            Mine, His, and Thine.

CHORUS.   Soon slips, I fear me,   9735
                 The knot benign!

HELENA AND FAUST.
                 Bridle, oh, bridle,
                 Your parents urge,
                 Impulses' idle
                 Vehement surge!   9740
                 Grace our lonely
                 Rustic purlieus.

EUPHORION.   For your sakes only
                 Patience I use.
              [*tracing a winding path through the* CHORUS *and drawing it away to dance*]
                 This merry tribe I ring,   9745
                 Airy and light.
                 Now is the tune I sing,
                 My movement right?

HELENA.   Yes, you do well to dance,
                 Leading these lovely ones,   9750
                 Your arts employ.

FAUST.   Would we were done with this!
                 I in this flightiness
                 Can take no joy.

              [EUPHORION *and* CHORUS, *dancing and singing, move in intricate evolutions.*]
CHORUS.   Ah, as you wave your arms'   9755
                 Well-shapen pair,
                 Your shining ringlets' charms
                 Shake in the air,
                 As to the ground you put
                 Lightly your tender foot,   9760
                 As limb on limb repair
                 Gracefully here and there,
                 You have achieved your goal,
                 Enchanting child;
                 Have all our hearts beguiled,   9765
                 Won every soul.
              [*Pause.*]

EUPHORION.   You be as many
                 Does of light tread,
                 Be from this cranny
                 To new game led;   9770

　　　　　　　I'll do the hunting,
　　　　　　　You make escape.

CHORUS.　　　You, to disarm us,
　　　　　　　Need not be lithe,
　　　　　　　Nothing would charm us　　　　　　　9775
　　　　　　　Or seem as blithe,
　　　　　　　As to embrace you,
　　　　　　　Beauteous shape!

EUPHORION.　Through arbors scurry,
　　　　　　　By boulders hurry,　　　　　　　　　9780
　　　　　　　What's lightly gathered,
　　　　　　　That I disdain,
　　　　　　　But danger weathered
　　　　　　　I count for gain.

HELENA AND FAUST.
　　　What self-will! What reckless bounding!　　9785
　　　Hopeless to contain his daring.
　　　There, like hunting-horns resounding,
　　　Din through woods and valleys blaring;
　　　What abandon! Wanton roar!

CHORUS.　　[hurrying up one by one]
　　　Racing on, he left us lagging,　　　　　　9790
　　　Passed us by with scorn uncaring,
　　　There he now approaches, dragging
　　　Just the wildest in the score.

EUPHORION.　[carrying up a young girl]
　　　Here this sturdy lass I carry,
　　　For my pleasure and enjoyment,　　　　　　9795
　　　Her reluctant breast I press
　　　In delightful forced caress,
　　　Her resisting lips I kiss,
　　　Proving strength and willfulness.

GIRL.
　　　Stop! Within this body, pirate,　　　　　　9800
　　　Pluck and strength are not at bay,
　　　Spirits like your self-will fire it,
　　　Not so lightly brushed away.
　　　He who thinks me lost and cringing,
　　　On his arms too much relies!　　　　　　　9805
　　　Hold me fast, here I go singeing
　　　Striplings for a lark—surprise!
　　　　[She kindles and flares up as a flame.]

Follow me to regions aerial,
Follow me to somber burial,
Catch me, catch the vanished prize.   9810

EUPHORION.   [*shaking off the last of the flames*]
Cliffside's confining press,
Forest and brush,
Pall in their narrowness,
Am I not young and fresh?
Winds, they go soaring,   9815
Waves, they are roaring,
These from afar I hear,
Fain would be near.

[*He leaps ever higher up the cliffs.*]
HELENA, FAUST, AND CHORUS.
Would you ape the chamois' ways?
Horrid downfall we are dreading!   9820

EUPHORION.
Ever upward am I heading,
Ever farther must I gaze.
        Now I know where I stand!
        In the isle's heartland,
        Pelops' domain within,   9825
        Mainland and ocean kin.

CHORUS.   Would you not gently
        Dwell amid wood and peak?
        Let us contently
        Vine arbors seek,   9830
        Grape-rows the hillocks bound,
        Fig-green and apple-gold;
        Fast to the lovely ground,
        Lovely one, hold!

EUPHORION.   Dream ye of peaceful day?   9835
        Let dream who may!
        War! does the watchword sound,
        Triumph! the hills resound.

CHORUS.   He who in peace invites
        Scourges of war,   9840
        Hope and all dear delights
        He must abhor.

EUPHORION.   Those whom this country bore,
        Dangers behind, before,
        Boundless and bold of mood,   9845

　　　　　Prodigal of their blood:
　　　　　To her undaunted sons'
　　　　　Sacred resource,
　　　　　To the embattled ones
　　　　　May it add force![4]　　　　　　　　　　　9850

CHORUS.　　Lo, aloft, and climbing higher!
　　　　　Yet his image never shrinks,
　　　　　Gleam of armor his attire,
　　　　　As of bronze and steel it winks.

EUPHORION.　No escarpment, no immuring,　　　　　9855
　　　　　Trust oneself is all one can;
　　　　　Fortress firm for sure enduring
　　　　　Is the iron breast of man.
　　　　　Lightly armed, field every human
　　　　　If unconquered ye would dwell;　　　　　9860
　　　　　Be an amazon each woman,
　　　　　Every child a sentinel.

CHORUS.　　Poesy pure, august,
　　　　　Heavenward rise it must,
　　　　　Glittering, starry bright,　　　　　　　9865
　　　　　Ever so far, its light
　　　　　Ever to reach us still,
　　　　　Hear it we ever will,
　　　　　Ever delight.[5]

EUPHORION.　No, not as child in arms arriving,　　9870
　　　　　As youth in armor let it be,
　　　　　In ardent spirit soon contriving
　　　　　To join the strong and bold and free.
　　　　　Forth fare!
　　　　　Now, there,　　　　　　　　　　　　9875
　　　　　To fame the open road I see.

HELENA AND FAUST.
　　　　　Into living ushered scarcely,
　　　　　Scarce to smiling day inured,
　　　　　Yet by dizzying stairs perversely
　　　　　Into parlous spaces lured?　　　　　　9880
　　　　　Are then we
　　　　　Naught to thee,
　　　　　Lovely bonds a fantasy?

---

4. An obscure passage syntactically. The opening subordinate phrases stand in opposition to the main clause of the last two lines ("resource" and "force"; "the embattled ones" and "undaunted sons"), and the pronoun of the final line presumably refers to the war, which Euphorion champions.
5. The only instance in the entire Euphorion sequence of his being explicitly associated with the spirit of poesy.

EUPHORION.   Across the ocean hear it thunder,
                There gorge on gorge reverberate,   9885
                Hear host on host, aclash, asunder,
                Deal thrust on thrust in throes of fate.
                And death's thrall
                Is duty's call,
                Fate decreed it once for all.   9890

HELENA, FAUST, AND CHORUS.
                What appalling, grim insistence!
                Is it death, then, duty wills?

EUPHORION.   Shall I watch at idle distance?
                No! I share their needs and ills.

THE FORMER. Death is by heady   9895
                Rashness foretold!

EUPHORION.   Still! And already
                Pinions unfold![6]
                Thither! I must! I must!
                Grant me the flight!   9900
[*He launches himself upon the air; his garments carry him for an instant, his head shines, a trail of light marks his wake.*]
CHORUS.   Icarus! Icarus![7]
                Piteous plight.
[*A beautiful youth plunges down at the parents' feet; one seems to recognize in the body a familiar figure;*[8]† *but the corporeal vanishes at once; the aureole rises like a meteor to the sky; robe, cloak, and lyre are left behind.*]
HELENA AND FAUST.
                Must agony overwhelm
                Delight so soon?

EUPHORION'S VOICE.   [*from the deeps*]
                Mother, in this dim realm   9905
                Let me not dwell alone!
   [*Pause.*]

CHORUS.   [*dirge*][9]   Never lonely—Wheresoever
                Dwelling (we do not mistake you),

---

6. Euphorion's assertion that his wings here unfold for flight is contradicted by the stage direction following, which indicates unambiguously that he is suspended momentarily by his garments only.
7. The son of Daedalus, a craftsman of ancient Crete, who tried to escape with his father on artificial wings that melted when he flew too near the sun.
8. George Gordon, Lord Byron (1788–1824). (See the conversation with Eckermann of July 5, 1827, below.) For Goethe, Byron embodied the modern spirit of poetry that we now call Romantic.
9. In his conversation with Eckermann of July 5, 1827 (below), Goethe noted that the Chorus here completely abandons its role. Nothing remains of Greek drama or even of the *Helena*, as Goethe pays his poetic tribute to the dead Byron. (See first note 1, p. 241.)

As you quit the day forever,
None of these our hearts forsake you.   9910
Tears and dirges gladly sparing,
Envious, we sing your praise:
Song and soul were fine and daring
Both in bright and dreary days.

Born to easeful earthly station,   9915
High of lineage, great of gift,
Soon, alas! his own damnation,
Youthful blossom roughly reft.
Worldly insight clearer, harder,
Tuned to every heartstring's tone,   9920
Finest women's loving ardor,
And a music all his own.

But you rushed most vehemently,
Heedless, into tangling flaw,
Fell afoul incontinently   9925
Of propriety and law;
Yet at last exalted yearning
Lent to native courage weight,
Splendid laurels to be earning
You were minded—not so Fate.   9930

Who succeeds? That query dismal
Muffled Destiny leaves moot,
When misfortune most abysmal
Strikes the bloodied people mute.
Yet afresh new anthems sow them,   9935
Stand in mourning bowed no more:
For the soil again will grow them
As it ever has before.
[*Complete pause. The music ends.*]

HELENA.   [*to* FAUST][1]
An ancient truth, alas, is proved once more through me:
That beauty and good fortune are but fleetly joined.   9940
Severed is now the bond of life like that of love,
Lamenting both, I grievingly pronounce farewell!
And one last time I fling myself into your arms.
Persephoneia, gather in the boy and me.
[*She embraces* FAUST; *her corporeal substance vanishes, robe and
veil are left in his arms.*]
PHORCYAS.   [*to* FAUST] Hold fast what of it all remains to you.   9945
Do not release the robe. Already demons
Are plucking at its corners and would like

---

1. Helena, implicitly acknowledging her break with Faust, speaks once again in iambic trimeter.

To snatch it down to Hades. Hold it fast!
It is the goddess, whom you lost, no more,
Yet godly still. Make use of the exalted   9950
Inestimable boon and rise aloft,
It bears you swiftly over all that is base
Across the ether, for as long as you may endure.
We meet again, far, passing far from here.
        [HELENA'S *garments dissolve into clouds, surround* FAUST, *lift him*
        up, and drift past with him.]

PHORCYAS.   [*gathers up* EUPHORION'S *robe, cloak, and lyre from the*
        ground, steps up to the proscenium, raises up the exuviae,
        and speaks]
Still fortunately these endure!   9955
The flame is vanished, to be sure,
Yet leaves the world in no distress.
Enough remains to consecrate the poet,
Stir guildsmen's greed, collegial pettiness;
And, ready talent lacking to bestow it,   9960
I can at least lend out the dress.
        [*She seats herself in the proscenium against a column.*]
PANTHALIS.
Make haste now, girls! now that we are well rid of spells,
The Old-Thessalian crone's chaotic thrall of mind;
Likewise the swirl of much-confounded tinkling notes,
Blurring the ear, more sorely still the inner sense.   9965
Downward to Hades! For you saw the Queen make haste
With measured pace that way. Let forthwith in her prints
The footsteps of her loyal maidens now be set.
We find her at the throne of the Inscrutable.
CHORUS.   Queens, to be sure, find their pleasure wherever;   9970
        In Hades, even, they take pride of place,
        Proudly joined to their peers,
        In Persephone's innermost counsels;
        But we, in the background,
        Deep in asphodel meads,   9975
        Companioned to lanky poplars
        And barren willows,
        What pastime have we?
        Whispering, bat-fashion,
        Twitters, unpleasing, eerie.   9980
PANTHALIS.
He who has earned no name, nor strives for noble things
Belongs but to the elements, so get you gone!
I yearn to join my Queen; in merit not alone,
But in our loyalty we live as persons still.
        [*Exit.*]

ALL.   Restored are we to the light of day,   9985
                Persons, indeed, no longer,
                That we feel, we know.
                But never to Hades will we return.
                Ever-live Nature
                Lays to us spirits   9990
                As we to her, full-valid claim.

A PART OF THE CHORUS.²†   We within these myriad branches'
          whispery quiver, breezy floating,
    Lure and dally, softly tempting, up the rootwork founts of living,
    To the twigs; and now with foliage, now with blossom all-
          abundant,
    We adorn the fluttering ringlets free to prosper in the air.   9995
    Falls the fruit, at once forgather lustily both flock and people
    For the grasping, for the tasting, briskly striding, keenly pressing,
    Bowing one and all about us as before the earliest gods.

ANOTHER PART.³   To these cliffsides' polished mirror gleaming far
          into the distance,
    Undulating, nestling gently and caressingly we cling;   10000
    Hearken, listen to each sound, the notes of songbirds, reedy
          fluting,
    Be it Pan's dread voice, reply is ever ready to go forth;
    Zephyrs breathe, we breathe in answer, roll the thunders, ours
          go rolling
    Stunning in reverberation, threefold, tenfold, after it.

A THIRD PART.⁴   Sisters! Livelier of spirit, we pursue the brooks'
          swift courses;   10005
    For the hillocks in the distance tempt us with their rich
          adornment,
    Down and ever down, we water, ever welling and meandering,
    Now the meadow, now the pastures, soon the garden round the
          house.
    There the cypresses' slim tapers point it out above the
          landscape,
    Rising to the ether over span of shore and watery mirror.   10010

<hr>

2. The first group of the Chorus is transformed into tree nymphs (Dryads) such as Mephistopheles encountered outside the cave of the Phorcyads in the "Classical Walpurgis Night" (lines
   7959 ff.).
3. The second group becomes mountain nymphs (Oreads) such as Mephistopheles also encountered
   in the "Classical Walpurgis Night" (lines 7811 ff.).
4. The third group becomes water nymphs (Naiads) such as those that appeared at several points in
   the "Classical Walpurgis Night": the Nymphs in the reeds at the Peneios (lines 7263 ff.); the
   Sirens of the Aegean (lines 7156 ff. and 7495 ff., and throughout the final section); and perhaps
   even the Nereids and Dorids who participated in the festival of Galatea.

A FOURTH PART.[5]   Range you others where you fancy, we
     encompass, cling with rustling
To the fully planted hillside where the vine greens on its staff;
There through days and hours the vintner's indefatigable
     passion
Lets us see the fondest fervor's ever dubious reward.
Now with hoe and now with mattock, now at heaping, pruning,
     binding,   10015
He will pray to all the gods, the sun-god, though, to most avail.
Bacchus stirs himself, the pampered, little for his loyal servant,
Rests in arbors, lolls in caverns, trifling with the youngest faun.
All that ever yet he needed for his daydreams' semi-trances
Ever waits for him in wineskins, kept for him in butts and
     pitchers.   10020
Right and left in coolness hidden for eternities of time.
But when all the gods have readied, Helios above the others,
Airing, moisting, warming, blazing, cornucopias of grape,
Of a sudden life resurges where the vintner worked in quiet,
Bushes swish and brush each other, rustles run from stock to
     stock.   10025
Baskets creaking, buckets rattling, shoulder-hampers groaning
     off,
All toward the mighty wine-press, for the treaders' sturdy dance;
That is when the sacred bounty of the luscious pure-born
     berries,
Rudely trampled, foams and splatters, all commingling foully
     squashed.
Smiting now the ear, the cymbals' and the timbrels' brazen
     clangor   10030
Hail the wine-god Dionysus out of mysteries revealed;
Forth he steps with goat-foot satyrs, whirling nymphs of goat-feet
     also,
All between, with strident braying blares Silenus' long-eared
     beast.
Naught is spared! The cloven talons trample down all chaste
     decorum,
Senses all are whirled a-stagger, stunned the ear to deafness
     dread.   10035
Drunken groping for the goblets, glutted sodden heads and
     paunches,
Still at pains is one or other, only to increase the turmoil,
For to garner fresher vintage, older skins are swiftly drained![6]

---

5. The fourth group of the Chorus enters directly into the vines and the grapes, grows to ripeness, and becomes the spirit of wine produced from the harvest, identical with the god Bacchus, or Dionysus.
6. In the closing section of the passage, Dionysian revels burst loose in overwhelming force, complete with all the drunken company of the god, the satyrs and nymphs, the fat-bellied Silenos and his ass. A totally new tone enters the choral song, as all order and control is destroyed and drunken chaos ensues.

[*The curtain falls.*]

[PHORCYAS, *in the proscenium, rears herself to giant stature, but steps down from the buskins and casts off mask and veil, revealing herself as* MEPHISTOPHELES, *in order to provide in an epilogue such comment on the play as might be necessary.*][7]

---

7. Mephistopheles seems to intend an epilogue, which he would speak as he removes his costume, buskins, mask, and veil, rearing up to gigantic proportion—one recalls the monster that emerged from the poodle, and the devil from the monster, in the first study scene of Part One.

ACT IV

High Mountains

Sheer, jagged pinnacles. A cloud drifts up, settles against the cliff, sinks down onto a projecting ledge. It divides.[1]

FAUST. [*steps forth*]†
    The most profound of solitudes beholding underfoot,
    I circumspectly tread the margin of these peaks,   10040
    Dismiss my aerial engine, which on cloudless days
    Has spirited me gently over land and sea.
    It slowly separates from me without dispersing.
    The essence forges eastward in compacted train,
    The admiring eye pursues it, in amazement lost.   10045
    It parts in floating, undulating, changeably;
    Yet would adopt a shape . . . Yes! I am not deceived!
    On sun-gilt holstery in wondrous splendor laid,
    Of titan size, indeed, a godlike female form,
    I see it well! Resembling Juno, Leda, Helena,   10050
    In what majestic loveliness it wavers in my sight.
    Alas, too soon deformed! Distended, shapelessly amassed,
    It hulks at orient like a distant arctic range,
    Its glamor mirroring deep sense of fleeting days.[2]

    About my breast and brow a shining band of mist   10055
    Still hovers, though, exhilarating, tender, cool.[3]
    Now lightly, hesitantly, it ascends, higher and higher,
    Takes form. Am I received by an enchanting shape,
    As of long-lost, most cherished boon of earliest youth?[4]
    The inmost heart's primordial treasures rise again,   10060
    Aurora's[5] love, winged impetus it means to me,
    The swiftly felt, first, scarcely comprehended glance,
    That, caught and held, outglittered any gem.
    Like beauty of the soul, the lovely image is enhanced
    And, undissolving, wafts aloft into the ether,   10065
    Drawing away with it the best my soul contains.[6]

---

1. The cloud formed from Helena's garments has carried Faust to high rocky peaks somewhere in the Alps. Compare the setting of this scene to "Charming Landscape," which begins Part Two. Faust's monologue also recalls his comments there, lines 4679–727.
2. The form of the Feminine has withdrawn to the eastern horizon, where it hovers over icy summits in the shape of a gigantic woman.
3. In contrast to the cumulus, this cloud is a cirrus.
4. A schema to Act IV indicates that the contrast of these two clouds is intended to symbolize for Faust the contrast between Helena and Gretchen. (See interpretive notes.)
5. Aurora, goddess of the dawn, signifies Faust's first love, Gretchen.
6. The ascent of this cloud prefigures the final ascent in "Mountain Gorges" (lines 12094–5), where Faust's spirit follows the penitent soul of Gretchen.

[*A seven-mile boot*[7] *pads onstage; another follows presently:* MEPHIS-
TOPHELES *dismounts. The boots hurry on.*]

MEPHISTOPHELES.†   Now that was rapid transport for us![8]
But tell me, what are you about?
Debarking in the midst of horrors,
In grimly yawning rock redoubt?   10070
Though not this very spot, I know it well,
For properly this was the pit of hell.[9]

FAUST.   Of foolish legends you are never short;
We're in for yet another weird report.

MEPHISTOPHELES.   [*seriously*]
When the Almighty—I know well wherefore—   10075
From air did banish us to depths of wrath,[1]
Where all about us from a glowing core
Eternal blazes ate their flaming path,
We found ourselves amid excessive brightness
Pent up in most uncomfortable tightness.   10080
The devils all together started coughing,
Blew out from upper and from nether offing;
Hell swelled with acid stench and sulfur reek,
What press of gas there was! It reached a titan peak,
So that at last the level earthen crust,   10085
Thick as it was, burst with the rending thrust.
The cloth has now been given a new tweak,
What was the base one time, is now the peak.
On this the proper recipes are grounded
By which the top and bottom are confounded.   10090
For we escaped the seething servile pool
To supereminence of aerial rule.
It is an open secret closely sealed,
To gentiles only late to be revealed. [*Ephesians vi.12*][2]

FAUST.   To me the mountain mass lies nobly mute,   10095
The whences and the whys I don't dispute.
When Nature by and in herself was founded,
In purity the earthen sphere she rounded.
In summit and in gorge did pleasure seek,
And threaded cliff to cliff and peak to peak;   10100
Then did she fashion sloping hills at peace
And gently down into the vale release.

---

7. A fairy-tale device borrowed from the seven-league boots in the story of Tom Thumb by Charles
   Perrault (1628–1703).
8. An ironic allusion perhaps to Luke 1.39, "Mary rose in these days and went into the hill country
   with haste."
9. According to popular superstition, mountains were formed when devils coughed in hell. Recall
   the theme of volcanic explosion in the "Classical Walpurgis Night."
1. An allusion to the fall of the angels with Lucifer after they rebelled against God, for which see
   Milton's *Paradise Lost* (Books 1 and 6).
2. "For our wrestling is not against flesh and blood, but against the powers, against the world rulers
   of this darkness, against the spiritual hosts of wickedness in the heavenly places." The biblical
   references in the last two acts of Part Two were added by Goethe's associate and literary advisor,
   F. W. Riemer (1774–1845).

All greens and grows, and to her gay abundance
Your swirling lunacies are sheer redundance.

MEPHISTOPHELES.   Oh yes! . . . that seems as clear as day to you,   10105
But to a witness it is just untrue.
Why, I was there when down below us, scalding
With tumbling streams of flame the chasm swelled;
When Moloch's hammer,[3] cliff to boulder welding,
Whole mountain fragments far abroad propelled.   10110
And still the lands with alien masses stare;
Who can explain the force that hurled them there?
Philosophers have shaped no concept for it,
There lies the stone, they simply must ignore it.
And quite in vain the best of brains were racked.—   10115
Alone the artless common people know
And are not fooled by intellect;
Their wisdom ripened long ago:
A wonder! here the Devil's in respect.
My wanderer, with simple faith for crutch,   10120
To Devil's Rock, to Devil's Bridge[4] will trudge.

FAUST.   It's quite a fascinating thing to hear
How devils look upon the natural sphere.

MEPHISTOPHELES.   Be Nature as it is! What do I care?
It's *point d'honneur!*—Beelzebub[5] was there.   10125
It is by us great things are made and broken,
Upheaval, chaos, violence! this be your token!—
No more with ambiguities to tease you—
Tell me, did nothing on our surface please you?
You have surveyed immeasurable stretches,   10130
The kingdoms of this world and all their riches; [*Matthew iv*][6]
And yet, insatiable as you are,
You've felt no appetite so far?

FAUST.   Yes! One great thing did tempt me, one.
You guess at it!

MEPHISTOPHELES.   That's quickly done.   10135
I'd choose a typical metropolis,
At center, bourgeois stomach's gruesome bliss,
Tight crooked alleys, pointed gables, mullions,
Crabbed market stalls of roots and scallions,
Where bleeding joints on benches lie,   10140
Prey to the browsing carrion-fly;
For there at any time you'll find
Ado and stench of every kind.
Then boulevards and spacious squares

---

3. Moloch, god of the Ammonites (Leviticus 18.2), is the most warlike of the devils in Milton's
   Paradise Lost (1.392 ff., 2.43 ff.); in Klopstock's *Messiah* (2.352 ff.), he dwells in the mountains.
4. An allusion to the natural geological formation of this name in the Alps on the road through the
   St. Gotthard pass.
5. See note to line 1334.
6. "Again, the devil took him to a very high mountain, and showed him all the kingdoms of the
   world and the glory of them" (4.8).

To flaunt aristocratic airs;   10145
And on, past any gate's resistance,
The suburbs sprawl into the distance.
There I'd rejoice in coaches gliding,
The noisy here-and-thither-sliding,
Eternal forward-backward hustle,   10150
The scattered ant-heap's teeming bustle.
And when I rode, and when I strolled,
By myriads I should be extolled,
Be ever central, ever lead.
FAUST.   You offer me not bread but pebbles.   10155
One cheers to see the people breed,
In snug accustomed manner feed,
Grow lettered even, start to read—
And all one does is raising rebels.
MEPHISTOPHELES.   Then I would build myself, as grandees ought,   10160
A pleasance at a pleasant spot,
Hill, forest, lowland, lea, and grange
To splendid gardens rearrange.[7]
In foils of foliage, velvet meadows,
Perspective pathways, artful shadows,   10165
Cascades through rock with rock combined,
And waterworks of every kind;
Where here will soar the awesome central fountain,
There hiss and piss wee bagatelles past counting.
Snug little cabins then I'd have them build,   10170
With fairest ladies to be filled,
And timeless pleasures to be wooed
In charmingly gregarious solitude.
Ladies, I say; for to me, once for all,
But in the plural women count at all.   10175
FAUST.   Tawdry and up-to-date! Sardanapal![8]
MEPHISTOPHELES.
What goal then, let me guess, won your allegiance?
A high and bold one, I surmise.
Much closer as you soared to lunar regions,
They must be where your fancy flies?   10180
FAUST.   By no means! Still this planet's soil
For noble deeds grants scope abounding.
I sense accomplishments astounding,
Feel strength in me for daring toil.
MEPHISTOPHELES.   So now you crave a hero's fame?   10185
This tells from whose high company you came.
FAUST.   Sway I would gain, a sovereign's thrall!
Renown is naught, the deed is all.

---

7. The following description suggests the formal gardens of Baroque and Rococo estates, as in the
   park at Versailles during the eighteenth century.
8. The king of Assyria, a legendary reveler and debaucher and the titular hero of Byron's play
   Sardanapalus (1821), which had been dedicated to Goethe.

MEPHISTOPHELES.   Yet poets will arise to render
    Unto posterity your splendor,   10190
    Praise folly, folly to engender.
FAUST.   Of all this nothing I concede.
    What do you know of human need?
    All sting and gall, what can your mind
    Know of the longings of mankind?   10195
MEPHISTOPHELES.   Have it according to your bent!
    Confide to me your crotchets' full extent.
FAUST.   On the high sea my eye was lately dwelling,
    It surged, in towers self upon self upwelling.
    Then it subsided and poured forth its breakers   10200
    To storm the mainland's broad and shallow acres.
    This galled me—showing how unbridled blood
    By passionate impulse in rebellious flood
    To wry perversity of temper blights
    The liberal mind which cherishes all rights.   10205
    I thought it chance, gazed on with sharp intent,
    The wave held on, then rolling backward went,
    Back from the proudly conquered goal it came;
    An hour would lapse, but to repeat the game.
MEPHISTOPHELES.   [ad spectatores]
    These are not novel tidings to my ears,   10210
    I've known of it these hundred thousand years.
FAUST.   [continuing, with passion]
    Forward it steals, and in a myriad starts,
    Sterile itself, sterility imparts;
    It swells and grows and rolls, and spans
    The noisome vacancy of dismal strands.   10215
    There wave on wave imbued with power has heaved,
    But to withdraw—and nothing is achieved;
    Which drives me near to desperate distress!
    Such elemental might unharnessed, purposeless![9]
    There dares my spirit soar past all it knew;   10220
    Here I would struggle, this I would subdue.

    And it is possible!—Surge as it may,
    Past every hill it winds its pliant way;
    However boisterously it cavorted,
    Small height will proudly loom to thwart it,   10225
    Small depth profound attraction holds.
    Straight in my mind plan upon plan unfolds:
    Earn for yourself the choice, delicious boast,
    To lock the imperious ocean from the coast,
    To shrink the borders of the damp expanse,   10230

9. Faust's concern with the waste of energy involved in the flux of the tides echoes the argument of
    a work that Goethe read while composing this scene, *Tableau of the Baltic Sea* by Catteau-
    Calleville (1812).

And gorge it, far off, on its own advance.
This, step by step, my mind led me to see;
This is my wish, in this dare further me!

[*Drums and warlike music at the audience's back in the distance,
from the right.*]

MEPHISTOPHELES.   How easy! Do you hear far drums resound?
FAUST.   War once again! The sane detest the sound.   10235
MEPHISTOPHELES.   War, peace, what matter. The endeavor
To feather one's own nest is clever.
You watch, you crouch, you pounce upon your rabbit:
The opportunity is there, Faust—grab it!
FAUST.   That puzzle-box put back upon the shelf!   10240
In plain and brief, what's up? Explain yourself.
MEPHISTOPHELES.   Upon my tour I could not help observing
That the poor Emperor's plight is most unnerving;
You know him—when we entertained him,
With counterfeit of wealth sustained him,   10245
He thought the world his for a song.
You see, he came into his title young;
He ventured to conclude at random
It would be easy to combine,
Desirable, and altogether fine,   10250
To govern and enjoy in tandem.
FAUST.   A grave mistake. Who is to order ought
In ordering his bliss to find.
His soul with high design is fraught,
But what—must be revealed to no man's mind.   10255
What to his trustiest in whispers is propounded
Is brought about, and all the world's astounded.
Thus he remains the one on whom all leans,
The worthiest—; incontinence demeans.[1]
MEPHISTOPHELES.   No fear! He did not stint himself—not he!   10260
Meanwhile the realm broke up in anarchy,
Where large and small made war the length and breadth,
Where brother brother put to flight, to death,
Where castle warred on castle, city on city,
Burgher on noble, feuding without pity,   10265
The bishop even with his chapter and flock.
They would draw arms as soon as look.
Churches knew blood and death, town gates once crossed,
Merchant and wanderer were as good as lost.
And all grew vastly bold, for living meant   10270
Dog must eat dog—and so, somehow, it went.
FAUST.   Went, limped and fell, stood up once more to reel

---

1. The final phrase here has been much disputed, on the incorrect assumption that Faust here rejects the principle of enjoyment (*Geniessen*: here, "incontinence"), which has motivated his activity from the outset of the drama. The contrast intended is no different from that between government and enjoyment mentioned in line 10251.

And took a clumsy tumble, head over heel.

MEPHISTOPHELES.   This state of things no one was to deplore,

Each one was able, each one meant to score.   10275

The merest pawn would for a rook show off;

Until at last the best had had enough.

The most resourceful rose with one accord

And said: "He who can give us peace is lord.

The Emperor cannot, will not—let us choose,   10280

Let a new Emperor new life infuse,

Make fresh the world and safe for men

So none will suffer, none abuse;

And peace and justice wed again."[2]

FAUST.   Sounds holy.

MEPHISTOPHELES.   Right! Such moves the clergy launches,   10285

They were securing their well-nourished paunches.

The clergy more than others took their side.[3]

Revolt swelled up, revolt was sanctified.

So that our Emperor, whom we gave delight,

Is here drawn up, perhaps for his last fight.   10290

FAUST.   I feel for him, he was so good and open.

MEPHISTOPHELES.

Come, let's look in; while there is life, there's hoping.

Let's free him from this narrow valley!

A thousand rescues brings a single sally.

Who knows how yet the cards may stack?   10295

And back in luck, he'll have his vassals back.

      [*They climb across the foothills and inspect the disposition of the
      troops in the valley. Drums and warlike music resound from below.*]

MEPHISTOPHELES.   I see that the position's well secured;

We add our bit, and triumph is assured.

FAUST.   What could our intervention mend?

It's fraud! Vain magic, sleight of hand!   10300

MEPHISTOPHELES.   It's stratagem that wins the battle!

You'll keep yourself in higher mettle

If you consider your ambition.

If we preserve the Emperor's throne and land,

You may kneel down here and petition   10305

As fief from him the boundless strand.

FAUST.   As many things as you've been through—

Go on and win a battle, too.

MEPHISTOPHELES.   No—you shall win it! For this show

You are the Generalissimo.   10310

FAUST.   Yes, that would be the proper rank!

Give orders where my knowledge is a blank.

---

2. An allusion to Psalms 85.10, "Righteousness and peace have kissed each other."
3. The clergy oppose the Emperor because their possessions are threatened by anarchy. In the outline of Part Two dictated in 1816 (see below), Goethe indicated that Faust would wage war against the monks after the death of his and Helena's son. A remnant of that original plan may be apparent in the dilemma of the Emperor as described here.

MEPHISTOPHELES.   Leave to the General Staff the worry,
   And the Field Marshall won't be sorry.
   Battle disorder—long I sensed it,   10315
   And battle order promptly drew against it,
   From primal mountains, primal human force;
   Happy the man who garners this resource.
FAUST.   What moves in arms there down the glen?
   Did you stir up the mountain men?   10320
MEPHISTOPHELES.   No, no—like Quince I just withdrew
   The quintessence of the whole crew.[4]
      [*Enter* THE THREE MIGHTY MEN (*Samuel ii. 23.8*).][5]
MEPHISTOPHELES.   Why, there my lads are coming, see?
   Of much disparate ages, you can tell,
   Of different garb and panoply;   10325
   They ought to serve you pretty well.
   [*ad spectatores*] The kids now fancy the historic
   Knight's armor and the vizor's clatter;
   And as the louts are allegoric,
   You all will like them that much better.[6]   10330
PUGNACIOUS.   [*young, lightly armed, colorfully dressed*]
   Let anyone as much as eye me,
   Right in the kisser I will blip 'em,
   And those that chicken out and fly me,
   I catch by their back hair and flip 'em.
RAPACIOUS.   [*mature, well armed, richly dressed*]
   Just picking fights is nursery stuff,   10335
   You might as well be bashing boards;
   Just go for pickings fat enough
   And ask the questions afterwards.
TENACIOUS.   [*elderly, heavily armed, unclothed*]
   With that affairs are hardly bettered,
   A goodly pile is quickly scattered,   10340
   And life will wash it down the drain.
   Takers are smart, but keepers saner;
   Rely upon the old campaigner,
   You won't be clipped of it again.
      [*They descend as a group.*]

---

4. An allusion to Peter Quince in Shakespeare's *Midsummer Night's Dream*, who, as author, director, and manager of the play performed by the tradesmen of Athens, was its "quintessence"; stressed on the first syllable.
5. An allusion to "the three mighty men" who are named as fighting in the army of King David: Jashobeam, Eleazar, and Shammah. They have apparently been summoned by Mephistopheles from hell.
6. An allusion to modish chivalric and Gothic novels and plays popular during the later Romantic period in Germany.

In the Foothills†

Drums and martial music from below. The EMPEROR'S *tent is being pitched.*

EMPEROR. COMMANDER-IN-CHIEF. AIDES.[1]

COMMANDER-IN-CHIEF.   The concept still appears well-grounded   10345
  To have withdrawn to this convenient dale
  The whole force, tightly massed and bounded;
  I firmly trust we shall prevail.
EMPEROR.   We now must see how it turns out;
  This yielding irks me, though, this all-but-rout.   10350
COMMANDER-IN-CHIEF.
  Be pleased to look at our right flank, o Sire.
  Just such terrain as strategists admire;
  Passable hills, yet not unduly so,
  Advantageous to us, traps to the foe.
  We, half concealed, on wavy ground at large;   10355
  The cavalry dare not attempt a charge.
EMPEROR.   This leaves but praises for my part;
  Here may be tested brawn and heart.
COMMANDER-IN-CHIEF.   Here, in the central meadow's flat terrain
  You see the phalanx[2] poised in fighting vein.   10360
  High in the air the halberds glint and blaze,
  Catching the sunbeams through the morning haze.
  How ominously heaves the mighty square
  With thousands all afire to do and dare!
  This should attest their massive force for you;   10365
  I look to them to cleave the foe in two.
EMPEROR.   This handsome view I never had before.
  Worth double of its strength is such a corps.
COMMANDER-IN-CHIEF.   Of our left flank I offer no report,
  Stout heroes occupy the rocky fort.   10370
  The cliffs which now with glittering armor stare
  Protect the stronghold's vital thoroughfare.
  I see an unsuspecting hostile force
  Already founder on a bloody course.
EMPEROR.   There they come marching up, my two-faced kin,   10375
  Who called me uncle, cousin, brother then,
  And robbed, by mounting licence of their own,
  Of might the scepter, and of awe the throne,
  Laid waste the realm by mutual enmity,

1. This battle scene, like the funeral games in Homer's *Iliad* or the war in Heaven in Milton's
   Paradise Lost, imposes a sense of spectacle and cosmic show upon the reader. Here, as elsewhere
   in *Faust*, Mephistopheles (with his three infernal henchmen) unleashes the demonic powers in
   the battle. Much of the dramatic and poetic technique of this scene reflects the tradition of
   Baroque drama and, especially, Shakespearean history plays.
2. A body of heavily armed infantry formed in close, deep ranks and files with joined shields and
   long lances.

And now in rebel concert fall on me.   10380
The rabble wavers in uncertain spirit,
Then breaks and rushes where the currents steer it.
COMMANDER-IN-CHIEF.
Here hastes a good man down the rocky slope,
Sent for intelligence; success, I hope!
FIRST SCOUT.   Yes, our mission is well ended,   10385
            And it was by ruse and pluck
            That both there and back we wended;
            But we bring but little luck,
            Many swear pure dedication,
            As some loyal bands do still;   10390
            But excuse for hesitation:
            Inner ferment, civil ill.
EMPEROR.   To save its skin is egoism's all,
Not debt of love, not duty's, honor's call.
Do you not judge, when your account is due,   10395
That neighbor's fire³ will leap to your house too?
COMMANDER-IN-CHIEF.   Down climbs the second in the interim,
But wearily—he shakes in every limb.
SECOND SCOUT.   First we smilingly detected
            Rank disorder's riotous throes;   10400
            Then abruptly, unexpected,
            A new Emperor arose.⁴
            Now in predetermined manner
            Trots the multitude to battle;
            Once unfurled the lying banner,   10405
            All come flocking.—Sheep and cattle!
EMPEROR.   A rival Emperor profits me—I feel
My sovereignty's never been more real.
The armor, first but as a soldier borne,
With more exalted purpose now is worn.   10410
At every feast, as brilliant as it was,
Danger I missed, for lack of other flaws.
When you advised to tilt at ring and hole,
My heart beat high, for jousting throbbed my soul.
And had you not dissuaded me from war,   10415
A hero's aureole had graced me long before.
I felt my spirit sealed with hardihood
When mirrored in that realm of fire I stood.⁵
The force blazed out at me with hideous clutch,
It was but make-believe—but grand as such.   10420

---

3. See Horace, *Epistles* 1.18.84: "It's your concern when your neighbor's wall is ablaze."
4. The appearance of a rival emperor to challenge the authority of the true Emperor may be
   borrowed from a corresponding theme in Shakespeare's *Richard III* and *Richard II*, where in each
   case the king is challenged and overthrown by a rival for the throne because of an abuse of royal
   privilege and power.
5. See the Emperor's disguise as Pan in the Carnival Masque (lines 5987–6002).

Of feats and fame I have been dimly dreaming,
Now I make up the fault of wanton seeming.

[*The heralds are dispatched to challenge the* RIVAL EMPEROR. *Enter* FAUST *in armor, with half-closed visor,* THE THREE MIGHTY MEN,[6] *armed and attired as earlier.*]

FAUST.   We join you, and I hope, unblamed; indeed,
Precaution counts no less without a need.
You know the mountain folk[7] reflect and pore,   10425
Versed in the scripts of rock and nature lore.
The spirits, long estranged from lowland sites,
Prefer more than before the craggy heights.
They mutely toil through intricate crevasses
In rich metallic vapors' noble gases;   10430
In ceaseless separating, testing, blending
Their every urge to new invention bending.
With the fine finger of spiritual passion
Their delicate transparent shapes they fashion;
Then, in the crystal's timeless silence furled,   10435
They see the progress of the upper world.
EMPEROR.   I've heard this and believe it true, but how,
My worthy man, can this concern us now?
FAUST.   The Sabine sorcerer of Norcia,[8] Sire,
Is your devout and honorable squire.   10440
What hideous doom on him was grimly calling,
The faggots crackled, flames flicked up, appalling;
The well-dried logs, heaped criss-cross all about,
With pitch and sulfur-covered rod eked out:
All hope, from man, God, devil was in vain,   10445
But Highness burst apart the glowing chain.
In Rome it was. Still deeply in your debt,
His heart is ever mindful of you yet.
He quite forgot himself from that hour on,
He asks the star, the depth, for you alone.   10450
He urged as foremost care, and made it ours,
To stand by you. Great are the mountain's powers;
There Nature acts prepotently and free,
Thick-witted clergy scolds it sorcery.
EMPEROR.   On days of feasting, when the guests we hail,   10455

6. See note preceding line 10323. The supernatural devices in the battle that follows were borrowed in part from Sir Walter Scott's *Letters on Demonology and Witchcraft* (1831), which Goethe was reading in December, 1830, and January, 1831.
7. An allusion to creatures of folk superstition such as goblins, gnomes, elves.
8. This story of the Sabine sorcerer of Norcia (an Italian town infamous for sorcery) is presumably invented by Faust (and Mephistopheles) to deceive the Emperor into accepting their demonic assistance. Reference to this is also made on two later occasions (see lines 10606 and 10988). Supposedly the Emperor, on the occasion of his coronation in Rome, pardoned this sorcerer, who was about to be burned to death. For this reason—so Faust claims—the sorcerer has since been devoted to the Emperor and now has conjured the mountain spirits to come to his aid.

The gladly entering gladly to regale,
We gaily see each new one's forward thrust
Compress the dwindling floor-space as it must.
How much more welcome still the honest figure
Who proffers for most present help his vigor   10460
At morning hour of such ambiguous valence
Because fate's scales hang over it in balance.
Yet at this solemn moment here, repeal
The valiant sword-arm from the willing steel,
Honor the hour which many thousands draws   10465
To march in arms for or against my cause.
Man trust but self! Who craves for throne and crown,
Let him in person merit such renown.
Be what arose against me now—the ghost
Which "Emperor" styles itself, duke of the host,   10470
Lord of our lands, our vassals' suzerain—
By My hand thrust among the dead again!
FAUST.   However turns the course of nemesis,
You do not well to stake your head like this.
Is not the helm adorned with plume and crest?[9]   10475
It shields the head which crowns our pluck with zest.
What could the limbs effect without the head?
For when it slumbers, all are laid abed,
If it is hurt, it lames the others' lives,
Who rise afresh when swiftly it revives.   10480
With speed employs its solid right the arm,
It lifts the shield to guard the skull from harm,
The sword observes its duty, nothing slow,
It strongly parries and returns the blow;
Part in their luck the sturdy foot is granted,   10485
And on the victim's neck is briskly planted.
EMPEROR.   Such is my wrath, the proud head I would treat
But as a new-made footstool for my feet![1]
HERALDS.   [returning]
                    Little honor, scant audition
                    We encountered in our questing,   10490
                    Of our nobly forceful mission
                    They made scorn as feeble jesting:
                    "Dust are all your Emperor's glories,
                    Valley echo's vacant chime;
                    To recall him smacks of stories   10495
                    Starting 'once upon a time' "
FAUST.   Now have their wish those ever, firm and true
Who were the best and took their stand with you.

---

9. There is a playful association here of the Emperor as head of state with the elaborately adorned
   helmet he wears in battle. (See the Pygmy Generalissimo in the "Classical Walpurgis Night,"
   lines 7644–53.)
1. An allusion to Psalms 110.1, "The Lord said unto my Lord [i.e., King David], sit thou at my right
   hand, until I make thine enemies thy footstool."

There nears the foe, yours keenly bide your wishes,
  Bid them attack, the moment is propitious.   10500
EMPEROR.   At this point I relinquish the command.
  [*to the* COMMANDER-IN-CHIEF]
  Let now your duty, Prince, be in your hand.
COMMANDER-IN-CHIEF.
  Then let the right dress lines and take the field!
  The enemy's left wing, just now ascending,
  Before their final step is done, shall yield   10505
  To youthful strength of loyalty defending.
FAUST.   Give your permission, then, for this live blade
  To step into the ranks of your brigade,
  To fuse with them in most pervasive way,
  And so allied, his robust sport display.   10510
  [*He points to the right.*]
PUGNACIOUS.   [*steps forward*]
  Who shows his face to me won't turn his back
  But with both jowls on him well-minced with mangling,
  Who turns his back will find a grisly slack
  Of neck and head and top-knot down it dangling.
  And if yours lay about them then   10515
  With swords and maces as I scythe,
  Then watch the foe, man over man,
  Drown in their own gore where they writhe.
  [*Exit.*]
COMMANDER-IN-CHIEF. Now let our center phalanx follow, steady,
  Launch shrewd assault with all the strength it can,   10520
  A little rightward, where our force already
  With fierce attack has discomposed their plan.
FAUST.   [*pointing to the middle one*]
  Accept this fellow, too, beneath your sway;
  He's lithe and sweeps all obstacles away.
RAPACIOUS.   [*steps forward*] High daring of the imperial side   10525
  With thirst for plunder be allied;
  And on one goal let all be bent:
  The rival Emperor's costly tent.
  He shall not long be boasting of his throne,
  I make the phalanx' forward edge my own.   10530
GRAB-SWAG.   [*sutler-woman, nestling against him*][2]
  Though I'm not spliced with him, for sure,
  He stays my dearest paramour.
  What harvest's ripened for our craws!
  Woman's a wild thing when she claws,
  In looting knows no law or shame;   10535
  In victory on! and anything's fair game.

---

2. No explanation is given for the appearance of this sutler-woman (though Goethe may have borrowed her from the corresponding figure in Schiller's verse prologue to the drama *Wallenstein*,
   "Wallenstein's Camp").

[*Exeunt both.*]
COMMANDER-IN-CHIEF.   As was to be foreseen, on our left flank
  Their right now falls in strength. Each man, each rank
  Will now repulse them as they fiercely mass
  To gain the rocky narrows of the pass.   10540
FAUST.   [*gesturing to the left*]
  Then, Sir, note this one too; for the strong arm
  To reinforce itself can do no harm.
TENACIOUS.   [*stepping forward*]
  Now finds the left all care dispelled!
  Where I am, what is gained is tightly held;
  In this my strength resides of old: 10545
  No lightning-bolt can break my hold.
      [*Exit.*]

MEPHISTOPHELES   [*descending from above*]
  Now watch how, in the background, masses
  From all the jagged rock crevasses
  Pour forth in arms, for space contesting,
  The narrow mountain paths congesting,   10550
  With helm and harness, sword and spear
  They form a bulwark in our rear,
  Poised to receive their battle task.
  [*under his breath, to those in the know*]
  Whence it all came, you must not ask.
  Of course, I was not slow to clear   10555
  The armories of all their gear;
  There they all stood, on foot or mounted,
  As if still lords of earth accounted;
  What knight, king, emperor was before
  Is empty snail-shell now, no more;   10560
  Specters caparisoned in many a piece
  Lend medieval times a pert new lease.[3]
  Whatever little imp hides up each cuff—
  For this time it looks genuine enough.
  [*Aloud*] Hear them beforehand seethe in anger,   10565
  And, jostling, clash with tinny clangor!
  The tattered flags surmounting the formations
  Have waited for fresh breezes with impatience,
  An ancient tribe stands by here, after all,
  Glad to be mingling in a modern brawl.   10570
      [*Fearful flourish of trumpets from above, noticeable wavering in the
      enemy army.*]
FAUST.   There glimmers the horizon darkling
  But here and there with telltale sparkling,
  A radiance ominously ruddy;

---

3. An anachronistic allusion to the early-nineteenth-century fad, especially among wealthy aristocrats,
of collecting medieval armor.

The weapons glint, already bloody,
The crags, the woods, the atmosphere,   10575
The whole of heaven interfere.
MEPHISTOPHELES.   Our right maintains its firm array;
I see, though, from among them jutting,
Our lithe Audacious, hugely strutting,
Abustle in his private way.   10580
EMPEROR.   A single arm I first saw flying,
Now there's a dozen flailing, plying,
This is not done in Nature's way.
FAUST.   Have you not heard of vapor bands[4]
Which waft along Sicilian strands?   10585
There, wavering clear, in light of day,
On mists of middle air projected,
By special redolence reflected,
A sight to marvel at appears:
Of cities here and thither shifting,   10590
Of gardens up and downward drifting,
As view on view the ether clears.
EMPEROR.   How suspect, though! I see appear
The glittering tip of each tall spear;
I see our line—on their bright lances,   10595
Each one, a flickering flamelet[5] dances.
This has too fey an air, I fear.
FAUST.   Your pardon, Sire, these are the last
Of spirit natures of the past,
The Dioscuri's lumen cast,   10600
By whom all mariners swore fast;
Their final strength they muster here.
EMPEROR.   But say: to whom are we beholden
For Nature's patently unfolding
For us enigmas without peer?   10605
MEPHISTOPHELES.   To whom but him, the lofty master[6]
Who in your destiny takes part?
Your foes' designs of dire disaster
Have exercised him deep at heart.
His gratitude will see you saved,   10610
Let even his own death be braved.
EMPEROR.   They were parading me with pomp and shout,
I counted now, and meant to try it out,
So I saw fit, without much thought or care,
To help that whitebeard to some cooler air.   10615
The thwarted clergy took it with long faces,
That caper scarcely raised me in their graces.

---

4. Fata morgana, familiar to Goethe from such works as Athanasius Kircher's *Great Work of Light and Shade* (1646).
5. Electrical discharge known as St. Elmo's fire, visible at the tips of masts of ships when they are struck by lightning in storms.
6. The sorcerer of Norcia, referred to below as "whitebeard" (line 10615). (See note to line 10439.)

Years after, am I to detect
This cheerful action's late effect?
FAUST.   You cast your bread upon the waters;   10620
Now heavenward your gaze incline!
Methinks He will despatch a sign,
Attend, its sense will soon be taught us.
EMPEROR.   An eagle drifts high in the firmament,
A griffin after him with dire intent.[7]   10625
FAUST.   Attend! this augurs well, I say.
The griffin is a beast of fable;
How could he flatter himself able
To match true eagles in the fray?
EMPEROR.   As I look on, they interloop   10630
In spacious circles—now, one swoop,
They're flying at each other's craws,
Rake breast and neck with cruel claws.
FAUST.   Mark how, bedraggled with his mauling,
The wicked griffin reaps but woe,   10635
And lion-tail adroop, is falling
From sight to high-woods far below.
EMPEROR.   May sign be equalled by event!
I mark it with astonishment.
MEPHISTOPHELES.   [*toward the right*]
Our assault, by much repeating,[8]   10640
Has the enemy retreating,
And, their fighting spirit failing,
To the right their lines are trailing,
Causing turmoil as they enter
Units of their leftward center.   10645
Our own phalanx' armored edges
Draw to right and drive their wedges
In that gap like lightning flashing.—
Now, like waves to tempest's lashing,
Foams the rage of equal forces,   10650
Fiercely clenched with matched resources;
When was stratagem more splendid?
Ours the battle-day here ended!
EMPEROR.   [*on the left, to* FAUST]
Watch! That side wakes grave suspicion,
Hazardous seems our position.   10655
No more stones flung down the edges,
Foes have gained the lower ledges,
Crests already stand deserted.

---

7. The eagle and the griffin represent, respectively, the Emperor and his rival, in the manner perhaps
   of heraldic coats of arms. For a similar augury predicting the outcome of battle, see Homer, *Iliad*
   12.200–9.
8. The following two speeches (lines 10640–63) are in four-stress trochaic meter, borrowed by
   Goethe from Spanish Baroque drama. This meter is also used in the opening scene of Act V,
   "Open Country" (lines 11043–142).

Now!—The foe, in mass concerted,
Nourishing his uprush steady,   10660
May have gained the pass already.
End result of impious striving!
Vain was all your arts' contriving.
  [*Pause.*]

MEPHISTOPHELES.   I see my ravens homing yonder,
What message might they bear, I wonder?[9]   10665
I greatly fear our issue fails.
EMPEROR.   What are these birds of ill about?
The struggle for the rock redoubt
Was where they set their sooty sails.
MEPHISTOPHELES.   [*to the ravens*]
Sit down, quite close, where I can hear.   10670
He is not lost who has your ear,
Your counsel, being sound, prevails.
FAUST.   [*to the* EMPEROR] You are aware of course of pigeons
Returning from remotest regions
To brood and food they cherish most.   10675
So here, but with a change of lease;
The pigeon mail may serve in peace,
But war commands the raven-post.
MEPHISTOPHELES.   A heavy bane appears to loom,
Look there! observe the signs of doom   10680
About our heroes' rocky rim.
The nearest heights have been percoursed,
And should the pass itself be forced,
Our chance of holding out is slim.
EMPEROR.   So I am swindled after all!   10685
I have been quailing in its thrall
Since first you snared me in that net.
MEPHISTOPHELES.   Take heart! We are not beaten yet.
Cool wins the final trick, not nervous;
Just near the end things may seem out of hand;   10690
I have my trusty scouting service,
Command that I may take command.
COMMANDER-IN-CHIEF.   [*who has joined them meanwhile*]
Your bond with these and close alliance
I bore with long and pained compliance,
No lasting luck can magic earn.   10695
I cannot turn this fight or mend it,
As they began it, let them end it,
And so my baton I return.
EMPEROR.   No, keep it for the better hours
That fortune may yet bless us with.   10700
That gargoyle makes me shrink and cower,

9. On the mythological source of the ravens, see note to line 2491.

He and his cozy raven kith.
[*to* MEPHISTOPHELES] The baton I can't award you,
You do not seem the proper man,
Command what help your arts afford you,   10705
And let things take what course they can.
    [*Exit into the tent with the* COMMANDER-IN-CHIEF.]

MEPHISTOPHELES.   I hope the bludgeon keeps him fit!
  We others would have little use for it,
  It had a cross of sorts stuck on.
FAUST.   What shall we do now?
MEPHISTOPHELES.   It's all done—   10710
  Now, cousins swart, to service fleet,
  Off to Great Mountain Lake, the Undines[1] greet,
  And ask them for the semblance of their flow.
  By arts inscrutable and feminine,
  They split the semblant from the genuine,   10715
  And all would swear that what is not is so.
    [*Pause.*]
FAUST.   The devastating way our ravens
  Must have beguiled those water maidens!
  Some rills already run, I see.
  From many a spur of rock all bare and arid   10720
  A scampering full-bodied spring is carried,
  All done for is their victory.
MEPHISTOPHELES.   This is the weirdest welcome yet,
  The boldest climbers are upset.
FAUST.   Already stream to stream roars strongly coupled,   10725
  From gorges they return once more redoubled,
  One flow now casts an arching swell,[2]
  At once it flattens to the rocky coaming,
  Now this, now that way thundering and foaming,
  And hurls itself by steps downhill.   10730
  What use their resolute, heroic lunging,
  The mighty flood engulfs them in its plunging.
  Its fury makes me shudder, too, and stare.
MEPHISTOPHELES.   I can see nothing of these watery lies,
  The spell bewilders only human eyes,   10735
  I am amused by the bizarre affair.
  In masses, whole platoons, away they bound,
  The fools think they are being drowned,
  They pant and snort while walking safe and sound,
  And ludicrously paddle on dry ground.   10740
  Now there's confusion everywhere.
    [*The* RAVENS *have returned.*]

---

1. Water spirits (see note to line 1272).
2. This passage (*Bogenstrahl*) indicates the formation of a rainbow, as in Faust's monologue in
"Charming Landscape" (lines 4721–7).

I shall commend you at the Master's[3] throne;
If now you would prove masters of your own,
Then hurry to the glowing smithy
Where sparks by dwarf-folk ever busy   10745
From stone and metal are retrieved.
Demand, with much persuasive chatter,
A fire, to glow, to beam, to spatter,
As in a lofty mind conceived.
True, summer lightning in the distance winking,   10750
Stars plunging down too fast for eyelid's blinking,
May happen any summer's night;
But summer lightning in the tangled briar,
Stars sizzling on wet ground and spitting fire,
That's hardly such a common sight.   10755
So don't you put yourselves to undue strain,
First make request for it, and then ordain.
    [*Exeunt the* RAVENS. *Things take the prescribed course.*]
MEPHISTOPHELES.   To foes obscurities profound!
And step by step on unknown ground!
On every hand an errant spark,   10760
Quick glare, to plunge in sudden dark.
All this is very fair and right,
Now for some noise to stoke the fright.
FAUST.   From musty halls the hollow weaponry
In open air feels newly strong and free;   10765
It's clanged and rattled up there for some time,
A wondrous and deceptive chime.[4]
MEPHISTOPHELES.
Quite right! there's no more holding them, it looks,
The air resounds with knightly donnybrooks,
As in idyllic times of yore.   10770
Pallettes' and brassarts' steely sheens,
Embodying Guelfs and Ghibellines,[5]
Renew at once their feuding hoar.
Fixed in hereditary groove,
Irreconcilable they prove,   10775
Now far and wide resounds the roar.
When all is said, it's party hate
Works best in every devil's fête,
Down to the very utmost horrors;
With sounds now hideously Panic,   10780
Now shrill and stridently satanic,
It spreads alarm through vale and forest.
    [*Sounds of warlike tumult in the orchestra, eventually changing to gay martial airs.*]

---

3. This reference to a "Master" is obscure. Some commentators claim it is Satan.
4. See lines 10554–64.
5. See note to line 4845.

The Rival Emperor's Tent†
A Throne, Rich Appointments

RAPACIOUS, GRAB-SWAG.

GRAB-SWAG. So we were first to get here, see?
RAPACIOUS. No raven flies as fast as we.
GRAB-SWAG. My, what a hoard is here piled up!   10785
  Where do I start? Where do I stop?
RAPACIOUS. The room is loaded fit to burst!
  I don't know what to reach for first.
GRAB-SWAG. That rug would suit me well, for sure;
  My pad is often sadly poor.   10790
RAPACIOUS. Here hangs a mace of steel with spikes;
  I have long hankered for the likes.
GRAB-SWAG. This scarlet cloak with golden seam,
  Of such I often used to dream.
RAPACIOUS. [taking the weapon]
  With this the job is quickly done.   10795
  One strikes him dead and passes on.
  You've piled so much upon your hunch,
  And nothing useful in the bunch.
  Leave all that rubbish in its place
  And take away this little case,   10800
  Or that one; nothing but pure gold,
  For army-pay, their bellies hold.
GRAB-SWAG. This thing is murder just to shift;
  I cannot carry it or lift.
RAPACIOUS. Hunch over, quickly! Bend your rump,   10805
  I'll heave it on your sturdy hump.
GRAB-SWAG. It's fit to break my back in two.
  Oh no! that's done it now for you!
      [The coffer falls and bursts open.]
RAPACIOUS. There lies the yellow gold in heaps;
  Jump to it, rake it up for keeps!   10810
GRAB-SWAG. [crouching down] Quick, fill my apron with the stuff!
  We still can carry off enough.
RAPACIOUS. Enough of that! Don't dawdle so!
      [She gets up.]
  That apron has a hole—oh no!
  Wherever you may stand or go,   10815
  Our treasure lavishly you sow.
AIDES. [of our EMPEROR] Who let you in this place of homage,
  In the imperial hoard to rummage?
RAPACIOUS. We risked our limbs, and life to boot,
  And claim our honest share of loot.   10820

Such is the rule in enemy tents,
We're soldiers, see, at all events.
AIDES.   That's not our view of soldierdom,
　Both fighting-men and thieving scum;
　To join our Emperor's company,   10825
　An honest soldier one must be.
RAPACIOUS.   That honesty's a windy thing,
　You call it "requisitioning."
　You, one and all, end up in clover,
　The trade salute is "hand it over."   10830
　[to GRAB-SWAG] Tote what you can, and on your way!
　We are unwelcome guests today.
　　[Exeunt.]
FIRST AIDE.   Say, why did you not promptly trim
　That fellow's shameless snout for him?
SECOND.   Somehow I lost my strength to clout him,   10835
　There was a spooky air about them.
THIRD.   Me too, my eyes gave out on me,
　It flickered so I could not see.
FOURTH.   There's something up, I don't know what:
　The whole day long it was so hot,   10840
　With such a sultry, dismal pall,
　The one would stand, the other fall,
　You groped about and struck a blow,
　And every lunge would fell a foe,
　Your eyes were hung about with mist,   10845
　Your hearing hummed and buzzed and hissed.
　And so it went, and now we're here,
　And how it came about, we've no idea.
　　[Enter the EMPEROR with FOUR PRINCES. The AIDES withdraw.]⁶
EMPEROR.   Be that as it may be! The enemy is shattered,
　The remnants of his rout in level country scattered.   10850
　Here stands the vacant throne, and treason's treasure-mound,
　Smothered in tapestries, constricts us all around.
　We, by our palladins in honoured ease protected,
　Imperially await the commonwealth's elected;
　Tidings of happiness arrive from every side: 10855
　Of cheerful loyalty and Empire pacified.
　Though interwoven with our fight there was some juggling,
　In essence it was still ourselves who did the struggling.
　Strange cases often favor fighting-men just so,
　A stone falls from the sky, blood rains upon the foe,   10860
　From rocky caverns issue wondrous chords resounding,

---

6. In this final scene of Act IV, the last part of *Faust* to be composed, Goethe makes use of the
　Alexandrine, consisting of a six-stress iambic line in rhymed couplets with a caesura after the third
　stress. The standard verse form of Baroque and neoclassical tragedy in the seventeenth and early-
　eighteenth centuries, derived from French drama, the Alexandrine had become associated with
　pompous and ceremonial public or political action. This scene complements the initial appear-
　ance of the Emperor with his counselors in Act I ("Imperial Residence," lines 4728 ff.).

Which have the foe's heart quailing, but set our hearts
     bounding.
The adversary lies, by lasting mockery chafed,
The victor, as he triumphs, lauds the grace vouchsafed.
And all intone, unasked, by their spontaneous choices,   10865
"Now let us praise the Lord," sung by a million voices.[7]
Yet for the highest prize, my pious glance I bid
Turn back into my heart, as else it seldom did.
A young, vivacious prince may have glad days to squander;
The years will teach him, though, the moment's weight to
     ponder.   10870
Hence I ally myself forthwith, without delay,
With you four worthy ones for house, estate, and sway.[8]
[to the first]
Yours was, o Prince, the host's astutely wrought complection,
Then, at decisive point, heroic bold direction;
Be active then in peace as may with peace accord,   10875
I name you Arch-Marshal, bestow on you the sword.

ARCH-MARSHAL.

Your trusty host, of late engaged on home disorders,
When it confirms Your throne and person at the borders,
Be it our privilege 'mid festive revelers massed,
In the ancestral hall to order your repast.   10880
Before you borne, beside you held, its shining splendor
Exalted majesty unceasing escort render.

EMPEROR.   [to the second]

He who with gallantry combines a gentle grace,
You! be Arch-Chamberlain; it is no easy place.
O'er all domestic staff you wield supreme observance,   10885
In whose internal strife I find indifferent servants;
Be henceforth honored your example and held blest
How one may please one's lord, the Court, and all the rest.

ARCH-CHAMBERLAIN.

It earns one grace to speed the lord's design exalted,
Be helpful to the best, nor even hurt the faulted,   10890
Be calm without deceit, clear without trickery,
If You see through me, Sire, that is enough for me.
May fancy in advance that feast-to-come engender?
At table, mine will be the golden bowl to tender,

---

7. A reference to Luther's German version of the Latin hymn "Te Deum laudamus," ascribed to St. Ambrose.
8. The following lines recapitulate the traditional investiture of the Holy Roman Emperor by the princes responsible for electing him: the Elector of Saxony serves as Chief Marshal, the Elector of Brandenburg as Chief Chamberlain, the Elector Palatine as Chief Steward, and the Elector of Bohemia as Chief Cupbearer. Traditionally, the three spiritual princes—the Archbishops of Mainz, Trier, and Cologne—also participated in the election, though only one Archbishop appears in this scene (the Chancellor of Act I, lines 4847 ff.). These princes correspond to the counselors who appear in Act I (the Chief Marshal would have been the Quartermaster; the Chief Chamberlain the Marshal; the Chief Steward the Treasurer; and the Chief Cupbearer, whose youth is emphasized, perhaps the Herald of the Carnival). Goethe was familiar with this ceremonial procedure from personal experience, having witnessed the coronation of Joseph II in Frankfurt in 1764.

Mine to receive Your rings, so at the jubilee   10895
Your hand refresh itself, as Your regard does me.
EMPEROR.   I am too grave of mind to ponder gay distraction,
But be it so! It too will further cheerful action.
[to the third]
You I appoint Arch-Steward! Thus henceforward be
Lord of the hunt, the game preserves and fowlery;   10900
At all times serve the choice of favorite dish I mention
As proffered by the month, prepared with due attention.
ARCH-STEWARD.   Most pleasant duty be for me a rigid fast
Till You enjoy the cheer of a select repast.
Your kitchen staff and I shall seek by joint persistence,   10905
To hasten on the season, nearer draw the distance.
You spurn the far and early which the board may boast,
It is the plain and hearty that You look for most.
EMPEROR.   [to the fourth]
Since unavoidably we talk of feast and revel,
The goblet-bearer you become, my young daredevil.   10910
Arch-Cupbearer, make sure now that our cellars stock
In lavish quantity fine malmsey, claret, hock.
But use restraint yourself, see that you are not tempted
By moment's chance and mirth to think yourself exempted.
ARCH-CUPBEARER.
Why, even youth matures to man's estate, my Prince,   10915
Before You are aware, once given confidence.
I too transport myself to that great festive morning,
The Emperor's serving board most fittingly adorning
With gold and silver bowls of state and circumstance,
For You the loveliest cup, though, choosing in advance: 10920
A lucent Venice-shell, wherein contentment huddles,
The wine's aroma gains in strength, but not befuddles.
Upon such wondrous gift one well may lean too hard,
Your Majesty's restraint, though, is superior guard.
EMPEROR.   What by unquestionable pledge I made your dower   10925
You heard with confidence upon this solemn hour.
The Emperor's word is great and any gift ensures,
Yet noble writ is needful for investitures,
Needful his hand and seal. For its due formulation
The moment brings the proper man to his right station.   10930
[Enter the ARCHBISHOP (ARCH-CHANCELLOR).]
EMPEROR.   When to the keystone is entrusted the great arch,
Then it is made secure against the ages' march.
Behold four Princes here! Already We expounded
Whereon the welfare of estate and house is founded.
Now shall what in Our realm at large may live and thrive   10935
Be laid, with weight and force, upon Arch-Princes five.
In lands they shall stand out above all other orders,
Wherefore I here and now extend their feudal borders
Out of the fiefs of those who turned from me of late.

I allocate to you many a fine estate,   10940
As well, the privilege to stretch afar your charter
As chance may offer, through reversion, purchase, barter;
Then, you shall wield untrammeled in your own domain
Whatever territorial rights to lords pertain.
Your verdicts passed as Lords Appellate shall be binding: 10945
There shall no recourse lie from your judicial finding.
Then, tax, rent, levy, impost, yours be without stint,
Royalties from safe-conduct, mining, salt, and mint.
For as my gratitude's most signal demonstration,
I raised you little short of the Imperial station.   10950
ARCHBISHOP.   Let me in all our names profoundest thanks intone,
    You make our might more firm and fortify your own.
EMPEROR.   Still higher trust the five of you I thought on giving.
    I live yet for my realm, and while I relish living,
    My noble forebears' chain draws thoughtful gaze instead   10955
    From active enterprise to what must loom ahead.
    I, too, in course of time must part from what I cherished:
    Then be the realm's Electors, and, old liege-lord perished,
    On sacred altar raise the new one, crown on brow,
    And peaceful then may end what was so stormy now.   10960
ARCH-CHANCELLOR.
    With humble bow, yet pride in depth of soul, we princes
    Obeisance make to you, earth's premier eminences.
    While loyal blood our veins amply percourses still
    We are the body which you animate at will.
EMPEROR.   Thus, in conclusion, be all hitherto instated   10965
    For every age to come, by writ perpetuated.
    Your sovereign tenure shall be absolutely free,
    Yet indivisible be it by Our decree.
    However you increased what by Our will was tendered,
    All shall to eldest sons in fullness be surrendered.   10970
ARCH-CHANCELLOR.
    I cheerfully confide this grant of gravest powers
    Forthwith to parchment, for the Empire's weal and ours;
    Our busy Chancery shall copy, seal, and date it,
    Your sacred signature, o Sire, corroborate it.
EMPEROR.   And so I give you leave, that each may go his way   10975
    In privacy to ponder this auspicious day.
        [*The* LAY PRINCES *depart. The* ARCHBISHOP *remains and speaks with
        rhetorical fervor.*]
ARCHBISHOP.
    The Bishop stays behind upon the Chancellor's leaving,
    Impelled to seek Your ear by most severe misgiving.
    His fatherly concern relief for you would seek.
EMPEROR.   At such a joyful hour, what apprehensions? Speak!   10980
ARCHBISHOP.   What bitter grief to me to find, at such an hour,
    Your consecrated head in league with Satan's power.
    Secure indeed upon the throne, as one may hope,

Yet woefully in scorn of God and Father Pope.
Apprised of it, his sacred judgment's swift conviction   10985
Will blight your sinful realm with bolts of interdiction.
He still has not forgotten how Your word unbound
That doomed magician[9] on the day that you were crowned.
To Christendom's great harm, your diadem's effulgence
Shed on that head accursed the ray of first indulgence.   10990
Beat, then, Your breast, divert from the ill-gotten bliss
Forthwith a moderate mite back unto holiness.
That sweep of hills whereon your tent was then erected,
Where by pernicious spirit-league you were protected,
Where avid ear you leant unto the Prince of Lies,   10995
This consecrate to sacred cause in pious wise;
With mountain and dense forest to their furthest bounding,
With sloping alps of green to pastures lush redounding,
With limpid lakes ateem with fish, with countless rills
Which, busily meandering, plunge down the hills;   11000
Then the broad dale itself, with paddocks, meadows, shires;
You will find mercy if contrition thus aspires.
EMPEROR.   By my grave fault I am so grievously dismayed,
At your discretion let the boundary be laid.
ARCHBISHOP.   Firstly! the space by such iniquity polluted   11005
Be forthwith for Our Lord's high service instituted.
Its sturdy masonry the mind's eye swiftly builds,[1]
A shaft of morning sun the choir already gilds,
The edifice expands and grows, the cross-shape forming,
The nave looms up and on, the faithful spirits warming,   11010
There, to the worthy portals cluster the devout,
As first through hills and dales the call of bells rings out.
From heavenly spires it rings, as they to Heaven aspire,
The penitent approach, rebirth their pure desire.
To that great consecration—may the day come soon!—   11015
Your presence, Sire, will add the highest grace and boon.
EMPEROR.   May such a lofty work be pious mind's profession,
To praise the Lord our God, and cleanse me of transgression.
Enough! Some surge of spirit I already feel.
ARCHBISHOP.
As Chancellor now I urge due form, to sign and seal.   11020
EMPEROR.   A formal deed of transfer to the Church—design it,
Lay it before me and I shall be pleased to sign it.
ARCHBISHOP.   [has taken his leave, but turns back at the exit]
Then you devote to the emerging work's intent
All land appurtenances, impost, tithe and rent,
Forever. Worthy maintenance exacts high levy,   11025
And costs of careful governance are no less heavy.

---

9. The sorcerer of Norcia (see note to line 10439).
1. The Archbishop describes the construction of a Gothic cathedral, which serves as an analogue to
   Faust's reclamation of land in Act V. Goethe may here allude to the plans of his friend Boisserée
   to secure support from the Prussian king to complete the Cathedral of Cologne.

To speed construction even on such desert spot,
Some requisitioned booty-gold you will allot.[2]
Besides all this, it needs, I cannot but remember,
Divers remote supplies as lime and slate and timber.   11030
The people do the hauling, from the pulpit taught,
The Church commends him who fares forth in her support.
    [*Exit.*]
EMPEROR.   The sin I shouldered is a great and irksome yoke,
I reap sore damage from the odious conjuring-folk.
ARCHBISHOP   [*returning once again, with a most profound
        obeisance*]
Your pardon, Sire! You granted that most ill-famed man   11035
The Empire's coastline; yet on this shall fall the ban
Unless you grant the Holy Purse, as contrite truant,
There, too, the tithe and rent and bounties thence accruant.[3]
EMPEROR.   [*peevishly*]
The land's not there, it lies beneath the ocean swell.
ARCHBISHOP.
Who has the right and patience, wins his day as well.   11040
Your word shall be our bond, may lapse of time not flout it!
    [*Exit.*]
EMPEROR.   [*alone*]
Why not sign over all the realm while we're about it!

---

2. See Rapacious's remark, lines 10827 ff.
3. This is the only reference to the bestowal of land upon Faust, earlier mentioned as a plan by
   Mephistopheles (lines 10305–6), which had presumably been one of Goethe's original motives
   for writing Act IV.

ACT V†

Open Country[1]

WAYFARER.[2] Aye, the same dark linden swaying,
　　Now matured to aged strength,
　　Welcome, after years of straying,　　　　　　　　　11045
　　They salute me back at length!
　　Aye—the selfsame humble acres!
　　To that hut of refuge fair
　　I repaired when storm-lashed breakers
　　Cast me on the sand-dunes there.　　　　　　　　　11050
　　Who received me when I foundered,
　　I would bless the honest pair,
　　Hardly to be still encountered,
　　Old as even then they were.
　　Those were folk of pious living!　　　　　　　　　11055
　　Should I knock, call out? All hail!
　　If you know the bliss of giving
　　As of old, and never fail.

BAUCIS. [a little granny, very old] Hush! Keep quiet, dear arrival,
　　Let him rest, my frail old man!　　　　　　　　　11060
　　Lengthy slumber grants revival
　　For brief vigil's active span.

WAYFARER. Is it you, then, Mother, living
　　To receive my second thanks,
　　For the life-gift jointly given　　　　　　　　　　11065
　　To the youth cast on your banks?
　　Are you Baucis who devoutly
　　Quickened once this faltering lip?
　　　　[The HUSBAND enters.]
　　You Philemon, who so stoutly
　　Snatched my hoard from water's grip?　　　　　　　11070
　　Silvery pealing from your arbor,
　　From your hearth the nimble flame—
　　You in gruesome plight were harbor
　　Whence relief and comfort came.
　　Let me scan the boundless ocean,　　　　　　　　　11075
　　Kneel upon the sandy crest,
　　Pour in prayerful devotion
　　What would burst my crowded breast.
　　　　[He strides forward upon the dune.]

1. Goethe here adapts a tale from Ovid's *Metamorphoses* (8.611–724; see his conversation with
Eckermann of June 6, 1831, below).
2. Ovid's gods in disguise are replaced by an anonymous traveler, returning to this place to receive
hospitality from the aged couple after years of absence since an earlier visit.

PHILEMON.   [*to* BAUCIS] Lay the table for us, hurry,
  In our little garden bright.   11080
  He will start aback and scurry,
  See and not believe his sight.
  [*standing beside the wayfarer*] What so fiercely overbore you,
  Rolling breakers, foam-bespewed,
  See as garden-land before you,   11085
  Glimpse of paradise renewed.
  Older, slower to be aiding
  Ready-handed as of yore,
  I beheld, my powers fading,
  Surf already far offshore.   11090
  Clever masters' daring minions
  Drained and walled the ocean bed,
  Shrank the sea's entrenched dominions,
  To be masters in her stead.
  Gaze on hamlets, common, stable,   11095
  Luscious meadows, grove and eave,—
  But enough—let us to table,
  For the sun would take his leave.
  See the sails from farthest westing
  Safe to anchorage repair!   11100
  Well the seabirds know their nesting,
  For the harbor now is there.
  Outward pressed to distant spaces
  See the ocean's azure sheen,
  Breadth of densely settled places   11105
  Right and left and all between.[3]

[*The three at table in the little garden.*]

BAUCIS.   Silent? And, it seems, unable
  To relieve your hunger, too?
PHILEMON.   He would hear the wondrous fable;
  Tell him, as you like to do.   11110
BAUCIS.   Well! A wonder, do not doubt it!
  Still it makes my reason fret;
  Something wrong was all about it
  That I cannot fathom yet.
PHILEMON.   On the Emperor dare one blame it, 11115
  Who conferred on him the shore?
  Did a herald not proclaim it,
  Trumpets flourishing before?
  Here a footing first was grounded,
  Not far distant from our bluff,   11120

---

3. Philemon surveys the city that has been built, at Faust's command, on the land reclaimed by pushing the sea behind dikes located far off, near the horizon.

Tents and huts—but green-surrounded,
Rose a palace soon enough.
BAUCIS.   Vainly in the daytime labored
Pick and shovel, clink and strike,
Where at night the elf-lights wavered,   11125
By the dawn there stood a dike.[4]
Human victims bled and fevered,
Anguish on the night-air borne,
Fiery torrents pouring seaward
Scored a channel by the morn.   11130
Godless is he, he would savor
This our grove and cabin here;
Now the newly strutting neighbor
As his subjects we should fear.
PHILEMON.   Yet he pledged, you have forgotten,   11135
Homestead fair on new-won land!
BAUCIS.   Do not trust the ocean bottom,
Steadfast on your hill-brow stand!
PHILEMON.   To the chapel let us wander,
Greet the parting sun once more;   11140
Ring and kneel in worship yonder,
Trusting God as heretofore.

---

4. Baucis indicates her awareness that devilish powers have been employed in the dark of night. The
technology of such dike and dam projects, recalling the labors of lowland Friesen and the Dutch
in the late Middle Ages, also reflects Goethe's interest in similar projects during his own day,
such as plans for the harbor in Bremen or the Panama Canal.

Palace
Spacious Ornamental Gardens; Large, Straight Canal

FAUST *in extreme old age,*[1] *walking about in meditation.*

LYNCEUS, THE KEEPER OF THE WATCHTOWER,[2]†
    [*through a speaking-tube*]
    The sun is down, the last few vessels
    Are briskly coursing harborward.
    A sailing lighter slowly nestles   11145
    Up-channel from the open port.
    The colored streamers flutter gaily,
    The rigid davits stoutly rise;
    With you for patron, blest the sailor,
    And blessing yours for late-won prize.   11150

    [*The little bell tolls on the dune.*]

FAUST. [*starting violently*]
    That cursed peal! Malign and groundless,
    Like shot from ambush does it pierce;
    Before my eyes my realm is boundless,
    But at my back annoyance leers,
    Reminding me with envious stabbing: 11155
    My lofty title is impure,
    The linden range, the weathered cabin,
    The frail old church are still secure,
    And should I seek my ease there—crawling
    At alien shades my flesh would rear,   11160
    Thorn in my side, encumbrance galling,
    Oh, were I far away from here!
KEEPER OF THE TOWER. [*as above*]
    To port the flag-gay bark does ride
    On the fresh breeze of eventide!
    How high its nimble course is stacked   11165
    With riches crated, cased, and sacked!

    [*Splendid bark, richly and colorfully laden with products of exotic
    regions.*]

    [*Enter* MEPHISTOPHELES, THE THREE MIGHTY MEN.]

---

1. See Goethe's conversation with Eckermann, June 6, 1831 (below), concerning Faust's age.
2. Presumably the same figure who served as watchman of the tower in the middle section of the
   Helena. (See note to line 7377.)

CHORUS.   There, overboard
           And we're ashore.
           Hail to our Lord.
           And Patron here!   11170

[*They disembark, the goods are moved ashore.*]

MEPHISTOPHELES.   With credit we have met our task,
   In Master's praise we'll gaily bask.
   With just two ships we started then,
   With twenty we are back again.
   What great things we achieved, behold,   11175
   Here by our cargo can be told.
   Free ocean makes you scruple-free,
   Cobwebs of caution swept to sea.
   There only counts the timely grip,
   You catch a fish, you catch a ship,   11180
   And once of three the masters now,
   You hook the fourth one anyhow;
   The fifth will be in sorry plight,
   You have the force, and might is right.
   You tend the what and not the wise,   11185
   If I know naval enterprise:
   For commerce, war, and piracy,
   They form a seamless trinity.
THE THREE MIGHTY MEN.
      Not thanked or hailed,
      No hail or thanks,   11190
      Why, did we sail
      A stench to banks?
      His face is wry,
      His brow is grooved,
      The regal loot   11195
      Is not approved.
MEPHISTOPHELES.
      Do not expect
      A wage to spare,
      You know you took
      Your proper share.   11200

THE MEN. The part we had
      Was just for fun,
      We all demand
      An equal one.
MEPHISTOPHELES.
      First sort upstairs   11205
      In hall on hall
      The precious goods
      Assembled all.

When he takes in
The stately show,   11210
And reckons up
The loot just so;
I bet it's you
He'll stint the least,
He'll give the squadron   11215
Feast on feast.
The pretty birds³ arrive tomorrow,
You'll find my service prompt and thorough.

[*The cargo is hauled away.*]

MEPHISTOPHELES.   [*to* FAUST]
  With clouded brow and somber-gazed
  You hear your lofty fortune raised.   11220
  Exalted wisdom now is crowned.
  At peace are sea and solid ground;
  From harboring shore, to speed at large,
  The willing sea received the barge;
  Say, "from this palace, from this beach,   11225
  The world is wholly in my reach."
  All started from this very spot,
  Here stood the earliest wooden hut;
  A shallow groove was scratched before
  Where now they ply the busy oar.   11230
  Your noble mind, their toiling hands,
  Secured the prize of seas and lands.
  From here—
FAUST.   That blasted *here*! you see?
  That's just what sorely weighs on me.
  To your great cunning I confide it,   11235
  I feel my heart is stabbed and maimed,
  My mind unable to abide it—
  Yet as I say it, I'm ashamed.
  That aged couple must surrender,
  I want their linden for my throne,   11240
  The unowned timber-margin slender
  Despoils for me the world I own.
  There, for the eye's untrammeled roving,
  I wish a scaffold to be woven
  From branch to branch, for vistas deep   11245
  Of my achievement's fullest sweep,
  With all-embracing gaze to scan
  The masterpiece of sapient man,
  As he ordains with thoughtful mind
  New homestead for his teeming kind.   11250

3. Sailors' slang for women of easy virtue who gather at ports of call.

Thus we are stretched on cruellest rack,
In riches sensing what we lack.
The tinkling chime, the linden bloom
Close in like sanctuary and tomb.
The will's omnipotent command,   11255
Like surf it breaks upon this sand.
How can I rid myself and breathe!
The bell but tinkles, and I seethe.

MEPHISTOPHELES.   Of course! Such chief annoyance must
Turn all one's life to ash and dust.   11260
The finer ear, who would deny it,
Recoils from this repulsive riot.
Does not that noisome ding-dong-dingling
Befoul the sky of evening, mingling
With all events its souring ferment,   11265
From first immersion to interment?
Till life seems but a shadow throng
Parading between ding and dong?

FAUST.   That stubbornness, perverse and vain,
So blights the most majestic gain   11270
That to one's agonized disgust
One has to tire of being just.

MEPHISTOPHELES.   Why should you scruple here and wince?
Have you not colonized long since?

FAUST.   Go, then, and clear them from my sight!—   11275
The handsome little farm you know
That I assigned them long ago.

MEPHISTOPHELES.   One hauls them off and makes them settle,
And in a trice they're back in fettle;
For, once sustained the rude offense,   11280
A pretty place is recompense.
      [He gives a strident whistle.]

      [Enter THE THREE.]
MEPHISTOPHELES.   Come! As the Master bade to say,
Tomorrow will be Navy Day.

THE THREE.   The old gent's welcome was a slight,
A rousing feast will do us right.   11285
      [Exeunt.]

MEPHISTOPHELES.   [ad spectatores]
What passes here is far from new;
There once was Naboth's vineyard, too. [Kings i.21][4]

---

4. King Ahab coveted Naboth's vineyard and tried unsuccessfully to buy it from him. The king's
wife, Jezebel, therefore plotted against the life of Naboth, after whose death Ahab seized the
vineyards, only to be confronted there by the prophet Elijah, who accused him of the murder.

Deep Night

LYNCEUS, *the keeper on the watchtower of the palace, singing.*

LYNCEUS.   To seeing born,
To scanning called,
To the watchtower sworn,   11290
I relish the world.
Sighting the far,
Espying the near,
Moon-disc and star,
Forest and deer.   11295
In all I behold
Ever-comely design,
As its virtues unfold
I take pleasure in mine.
You fortunate eyes,   11300
All you ever did see,
Whatever its guise,
Was so lovely to me!

[*Pause.*]

Not for pleasure, though, my master
Placed me on this lofty stand;   11305
What a hideous disaster
Threatens from the darkened land!
Spattering sparks are winking, glaring
Through the linden's doubled gloom,
Fanned by rushing air, the flaring   11310
Burrows deeper and gains room.
Woe! the inner hut's afire
That was moist and mossy green,
Instant rescue would require,
Yet no help is to be seen.   11315
Ah, the poor old pair that tended
Else so watchfully their fire,
Must their age in smoke be ended,
Snuffed in conflagration dire!
Like a glowing fiery steeple   11320
Redly soars the mossy frame,
Scarcely could the honest people
Flee this raging hell of flame!
Through the boughs, their leafy tracing,
Soaring tongues of fire are racing,   11325
Branches furnish ready fuel,
Flash and tumble down the trees;

Ah, the gift of sight is cruel
Showing horrors such as these!
There, the chapel in their falling   11330
Ponderous boughs have battered down,
Pointed serpent tongues appalling
Now engulf each leafy crown.
To the roots agape and trembling
Melt the trunks in scarlet blaze.—   11335

[*Long pause; sound of singing.*][1]
    To dead centuries assembling
    What throughout them pleased the gaze.

FAUST.   [*on the balcony, facing the dunes*]
  Up on the keep, what crooning whimper?
  The tone's outhurried by the fact;
  My watchman wails; my inmost temper   11340
  Is soured by the impatient act.
  But where the linden stand is wizened
  To piteous ruin, charred and stark,
  A look-out frame will soon have risen
  To sweep the world in boundless arc.   11345
  Thence I shall view the new plantation
  Assigned to shelter the old pair,
  Who, mindful of benign salvation,
  Will spend life's happy evening there.
MEPHISTOPHELES AND THE THREE.   [*below*]
  Here we return in full career;   11350
  It was not smoothly done, I fear.
  We knocked, we rapped, we knocked in vain,
  No one would open up; again
  We knocked and rattled somewhat more,
  And inward fell the brittle door.   11355
  We called and threatened more than once,
  And still we met with no response.
  As at such times it will occur,
  They wouldn't hear, so didn't stir.
  So we fell to without ado   11360
  And nimbly moved them out for you.
  The couple did not suffer much,
  From fear fell lifeless at our touch.
  A lurking stranger who was found
  And offered fight, was laid aground.   11365
  Live embers, knocked about a bit
  In brief but furious struggling, lit

---

1. The opening section of Lynceus's monologue was sung, his description of the burning of hut and chapel was spoken, and here he commences again with his song, only to be interrupted by Faust, who objects to the sound.

Some straw—and now it blazes free,
A funeral pyre for those three.
FAUST.   So you have turned deaf ears to me!   11370
I meant exchange, not robbery.
This thoughtless violent affair,
My curse on it, for you to share!

CHORUS.   That ancient truth we will recite:
Give way to force, for might is right;   11375
And would you boldly offer strife,
Then risk your house, estate, and—life.
     [*Exeunt.*]

FAUST.   [*on the balcony*]
The stars withdraw their gleam and wink,
The fiery blazes dwindle, sink;
Still hither, fanned by vagrant drafts,   11380
A veil of smoke and vapor wafts,
Too rashly bid, too swiftly done!—
What wanders here, of shadows spun?[2]

---

2. Faust observes the spirit figures that appear in the following scene, as they form themselves out
of the smoke and vapor of the burning ruins.

Midnight†

[*Enter* FOUR GRAY CRONES.][1]

THE FIRST.   My name, it is Want.
THE SECOND.   My name, it is Debt.
THE THIRD.   My name, it is Care.
THE FOURTH.   My name, it is Need.   11385
THREE TOGETHER.   We cannot gain entry, the portals are locked,
   A wealthy man lives here, our entrance is blocked.
WANT.   I pass into shadow.
DEBT.   I pass into naught.
NEED.   The pampered dismiss me from sight and from thought.
CARE.   You sisters, you never may enter therein.   11390
   But Care—she will creep through the keyhole unseen.
      [CARE *disappears.*]
WANT.   Away, my gray sisters, we may not abide.
DEBT.   I, sister, will join you and cleave to your side.
NEED.   And Need follows close on the heel of the other.
THREE TOGETHER.   Clouds drifting, enveloping star upon star!   11395
   Back yonder, remote, from afar, from afar
   We see him approach, it is——Death, our brother.

FAUST.   [*in the palace*] Four I saw enter, go but three;
   Unfathomable was their speech to me.
   Like "Need" it lingered on the breath,   11400
   Then, like a somber echo—"Death."
   It droned as with a muffled ghostly threat.
   I have not fought my way to freedom yet.†
   Could I but clear my path at every turning
   Of spells, all magic utterly unlearning;   11405
   Were I but Man, with Nature for my frame,
   The name of human would be worth the claim.

   And such I was, before I fell to searching
   The dark, with curses world and self besmirching.[2]
   So thick is now the air with spook and elf   11410
   That no one knows how to extract himself.
   Though smiling day with light of reason gleams,
   The night entangles us in webs of dreams;
   We gaily turn from meadows lush with sap,
   A bird will croak; what does it croak? Mishap.   11415
   Enmeshed on every hand by superstition,
   Events of omen, portent, premonition . . .

1. These four allegorical hags recall the Witches in Shakespeare's *Macbeth*, who confront Macbeth
   and Banquo on the Scottish heath.
2. Recall Faust's curse before his pact with Mephistopheles, lines 1583–606.

Abashed we stand, alone with but our fear.
The door has creaked—and no one enters here.
[*shaken*] Is someone here?

CARE.   The question calls for Yea.   11420
FAUST.   And you—who are you?
CARE.   I am here, I say.
FAUST.   Remove yourself!
CARE.   I am where I should be.
FAUST.   [*incensed at first, then mollified, to himself*]
Restrain yourself and speak no conjury.

CARE.   If there were no ear to hear me,
                  Still the pounding heart would fear me;   11425
                  In most manifold array
                  I exert relentless sway,
                  Haunt the seaways, haunt the canyon,
                  Ever timorous companion,
                  Ever found and never sought,   11430
                  Ever paid both curse and court.
       Gray Care—am I unknown to you?
FAUST.   I only sped the whole world through,
Clutched any stray temptation by the hair,
And what fell short, abandoned there,   11435
And what eluded me, let pass.
All that I did was covet and attain,
And crave afresh, and thus with might and main
Stormed through my life; first powerful and great,
But now at pace more prudent, more sedate.   11440
I know full well the earthly sphere of men—
The yonder view is blocked to mortal ken;
A fool who squints beyond with blinking eyes,
Imagining his like above the skies;
Let him stand firm and gaze about alert;   11445
To able man this world is not inert;
What need for him to roam eternities?
What he perceives, that he may seize,
Let him stride on upon this planet's face,
When spirits haunt, let him not change his pace,   11450
Find bliss and torment in his onward stride,
Aye—every moment stay unsatisfied.[3]

CARE.   Once I mark him and assail him,
                  Nothing earthly will avail him,
                  Never-ending gloom descending,   11455
                  Sun his rise and fall suspending;
                  Unimpaired all outer senses,
                  Dark on dark the soul enfences,
                  Stays his hand of any treasure
                  To possess himself at leisure.   11460

---

3. Recall the terms of Faust's wager with Mephistopheles, lines 1699–706.

Weal and woe of like redundance,
He must famish in abundance,
Be it gladness, be it sorrow,
He defers it to the morrow,
Of the future ever heedful,   11465
Ever laggard of the needful.
FAUST.   Desist! This will not work on me!
Such caterwauling[4] I despise.
Begone—your wretched litany
Might well unnerve a man, however wise.   11470
CARE.   Be it going, be it coming,
All resolve is taken from him,
Down the highway's level coping
Staggering he trips and groping,
Deeply mired and farther erring,   11475
Senses mocking, vision blurring,
Burden to himself and others;
Breath sustains no more than smothers,
Fails to strangle or revive him,
Hung between despair and striving.   11480
Thus a langorous pursuing,
Hard refraining, nauseous doing,
Now reprieving, now molesting,
Hollow sleep and shallow resting,
Keep him shackled to his station   11485
And prepare him for damnation.
FAUST.   Unholy wraiths! For eons you exerted
Your hateful sway on humankind just so;
The most indifferent days you have perverted
To loathsome coils of involuted woe.   11490
Not lightly is the demon net uncast,
Strict spirit-bond, I know, is hard to sever;
And yet your power, o Care, insidiously vast,
I shall not recognize it ever.
CARE.   Taste of it forthwith, then, as rife   11495
With curse I turn away offended!
Man commonly is blind throughout his life,
My Faust, be blind then as you end it.
[*She breathes upon him. Exit.*]
FAUST.   [*blinded*]
The night, it seems, turns deeper still—but shining,
The light within continues ever bright,[5]   11500
I hasten to fulfill my thought's designing;
The master's word alone imparts his might.

---

4. As indicated by the sustained use of feminine rhymes in the speeches by Care, she addresses Faust
in a kind of chant and wailing lament, as if to cast a spell.
5. That blindness brings a deeper, more authentic insight is an ancient literary motif, as in Sophocles'
Oedipus the King (which Goethe may have had in mind here), where the prophet Tiresias, though
blind, sees the truth, and the effect of such true sight on Oedipus is to blind him.

Up, workmen, man for man, arise anew!
Let blithely savor what I boldly drew.
Seize spade and shovel, each take up his tool!   11505
Fulfill at once what was marked off by rule.
Attendance prompt to orders wise
Achieves the most alluring prize;
To bring to fruit the most exalted plans,
One mind is ample for a thousand hands.   11510

Great Outer Precinct of the Palace†
Torches

MEPHISTOPHELES.   [*as supervisor, in the lead*]
>Step up, step up! Come on, come on!
>You quivering lemur creatures,[1]
>Patched up from sinew, band, and bone,
>Exiguous demi-natures.

LEMURES.   [*in chorus*]
>We are aware and are at hand,   11515
>Here at your service find us,
>Was it a broad expanse of land,
>They said had been assigned us?

>A measuring chain is ready too,
>And stakes to mark the plotting,   11520
>What we were summoned here to do
>We knew but have forgotten.

MEPHISTOPHELES.   No call here for artistic grace;
>The dig is measured by the digger;
>Your lankiest lie down upon his face,   11525
>The rest cut out the turf to suit his figure;
>As for our forebears it was done,
>Scoop out an oblong tetragon!
>From palace down to narrow stall,
>That's the inane conclusion, after all.   11530

LEMURES.   [*digging with teasing gestures*][2]
>When I was young and lived and loved,
>It seemed like honey-sipping,

---

1. *Lemures* (Latin), spirits of the evil dead in classical mythology, depicted like skeletons on a bas-relief excavated in a grave near Cumae in southern Italy, which was known to Goethe. (Not to be confused with "lemurs," a nocturnal lower primate.)
2. The song of the Lemures is adapted from the Gravediggers' song in Shakespeare's *Hamlet* 5.1:

>In youth when I did love, did love,
>>Methought it was very sweet
>To contract-O-the time for-a-my behove,
>>O methought there was-a-nothing-a-meet.

>But age with his stealing steps
>>Hath caught me in his clutch,
>And hath shipped me intil the land,
>>As if I had never been such.

Goethe also was familiar with Shakespeare's source, a poem attributed to Lord Nicholas Vaux (d. 1523), later included by Bishop Percy in his *Reliques of Ancient English Poetry* (1765) as a ballad entitled "The Aged Lover Renounceth Love" (Vol. 1, Book 2.2).

Where pipers skirled and dancers shoved
My feet went tripping, skipping.

Now age with its insidious crutch   11535
Hit me and sent me groping;
I tripped the grave-door, just a touch,
What fool had left it open?

FAUST.
    [*issuing from the palace, groping his way by the door-jambs*]
How gaily ring the spades, a song of mirth!
It is my host of toiling slaves,   11540
That renders self-content the earth,
Ordains a border to the waves,
The sea with rigid bonds enchains.
MEPHISTOPHELES.   [*aside*] For us alone you are at pains
With all your dikes and moles; a revel   11545
For Neptune, the old water-devil,
Is all you spread, if you but knew.
You lose, whatever your reliance—
The elements are sworn to our alliance,
In ruin issues all you do.   11550
FAUST. Ho, overseer!
MEPHISTOPHELES.   Here!
FAUST.   From every source
Find me more hands, recruit with vigor
Spur them with blandishment and rigor,
Spare neither pay nor lure nor force!
I want a tally, daily to be rendered,   11555
How much the trench in hand is gaining room.
MEPHISTOPHELES.   [*under his breath*]
The question, as I understand it,
Is not of room so much as tomb.
FAUST.[3] A chain of marshes lines the hills,
Befouling all the land retrievement;   11560
To drain this stagnant pool of ills
Would be the crowning, last achievement.
I'd open room to live for millions
Not safely, but in free resilience.
Lush fallow then to man and cattle yields   11565
Swift crops and comforts from the maiden fields,
New homesteads near the trusty buttress-face
Walled by a bold and horny-handed race.
A land of Eden sheltered here within,
Let tempest rage outside unto the rim,   11570
And as it laps a breach in greedy riot,
Communal spirit hastens to defy it.

---

3. Faust's final speech replaces an earlier, shorter version (cited in the interpretive notes).

Yes—this I hold to with devout insistence,
Wisdom's last verdict goes to say:
He only earns both freedom and existence   11575
Who must reconquer them each day.
And so, ringed all about by perils, here
Youth, manhood, age will spend their strenuous year.
Such teeming would I see upon this land,
On acres free among free people stand.   11580
I might entreat the fleeting minute:
Oh tarry yet, thou art so fair!
My path on earth, the trace I leave within it
Eons untold cannot impair.
Foretasting such high happiness to come,   11585
I savor now my striving's crown and sum.

[FAUST *sinks backward; the* LEMURES *break his fall and lay him on
the ground.*]

MEPHISTOPHELES.   No joy could sate him, no delight but cloyed,
For changing shapes he lusted to the last;
The final moment, worthless, stale, and void,
The luckless creature, he would hold it fast.   11590
Here he who fought me off so well—
Time triumphs—stranded lies, a whitened shell.
The clock is muted—
CHORUS.   Mute! Like midnight it is stilled.
The hand is falling,
MEPHISTOPHELES.   Fell—it is fulfilled.[4]
CHORUS.   It is all over.
MEPHISTOPHELES.   Over! Stupid name.   11595
Why over?
All over and pure nothing—just the same!
What has this constant doing ever brought
But what is done to rake away to naught?
So it is over! How to read this clause?   11600
All over is as good as never was,
And yet it whirls about as if it were.
The Eternal-Empty[5] is what I prefer.

---

4. A parody of Christ's last words on the cross, "It is finished" (John 19.30).
5. This phrase anticipates the final couplet of the Chorus Mysticus (lines 12110 f.).

Entombment[1]†

LEMUR.   [*solo*][2] Who was it built this house so ill
               With shovel and with spade?   11605
LEMURES.   [*in chorus*]
               For thee, dull guest in hempen twill
               It's far too neatly made.
LEMUR.   [*solo*] Why is the hall so ill supplied,
               No board or chairs, how came it?
LEMURES.   [*in chorus*]
               It is but briefly occupied;   11610
               So many wait to claim it.

MEPHISTOPHELES.
     There lies the corpse, and when the soul would flit,
     I'll show it straight the bond with blood cemented;
     Yet tricks galore have lately been invented
     To cheat the devil of his writ.   11615
     On novel routes we're yet unknown,
     The former one offends opinions;
     I used to do it all alone,
     Now I am forced to call on minions.
     All round, we are in sorry plight!   11620
     Tradition, custom, old-established right,
     There's nothing to be trusted as it was.
     With its last breath it used to slip the house,
     I'd lie in wait, and like the nimblest mouse
     Snap! I would hold it fast in clenched-up claws.   11625
     Now it hangs back, is loth to leave the place,
     The body's wretched shack, noisome and brooding;
     The elements by their own feuding,
     They must at last evict it in disgrace.
     And though for days and hours I rack my brain,   11630
     The plaguy questions, when? how? where? remain:
     Why, even old man Death's swift pounce runs out,
     The very whether? long remains in doubt;
     I've often lusted at stiff limbs—in vain,
     It was all sham, they stirred, they moved again.   11635

1. An intentional allusion to the iconography in medieval art of Christ's entombment. It has been
   argued that Goethe was influenced in particular by fourteenth-century frescoes of the Camposanto
   in Pisa depicting the Triumph of Death, the Last Judgment, and Hell.
2. Again the Lemures' song echoes the Gravediggers' song in *Hamlet* 1.5:

               A pickaxe and a spade, a spade,
               For and a shrouding-sheet;
               Oh, a pit of clay for to be made
               For such a guest is meet.

[with fantastic gestures of conjuration, fugleman-fashion[3]]

Step lively! make your paces double-long,
Knights of the straight, knights of the crooked horn.
Chips off Old Nick's block, to the manner born,
And mind you, bring up Hell's jaws[4] right along.
Hell's jaws are many, many! to be sure,   11640
It swallows them by rank and etiquette;
Yet even on this final guided tour
We'll all become less formal soon, I bet.

[The ghastly jaws of Hell open at left.]

With tusks agape, the arching gullet breathes
A raging cataract of flame eternal,   11645
See, in the smoldering distance fumes and seethes
The citadel of flame in blaze infernal,
Up to the fangs the scarlet floodtide surges,
Some of the damned swim up, on rescue bent,
The vast hyena mauls them and engorges,   11650
And they resume their anguished hot descent.
The corners, too, are worth exploring, brim-full
Of greatest horrors in least space confined!
Try as you like to terrify the sinful,
They count it fraud and figment of the mind.   11655

[to the FAT DEVILS *of the short, straight horns]*

Now, paunchy rascals, with your cheeks all burning!
Who stuffed with hellish sulfur fairly glow;
You clumsy cloddish bullnecks never-turning,
You watch for glint of phosphor here below:
That is the little soul, winged psyche, land her   11660
And pluck the wings, it leaves a sordid worm;
Then with my stamp of lordship I will brand her,
And off with her in whirling fiery storm.

So, to patrol the lower station,
You bellows, is your duty, mark;   11665
If that's her chosen habitation,
The matter's somewhat in the dark.
The navel's where she likes to stay,
Look sharp, she may give you the slip that way.

[to the LEAN DEVILS *of the long, crooked horns]*

3. A reference to the leader of a file of troops in a marching army who would direct the movements
of his group.
4. The traditional hell-mouth of the medieval stage (see note to line 242).

You, guardsmen loons, great jackanapes unsteady,   11670
Rake through the air with unremitting tries;
Arms stretched aloft, sharp talons at the ready,
To catch the fluttering flibbet as it flies.
She's ill at ease in her old house, I'd say,
And genius seeks the straight and upward way.   11675

        [*Aureole from above, right.*]

HEAVENLY HOST.   Follow, ye envoys,[5]
                Heaven-born convoys,
                On leisured wing coast:
                Sinful ones shriving,
                Dust to enliven;   11680
                Bounteous giving
                To all things living
                Waft in its striving
                The hovering host.

MEPHISTOPHELES.   A tuneless jangling, nauseous and churlish,   11685
      Comes from above with the unwelcome day;
      The kind of mincing medley, boyish-girlish,
      As unctuous taste may relish, I daresay.
      You know how we in heinous hour allotted
      Annihilation to the human brood: 11690
      The blackest infamy we plotted
      Just suits their bland beatitude.

      Look at the canting holy-oilers!
      Thus they have snatched from us so many a prize,
      With our own weapons they would foil us;   11695
      They too are devils, only in disguise.
      If you want shame eternal, lose today!
      On to the graveside, hold it come what may!

CHORUS OF ANGELS.   [*strewing roses*][6]
                Roses, you glowing ones,
                Balsam bestowing ones!   11700
                Floating and flickering,
                Stealthily quickening,
                Rose-twiglet-whirling ones,
                Rosebud-unfurling ones,
                Hasten to spread.   11705

5. *Angeloi* (Greek), "messengers," i.e., angels, surrounded by the heavenly "glory" (Aureole).
6. The association of roses with Heaven was traditional. In a fresco by Luca Signorelli (1441–1523) in the Cathedral of Orvieto, angels are depicted strewing roses on the blessed. In the final scene (lines 11942 ff.), we learn that the angels have received the roses from the souls of the penitent, one of whom is Gretchen.

> Spring, burst out blooming,
> Emerald, red;
> Send grace perfuming
> The sleeper's bed.

MEPHISTOPHELES. [*to the* DEVILS]
Why hunch and flinch? Is this my hellish host?   11710
Let them strew on and show your mettle.
Back, every lubber, to his post!
To snow in with their childish catch-a-petal
The red-hot devils, seems to be their boast;
It melts and shrivels at your puff—   11715
Now, blowhards, blow!—Enough, enough!
Before your frowst the whole swarm withers off.—
Come, not so wildly! shut your snouts and noses!
There—you have blown too strongly for the roses.
The proper dose you never seem to learn.   11720
They shrivel; more, they darken, curl up, burn!
Now it drifts up in flames, pernicious, clear,
Thrust out against it, close together here!
The spirit drains away, all valor spent!
The devils sense a flattering alien scent.   11725

CHORUS OF ANGELS.   Blossoms of blessing,
                     Gay flames caressing,
                     Love they are spreading,
                     Ecstasy shedding,
                     As heart would pray.   11730
                     Message of verity,
                     Ether all clarity.
                     To Heaven's company
                     Everywhere day.

MEPHISTOPHELES.   O curse! O shame upon such bumpkins!   11735
Here's devils standing on their pumpkins,
Cartwheel on clumsy cartwheel turned,
They plunge to Hell arse-over-face.
My blessings on the scalding bath you earned!
But as for me, I keep my place.   11740
[*battling the fluttering roses*]
Off, will-o'-the-wisps! you too! shine ever so much,
You're just some nauseous jelly to the touch.
What, are you fluttering still? Will you be off!—
It grips my neck like pitch and sulphur stuff.

CHORUS OF ANGELS.   What is not yours to keep,   11745
                     Leave it aside,
                     What mars your inmost deep,

You must not bide.
Thrusts it with mighty force,
Hold to the stronger course.   11750
Love leads but loving ones
In to the source.

MEPHISTOPHELES.   My liver burns, my heart, my head as well,
Some super-devilish element!
More pointed far than flames of hell.—   11755
That's why you so prodigiously lament,
Unhappy lovesick lads, who wander, spurned,
Their craning necks to the belovèd turned.

I too! What draws my head that way for me?[7]
Do we not stand in sworn, inveterate enmity?   11760
The sight was else so bitterly averse.
Did something alien steep me through and through?
Those captivating youths, I quite enjoy the view;
What hinders me from uttering a curse?—
And if I get infatuated,   11765
Who will in future be the dunce?
The lawless rascals that I hated,
They seem so very lovely all at once!—

You pretty children, let me quiz you:
Are you not too of Lucifer's own kind?   11770
You look so sweet, why I would like to kiss you,
You turn up just in time, I find.
Somehow I feel so natural, so trustful,
As if a thousand times I'd watched your ways,
So stealthy-kittenishly lustful;   11775
Fair still, more fairly fair, with every gaze.
O, do approach, o grudge me not a glance!
ANGELS.   We're coming—why retreat as we advance?
We are approaching, stay then if you can.

[*The* ANGELS, *drifting all about, occupy the entire space.*]

MEPHISTOPHELES.   [*who is being crowded into the proscenium*]
You who berate us fiends and elves,   11780
You are arch-conjurers yourselves;
For you seduce both maid and man.
Ah, what a damnable affair!
Is this love's essence that appeared?
My body is a single blazing flare,   11785

---

7. As a final ironic twist to the devil's role, Mephistopheles is distracted by sexual desire in response
   to the naked bodies of the young angels, thus abandoning his opposition to them.

I hardly notice that my neck is seared.—
You waver to and fro, please try descending,
A bit more worldly-like your sweet limbs bending;
Though gravity, I grant, sits well on you,
I'd like, just once, to catch you smiling, too;   11790
I'd cherish the delight of it always;
I have in mind the way that lovers gaze,
A dimpling near the lips, and it is done.
You, lad, I like the best, so lean and tall,
That curate's mien becomes you not at all,   11795
Give me a little wanton wink, come on!
You need a decent naked fashion, too,
That long enfolding robe is over-prim—
They turn around—now for a backward view!
I could just eat them up, the lot of them.   11800

CHORUS OF ANGELS.   On to the Light,
                     Loving flames, stream,
                     May Truth redeem
                     Self-damned from blight,
                     That, gladly weaned   11805
                     From evil and cleaned,
                     In the All-Unity
                     Blessèd they be.

MEPHISTOPHELES.   [coming to his senses]
     What ails me!—Job-like, boil on boil my skin,
     All sores I stand and shake with self-disgust,[8]   11810
     And yet triumphant, as I come to trust
     In my firm inner self and in my kin;
     I know the noble devil parts are safe,
     It's only skin the love-spook knows to chafe;
     Extinguished are the vicious flames I fought,   11815
     And now I curse you all together, as I ought!

CHORUS OF ANGELS.   Sheltered by glows
                     All-holiest, mightiest,
                     Bliss with the righteous
                     Living, he knows.   11820
                     In unison fair
                     Soar now and quire,
                     In purified air
                     May the spirit respire!

[They soar up, carrying off FAUST'S immortal essence.]

8. An allusion to the suffering Job, beset by diseases inflicted at Satan's behest, suggesting an ironic
   connection with the earlier use of Job in "Prologue in Heaven" (see interpretive notes).

MEPHISTOPHELES.   [*looking about him*]
   How can this be? Where are they gone away?   11825
   You half-baked tribe, you have made off with it,
   To heaven they are spiriting my prey;
   That's why they came to buzz about this pit!
   I have been robbed of costly, peerless profit,
   The lofty soul pledged me by solemn forfeit,   11830
   They've spirited it slyly from my writ.

   Where do I sue now as complainer?
   Who will enforce my well-earned right?
   You have been fairly cheated, old campaigner,
   You have deserved it, grim enough your plight.   11835
   This thing was wretchedly mishandled,
   A great expense, for shame! is thrown away,
   A vulgar lust, absurd amours have dandled
   The seasoned devil of his prey.
   If to this childish-fatuous spree   11840
   One so experienced could descend,
   Then no mean folly it must be
   That seized upon him in the end.

Mountain Gorges[1]†
Forests, Cliffs, Wilderness

HOLY ANCHORITES,[2] *scattered up the mountainsides, dwelling among rock-clefts.*

CHORUS AND ECHO.†
>Wild-forest swaying near,
>Ponderous boulders here,   11845
>Tree roots entwine and close,
>Tree trunks in serried rows.
>Gushing up, wave on wave,
>Shelter, the deepest cave.
>Lions, they slink around,   11850
>Kindly, without a sound,
>Honor the hallowed grove,
>Refuge of sacred love.

PATER ECSTATICUS.[3] *[floating hither and thither]*
>Joy ever searing on,
>Love's ever-glowing bond,   11855
>Seething with ache the breast,
>Foaming of God-lust blest.
>Arrows, pierce through me,
>Lances, undo me,
>Bludgeons, come batter me,   11860
>Lightning, come shatter me,
>That dross might separate
>All and evaporate,
>Shine but the lasting star,
>Timeless love's core.   11865

PATER PROFUNDUS.[4] *[in a deep region]*
>When at my feet, with boulders teeming,
>Gorge leans on chasm in ponderous sprawl,
>A thousand glittering brooklets streaming
>To join the flood-spate's gruesome fall,
>When, by its own stout urge directed,   11870
>The tree thrusts upward, straight and tall,

1. The several possible visual sources for this final scene are discussed in the interpretive notes.
2. Hermits of the first centuries of the Christian era who lived in the wilderness and practiced self-mortification to attain a mystical union with God.
3. The first of four titles assigned to the anchorite fathers: *Ecstaticus, Profundus, Seraphicus,* and *Marianus.* These titles indicate a hierarchy of ascending degrees of divine knowledge. Historically, the title *Ecstaticus* had been used for St. Anthony, Johann Ruysbroek, and Dionysius the Carthusian; levitation had been attributed to, among others, St. Francis Xavier.
4. Traditionally, an epithet applied to St. Bernhard of Clairvaux (1091–1153), who appears in Dante's *Paradiso* (Cantos 31 ff.), replacing Beatrice as the poet's guide, to lead him toward a mystical vision of God.

'Tis by all-potent love effected,
Which fashions all, and fosters all.

As though ravine and woods were waving,
A clamor thunders all about,   11875
And yet, still gracious in their raving,
The floods go plunging down the spout,
To moist the dale their urgent calling;
The lightning's, as it flared and hissed,
To carry freshness in its falling   11880
To ether charged with noisome mist.

Love-envoys, they proclaim what merit
Here works its all-creative will.
O may it also light my spirit;
Now chafes the mind, confounded, chill,   11885
In curbs of torpid senses shrinking,
In sharply tightened chains that smart.
Almighty Lord! O soothe my thinking,
Illumine Thou my needy heart.

PATER SERAPHICUS.[5]   [in a middle region]
What a wispy dawn-cloud hovers   11890
In the spruces' swaying hair;
Do I fathom what it covers?
A young spirit band is there.

CHORUS OF BLESSED BOYS.[6]
Tell us who we are, dear Father.
Tell us, Father, in what place?   11895
We are happy, all together,
Life to us is such mild grace.

PATER SERAPHICUS.
Boys! born at the midnight sleeping,
Scarce unfolded sense and brain,
For their parents, early weeping,   11900
For the angels, cherished gain.
That a loving heart is present,
Well you sense, so closer glide;
Yet earth's jagged paths a pleasant
Fate vouchsafed you not to stride.   11905
Sink into my eyes, employ them,

---

5. Traditionally, an epithet ascribed to St. Francis of Assisi (1182–1226), founder of the Franciscan order, who led a life of exemplary simplicity.
6. Unbaptized children who died immediately after being born and are thus without sin, yet also without experience of life. Their relation to Pater Seraphicus may be compared with that of Homunculus to Proteus in the final scene of the "Classical Walpurgis Night."

Fit at world and earth to peer,
As your own you may enjoy them,
Gaze at these environs here.
[*He assumes them within himself.*]
    These are trees, and yonder, boulders,   11910
Waterfalls that downward shoot
And with heaving giant shoulders
Further tilt their dizzying route.

BLESSED BOYS.   [*from within*]
    Mighty vistas strike our gazes,
But too somber is the spot,   11915
Thrills of fear and awe it raises,
Noble, kind one, hold us not.

PATER SERAPHICUS.
    To a higher sphere ascending,
Ever grow in hidden wise,
As, in purity unending,   11920
Godly presence fortifies.
For this is the spirit ration
Found where ether is most free,
Timeless loving's revelation,
Which unfolds to ecstasy.   11925

CHORUS OF BLESSED BOYS.   [*circling the highest peaks*]
        Hand to hand sealing,
        Join a gay roundelay,
        Reverent feeling,
        Make it resound away;
        Holiest teaching   11930
        Trust without fear,
        Know you will reach him
        Whom you revere.

ANGELS.   [*floating in the higher atmosphere, bearing* FAUST'S
    IMMORTAL ESSENCE]
    Pure spirits' peer, from evil coil
He was vouchsafed exemption;   11935
"Whoever strives in ceaseless toil,
Him we may grant redemption."
And when on high, transfigured love
Has added intercession,
The blest will throng to him above   11940
With welcoming compassion.[7]

---

7. Concerning this important speech as the key to Faust's salvation, see Goethe's conversation with Eckermann, June 6, 1831, below. (Lines 11936–7 were enclosed in quotation marks in Goethe's manuscript and in all subsequent editions.)

THE YOUNGER ANGELS.
> From the hands of pure contrition,
> Holy love, those roses showered
> Help us to prevail, empowered
> To fulfill the lofty mission,   11945
> Of this soul-prize to delude them.
> Devils scattered as we strewed them,
> Fiends inured to hellish anguish
> With love's torment learnt to languish;
> Petals stung the spawn of evil,   11950
> Why, the very Master-Devil
> We have pierced with stabbing pain.
> Triumph! it was not in vain.

THE MORE PERFECTED ANGELS.
> Earth remnants molest us,
> To bear them is toil,   11955
> Were they asbestos,
> They still would soil.
> When spirit strength has surged
> And the elements to communion
> With itself has merged,   11960
> No angel could sever the union
> Of two fused in one,
> Of twin natures blended,
> Eternal love alone
> Has strength to end it.[8]   11965

THE YOUNGER ANGELS.
> Swathing the lofty cliff,
> I divine, stirring near,
> Wafting like mist adrift,
> Spirit life here.
> Now thins the fleece of cloud,   11970
> I see a lively crowd
> Of blessed boys,
> Rid of the weight of earth,
> In a circle curled,
> They relish the joys   11975
> Of fresh spring, rebirth
> In the glad upper world.
> For a beginning,
> Rising bliss winning,
> Let him join these!   11980

8. Recall Faust's comments on the two souls within his breast (lines 1112 ff.).

THE BLESSED BOYS.

> Gladly we gather in
> Him in the pupal stage;
> Glad by the same to win
> Angelic gage.
> Loosen the flaking film   11985
> Left yet to bind him,
> Life in the sacred realm
> Has grown and fined him.

DOCTOR MARIANUS.   [*in the highest, purest cell*]⁹

> Here is the prospect free,
> Spirit uplifting.   11990
> Womanly shapes I see
> Heavenward drifting.
> Star-garlands burgeon,
> High at their center
> Heaven's crowned Virgin,   11995
> Known by her splendor.

[*rapt*]¹

> Sovereign Mistress of the World,
> On the azure awning
> Of the Heavens fresh-unfurled,
> Let Thy grace be dawning.   12000
> What the breast of man doth move,
> Tender, earnest feeling,
> Deign to sense it and approve
> Sacred love's revealing.

> As invincible we stood   12005
> When Thou badest the pious,
> Of a sudden melts our mood
> As Thou pacifiest.
> Virgin Thou immaculate,
> Rich in grace maternal,   12010
> Chosen for divine estate,
> Crowned our Queen Eternal.

> About Her swathing
> Cloud wisps tremble,
> Expiant maidens'   12015
> Airy assembly,
> Humbly Her knees in

9. As a sublime counterfigure to Doctor Faustus in his study at the outset of the drama, this mystical devotee of the Virgin represents the highest level of spiritual perfection attainable within the human sphere.

1. The following prayer of rapture addressed to the Mater Gloriosa echoes the prayer to the Virgin Mary by St. Bernhard in Dante's *Paradiso* 33.1–39, which apparently served Goethe as a model for the latter part of this scene.

> Penance seeking
> Pardon bespeaking.

> Nor to Thee the Lord denied it,   12020
> Pure Thyself and peerless,
> That the easily misguided
> Should approach Thee fearless.

> In their carnal weakness nursed,
> Hard is their salvation;   12025
> Who unaided ever burst
> Shackles of temptation?
> How the foot so swiftly slips
> Down the glassy reaches!
> Who resists bold eyes and lips   12030
> And endearing speeches?

[MATER GLORIOSA[2] *floating on high.*]

CHORUS OF PENITENT WOMEN.
> Thou who art soaring
> In realms undying,
> Hear our imploring,
> Thou past all vying,   12035
> Rich mercies pouring!

MAGNA PECCATRIX.   [*Luke vii. 36*][3]
> By the love that at the feet
> Of Thy son and Savior lying,
> Poured them tears for unguent meet,
> Scorn of Pharisees defying;   12040
> By the vessel whence so amply
> Fragrance overpoured the rims,
> By the ringlets that so gently
> Served to dry the sacred limbs—

MULIER SAMARITANA.   [*John iv*]
> By the wellspring whither erstwhile   12045
> Herds of Abraham were driven,
> By the pail whence to the thirsting
> Savior's lips cool drink was given,
> By the pure and plenteous fountain
> Thence forever outward streaming,   12050
> Ever sparkling and abounding
> Flows for all the world's redeeming—

MARIA AEGYPTIACA.   [*Acta Sanctorum*]
> By the shrine where what was mortal

---

2. The Virgin Mary appears in Glory, accompanied by female attendants, a counterpart to the statue of her as the Mater Dolorosa to whom Gretchen prayed in Part One, "By the City Wall" (lines 3587 ff.; see also the interpretive note for that scene). Suggested iconographic sources for this vision are paintings of the ascension of Mary, for instance by Titian, in Venice.
3. The sources for the three penitent female sinners are discussed in the interpretive notes.

Of the Lord was laid in mourning,
By the arm that from its portal   12055
Spurned me back with voice of warning;
By my forty years' repentance
Humbly served in desert land,
By the blissful parting sentence
I inscribed upon the sand—   12060
THE THREE TOGETHER.
Thou who those of great transgression
From Thy presence dost not banish,
And their treasures of contrition
Through the eons still replenish,
Grant this soul, we join in praying,   12065
Who but once misstepped, unwitting,
Unaware that she was straying,
Such forgiveness as is fitting!
UNA POENITENTIUM, ELSE CALLED GRETCHEN.   [nestling]
Incline
Thou past comparing,
Thou radiance bearing,   12070
Thy grace upon my happiness.
The early-cherished,
No longer blemished,
Returns to bliss.[4]   12075
BLESSED BOYS.   [circling closer]
He already outgrows us
In bodily might;
True care that he owes us
Will richly requite.
We early were riven   12080
From earthly creatures,
He, wise in living,
Will fitly teach us.
THE ONE PENITENT, ELSE CALLED GRETCHEN.
'Mid spirit choirs fresh life commencing,
The novice scarce regains his wit,   12085
The heavenly host but dimly sensing,
Already he has merged with it.
Behold! how, all terrestrial cumbrance,
A worn-out guise, cast off at length,
In first ethereal adumbrance   12090
He issues forth in youthful strength.
Vouchsafe me through new morn to lead him,
Too bright as yet for him to see.[5]

---

4. An adaptation of Gretchen's earlier prayer of despair to the Mater Dolorosa (see lines 3587 ff.).
5. The theme of a blinding brightness recalls the Earth Spirit (lines 481 ff.) and the rising sun in
   "Charming Landscape" (lines 4702–3). A corresponding theme of developing vision of a purer
   light is also central to Dante's progress in the company of Beatrice in the *Paradiso*.

MATER GLORIOSA.
         Come, soar to higher spheres, precede him,
         He will divine and follow thee.   12095

DOCTOR MARIANUS.   [*prostrate in adoration*]
         Gaze to meet the saving gaze,[6]
         Contrite all and tender,
         For a blissful fate your ways
         Thankfully surrender.
         May each noble mind be seen   12100
         Eager for Thy service;
         Holy Virgin, Mother, Queen,
         Goddess, pour Thy mercies!

CHORUS MYSTICUS.†
         All that is changeable
         Is but reflected;   12105
         The unattainable
         Here is effected;
         Human discernment
         Here is passed by;
         The Eternal-Feminine[7]   12110
         Draws us on high.

FINIS

---

6. The German of this line, *Blicket auf zum Retterblick*, recalls the theme of the "moment" to which Faust aspired: *Augenblick*. It is ironic and important that such affirmation is spoken by an ecstatic devotee of the Virgin who is "prostrate in adoration."
7. This often-discussed phrase should be referred back to the counterphrase used by Mephistopheles in line 11603. (See interpretive notes.)

Interpretive Notes

Goethe's *Faust* has been discussed and interpreted by a wide diversity of scholars and critics for an equally wide range of purposes from the time the poet first began to publish the drama to the present day. The historical and critical materials assembled in this edition bear partial witness to this ongoing endeavor. The most daunting challenge for such interpretive response, however, has long been demonstrated by the numerous commentaries that have accompanied various editions of the play. For the most part these commentaries are in German, and to a considerable degree they address primarily, if not exclusively, questions of obscure and difficult details in the text of *Faust*. This remains true for the most recent editions in Germany (by Albrecht Schöne, by Dorothea Hölscher-Lohmeyer, and by Ulrich Gaier), where exhaustive erudition and patience in details yields clarification of seemingly limitless particulars. What is needed for a readership in English, however, as intended by this critical edition, usually within the limits of the study of literature in translation at university level, is assistance with the many crucial questions of meaning and significance that arise in response to virtually every scene in the drama. These interpretive notes are intended to address specifically these needs in ways that may be helpful for both students and teachers of *Faust* at all levels of experience and sophistication.

The inclusion of interpretive notes in the first edition of the Norton *Faust* (1976) was regarded by both editor and publisher as an experiment in supplementary commentary beyond the normal format of the Norton Critical Editions. Generous response from many friends and readers has provided encouragement for expanding and strengthening these notes for the new edition. The editor is especially grateful to the publisher for approving such expansion, since the experience of working on *Faust* and teaching the drama under every conceivable circumstance over the past quarter century has led to a strengthening of conviction and, it is hoped, insight on almost every point. The notes emphasize, as in the first edition, above all the wide range of literary allusions, which constitute the intricate fabric of Goethe's drama, and also the complex thematic and structural interaction back and forth among the various scenes of the drama, frequently in symbolic and self-reflective ways. Particular attention has been given in these revised notes to Part Two on the conviction that the majority of the interpretive problems for a reading arise here and because this uniquely creative and wide-ranging portion of the work has come increasingly to fascinate readers at the end of the twentieth century and beginning of the twenty-first. It is the sincere hope of the editor that these notes will assist new readers of *Faust* without diminishing in any way the challenge and the pleasure of arriving at an understanding of Goethe's uniquely fascinating great play of the world.

"Dedication" (lines 1–32)

Composed on June 24, 1797 (according to Goethe's diary entry), two days after the poet wrote to Schiller of his plans to recommence work on the uncompleted drama. Apart from intermittent efforts in Italy in 1788 and shortly thereafter to prepare the play for publication as A *Fragment* in his collected works in 1790 (*Schriften*, vol. 7), over two decades had passed since Goethe had written the various drafts, which we know as the *Urfaust* from the transcript prepared by Luise von Göchhausen shortly after Goethe arrived in Weimar in 1775. The dedicatory poem of 1797 thus describes the poet's response to this earlier material as he prepares to pick up where he had left off. The characters of the drama haunt him like spirits half-realized from his past, and this calls to mind the days of his youth and the departed friends who were close to him when he was first writing the play. This sense of distance from the world of *Faust*—even the world partially created in the earlier manuscripts—combined with feelings of nostalgia and regret, is crucial for understanding the point of view established in the completed drama (at least in Part One). "Dedication" was first published with the completed Part One in 1808, in the position it has occupied ever since as the first of three prefatory texts to the drama as a whole.

Critics have noted that Goethe returned to *Faust* from writing ballads during the spring of 1797 for Schiller's journal of poetry, *Musenalmanach*, and that the spirit world of his ballads is closely akin to the attitude and mood that Goethe associates with *Faust* in the "Dedication." The form of the "Dedication" is the stanza in ottava rima (eight lines of iambic pentameter with the rhyme scheme a-b-a-b-a-b-c-c), derived from Italian romances of the sixteenth century (e.g., by Ariosto, Tasso, etc.). Goethe used this form earlier for his incomplete epic *Die Geheimnisse* (which begins with a longer poem also entitled "Dedication," which Goethe subsequently placed at the very beginning of his collected works). Goethe associated this poetic form with reflective and melancholy moods and with a certain formality of emotional expression. The importance of Schiller for Goethe's attempt to renew work on the drama, as documented from his persistent inquiries in their almost daily correspondence at the time, should also be considered. Schiller shared with other readers of the published *Fragment* of 1790, such as Wilhelm von Humboldt, Friedrich Schlegel, and the philosopher Schelling, a fascination with the philosophical implications of the tragedy.

In the final stanza of "Dedication," Goethe describes his response to the encounter with his earlier work in terms of a long-neglected desire. Such a response of longing to the realm of spirits anticipates the most characteristic trait of Faust himself as a boundless and insatiable "striving" (*Streben*). The intensity of this emotion for the poet includes, as intended, a renewal of the creative poetic process. The successful re-creation of the poetic world of *Faust* for the poet thus constitutes an eminently "Faustian" experience and serves as a paradigm for the drama as a whole.

Of interest also is the fact that Goethe composed a verse epilogue to *Faust*, presumably at about the same time as "Dedication," entitled "Farewell" (*Abschied*), also a poem in four stanzas of ottava rima. This poem is preserved in a manuscript for *Faust*, dated approximately 1825/26, when work on Part Two had already advanced significantly. The poem was never published with the drama (perhaps only through oversight by Goethe's literary executors?) and was subsequently included among the Paralipomena for *Faust* in the complete Weimar edition of Goethe's works (Para. 98; vol. 15, 1, 344 f.).

"Prelude in the Theater" (lines 33–242)

Composed presumably in the period from 1798 to 1800 (perhaps soon after the renovation of the Weimar Theater in the summer and fall of 1798), the "Prelude" offers a general view of the theater from the threefold perspective of the Theater Manager, the Dramatic Poet, and the Actor (or Comedian). All three perspectives were, of course, familiar to Goethe— indeed, he had performed all three functions himself at different times— though he should not be identified with any of the three speakers in the "Prelude," least of all with the Poet. Goethe offers here a playfully ironic picture of the theater of his time, juxtaposing its several concerns in such a way that broader, ultimately universal implications are defined, which pertain not only to *Faust* but to all drama and performance in any theater.

Sources for the "Prelude," especially in the tradition of plays-within-plays, where ironic comments on the performance of plays can be made, as in the *Mousetrap* of Shakespeare's *Hamlet*, or the actors' comments in *The Knight of the Burning Pestle* by Beaumont and Fletcher, Calderón's *Great Theater of the World*, or Ludwig Tieck's Romantic comedies, such as *Puss in Boots* (*Der gestiefelte Kater*), are less important than the more general sense of theater established by the "Prelude" for the drama of *Faust*. This diversity of views is both pragmatic—as demonstrated by the arguments of the Director and the Comedian concerning the necessity of, respectively, a popular success to bring in money and immediacy of response as measured by applause—and theoretical—as indicated by the attitude of the Poet toward art and poetry, which reflects familiar positions toward aesthetics at that time (as in the essays of Schiller, whose views Goethe largely shared).

Some critics have questioned the relevance of the "Prelude" for *Faust*, yet each of the three speakers expresses characteristically "Faustian" views concerning, respectively, the meaning, the effect, and the institution of theatrical art. The Manager favors spectacle and diversity of effect so that the audience will be captivated by the show. The Clown favors fantasy and foolery for a laugh, in ways that are not incompatible with the motives of the Manager. The Poet, by contrast, is a kind of idealist, who wishes to convey eternal truths through his art; but he, too, indicates a concern for the way in which theater can put such ideas into practice as external events. There can thus be no question that Goethe intended the "Prelude" to establish a conscious sense of "theater" and performance as central to the drama of *Faust* as a whole, including also Part Two, which was not written until much later. Despite its playful and satirical tone, the "Prelude in the Theater" remains a valuable document for theater history and for the theory of drama in relation to theatrical production. The burden of its argument should also discourage any preoccupation among its readers with the philosophy of *Faust* at the expense of its theatricality.

"Prologue in Heaven" (lines 243–353)

Composed when Goethe was completing Part One of the drama, presumably in late 1799 or 1800, the "Prologue in Heaven" introduces an important transformation of the traditional Faust legend. Faust's pact with Mephistopheles—the central feature of that legend—now proceeds not only from Faust's own decision to work with magic but also from a wager contracted independently between Mephistopheles and the Lord within a transcendent context beyond the limits of human knowledge and existence. Neither the use of black magic nor the question of damnation thus stands at the center of Goethe's drama, but rather the fundamental question of human nature itself, the existential question of the human condition. And it is the Lord in the "Prologue," not Mephistopheles, who first mentions Faust as the representative exemplum for that which constitutes the human condition.

Goethe borrows here a central feature of the biblical tradition, namely the prologue to the Book of Job (1.6–12), thus superimposing upon the drama of Faust the traditional philosophical and existential, as well as theological, implications of Satan's testing of Job. In a comment to Eckermann later in his life (dated January 18, 1825), Goethe expressed his satisfaction with regard to this bold association of Faust with the biblical figure of Job. There is of course, a crucial contrast between Job, who serves in the Bible as the model of a just and upright man, and Faust, who (in the words of Mephistopheles, 300) serves the Lord "in a curious fashion." The terms of the wager and its working out are thus very different in Goethe's drama.

Goethe's "Prologue" also derives certain theatrical qualities, in particular the representation of the Lord upon his throne within the court of Heaven before the "heavenly host," from another poetic attempt to "justify the ways of God to man," namely Milton's *Paradise Lost*, especially the scene in Heaven in Book 3 of that epic. The role of Goethe's Mephistopheles remains, of course, very different from the role of Milton's Satan, as indicated by the fact that Christ is the interlocutor of God in Milton's scene, whereas Mephistopheles (like Satan in the Book of Job) assumes that role in Goethe's "Prologue," essentially in the manner of a court jester, called "rogue" (*Schalk*, 339) by the Lord (a role that Mephisto later also assumes in the court of the Emperor in Act I of Part Two).

Equally important for the "Prologue in Heaven" is the implication that Faust will ultimately be saved rather than damned in Goethe's drama. This constitutes another fundamental change in the traditional legend, to which Goethe here commits himself. Mephistopheles' role is thus also made subordinate to the will of the Lord. The devil in Goethe's "Prologue" thus assumes the somewhat playful and congenial function of reporting to the court of Heaven about the state of the world and the condition of mankind (271–92). Mephisto's complaint that he finds the condition of mankind to be "wretched" and of "precious little worth" (296–7) is mollified by the ironic tone of his entire exchange with the Lord. Goethe thus establishes for his drama a transcendent perspective of tolerance, which the reader is invited to share. In the tradition of medieval and Baroque allegorical drama, the "Prologue in Heaven" introduces a superior playful tone that purposefully offsets the high tragic manner of Faust's existential tragedy as scholar discontent with the limits of human knowledge and experience. On the authority of the "Prologue," furthermore, we learn to take Mephistopheles' subsequent self-definition as true, when in his first conversation with Faust he calls himself a "part of that force which would / Do ever evil, and does ever good" (1335–6), a statement also borrowed from Milton's Satan (*Paradise Lost* 1.162–3 and 217–8), though Mephisto does not in that conversation with Faust in his study acknowledge the Lord as the ultimate source of this good.

Critics of Goethe's *Faust* have correctly pointed out that the purposefully theatrical and allegorical quality of the court of Heaven as represented in the "Prologue" should not be understood in terms of Christian theology or any other religious doctrine. The exchange between Mephistopheles and the Lord takes place within the setting of a feudal court, very much in accord with traditional ceremonies of state as represented in Renaissance and Baroque drama, familiar, for example, from Shakespeare's history plays. The Lord is presented as a benevolent monarch surrounded by his subjects, the hosts of Heaven (see stage direction preceding line 243). The Archangels represent vassals who celebrate the cosmos as the Lord's domain. Mephistopheles' role thus corresponds to that of a court jester, resembling the role of the Comedian in the "Prelude in the Theater" and anticipating his disguise as jester in the court of the Emperor in Act I of Part Two. Indeed, the entire setting of the Emperor's court in Part Two may be read—and presumably was so intended by Goethe—as a parody of the rule of justice represented by the heavenly court of the "Prologue." Also important is the structural balance of transcendent perspectives between the "Prologue in Heaven" and the final scenes of Part Two, "Entombment" and "Mountain Gorges," which thus constitute a kind of epilogue for Goethe's drama with an equally transcendent though ironic tone.

Hymn of the Archangels (lines 243–70)

This hymn is a celebration of the cosmos in its dynamic yet all-inclusive harmonious activity, addressed to the Lord by his chief vassals in direct response to the life and work of the cosmos as they perceive it from their heavenly vantage point. Yet the poetic implications of the hymn extend beyond celebration, establishing implicitly an identity between speaker, statement, and referent. Through this hymn of celebration Goethe introduces to his drama a mode of poetry that imitates the life process itself, using imagery of sight and sound to equate the action of the cosmos with its own statement. Comparable also to such poetic discourse is the speech of the Earth Spirit in the opening scene, "Night" (from the *Urfaust*; 501–9), in which the Spirit presents itself—and thus identifies itself—by describing its activity. A more complex instance of such self-referential *poiesis*, composed a full quarter century after the "Prologue in Heaven," occurs in the scene "Charming Landscape," which opens Part Two of the drama, where the spirit chorus recites—and thus bears witness to and itself performs—the watches of the night (4634–65).

The three Archangels presumably derive from their counterparts in Milton's *Paradise Lost* (since biblical references to these figures are obscure). All three celebrate cyclical processes within the cosmos from different perspectives: Raphael, the circular path of the sun; Gabriel, the cycles of night and day and the changing tides of the Earth; Michael, the motion of storms with their lightning and thunder, as well as the gentler activity of good weather. In their refrain (which restates the final lines of Raphael's stanza) all three affirm the glory of the Lord, himself incomprehensible, as manifested in the permanent life of his creation. The Archangels employ a lyric stanza with regular four-stress iambic lines, alternating feminine and masculine endings, and alternating rhymes. The exalted tone and measured cadence of this opening hymn stands in purposeful contrast to the more familiar, colloquial, and ironic speech of Mephistopheles that follows it.

The Lord's Hermeneutical Mandate (lines 344–9)

In the final lines of the concluding speech by the Lord in the "Prologue in Heaven," a directive is given to the host of angels, "true scions of the godly race" (344), in contradistinction to the largesse granted to Mephistopheles, whose function on Earth is to goad and provoke humankind— Faust in particular!—to sustained activity as preferred alternative to an all-too-human predilection for "repose at any price" (341). The Lord's instructions for his authentic offspring (*die echten Göttersöhne*, 344), by contrast, may be referred implicitly also to the audience of Goethe's play—indeed, to ourselves as readers—with regard to our reception and interpretation of the drama to come. Three distinct modes of aesthetic and cognitive interplay are stated: 1) to enjoy the beauty of that which lives in all its diversity (*der lebendig reichen Schöne*, 345); 2) to be embraced by that which comes to be (*das Werdende*) in its eternal life and influence (*das ewig lebt und wirkt*, 346); and 3) to seize and grasp in abiding thought (*befestiget mit dauernden Gedanken*) that which hovers before us in "wavering revelation" (*was in schwankender Erscheinung schwebt*, 348). It may be argued that Goethe here summarizes in the Lord's instructions his own philosophy of human experience and his view of the function of art in general. Juxtaposing this threefold mandate with the message conveyed earlier by the "Dedication" and the diverse views of the Poet, the Actor, and the Theater Manager in the "Prelude in the Theater" makes apparent that the instructions conveyed by the Lord to his angelic hosts as they observe and respond to the activities of the cosmos also define precisely the kind of experience to be conveyed by *Faust* as drama performed in the theater to its audience. Above all, the third and most challenging mandate of the Lord provides a sense of hermeneutical obligation for us, namely to translate that which appears upon the stage as diverse shadowplay into knowledge and thought that endures as meaning. (This hermeneutical mandate from the Lord in Heaven should also be compared with the four couplets by the Chorus Mysticus, composed at the end of Goethe's life, which bring the final scene of Part Two to a close.)

"Night" (lines 354–807)

The opening scene of Goethe's drama imposes two specific challenges for interpretation: 1) two quite disparate stages of composition, separated by a distance of more than a quarter century, are joined together here, not without considerable effort on the part of the author's synthesizing powers; and 2) the scene as a whole, modeled by implication on the subgenre of monodrama, which was popular in the eighteenth century and well known to Goethe (especially from French sources), presents within its limited scope a programmatic survey in miniature of the essential Faustian dilemma, from which the entire drama proceeds. In contrast to the Aristotelian plot of drama, familiar from the conventional five-act play in the French neoclassical tradition, the opening scene of *Faust* serves as paradigm for the drama as a whole.

The opening section of the scene—including Faust's initial monologue in his study, his contemplation of the Sign of the Macrocosm in the book of magic, and his conjuring of the Earth Spirit, using a formula from the same book, along with the visit from his famulus, Wagner (354–605)— belongs to the earliest stage of composition and coincides (with only minor revisions) with the text contained in the *Urfaust*, dating from the early 1770s. Of particular interest are the terms with which Faust initially makes use of magic, attempting to achieve an experience of life's totality with no thought of evoking the powers of the devil for assistance (as had always been the case in the traditional Faust legend). The distinction between the Sign of the Macrocosm and the Earth Spirit also introduces a crucial contrast between two opposing forms of semiosis; a pictorial sign in the case of the former, where the cosmos is represented schematically as a kind of picture; and a verbal sign in the latter instance, where Faust by uttering a magic formula from the book conjures the Earth Spirit to appear before him.

The contrast between these two kinds of sign also results in a twofold failure. The Sign of the Macrocosm fails to satisfy Faust because it is only an artificial representation of life, an empty *Schau-spiel*, a play or show for the eye (454), which, however impressive as a self-contained harmonious interactivity, does not provide the viewer with the actual experience of life that he seeks. The Earth Spirit, by contrast, is all fire and force, overwhelming Faust and threatening to destroy his mortal self. Despite his hybristic claim to the Spirit that he is akin to it ("I am Faust, . . . I am the same!," 500), the Spirit mockingly rejects him with a threefold internal rhyme in the German: *"Du gleichst dem Geist den du begreifst, / Nicht mir!"* (512–3). There is no equality—indeed, no similitude or kinship—here, and Faust is left bereft in solitude as his assistant, Wagner, knocks on his study door, thinking that his master has been declaiming speeches from Greek tragedy.

Particularly important in the earlier portion of "Night" is the strongly satirical aspect of the scene, directed especially against the pretensions of academic and scientific learning. The character of Faust as scholar and professor was for the young Goethe, himself a somewhat reluctant student newly exposed to such learning at the University of Leipzig, a source of amusement and a focus for polemical critique. The language of Faust's opening monologue is purposefully archaic and simplistic, as is made apparent by the use of doggerel verse (*Knittelvers*), a form derived from popular literary conventions associated with the era (early-sixteenth century) when the historical Dr. Faustus lived. The trappings of the scholar's study furthermore, its dusty books, manuscripts, and various kinds of scientific equipment, suggest a sterile intellectual or indeed existential prison for the self. To this satirical element should be added a consciously sentimental desire—within familiar conventions of sensibility in the mid-eighteenth century—to escape from the realm of dead learning and to commune with nature as a living reality. This is particularly apparent in Faust's response to the moonlight that shines through his stained-glass window (386–409), where he instantly imagines himself to be out in the open countryside, absorbing the mood and emotion of nature. The image he introduces in response to the Sign of the Macrocosm also fits this desire (455–9), as Faust expresses a longing to suck nourishment from nature as from the breasts of a mother.

Equally forceful as satire is the portrayal of Famulus Wagner, for whom the pleasures of dry, lifeless learning are fully adequate to the fulfillment of his pedantic desires: "Though I know much, I would know everything" (601). Particularly appropriate to such satirical concern is the error of judgment that brings Wagner to knock on Faust's door in the first place: he mistakes the sounds of his master's confrontation with the Earth Spirit for a recitation from the text of some Greek tragedy. This satirical strain in Goethe's drama is further developed in the scene with the student just following the pact scene (1868–2050) and the scene of drinking and carousing among the students at "Auerbach's Tavern in Leipzig" (both scenes also composed as part of the *Urfaust*).

The Influence of Rembrandt's Faust Etching

When Goethe first prepared the fragment of his *Faust* for publication in 1790, he commissioned from the young Swiss artist Johann Heinrich Lips, whom he had met in Italy and subsequently invited to Weimar, as illustration for the frontispiece a copy of Rembrandt's well-known etching of the scholar in his study contemplating a spirit (c. 1650), which was already associated with the Faust legend in the mid-eighteenth century. Scholars of Goethe's *Faust* have paid curiously little attention to this significant visual signal by the poet. Goethe is known to have been fascinated by the work of Rembrandt from an early age. He also possessed a copy of the Faust etching (still contained in his collection of art, preserved in the Goethe Archives at Weimar), possibly already at the time when he first conceived the plan for *Faust*. It is therefore likely that the spirit figure that appears before the scholar in Rembrandt's etching, however Goethe may have interpreted the meaning of this cryptic image, provided the initial stimulus for the conjuring of the Earth Spirit in the scene "Night." The implications of this source, especially with regard to Goethe's substitution of the Earth Spirit for the devil in the traditional scene of conjuring by magic from the Faust legend, should be carefully considered. The fact that Goethe later omitted the illustration from Rembrandt when he published the completed Part One in 1808 does not diminish the significance of its inclusion for the initial publication of the *Fragment* in 1790.

The Later Addition to "Night" (lines 606–807)

When Faust continues his monologue after Wagner leaves, an apparent recapitulation of the preceding events occurs, in particular a review by Faust of his confrontation with the Earth Spirit. This transitional section of the scene indicates the process of re-creation and transformation undertaken by Goethe around 1800 as he worked himself back into the mood of the earlier fragment and, simultaneously, carried its perspective forward into his later, more mature view of Faust's dilemma. The more universal, indeed archetypal, tragedy of the human condition is thus fully established within this later monologue, at least by the introduction of the suicide motif (686 ff.), followed by Faust's existential crisis of despair and his subsequent renewal of spirit in response to the celebration of Christ's Resurrection on Easter morning. There is no indication in the text of the *Urfaust*, which is far more satirical and purposefully archaic in style and tone, that Goethe initially intended Faust to be associated in any way with Christ, or even that the scene "Night" originally coincided with Easter.

Concerning the structure of the scene as a whole, it should be noted how boldly Goethe exploits his most radical departure from the traditional legend of Faust. Having abandoned the devil entirely in the opening scene of conjuring by magical sign, substituting the Earth Spirit for Mephistoph-eles, Goethe juxtaposes Faust's despair at his failed encounter with the Spirit with the liturgical celebration of Christ's Resurrection, overheard in the singing of the Chorus at Easter Mass in a nearby cathedral. The Res-urrection of Jesus at Easter is associated both with the renewal of life in nature at springtime (as the following scene, "Outside the City Gate," demonstrates) and with the renewal of spiritual energy in Faust himself through his creative recollection of the faith he enjoyed as a child. A twofold transformation of the traditional magus thus occurs in this scene: first, in accord with the boundless striving of the Romantic (or pre-Romantic) power of will, Faust attempts to challenge the spiritual power of the world by confronting the Earth Spirit; and, second, by association and analogy with the Christian myth of Resurrection, Faust's state of mind is transformed and his spirit renewed. The opening scene of the drama thus demonstrates how Goethe, at the initial stage of composition, radically transformed the Faust of popular legend into a prototypical Romantic hero and, at the later stage of composition, subsequently modified the hero's stance in such a way that his ultimate salvation is prefigured by analogy to Christ's Resurrection at Easter.

The inner psychological motivation of Faust's second monologue is crucial to the drama yet difficult to follow. In less than one hundred lines of verse, spoken after Wagner leaves, Faust works himself into a suicidal despair, purely through reflection upon the incidents that have preceded. If Faust were actually to drink the poison he pours into the chalice, the result would be identical to the annihilation of his mortal existence, with which he was threatened through his encounter with the Earth Spirit. The rec-ollection of his encounter with the Earth Spirit brings Faust face to face with futility, not only because he is incapable of confronting the Spirit as an equal but also because as a human being he is subject to time and the limitations of his mortal life, as represented by the existential prison cell of his study.

The conditions or contingencies of his life are referred to, in what ap-proaches a mythical personification, as "gray Care" (644). Goethe here anticipates the appearance, in Act V of Part Two, of the spirit figure of Care, who approaches Faust after the death of Philemon and Baucis and who blinds him just before he dies. This spirit figure at the end of the drama should thus be regarded as a counterfigure to the Earth Spirit at the beginning. Faust's dilemma, which assumes an existential despair in the final version of the opening scene, is thus defined by the fact that he stands suspended between these opposing spiritual forces—the Earth Spirit and Care—juxtaposing the two in his mind in an irreconcilable tragic conflict. Interpreted in this way, the second monologue in "Night" as-sumes symbolic significance beyond the particular terms of the Faust leg-end. Goethe establishes in the opening scene of his drama a paradigmatic demonstration of what later came to be called Romantic despair. Goethe's

Faust thus articulates the fundamental tragic dilemma of the human condition.

The Easter Chorus (lines 737–807)

Faust responds to the music of the Easter liturgy as to a heavenly visitation. What he overhears is a Choir performing the story of the Resurrection from the Gospel narratives as part of the celebration of the Easter Mass in a nearby church. This liturgy, involving three distinct voices—the angels, the disciples, and the three Marys at the empty tomb of Jesus—belongs to the oldest tradition of liturgical drama in the Christian church, thus providing another example of a play within the play. Though Faust denies all Christian faith for himself (765–8), as Goethe would likewise have done, he nonetheless acknowledges the validity of the Easter ritual as a miracle of rebirth for the faithful. Such faith, he admits in recalling his own childhood, was once shared by him as well. More important for the drama is the function of this visitation within the larger structure of the scene.

In contrast to the appearance of the Earth Spirit, which was conjured by Faust through uttering the magical sign, the Easter Chorus occurs unexpectedly and by surprise, a gift of grace at the moment when he is about to drink the poison. The poison as "quintessence of all subtly lethal power" (694) is implicitly offset by the eucharist of bread and wine, which the participants at the Easter Mass partake in symbolic commemoration of the new covenant of Christ with the faithful. In contrast to the poison, which would have caused Faust's death, the eucharist brings new life to those who believe. The juxtaposition of these two spiritual visitations—the Earth Spirit and the Easter Chorus—is thus central to Faust's experience both in this opening scene and in the drama as a whole. The Resurrection of Christ at Easter also prefigures Faust's ultimate salvation at the end, confirming the earlier prophecy of the Lord in the "Prologue in Heaven" (308–9 and 328–9). And both these visitations, as mentioned, constitute a radical departure by Goethe from the traditional Faust legend, which had always begun with the conjuring of Mephistopheles by Faust.

"Outside the City Gate" (lines 808–1177)

This scene follows without interruption the conclusion of "Night" on Easter morning. Goethe also composed the scene more or less sequentially with the completion of "Night," probably early in 1801. In its opening sequence, "Outside the City Gate" provides a panoramic mode of dramatic action, showing the general activity of the town in celebration of Easter (perhaps resembling the Frankfurt that Goethe knew from his childhood). Goethe here introduces a mode of theatrical tableau, which functions like a genre painting, possibly with traditions of seventeenth-century Dutch painting consciously in mind. An informal procession of figures moves across the stage, representing typical citizens of the town from various levels of society and at various ages and engaged in various activities. Until the appearance of Faust and Wagner (after 902), nothing in the scene pertains directly to the drama except insofar as the procession provides a general thematic overview of human concerns and desires. A somewhat playful, even satirical tone pervades the entire procession, as if the various activities and preoccupations of human society were being exposed as a source of ridicule and folly. Such a satirical theatrical display of human behavior, often quite unrelated to the character of Faust himself, occurs frequently later on in Goethe's drama, e.g., in the procession toward the witches' Sabbath on the Brocken in the Harz Mountains on Walpurgis Night. Especially in various allegorical and symbolic scenes of Part Two, notably in the Carnival Masque in Act I and the "Classical Walpurgis Night" in Act II, Goethe later expanded his theatrical vision in *Faust* to include all of humankind within the scope of a universal satire. To this extent, "Outside the City Gate" assumes a paradigmatic status for the social dimension of Goethe's great theater of the world.

In this scene, the beneficial effects of Easter are displayed, specifically through the return of spring to the land with a corresponding sense of new life and renewed spirit, as manifested in the behavior of all the people who come through the city gate, young and old, rich and poor. The setting and the structure of the scene thus demonstrate the effects of this renewal as an emergence, or an opening outward, of a communal spirit. The citizens of the town proceed out of the narrow city gate and into the open countryside, as if they were being released from the imprisonment of winter within the oppressive confinements of society. The speech Faust addresses to Wagner as they also join the excursion into the country (903–40) is justly famous as a celebration of nature in its renewal at springtime and the response of all living creatures to this sense of new life. His concluding assertion, addressed to all who participate in this celebration—"Here I am Man, am free to be me!" (*Hier bin ich Mensch, hier darf ich's sein*, 940)—if applied specifically to Faust himself, would provide a solution to his sense of existential imprisonment within the confinement of learning and science as symbolized by his study in the opening scene of the drama. The Easter walk thus functions implicitly as a model for the affirmation of human existence, as had the symbol of the resurrection in the celebration of the Easter Mass by the Choir at the end of "Night."

Initially, the perspective of the scene is fixed at a convenient vantage point near the city gate. We witness the procession of citizens, which emerges through the gate and passes across the stage. Later on, however, following Faust's opening speech describing the vista spread before him, the scene moves almost cinematically with Faust and Wagner through the landscape. They make their way, first, to the village with its rustic festival, then to the top of a hill, where they watch the sun go down, and finally back to the city gate, accompanied at the end by the black poodle (Mephistopheles in disguise), returning at evening to the protection and enclosure of house and study. The scene thus assumes a cyclical structure, moving with Faust as he makes his way outward from the city to the limits of human habitation and activity in nature and then back to the gate and the protection of the city. The circular structure of this Easter walk outward and back establishes a symbolic form for human life and experience in general, as also for the career of Faust himself as it will unfold through the drama in its activity and involvement with the open world at various levels of complexity.

Faust's Participation in the Village Festival (lines 945–1010)

A sign of the symbolic form of the Easter walk at its simplest level is the celebration of the peasants in their village, to which Faust is also made welcome. The dance of the young men and maidens to the song *Der Schäfer putzte sich zum Tanz* (949–80), which Goethe had composed perhaps twenty years or more before including it in this scene for *Faust*, offers a secular analogue to the Choir celebrating the Resurrection at the Easter Mass at the end of the preceding scene. This sense of analogy and contrast is made explicit when the Old Peasant welcomes Faust to their company by inviting him to share their drink with them, which may be regarded as a secular equivalent to the eucharist in the Mass. The Peasant thanks Faust for having saved many of them from the plague at an earlier time, when he tended them in their sickness along with his father, a medical doctor. Faust subsequently indicates to Wagner (1026–55) that his ministrations had been futile, that the medicines created by his father had been the product of alchemical experiments that produced poisons rather than cures for the plague. Such recollections recall the poison Faust himself was about to drink at the moment he heard the Easter Chorus and only add to the sense of positive, restorative value of both the eucharist of the Mass and the festival of the village with its communal drink, song, and dance. Faust's own central concerns, however, lie elsewhere, as indicated in the latter part of the scene through his soliloquy at the setting of the sun and his speech about the two souls dwelling in his breast.

Faust's Sunset Speech (lines 1064–99)

Faust's speech in response to the setting sun, in effect a monologue or soliloquy, may be regarded as a central programmatic poetic text for European Romanticism. His mood, as in the opening scene, is a mixture of frustration at his own condition as human being and his desire for infinite satisfaction. His response to the sunset also resembles his response in the opening scene to the moonlight shining through the window of his study (386–409). There as here Faust responds to the visitation of a heavenly light through an imagined projection of his spirit beyond himself into a communion with nature and divinity. Correspondingly, both these imagined flights of the spirit result in an abrupt return to consciousness and the disillusioning recognition that it was all a kind of dream or fiction, created by the power of the imagination in response to the light.

Watching the sun as it sets over the horizon, Faust projects his desire to sustain the light through an image of spiritual flight. By imagining himself moving in the company of the sun, which increasingly assumes the guise of a divinity, Faust also comes to identify himself with this god. He imagines himself moving above the Earth, surveying the whole of it from his transcendent vantage point. He conceives of himself as the mythical center of a cosmic activity (1085 ff.), poised between Heaven and Earth, day and night. As the sun departs and evening begins to come on, however, Faust returns to consciousness of himself and an awareness of his earthly stance upon the hill, acknowledging that his "fancy" (1089) was no more than that. The concluding lines of his speech affirm through generalization the validity for all mankind of such transcendent longings and imaginings, that preeminently Faustian feeling of infinite desire, associated in the sequence of concluding couplets with flights of birds in the sky: the lark in its jubilation, the eagle in its heights, and the crane in its migrations.

The Doctrine of Two Souls (lines 1110–7)

Faust's comments concerning the two opposite impulses of the human mind have been much discussed by scholars of *Faust*. It would be an error to assume, as some have done, that Goethe here intended to introduce a philosophical doctrine to his drama. What comes most readily to mind is the myth of the soul developed in the "palinode" of Socrates in Plato's *Phaedrus*, where the soul is described as a chariot being pulled by two horses that seek to go in opposite directions, with reason as charioteer attempting to keep both under control. Much closer at hand when Goethe composed this scene would have been a corresponding philosophical doctrine from Fichte's *Wissenschaftslehre* (1794), in which knowledge and even consciousness itself are defined as the result of a reciprocal opposition in the mind between a polarity of impulses, or "drives" (*Triebe*). Closely related to Fichte's theory of a reciprocity of opposing impulses (and directly influenced by it) is the argument in Schiller's *Letters on the Aesthetic Education of Man* (1795), in which a dichotomy of forces in the self is defined between what is called the "material drive" (*Stofftrieb*) and the "formal drive" (*Formtrieb*). Schiller's theory of aesthetic experience may be regarded as a conscious application of the epistemology of idealist philosophy, where the ideal of beauty constitutes a harmonious balance between these opposing drives, in what is termed a third drive uniting both the others: the "play drive" (*Spieltrieb*), corresponding essentially to the poetic imagination. Goethe was familiar with such theories, especially that of Schiller, and was essentially in agreement, so that Faust's assertion that two opposing "souls" reside within his breast may reflect the influence of such philosophical doctrines without being dependent upon them.

More important is the role of such a duality in the self throughout *Faust* as a dramatic theme that recurs again and again in various guises. One need recall only Mephistopheles' description of human desire to the Lord in the "Prologue in Heaven" as analogous to the leapings of a grasshopper (287–90; also 304–5), or the polarity between the Sign of the Macrocosm and the Earth Spirit in Faust's initial attempt to achieve satisfaction of his desire for comprehensive knowledge and experience through magic (429–513). Similarly, in the present scene and the one that follows, Faust's desire to follow the path of the sun is offset by his contentment when he returns again to his study and begins to read his Bible. Note that Wagner, in apparent contrast to Faust—as Faust himself here emphasizes (1110 f.)—is aware only of the second of the two opposing forces, never having felt any longing for infinite vision.

Mephistopheles, who is about to enter the drama and will not again depart until after Faust's death, seems to ignore this duality, though his own role in opposition to the character of Faust may well symbolize through the contrast of their respective roles a further instance of it. In the wager he offers to Faust in the second study scene (1688–707), Mephistopheles anticipates the possibility that Faust may overcome his inner conflict of opposing desire and thus by achieving satisfaction and contentment finally fall victim to his devilish stratagems. The drama of course proves Mephistopheles to be mistaken, in this as in other respects. In what ways his attempt succeeds or fails remains one of the central issues for Goethe's drama. Nonetheless, Mephistopheles chooses precisely the right moment to enter the drama, disguised as a poodle, immediately following Faust's speech about the two souls in his breast. Bear in mind, however, that the devil does not appear—as in the traditional Faust legend—because Faust has conjured him, but rather because of the wager he made with the Lord in "Prologue in Heaven."

The First Study Scene (lines 1178–529)

The scenes in Faust's study, where Mephistopheles first reveals himself, and where the pact with Faust is established, were composed in close proximity to "Outside the City Gate," probably late in 1800 or early in 1801. Here Goethe finally set himself the task of making his peace with the popular legend of Faust. No single feature of the Faust tradition, not even the damnation of Faust (which Goethe already planned to replace with Faust's salvation), imposed such unyielding and archaic demands on the author as the initial terms of the meeting with Mephistopheles. Here Goethe also had to establish the nature and the function of the devil for his *Faust* in a manner that would be suitable for the rest of the drama, both for what had already been written (i.e., the Gretchen tragedy) and for what was yet to come. Goethe therefore determined to juxtapose in these scenes two radically contrary motives, which unavoidably elicit quite opposite responses from readers, leaving an impression of profound ambivalence. On the one hand, almost by force and with a strong dose of poetic irony, Goethe transports us back into the remote context of the popular legend, as if he were again (as in the opening monologue of Faust) imitating the style and tone of the sixteenth-century chapbook or some subliterary late-medieval ballad. On the other hand, both the character of Mephistopheles and the terms of his pact with Faust are accommodated and transformed to accord with Goethe's new, more sophisticated and complex intentions for the drama.

For these separate motives Goethe also provided quite separate poetic effects. The archaic material of Mephistopheles' appearance and the signing of the pact, much of it derived from the popular version of the Faust story adapted by Johann Nicolaus Pfitzer (1674)—which Goethe knew—assumes a playful, almost satirical tone, as if the magic and supernaturalism were not to be taken quite seriously. There is a sense of hocus-pocus to these scenes, as in a spectacular magic show, as if we were attending a performance of the folk play or puppet show of Faust, which was also familiar to Goethe from his childhood. In this, Goethe also accommodated himself to expectations raised by the published Fragment of 1790, in which basic questions concerning the role of Mephistopheles and the nature of his pact with Faust were left wide open.

But Goethe had little sympathy with mere magic and the supernatural in accord with the popular legend. His playful, ironic style, willfully archaic and overly simplistic, makes this all too apparent. Far more serious and far more difficult, on the other hand, was the integration of this traditional material into the drama of Faust as Goethe conceived it, as his various friends and critics had responded to it—Schiller and the philosophers at Jena above all—from the text of the published Fragment, and as the universal and even philosophical concerns of the drama were developed by the poet through the other scenes composed since he had recommenced work on the drama in 1797. Goethe needed to accommodate these scenes with Mephistopheles to the implications of his Faust as he understood them around 1800, while at the same time paying ironic lip service to the popular legend. Above all in those sections of the two study scenes that are new to Goethe's version—Faust's initial mood after his Easter walk and his attempt to translate from the Bible, several aspects of Mephistopheles' self-definition, the song sung by the spirits conjured by Mephisto to lull Faust to sleep, Faust's curse against human existence, and especially the wager that emerges from the traditional pact with the devil—these aspects of the scenes indicate the direction in which Goethe was moving away from the popular legend. These are also the aspects that demand the reader's careful attention.

Faust's Translation of the Bible (lines 1210–37)

Faust here introduces the theme of Christian revelation as a valid analogue to his own intellectual concern. From Goethe's point of view this would not necessarily indicate the perspective of organized religion. Historically, Faust was a contemporary of Martin Luther, whose translation of the Bible into German (New Testament, 1524) includes the familiar version of the opening verse to the Gospel of John, with which Faust begins: "In the beginning was the Word" (Im Anfang war das Wort). Here Faust, in effect, shares (or imitates) Luther's labor of translation, though he immediately transforms the text to accord with his own philosophy of life. Within the context of Goethe's drama, the translation of Scripture provides an ironic parallel to the appearance of Mephistopheles: both the devil in his guise as poodle and the text of the Gospel as Word of God provide instances for the incarnation of spirit, for which Christ himself serves theologically as paradigm. Mephistopheles apparently recognizes this exercise in translation as a kind of competition for his own role and grows increasingly violent in his barking. The reader should consider the irony implicit in these two simultaneous though radically different forms of translation: Word into Deed and dog into devil.

Faust's sequence of terms for the Greek *Logos* reflects the intellectual background to Romantic thought to which Goethe himself contributed during the latter half of the eighteenth century. The rejection of "Word" for "Sense" (*Sinn*) corresponds to the rejection of traditional rhetorical views of language as mere form or artifice in favor of the sense, the meaning, the feeling that language represents. An analogue to this is provided by Faust himself in the scene from the Gretchen tragedy (composed before 1775), "Marthe's Garden," in which Faust discusses religion and refuses to accept any name for God, asserting instead that "Feeling is all" (3456). The second alternative choice of terms, "Force" (*Kraft*), corresponds to a basic view of life in the era of the German Sturm und Drang during the 1770s, which in large measure Goethe himself established through such works as *The Sorrows of Young Werther* and *Götz von Berlichingen*. The final choice of term, "Deed" (*Tat*), is clearly the most Faustian, the most valid for Goethe's drama as a whole, corresponding to the famous couplet in Faust's last monologue in Part Two: "He only earns both freedom and existence / Who must reconquer them each day" (11575–6). (See also the Lord's statement about the need for humankind to be active even if the devil must drive people to it, 340 ff.) *Logos* as "Deed" also corresponds to the philosophy of idealism, as in Fichte's *Wissenschaftslehre* (1794), which argues that experience, consciousness, and even life itself originate when the self posits itself through action (*Tathandlung*) and self-assertion. Thus, whether Faust himself is aware of any such implications, Goethe here transforms the biblical Word from the context of Luther and the historical Faust to the context of Romantic idealism, the context in which Goethe was writing and the context to which his *Faust* was addressed.

The Song of the Spirits (lines 1447–505)

The entertainment promised by Mephistopheles provides, of course, his means of escape. The spirits he conjures (presumably the same as were heard earlier, in the corridor, 1259–70) offer a magical vision that affects all the senses (sound, 1439; sight, 1440; smell, 1442; taste, 1443; touch, 1444). The devil's irresistible art thus lulls Faust to sleep. The spirit song that follows, apart from being one of Goethe's most brilliant lyric poems —employing trochaic meter in two-stress short lines and varying rhyme scheme—establishes a mode of verse with crucial implications for the entire *Faust* drama, especially Part Two. The magic of Mephistopheles manifests itself to the senses as demonic art; the expression of this art in the drama, perforce, is verbal, poetic, dependent on Goethe's own art; and the medium of expression is the voice of spirits, a kind of demonic chorale, representing presumably the voice of nature itself (assuming that these, as with others later on, are spirits of nature). The fact that they deceive Faust and hypnotize him is itself perhaps a part of this theme. At the outset of Part Two, the song of the elves will transform and renew Faust (4634 ff.); the spirit show of Helena and Paris will inspire his love for her (6427 ff.); and much of the "Classical Walpurgis Night" and the Helena act may be regarded as supreme examples of such poetic-mythical phantasmagoria. Further instances of spirit song as the voice of nature are the hymn of the Archangels in the "Prologue in Heaven" (243 ff.) and the song of meta-morphosis by the Chorus in Act III of Part Two (9992 ff.), in which the singers actually become spirits of nature.

During the present song, the mind of the reader, sharing in the response of Faust as listener, moves through a poetic-visionary process, like a mental journey that creates its own reality as it goes along. Initially a sense of transcendence is affirmed, as if the walls of Faust's study opened up to reveal the whole of nature and the cosmos (1447–56). Within this open domain a sense of spiritual beauty (*Geistige Schöne*, 1458; here: "graces uplifting") is asserted to overwhelm the participant, soliciting a response —eminently Faustian—of "lovelorn yearning" (*Sehnende Neigung*, 1461), which leads to a flight across lands, moving swiftly to a kind of garden enclosure or "arbor" (1466, 1470), where lovers exchange vows (1467 ff.). From this retreat of love, apparently through association with the arbor as a grape vine, a Dionysian revel is conjured in which the wine flows forth from the pressed grapes in broad streams, permeating the landscape itself, like rivers flowing to the sea (1471–83). The poem—or whatever spirit participates in what the song says—then moves as a bird in flight, following the sun outward across the sea to blissful islands, where singing choirs are heard and dancers are seen on meadows (1484–96). From here, activity extends in every direction, climbing mountains, swimming lakes, hovering in the air, ascending finally as a blissful celebration (*Seliger Huld*, 1505; here: "blessed requital") of life itself and of the distant loving stars (1497–505). (Such visionary experience should also be compared to earlier in-stances for Faust, e.g., his response to the moonlight shining into his study, 386–97, and his response to the sunset during his Easter walk, 1068–99.)

The (Abandoned) Disputation Scene (between Study [I] and Study [II])

As late as April, 1801, as indicated in a letter to Schiller, Goethe intended to write an additional scene, the "Disputation," which would have been placed between the two study scenes. Ultimately he abandoned the plan, leaving only a sketch for its structure and a draft for the opening lines (see Paralipomena Nos. 11 and 12 to *Faust I*, Weimar edition, vol. 14, 290 ff.). This academic debate, so far as can be construed from the frag-ments, was to have occurred in a large auditorium with students and fac-ulty in attendance. In his guise as wandering scholar, Mephistopheles was to challenge Faust in the debate concerning the respective value of experience and intuition versus imaginative vision, Mephistopheles defending the former and Faust—despite his central preoccupation with the experience of life—the latter. With reference to a philosophical concern for self-knowledge ("*Gnothi seauton* [Gk.] *in schönem Sinne*," Para., 11) and something called a "creative mirror" ("*schaffender Spiegel*," ibid.), Faust was to celebrate the inner life of the mind, perhaps sustaining the mood that resulted from the first study scene, especially the vision evoked by the song of the spirits. Mephistopheles was to speak as a man of the world, offering information about various natural phenomena (derived apparently from Goethe's own preoccupation at that time with the natural philosophy of Schelling and others). Apparently, Mephistopheles was to win a resounding triumph in the debate, causing Faust once again to fall into a profound despair.

When composing the second study scene, Goethe still intended to write this "Disputation," and the radical reversal of roles and attitudes between Faust and Mephistopheles that takes place between the first scene and the second in the text as it stands—totally without explanation or apparent cause—can be understood only with reference to the abandoned scene. Some sense of participation in the academic life of Faust's university is still indicated by Mephistopheles at lines 1712–3, where he speaks of the "doctoral feast" to take place that evening. The effect of this change in mood and relationship between the two protagonists for the second study scene is that Faust assumes the stance of negator and denier, even uttering a categorical curse against life itself, while Mephistopheles, who is now dressed like a Spanish cavalier—a figure borrowed from the Don Juan legend, ready to lead Faust into the world according to the pact he proposes—must play a conciliatory role, cajoling and encouraging Faust to take up life with him on his (the devil's) terms. It is regrettable that Goethe did not complete the "Disputation" scene, since it would no doubt have been a powerful theatrical event, further clarifying the dialectical opposition between Faust and Mephistopheles, and would have prepared the reader for the pact scene far more effectively.

Faust's Curse (lines 1587–606)

In his mood of despair at the outset of the second study scene, Faust curses every basic aspect of human existence. Even though seemingly unmotivated, this sequence constitutes one of the earliest and most powerful expressions of absolute nihilism in European literature. The initial metaphor defines the mind, or soul (*Seele*, 1587; 1588 in Arndt's translation), as bound within the body as a "cave of grief," for which the data received from the senses serve as "lures and blandishments." First, Faust curses what is termed "smug delusion" (1591), apparently the intuition of higher things through the phenomena of the natural world, which Mephistopheles in the "Prologue in Heaven" mockingly called the Lord's gift of reason, "of Heaven's light a glitter" (284). Faust then curses the world of phenomena itself, as perceived by the senses (1593–4). The "lying dreams" (1595–6), which next receive his curse, include not only the visions of sleep—mentioned just above in Faust's lament (1562 ff.)—but also the illusions and ideals of humankind regarding immortality. Next, in quick survey Faust adds to his curse those aspects of life earlier referred to as Care (644 ff.): property, family, and labor (1597–8), also wealth and the particular deceptive pleasures it provides (1599 ff.). The curse against wine and love (1603–4) calls to mind the vision that the spirits' song conveyed to Faust in the preceding scene (1463–83). Faust thus rejects the vision that so recently exerted such hypnotic power over him and that will constitute his central preoccupation during much of his subsequent career throughout the drama. Finally, rejecting the primal Christian virtues of faith, hope, and patience (*spes, fides, patientia*), Faust extends his curse to include those positive and redemptive qualities of mind he demonstrated at the outset of the first study scene, after he returned from his Easter walk, when he turned to the Bible, attempting to translate the *Logos* of the Gospel of John into German. For Mephistopheles, to whom this curse upon everything that might have value for Faust's existence must seem most welcome, it is apparent that the learned doctor is now ready to enter into a pact with the devil.

Faust's Wager with Mephistopheles (lines 1699–706)

The concept of the "moment" (*Augenblick*, literally: "blink or glance of an eye") is crucial for *Faust* as a whole. Nor does Goethe subsequently allow the reader to forget the terms of the wager that Faust here proposes and that Mephistopheles accepts. The question of the moment recurs, for instance, in several climactic scenes of Part Two (for example, in the "Classical Walpurgis Night" of Act II, when Galatea appears at the climax of the festival at the Aegean Sea, 8424–5; in the central section of the Helena act, when Faust and Helena are united in marriage through the exchange of rhymes for love, 9411 ff.; and in Faust's final speech in Act V, when the terms of the wager seem to be fulfilled, 11585–6). What Faust has in mind as the condition for his wager is not only a sense of satisfaction, which would complete and negate his striving (consider Mephistopheles' contrasting view, 1688–91), but also an absolute fulfillment of all desire, where the temporal and experiential process involved in such striving would be gathered together within such a single moment, so that time itself would be transcended.

Ultimately, this concept of an absolute moment is understood by Faust to be aesthetic, in basic agreement with idealist theories of beauty in art (as indicated by Faust's use of the term "fair"—*schön* in the German, 1700). Appropriately, therefore, Part Two offers more authoritative demonstrations for such beautiful moments along with the impossibility of sustaining such moments as the basis for a permanent reality in the world. At the same time, with regard to the question of Faust's salvation and the redeeming power of Gretchen's love as its precondition, the nearest instance of such a fulfillment in the moment that Faust envisions is found in the ultimate self-sacrifice of love. Gretchen demonstrates this in an intuitive manner; Homunculus at the end of the "Classical Walpurgis Night" demonstrates it as a conscious principle of organic life itself. At this point in the drama such possibilities cannot be anticipated, above all since Mephistopheles has no comprehension of love and does not himself participate at all in the instances mentioned. The reader is thus left to clarify the meaning of the "moment" for *Faust* as a whole through a critical reading of the drama itself. The devil proves to be incapable of understanding the ultimate meaning of Faust's wager, just as he is also incapable of preventing Faust's ultimate salvation.

The Fragmentary Dialogue Between Faust and Mephistopheles in the Fragment of 1790 (lines 1770–850)

During his stay in Italy (1786–88), Goethe returned to the earlier manuscript material for his *Faust* in order to prepare the drama for publication in his collected works. This material became the *Fragment* of 1790, which for nearly two decades (until the appearance of the completed Part One in 1808) was the only text of *Faust* known to such readers as Schiller, the Schlegels, Schelling, and Hegel. For inclusion in this *Fragment* Goethe composed three new scenes: the "Witch's Kitchen," "Forest and Cave," and the fragmentary dialogue between Faust and Mephistopheles that follows the (at that time unwritten) pact in the second study scene. This brief fragmentary scene proved to be crucial for early readings of *Faust* because Mephistopheles there appears for the first time in the *Fragment* (the "Prologue in Heaven" was yet even to be conceived). In effect, the exchange between Faust and Mephistopheles in this dialogue stood as conscious parallel to and contrast with the crucial encounter between Faust and the Earth Spirit in the early, incomplete version of "Night." Goethe thus intended the scenes to be juxtaposed and to that end reformulated Faust's basic existential demand, which had earlier been rejected so categorically by the Earth Spirit and now in singularly ironic fashion is received by Mephistopheles as his essential mandate.

The six lines spoken by Faust at the outset of their exchange (1770–5) sum up in absolutist terms everything he demands of life. Mephistopheles responds in a sequence of three speeches that so deflate and undermine Faust's resolve that his mood is totally reversed and he is thrown into a sense of defeat. Faust's subsequent reply—also consisting of only six lines (1810–5)—expresses the kind of existential despair that the more elaborate and categorical curse on all human values later included at the opening of the completed scene (1587–606; discussed above) constitutes as an incipient nihilism.

Mephistopheles responds to this categorical reversal of mood in a speech that launches the most sardonic attack ever made against idealism. His most fundamental stance as devil in Goethe's drama is defined by the simple assertion "Throw over all reflection / And off into the world posthaste!" (i.e., "stop thinking about yourself and just go for it," 1828–9). He offers a devastating image for all speculative thought in its essential ineffectiveness: that of a beast tied to a stake on arid grazing land with no other option than to go round and round in a circle. This may be regarded as the devil's ultimate response to the claims of the scholar in his study, no less negative and no less categorical than the Earth Spirit's rejection of Faust in the opening scene of the drama.

Mephistopheles' Monologue (lines 1851–67)

This monologue by Mephistopheles, virtually the only one of its kind in the entire drama, addressed to Faust in his absence as the devil dons the professor's academic robe, is crucial for clarifying the relationship between them from the devil's perspective at this stage in the drama. The speech is also important because it was singled out by the early philosophical critics of the Faust *Fragment*. Both Schelling (in his brief discussion of *Faust* from the *Philosophy of Art*, c. 1804) and Hegel (in the section on "Desire and Necessity" in *The Phenomenology of Spirit*, 1807) quote from this speech.

Faust will fall victim to Mephistopheles, so the devil believes, because, following Mephistopheles' bidding (1835–41), he has abandoned "intelligence and science" (*Vernunft und Wissenschaft*, 1851) and is now subject to the deceptions and illusions of the "liar-in-chief" (literally, "spirit of lies," *Lügengeist*). The description of Faust's infinite striving (1856–9) corresponds essentially to Faust's nature as we have witnessed it thus far. Mephistopheles' motive for dragging him through the realm of sensuous experience, as expressed in 1860–5, goes directly contrary to the terms of their wager (as formulated in the portion of the scene composed around 1800, 1692–706). Using a figurative allusion to the legend of Tantalus, who was tortured in hell by having food and drink close at hand that he could see and smell but never enjoy, Mephistopheles reverses the torture and imagines Faust—"sticking, writhing, flagging"—yearning in vain for relief.

Such relief, however, is precisely the opposite of the goal that Faust defines for their wager. Mephistopheles will win only if he enables Faust to achieve the beautiful moment of fulfillment. As this statement stands within the larger context of the second study scene, Mephistopheles can be regarded only as having misunderstood the terms of the wager. The most likely explanation, however, is that Mephistopheles here speaks from a perspective far closer to the traditional pact from the Faust legend, a perspective valid for the *Fragment* of 1790, which was still a long way from the more sophisticated philosophical position defined by the wager in the final text of *Faust*, Part One. The concluding lines of the monologue (1866–7) seem to assume that Faust will be damned in the end even without the devil's intervention, which, given the wager made with the Lord in the "Prologue in Heaven" (composed twelve years later, of course), ought to make Mephistopheles more cautious, even in the context of his monologue.

The Scene with the Student (lines 1868–2050)

By every indication, this scene of broad academic satire, which is contained in the *Urfaust* (with an even stronger doggerel tone) immediately following the scene with Wagner in "Night," must have originated at the earliest stage of composition for the drama. The confrontation of such a naive and gullible freshman, who has come to consult the learned doctor for advice on his course of study, with the devil wearing Faust's robes and thus pretending to offer such advice, provides a comic interlude that is always a source of amusement for students studying Goethe's *Faust*, who can usually feel some sympathy for the Student and the way he is treated by Mephistopheles. Later in Act II of Part Two, however, Goethe brings the Student back to Faust's study as a Baccalaureus (6689–806), when he has completed his university studies, and the burden of satire is turned back on the Student, who presumes to dictate with considerable bluster his own radical philosophical convictions to the devil, who is once again in academic disguise.

Along with the humor of Goethe's satirical survey of the four faculties in the traditional university, whose dominant features are outlined for the Student by Mephistopheles, there is at least one serious theme that recalls a central concern from the opening of the drama (and which was only introduced to the Student scene in the final text of Part One). In discussing theology with the Student (1982–2000), who confesses to some bewilderment at the abstruse terminology of this science, Mephisto emphasizes that it is all merely words. The student believes, however, that some concept (*Begriff*) must be standing behind each word. Mephisto's categorical rejection of this claim, asserting that words in themselves can serve to build a system without worrying about the sense, recalls the exchange between Faust and Wagner in "Night" concerning the art of rhetoric (534–47), where Faust insists that words must proceed from the heart. Subsequently, in his discussion of religion with Gretchen (3414–58), Faust will insist that the names for God are irrelevant, since "Feeling is all; / Name is but sound and fume." Mephistopheles holds to his doctrine of arbitrary signifiers, however, as becomes even more apparent, for instance, in Part Two, when he proposes his scheme of fiscal reform to the Emperor by introducing paper money. Also on Mephisto's side are the monkeys serving the Witch in her kitchen, who speak human language (they "ape" words), without any sense of what they might mean (2453–60).

Mephistopheles on the "Iota" (line 2000)

The phrase "no jot or tittle" (*kein Jota* in the German) alludes to Matthew 5.18, "For verily I say unto you, Till heaven and earth pass, one jot or one tittle shall in no wise pass from the law, till all be fulfilled" (King James Version). Mephistopheles' response to the Student's claim that every word must stand for a concept provides an ironic defense for the autonomy of words as words. Mention of the "jot" (*iota*, the Greek letter *i*) alludes —ironically in the mouth of the devil!—to the conflict between the Arians and the Athanasians at the Council of Nicaea (A.D. 325) concerning the relation between the Father and Son in the Trinity. The issue turned on the distinction between two Greek words, identical except for the iota: *homoousios*, "of the same nature" (argued by the Athanasians), and *homoiousios*, "of similar nature" (argued by the Arians). The Athanasians prevailed, and the resulting creed, generally adopted by both the Greek and Roman churches, dropped the iota, thus asserting the identity of Father and Son. This goes directly contrary to Mephistopheles' claim, however, suggesting that from the ironic perspective of the author, whose views on language would have supported Faust's concern to go beyond the word (*Logos*) and even beyond its meaning (*Sinn*) to the force (*Kraft*) and the deed (*Tat*), the Student is correct in his conviction that for every word there should be a concept. The irony of the scene is heightened, of course, by the fact that the Student is not able to defend himself, does not know who Mephistopheles is, and probably does not understand what he is saying anyway.

"Auerbach's Tavern in Leipzig" (lines 2073–336)

The visit to Auerbach's Tavern, a well-known and time-honored drinking place in the city of Leipzig (founded in 1438), especially frequented by students from the university, offers relatively little that seems directly related to Faust's central concerns. The significance of the visit for Faust is primarily negative, indicated by his apparent disdain for such drinking and debauch. He speaks only two short lines in the entire scene (2183 and 2296), spending the rest of the visit apart as a detached, ultimately even a bored observer. Mephistopheles' justification for the visit (2158 ff.), in a speech added to the revised version of the scene published in the *Fragment* of 1790, seems indifferent and unpersuasive, as if it were an afterthought by Goethe. The corresponding speech in the *Urfaust* is: "Now watch how they carry on here! If you enjoy it, I can provide this kind of society every night." Neither the drunken carousing nor the magical hocus-pocus seem to contribute more than a sense of satire and slapstick theater to Goethe's drama. Yet precisely at this level the scene has proven to be singularly effective on the stage, as more than a century of theater productions can attest. In particular the songs and the use of music, but also the magic tricks played on the drinkers by Mephistopheles, provide a colorful sense of show and spectacle.

Traditionally for performances, the four drinkers constitute a male quartet (two tenors and two basses), and the several kinds of songs, which are at least briefly introduced, provide a sense of the music hall or light comic opera. The four drinkers are also academic stereotypes: Frosch ("frog") being the traditional nickname—in both Germany and the United States —for a beginning student; Brander (or Brandfuchs; "fire-fox") being the designation for a disillusioned "sophomore." The name Altmayer may indicate an older, former student (*alter Herr*, i.e., alumnus), as Siebel may be the bartender or tavern keeper (whose name suggests a "sieve"). From the banter about intrigues of love (2101–18), it appears that Frosch has stolen Siebel's mistress from him. Brander sings the song of the rat who eats poison and behaves "as if the love-bug bit her," and subsequently Mephistopheles sings the song of the flea who becomes a favorite at court. Both songs convey a sharp sense of satire—the one addressed to conventions of love, the other to the politics of the ancien régime—where animals are substituted for social types. The theme of drunkenness and physical violence that pervades the magic tricks Mephistopheles plays on the drinkers further heightens a sense of bestiality for the scene as a whole, emphasized above all in the drinkers' raucous carousing in response to the wine that flows from the false spigots: "Carouse like aborigines [cannibals in the German], / Five hundred wallowing swine!" (2293–4). The theme of drinking, especially with a false wine conjured by magic that turns into flames when spilled (2299 ff.), recalls the poison Faust almost drinks at the end of "Night" and anticipates the magic brew of the "Witch's Kitchen," which Faust will drink in order to be rejuvenated in the following scene.

Of particular interest is Goethe's concession in this scene to the popular tradition of the Faust legend. "Auerbach's Tavern in Leipzig" is the only scene in Faust, Part One, located with geographical specificity in an actual place. This drinking locale also joins together the widely disparate eras separating the historical Dr. Faustus from the author of the drama. According to tradition, Faustus actually visited Auerbach's Tavern when he was in Leipzig in the year 1526; Goethe, as student at the University of Leipzig during the mid-1760s, also frequented the place, especially during the time when his friend Behrisch—apparently an enthusiastic participant in such drinking bouts as here portrayed—lived in a rented room at the inn there. Two rather primitive frescos had been painted on the walls of the tavern about a century after the supposed visit by the historical Faustus (i.e., c. 1625), and both were still there in Goethe's day (and in much restored versions are still there today): the one shows Faust at a table with a group of students drinking and playing music; the other depicts Faust riding out the door on a wine cask, to the amazement of his drinking partners (cf. 2229 ff.). Goethe intentionally incorporated these incidents from the frescos in his scene, thus using the place in accord with the artistic representations from popular tradition associated with it.

Yet he also made some important changes. Mephistopheles does not figure in the paintings nor in the traditional tale of Faust's visit to the tavern; Faust himself is both the drinker and the magician. In the Urfaust, Goethe acknowledges this by having Faust himself perform the tricks of magic at the end of the scene (tricks that also derive from the popular legend of Faust); in the revised version published in 1790, it is Mephistopheles who performs both Faustian roles, playing the tricks of the wine and the hallucination that causes the drinkers to grab one another by the nose, as well as singing the song of the flea (which he already did in the first version). A continuity of tradition is thus preserved by Goethe, but a radical transformation in the nature and role of Faust is implicitly acknowledged. The devil serves as a substitute for the learned doctor in performing the

magic tricks—something that also holds true later, in the court of the
Emperor in Part Two, where Mephistopheles assumes the guise of court
jester and assists Faust in performing the spirit show of Paris and Helena.

"Witch's Kitchen" (lines 2337–604)

Goethe must have recognized from the earliest stages of work on his *Faust*
a radical discrepancy between the roles his character plays in the two
sections that ultimately became Part One. The entire opening sequence
of scenes—including those written much later, around 1800—from the first
monologue through "Auerbach's Tavern," emphasize the intellectual and
existential disillusionment of an aging academic, a scholar who is fed up
with learning and science, requiring a degree of sterile frustration in a
figure generally assumed to be about fifty years old (see 2055 ff., as also
"Witch's Kitchen," 2341–2). The encounter with Gretchen, however,
which fills the latter half of Part One, demands that Faust play the role
of seducer and libertine, a kind of Don Juan, who must be physically
attractive to a very young woman. Magical rejuvenation through the devil's
powers—a device not otherwise contained in the popular Faust legend at
all—must have been planned by Goethe even when he was composing
the *Urfaust*. The primary dramatic function of the scene is thus Faust's
drinking of the magical brew prepared by the Witch and her simian assistants in the bubbling pot (presumably at the command of Mephistopheles,
who here serves as the traditional devil of medieval superstition, even to
the point where the Witch calls him "Satan," 2504).

When Goethe came to compose this scene, however, the demands it
placed upon him were totally alien to his poetic inclinations. He wrote it
during the early spring of 1788, under pressure of a publisher's deadline
for his collected works, to be included in vol. 7 as part of A *Fragment.*
Goethe was then in Rome, nearing the end of his Italian journey, steeped
in classical art and culture to a degree unequaled in his subsequent career.
He wrote the scene, according to his remarks to Eckermann over forty
years later (April 10, 1829), in the gardens of the Villa Borghese, where
the atmosphere of primitive, Nordic witchcraft demanded by the scene
must have seemed the true antipode of the Eternal City and the Italian
spring. Such a radical contradiction of mood is appropriately demonstrated
in Faust's own state of mind, perhaps as a reflection of Goethe's situation
while writing the scene: he is appalled by the Witch, her kitchen, and her
companions and disgusted by her brew, to the point (2337–46) where he
almost refuses to submit to Mephistopheles' youth cure.

At the same time, apparently without any assistance by Mephistopheles, as
an ironic alternative to drinking the Witch's brew, Faust is transfixed by
the magic mirror, in which he perceives the image of a woman, presumably in the manner of paintings depicting the nude Venus by such Italian
masters as Giorgione or Titian (the former known to Goethe from the
gallery in Dresden; the latter—which Goethe later often praised—in the
Uffizi Gallery, Florence). We are provided only with Faust's response to

the image in a speech that praises the beauty of the woman and indicates the awakening of a powerful erotic desire (2429–40). In a paradox that is clearly intentional to the scene, Faust is thus rejuvenated in spirit through the unexpected contemplation of the classical ideal of feminine beauty, which elicits an appropriate erotic response from him, before he is rejuvenated magically in body by drinking the Witch's brew. Is Goethe not playing a joke on the devil here by showing that the image in the mirror, which may be a projection of Faust's own imagination and desire, is far more effective in rejuvenating him than the Witch's magic brew?

A further difficulty this scene has presented to generations of critics pertains to the incantatory verses of the Witch and her Marmosets (especially 2394–428, 2450–60, 2540–52). The animals engage Mephistopheles in a kind of carnival show, where they perform a parody of world government with the devil as regent, a Lord of Misrule. Their props include a glass globe, a sieve, a pillow for a crown, and a feather duster as scepter. Mephisto is placed on a settle as throne, while the Marmosets pay him homage in a kind of singsong verse. Their final lines indicate that they merely utter the sounds of their rhyming without any sense or meaning (2454–5 and 2458–60). Efforts to extract some secret symbolic significance from these jingles with their accompanying objects of rule have yielded little more than a kind of arbitrary slapstick.

The appearance of the Witch adds little to the action apart from her rage and violence, until she recognizes the presence of her infernal master and becomes accommodating and acquiescent. The Witch's rite of bell, book, and candle, complete with a magic circle into which Faust must step, also seems at best a kind of degenerate parody. The consensus of modern readers is that Goethe here imposes a procedure that is mere nonsense, having no further significance and authority for the drama than had been the case with the magic spells cast by Mephistopheles upon the drunken students in "Auerbach's Tavern." The language begins at the level of children's jingles and degenerates to a random number game in the Witch's arithmetic chant (das Hexen-Einmaleins, 2540–52). Much of the language serves no greater function than mere incantation, as its sound suggests. In this, Goethe was no doubt borrowing from the well-known verses intoned by the Witches in Shakespeare's Macbeth 4.1: "Double, double, toil and trouble; / Fire burn, and cauldron bubble." Indeed, the cauldron scene in Shakespeare's play probably provided Goethe with his most vivid dramatic source for the "Witch's Kitchen," along with popular pictorial examples of such witches that he may have known from seventeenth-century Dutch painting.

Goethe is also concerned here again with the theme of bestiality, presumably in direct juxtaposition with "Auerbach's Tavern," especially through the role of the Marmosets and their use of language. Just as the drinkers in the tavern become more and more bestial in their debauching, so here the animals, who behave like human beings, particularly in their ability to speak, demonstrate a perversion of pretense. In this regard, the

Marmosets bear out the earlier assertion by Mephistopheles to the Student (1994 ff.) that words need not be accompanied by concepts to which they correspond. Here we have an extreme instance of empty semiosis, perhaps beyond even the limits that Mephistopheles envisioned, where words are used purely for the sound, totally devoid of sense.

From such a perspective, the magical rite that the Witch imposes on Faust at the end of the scene assumes dubious implications. With its use of music, book, torches, and brew it clearly serves as a parody of a religious rite, in particular of the Christian Mass, suggesting that the drinking of the magic potion by Faust should be juxtaposed with the eucharist of the Easter service in "Night," which itself was contrasted with the poison that Faust was about to drink. Goethe seems to be working against himself on purpose. The magic potion that rejuvenates Faust, according to a folk belief with which the poet was not much in sympathy, is placed in association with other symbolic, spiritual acts in the drama that have far greater significance and authority than this event. Apart from the vision of the feminine in the magic mirror, which establishes the central theme of woman as the embodiment of ideal beauty and the erotic as a legitimate aspect of Faust's essential striving, this scene may be taken as arbitrary theatrical display, providing a pervasive sense of comic self-parody.

"Highway" (in Urfaust, before the Gretchen Sequence)

Highway

A wayside cross, on the hill at right an old castle, in the distance a little peasant hut.

FAUST.   What's this, Mephisto, are you pressed?
  Why drop your eyes before the shrine?
MEPHISTOPHELES.   I don't deny that I am prejudiced,
  But I detest it—just a quirk of mine.
              —Translated by Walter Arndt

In the text of the *Urfaust*, copied from Goethe's manuscripts by Luise von Göchhausen in 1775, a short scene occurs between "Auerbach's Tavern" and the opening of the Gretchen sequence ("Witch's Kitchen," of course, had not yet been written). This scene, which Goethe later cut from the text of the *Fragment* of 1790, is the only portion of the original *Faust* preserved from Goethe's own manuscript. The scene deserves consideration, especially insofar as it offsets and balances the later short scene in prose from the *Urfaust*, which Goethe did retain in Part One, "Night. Open Field" (4399–404).

The Gretchen Tragedy (lines 2605–3834 and 4405–612)

The sequence of scenes concerned with Faust's seduction of Gretchen (or Margarete; both names are used in the text, Gretchen being the diminutive and more familiar version of the name), composed as part of the *Urfaust*, probably in early 1775, constitutes the latter half of Part One. This sequence has always fascinated readers of Goethe's *Faust* and has been largely responsible for the widespread popular appeal of the drama, especially in the theater. The impact of the so-called Gretchen tragedy on the popular imagination, as measured by subsequent imitations (as in the musical scenes and operas by Berlioz, Gounod, and Boito, among others), has established Faust's role as libertine with equal importance alongside the tradition of his pact with the devil. Here, more even than in the encounter with the Earth Spirit, the author of the *Urfaust* departed radically from any sources in the popular legend. All attempts to locate an analogue to Gretchen in the Faust chapbooks have been futile.

In two important ways Goethe introduced a perspective to his drama that was entirely removed from the antiquarian and hocus-pocus qualities of the traditional Faust and that addressed central concerns of later-eighteenth-century thought and sensibility. First, the theme of seduction, predominant in domestic, middle-class drama and a preoccupation of the age—from Rowe's *The Fair Penitent* to Lessing's *Emilia Galotti*, from Casanova's *Memoirs* to Beaumarchais's *Marriage of Figaro*, from Laclos's *Liaisons dangereuses* to Mozart's *Don Giovanni*—was united with the essential dynamic power of will in Faust, his striving for infinite knowledge and experience. The philosopher Kierkegaard recognized this when he chose the Gretchen episode alongside *Don Giovanni* as his central examples, in *Either/Or* (1843), for the aesthetics of the erotic. Second, a dimension of social realism was introduced to *Faust* that carried profound legal and moral implications for Goethe's own time. The theme of infanticide, often involving the seduction of innocent girls who subsequently fell victim to the intolerance of eighteenth-century middle-class society, usually leading to their execution, while their seducers escaped without penalty, attracted many writers, especially among the German Sturm und Drang, all of whom sought to denounce a barbarous injustice. It has been persuasively argued that Goethe first conceived the Gretchen tragedy in direct response to the execution for infanticide in Frankfurt on January 14, 1772, of Susanna Margaretha Brandt. Such external evidence also lends support to the impression any reader will receive from the Gretchen tragedy that she, not Faust, is the central figure of the sequence; that it is her "tragedy"; and that he functions above all as the instrument of her destruction, however authentic his erotic motives may be.

Within the larger context of the drama, however, especially in the later published versions (the *Fragment* of 1790 contains the entire sequence through Gretchen's collapse at the end of the cathedral scene; the conclusion, with a revision of the dungeon scene from its initial prose to verse, was added in Part One), the Gretchen tragedy came to assume a significance for Faust and his ultimate salvation that went far beyond the themes of libertinism and infanticide. Gretchen, in her authentic love for Faust, emerges as the most powerful embodiment of the Feminine in the drama, the principle that defines the highest object of Faustian desire and ultimately serves—through a recollection of Beatrice's intercession on behalf of Dante in *The Divine Comedy*—as the instrument of Faust's salvation. The essential triangular relationship of the figures in this sequence —seemingly a parody of an eighteenth-century literary cliché: Faust as libertine, the agent of erotic desire; Gretchen as the appropriate object of seduction; and Mephistopheles as the instrument of fulfillment, or the "go-between"—establishes an archetypal or mythical pattern that is central to the entire drama. In one sense this constitutes the transformation of a traditional demonic seduction (used, for instance, by Thomas Mann in his novel *Doctor Faustus* [1947], and hinted at by Goethe later in the "Walpurgis Night," when Faust dances with the youthful, naked witch), where sexual enticement through a seemingly beautiful girl, who subsequently proves to be a monster in disguise, serves the devil as the means of trapping the wayward sinner (see in this regard 3324–5, in "Forest and Cave," where Faust associates Mephisto with the serpent).

At a deeper level, however, this pattern establishes a dramatic reenactment of the biblical myth of the Fall, though also with a crucial difference. Contrary to the biblical account and in opposition to Milton's dramatization of it in *Paradise Lost*, Eve becomes the innocent victim of Adam's erotic desire, not the mediator of Satan in eating the forbidden fruit. Yet Mephistopheles is true to his traditional role as the tempter, however complicated by literary tradition as a pander or conniving servant (recall Sganarelle and Leporello in versions of the Don Juan legend), and his presence legitimizes the mythical analogue to the Fall, which might otherwise seem far-fetched. Goethe later acknowledged such implications retrospectively, at the end of "Dungeon," when the voice from above announces that Gretchen is saved (4611), and in the reappearance of Gretchen in Part Two as the "shining band of mist" (10055), which Faust observes ascending heavenward at the outset of Act IV, and lastly as the Penitent Spirit ("Una Poenitentium," 12069–75) in the final scene of the drama, where she intercedes with a prayer to the Mater Gloriosa on behalf of Faust's salvation, echoing Gretchen's earlier prayer to the Madonna in "By the City Wall" (3587 ff.).

Most important for the dramatic technique of the Gretchen episode is the influence of Shakespeare, apparent throughout, both in the scenic technique and in the psychology of character. Here Goethe writes as the representative dramatist of the Sturm und Drang, a movement steeped in Shakespeare and that in this instance achieved an imitation of the master that is worthy of him. Apart from various specific borrowings throughout the sequence of scenes (as mentioned in the footnotes), Goethe also adapts to his purpose the radically anticlassical (or anti-neoclassical) technique of brief lyrical and emotional scenes, which was felt at that time to be eminently Shakespearean. Far more important is the dialectical contrast of dramatic moments that Goethe achieves through this sequence, establishing a complex and varied mood for the Gretchen tragedy that accompanies and itself elicits the appropriate response to its advance from innocence to surrender to despair and, finally, to madness and destruction. Also derived from Shakespeare, however eighteenth-century in its guise, is the psychology of the heroine, who clearly blends various positive attributes of Shakespeare's female characters with great force and attraction, from Juliet and Ophelia to Desdemona and Imogen, with less apparent parallels to numerous others (such as Lady Anne in *Richard III* or Isabella in *Measure for Measure*). Above all through an intensive, lyrical focus on his heroine, Goethe establishes a direct revelation of her emotional state of mind, externalized, often with great dramatic power, in scenes that otherwise would seem to be no more than brief songs or monologues (as in "Gretchen's Chamber," with the song at the spinning wheel, 3374 ff., or in "By the City Wall," with her prayer to the Virgin, 3587 ff.). Through this mode of lyrical drama from within, the entire sequence assumes an intensity and an authority of mood that ultimately, in "Dungeon," goes beyond even the limits of Shakespeare and perhaps to the limits of what is tolerable in pathos for any theater audience.

A word also should be said about Gretchen's character as woman in the context of feminist-critical interest in the literary portrayal of women. Gretchen is far more complex than a mere innocent victim. Her social status, however little we see of it, as in her relation to her mother (who never appears) and to her neighbor Frau Marthe Schwerdtlein, clearly reflects all the virtues of bourgeois life, even if under simple circumstances. She also represents genuine Christian virtues, presumably Catholic (if only because those scenes set within the church, such as the Easter Chorus in "Night" or the cathedral scene, suggest that the Protestant Reformation has no validity here), since we first meet her as she comes from confession, where, as Mephisto emphasizes, she had no sins to confess (2621 ff.). Yet Gretchen proves susceptible to temptation in response to the jewels secured by the devil as a gift to her, even if she gives the first casket to her mother, who passes it on to the church (cf. "On a Walk," 2805 ff.); she keeps the second casket a secret and wears the jewelry at the home of Frau Marthe. Even more, she is subject to Faust's flattery and apparent devotion, as manifested in the banter between them in "Garden" (3074 ff.). When she flees from Faust into the "Garden Pavilion," fully expecting him to follow her, she returns his kiss and declares, "Dearest man, I love you with all my heart" (3206). She responds to his request to sleep with her by putting into her mother's evening drink the sleeping potion (poison?), which Faust gives her (having received it from Mephisto?) and which causes her mother's death. And, of course, she becomes pregnant at precisely the stage in their relationship where Faust seems to withdraw from further contact, abandoning her completely after he kills her brother Valentine in a duel, in which Mephistopheles guides his sword. From that point, when the dying Valentine denounces her in the presence of her neighbors, until "Dungeon," Gretchen is submitted to public abuse and scorn, most of which we do not directly witness; and after she drowns her newborn child, she is condemned to death by a court of law. Goethe himself commented that, however much she may be the victim of Faust's seduction, she is nonetheless guilty of infanticide. The effect of her suffering is measured by her apparent derangement—modeled on Ophelia in Shakespeare's *Hamlet*—in "Dungeon." Her irresistible power and fascination as dramatic character, however, resides in the manner in which she grows and is transformed by her love for Faust and by the suffering it causes her. She is in truth the only character in the drama who evolves and develops in the course of the action. There can be little question that Goethe achieves in the portrayal of Gretchen, in all her complexity and pathos, the most powerful female character in German literature. That Gretchen also serves as a categorical indictment of the injustice of eighteenth-century society toward such victims of love and seduction is also beyond question. Yet when all is taken into account, it is apparent to every reader, as also to Faust himself, that Gretchen is much more than simply a victim and that her love for him proves to be a redemptive force, which is finally stronger than the devil's wager with Faust.

Ballad of "The King of Thule" (lines 2759–82)

Scholars generally assume that Goethe composed this ballad, which Gretchen sings in the privacy of her bedroom in "Evening," independently of the drama and subsequently decided to include it (already in the *Urfaust*), since it heightens so powerfully and ironically Gretchen's situation. Apparently without conscious motive, as she undresses, she sings the ballad as a song she has somewhere learned. It tells the tale of an ancient Nordic king who remains faithful to his mistress (*Buhle* in the German) long after her death by always drinking from the golden chalice she gave to him when she died. At the moment of his death, he drinks from it once more and hurls it into the sea. The ballad thus symbolizes an ideal of constancy in love, specifically with reference to the man for the woman who is not his wife, until the moment of his death.

No reader of *Faust* will fail to note the irony in Gretchen's singing this ballad at the moment when she is about to expose herself to the attraction of the jewelry that Faust and Mephisto have secretly placed in her cabinet. The seduction intended by Faust brings no option for constancy, least of all with regard to the wager he made with Mephisto concerning the moment he might wish could tarry (recall 1699 ff.). Gretchen sings the song, furthermore, as she undresses on the stage, thus exposing herself (with appropriate limits, though several modern productions of the play have actually had the actress undress to complete nudity) as vulnerable to the erotic temptations of her seducer. This unconscious striptease (in its effect on the audience in the theater) presents Gretchen in a very different light than Faust's highly sentimental praise for the innocence of the furnishings in her room, in particular her bed (2709–16), where he will soon seduce her and bring her ruin. In the final image of the scene, after Gretchen discovers the box of jewels, she tries them on, seated before her mirror in her shift or nightdress, lamenting the lot of the poor, for whom everything depends on gold (2802 ff.). Goethe thus combines to great theatrical effect the musical and poetic power of his ballad with the implicit visual symbolism of Gretchen's body exposed on the stage as image of vulnerability for seduction.

"Forest and Cave" (lines 3217–373)

The concluding section of this scene (3342–69), was already contained in the *Urfaust* as the latter part of a scene immediately following "Cathedral." The scene began with what ultimately became the opening of the Valentine scene (3620–59). "Forest and Cave" as it now stands was composed in Rome early in 1788, as indicated in part by the use of blank verse for Faust's monologue, a verse form at that time only recently introduced to German drama from the model of Shakespeare (e.g., in Goethe's *Iphigenie auf Tauris* and *Torquato Tasso*, also composed in Italy and shortly thereafter). In the *Fragment* of 1790, the scene is located later in the Gretchen sequence, just following "At the Well." In its final position in the drama, it serves to interrupt the continuous sequence of scenes leading to the declaration of love in "A Garden Pavilion" and is purposefully juxtaposed with Gretchen's soliloquy at the spinning wheel in "Gretchen's Chamber," immediately following.

This scene constitutes the center of the Gretchen tragedy, its focal point and high point within the thematic concerns of the Faust drama as a whole. Indicative of this is the extent to which the reflective self-analysis by Faust in his monologue reestablishes an awareness of his existential condition, his Faustian nature, totally removed from the specific context of his involvement with Gretchen. Goethe thus connects this monologue thematically with the opening monologue of Faust in his study (hence his direct address here to the Earth Spirit). Such thematic connections were subsequently strengthened when the scenes for the so-called great lacuna (*große Lücke*, i.e., from the original version of "Night" through the pact scene in the second "Study") were composed around 1800. Much of what is stated there, especially in the *Logos* scene, when Faust returns to his study after the Easter walk (1178 ff.), and in the pact scene, especially just following the wager with Mephistopheles (lines 1742–867, part of which was also composed for the *Fragment*), bears directly on what Faust here asserts about himself in "Forest and Cave."

Critics have been bothered by the question of whether the Earth Spirit is indeed responsible in any way for what Faust has achieved and received. One cannot forget that the Spirit turned its countenance toward Faust in the fire only to overwhelm and reject him. One hypothesis has held that Goethe intended at this stage of composition (the "Prologue in Heaven" had not yet been conceived) to make the Earth Spirit responsible for the appearance of Mephistopheles, as Faust here assumes (in 3243 ff.). Within the perspective of Part One, however, it makes more sense to argue that Faust is merely in error (once again), since he can have no knowledge of the "Prologue in Heaven" anyway nor even surmise how Mephistopheles was motivated to appear to him in the guise of the poodle. Such ironic discrepancy between the perspective of Faust the character and the drama *Faust* as a whole must be recognized as an essential aspect of Goethe's work.

The crucial significance of this scene resides in the contrast between Faust's philosophical monologue, which he addresses directly to nature, defining a mode of self-consciousness through his confrontation with the storm, the moonlight, the "rocky cliffs" and "moisty foliage" (3237), and the subsequent dialogue with Mephistopheles, in which the devil once again mocks Faust's manner of self-reflection in contrast to the seduction of Gretchen, which is now all but complete. The result is an agony of conscience for Faust, which does not, of course, prevent the destruction of Gretchen about to take place. Particularly powerful is the image introduced by Faust in his final speech in the scene (3345–65), where he as "homeless" force (*der Unbehauste*, 3348) affects the domestic bliss of Gretchen like a waterfall in an Alpine meadow, undermining her small cabin and dragging it downward into the abyss of his own perdition (*zu-grunde gehn*, 3365). A related though very different use of the waterfall in an Alpine landscape will serve as setting for the opening scene of Part Two ("Charming Landscape," 4613 ff., esp. 4717–27). In general, "Forest and Cave" provides a programmatic reformulation of the central existential problem of *Faust*, just as powerful and comprehensive as was the case in the opening scene, "Night."

"Gretchen am Spinnrade" *(lines 3374–413)*

The brilliant and irresistible musical setting of Gretchen's monologue at the spinning wheel by Franz Schubert in 1814 has made this text known to all the world as a lyrical effusion—indeed, as a song. There is some justification in regarding the text as such, especially since Gretchen has several other songs, from "The King of Thule" to the lyrical version of the fairy tale of the juniper tree, which she sings in the final dungeon scene of Part One. The stage directions here do not mention singing, however, and despite the short two-stress lines in four-line stanzas with rhyme in the second and fourth lines, the outburst may be regarded as spoken—or better, chanted—by Gretchen in keeping with the rhythm of the treadle on her spinning wheel (which Schubert's piano accompaniment also imitates), a powerful symbol of a repetitive and empty passing of time.

Her soliloquy should also be compared and contrasted with the far more cerebral monologue by Faust in "Forest and Cave," the scene that immediately precedes it. No greater contrast in manner of speech and style could be imagined; nor is there even a correlation between them in content and mood. Faust directs his concern toward nature in general, and he regards his communion with nature as a gift from the Spirit, yielding above all self-reflection for the speaker. Gretchen, by contrast, focuses exclusively on her sense of isolation and her sexual desire, a loss forever of the innocence and peace she enjoyed before meeting Faust. She even repeats the opening stanza twice again as a refrain to her effusion. Her desire also overwhelms her in physical—indeed, sexual—terms. Following her litany of praise for the man she desires, specifically for his body, in the sixth stanza (3394 ff.), she reaches an initial climax to her utterance in the phrase "And oh, his kiss!" (*Und ach, sein Kuss!*, 3401). The last two stanzas also carry the sense of physical longing even further. In the earlier version of her soliloquy (in the *Urfaust*), Gretchen asserts that her "lap" (*Schoos!*, a euphemism for her sexual organs), rather than her "bosom" (*Busen*), "strains" toward him (*drängt sich nach ihm hin*), and she follows the monosyllable *Schoos!* with the equally powerful exclamation *Gott!* In the final, climactic stanza she even imagines that she will "die" from his kisses (*vergehen;* "swoon and melt!" in Arndt's version), which recalls the traditional poetic designation for sexual orgasm as a kind of dying, suggesting that she has more than only kisses in mind as the cause. Goethe could not have created a more powerful contrast between the two lovers than these respective soliloquies, which further affirm for the audience that Gretchen will ultimately be deceived and abandoned by Faust.

Faust's "Credo" (lines 3431–58)

This speech by Faust to Gretchen in response to her inquiry about his attitude toward religion is often referred to as Faust's "credo." Goethe again employs a free rhythmic verse form that also quickly abandons rhyme. In this way, recalling the manner of the Earth Spirit in its self-presentation (501–9), the language imitates, and to a degree becomes identical with, the emotions it expresses. This is all the more striking because the speech directly addresses the problematic status of language in naming what is ineffable. Goethe here indicates once again the central thematic concern in *Faust* with the relation between word as sign and that which it signifies, specifically the relation between rhetoric and spirit, as indicated (already in the *Urfaust*) by the conversations between Faust and Wagner (530–57) and between Mephistopheles and the Student, especially where theology is discussed (1983–2000). This theme is represented at a later stage of composition above all in the *Logos* scene (1224–37). Despite the emphasis placed throughout on a personal experience of the divine, an emotional intuition of the God within, the concluding lines—in which Faust utters his now-famous tag "Feeling is all" (*Gefühl ist alles*)—consciously call to mind a venerable tradition of theological debate concerning the validity of names for God. It may also be inherent to the ironic technique of such verbal performance concerning the artifice of words that Faust is equally caught up in his own rhetoric, which constitutes after all yet another strategy of seduction.

The Valentine Scene (3620–775)

The opening section of this scene (3620–59, excluding 3646–9) is contained in the *Urfaust*, located immediately following (rather than before) the scene "Cathedral." It was omitted entirely from the *Fragment* of 1790. The expanded version in Part One was composed presumably around

1800, though completed only at the end of March and April, 1806, shortly before Goethe finally released the manuscript to his publisher Cotta. The final text of the entire scene is preserved in Goethe's own hand. In addition to the death of Gretchen's brother Valentine and his public denunciation of her before he dies, this scene provides the motive for Faust's flight from the city to avoid arrest for the killing (3712 ff.). Goethe has Mephistopheles mention explicitly that this is the evening two nights before the Walpurgis Night (3660 ff.), thus anticipating his visit there with Faust (which he presumably intends even before Valentine is killed). This scene brings Faust in his role of libertine, seducer, and lover of Gretchen into close proximity with the Don Juan legend. Whether or not Goethe had Mozart's opera *Don Giovanni* (1787) in mind when he composed the final version of this scene, it is interesting to compare with this scene in *Faust*, first, the nighttime duel in the opening scene of the opera between Don Giovanni and the Commendatore, father of Donna Anna, whom Don Giovanni has just attempted to seduce, and, second, the canzonetta that Don Giovanni, disguised as Leporello, sings beneath the balcony of Donna Elvira at the beginning of Act II, accompanying himself on a guitar, as he attempts to seduce Donna Elvira's servant girl. The role of Don Juan in both its aspects is assumed here more by Mephistopheles than by Faust, since it is the devil who sings the song—borrowed from Ophelia's mad song in Shakespeare's *Hamlet* 4.5—beneath Gretchen's window (3682–97) and who subsequently in the duel manipulates the sword that kills Valentine (3704–11).

"At the Well" (lines 3544–86), "By the City Wall" (3587–619), and "Cathedral" (3776–834)

In the published *Fragment* of 1790, these scenes assume a crucial role as the conclusion of the Gretchen sequence, even though the final scenes of what later became Part One had already been composed for the *Urfaust*. In effect, the crisis of conscience and emotion for Gretchen in this scene, culminating in her collapse into a faint at the end, marked at that stage in the drama the moment when her sin and her pregnancy became public, the moment also when Gretchen's condemnation by the church and by her society began. In the original sequence of scenes in the *Urfaust*, three consecutive moments of subjective pathos for Gretchen in her guilty state of mind, knowing that she is pregnant out of wedlock, follow directly on each other.

1. "At the Well," in which Lieschen talks mockingly to Gretchen of a common friend, Barbara, who has also become pregnant. This scene leaves Gretchen with an overwhelming sense of the fate that now awaits her. This guilt is marked in particular by the final lines in her concluding speech to herself: "Now I myself am bared to sin! / Yet all of it that drove me here, / God! Was so innocent, was so dear!" (3584–6).
2. "By the City Wall," in which Gretchen appears alone, kneeling before the statue of the Virgin in her role as Mater Dolorosa, protectress of women in need. Gretchen prays to the Virgin for help, using the opening of the *Stabat Mater*, a thirteenth-century Latin hymn attributed to Jaco-

pone da Todi. Gretchen repeats her opening prayer at the end of her appeal: "Incline, / Thou rich in grief, oh shine / Thy grace upon my wretchedness!" (3617–9). (Note that in the final scene of Part Two, "Mountain Gorges," the Virgin Mary appears soaring high in the heavens as Mater Gloriosa, and the spiritual apotheosis of Gretchen, as Una Poenitentium, appeals to her on behalf of the now dead Faust to secure his salvation, using a variant of these same traditional verses: "Incline / Thou past comparing, / Thou radiance bearing, / Thy grace upon my happiness" [12069–72].)

3. "Cathedral," in which Gretchen is confronted by an Evil Spirit that plagues her for her sins. In the *Urfaust*, this scene is indicated by a stage direction that calls for Gretchen to attend a Requiem Mass for her mother, who died apparently from the sleeping potion administered to her by Gretchen at Faust's bidding so that he could come to Gretchen's bedroom by night. The scene achieves particular theatrical power through a complex sequence of three voices in alternation: the cathedral choir, which intones the traditional Latin text of the Requiem Mass; the Evil Spirit, which whispers in Gretchen's ear, adapting aspects of the same text into a personal warning about her eternal damnation at the Last Judgement; and Gretchen's increasingly agonized outbursts as she loses all control of herself, cannot even breathe, and finally falls into a faint, appealing to her neighbor in the pew for her smelling salts ("Neighbor! Your salts!," 3834) as she collapses.

In the final version of Part One, Goethe complicates the sequence of Gretchen's passion and fall by inserting the Valentine scene just before "Cathedral." This interrupts the heightening intensity of Gretchen's agony, adds the public denunciation of Gretchen by Valentine as he dies, and also makes it unclear whether the Requiem Mass being celebrated in the cathedral is in commemoration of her mother or her brother (or perhaps even both). We also remain uninformed about the nature of the Evil Spirit, which is certainly quite unrelated to Mephistopheles, who by this time has departed with Faust for the Walpurgis Night. It may be helpful at this point to recall the transcendent perspective established for the drama by the "Prologue in Heaven," with its representation of the court of the Lord, and to look ahead to the final moment of "Dungeon," in Part One, in which a voice from above responds to Mephisto's assertion that Gretchen is condemned by answering that she is "Redeemed!" (4611). The Evil Spirit may well constitute a theatrical externalization and embodiment of Gretchen's own guilty conscience, but it also serves to remind us that there is indeed a transcendent perspective to Goethe's theater of the world and that Gretchen, who appears here to be the victim of Faust's love, will ultimately serve as the instrument of his salvation at the end of Part Two.

"Walpurgis Night" (lines 3835–4222)

No other scene in Goethe's *Faust* places such difficult demands on the reader for understanding its place and significance in the drama. The essential meaning that Goethe wished to convey resides in the Walpurgis

Night revels themselves, quite apart from any necessary association with Faust and his pact with Mephistopheles. Indeed, apart from a few obscure eighteenth-century sources (such as the poem "Die Walpurgis Nacht" of 1756 by the poet Johann Friedrich Löwen [1729–1771], which Goethe knew), no material in the Faust tradition associated him with the legends of the May Day witches' Sabbath. When Goethe returned to work on *Faust* in 1797, however, this scene attracted his attention above all, and it may have been the first new section for Part One that he attempted to add to the drama, though without initial success. At that time, Goethe associated Faust with the murky spirit world of Nordic, Germanic legend, represented also by several of the ballads he had recently composed for Schiller's journal of poetry, *Musenalmanach*. The "Walpurgis Night" therefore provided a logical extension of the hocus-pocus and superstition established in "Witch's Kitchen" (in which the event on the Brocken is also mentioned; see 2589–90. It is also alluded to in "Auerbach's Tavern" [*Blocksberg*; translated "Hallowe'en" by Arndt], 2113–4). By temper and mood, the poet in the 1790s strongly preferred classical art—which he had assimilated in Italy and which is manifested in such a work as the then recently completed short epic *Hermann und Dorothea*, in Homeric hexameters—rather than the dark, supernatural Nordic world of witches and demons.

A clear distinction can be made between the initial purpose of the "Walpurgis Night," as derived by Goethe from various literary sources and outlined in his first drafts for the scene, which survive among the Paralipomena published in the apparatus of the Weimar edition of Goethe's works, and the function of the final text in *Faust* as published in 1808. This distinction is important for understanding both the "Walpurgis Night" and Goethe's evolving view of the drama during the years when Part One was completed (i.e., 1797–1806). The sources used for the scene have been traced by scholars to several books borrowed by Goethe from the ducal library in Weimar at the time when he was working on the scene, especially from 1799 to 1801. For the most part, these books consist of obscure, pseudoscientific compendia of medieval folklore from the seventeenth century. The accounts offer a fantastic view of Sabbath rituals in medieval witch cults, colored by a mixture of popular superstition and moralistic outrage. These annual revels, supposed to take place during the night before May 1, involved a procession of witches and warlocks in the darkness to the summit of the Brocken, the highest peak in the Harz Mountains of central Germany, where orgies were held in celebration of Satan, including communal sexual intercourse and an act of obeisance to Satan that involved kissing the anus of a goat. That Goethe initially planned to follow the accounts of such satanic debauchery, even including an appearance by Satan himself—who figures nowhere else in *Faust*!— upon his throne at the summit of the mountain, is apparent from these manuscript drafts for the earliest version of the scene, dating from about 1798–99. (Scholars have occasionally made much of these drafts for a scene of wanton sexual debauch, as does most recently Albrecht Schöne in his book *Götterzeichen, Liebeszauber, Satanskult* [Munich, 1982] and in his apparatus for the edition of *Faust* in the *Bibliothek Deutscher Klassiker* [Frankfurt, 1994], but these drafts need be of no further concern here.)

What led Goethe to change his mind about the nature and function of the "Walpurgis Night" for his drama and to curtail so drastically the scene of debauch that he had initially planned for Part One? Critics have tended to read Goethe's *Faust*, especially Part One, from the perspective of the central character and with regard to the problem of the pact and wager with Mephistopheles. The drama has been viewed, in other words, essentially as a tragedy of character, even if that character comes to assume a representative, even universal significance for mankind in general. More recent discussions, however, especially those that take Part Two adequately into account, have come to recognize that Goethe's interest in *Faust* ultimately extends far beyond an immediate concern with character. That this is so in Part Two—in the Carnival Masque of Act I, the "Classical Walpurgis Night" of Act II, and the *Helena* (as Goethe referred to it) of Act III—need hardly be defended. It also holds true in Part One, at least tentatively, for those scenes in which the scope of the drama extends to a more general satirical panorama of human folly, as in the procession of citizens in "Outside the City Gate," the drinking songs and magic tricks in "Auerbach's Tavern," the play of Misrule with the Marmosets in "Witch's Kitchen," and most of all in the chaotic business of the "Walpurgis Night" and "Walpurgis Night's Dream." Goethe's presentation of the witches' Sabbath on the Brocken shifts away from any interest in the orgiastic revels at the summit, as these were imagined by the popular imagination, toward a very different kind of festival on May Day night that has much more positive and serious implications for the drama of *Faust* as a whole. For this less extreme view of the rites of May, which are just as pagan in origin as the cult of Satan yet are far more suitable to social satire and to theatrical spectacle, Goethe's chief source for the "Walpurgis Night's Dream" eminently served his purpose: the fairy world of Shakespeare's *Midsummer Night's Dream*. (The implications of this shift in theatrical models is discussed in more detail in the note to the "Dream," which follows.)

Much of the satirical material contained in "Walpurgis Night," it must be admitted, holds little interest for a modern reader. This is true especially for the entire sequence with the Proctophantasmiac near the end of the scene (4144–75), a cutting satire directed against the aging leader of the Berlin Enlightenment, Friedrich Nicolai, an arch-rationalist, who had recently (in 1799) published a treatise debunking claims that spirits were haunting the area of Tegel, north of Berlin. He claimed that he had been cured of any such hauntings by having leeches applied to his anus, hence the name that Goethe assigns to him here (deriving from the Greek word for anus, *proktos*). Perhaps worth noting in this otherwise uninteresting jab at the older and rather cranky author, who had first run afoul of Goethe in 1775, when he published a parody of Goethe's novel *The Sorrows of Young Werther*, is the association (perhaps?) of his symbolic name in this scene with the ritual obeisance to Satan in the form of a goat (which Goethe of course decided to omit), requiring that his devotees kiss its anus. Equally arcane is the group of old men seated around a campfire on the meadow to which Mephisto leads Faust when they turn away from the procession advancing toward the summit of the Brocken: the General, the Cabinet Minister, the Social Climber, and the Author (4072–95). The identity of these figures has still not been clarified by scholars.

More appropriate to the sense of the "Walpurgis Night" as demonic festival in general are the opening sequence, in which Faust and Mephistopheles are led around the mountain in confusion by a Will-o'-the Wisp (3855–911), even joining in to sing what appears to be a kind of operatic trio or chant (3871–911); and the complex interlude involving a varied crowd of witches and warlocks in a diverse chorus, much of it presumably also sung, as they ascend the mountain (3956–4015). This chaotic procession survives as a vestige of the original draft for the scene as an orgy and a wanton debauch. Even these portions of the scene, however, are likely to seem merely antiquarian curiosities presented in almost arbitrary confusion.

What remains of significance for the drama, therefore, are those activities directly involving Faust as he makes his errant way with Mephistopheles, first in approaching the setting of the festival (3835–54), next in attempting to join the procession (3935–55), then as Faust quickly becomes separated and in danger of getting lost (4020–9), so that Mephisto proposes they turn aside to observe the related activities on a safer middle ground: "Let us escape the crush and flee" (4025). Faust immediately acquiesces, and this results in a far more effective satirical focus in the exchange between these two travelers (4030–71). Of interest in particular is the vivid description of the mountain landscape as a version of Mammon's palace flashing with gold (3913–31; presumably borrowed from the description of Pandemonium in Milton's *Paradise Lost*, Book 2). Central thematic interest here pertains to the encounter with and response to a series of female figures, where increasingly wanton sexual excess plays a role: from the Peddling Witch selling her wares (4096–117) to the figure of Lilith, Adam's first wife according to a legend in the Jewish Talmud, based on the twofold account of creation in Genesis the name meaning "night hag" in Hebrew; see Isaiah 34.14), and thought to be a consort of the devil who threatens pregnant women and small children (4118–23). Third in this sequence is the pair of naked witches, one young and sexually attractive, with whom Faust dances (a kind of surrogate Gretchen), the other an elderly hag (possibly the same Witch earlier encountered in "Witch's Kitchen"), with whom Mephisto dances. Their brief exchanges in four-line stanzas, involving increasingly lewd jokes and presumably sung in the manner of a bawdy backroom ballad (4126–43), are broken off when Faust reacts in disgust to a little red mouse that jumps out of the mouth of the witch with whom he is dancing (4176–82).

The climax and turning point of the entire scene occurs when Faust is confronted by the strange spirit that Mephisto calls a "wraith" (*Idol*, or *eidolon* [from the Greek], 4190), which assumes the guise of Gretchen. The creature apparently appears before him completely naked—in the original draft of the scene it performs a lewd dance, exposing its sexual organs—but has a thin red slit across its throat, indicating that it has been beheaded, as Gretchen is shortly to be executed at the end of "Dungeon" (4204–5). This vision may be regarded as a projection by Faust's own imagination or conscience, perhaps in the same way that the Evil Spirit whispering in Gretchen's ear in the preceding scene, "Cathedral," symbolizes an objective manifestation of her own sense of guilt. More to the point, however, is a sense of parallel form and function between this "Idol" as it appears to Faust and his vision of the female figure in the magic mirror in "Witch's Kitchen." These images, both apparently representing the nude body of a woman—though only the latter resembles Gretchen— serve to frame the entire seduction of Gretchen for Faust like a prologue and an epilogue, constituting in the latter instance a cry of conscience set against his initial erotic desire. This vision also breaks the spell of the Walpurgis Night for Faust once and for all, even though Mephistopheles insists that it is all a delusion and a dangerous one at that (he associates the wraith with Medusa, 4192 ff.). Faust subsequently falls silent through the entire "Intermezzo" that follows, not speaking again until he does so in a rage directed at Mephistopheles concerning the fate of Gretchen in the following scene, "Dreary Day. A Field."

"Walpurgis Night's Dream or the Golden Wedding of Oberon and Titania. Intermezzo" (lines 4223–398)

Critics have been embarrassed by the apparent lack of any direct relevance to the Faust story demonstrated by this "Intermezzo." Even its function as an intermezzo, or entr'acte, is unclear, due primarily to Goethe's decision not to conclude the "Walpurgis Night," as first planned, with a climactic scene to follow the "Dream" at the Brocken (that is, the summit of the Blocksberg) in the presence of Satan. Goethe had originally intended the entire dream sequence to serve as a true interlude both for the Walpurgis Night generally and for the activities of Faust and Mephistopheles as they ascend the mountain. Instead, as the text now stands, the intermezzo brings the "Walpurgis Night" to a close, thus assuming perforce the role of a surrogate and ineffective climax, in place of the scene with Satan. It consists of nothing more than a sequence of single speeches, or short stanzas in verse, presented as a kind of pageant before Oberon and Titania, the king and queen of the fairies. These fairy monarchs are, of course, borrowed from Shakespeare's *Midsummer Night's Dream*, which Goethe knew in the original and which had at that time been newly translated into German by August Wilhelm von Schlegel, shortly before the "Intermezzo" was composed. Several late-eighteenth-century operatic versions of Shakespeare's story may also have had some influence, in particular an opera by Paul Wranitzky, *Oberon, or the King of the Elves*, staged by Goethe in Weimar in 1796, based on an epic poem in ottava rima by Christoph Martin Wieland, also entitled *Oberon*. These versions served much later as the sources for Carl Maria von Weber's opera *Oberon* in

1826, but none of them need concern us further here. The speakers in the interlude include a number of figures who represent various modes and schools of thought and writing in Goethe's own day, represented as objects of satire in schematic, allegorical manner. Some of these figures are so obscure that even Goethe's own audience would not have recognized them. What, then, does such a piece have to do with *Faust*, if anything?

Above all, one must consider how the source from Shakespeare has been adapted here and how the "Dream" itself is incorporated into the "Walpurgis Night." A group of amateur actors (*dilettantes* in the original, 4217–8) perform a story that one of them has written. The amateurs thus resemble the group of tradesmen, or mechanicals, in A *Midsummer Night's Dream*, including Peter Quince and Bottom the Weaver, who in the final scene present their dramatic version of Pyramus and Thisbe before Duke Theseus and his bride, Hippolyta, at the Athenian court. Goethe thus imposes on his "Intermezzo" an intentional irony of ineptitude, borrowed from his source, though he does not indulge in the same kind of Shakespearean slapstick. By instead focusing his satire on themes of poetry and letters, of philosophy and politics, Goethe exposes, through the inadequacy of what is said, characteristic failings of human culture and society, specifically in later-eighteenth-century Germany. For whom and for what motive, however, is this exposé presented?

In Shakespeare's play, the patrons and audience of the mechanicals' entertainment are the rulers of the city and their court, human beings who are celebrating a threefold marriage. The spirits of the wood, furthermore, who figure so centrally in the play, have nothing to do with this slapstick performance and remain invisible in their natural domain until the epilogue, when Puck, along with Oberon and Titania and their fairy train, enters the palace to bring blessings of fertility to the marriages being consummated. In Goethe's "Intermezzo," the fairy king and queen are themselves the recipients or designated audience of such an entertainment, presented to them as part of the celebrations for their golden wedding anniversary. At the same time, however, these fairies (apparently) are themselves part of the "Intermezzo," part of the theatrical show performed on the fairy stage. The "Dream" thus consists of a play within a play, or—to be more precise with reference to readers of Goethe's *Faust*—it involves a play within a play within a play. At the outer level is the witches' Sabbath of the "Walpurgis Night"; at the center is the satirical exposé of human folly and failure through the bungling procession of the amateur players on the fairy stage; and in between is the golden wedding festival of Oberon and Titania. It all seems rather more complicated than the text of the interlude could justify.

The "Dream" also shares another aspect of Shakespeare's play. The spirits in A *Midsummer Night's Dream* enjoy a privileged status as powers of nature, powers that may be playful—as demonstrated by Puck, or Robin Goodfellow (the mischievous poltergeist, who also appears in Goethe's

"Dream," essentially playing the same role)—but that may also be dangerous to the human community, especially when there is dissension or conflict among them, as there is in Shakespeare's play between Oberon and Titania. Critics have noted that a more exalted tradition of pagan folk belief stands behind these fairy monarchs, and we may assume Goethe to have been at least intuitively aware of it as well. Oberon is a variant of the Lord of the May Day rites, a powerful demonic force that was often identified, especially in the context of Christian polemics against such pagan survivals, with Satan himself. As such, Oberon also qualifies as a surrogate for the demonic patron (i.e., Satan) of the "Walpurgis Night." Titania, on the other hand, is a kind of nature goddess, the embodiment of that power of growth and fertility associated with the green world of woods and fields and with the summer as a season of warmth and recreation. In Shakespeare's play, strife between these two powers threatens to divide and even destroy the natural world. Their reunion and reconciliation is crucial to the successful conclusion of the comic plot. Goethe presents the "Walpurgis Night's Dream" as an ironic commemoration of the resolution of that strife at the end of A Midsummer Night's Dream, but he purposefully confuses the resolution of strife in nature with the human marriages celebrated in Shakespeare's comedy. The golden wedding anniversary of Oberon and Titania marks the resolution, so they themselves emphasize (4243–50), of fifty years of domestic squabbling in the realm of natural spirits that they rule. The present festival thus celebrates a universal harmony and peace, a sense of fulfillment and bliss, clearly at odds with both the amateur quality of the theatrical show and the sense of excess and debauch taking place simultaneously in the witches' Sabbath on the Brocken. Also indicative of this resolution in the realm of natural spirits is the appearance alongside Puck of Ariel, a spirit of the air derived by Goethe from Shakespeare's Tempest and subsequently employed in the opening scene of Faust, Part Two, who seems to embody that ministry of harmonious interaction that the fairy festival is meant to signify. In this regard, the "Intermezzo" has nothing in common with either the human world of Faust or the demonic domain of Mephistopheles; yet ironically, it reflects on both, if only through contrast.

Completely by surprise, therefore, Goethe affirms a positive and creative order to the natural world in the midst of apparent categorical denials of such order, as demonstrated both in the human setting of the Gretchen story and in the demonic setting of the "Walpurgis Night." Yet the poet also knew that the May Day rites celebrated in Shakespeare's play, where all strife between Oberon and Titania is resolved, were essentially identical with the traditional pagan festival of the Walpurgis Night itself, the night from April 30 to May 1, and that the essential meaning of this festival is not sexual debauch but rather the regeneration and renewal of life and spirit in the natural world. Indeed, the festival signifies a secular form of salvation, both in the sense of redemption, as declared by the voice from above for Gretchen at the very end of Part One (4611), and in the sense of new life in nature, as subsequently performed poetically and musically by the elfin chorus directed by Ariel at the outset of Part Two, which incidentally transforms and revives Faust's agonized state of mind following the execution of Gretchen. Intentional parallel and repetition are also included here with regard to the Easter Chorus celebrating the Resurrection of Christ on Easter Sunday morning at the end of "Night."

A contrast between failure and creativity at the outset of Part One may also be perceived within the "Walpurgis Night's Dream." The festival of golden harmony among the spirits transforms, at least in part, and offsets the satirical bungling of the amateur performers and the objects of their satire, through a reflection, however distant and with a sense of irony, upon the authentic art and poetry appropriate to the realm of spirits. This process of transformation and renewal is associated also with nature and, subsequently, in Part Two, with classical myth, culture, and art. The figure of Ariel especially introduces such redemptive powers of the heavenly spirit into the "Dream" and at the end invites everyone, including presumably the audience of *Faust*, to the palace of Oberon on the hill of roses (4393–4), which proves to be the setting of the "Charming Landscape," where the same Ariel introduces the scene that begins Part Two.

Finally, all distinctions in the "Dream" between internal and external perspective, between actors and audience, dissolve into a general confusion that results from reading the sequence of its short speeches. This confusion is due in large measure to the uniformity and willful inadequacy of the poetic form employed throughout, a short four-line stanza in doggerel ballad style. Goethe thus imposes upon his "Intermezzo" the illusion of a linear progression through this sequence of cumbersome and isolated utterances, as if the entire show were a ceremonial procession, or masque, not quite under control, or a narrative structure consisting of unrelated units of discourse. In contrast to the form, however, the entire complex establishes multiple layers of ironic self-reflection that constantly shift and undercut all sense of dramatic illusion. What Goethe here achieves, then, is a play within a play within a play that is totally devoid of coherent plot and that purposefully juxtaposes various voices at different levels of perspective. It may even be argued that the language of the "Dream" itself is intentionally perverse. Not only are the separate statements inadequate as expressions of the meaning to be conveyed, but the nature of the "Dream" itself resists any correlation between statement and meaning, between signifier and signified, except in terms of the irony of theatrical performance. And we also are caught up in that irony, since we, like Faust and Mephistopheles, witness that performance and come to recognize that the object of satire is indeed the world of human society, in which we also dwell. The entire "Dream" thus functions as a sequence of self-reflecting mirrors, which may finally project only the images of the spectators back upon themselves, functioning as a kind of *mise en abime*.

Perhaps this is after all an essential characteristic of spirit shows and dream sequences. We emerge with a sense of radical ambivalence, where the separate realms of spirit and humanity are intentionally confused, as also are all distinctions between good and evil, nature and the demonic, authentic poetry and incompetent dilettantism. Only through such ironic confusion can the "Dream" finally serve as a substitute for the climax of the "Walpurgis Night," in the satanic orgy that Goethe originally planned to write. The "Dream" provides an ironic alternative to the scene with Satan on the Brocken; but it also provides equally—if only in miniature—an ironic analogue to *Faust* itself, with regard to both the general condition of Faust's relation to Mephistopheles and the particular situation at this point in the drama concerning Faust's love for Gretchen, which now approaches its final catastrophe and tragic collapse. These thoughts about the "Walpurgis Night's Dream" may well suggest the kind of strategy that led Goethe to include it in his *Faust*, but that does not mean that the text of the "Intermezzo" could ever in itself summon much interest for a reader of the drama.

"Dreary Day. A Field" and "Night. Open Field" (lines 4399–404)

These two brief scenes, the one in prose (the only section in the entire published drama written in prose) and the other in irregular unrhymed verse, both derive, virtually without change, from the *Urfaust*. Scholars of Goethe's *Faust* generally agree that "Dreary Day" must represent one of the earliest scenes to have been composed for the drama, perhaps composed very soon after the execution of Susanna Margaretha Brandt in Frankfurt in 1772, at the time when Goethe first conceived the plan for the seduction of Gretchen as part of his *Faust*. The language of this prose text is violent and fragmented in its syntax, reflecting the extreme of anger and despair in Faust and the apparent sarcasm and indifference of Mephistopheles. The line spoken by the devil—"She is not the first"—occurs verbatim in the legal documents from the trial of Susanna Margaretha Brandt for infanticide. Four times in the opening two speeches by Faust the term *Elend* ("misery") occurs—translated by Arndt as, respectively, "In misery!", "In unredeemable ruin!", "this depth of misery," and "this single one's suffering." This is the prose style characteristic of Goethe's early, so-called Sturm und Drang period. The scene is inserted in Part One following the "Walpurgis Night" and "Dream," where it may originally have had no logical place. Faust has apparently just learned about Gretchen's arrest for infanticide and that she has been condemned to death. How he has secured this information, whether from Mephisto or some other source, is not clear, since nothing in the preceding scenes, apart from the vision of the wraith in the guise of Gretchen with its throat slit, could have indicated to him what has happened. A brief reference in the fragmentary drafts for the "Walpurgis Night" suggests that Goethe may have intended at one stage while composing the sequence to have had Faust overhear comments about Gretchen's fate from gossiping "toads" (*Kielkröpfe*). At any rate, the concluding sequence of scenes for Part One, even if chronologically in correct order, imposes such extreme contrasts of style and such radical gaps in logic and narrative continuity that a reader is bound to feel that Goethe has contented himself here with a kind of dramatic patchwork.

The brief scene in which Faust and Mephisto ride on the magical black steeds (mentioned by the devil at the end of "Dreary Day") past the place of execution—apparently a raised stone surface, called "raven-stone" (*Rabenstein*), upon which Gretchen is to be beheaded at dawn—is justly famous from subsequent visual and musical settings (e.g., in the engraving by Delacroix and the frenzied orchestral ride to hell composed by Berlioz for his *Damnation of Faust*). Yet Goethe provides little information about these magical black steeds and about the creatures—witches or evil spirits? Mephisto calls them "a witches' guild"—who are seen lying in wait at the place of execution. Perhaps they are preparing to seize the soul of Gretchen after her death (despite the fact that the final version of "Dungeon" includes the voice above that proclaims her salvation). In effect, the scene is a youthful instance of dramatic mood painting by Goethe.

"Dungeon" (lines 4405–612)

This scene is contained in the *Urfaust* in a prose version but omitted, along with the two scenes just preceding, from the published *Fragment* of 1790. Presumably, Goethe was uncertain at that time how to organize the material for the ending of Part One, as the discontinuities of the final text suggest. "Dungeon," however, may justifiably be regarded as the dramatic high point of the entire Gretchen sequence. Indeed, the emotional power of the scene surpasses anything else Goethe ever wrote and achieves a pathos and intensity unsurpassed in European drama, equal to the several scenes from Shakespeare to which it is indebted. The organization of the scene is built to a large degree upon the shifting dynamics of interaction between the two central characters, achieving a rhythm of opposing moments and mood that approximates a musical form. The setting of the scene is arranged with a precise visual sense of symbolic space, employing a frame or threshold between the outer corridor of the prison with the door leading into Gretchen's cell and the narrow, confining cell itself. This dark enclosed space, where Gretchen cowers in chains, is entered by Faust with keys and a lamp secured by Mephistopheles. Her space of confinement offsets and contrasts with corresponding scenes earlier in the Gretchen episode, which were also small and confining but which conveyed a more positive mood appropriate to her character and to her love: her bedroom, which Faust entered with Mephistopheles in order to place the casket of jewels, and the garden pavilion, in which the lovers first exchanged vows of love. A thematic though more distant and ironic parallel is also established with the confinement of Faust's own Gothic study at the outset of the drama, a setting that provided a quite different sense of imprisonment for the scholar confined by his academic learning.

Gretchen's state of mind, a derangement that indicates a complete withdrawal into herself, complements the enclosure of the cell. Goethe modeled her madness on Ophelia's mad scenes in *Hamlet*. The song that Gretchen sings (4413–20) derives from a popular though gruesome fairy tale, which was later included by the brothers Grimm in their *Kinder- und Hausmärchen* (1810–12) in a Low German version entitled "The Juniper Tree." As alluded to by Gretchen's ditty, the wicked stepmother in the tale kills the young boy, then cooks and serves up his flesh in a stew to his father. The boy's sister gathers up his bones and buries them beneath the juniper tree, where their real mother is buried, whereupon a beautiful bird appears in the tree singing this song. The voice singing here is in effect that of Gretchen's drowned baby, indirectly accusing its own parents of its death. When Faust tries to speak to Gretchen, she thinks he is her executioner come prematurely to take her to her death (4427–40). She ignores Faust's repeated appeal to escape with him and instead describes in vivid though deranged language the events that have occurred, including the drowning of her child, which she imagines still to be struggling to live (4552–62). Faust, it should be noted, never mentions the child or even acknowledges its existence. Gretchen, in outlining her wish to be buried next to her mother and brother with her baby at her right breast (4521–9), also insists that "no one else will lie by me!" Faust is already excluded implicitly by her from the scenario of her execution and final repose.

Two moments of recognition are crucial for the dynamics of Gretchen's response to Faust's visit in her dungeon cell. The first occurs following his loud calling of her name (4460–1), when her chains miraculously fall from her and she recognizes his voice. This is also the only time in the entire drama that Faust calls her "Gretchen." She tries to kiss him and caress him but finds his lips to be cold and concludes, despite his protests, that his love for her is gone. The second moment, even more powerful, occurs when Mephisto enters the cell, urging that they leave immediately. Gretchen, recognizing the devil, cringes from him and turns away from Faust once and for all, with a cry that indicates her disgust: *Heinrich! Mir graut's vor dir!* (4610; Arndt: "Heinrich! I shrink from thee!")

In the last section of Part One to be published, Goethe reintroduces a transcendent perspective—recalling the Lord's promise of redemption in the "Prologue in Heaven"—as Gretchen submits herself entirely to the judgment of God (4605). Mephisto asserts that "She is condemned!", but a voice from above corrects him to announce that she is "Redeemed!" Mephistopheles drags Faust away, as if the devil were here taking him to hell, as in the traditional legend. We hear the voice of Gretchen within her cell, calling Faust's name, "Heinrich! Heinrich!", as the curtain closes. Goethe thus concludes Part One with a tentative sense of an ending that will be offset and revised by the ultimate conclusion of Part Two, even though the execution of Gretchen here proceeds despite Faust's attempt to prevent it. Readers of Part One should consider the implications of this ending for Goethe's generic designation of his *Faust* as *A Tragedy*.

"Charming Landscape" (lines 4613–727)

This short scene, poetically complex and dramatically autonomous, provides a programmatic demonstration at the outset of Part Two of the radically new and wide-ranging poetic and symbolic scope that the subsequent five acts of the drama will achieve. Through the twofold perspective of Ariel with his elfin chorus and Faust in his monologue, Goethe once again presents the central insight of his drama as a whole concerning human life and its relation to the dynamic processes of great creating nature. "Charming Landscape" thus assumes at the level of poetic form a degree of autonomy that frees it from all obligation to dramatic continuity. Efforts by critics to explain how Faust came to this mountain meadow, how much time has elapsed since the execution of Gretchen, where Mephistopheles has gone and why, and especially how this scene can be justified morally in light of Gretchen's death and Faust's apparent guilt in both a legal and an existential sense are inappropriate and futile, since the scene itself takes no cognizance of them. Nor is there any direct relation of this scene to the action that follows in the court of the Emperor. It stands apart and above the drama proper and reflects upon its entirety as a kind of paradigm for the Faustian dilemma as such from the perspective of the author at the time when he returned to work on the drama in the mid-1820s.

The only legitimate continuities for this scene within the rest of *Faust* are found in other programmatic moments, above all in the scene "Night," which begins Part One and with which this scene thus stands in an important correlation. "Charming Landscape" performs a symbolic transformation in Faust's state of mind, which stands in purposeful contrast to his initial attempt to conjure the Earth Spirit in his study at night. Also important for comparison are other monologues by Faust, such as his sunset speech in "Outside the City Gate" (1064–99), his address to nature in "Forest and Cavern" (3217–50), or—looking ahead to Part Two—his farewell speech to the vision of Helena at the outset of Act IV (10039–66) and his final speech in Act V, where he imagines the utopian future realm that he has tried to construct on the land claimed by pushing back the sea (11559–86). What unites these other moments in the drama with this scene, and indeed unites the drama of *Faust* as a whole, is the fundamental attempt by Faust to comprehend human existence in its constantly varying temporal dimensions and its constant dependence on shifting forces of mind and will, which motivate all action and thought, with reference to some ultimate and absolute power of spirit or divinity, either within nature and thus accessible to human experience or else above and beyond the natural world, transcending all knowledge and understanding.

By borrowing and adapting alien poetic forms Goethe here also accommodates to his drama—as so often in his literary work—resources and resonances from European cultural tradition. The spirit Ariel, familiar from Shakespeare's last play, *The Tempest*, who appeared earlier at the end of "Walpurgis Night's Dream" (4391–4), is here reintroduced as the manager or orchestrator of nature's spectacle of redemption. This congenial spirit of the air rejoices in his native element along with the chorus of elves that attends his bidding. Their function is to articulate the natural process of time—through the night to the dawn of a new day—in a lyrical mode where natural process and song are identical.

Particularly striking is the similarity of form, tone, and diction in the lyrics sung by Ariel in both *The Tempest* and "Charming Landscape." The dominant meter of these songs is trochaic, usually in four-stressed lines with alternating rhyme or rhyming couplets. The famous song that Ariel sings to Prince Ferdinand about his supposedly drowned father, "Full fathom five thy father lies" (*The Tempest* 1.2.400 ff.), consists of a single stanza of eight lines, corresponding precisely to the form of Ariel's opening song in "Charming Landscape" (4613 ff.) and the night song of the elfin chorus that follows (4634–65). Poetic effects used in Shakespeare, especially involving phonetic patterns of internal rhyme, alliteration, and the repetition of consonants, to achieve a musical, almost magical sense of chant or charm, are also imitated by Goethe. In Shakespeare, Ariel is the voice of the air, the element to which he is freed by Prospero at the end of the play. In Goethe, he speaks with the same voice and indeed represents or embodies a spiritual element of nature itself. Ariel thus affirms in "Charming Landscape" the ultimate triumph of his liberation as spirit, as if nature itself were singing these songs in a poetic language that perfectly fuses sense and sound.

Ariel and the spirit chorus are themselves identical with the redemptive, healing forces they describe and celebrate in their song. These forces restore and renew Faust's spirit through a therapy of sleep, while the cycle of day and night passes through its four traditional watches as articulated in the choral song of the elves. In a draft for this scene, Goethe originally labeled the individual stanzas of this song in accord with the traditional names of the watches through the night—*Serenade, Notturno, Matutino,* and *Réveille*—thus indicating the stages of time passing that the song demarcates. Symbolic echoes also resonate here from the hymn of the Archangels in "Prologue in Heaven" and the Easter Chorus at the end of the scene "Night." An even closer analogue to such spirit song as the unmediated voice of nature is the visionary dream trip performed by the spirit chorus in the first study scene, a performance that hypnotizes Faust and puts him to sleep, just as here he sleeps through the choral watches of the night.

Goethe's second literary source is equally powerful and eloquent in its implications for the scene. Faust's monologue after he awakens at dawn is written in terza rima, the meter of Dante's *Divine Comedy,* a complex form of interlocking rhymes in a continuous sequence of iambic pentameter. Goethe imitated this verse form in the monologue for the first time in his career (using it subsequently only for the poem he wrote in response to the contemplation of Schiller's skull, "*Im ernsten Beinhaus wars . . .*"). The persistent forward motion of Dante's poetic meter through a continuous circling and interlocking chain of rhyme demands (as Goethe stated in a conversation on September 29, 1823, as recorded by Chancellor Fr. v. Müller) a "broad and rich subject matter as its basis, if it is to give pleasure." *The Divine Comedy,* in its massive architectonic structure through one hundred cantos, employs terza rima to trace the journey of the visionary mind through the entire range of the cosmos, in analogy to the movement of the drama described by the Stage Director at the end of

Goethe's "Prelude in the Theater": "From Heaven through the World to Hell" (242). Dante's journey is more or less continuous from canto to canto: from Hell through Purgatory to Paradise. Faust's monologue may be interpreted as imitating in miniature the progress of Dante's vision, as articulated by the advance of Faust's statement from the moment of his reawakening and the renewal of his desire or will, leading to the direct encounter with the power of divinity, represented by the rising sun. Dante's poem also begins with the poet "coming to himself" (*mi ritrovai, Inferno* 1.2) in a dark wood, just as the sun is rising over a high hill following a dark night of the soul.

Particularly important as a structural feature of Faust's monologue, in contrast to Dante's poetic journey, is the decisive interruption of continuity in Faust's thought process, breaking the flow of the terza rima at two crucial moments in the speech. This twofold reversal and caesura in Faust's discourse is indicated by the use of dashes in the printed text, first in mid-line at 4695 ("Raise up your gaze!—") and second at 4702 ("He clears the rim!—"). Such a breakdown of continuity thematizes Faust's failure to achieve a direct and unmediated vision of the absolute, a failure that recapitulates the initial attempt in Part One by Faust to confront the Earth Spirit. Despite the limited scope of Faust's monologue in terza rima, comparison and contrast with Dante's epic journey toward his successful vision of God at the end of the *Paradiso* signals a fundamental feature of Goethe's drama as tragedy with regard to Faust's boundless striving and the inevitability of his failure to achieve satisfaction and fulfillment. This pattern of striving and error, first mentioned by the Lord in "Prologue in Heaven," repeated in the wager between Faust and Mephistophiles in the pact scene, and demonstrated at crucial moments of encounter throughout the drama—from the encounter with the Earth Spirit to the final vision of the blind Faust in his last speech—is here presented programmatically within the poetic form and structure of the monologue itself.

Faust's monologue is so central to an understanding of Part Two as a whole that more detailed scrutiny of what it says is justified. The speech begins at the moment of awakening consciousness after Faust's sleeping cure through the nighttime ministrations of the spirit chorus. The arrival of dawn solicits in Faust's mind a reciprocal response, which manifests itself in his renewed desire, indeed, in his *(Faustian)* "striving" toward the highest mode of existence (*Zum höchsten Dasein immerfort zu streben*, 4685). His speech is divided into four separate verse paragraphs, which articulate four distinct cognitive stages of response.

The first stage is an unfolding, an opening outward of his desire, which advances into the morning and seeks to permeate the whole of animated nature, regarded as a garden, a "paradise" (4694; translated by Arndt as "Eden's bower"), in which Faust will live and act. The second stage delineates the heroic, ultimately tragic thrust of Faust's mind toward a confrontation with divinity as it manifests itself in the light of the rising sun. Instantaneous blindness results from the overwhelming brightness of the sun, forcing Faust to turn away his gaze, thus reversing his basic stance in what amounts to a tragic turn of the mind.

This retreat manifests itself in the reflective discourse of the third verse paragraph: Faust thinks over what has happened and formulates his thoughts in a language that assumes an intentional generality. At the end of the second paragraph (4703), he refers to himself using an emphatic first-person singular, the first occurrence of such a pronominal subject in the monologue. In the third paragraph, by contrast, he employs the first-person plural, as if he were here speaking for all humankind, passing a judgment that goes beyond the authority of personal experience and assumes the status of a universal law. When he confronts the sun, Faust retreats, not to escape exposure, as was the case with Ariel and the spirits of nature, but to secure the conditions for reflective thought, which—as Goethe knew from the entire history of German idealist speculation—is the necessary condition for all conceptual knowledge and understanding. In this way also, Faust exemplifies that nobility of mind mentioned at the conclusion of the song by the elfin spirits, a nobility that "perceive[s] and swiftly grasp[s]" (*versteht und rasch ergreift*, 4665).

The final section of the monologue introduces one of Goethe's most archetypal images for human experience. The life of a human being is symbolized by the waterfall as it plummets downward, crashing from rock cliff to rock cliff. (Readers should recall the similar image Faust uses to describe his destructive effect on Gretchen at the end of "Forest and Cave," 3350–73). The force of the flowing water corresponds to the will or drive that constitutes Faustian striving. The clash of water and rock, however, produces a spray or mist that hovers above the waterfall. The fine water droplets, though in constant motion, are suspended as a constant veil, indistinguishable by the eye as either rise or fall. The term *Wechseldauer* (4722; translated by Arndt as "in variance lasting"), applied to the resulting rainbow, indicates a central concept for Goethe with regard to the value of art as permanence in change (see his philosophical poem "*Dauer im Wechsel*" and the image of the veil of poetry received from the hand of truth in the programmatic poem "*Zueignung*," which Goethe placed as dedication to his collected works: *Der Dichtung Schleier aus der Hand der Wahrheit*). This mist is described as life's "most youthful veil" (*jugendlichstem Schleier*, 4714; translated by Arndt as "most young of youthful hazes")—the concept of a veil is central to Goethe's view of art, as indicated at the end of Act III, when Helena's veil is transformed into a cloud that carries Faust back from Greece to Germany.

In this mist Faust discovers the ultimate symbolic sign for his reflections on the meaning of human existence. The mist catches the light of the sun as it shines through the air, each tiny droplet of water serving as a crystal from which the light is mirrored back and refracted, forming for the perceiving eye in the totality of this process a rainbow in its varied color. The image of the rainbow serves as symbol for the aspect of human creativity that constitutes art and poetry, indeed, human culture in the most general, all-inclusive sense of the term. This form of visual experience also remains accessible to Faust after he has turned away from the blinding light of the sun, providing a comprehensive and reliable mirror or "reflection" of human striving (*Der spiegelt ab das menschliche Bestreben*; "This mirrors all aspiring human action," 4725). The depiction of the rainbow in its accurate scientific detail reflects Goethe's extensive study of optics and color theory, culminating in his *Farbenlehre* of 1810.

The striving that constitutes Faust's essential nature is thus sublimated into a reflection upon itself, a representation of itself as model or analogue for the work of art, in and through which the authentic light of the divine, which—like the sun—overwhelms human vision in direct confrontation, is refracted into the many-hued spectrum of the rainbow. In this sense, the final line of Faust's monologue describes the highest possible achievement of human art and culture, in Goethe's view. That quality or aspect of life accessible to human experience—the same force that beat again anew in Faust's pulse at the dawn of this new day, affirmed at the outset of his monologue (4679–80)—is this multicolored refraction, which we may have and hold: *Am farbigen Abglanz haben wir das Leben* (4727). Three levels of reflectivity are thus included in the symbol of the rainbow: 1) the mirroring and refracting of the sun's light; 2) the cognitive perception of the refracted colors by the human eye; and 3) the conceptual comprehension of this visual experience by the mind, as demonstrated by the several reflective structures in the language of Faust's monologue.

"Imperial Residence" (lines 4728–5064)

The actual drama of *Faust*, Part Two, commences with the entrance of the central characters, Faust and Mephistopheles, into the world of public political affairs at the court of the young Emperor. Only Act I takes place within the imperial palace; yet virtually everything that follows—including the search for Helen of Troy, which fills Acts II and III with its peculiar mythical-psychological action; the war against the Rival Emperor in Act IV, which involves both Faust and Mephisto in a supreme test of magic in action so that the Emperor emerges victorious; and, finally, the land reclamation project undertaken by Faust along the tidal shores in order to build his new modern city, an action nearing completion in Act V—proceeds directly from Faust's involvement in the affairs of state. No greater contrast with the far more intimate and domestic world of Gretchen in Part One could be imagined, as Goethe no doubt intended when he returned to serious work on *Faust* during the last years of his life. The general subject of Faust's involvement in the world of the Holy Roman Empire of the German Nation had always figured in the popular legend of Faust from the initial chapbook of 1587 through all subsequent versions. Goethe intended from the earliest stages of composition for his drama to include such material in the work; yet how radically different the world of Part Two finally proved to be: different not only from Goethe's own Part One but also in every way from all earlier versions of the Faust legend. This sense of radical difference is crucial to the unique manner and style of Part Two as drama, a point that has been noticed by critics from the time of publication, soon after Goethe's death, until the present. The challenge of evaluating the nature of this difference in terms of literary style and dramatic mode has been a continuing source of controversy and fundamental disagreement among the scholars.

Goethe's prose outline of Part Two, dictated in 1816 for inclusion in his autobiography (see below), gives attention to details of place and motive, even to historical reference, very much within the conventions of traditional historical drama. Faust's visit to the Emperor is there said to take place at the Imperial Parliament at Augsburg; the Emperor is identified as Maximilian I, who reigned from 1493 to 1519 and was indeed on the throne during the lifetime of the historical Faustus; and their meeting is said to occur—as was the case in the popular chapbook version of the legend—because the Emperor has heard of Faust's magical powers and wishes to meet him (or so, according to the outline, Mephistopheles reports to Faust). The plan for the visit, furthermore, is to be discussed in the opening scene of Part Two, when Mephisto joins Faust in "Charming Landscape," following Faust's monologue in response to the sunrise. The initial encounter with the Emperor—still according to the outline—is to occur in the absence of Mephistopheles, so that Faust himself has to respond to the Emperor's questions, with Mephisto interceding only when Faust becomes flustered and confused. The interview is to conclude with a request from the Emperor to witness a show of apparitions and spirits, among them presumably Helen of Troy. If this outline were all that Goethe had completed of Part Two, we would have no idea of the thematic significance that the encounter with the imperial court subsequently assumes for the drama. From a reading of the prose outline we may well ask whether Goethe himself had any clear idea at that time what would ultimately emerge for Part Two.

Particularly troubling is the seemingly laconic dismissal of all particulars concerning time and place for the action in the court, even to the point where all proper names are abandoned and characters are defined only by the office each holds. No preparation or transition to the court is provided, since Mephisto does not even appear in "Charming Landscape." This absence contrasts with his behavior both in "Forest and Cave" in Part One (3251 ff.) and in "High Mountains," the opening scene of Act IV in Part Two (10067 ff.), in which the devil joins Faust in the Alps after they have returned from Greece. And why is Faust missing from the opening scene of court, in which the Emperor consults his several counselors on affairs of state, only to be joined by Mephistopheles in his disguise as court jester, unknown to any in the court but presumably recognizable as the devil to an audience in the theater? No explanation is offered for his presence, and the Emperor accepts him at his side with no questions asked. Faust himself does not appear until the middle of the elaborately allegorical scene that follows, the Carnival Masque or *Mummenschanz* ("Spacious Hall"), where he is disguised as Plutus, god of wealth, unknown to and unexpected by the Herald (see 5494 ff.) and perhaps even unrecognizable at first to us. There is thus little indication at the level of plot and character of any thematic connection between the political world of the Emperor and the central concerns of Faust.

The explanation for all this is found in Goethe's allegorical technique through the whole of Part Two, where literally everything that happens participates in an elaborate symbolic action in which Faust himself no longer holds an exclusive place. The entire world of the drama assumes Faustian qualities that are represented in general, even universal terms, which translate all individuality into generic political or even mythological terms. The role of theater as spectacle and as festival is also greatly enhanced, to the point where all historical and mimetic frames of reference disappear. Goethe thus begins an elaborate exploration of public issues, including questions of both political philosophy and economic reform, which extend throughout the rest of the drama in the form of various symbolic transformations and theatrical or mythological excursions along the way.

The Emperor and His Politics

Within the public dimension of the drama, the Emperor serves as an analogue to Faust himself. At the outset, he is immature and politically irresponsible, newly returned from his coronation in Rome (see 5068 ff. and 10439 ff.) and anxious to introduce the customs of the Roman carnival to his German court (see 5065 ff.). He proves inept as a ruler, failing to organize the finances of his realm, failing to assert adequate leadership over his vassals and counselors, and later (in Act IV) failing to provide effective leadership in warfare. Mephistopheles' intervention provides an infernal solution to the Emperor's ineptitude, for which, beyond all comprehension by the Emperor himself, a devilish price is exacted. Both the financial reform proposed by Mephisto as court jester and the military assistance he later provides in the war are fraudulent, despite apparent initial success at the level of deceit and illusion. The paper money introduced to cover the debts of the realm, despite the elaborate claim by Mephisto that it will be sustained by the wealth of buried treasure beneath the ground, has no real value whatsoever and provides only a temporary illusion of relief, followed by drastic inflation and a collapse of credit. In Act IV, the outcome of the devil's fiscal reform is anarchy, rebellion, and open warfare (see 10234–96). Nor would the Emperor stand a chance of victory in that war without the aid of Faust, who releases the deceptive powers of Mephisto and his three infernal companions (see 10323 ff.) to rout the forces of the Rival Emperor through the use of elemental magic, the power of fire and water (see "In the Foothills," 10345–782). The effect of such a political alliance with the devil is apparent at the end of Act IV, where the Emperor attempts to reward his chieftains, including Faust, who claims ownership of the tidal lands, which he will use for his reclamation project (shown in Act V). The Emperor quickly falls victim to oppressive moral and material demands from the church, which through the Archbishop exacts a heavy penalty for the Emperor's dubious involvement with the powers of darkness (see 10931–11042). Our last view of the Emperor, at the end of Act IV, suggests that he emerges from his involvement with Faust and Mephistopheles both sadder and wiser, no longer free to rule with any legitimacy or authenticity but at last truly aware of what the responsibility of imperial rule requires. Readers of Goethe's *Faust* have always recognized that this complex economic and political action signifies at the level of allegory a categorical negative judgment by the author of the drama against developments in Europe during the restoration following the fall of Napoleon and the establishment of the so-called Holy Alliance.

The Emperor himself has no explicit historical counterpart, but an implicit literary model for his role may be found in the history plays of Shakespeare. In this we may observe once again how freely Goethe departed from the popular legend of Faust—a departure not even hinted at in the 1816 prose outline for Part Two—in order to establish a more universal basis for the symbolic action of his drama. Essential parallels of structure and theme may be detected above all in the later history cycle of Shakespeare, sometimes referred to by critics as the Henriad, consisting of the four plays *Richard II*; *Henry IV, Parts I and II*; and *Henry V*. These connections have not often been noted by scholars of *Faust*, but once they are recognized, it becomes difficult to ignore them. We should not forget how important Shakespeare was for Goethe at all stages of his career, not only in *Faust*.

Shakespeare dramatizes a comprehensive revolution in the rule of the English kings at the end of the Middle Ages through a cycle of corruption, usurpation, violent civil disorder, and final restoration. A grand panorama is portrayed through the reign of three monarchs: Richard II, who abuses the privileges of his office and is deposed by his rival, Henry Bolingbroke; the latter, as Henry IV, who must rule under the burden of his guilt for having usurped the throne through civil war and murder; and, finally, Henry V, whose role as Prince Hal with his companion Falstaff throughout the central plays prepares for his triumph as warrior king against the French at the battle of Agincourt as well as his subsequent betrothal to Princess Katherine of France. All this may seem very distant to the action of Goethe's *Faust*, but the sweep of Shakespeare's historical panorama is transformed by Goethe into the various public events that focus on the single figure of the young Emperor. This monarch displays a number of attributes seemingly in common with Shakespeare's Prince Hal, in particular his frivolous pleasure in feasting and entertainments, including his disguise at the Carnival Masque as the great god Pan. Yet in contrast to Shakespeare's Hal, the Emperor fails to develop a realistic sense of political power and of his own obligations as monarch. Attributes of both Richard II and Henry IV, furthermore, may also be perceived in the Emperor, suggesting that Goethe consciously combined all three rulers from Shakespeare into one. Richard II abuses the privileges of his inherited throne by frivolous and irresponsible behavior, in a manner that closely corresponds to the role of the Emperor in accepting Mephisto's fiscal reform. Open rebellion and war are the outcome in both cases. The Rival Emperor in Act IV of *Faust*, Part Two, though he remains curiously out of sight in Goethe's drama, closely resembles the figure of Henry Boling-broke in *Richard II*, who opposes the legitimate king and, in that case, successfully seizes the throne. In *Faust*, the rebellion fails due solely to the intervention of Faust and Mephistopheles, so that the Emperor finally retains his throne. Yet at the end his rule is compromised and plagued by guilt, very much in the manner of Shakespeare's Henry IV, who spends his time as ruler in penance and prayer. Henry IV's most famous line could well apply to the Emperor in *Faust* as we see him at the end of Act IV: "Uneasy lies the head that wears a crown" (2 *Henry IV* 3.1.31). Such echoes of Shakespeare in the characterization of the Emperor remain no more than that, yet they suggest the degree to which the symbolic action at a political level in *Faust* should not be read simply as an allegory for the events in Europe during the era of Napoleon and the restoration.

Carnival Masque ("Spacious Hall," lines 5065–986)

The "masquerade" (line 4767; *Schönbärte mummenschänzlich* in the German), celebrating the traditional pre-Lenten Carnival, extends for more than nine hundred lines, thus occupying fully one-eighth of *Faust*, Part Two. Most readers are likely to wonder what Goethe is trying to do with such a seeming digression, much of which commands little interest either as poetry or as drama. Nor is it always quite clear precisely what is happening and why, least of all who is in control of an event so varied and confusing. The most immediate parallel from Part One is, of course, the "Intermezzo" to the "Walpurgis Night," the celebration of the golden wedding anniversary of Oberon and Titania by the amateur theatricals. This analogy is significant—despite the danger that the reader will lose patience with both digressions from the central focus on Faust—primarily with regard to a technique of theatrical spectacle and its use for purposes of social satire. Goethe's great allegorical theater of the world here unfolds in ways that subsequently—above all, in Acts II and III—become all-inclusive for the symbolic and mythological implications of the drama. The sheer length of this scene so early in the action of Part Two suggests that for Goethe the Carnival Masque is no digression at all but rather a gateway into the strange medium of his art. The masquerade staged by the court of the Emperor thus quickly becomes an ironic commentary on the theatrical technique of *Faust*, Part Two, in general.

Scholars have often pointed to specific documentary sources for Goethe's revival of a form of entertainment associated above all with festivals in the aristocratic courts of the Renaissance, such as the book by Antonio Francesco Grazzini on triumphs, masques, and carnival entertainments staged in Florence during the mid-sixteenth century at the court of Lorenzo de Medici, published in Italian in 1750 and borrowed by Goethe from the ducal library in Weimar in August, 1827; or the *Triumphal Procession of the Emperor Maximilian* by Dürer, which also depicts an elephant. This research has led to various arguments about the historicity of the Masque, as if it were actually being staged in the imperial court in Germany at the time when Dr. Faustus lived. In addition, Goethe's own experience of carnival during his stay in Italy, documented above all in the monograph he published on the Roman carnival soon after he returned (1790), also influenced the kind of scene he here introduces to his drama. Equally significant, though never even remotely as elaborate, complex, and fantastical as the scene staged in *Faust*, were the theatrical entertainments and masques that Goethe himself created and directed for particular occasions of state at the Weimar court. These sources and influences, however, though interesting and helpful, do not clarify just what the Carnival Masque in *Faust*, Part Two, signifies for Goethe's drama.

The essential mode of performance in the Masque is that of procession, where a seemingly endless sequence of figures in elaborate costume makes its way across the stage. We are to assume that the actors in the Masque are members of the court who have taken on specific roles for the occasion. As at a kind of cosmic costume ball, each group presents itself and identifies itself to the audience through a spoken (or sung) poetic text. The procession is conducted and controlled—at least up to a certain point—by a Herald, a character otherwise unknown to us, who serves as master of ceremonies and introduces each group as it arrives on stage. The texts spoken by each group serve only as partial supplement to what in a theatrical performance—assuming such a performance were ever to be achieved—would be conveyed visually through costume and choreography and musically through accompanying orchestration, with the specific instruments often specified. The figures themselves also appear quite free to perform certain improvised actions, possibly in conscious imitation of the popular Italian comedy (commedia dell'arte, which was also well known to Goethe). At several points, Goethe's stage directions assume quite elaborate descriptive form, almost in the manner of a prompt book. This Masque thus abandons any pretense of traditional mimetic drama by collapsing all action into show and translating all characterization into external surface as costume and mask. So what, we may ask, is the point?

Satire is the dominant mode, directed outward toward the audience as a form of exposé or indictment. What we witness as audience is a highly mannered and stylized image of human life and behavior that assumes ever more encompassing claims. In this regard, we should also recall the procession of citizens that comes out through the city gate, enjoying the pleasures of springtime, in the scene on Easter Sunday in Part One. Equally valid as precursor, however extreme, is the procession of witches and warlocks that ascends the Brocken to participate in the demonic revels of May Day in the "Walpurgis Night" of Part One. In the Carnival Masque sequence, a twofold thematic concern may be traced, in which display for the purpose of buying and selling coincides with the erotic allure of young women and men—flower girls and farmers—who in hawking their wares are also implicitly presenting themselves as potential produce for barter. This is particularly apparent following the song of the Gardeners, when the Mother encourages her Daughter to present herself as a commodity and to catch a husband (5178–98). The stage directions after the Mother's three stanzas indicate a general confusion of courting and flirting, as "Playmates, young and beautiful, join the scene" with "unconstrained chattering." Fishermen and Birdcatchers (one is reminded of Papageno, the birdcatcher who wishes he had a net with which to snare himself girls, in Mozart's opera *The Magic Flute*) "mingle with the pretty girls," and the verbal activity between both sexes is granted a general license to improvise: "Efforts on both sides to attract, captivate, evade, and detain occasion most agreeable dialogues." All of this is, of course, left entirely to the imagination of the reader, although an effective stage performance would need to put it all into practice.

The sequence of allegorical figures advances through several stages of heightening and intensification, as the initial groups of Flower Girls and Gardeners are replaced by the more rough-hewn and even violent Woodcutters, Pulcinelli, and Parasites, followed even by a drunkard, who entices all to join him in an excess of drink. Readers may recall the drunken students in "Auerbach's Tavern" as an analogue, though the implications of this behavior and the accompanying commentary extend beyond the more limited convention of satirical songs used in the earlier scene, as in Brander's "Song of the Rat" and Mephisto's "Song of the Flea." Mythological figures quickly follow in ways that presumably heighten the sense of allegory and abstraction, perhaps in the manner of modern imitations of classical sculpture and painting, in order to convey a moral lesson or a sense of the essential human condition. The Graces, the Fates ("Parcae") and the Furies—all familiar from the mythological subject matter of rococo and neoclassical art—lead directly to what appears to be the high point of the Masque, at least as planned and staged by the Herald: the pageant of Victory. Goethe here introduces an elephant onto the stage, accompanied by several allegorical female figures. In all likelihood, the idea for such a spectacle derived not only from depictions of similar triumphant processions from traditions of antiquity—as in the painter Andrea Mantegna's depiction of the triumph of Julius Caesar (1490), which Goethe owned in a woodcut by Andrea Andreani—but also from the stages of grand opera as it had developed in Paris during the 1820s through the work of such composers as Rossini and Spontini. (The production of Spontini's opera *Olimpie* in Berlin in 1821, with a German translation of the libretto by E. T. A. Hoffmann and sets by the architect Karl Friedrich Schinkel, was the first time an elephant appeared on the stage of the opera house Unter den Linden.) The women accompanying Victory—who is portrayed as a woman seated upon a throne on the elephant's back—personify Fear, Hope, and Intelligence, the first two in chains at the side of the elephant, the last serving as the leader walking in front (5407–56). Even though we as readers of *Faust* can only imagine the effect this triumphant pageant was intended to achieve on stage, we cannot fail to see how theatricality and allegory here work together to enhance the specific significance of the Carnival Masque. For the Herald, this moment, like the climax of a fireworks display, provides the appropriate affirmation of his role as master of ceremonies. Yet much more follows, with surprise upon surprise, quickly bringing into question the degree of control and coherence involved.

The turning point of the Masque is signaled by the appearance of the twofold costume worn (apparently—there is no hint in the stage directions) by Mephisto, still in his role as court jester, now in the guise of an anti-masque representing the two debunkers of antiquity, Thersites and Zoilos, to undermine the illusion of the procession. Following the example of Odysseus, who in Book 2 of Homer's *Iliad* beats Thersites into a bloody mess, the Herald strikes the jester with his mace, whereupon—through what may be surmised as the devil's magic—the figure transforms into an egg, from which are hatched an adder and a bat. We are reminded of the transformation of the poodle into a hippopotamus, from which Mephisto first emerged, back in Faust's study after the Easter walk in Part One. The Herald senses that supernatural forces may be at work ("ghostly raiders," "spooks and spells," 5500 and 5502), over which he has no control. His response to the elaborate pageant that now appears indicates, in a way that signals also the central task imposed on the audience—and, indeed, on ourselves as readers—that he must interpret (*erklären*, 5507) that which he cannot comprehend (*begreifen*, 5508). We may surmise that Goethe here takes the allegory of the Carnival Masque into a dimension that transcends the occasion for the Emperor's court in order to thematize the problematic significance of the fiscal strategem imposed by Mephisto upon the court. This proves to be the case in ways that also call into question the control that Mephisto, and Faust as well, may be capable of imposing on the remainder of the scene. Goethe provides ironic signals concerning the challenge of interpretive response through several passages scattered throughout the sequence, in which members of the crowd on stage (participants in the Masque, who also serve as spectators) express their bewilderment in various configurations: "Muttering" (*Gemurmel*, 5484–93); "Female Gossip" (*Weibergeklatsch*, 5640–5); "Women en Masse" (*Weiber in Masse*, 5670–4); "Cries of the Crowd, alternating" (*Wechselgeschrei der Menge*, 5715–26); "Tumult and Shouts" (*Geschrei und Gedräng*, 5748–56); "Turmoil and Song" (*Getümmel und Gesang*, 5801–6).

The immediate challenge imposed by this new pageant—a float of dragons pulling an opulent carriage—is made by the Boy Charioteer (*Knabe Wagenlenker*), a congenial guide for the spectacle, who enters and leaves the drama in this episode with no rational explanation whatsoever. He emphasizes that all the figures are "allegories": "And as such you ought to know us" (5531 f.). He presents his master seated on the carriage, described by the Herald as he appears in a costume of turban and luxurious robe, and assigns him the name "Plutus, the god of opulence" (5569). Whether an audience in the theater would recognize Faust, who here makes his first appearance at the court, in this costume is difficult to say; but the reader of the drama could certainly not know him without a footnote of explanation, or at best only by retrospective surmise at the end of the scene. The Boy Charioteer also identifies himself as "profusion" and "poetry," one who fulfills himself only "by squandering his inmost wealth"

(*Bin die Verschwendung, bin die Poesie; / Bin der Poet, der sich vollendet, / Wenn er sein eigenst Gut verschwendet*, 5573–5). The third figure in the pageant, who perhaps enters the stage somewhat later, calls himself in his first speech *Avaritia* (in Latin; 5650) and, subsequently, "Greed" (5665). It is perhaps less difficult to recognize Mephisto in yet another of his many disguises. His actions also reveal him to us, if not to the assembled crowd.

What happens during this allegorical appearance? The Boy Charioteer, in addition to his dialogue with the Herald and with Plutus, constantly snaps his fingers, sending among the crowd what seem to be varied jewels that quickly are transformed into flickering flames or into insects, such as beetles and butterflies (see 5583–605). Even the Herald recognizes that this is a deception, though the crowd continues to grab for what they take to be valuable gems and gleaming gold. To what extent this kind of fraudulent and deceptive squandering may also be characteristic of poetry, as here embodied in the Boy Charioteer, is left to open speculation. Plutus, however, declares the Boy to be "spirit of my spirit" (5623) and even echoes the voice of the Lord in the Gospel account of Jesus' baptism (Matthew 3.17), when he declares, "My cherished son, I take delight in thee" (5629). In what way would Poetry be the legitimate son of Plutus, god of wealth? And is there any thematic validity to Faust's association— assuming we have recognized him in the latter disguise—with this enigmatic allegorical figure? No answers to these questions are provided, as the Boy Charioteer departs in response to instructions from Plutus that he retreat into solitude, where he may create his own world (5690–6), never to return again—at least not in the costume of Boy Charioteer. Goethe himself, in conversation with Eckermann (December 20, 1829; see below), identified this figure with Euphorion, the offspring of Faust and Helena who, of course, is born two acts later in the drama. We may take a clue from this remark concerning the relative ease with which the symbolic figures in *Faust*, Part Two, make their way from one guise to another.

Just prior to the departure of the Boy Charioteer, Plutus descends from his carriage and lifts onto the stage a huge chest, which appears upon his opening it to be full of treasure (5683–9 and 5709–14). The crowd rushes in to grab whatever comes to hand, despite the Herald's warning that this is all clearly a fraud. The result, predictably, is that the gold instantly turns to fire, threatening to burn those who grab for it. We may recognize once more the kind of magic used by the devil on many occasions in the drama, as in the wine trick in "Auerbach's Tavern," where the spilled wine turns into flames, and in the chest of jewels used to seduce Gretchen. The theme of a demonic false fire subsequently returns in the earthquake episode of the "Classical Walpurgis Night" and in the magic used to win the war in Act IV. The building of Faust's city in Act V also appears to require the use of Mephistophelian fire by night (see 11123–30). Yet the devil has one additional trick to play, borrowing perhaps from the theme of sexual orgy introduced in the "Walpurgis Night." The figure of "Greed" (as he is now called, 5767) gathers the false gold from the chest and molds it into a huge phallus, with which he threatens and frightens the women

in the crowd, who earlier had abused and insulted him in his guise as
"Starveling" (see 5670 ff.). It seems that the theme of wealth combined
with sexual bravado provides a key to the allegorical significance of the
entire pageant. What is not yet clear is whether Faust and Mephisto intend
this display to serve as a lesson to the Emperor, who is about to introduce
the scheme for fiscal reform through paper money and who is also about
to enter the stage disguised as the great god Pan with his wild entourage.
We may repeat the questions: who is in charge here? and what is the
point?

The final section of the Masque focuses on the Emperor, disguised as Pan,
later referred to by his attendant Nymphs as "the whole world" (*das All
der Welt*, 5874), which associates the name of the god with the adjective
pan in Greek, meaning "all." Presumably, those assembled on stage are
aware of this disguise, as Faust-Plutus indicates that he knows who is here
(5807–10), so we as audience or readers of *Faust* should also be aware of
the Emperor's presence—even though, curiously, he never speaks a line
during the entire sequence. The attendants of Pan, who enter in procession
one group after another, perform in accord with the convention of the
masquerade established at the outset of the scene. They identify themselves
through their speeches, describing their masks and costumes, their actions
and functions within the allegory of the "savage host" (5801) of both classical and Germanic folklore: Fauns, Satyrs, and Gnomes, followed by Giants (the bodyguards of the Emperor) and Nymphs (apparently a chorus
of women from the court). In the sequence of descriptive statements, an
apparent decorum of disorder is maintained, suggesting that—once again,
as at the outset of the Masque—all is proceeding according to plan. We
may also assume that this plan reflects the Emperor's own wishes in his
capacity as the patron of the festivities.

Of particular interest in this procession is the role of the Gnomes, diminutive figures from Germanic mythology (elves, hobglobins, and dwarfs),
whose traditional function is to mine the precious metals and stones out
of the depths of the Earth. In describing this function for themselves
(5848–63), they also assert their innocence of the consequences, wherein
gold causes scheming and criminal violence among humankind. The
danger of burning by fire from the false gold in Pluto's chest is thus
complemented by the consequences of the Gnomes' mining of real gold.
Yet the theme of mining connects with the plan for fiscal reform proposed
by Mephisto in his guise as jester to the Emperor, whereby the financial
crisis of the realm would be resolved by digging up the treasures of the
Earth. The presence of the Gnomes in the Masque, especially in the
speech of their Deputation directly to the Emperor (5898–913), in which
they celebrate the intended outcome of their mining activity as the placing
of the treasure they unearth in the hands of the Emperor for his good use
and safekeeping, thus symbolizes the expected consequences of this proposed reform. In truth, however, Mephisto never intends to dig up this
treasure but only to issue certificates of credit ("paper money") as legal
tender for what hypothetically might exist. The Emperor and his Court

are unaware of this fraud within the allegorical representations of the Carnival Masque.

Meanwhile, Mephisto, who is presumably still on stage in his guise as *Avaritia*, or the Starveling, or Greed, during the final section of the Masque, does not speak a word, nor does any stage direction indicate what his role may be during the action that follows, though we surmise that he is directly responsible for the magic tricks about to be performed. Faust in his guise as Plutus, however, clearly knows what is to come, as indicated in his two short speeches to the Herald in response to the appearance of Pan (5807–14 and 5914–19). He warns the Herald about the "gruesome riot" (5917) about to transpire and urges the Herald to mark it well and take it all down as protocol for future ages. This the Herald proceeds to do through his elaborate description of the ensuing catastrophe (5920–69). Goethe's source for the conflagration, as often noted by scholars, is the account he read as a child, in the *Historischer Chronica* by Johann Ludwig Gottfried (1642), of a festival in the court of Charles VI of France, where the king and a number of courtiers were dressed as wild men and satyrs. A torch set fire to the king's costume, and the fire then spread to the courtiers when they tried to extinguish the flames. As a result, four of the courtiers died of their burns and the king reverted to a former state of insanity.

As the Emperor in his costume as Pan approaches the chest of Plutus with its false treasure, the question inevitably arises as to the purpose and significance of what ensues. There can be no doubt that Mephisto and Faust are responsible for the fire, just as there appears to be no doubt that the fire itself is only a magic trick and thus an illusion, just as the water spray—a kind of demonic sprinkler system—that quenches the fire at the very end of the scene is also only a trick or an illusion. But do these intruders into the affairs of state intend to teach a lesson to the Emperor, which would in effect amount to an exposé of their own fraud in the proposed fiscal reform? It hardly seems likely that the devil would want to give the trick of his strategem away before the event, nor could any legitimate motive be attributed to Faust—who, after all, was not present in the Throne Room, where Mephisto as jester made his proposition—for here staging an allegorical warning to the Emperor about getting burned by the devil's gold. More likely and in keeping with the didactic-pedagogical satire of the Masque as a whole is that the lesson of this conflagration is directed toward ourselves as audience or readers of the drama. The final speech of Plutus (5970–86), in which Faust seems to remove his mask and speak *in propria persona* as he brings the entire Carnival to a close, seems to indicate the degree to which the central character of the drama, here functioning as master magician and master of ceremonies (having usurped the Herald's role), brings the allegorical show to its proper conclusion. In doing so he also speaks for the author of the entire spectacle, much in the manner that Prospero in Shakespeare's *Tempest*—a work that may well have influenced Goethe in conceiving his allegorical masque—acts in his capacity as magus on behalf of the playwright himself. The message of the spectacle is directed toward the audience of the drama, and the character who possibly stages the action and certainly interprets it serves as the vehicle for the author's own intention. At any rate, we may be certain (from the evidence of the scene immediately following) that the Emperor learns nothing from his near miss with death by "pyromantic sport" (*Flammengaukelspiel*, 5987). Mephisto, who has been craftily silent during the spectacle of flames and water spray, which he himself possibly has staged, offers no indication whatsoever concerning his motive here, though we may detect an apparent analogue between the catastrophe of the Carnival and the outcome of the fiscal reform about to be set in motion. Faust's role remains the most enigmatic of all. If indeed he serves as agent and spokesman for the playwright, then we are still left to wonder why he is doing so and how it should be interpreted within the larger context of *Faust*, Part Two. Perhaps the monologue by Faust in the scene "Charming Landscape" provides our best clue, namely that the entire allegorical spectacle of the Carnival Masque should be viewed as similar to the symbol of the rainbow: the colorful hue of refraction, through which alone we may have, or grasp, the meaning of human life.

"Pleasance" and Paper Money (lines 5988–6172)

This scene divides into two sections, both by its content and from the history of its composition. The opening speeches (through 6036) were written in immediate sequence with the Carnival Masque, probably in the last weeks of 1827 or early in 1828, and included with the text of Act I in its entirety up to this point (6036), which Goethe sent to his publisher in mid-February to be included with *Faust*, Part One, in vol. 12 of his *Collected Works* (*Ausgabe letzter Hand*). The remainder of the scene, which constitutes the so-called paper-money scheme, was written somewhat later, perhaps near the end of 1829, when the remaining parts of Act I were completed. The shift of focus from the Emperor's concern for entertainment to the news of the impact of the paper currency is thematic to the entire sequence in the Emperor's court. His preoccupation with amusement constitutes a drastic neglect of duty in the face of the financial crisis in his realm. He appoints Faust to be his chief entertainer, Master of the Revels, a kind of "Shehrazade" (6033), as if this were *The Thousand and One Nights* (from the collection of Arabian tales that had become popular in Western Europe during the eighteenth century). He wants to be entertained with daily magic shows. Of interest also is the vivid description the Emperor provides in his opening speech of his experience in the conflagration at the end of the Masque (5989–6002). The vision of an infernal realm of fire, where the Emperor imagines himself Pluto, the ruler of the dead (not Plutus, the god of wealth, played by Faust in the Masque), assumes mythical proportions, anticipating the theme of volcanic creation and destruction that will be more fully developed in the "Classical Walpurgis Night." The Emperor's final assertion that he seemed to be ruler over a thousand salamanders recalls the association of salamanders with fire in Faust's initial confrontation with Mephistopheles as infernal monster in the first study scene of Part One (1273, 1283 f.). Mephisto responds to the Emperor's evocation of the realm of fire by conjuring an equally powerful counterrealm of water (6006–27), where the movement of ocean also constitutes a mythical realm for the Emperor as a second Peleus (6026), united with Thetis—the mother of Achilles—according to the ancient legend. These images also anticipate the "Classical Walpurgis Night," where in the final scene at the edge of the Aegean Sea various "wonders of the sea" (*Meerwunder*; 6015, translated by Arndt as "portents of the ocean," and stage direction before 8044, where the Nereids and the Tritons are assigned the same label) appear as participants in the mythical celebration that culminates in the appearance of the nymph Galatea. The unusually vivid poetic language used in both these speeches—the Emperor's on the realm of fire and Mephisto's on the realm of water—may consciously imitate the fantastic fairy-tale idiom of *The Thousand and One Nights* (or *Arabian Nights*, mentioned in 6032). The juxtaposition of fire and water in these opening speeches thus establishes a thematic contrast that will assume far more cosmic implications in the mythological festival yet to come.

Mephistopheles turns the Emperor's neglect of his political responsibilities to his own purpose by manipulating the fiscal crisis in the realm through a devilish entertainment of his own devising. Indeed, the introduction of the new paper currency proves to have already occurred in the midst of the Carnival Masque, though no one, least of all the Emperor himself, was aware at the time what was happening. Goethe seems by this stratagem to invite a reconsideration of the thematic material pertaining to wealth, treasure, and exchange that permeates the entire Masque, particularly with regard to the meeting of Faust as Plutus and the Emperor as Pan. As Goethe indicated to Eckermann in discussing this scene (December 7, 1829; see below), Mephistopheles had arranged that in the midst of the Masque the Emperor sign a paper authorizing the bill to serve as money. (It may be that the Deputation of Gnomes, 5898–913, presented the Emperor as Pan with the document for his signature; otherwise, it must have occurred offstage.) Subsequently, it appears that Mephisto caused the paper to be copied and reproduced a thousandfold, then circulated throughout the realm as legal tender. The Emperor suspects fraud so long as he doubts the signature. The assurance of his Treasurer (6066–82) puts him at ease, however, so that the larger question of legitimacy for the paper money never arises. It is not only that the supposedly limitless buried treasure that is to cover the monetary value of the paper bills has not been (and will not be) secured, but also that by multiplying these bills Mephistopheles perpetrates a potentially unending extension of the supposed resources of the treasury. In effect, he thus becomes a counterfeiter, at the same time that he surreptitiously invents printing (assuming the historical setting of the Faust legend to stand in close proximity to Gutenberg). To what extent Goethe intends this entire experiment with paper money to reflect on fiscal strategies developed during the eighteenth century (beginning with the Scotsman John Law, who attempted a similar scheme in France in 1721 with disastrous results, and continuing above all with the inflation caused by the so-called *assignats* used in France following the

Revolution) is difficult to say. The ultimate consequence of this strategem will be, of course, rampant inflation that results in open rebellion and warfare in Act IV.

Particularly important for the drama is the characteristic quality of this Mephistophelian tactic. The written text of the bill with the Emperor's signature may be regarded as duplication in kind, if not in specific intent, of the written pact that Faust once signed in his blood with the same devil. More than this, the technique of reproduction suggests the same disrespect for the relation of word to sense, of text to substance, of medium to essence, that Mephistopheles displayed in his initial appearances in Part One. The lack of an authentic base in gold for the paper money is no different from the lack of an authentic sense for the words in which this devil deals. (Of interest as comic grace note is the fact that only the Fool, who returns at the end of the scene, after Mephisto has usurped his place at court, decides to convert the value of the paper notes he receives into land and property, that is, into real estate, which will of course retain its value after the inflationary collapse of the imperial economy [see 6155–60].) Nor would the final judgment against the Emperor be any less condemning than that against Faust, were it not for the ultimate ironic turn of the drama against Mephistopheles and damnation. In this, also, we may contrast the manner in which the Emperor manages the political affairs of his court with that of the Lord's rule over his cosmic realm in the "Prologue in Heaven." The transcendent source of salvation, like the transcendent source of love, ultimately legitimizes the fraudulent medium imposed by Mephistopheles upon his all-too-willing human agents. A thematic parallel is also implied between the paper money and the theatrical medium within which the spirit of Helena is subsequently embodied. The difference, of course, resides in the authenticity of Faust's spiritual journey to secure her and bring her back into the realm of his own experience. For that, as Mephistopheles himself acknowledges, the power of the Mothers offers special privilege.

"Dark Gallery" (lines 6173–306)

With casual abruptness, as a direct result of the Emperor's new office for Faust as Master of the Revels (see 6035–36), the theme of Helena from the traditional Faust legend is introduced as the subject of an occasional entertainment. Faust clearly regards the proposal at first as no more than this, as his initial speech to Mephistopheles makes clear. But the latter describes the task with unexpected seriousness, contrasting the world of Nordic witchcraft, familiar from the "Witch's Kitchen" and "Walpurgis Night" in Part One, with the more awesome realm of mythical archetypes within which the classical spirit of Helena resides. Faust initially associates this new mode of hocus-pocus with the rituals of the "Witch's Kitchen" (see 6229–30), forgetting that the vision of the Feminine had also appeared to him there in the magic mirror. Yet even the sound of the word *Mothers* indicates the emergence of something radically new for Goethe's drama. Faust's emotional response to the word supports this change, particularly as indicated by the use of stage directions for his state of mind at three separate moments in the scene ("starting," 6216; "with a shudder," 6265; "enraptured," 6281), a descriptive device that Goethe only rarely employs in this drama.

Critics and scholars have also been struck with a ponderous awe in response to the name *Mothers*, and this response has led to an enormous body of erudite speculation concerning both the doctrine implied by the name and its possible sources. What has often gone unnoticed is the characteristic ironic tone of the entire scene, an instance once again of Mephistopheles' role as manipulator and trickster. This tone seems particularly apparent in his instructions to Faust, not only concerning the need to strike the magical key against the tripod in the midst of the silent Mothers, who are strangely declared unable to see anything but spirits (see 6290–3), but also in Faust's heroic posing in rehearsal of his quest (stage direction after 6293). Freudian critics have, not surprisingly, made much of the implicit sexual imagery in the key and the tripod, raising the somewhat problematic question of psychological incest with regard to Faust's quest. The final couplet of the scene, furthermore, spoken *ad spectatores* by Mephistopheles after Faust has stamped his foot and disappeared, indicates that no very reliable clarification of mystical doctrine is likely to be forthcoming from this instructor.

In a conversation with Eckermann (January 10, 1830; see below), responding to an inquiry concerning the origin of the Mothers, Goethe referred to Plutarch as his source for the name but claimed the rest as free invention. He also quoted a line from the scene, "Why, it strikes a singular chord" (6217), suggesting that the playful air of mystery—at the ironic expense of Eckermann's serious concern—may have been precisely the effect he intended for the entire scene. The source in Plutarch has been identified as the *Life of Marcellus*, chapter 20, or (less likely) the treatise *On the Decline of Oracles*, chapter 22. The former concerns the cult of mother goddesses in Engyon, of ancient Cretan origin, discussed in relation to a certain Nikias, a refugee of the Carthaginian dominance at Engyon and a friend of the Romans in the time of Marcellus (late third century B.C.). Plutarch emphasizes the service of Marcellus as civilizer of Rome, one of the first to bring Greek art and learning to the Italian city (as Faust subsequently brings the forms of Helena and Paris to the Emperor's court). These mother goddesses were identical (according to the world history of Diodorus Siculus, also known to Goethe) with the Corybantes of Crete, associated with the Great Mother, Rhea, or Cybele, or Demeter. There is a significant mythological connection here with materials used by Goethe in the concluding festival of the "Classical Walpurgis Night," in particular the rites of the Cabiri (see footnote to 8074), as also with the myth of the rape of Demeter's daughter Persephone by Hades and her subsequent role as queen of the underworld. It had initially been Goethe's intention that Faust participate in the "Classical Walpurgis Night" in order to visit the underworld and plead through Manto with Persephone for the release of Helena. All this material suggests, as any perceptive reader of *Faust* will note, that the initial descent to the Mothers, despite its appropriately ironic and mystifying quality, prefigures the more authentic search for Helena that occurs subsequently in the "Classical Walpurgis Night." Apart from this, all else in "Dark Gallery" should be interpreted within the dramatic context of Faust's relation to the Emperor. Goethe may also have intended a pun on the name *Mothers*, which in German (*die Mütter*) sounds virtually identical to the word for "myth" (*die Mythe*).

In addition, Goethe makes playful use throughout this scene of terms appropriate to initiation into a mystery rite. Mephistopheles speaks of steeper steps into a more "deeply alien" realm (6194–5), which evokes the procession into a sacred precinct or into the temple of the mysteries. His initial speech on the Mothers indicates what he calls a reluctance to reveal, or "touch on" (*entdecken*), a more exalted mystery or secret (*Geheimnis*, 6212). Above all, the phrases describing the path into the Mothers' realm, despite the willful obscurity of abstractions, suggest the vocabulary of mystery: "Into the unacceded, / The inaccessible; toward the never-pleaded, / The never-pleadable" (6222 ff.). Also, the emphasis on "wastes . . . solitude," "wilderness and dereliction" (6227, 6236) contributes to this sense of participation in a separate and alien realm of experience. Faust acknowledges these implications when he addresses Mephistopheles, not without irony, as "mystagogue in chief," associating his own role with that of a "neophyte" (6249–50). Such implications are further strengthened by the use of symbolic objects traditionally associated with such mystery rites: the key (6259), which will unlock the secret, and the tripod (6283 ff.), glowing with a substance associated with fire and aromatic fragrance. All this evidence has invited scholarly speculation, especially with reference to Jungian archetypes, concerning the precise nature of this mystery rite. A reader of *Faust* should bear in mind, however, that such evidence in this scene is limited to what is reported by Mephistopheles, who is a highly questionable source of information and whose role as mystagogue is equally dubious. Similarly, Faust as neophyte, who at this point has no awareness at all of what to expect, can hardly be looked to for guidance. Nor does the setting of the scene within the Gothic halls of the Emperor's palace provide anything but an ironic opposition to the ancient and mysterious mystery referred to as the Mothers. Only further developments within the drama can provide valid clarification of what this mystery portends. One should also bear in mind that the entire Helena act had already been completed and published when this scene was written, as had the detailed outline of the "Classical Walpurgis Night" contained in the "Second Sketch for the Announcement of the *Helena*" (see below).

"Hall of Chivalry," with The Rape of Helena (lines 6377–565)

This scene, which unexpectedly concludes Faust's stay at the court of the Emperor and also completes the first stage in his developing search for Helena, constitutes a superb climax to the theme of the theater in *Faust*. That is, it demonstrates in eminently theatrical terms how the performance in the theater relates, on the one hand, to visionary experience, both in dreams and in myth, and, on the other, with consummate irony, to the complex, essentially conflicted relation between art and society. Composed quite late in the process of writing Part Two, probably near the end of 1829 (see the conversation with Eckermann on December 30, below), the scene presupposes the Helena act (actually completed three years earlier) and thus consciously prefigures much that is achieved there. It also anticipates the great poetic challenge still to be faced by the poet during the first half of 1830, the "Classical Walpurgis Night," and provides the only valid mode of transition into that fantastic mythical realm for Faust, namely the medium of dream vision, which begins in immediate response to this spirit show at the Emperor's court, proceeds during his state of unconsciousness at Wagner's laboratory—where he dreams of the encounter between Leda and the swan, as described by Homunculus (6903–20) —and achieves fulfillment in the immediate vision of Leda at the banks of the Peneios, after Faust arrives in Greece and recovers consciousness (7271–94). The sense of theater established in "Hall of Chivalry," furthermore, relates directly to earlier instances of this mode of representation in *Faust*, above all to the sense of cosmic theater, or *theatrum mundi*, in "Prelude in the Theater" and, even more, in "Prologue in Heaven," as also to the more satirical sense of spirit show with all its negative implications in the "Walpurgis Night's Dream," and in the more sublime musical performance of Ariel and the elfin chorus in "Charming Landscape," where theatrical show is transformed into natural event. Closer at hand, finally, and thematically sequential to the social satire of the spirit show in "Hall of Chivalry," as measured by the responses of the members of the court in the audience, is the Carnival Masque, which first introduced Faust to the Emperor and secured his appointment as master of court entertainments. All these various connections and interrelations concerning the importance of theatrical performance come together in this scene, as Goethe intended they should, to establish the legitimate centrality of the spirit show of Paris and Helena for *Faust* as a whole.

Also important for understanding Goethe's theatrical technique in this scene is the crucial use he made of Shakespearean models, which has not hitherto been acknowledged by commentators. On the one hand, with regard to the ironic, ultimately disruptive impact of the theater on society, *The Mousetrap* in *Hamlet*, the play within the play staged by the players in accord with Hamlet's instructions before King Claudius and the court at Elsinore (3.2), provided the closest analogue to the effect Goethe wished to achieve in this scene. Other possible examples for such a play within a play could easily be found, both from the Baroque theater generally, with its fascination for illusion and spectacular effects, and from Romantic comedy in particular, such as the comedies by Ludwig Tieck written in the late 1790s. Nowhere, however, is the manipulation of audience response in direct relation to a dumb show so crucial to the central meaning of a theatrical performance as in *Hamlet*. The impact of the spirit show in *Faust* resembles that of *The Mousetrap* in *Hamlet*, yet with a crucial ironic difference. In *Hamlet*, in addition to the various sardonic responses elicited

by the show from members of the audience, Hamlet included, the entire
performance is directed toward Claudius as a trap with which to expose
his guilty conscience for the murder of Hamlet's father. The play functions
as a strategy of exposure: "The play's the thing [says Hamlet] / Wherein
I'll catch the conscience of the King" (2.2.581–2). In *Faust*, the impact
of the performance turns against its instigator, and Faust himself falls victim to the power of theatrical illusion. This shift of effect is central to
Goethe's drama, especially as the theme of vision pertains to the developing quest for ideal beauty embodied in the Feminine. Faust's surrender
to theatrical illusion, which also recalls Don Quixote's famous encounter
with Master Peter the puppet player in Cervantes's novel (Part 2, chapter
26), is in itself a profoundly Faustian gesture, recalling explicitly his response to the vision of the Feminine in the magic mirror of "Witch's
Kitchen" in Part One (2429 ff.), a vision that sent him into raptures of
erotic desire.

Another source in Shakespeare, however, deserves mention. In *The Tempest*, Prospero provides a theatrical entertainment for his daughter, Mir-
anda, and her lover, Prince Ferdinand, to celebrate and solemnize their
betrothal through the offices of spirits, the goddesses Iris, Juno, and Ceres,
who appear as players in the entertainment, serenading the lovers with
music. Especially considering Prospero's use of magic, which alone makes
his pageant possible, the parallel to Faust's presentation of Helena and
Paris is striking; but Goethe goes even further in adapting his source to
the purpose of *Faust*. Toward the end of the spirit masque in *The Tempest*,
Prospero suddenly remembers that intruders are approaching his cave,
breaks the theatrical illusion of his own show, and disperses the spirits with
a single quick command. The consternation of the lovers at the sudden
conclusion of the pageant results in his famous speech about the world as
theater, *theatrum mundi*: "Our revels now are ended. These our actors /
As I foretold you, were all spirits, and / Are melted into air, into thin air"
(4.1.148 ff.). Goethe imposes precisely the same sense of insubstantiality
upon Faust's spirit show but also, as in his use of *Hamlet*, turns his Shakespearean source ironically against his hero. Faust, in contrast to Prospero,
loses his sense of reflective distance on the spectacle he has created and
abandons his self-control in response to the illusion by committing an act
of violence, as he tries to seize the spirit of Helena away from the spirit
of Paris. Mephistopheles intrudes with a reminder, which is worthy of such
a demonic Prospero: "It's your own work, this ghostly mask, you dunce!"
(6546; in German, *das Fratzengeisterspiel!*). The effect, however, is a violent explosion, which causes the spirits of the dumb show to dissolve into
air—precisely as it happens in *The Tempest*—but leaves Faust unconscious;
indeed, his conscious mind has fallen completely, as we subsequently
learn, under the visionary spell of the dream that constituted the spirit
show in the first place. Only by pursuing this vision beyond the realm of
social reality into the mythical domain of the "Classical Walpurgis Night,"
leading finally to his confrontation with Persephone in the underworld,
can Faust recover himself again and incidentally achieve a meeting with
Helena on equal (theatrical) ground. The events of Acts II and III thus

proceed directly as consequence to Faust's loss of imaginative control in the final scene of Act I.

What is the content of the spirit show itself? The Astrologer, who seems to function as vehicle for the sardonic opinions of Mephistopheles, calls it *The Rape of Helena* (6548). Yet from all descriptions of what happens, it hardly seems appropriate to describe this action as rape (the German term *Raub* may mean more precisely "theft" or "robbery"). Indeed, Paris, who enters first, is said to fall asleep (6471), after which Helena approaches and awakens him with a kiss (6511–2)—like an ironic reversal of the kiss in the fairy tale "Sleeping Beauty"—and she then erotically entices the youth to follow her. He appears amazed at the sight of her, approaches and embraces her, and prepares to carry her off with him. At this point, Faust intrudes and disrupts the show. The scene clearly depicts a version of the familiar myth of Paris, who as a shepherd on Mount Ida was approached by the goddesses Hera, Athena, and Aphrodite and asked to give the golden apple of Eris to the most beautiful of them. Aphrodite promised Paris the most beautiful of mortal women, Helena, and for that received the apple. According to a more realistic version of the myth—as contained, for instance, in the Homeric epics and Greek tragedy—Paris, as a guest, subsequently visited the court of Menelaus in Sparta, where he seduced Helena and persuaded her to leave with him for Troy, thus causing the Trojan War. In Goethe's version, more fairy-tale-like, as befits a dream vision, Helena apparently appears to the sleeping youth from nowhere, indeed, as if in a dream, which Faust himself, with the dubious dispensation of the Mothers, has himself conjured; representing the ideal of beauty, she purposefully arouses Paris's erotic desire. In this, the power of Aphrodite herself is manifested, as also will be the case in the Triumph of Galatea at the end of the "Classical Walpurgis Night." No wonder that Faust reacts as he does and intervenes, forgetting—despite Mephistopheles' reminder—that the entire spirit show is the projection of his own mind, a dream image he himself is dreaming. Such implications indicate how the spirit show prefigures the actual encounter between Faust and Helena that is to take place in Act III.

Readers should also attend to the complex orchestration of responses by members of the court in this scene and in the short scene immediately preceding. "Brightly Lit Ballrooms"—to contrast in setting presumably with "Dark Gallery," in which Mephisto introduces Faust to the Mothers—takes place in rooms of the palace that lead to the Hall of Chivalry, where Faust's theatrical show is about to begin. The several members of the court who approach Mephisto for advice are all concerned with appearances and the cosmetics of love. These encounters constitute an ironic repetition, perhaps, of the scene back in Faust's study in which the Student approaches Mephisto (dressed in Faust's academic robes) for advice. This thematic focus anticipates the motives of response by the courtiers in the audience to the figures of Paris and Helena in the spirit show. All the courtiers are concerned with appearance as the basis for erotic attraction, offering a diverse range of opinions in response to what they see. No fewer than six women of the court express their views, followed by several male respondents and concluding with a Young Lady, an Older Lady, and an Oldest Lady (6453–78), all of whom comment, however superficially, on the sexual attraction of the youthful Paris. Helena elicits comments from an equal range of observers with a corresponding diversity of judgment, beginning with Mephisto, the Astrologer, and Faust (6479–501). Faust's speech in particular provides an enthusiastic tribute to the beauty of Helena and thus directly recalls—as it also alludes to—his speech in response to the vision of the Feminine in the magic mirror of "Witch's Kitchen" (2429–40). He asserts that the figure of Helena surpasses by far the image he had viewed then, perhaps suggesting that Helena's beauty far exceeds that of Gretchen, if only in terms of external attraction. But the nature of Faust's response—which Mephisto immediately recognizes as excessive and inappropriate (6501)—leaves no doubt that his motivation is erotic desire: "To thee I vow the stirring of all force, / All passion's sum and source, / Desire, love, worship, adoration, frenzy!" (6498 ff.). Such emotional extremes may well be characteristic of Faust's temperament in response to the Feminine. The larger spectrum of satirical responses by the audience of courtiers thematizes the significance of theater and performance. This sequence of responses continues up to the moment when Faust intrudes into and destroys the show. We ourselves, of course, were we attending a performance of *Faust*, would also participate in such a spectrum of response, within which Faust's extreme finds its appropriate place—however misguided and destructive—as the measure of feminine beauty in its capacity to elicit erotic desire.

"Narrow, High-Vaulted Gothic Chamber" (lines 6566–818)

The opening scene of Act II, which returns us to the location of Faust's academic career (familiar from the outset of Part One), provides a valuable sense of repetition and contrast, especially after the elaborate spectacles staged in the court of the Emperor in Act I. Completed early in December, 1829 (see the conversation with Eckermann on December 6, below), this scene thus serves an important thematic and structural function, which has not always been recognized. In a sense, Goethe here also recapitulates exactly the situation of "Charming Landscape" at the outset of Part Two, where Faust was sleeping in an Alpine field after his catastrophic encounter with Gretchen, just as later in Act IV a similar situation will recur (though Faust is there conscious) in the rocky peaks of the higher Alps after the encounter with Helena in Act III. The Gothic study of Faust the scholar conveys the sense of crisis and failure for academic learning from which Faust earlier escaped with Mephistopheles. For the poet of *Faust*, this return marked more than just closure for the structure of the drama, because it was over half a century earlier that he had written the opening monologue in "Night" and over twenty years earlier that he had published Part One. This sense of distance in time and experience is more important than any change within the character of Faust—assuming that any change has occurred!—since Faust himself is unconscious and unaware that Mephisto has brought him back. We have no precise idea how much time has elapsed within the drama; but Goethe himself had in the interim developed from a youthful radical, experimenting with the legend of Faust, into the leading literary figure of Europe, the elderly sage of Weimar. During this time, furthermore, Europe itself, which serves as the cultural and social basis for Faust's existential dilemma as man of learning, had been radically transformed by the French Revolution and the Napoleonic era into what might best be described as the new bourgeois world of the nineteenth century, an era of technological industrialization and conservative retrenchment. These historical changes are reflected in Acts IV and V of Part Two; in the meantime, Faust must follow an entirely different trajectory in his quest to achieve a union with Helena, a quest that, following the catastrophe of Act I, proceeds from the study, where Famulus Wagner is now the professor in charge, back to the mythical realm of antiquity, the world in which Helena herself originated. The action of the drama thus proceeds from this point to the conclusion of Act III as a continuous, if increasingly fantastic, mythical journey.

The representatives of academic learning in the earlier scenes in Faust's study, in addition to Faust himself, were Famulus Wagner and the Student. In Goethe's ironic return to the study, these same figures reappear. In place of Wagner, who has now assumed Faust's professorship, the new Famulus, named Nicodemus, appears, followed shortly by the same Student, who has now completed his studies and is called Baccalaureus. Here also Mephistopheles, as before, takes the place of Faust in his study, again donning his academic robes (6586–91), which in the interim have gathered much dust and house a colony of insects. Mephistopheles pulls a bell rope that causes a great clangor and opens all doors, signaling an epochal moment of great significance, in response to which both Nicodemus and the Baccalaureus enter sequentially (stage direction after 6619; see also 6667, 6727, and 6819–20). Both figures assume that nothing has changed in the study, despite changes in the world. The Famulus stands for the status quo of learning, a symbol of trivial pedantry, whose primary function is to preserve all Faust's scholarly materials as he left them; the Baccalaureus storms in with a blatant and boundless arrogance, measuring his own sense of growth against what seems to him a static world of dead learning. Goethe scholars generally recognize that the figure of the Baccalaureus parodies the attitude of radical student groups that developed at German universities after the Napoleonic wars (see conversation with Eckermann, December 6, 1829, below). The politics of the so-called *Burschenschaften* reflected a boundless self-confidence that quickly came into direct conflict with the conservative and even reactionary powers of the state. In the arrogance and aggressiveness of his speeches to Mephisto, the Baccalaureus demonstrates also an intensification of Faust's original rejection of all academic learning and authority. His assertion that all who have passed their thirtieth year are useless and might as well be put to death (6787–9) elicits an ironic aside from the devil, to whom this bluster seems all too familiar. In also asserting that the world did not exist until he created it (6794–806), the Baccalaureus unintentionally parodies the biblical myth of creation as well as a kind of blind, absolutist idealism. Elsewhere in his laboratory, as demonstrated in the following scene, Professor Wagner pursues his esoteric scientific experiment with characteristic pedantry, totally lacking Faustian qualities—as we would expect—and thus equally unresponsive to the conditions for Faust's return to consciousness. What makes the irony of this scene dramatically effective, especially through the agency of Mephistopheles in dealing with these figures—none of whom has any idea who he is—is the fact that Faust is present, though unconscious, concealed behind a curtain (which Mephistopheles conveniently raises as he enters, in order to make the audience aware of Faust's presence). We thus share with the devil a broader knowledge of what is happening and what is at issue than any of the characters, so that the perspective of the scene is turned against the assumptions of all those who inhabit this academic world. In writing this scene, particularly in contrast to what is shortly to take place in the "Classical Walpurgis Night," Goethe reaffirms his radical critique of academic learning in the context of the Faust legend, though here with a sophisticated and pertinent sense of the ways in which the modern university had developed during the great gap of time since he first began work on the drama. In 1770, the model university for Goethe would have been either Leipzig or Strassburg, where he had recently been a student; in 1829, the model had shifted to the University of Berlin, founded in 1810 by Wilhelm von Humboldt, which by this time had become the center of Hegel's philosophical school and where modern experimental science was quickly assuming a central place. More is thus at stake in the irony of Mephisto's return to Faust's study and his confrontation with the great experiment by Wagner than mere comic relief.

Epochal significance may be ascribed to Mephistopheles' ringing the bell, which shakes the entire structure of the Gothic hall with its sound and causes all the doors to fly open, doors hitherto locked and sealed shut, as if to symbolize the imprisonment of dead knowledge from which Faust first suffered. All three figures encountered in this and the following scene recognize the importance of this sound. Wagner associates the sense of epoch with the critical moment of his chemical experiment, in which—like a modern alchemist, closely resembling Dr. Frankenstein in Mary Shelley's novel, published less than a decade earlier—he seeks to synthesize a human being. The emergence of Homunculus in the next scene, which succeeds (we surmise) only because of the infernal assistance provided at the last moment by Mephistopheles, is merely the external sign of what this epoch signifies for the drama. The true liberation of the Faustian mind from imprisonment in itself is about to occur through a radical physical and spatial displacement into the festival of the "Classical Walpurgis Night," leading to the "Phantasmagoria" of the Helena act, in which Faust and the ideal of classical beauty are married and produce their offspring, Euphorion, the self-consuming spirit of poetry. Liberation of the reflective self through erotic longing for the Feminine, aided by Mephistopheles: this is the central theme of the Gretchen tragedy, as it is also prefigured in Faust's rejuvenation in the "Witch's Kitchen," when he views the Feminine in the magical mirror. Mephisto's ringing the bell is thus a signal of liberation, not only for the spirit of Homunculus in Wag-

ner's experiment but also for the unconscious Faust in his dream quest
for Helena. Mephisto's being aware of the developments that will ensue
seems unlikely. Goethe's drama thus establishes a realm of symbolic action
where all sense of motive and causality is unclear. Scholars have attempted
to explain what happens in this sequence of events with reference to various concerns and contexts in the life and thought of the author. Far more
important for the study of *Faust* is to consider carefully what happens in
all the diversity of its symbolic detail.

"Laboratory" and Homunculus (lives 6819–7004)

All the paraphernalia of the alchemist's laboratory, otherwise associated in
the popular legend with Faust himself, is here gathered visibly into a climactic parody of scientific experiment, for which Wagner, the pedant
turned professor, serves as the appropriate practitioner. The conventional
concerns of alchemy for such things as the philosopher's stone and the
creation of gold out of base metals are here united in the idea of Homunculus, the "little chemical man" in the test tube (as Goethe first referred
to him in the "Second Sketch for the Announcement of the *Helena*"; see
below). The setting of the scene recalls earlier descriptions by Faust of the
apparatus for his alchemical and medical experiments (see 668 ff., 1034–
49), which yielded, characteristically, either poison (686 ff.) or death
(1050–55). Thematic associations with the "Witch's Kitchen" are also apparent, especially due to the entrance of Mephistopheles, who serves as
an infernal catalyst for Wagner's experiment (as Goethe indicated to Eckermann on December 16, 1829; see below). Nor does Goethe abandon
the central thematic contrast between medieval and classical modes, related both to the contrast between Mephistopheles and Homunculus
(6923 ff.) and to the opposition of settings in the drama: the dark and
oppressive enclosure of the Gothic study and laboratory versus the open,
mythical realm of the "Classical Walpurgis Night" (in particular the festival at the Aegean Sea), to which Homunculus will shortly lead Mephistopheles and Faust. It is the same opposition established in the "Witch's
Kitchen" when Faust observes the Feminine in the mirror, a vision of
classical beauty, in total contrast to the medieval hocus-pocus of that scene.

Much discussion has been devoted to the figure of Homunculus, especially
with regard to possible sources. Generally, scholars now recognize that
Goethe was here developing the symbolic implications of his drama—in
a manner resembling the originality of the Earth Spirit in the *Urfaust*—
for which no specific source provides adequate anticipation. In addition,
no trace of this figure occurs in the outline of Part Two that Goethe
dictated in 1816 (see below), and the discussion of Wagner's creation in
the "Second Sketch for the Announcement of the *Helena*" of 1826 (see
below) does not use the traditional Latin term *homunculus* (literally, "little
man"). A large body of obscure material has been gathered in relation to
the idea of such an alchemical creation of life, of which the treatise by
Paracelsus (1493–1541) *On the Generation of Natural Things* is representative. It was thought that the proper blending in a glass container of male

sperm and organic material in an extreme state of putrefaction could, under the right conditions of time and warmth, create a living being. Such a source—and similar cabalistic works, such as the chapter on homunculi in Praetorius's *Anthropodemus Plutonicus* (1666)—may have been consulted by Goethe, in 1768, for instance, when he was studying the occult, or in 1798–99, when he was working on the "Walpurgis Night" for Part One. Also of interest as a possible source, particularly important for the role of Homunculus in the "Classical Walpurgis Night," are the scientific theories on the origin of life by contemporaries of Goethe, such as Lorenz Oken, who were associated with what became known as the philosophy of nature (*Naturphilosophie*), concerning the sea as the primal uterus in which the original seed of humankind came into being. Two aspects of the Homunculus episode are, however, unique to Goethe, as they are also central to *Faust*, in relation also to the predominant characteristics of the protagonist. First, Homunculus as created through alchemical experiment in a test tube is totally without material substance, that is, he is pure spirit, a state that explains his superior intellect and independent mind, even in comparison to Mephistopheles. As Goethe comments in the "Second Sketch" of 1826, Wagner's little chemical man contains within himself a universal historical world calendar, which provides him with knowledge of the "Classical Walpurgis Night," something even Mephistopheles has never heard of. Second, according to a natural impulse that is eminently Faustian, the disembodied spirit of Homunculus strives from the moment of its creation and appearance on the scene to achieve substantiality, to become material, that is, to find a body and become alive within the world of nature. In this regard, Homunculus's quest for physical existence is analogous to Faust's search for Helena, as the multiple structure of the "Classical Walpurgis Night" makes apparent.

The scene "Laboratory" also reiterates the central importance of the *moment* as thematic concern for Goethe's drama, in ways that recall the terms of the original wager between Faust and Mephistopheles. Wagner responds to Mephisto as he enters by welcoming him to "the hour's good star" (*Stern der Stunde*, 6832), indicating that the moment of fulfillment is at hand—signaled also by the ringing of the bell (6819–20), for which, as we know, Mephisto is responsible. The successful completion of this alchemical experiment occurs as an event within a single moment's time: "It swells, it gleams, piles up and on, / In just a moment [*Augenblick*] it is done" (6865–6). Similarly, Homunculus immediately recognizes Mephisto to be his "cousin," addressing him as "rogue" (*Schalk*—the same title assigned him by the Lord in "Prologue in Heaven," 339), and acknowledges that he is here "at the right moment" (*Im rechten Augenblick*, 6886; translated by Arndt as "right on cue"). We may surmise that this sense of the moment applies also to the precarious state of visionary unconsciousness in Faust, who lies dreaming of the mythological moment when Zeus, disguised as a swan, ravished Leda, who thus conceived Helena. Homunculus as pure spirit appears to be a kind of psychoanalyst, who, when invited by Mephisto to observe the unconscious Faust, is able immediately to penetrate his vision and interpret his dream. His description of Faust's vision (6903–20) constitutes a vivid retelling of this myth of origin, anticipating the festival of the Classical Walpurgis Night that takes place in the following scene. Goethe here translates into poetic narrative the image of this mythological event, which presumably derived from the famous painting by Correggio (c. 1530), purchased by Frederick the Great in 1770 and included in the paintings from the royal collection of Prussia exhibited in Schinkel's new museum of art in Berlin (opened 1830).

The point to emphasize here is that historical and experiential time are about to be collapsed into the continuum of myth, contained within what in effect constitutes only a single unit of time, an *Augenblick* in reality. As Faust is suspended in his dream, his psychological state—which Homunculus acknowledges might prove precarious, even dangerous, should he awaken here in the study (6930 f.)—transcends all temporal process and takes place in what can be described only as a sustained moment of vision. That moment coincides "just now," as Homunculus also points out (6940–3), with the celebration of the festival on the plain of the river Peneios in Greece on the anniversary of the battle of Pharsalus, fought in that place between Caesar and Pompey on August 9, 48 B.C. We can understand, perhaps, why Faust dreams of Leda and the swan following the explosion that caused him to lose consciousness, after he intruded on the spirit show of Paris and Helena. That this dream symbolizes a psychic vision coincident with the moment of fulfillment for Wagner's alchemical experiment in creation, however, appears purely arbitrary; yet for Goethe's drama such coincidence thematizes the transformation of time into the mythical and atemporal medium of the festival. The festival suspends historical time through its act of commemoration, a form of mythical repetition, itself completely out of time and contained within this complex moment of fulfillment. It is the moment in which Faust will confront his dream of Helena's conception as an actual event before his eyes (see 7249–312), and in which, through the agency of Manto as the fixed center of the festival, about whom time revolves (7481), Faust will descend into the underworld to appeal for the release of Helena from Persephone, queen of the dead. The juxtaposition of these several moments of fulfillment in the scene "Laboratory" through the creation of Homunculus thus prepares for the most radical transformation of the temporal medium in all of Goethe's *Faust*. No hint is yet offered that such fulfillment might be related to the terms of Faust's original wager with Mephisto concerning the "beautiful moment" that he might wish could be sustained: *Verweile doch! du bist so schön!* (1700). This thematic connection, however, may provide the key to interpreting the mythical action about to take place, which is the most complex and difficult sequence of events in the entire drama, a challenge to readers of *Faust* that we are still struggling to understand.

"Classical Walpurgis Night" (lines 7005–8487)

Nothing in Goethe's *Faust*—indeed, few texts in world literature—can match the "Classical Walpurgis Night" in complexity, obscurity, and overwhelming imaginative power. Above all, the tendency toward a symbolic form of action that leaves every convention of mimetic drama behind, including coherence of plot and character, here reaches a level of mythical vision that transcends every assumption a reader might make about Faust and the quest he undertakes in the company of Mephistopheles. Even the obsessive search for Helen of Troy through all the reaches of myth and legend extending back to the origins of Hellenic culture seems at best a partial motive for much that occurs in this sequence of scenes. Goethe indicated in conversations with Eckermann and in letters to Wilhelm von Humboldt at the time when he was writing this portion of the drama— during the first half of 1830, when most of Part Two had already been completed—that the process of composition, usually during the early morning hours before dawn, astonished even him, to the point where he feared that rational critics might judge him to have gone mad. In fact, after posthumous publication of Part Two in 1832, many of the leading scholars, such as Friedrich Theodor Vischer, argued that Goethe had become senile and lost his poetic powers, that these symbolic-mythological sections of the drama constituted a reduction of meaning and a loss of control.

Several documents make clear that Goethe came to the idea for the "Classical Walpurgis Night" very late. In his prose outline of Part Two, dictated for his autobiography in 1816 (see below), not a trace of this episode occurs. The transition to the Helena episode from the court of the Emperor takes place without any digressions into the realm of myth. A full decade later, when Goethe drafted his announcement for the *Helena* (see below), just after completing the third act of Part Two—the earliest to be completed and published—he provided a fascinating survey of the "Classical Walpurgis Night," perhaps because he was uncertain whether he would live to complete his drama. Readers who wish to understand the sequence Goethe finally composed should observe the many differences between it and the announcement for the *Helena* (which Goethe himself never published). The announcement does not mention, for instance, the festival at the Aegean Sea, which concludes the finished sequence. This portion of the "Classical Walpurgis Night" was thus conceived only after the sketch was written, perhaps when the scene itself was composed, in 1830. Much more emphasis is placed on Faust's quest for Helena in the sketch than in the final text, especially with regard to his descent into the underworld with Manto in order to plead for Helena's release before Persephone, queen of the dead. Goethe's decision not to include this scene in the final drama must also have occurred very late, perhaps only when it was displaced by the festival of Galatea. The role of Homunculus is correspondingly reduced in the sketch, and even Mephisto's adventures appear to be keyed much more closely to Faust in that stage of the poet's thinking. A number of factual details, such as the geographical layout of the plain of Pharsalus and the land of Thessaly, also the juxtaposition of the battle of Pharsalus with the festival of the "Classical Walpurgis Night," seem clearer in their rationale for the drama as described in the prose sketch. Above all, the contrast between prose description, which inevitably includes a degree of interpretive comment by the poet, and the poetic-spectacular events themselves as contained in the final drama, much of which takes place without any explanation whatsoever, indicates the extent to which Goethe's mythical vision left all rational discourse far behind. The sketch for the announcement of the *Helena* was published for the first time in 1888, among the Paralipomena for *Faust* in the Weimar edition (I, 15, 2, 198–212); no wonder that readers had been mystified by the "Classical Walpurgis Night," as indeed they continue to be.

Many disparate, often quite obscure sources in various mythological and poetic works from antiquity and about antiquity provided Goethe with the materials he wove together into the complex fabric of his scene. Yet in a fundamental sense the entire sequence is the imaginative creation of the poet, conceived as an analogue to the medieval-Germanic witches' Sabbath of the "Walpurgis Night" in Part One. Readers should consider the degree to which the structure of the earlier scene, however incoherent and fragmentary, served as the basis for the action in this later scene. Just as the earlier scene involved a procession of witches and warlocks ascending the Brocken in the Harz Mountains to encounter Satan on the summit, so also in the "Classical Walpurgis Night" the spirit figures of ancient myth are assembled to celebrate a corresponding festival. In this case, there is no ascent into the presence of a single demonic power, but rather a fundamental opposition between two primal symbolic yet natural events: the seismic eruption of the newly formed mountain from below the earth, leading to violent conflict and fiery destruction; and the procession upon the surface of the sea of fantastic creatures, who celebrate the triumph of the nymph Galatea as substitute for the goddess Aphrodite, thematizing the procreative power of Eros. On both of these mythical nights, Faust enters initially into the activity, only to pursue his own related though separate path. In each instance, that path also pertains directly to his conflicted relation to the two opposing manifestations of the Feminine, involving on the one hand his confrontation with the spectral vision of the naked Gretchen with her throat slit—the call of his conscience for his having caused her destruction—and on the other his descent into the underworld as a kind of latter-day Orpheus, pleading with Persephone for the release of Helena. In the Nordic "Walpurgis Night," the climax of the festival on the Brocken is elided and the banalities of the amateur theatricals that make up the "Intermezzo" and "Walpurgis Night's Dream" are substituted. In the "Classical Walpurgis Night," however, the climax of the festival at the shores of the Aegean is dramatized, as Faust's descent into the underworld is displaced by the encounter of Homunculus with Galatea and the fulfillment of his quest to achieve existence. These and similar correlations by contrast and comparison between the two "Walpurgis Nights," extending often to the details of both scenes, deserve careful exploration. This sense of relationship constitutes the most extreme example of what Goethe called "reflection by repetition" (*wiederholte Spiegelung*).

The events that take place in the "Classical Walpurgis Night" are for the most part representations of processes in nature that have been translated into symbolic and mythological forms. These forms are derived from various literary sources, selected by Goethe in what seems almost an arbitrary manner based on convenience. Scholars have managed to track down most of these sources, which will seem highly arcane and esoteric to the average reader of the drama. Many of the most unfamiliar figures from mythology derive from a compendium of ancient myths published by Benjamin erich, *Gründliches mythologisches Lexikon* (edition of 1770), which Goethe owned. One of the primary literary sources is the Latin epic by Lucan, *The Pharsalia*, which presents in detail the battle of Pharsalus between Caesar and Pompey and also includes the witch Erichtho, who is consulted before the battle to foretell its outcome. Goethe borrowed this figure to introduce his scene. In addition to describing the campfires at night before the battle, she establishes the appropriate verbal form for ancient tragedy, speaking for the first time in the drama in iambic trimeter, the meter of the spoken portions of Greek tragedy, thus assuming the role of a Euripidean prologue and anticipating the opening section of the Helena act. Scholars have given little attention to Goethe's use of Lucan, whose poem may be regarded as a kind of anti-epic (in contrast to the imperial privilege of Virgil's *Aeneid*), and what such a choice of source might imply. The historical battle that took place on the fields of Pharsalus does not figure directly in the action of the scenes to follow, though presumably the warfare that results from the emergence of Seismos from below ground establishes at the level of parody—through the battle of the Pygmies and the Cranes—the theme of warfare as central to *Faust*, Part Two, in general. The cause of the conflict on the slopes of the new mountain, a dispute over the gold that is thus unearthed, recalls the fraudulent plan for fiscal reform introduced by Mephisto to the Emperor's court in Act I, as it also anticipates the actual warfare that occurs in Act IV. The extent to which an allegorical allusion may also be intended to the wars in Europe during the Napoleonic era remains an open question. Clearly, Goethe's use of Lucan is more complex than might at first seem to be the case. Another literary source for some of the more blatant comic episodes in the "Classical Walpurgis Night" is Aristophanes. This applies in particular to the role of Mephistopheles in his involvement with the Thessalian witches, the Lamiae, and the Empusa (which appears with a donkey's head, borrowed from *The Frogs*; see 7676–800), leading to his encounter with the Phorcyads (7951–8033), where he discovers his proper disguise as ugly hag for the drama of Helena that follows. Goethe makes use here not so much of specific scenes in particular comedies by Aristophanes as the general style and manner of their social satire, where grotesque distortions of behavior are superimposed on sexual license, all of which is eminently suitable to Mephistopheles. The apparent analogy of this Northern devil's being out of his element among the mythical Grecian witches to the sexual debauchery of the witches' Sabbath on the Brocken in the "Walpurgis Night" of Part One leads primarily to a sense of contrast. The comic spirit of Aristophanes serves such contrast very effectively.

One of the most obscure yet central sources for the action in the "Classical Walpurgis Night" concerns the episode with Seismos and its significance for the entire sequence as a mythological festival. In a popular French novel by the Abbé Barthélémy, *Voyage du jeune Anarcharsis en Grèce* (1788), which Goethe knew, an annual festival is celebrated in Thessaly (3.35) in accord with accounts in classical sources cited in the novel, Athenaeus (14.45, 639 d–f) and Aelian (*Various History* 3.1). Goethe consulted both of these, the former with regard to the so-called Festival of Peloria (derived from a Greek word meaning "huge," "gigantic"), celebrated annually in commemoration of an ancient earthquake and upheaval of the landscape reported to have freed the waters originally covering this plain to flow out into the Aegean Sea; and the latter for an idyllic description of the Vale of Tempe, where the river Peneios flows, as a kind of earthly paradise. The geography of setting for Goethe's scenes and the mythological events that transpire during his festival are freely adapted to his own symbolic purpose. The earthquake that brings Seismos into view, as also the setting at the river's edge where Faust witnesses the encounter of Leda with the swan and where Chiron the centaur appears, is thus based, however loosely, on these remote literary sources.

Mythological Creatures of Origin:
Sphinxes, Griffins, Sirens (lines 7080–213)

The three alien travelers, who arrive in something resembling a spaceship (causing Erichtho to withdraw after speaking her prologue), quickly separate to explore this mythical Grecian terrain. Faust awakens as he lands, focused exclusively on his erotic quest for Helena ("Where is she?" [7056]), and Homunculus sets out on his corresponding quest to achieve physical being (i.e., to be born). This leaves Mephisto to confront a group of mythical monsters, whose presence constitutes one of the strangest scenes in the drama. The creatures assembled here—Sphinxes, Griffins, giant Ants, and the Arimaspians, later joined by the Sirens—indicate that they represent the primal era of antiquity, prior to anything we would regard as classical or even heroic, meaning the age of the legendary Greek warriors. Goethe thus purposefully depicts representatives of an originary mode of being. The Griffins growl and rasp at this alien visitor, angry because Mephisto casually refers to them as "grizzling sages" (*Greisen*, 7092—Arndt seeks to retain the crucial guttural sound in their name). Goethe plays with a peculiar ambiguity in the print type for German letters, where a single small horizontal line alone distinguishes between the letters *f* and *s* in German script (*Fraktur*), so that the terms *Greisen* and *Greifen* in German (7093) appear virtually identical. The Griffins express a theory concerning the origin of language according to the sounds of words—a kind of phonetic etymology—that they themselves symbolize. In one line they list six words that share identical consonantal sounds: *Grau, grämlich, griesgram, greulich, Gräber, grimmig* (7096; in Arndt, "Grey, grumbling, gruesome, graveyard, grimly, grunted"). A crucial pun, however, resides in their name itself, since "Griffin" (*Greifen*) in German also signifies the verb "to grasp" (*greifen*). The central function of these monsters, as quickly becomes apparent in their relations with the Ants and the Arimaspians, who greedily gather gold from beneath the surface of the

Earth, is to keep and hoard the treasure, i.e., to "grasp" it. Yet in accord with their emphasis on the origins of meaning in language on the basis of sound, the Griffins also symbolize the act of *grasping* that meaning. Mephisto has come face to face with mythical creatures who embody, and thus represent or signify, the origin of language.

The Sphinxes are more familiar to students of mythology, both from the legend of Oedipus and the riddle set him by the monster guarding the city of Thebes—mentioned subsequently by Faust (7185)—and from reports of the great statue of the Sphinx in Egypt, which Goethe in an early scientific essay on granite as the oldest (indeed, the original) stone of the Earth, believed to have been sculpted from this *Urgestein*. The Sphinxes themselves emphasize that their primary function is to endure, to abide in their place, unchanged and unmoved—as they indicate later with regard to their indifference to any disturbance ("We, by our Old Egyptian past affected, / Are long accustomed to millennial stays" [7241 f.]) and in response to the earthquake that brings Seismos into view: "Yet we shall not change our roost, / Not if all of hell were loosed" (7528 f.). Even more significant, in their opening statement (7114 f.) they breathe the tones of spirit (*Geistertöne*), which are then embodied (*verkörpert*), presumably as symbols of mythical identity. The meaning of the riddles they set for those who encounter them—in this case Mephistopheles, in the role Oedipus once played—resides in the recognition of such identity. In a sense, they challenge those who confront them with the obligation to demonstrate self-knowledge, which Mephisto proceeds to do by naming himself (in English) "Old Iniquity," a title borrowed from late-medieval morality plays. In addition, the Sphinxes provide Faust, when he subsequently stumbles on the scene (7181–213), with the crucial information that in order to find Helena he must inquire of the centaur Chiron. These ancient mythical creatures thus represent, like the Griffins, a primary, originary power.

The third group of mythical creatures who signify this power are the Sirens, known from Homer's *Odyssey*, where Odysseus (Ulysses) encounters them on his travels—as Faust also mentions in response to them (7186). The Sirens play a crucial role in the "Classical Walpurgis Night," especially in the festival at the Aegean Sea, where they function as a kind of musical chorus. Traditionally in mythology, the Sirens are regarded as dangerous and destructive powers, who seduce human beings to their death by their singing. In Goethe's drama, by contrast, the Sirens have a positive function, above all through the musical medium of their choral song. When we first become aware of the Sirens (stage direction before 7152), they are "tuning up for song above." At the outset of the festival at the shores of the Aegean, to which the Sirens repair just after the earthquake and the appearance of Seismos, they introduce the ceremonies thanks to a remarkably descriptive stage direction: "reclining here and there on the cliffs, piping and singing" (before 8034). We may surmise from the text that every speech assigned to the Sirens consists of choral song with instrumental accompaniment; indeed, the Sirens appear to symbolize music itself as artistic medium and song as a privileged vehicle of celebration. Much of the final festival, in fact, is orchestrated for music, with the Sirens playing the central role. In the opening choral sequence, where they are joined by the Nereids and Tritons (8034–82), the Sirens direct their hymnic praise to the moon as the goddess Luna, who appears to reside above in the heavens as patron of the festival—suspended at the zenith, symbolizing the moment of the festival as transcending time. The plea of the Sirens to "fairest Luna" (8043) that she "show us Grace" (*Schöne Luna, sei uns gnädig*) is essentially identical to the climactic appeal of Doctor Marianus to the Mater Gloriosa at the very end of the final scene of the drama: *Jungfrau, Mutter, Königin, Göttin, bleibe gnädig!* (see 12102 f.; translated by Arndt as "Holy Virgin, Mother, Queen, / Goddess, pour Thy mercies!"). The Sirens also sing a hymn of praise for Galatea just before she appears in triumph (8379–90), and subsequently they bring the entire "Classical Walpurgis Night" to its climactic conclusion, when they celebrate Eros, "who engendered it all!" (8474–83), opening the choral voice of the festival to the cosmos in the very last verses, sung by "All in Unison" (*All-Alle!*, before 8484–7—which is the only exclamation mark following the designation of a speaker in *Faust*). This cosmic chorale at the triumphant conclusion of this unique scene of praise stands in close sympathy with the famous Chorus Mysticus at the conclusion of the drama (see 12104–11), and indeed, scholars have determined that Goethe wrote both passages at virtually the same time, in the final weeks of 1830.

Faust's Path to the Underworld (lines 7249–494)

Faust's presence in the "Classical Walpurgis Night" is surprisingly compressed. Apart from his brief appearance in the scene where Mephisto confronts the creatures of origin (7181–213), which serves primarily to secure for Faust advice from the Sphinxes about how to find Helena, Faust has only one scene, labeled by editors "On the Lower Peneios" (Goethe omitted any title for the scene). Goethe's intention, which he seems to have abandoned only after concluding the "Classical Walpurgis Night" with the festival at the shores of the Aegean, had been also to portray Faust's visit to the underworld, where as a "second Orpheus" he would plead for the release of Helena in the presence of Persephone, queen of the dead. There has been considerable debate among scholars concerning Goethe's motive for abandoning this plan, though clearly he felt the "Classical Walpurgis Night" as it stands would suffice. Readers should keep in mind the simultaneity of the several events portrayed in this sequence— they are all aspects of the single mythical moment out of time that the festival signifies. In ways that demand careful interpretation, all three events (Faust's journey into the underworld with Manto, Mephisto's encountering the Phorcyads, and Homunculus's sacrificing himself in response to the Triumph of Galatea at the concluding festival) are closely related, however different the individual experience of the three alien visitors to Greece may be, and the climactic events of the final scene out at sea must serve as symbolic preparation for the appearance of Helena at the outset of Act III. Helena does appear because Faust has secured her temporary release from the underworld, but she also appears, according to the peculiar logic of this mythical action, as a consequence of the festival of Galatea.

In the single scene that dramatizes Faust's quest for Helena, three distinct and quite different encounters occur: 1) the repeat of his vision of Helena's conception, when Leda is seduced by Zeus (or Jupiter) in the form of a swan; 2) the meeting with the centaur Chiron, who is constantly on the move and allows Faust to ride upon his back; and 3) the arrival at the mysterious temple where the seer Manto resides, and Manto's subsequently leading Faust into the underworld. The contrast between these encounters is significant, yet their sequence also defines Faust's progress toward the successful completion of his quest. The vision of Leda at the banks of the Peneios (7277–312) recapitulates Faust's dream of this event when he lay unconscious in his study, a dream interpreted by Homunculus (6903–20). The fact that Goethe provides two versions of the same mythical act invites close comparison between them. The first is, of course, accessible to us only as verbal description by Homunculus and focuses almost exclusively on the figure of Leda herself and the single swan that approaches her as she bathes. The image fades—even for Homunculus— as the seduction begins. In the second case, by contrast, we must assume that Faust is describing a scene that actually takes place before his eyes upon the waters of the river Peneios. Recognizing that he has already witnessed this event in his dream, he even asks himself whether he is dreaming once again (7275 f.). Within the peculiar symbolic realm of the "Classical Walpurgis Night," however, we must assume that what Faust describes is actually happening, perhaps in a way that would also be visible to an audience in the theater (though the stage directions do not make this clear). The episode is introduced, furthermore, by the voice of the river itself—Peneios opens the scene with a single, ceremonial and incantatory speech, consisting of a series of commands in trochaic meter (7249– 56)—followed by the voices of the Nymphs who attend him and are apparently the manifestation of spiritual powers identified with the water (as later the voices of Oreas and Dryad will be identified as nymphs of the mountain and the trees; see 7811–20 and 7959–68). The river's words indicate that the Nymphs' voices are generated by the breeze blowing through the reeds at its banks, a kind of naturalistic aeolian harp. The river also indicates that he is being awakened by these voices from a sleep, "interrupted dream" (7253); whereas Faust responds to the initial song of the Nymphs by asserting that he is wide awake: *Ich wache ja!* (7271; "No slumber now!" in Arndt's translation). Faust's description of his vision here is longer and more elaborate than had been Homunculus's earlier account of the dream. Here the plurality of figures, both the young women who attend Leda, their queen, and the group of swans that approaches them, provides a sense of festive and communal event. Faust's description is interrupted, however, by the arrival of Chiron, described by the Nymphs (7313–80). Readers should also recall Faust's analogous visionary encounters in Part One, with manifestations of the Feminine in "Witch's Kitchen," where the image in the mirror faded when Faust approached it, and in the "Walpurgis Night," where the strange figure of the wraith appeared in the shape of Gretchen, naked and with her throat slit. The visual panorama described by Faust also seems much closer to Goethe's presumed pictorial source for the seduction of Leda and the swan, namely the painting by Correggio in the royal collection of Prussia, than had been the earlier description of Faust's dream by Homunculus.

The figure of Chiron assumes a singular importance for Faust in this scene, primarily because the dialogue between them as Faust rides on the centaur's back surveys both the substance and the form of mythical representation. Chiron is known in mythology (as emphasized also in Hederich, Goethe's primary source) as a teacher, specifically the teacher of famous heroes, whose development was influenced positively by this creature—half horse, half man—whose knowledge pertained above all to the lore of nature. Among those taught by Chiron (mentioned in the scene) were Achilles, Jason (who led the quest of the Argonauts for the Golden Fleece), Hercules, Orpheus the singer, the Dioscuri, Castor and Pollux (brothers of Helena), the Boreads (sons of the North Wind), and Lynceus (the steersman and watchman on the ship of the Argonauts, who subsequently appears in the central section of Act III as Faust's watchman on the lookout for the arrival of Helena and in Act V as watchman on the tower of Faust's palace). By engaging the centaur in dialogue, Faust joins the roster of his pupils, though here the form of instruction is exclusively verbal. It is of interest with regard to their dialogue as verbal form that Chiron rejects visual artistic representation, above all in sculpture (see 7395–405), preferring the living activity whereby beauty manifests itself as grace. This precisely is what he attributes to Helena, who also (he asserts) once rode on his back, exactly as Faust is doing. Chiron's tale of his encounter with Helena—which Faust as "philologist" (7426) reckons to have occurred when she was only ten years old—affirms her status as mythical model for the ideal of feminine beauty. Faust confirms this by articulating his obsessive longing to find Helena, and Chiron offers (7448–58) to help Faust by bringing him to Manto, the seer, daughter of Asclepios (god of healing; though in most sources she is the daughter of the blind prophet Tiresias), which immediately he does. The thematic contrast between Chiron and Manto—even though Manto has only a few lines to speak before she departs with Faust for the underworld—reaffirms a central aspect of Faust's mythical quest for Helena. Chiron is constantly in motion, moving about the spaces of the festival, whereas Manto, as seer or Sybil (7455), which title recalls the figure in the sixth book of Virgil's *Aeneid* who accompanies Aeneas to the underworld, resides motionless, indeed dreaming (see stage direction before 7471)—and thus asleep—within the temple of Apollo, which she serves as priestess. The descent to the underworld that she offers Faust, because she applauds his boundless longing for Helena, his striving beyond the limits of the possible (7488), consists primarily in a journey inward, as if to the realm of the unconscious, not unlike the strange journey that Faust earlier made in Act I to the Mothers.

Seismos and the War of the Pygmies and Cranes (lines 7495–675)

In letters written around the time when he was composing the "Classical Walpurgis Night," Goethe referred several times to his "very serious jests" (*sehr ernsten Scherze*). Few of these jests are both so comic and so serious as the parody of natural processes that the action of this scene contains. The violent earthquake that leads to the emergence of Seismos has nothing whatsoever to do directly with the actions of any of the three alien visitors to this mythical festival, not with Faust's quest for Helena, not with Mephisto's dalliance with the Thessalian witches, and not directly with Homunculus's search for existence, though the consequences of the earthquake do pertain by negative example to the last of these. The earthquake occurs without apparent warning to anyone and appears to take even the mythical creatures on the scene—the Sirens and the Sphinxes—completely by surprise. A reader of *Faust* is bound to ask just what is going on and what it signifies.

The most immediate answer to such a question derives from Goethe's scientific views and the contexts of natural science during his lifetime. The earthquake results from a subterranean volcanic explosion and demonstrates in miniature theatrical form the general theory of geological process designated by the term *Vulcanism*. This theory maintained that the surface of the Earth, above all in its diversity, its mountain ranges, peaks, and valleys, had been created by violent volcanic forces pressing forth from below. Goethe was familiar with this theory, in particular through the study published by Sir William Hamilton, member of the Royal Society in London, on the eruptions of Mount Vesuvius (1772), which Hamilton observed while ambassador from England to the Kingdom of Naples (where Goethe met him during his trip to Italy in 1786–8). Goethe also himself ascended Vesuvius to study the phenomenon of volcanic explosions. Seismos—the name is Greek for "earthquake"—demonstrates such creation by violence from subterranean infernal forces. Yet he also signifies much more for the drama.

Seismos emerges as a gigantic figure from chest and shoulder upward and is also in effect a new mountain resulting from this volcanic explosion, this earthquake. He has a voice and describes his own striving force of will, "with stupendous heaving, / I from the deeps thrust up and out" (*mit ungeheurem Streben, / Drang aus dem Abgrund ich herauf*, 7570 f.); yet he also becomes immediately a new surface or space, a landscape, upon which specific, characteristic events take place. As such, Seismos assumes thematic significance for the drama, both with regard to the boundless striving (*Streben*) that has motivated Faust from the outset and with more specific regard to the project of fiscal reform introduced in the court of the Emperor by Mephistopheles in Act I. Seismos is a living, if illusory, example of gold from below ground, revealed through the volcanic explosion. Initially, the primal creatures from the opening scene of the festival —the Griffins and the Ants (7582–605)—dig out the gold from metallic veins on Seismos's surface and hoard it as treasure. Yet at once and without causal explanation, open conflict and war break out on the mountain between the Pygmies and the Cranes. Such warfare derives from Homeric legend (*Iliad* 3.4–7), which was often represented in the visual arts in antiquity. The Pygmies, with their curious allies—Dactyls ("fingers"; from the Greek, as the term *pygmé* measures the distance from elbow to knuckles) and Emmets, the Pygmy Eldest and the Generalissimo—immediately call to mind the diminutive miners who accompany the Emperor in his costume as Pan at the Carnival Masque, the Gnomes and their Deputation (5840–63 and 5898–913). The conflagration, which there seemed to threaten the Emperor with death by fire, resembles the fiery subterranean force of the earthquake that brings Seismos to the surface. The war fought here, motivated primarily by greed for possession of the gold, anticipates the war that breaks out in the Emperor's realm in Act IV. Assuming that there is a thematic connection between these episodes, one may ask what the preoccupation with colorful military uniforms on the Pygmies signifies, especially since they slaughter the apparently innocent egrets to use the feathers for their helmets, as indicated in the speech by the Generalissimo (7644–53). This attack leads immediately to a counterattack by the Cranes of Ibycus, who are named for a legend (used by Schiller as the basis for one of his best-known ballads) in which the ancient Greek poet Ibycus is killed by thieves and subsequently avenged by cranes, who cause the murderers to reveal themselves. The name Ibycus as used here presumably indicates that the Cranes are avenging the slaughter of the egrets by the Pygmies, who are called by them "bowleg fat-paunch knaves" (*Fettbauch-Krummbein-Schelme*; 7669). All this violence and slaughter, which is not likely to elicit much interest from a reader, suggests that Goethe intends this entire sequence of volcanic force and its consequences to constitute an allegory for the violence and warfare in Europe during the era of the French Revolution and the Napoleonic campaigns. Precisely what such an allegory implies for the drama as a whole becomes clear only in light of the warfare of Act IV.

Homunculus and the Philosophers (lines 7851–95)

Anaxagoras and Thales, two familiar names from pre-Socratic philosophy, appear on the scene of this mythological festival to debate two conflicting doctrines of nature. It is precisely because of these doctrines that Homunculus seeks them out, as he says to Mephisto (7837), hoping the two ancient Greeks will assist him in his effort to come into being. In this he will not be disappointed, though these two figures do not necessarily speak for their historical namesakes. Anaxagoras, a friend of Pericles who lived and taught in Athens during the mid-fifth century B.C., developed a philosophy of nature as a constantly shifting system of material units or atoms motivated by an all-encompassing divine principle of mind (*Nous*). Goethe makes him the spokesman for the Vulcanist theory of creation through the force of fire, which the recent earthquake demonstrated. As he asserts: "That cliff [*Fels*; i.e., rock] exists by dint of swathes of flame" (7855). Thales lived a century earlier than Anaxagoras, in Miletus, and belongs to the earliest group of cosmologists in Greek culture. No writings by him are preserved (and perhaps were not preserved even in classical Athens), but he is known to have argued that all things derive from water as primal element, an idea that perhaps he brought to Greece after a sojourn in Egypt. Here he affirms precisely this idea in response to the assertion by Anaxagoras cited above: "It is in moisture [im Feuchten], though, that life became" (7856). In this, Thales speaks for the doctrine of natural creation opposing that of Vulcanism, namely Neptunism, to which Goethe subscribed. The concluding festival at the Aegean Sea will affirm the validity of Thales' theory, as the meteoric explosion about to occur will prove that fire is ultimately destructive and adverse to the creation of life. The basic theory of the Neptunists, represented above all in the writings of the geologist Abraham Gottlob Werner, Goethe's exact contemporary, argued that all forms of rock had resulted from sedimentation in water. Goethe's central concern in the "Classical Walpurgis Night" with regard to Homunculus's quest pertains instead to a principle of organic evolution through the element of water, as the concluding scene will demonstrate.

The conversation between Thales and Anaxagoras quickly reveals that they are rivals in their opposing models of natural creation. In their opposition, they also compete for the allegiance of Homunculus. Anaxagoras offers the speed of volcanic process, as well as the conflict and violence that accompany it; Thales insists that nature must take its own time for creative and innovative change through organic process. The war on Seismos between the Pygmies and the Cranes, which we witnessed, is described in vivid terms by Thales (7882–99) as an implicit warning to Homunculus, who has just been offered rule as king of the mountain by Anaxagoras. Anaxagoras then turns his attention toward the heavens and invokes the moon as goddess in her traditional threefold name: Diana, Luna, Hecate (7905). Alluding to the Thessalian witches' devotion to this goddess, Anaxagoras attempts to duplicate their supposed power to conjure her. When his prayer immediately appears to be answered by a heavenly body's swift descent toward the new mountain, Anaxagoras tries to retract his prayer and prevent the destructive impact: "For it was my doing" (7926–9). In this statement, he approaches the arrogance of the Baccalaureus in Act I, and clearly, through the boundless self-confidence of his claim, he is in error to an equal degree. In prostrating himself before the approaching heavenly body, furthermore (see stage direction after 7929), he seems to parody by anticipation the final prayerful attitude of Doctor Marianus before the epiphany of the Mater Gloriosa at the very end of the drama.

The heavenly body is a meteor, which strikes the summit of the mountain, killing all those who are fighting there regardless of which side they are on. Goethe here alludes to, but also parodies, theories of meteor crashes on the surface of the Earth, associating them with volcanic violence. Because of this outcome, Homunculus aligns himself with Thales, who proposes that they retreat to the shore, in order to participate in the "sea-feast" with its "wondrous guests" that is about to take place (7949 f.). As they depart, Thales emphasizes that the entire volcanic pageant has been a theatrical show, in which both the earthquake and the fall of the meteor were an illusion. The lesson of destruction, however, anticipates the war in Act IV, as it also does the pseudoheroic death of Euphorion in Act III, when he throws himself off a high cliff in an Icarus-like attempt to fly—another instance of boundless self-confidence in the manner of the Baccalaureus—and where his fall to Earth is also compared to a meteor (see stage directions before 9901 and 9903). The rejection of the doctrine of volcanic creation thus seems definitive for its various related manifestations in *Faust*, even though the political and existential implications of such violent processes extend to many different aspects of the drama, including even the technology of Faust's land-reclamation project in Act V.

Mephistopheles Among the Classical Witches (lines 7951–8033)

Given Mephistopheles's repeated insistence that he feels quite alien and out of place in the "Classical Walpurgis Night," it is remarkable that the role of this devil from the North in this spirit show of the South is so extensive and diverse. His encounter with such strange, even grotesque mythical monsters and witches calls to mind much of the freewheeling excesses and debaucheries from the "Walpurgis Night" in Part One. Above all, the emphasis on sexual license recalls Mephisto's involvement in that earlier demonic orgy, where he was clearly at home. Here in Greece, however, the devil is consistently the victim of deception and a perverse teasing by such figures as the Lamiae and the Empusa. His motive for coming had been his wish to encounter the Thessalian witches (see 6976–82); now that he does so, he finds his attempts to engage them in sexual activity repeatedly frustrated (7748–800). Following the departure of the Lamiae, Mephisto wanders through the landscape without apparent direction and motive. First, he comes to the mountain that speaks with the voice of the nymph Oreas, who juxtaposes the historical defeat of Pompey at the battle of Pharsalus with the earthquake that has just brought Seismos to light and will disappear again at dawn (7811–20); and, second, he happens upon Homunculus, who is seeking the philosophers Anaxagoras and Thales, whose views on nature he hopes will help him fulfill his quest for being. Neither of these episodes—the appearance of Seismos and the conversation with the philosophers—has anything directly to do with Mephisto. Only subsequently, when Mephisto, still feeling alienated from everything around him, encounters the tree nymph Dryad (7959–68), is he directed to the cave in which the three Phorcyads reside. These old gray hags, sometimes called the Graiae, daughters of Phorcys, were presumably introduced to this scene by Goethe from the description of them in Hederich's *Mythological Lexicon*.

In their dark and obscure cave, Mephisto finally finds his proper place in the "Classical Walpurgis Night," namely in the presence of these hags, who share one eye and one tooth between them and symbolize the ultimate extreme of ugliness in the midst of this classical mythical realm, the land of beauty (7978). In this encounter between the devil and ugliness, Goethe reverses the familiar view of antiquity that he had inherited from Winckelmann and others and in which he himself had invested deep aesthetic conviction, namely that the art and culture of classical Greece embodies the highest ideal of beauty. As a signal of this reversal, the Phorcyads themselves emphasize that they have never been represented in art, keeping out of sight "in stillest night and solitude confined" (8000). By borrowing their one eye and one tooth, Mephisto appropriates to himself the ugliness of the Phorcyads and thus achieves his proper and suitable guise for the act that follows, in which Faust encounters Helena, the true embodiment of that ideal of classical beauty, and in which Faust's erotic quest for union with that ideal is fulfilled. Mephisto's transformation into the symbol of ugliness thus stands as an appropriate opposing correlative to Faust's successful quest for Helena.

Festival at the Aegean Sea (lines 8034–487)

In Goethe's "Second Sketch for the Announcement of the *Helena*" (see below), no mention is made of the climactic festival that concludes the "Classical Walpurgis Night." This scene, nearly five hundred lines of diverse and constantly changing musical-lyrical celebration and philosophical commentary, is the boldest and the most obscure poetic sequence in the entire drama. This is also the symbolic high point of Goethe's work, despite the fact that neither Faust nor Mephistopheles is present during the scene. The idea for the festival must have occurred to the poet in the process of composing the "Classical Walpurgis Night" early in 1830. Ultimately, this scene also replaced Faust's visit to the underworld and his appeal to Persephone for the release of Helena, which was originally intended to conclude the sequence, though Goethe apparently decided to omit that scene only after Act II was finished. The mythical festival of life and love, procreation and organic evolution, at the shores of the Aegean Sea includes the fulfillment of Homunculus's quest for being, achieved when he shatters his glass against the shell of Aphrodite, which is being ridden by the nymph Galatea, whom this diminutive spirit chases out to sea in an erotic frenzy. This act of self-sacrifice and self-engendering in the sea serves as an analogy, if also a contrast, to the union of Faust and Helena in the act that follows: an analogy, insofar as the erotic desire of Homunculus resembles the striving of the Faustian will for ideal beauty; a contrast, insofar as the transformation and creation of Homunculus demonstrates nature's own process of generation and evolution, which contrasts with Faust's experience in his marriage to ideal beauty, as it also contrasts with human experience generally. What Goethe came finally to recognize, however, almost as if his mythical drama had taken its author by surprise, was that this festival-celebration of erotic fusion provides an adequate and appropriate alternative to Faust's visit to the dead. The ultimate result of Homunculus's self-sacrifice in response to Galatea is no less than the emergence of Helena, the embodiment of the classical ideal of beauty, at the outset of Act III, newly arrived (as she asserts) at the shores of her native Sparta and still dizzy with the motion of the sea (see 8488–93). Her journey from the underworld into the drama is identical with the journey from the sea to the land, from the domain of the festival of natural creation to the stage of Faust's all-too-human tragic drama. This connection is both subtle and crucial. In addition, within the symbolic medium of the "Classical Walpurgis Night," the events of the festival at sea fulfill the vision of Helena's conception when Leda is ravished by Zeus as swan in Faust's twofold dream of it.

The festival at the Aegean also contrasts intentionally with the geological events that occurred earlier inland on the plain of the Peneios, when the volcanic eruption brought the giant Seismos above ground. That event led to further violence, open warfare, wanton slaughter, and, finally, complete destruction when the descending meteor struck the summit of the new mountain. With these events, Goethe indicates his negative judgment concerning the volcanic theory of creation, whether that creation is defined in geological or in political and social terms. The poet, like Homunculus, prefers the teaching of Thales to that of Anaxagoras. The events of the concluding festival celebrate the slower, more evolutionary processes of creation that occur within the medium of water. As Thales asserts very near the end of the scene, in a hymn of praise for water as element and medium of life (and in an exclamation with double punctuation—the only instance of such punctuation in the entire drama): "From the water has sprung all life!!" (*Alles ist aus dem Wasser entsprungen!!*, 8435). According to this doctrine, life originated in the sea, as the elderly sages—Thales, Proteus, and Nereus—who witness the festival and comment on it agree, and from this original act of creation an evolutionary process commenced, which through time led to the emergence of ever higher, and more complex forms of life, culminating finally in human beings. When Homunculus shatters his glass against Galatea's shell and dissipates his spiritual flame into the water of the sea, he submits to this primal "neptunic" act of generation and enters into the process of organic evolution, which will lead eventually in the course of cosmic time to his emergence as a human being. As Thales says in his final speech to Homunculus: *Da regst du dich nach ewigen Normen, / Durch tausend, abertausend Formen, / Und bis zum Menschen hast du Zeit* ("You move there by eternal norms, / Through thousand, countless thousand forms, / There's time enough for manship still," 8324–6).

A few words should be said about the characters and roles of the two mythological figures to whom Thales leads Homunculus and who in crucial ways help bring the festival to its climactic close. Nereus, the first of the two old men of the sea to be approached (8082–159), proves to be a cranky grouch, though not without experience and wisdom in his dealings with humans. In his initial speech, he surveys two specific encounters with familiar heroes of Greek legend, both of which ended in failure: with Paris, who abducted Helena contrary to Nereus's advice and thus brought ruin on Troy (8110–19), and with Ulysses, whose wanderings—as recounted in Homer's *Odyssey*, though Nereus's contact with the hero is post-Homeric—brought suffering and loss from such destructive powers as Circe and the Cyclops, about whom Nereus had forewarned the hero. Nereus is also a father figure in accord with mythological tradition—fifty of his hundred daughters making up the Nereids, the other fifty being the

Dorids, all of them participating in the festival, perhaps by invitation from their father. Above all, Nereus is the father of Galatea, whose arrival at the climactic moment in substitution for the goddess Venus will also be signaled by the exchange of greetings as she rides past the shore where her father stands (8424–5). Nereus rejects Thales' request for assistance in Homunculus's search for being, though he does refer them to Proteus as someone who can provide the help they need. As a character, Nereus resembles Mephistopheles, above all in his negative ironic manner in conversation. Yet equally he may serve as a spokesman for Goethe in the wisdom of his old age. This holds true in particular for the final stance Nereus assumes, on the promontory at the edge of the sea, in response to his annual glimpse of his beloved daughter Galatea. Proteus is a more familiar figure from ancient literature, primarily due to the role he plays in the *Odyssey*, where Menelaus reports of his encounter with the old man of the sea at the shores of Egypt on his attempt to journey home from Troy (4.333–592). Proteus is an elusive shape-changer who must be tricked and captured before he will respond to questions. Once his favor is secured, however, he proves to be a reliable source of insight and prophetic truth. As in Homer, so also in Goethe. The scene in which Thales leads Homunculus to Proteus (8219–74) is filled with tricks and playful ruses and reversals, but Homunculus finally elicits the interest and support of the ancient by glowing brightly in his glass container and thus exerting an appropriate fascination, since his like has never before been seen. It is Proteus who reveals that Homunculus can find his true being only in the sea, where he must submit to the processes of evolutionary development (8260–4). In what proves to be a genuinely sympathetic act of assistance, Proteus transforms himself into a dolphin and invites Homunculus to ride with him out to sea (8271–4), where they join the procession, encounter Galatea on her shell, and find the opportunity for Homunculus to achieve his goal. Proteus thus also becomes an ally in the quest for being, as he is also an active agent and companion for Homunculus, more than is the case with Nereus and even Thales.

The festival scene at the Aegean is perhaps the most difficult in the entire drama to imagine being performed on stage, yet in its form and structure there is a strong sense of theatricality. Once again Goethe employs the form of procession as scenic structure, though in this case the procession passes by the shore with its rocky promontory. The lyrical and choral effusions by the varied participants are also separated by sections of dialogue that take place among those standing at the shore, namely Thales, Nereus, Proteus, and Homunculus. In addition, the Sirens as chorus, singing and fluting, are arrayed along the cliffs above the shore (as indicated in the initial stage direction; not to be confused with the Chorus of Telchines from Rhodes, 8275–84). This arrangement results in a dialectic of alternation between celebration and commentary. The perspective of the audience (or reader) remains at the shore, essentially alongside the commentators, looking out to the mythical procession as spectacle. The Sirens introduce the lyrical and ceremonial sequence of the scene in company with the Nereids and Tritons "in the shape of sea prodigies" (*Meerwunder;*

stage directions before 8044). The Nereids and Tritons swiftly depart for the island of Samothrace to bring the Cabiri, the so-called great gods of the traditional mystery rites celebrated there, to the festival (see below), and they shortly return with them, following the first section of dialogue (8082–159). The choral sequence in celebration of the Cabiri, again including the Sirens as chorus, establishes the basis for the epiphany to follow and concludes the role of these prodigies, who then depart (8160–218). The next group to appear in procession, even more fantastic and obscure, are the Telchines of Rhodes, riding "on sea-horses and sea-dragons" (stage direction before 8275) and carrying the trident of the god Neptune, which they forged in ancient times. Through their handiwork, the Telchines may also represent the earliest stage of human arts and crafts, thus thematizing implicitly a progression in the festival from lower, more primal and natural stages of culture toward higher forms of production and creation. They are followed by the Psylli and Marsi from Cyprus, riding "on bulls, calves, and rams of the sea" (stage direction before 8359). These obscure figures' primary function has been to tend the shell of Aphrodite, on which she rode to shore after her birth at sea and on which the nymph Galatea, who replaces the goddess in the festival, is shortly to ride past. Next to arrive are the Dorids, water nymphs and sisters of the Nereids (and thus of Galatea as well), who ride past on dolphins, carrying young sailors whom they have rescued from shipwreck (8391–424). Their misplaced erotic devotion to these humans, who by order from Nereus must be returned to land, anticipates the reverse erotic response of Homunculus to Galatea. The Dorids are the last figures to appear prior to the climactic moment of this festival procession, namely the epiphany of Galatea, riding in triumph on Aphrodite's shell and led by a flock of doves from the island of Paphos, who fly past the moon—first sighted as they approach by the Sirens (8339–46).

What does this sequence of mythical creatures riding past in triumphal procession signify, and how does this festival relate to the central concerns of Goethe's drama? On the one hand, these various groups of obscure participants, derived for the most part from entries in Hederich's *Mythological Lexicon* and virtually unknown to most readers, challenge us to locate a coherent motive in Goethe's otherwise seemingly arbitrary choice of participants. On the other hand, every reader will understand that the procession as a whole, extending from the sirens' initial prayer to the goddess Luna to the final epiphany of the nymph Galatea, is a celebration of love, specifically of Eros in its natural manifestations as a universal creative power. In certain ways, this procession recalls the theatrical technique of the Carnival Masque in the Emperor's court, in which diverse and colorful participants present themselves as they enter and cross the stage and for which the Herald provides a form of commentary and explanation that resembles the more elaborate role of the commentators here, namely Thales, Nereus, Proteus, and Homunculus. In the Masque, furthermore, the allegorical meaning of the floats becomes apparent through the involvement and response of the central characters—Faust as Plutus and the Emperor as Pan—just as here the response to and participation by Ho-

munculus in the Triumph of Galatea is crucial to the mythical significance of the procession. Also common to both sequences is the use of the
theatrical medium as artificial correlative for real events: political and social, even economic, in the case of the Masque; natural and mythical here.
The Masque at court, however, is staged by human agency and design,
even if Mephisto supplements the artifice of events through his demonic
power; in the festival at the Aegean, by contrast, we have no idea who is
staging the procession or how or even why, except that the mythical medium and the natural processes it represents appear to be fully integrated
and interdependent. What had earlier been part of an allegorical theatrical
show is here transformed into a festival celebration where nature and art
are one. Homunculus himself in his act of self-sacrifice and regeneration
symbolizes that fusion, as he also conveys the ecstatic comprehension and
affirmation of its all-encompassing significance.

The Cabiri from Samothrace (lines 8070–218)

In his treatise *On the Gods of Samothrace* (1815), the philosopher Schelling describes the Cabiri as a chain of ascending forces of divinity, extending from the primal depths of the Earth or the sea upward to the
heavens. Thought to be Phoenician in origin, these strange and remote
deities play a crucial role—so argues Schelling—in the mystery rites associated with the ancient religious center on the island of Samothrace. The
first of the Cabiri, named Axieros, is identified with the goddess Demeter,
or Ceres, the Great Mother, and is defined by a desire for growth or
creation. The second, Axiokersa, is identified with Persephone, or Proserpina, daughter of the first, who became queen of the underworld when
she was carried off by Hades. The third, Axiokersos, is the Egyptian Osiris,
or the Greek Dionysus, here thought to function in place of Hades as the
consort of the daughter. The fourth of the gods, called Kadmilos, is Hermes, messenger or guide, who leads the other gods up from the underworld
to the realm of Heaven. The interaction of these deities and their linear
ascent is understood by Schelling to signify a process of spiritual and cultural growth or the creation of consciousness, proceeding from the primal
urge of nature through erotic union toward complete consciousness and
intelligence. The final stage in this development consists of a recapitulation of the process of ascent at a higher level of intelligence in the Olympian realm, so that the actual number of the Cabiri in their hierarchy
would presumably be seven. Goethe makes fun of the uncertain number
of the Cabiri by suggesting that there could possibly be an eighth, whom
no one has yet thought of (8194–9). It may be that this unknown eighth
member would be Zeus himself. Goethe here offers a parody of Romantic
mythology in its speculation concerning the ancient mysteries, which had
occurred, for instance, in the elaborate and learned work by the classicist
Friedrich Creuzer, *Symbolism and Mythology of the Ancient Peoples*
(1810–12), as well as the treatise by Schelling specifically on the Cabiri.
Yet the summoning of the Cabiri to the festival of the "Classical Walpurgis
Night" is also very serious insofar as these strange and primitive gods, who
appear to Homunculus to be nothing more than earthenware jugs (8219–

24), thematize in the process of their hierarchical desire and ascent both Faust's visitation to the underworld and his appeal to Persephone for the release of Helena and also Homunculus's erotic response to Galatea at the climax of the festival, followed by his self-sacrifice and his procreative union with the element of water. Common to all three processes is the pattern of ascending creation and self-consciousness, so that in some highly elusive way the entire festival of Eros may be understood as an authentic recapitulation of the Cabiritic mystery rites from the ancient cult of the great gods on Samothrace, despite the fact that such disparate sources are here superimposed so playfully in Goethe's scene. The entire event is preeminently Faustian, despite the absence of Faust himself, in its essential and pervasive striving toward re-creation and self-fulfillment. The festival that the Cabiri are brought to bless thus constitutes in its primal act of procreation an appropriate prerequisite for the union of Faust and Helena that follows in Act III. The Cabiri's significance for this festival celebration, therefore, despite the satirical tone prevailing throughout, encompasses Faust's entire quest journey for the realization of Helena as the classical ideal of beauty.

The Triumph of Galatea (lines 8424–87)

There is a consensus among Faust scholars that the Triumph of Galatea, her appearance riding past on the shell of Aphrodite at the end of the festival at the Aegean Sea, is indebted to the famous wall painting of this subject in the Palazzo della Farnesina in Rome by Raphael, which Goethe knew from his stay in Rome during his Italian journey and an engraving of which he possessed. No other scenes in the drama are so closely dependent on an explicit visual source, with the possible exception of the conjuring of the Earth Spirit in the opening scene, which I have argued is a translation into dramatic form of Rembrandt's famous Faust etching. Goethe's Galatea enters the festival of the "Classical Walpurgis Night" directly from Raphael's powerful and mysterious image. Yet even this image contains a complex tradition in myth, legend, literature, and the visual arts, extending back to antiquity. For the purpose of interpreting Goethe's scene, a reader need not distinguish precisely the various sources that the poet may have used, but it is important to be familiar generally with the story of Galatea's Triumph, to which both Raphael and Goethe refer. Galatea, one of the daughters of Nereus, is known above all for the cumbersome and hopeless love she unwittingly inspires from Polyphemus, the giant Cyclops, whom Odysseus during his wanderings later blinds. Theocritus tells this story in one of his pastoral poems (Idyll 11), consisting of a monologue by the lovesick giant, who expresses his longing for the sea nymph as she frolics offshore. Ovid, in his *Metamorphoses* (8.719–897), tells a somewhat different story, in which Polyphemus's hopeless love for Galatea is contrasted with the genuine love the nymph shares with the young Acis. The Cyclops kills the youth by throwing a huge rock on him, and a spring of water bursts forth from the place of his death to flow out into the sea, where in effect within the medium of water the lovers are forever united. Other versions of this story, both from antiquity and from the Renaissance, elaborate on its implications. In relation to *Faust*, one of the most interesting and important of these versions appears in the *Eikones* (*Images*, or *Paintings*) of Philostratus, a Greek writer of the third century A.D., who provides detailed descriptions of a collection of paintings he claims is in Naples. Goethe worked intermittently for a number of years on a translation of these ecphrastic evocations of visual images—which may or may not have really existed as paintings—including a depiction of the Cyclops and Galatea. Goethe published this extensive essay in his journal *Über Kunst und Alterthum* (2.1) in 1818 (see Weimar edition, I, 49.1, 63–135, esp. "Cyclop und Galathee," 104–7). Philostratus's description of the giant Polyphemus in his attitude of grotesque erotic longing for the nymph derives in its details both from Homer's narrative in the *Odyssey* (Book 9) and from Theocritus's eleventh Idyll. No mention is made, however, of Ovid's alternative story about Acis. The description of Galatea frolicking upon the sea and riding her scallop shell, which is drawn by four dolphins with young Tritons holding the reins, suggests that Philostratus's text might have served as the basis for Raphael's depiction (though scholars have questioned whether the painter could have known the *Eikones* when he executed his painting, in the early years of the sixteenth century). Of interest also is the fact that Goethe, at the end of his translation of Philostratus's description, mentions the paintings on this subject by both Raphael and Carracci.

As so often in *Faust*, Goethe has radically transformed his sources, substituting Nereus, the father of Galatea, for Polyphemus and Homunculus for Acis. The former is positioned on the shore when the nymph passes by in her Triumph, just as the Cyclops was in the traditional story. In this case, however, instead of expressing a futile erotic longing, Nereus exchanges a greeting with his daughter, acknowledging her momentary presence at the climax of this annual mythical festival with the laconic call "It's you" (*Du bist es*, 8424), to which she replies with a futile command for her dolphins to stop, so that she may sustain this moment of meeting with her father. In contrast to Nereus, Homunculus responds to Galatea in an erotic frenzy, chasing after her out at sea as he rides on Proteus in the latter's guise as dolphin. Unlike Acis, he is not crushed by a rival for the nymph's love, but he does dissipate himself in the ocean by breaking his glass against her shell. These differences are significant for interpreting the responses of Nereus and Homunculus to the appearance of Galatea in Goethe's scene. Yet Raphael's painting contains neither Polyphemus nor Acis. In the room that contains Raphael's Galatea at the Palazzo della Farnesina, however, another wall painting, located immediately to the left and painted slightly earlier by the Venetian Sebastiano del Piombo, depicts the giant Polyphemus, who thus gazes toward Galatea in Raphael's image. In Raphael's painting, furthermore, three flying cupids hover above Galatea, aiming their arrows at her. Though perhaps unlikely to actually hit her, given the cupids' poor aim in the painting, presumably these arrows would inflame Galatea with passion for—whom else?—the Cyclops gazing at her from her left, at whom she perhaps glances back, as depicted by Raphael. Could Goethe also have intended Homunculus to serve as substitute for these cupids, thus reversing their attempt to shoot arrows at the nymph by turning the erotic passion evoked by her Triumph back upon the inflamed spirit chasing her as she retreats out to sea? Such questions indicate how productive and suggestive Goethe's transformation of Raphael's painting became.

Two further points should be made about the importance of Galatea for Goethe's *Faust*. First, following Galatea's call to Nereus as she is carried past him (*O Vater! Das Glück!*; "Dear Father, well met! / what bliss!" 8424 f.), her appeal to her dolphins to abide (*Delphine, verweilet! Mich fesselt der Blick*; "Oh my dolphins, do tarry just yet!") recalls the terms of Faust's wager with Mephistopheles. This meeting is the moment, the *Augenblick* (see 1699), that Galatea wishes would tarry (*verweilen*—the term used by Faust in his wager: *Verweile doch! du bist so schön!*, 1700); though of course the dolphins do not tarry and the moment does not abide, even though—paradoxically!—the entire festival at the Aegean takes place out of time, with the moon at its zenith, during a suspended mythical moment. Second, Homunculus's self-destruction is described by Nereus and Thales in terms of a fiery conflagration within the watery medium of the ocean (8464–73). The primal elements of fire and water are thus united in this sacrificial act of procreation. The final line of this description describes the event as it happens: "It's flaming, now flashes, already is scattered." The Sirens respond as final chorus, thus translating description into a form of dynamic musical and mimetic evocation: "It lightens and wavers and brightens the height: / The bodies, they glow on the courses of night, / And ringed is the whole by the luminous wall: / May Eros then reign who engendered it all!" (8476–9). Shortly before he completed the "Classical Walpurgis Night," Goethe had read a scientific treatise about phosphorescence in the waters of the North Sea caused by microscopic organisms when the surface became agitated. Here he superimposes this natural phenomenon on a symbolic event in which fire and water are united, which thus signifies literally an elemental, cosmic sexual climax, through which Homunculus achieves the fulfillment of his quest for life through the procreative power of Eros. This event of sacrifice and conception, death and rebirth, constitutes the high point and the conclusion of the "Classical Walpurgis Night."

The Helena Act (lines 8488–10038)

The conjuring of Helen of Troy by Mephistopheles to serve as a concubine for Faust was a traditional part of the Faust legend, which Goethe emphasized was part of the earliest plan for his drama. The first part of the *Helena* (as Goethe referred to Act III) was drafted in 1800, corresponding roughly to lines 8488–802. Concerning Goethe's difficulties in composing the episode at that time, see the exchange of letters with Schiller of September 1800 (below). In the surviving manuscript of this draft, the title is *Helena in the Middle Ages. A Satyr Play*. The prose sketch of Part Two dictated by Goethe in 1816 (see below) indicates the general function of the episode for the drama as envisioned at that time. The final text of Act III (written in 1825–26) was published independently in Goethe's final collected works, in 1827, with the title *Helena, Classical-Romantic Phantasmagoria, an Interlude to Faust*. The draft of Goethe's announcement for this publication is reprinted below. Unusual demands are made on the reader by the *Helena*, and the work has baffled many critics. As an interlude following the "Classical Walpurgis Night," this act assumes the same structural position in Part Two as the "Walpurgis Night's Dream," which follows the "Walpurgis Night" and is subtitled "Intermezzo," does in Part One. It is also important to bear in mind that Faust descended into the underworld with Manto during the "Classical Walpurgis Night" (after line 7494), and there he was to plead before Persephone, queen of the dead, for the release of Helena. Goethe planned to compose this scene in the underworld as a prelude to Act III and subsequently abandoned the plan only after the "Classical Walpurgis Night" was completed in 1830. The reader must assume at the outset of the *Helena* that Faust has been granted his request. Mephistopheles appears in Act III only in the guise of Phorcyas, which he assumed in the "Classical Walpurgis Night" (see lines 7951–8033). It becomes apparent, especially from the final stage direction to Act III (after line 10038), that Phorcyas-Mephisto functions as a kind of demonic stage manager for the entire interlude. Though he does not himself bring Helena to Faust, he is responsible for everything that happens after she arrives, especially for the setting and the transformations of scene: from the palace of Menelaus at Sparta, to the inner courtyard of a castle, to the pastoral grove in Arcadia. We are also to imagine (presumably) that all the characters who appear in the act are spirits: the Chorus accompanies Helena from Hades, and the attendants of Faust's castle (as also the dwarfs who appear after line 8937) are provided by Mephistopheles. (Possibly an exception to this is Lynceus.) The entire sequence of the *Helena* thus assumes the status of a theatrical show, a phantasmagoria of the poetic imagination, which not only serves to deceive Helena into believing she is really alive (as it does initially) but also establishes the only possible medium—a literary, poetic, artistic, and theatrical medium—within which it is possible for Faust to be united with Helena. The complexity and the power of Goethe's *Helena* derive from the thematic implications it assumes for the broader context of *Faust* as a whole. Helena embodies the ideal of classical beauty just as Faust represents the Germanic or Romantic spirit of infinite striving, and the offspring of their union, Euphorion, who was described by Goethe as the spirit of poetry, may be called the Byronic spirit of "modern" poetry. The historical scope and structure of the *Helena*, as Goethe emphasized (see his letter to Boisserée of October 22, 1826, below), extends across three thousand years of the Western cultural tradition, from the fall of Troy, at the time when the supposed historical Helen lived, to the battle of Missolonghi in 1824, when Byron died of fever (see note to lines 9907–38). The *Helena* must thus be understood as a mythical-poetic recapituation or re-creation of that cultural history, a theatrical event in symbolic terms: the marriage of Faust and Helena to produce the self-consuming spirit of modern poetry as the synthesis of the ancient and the medieval, the union of classicism and Romanticism.

Also important and difficult to follow through the *Helena* is the developing thematic self-awareness of this phantasmagoria as a mythical reality. The advance of dramatic action is more than a recapitulation of cultural history; a corresponding development of reflective understanding accompanies this action as a perspective or implied response imposed upon characters and audience alike. At the outset, for instance, Helena assumes that she really exists, as if she were arriving home from Troy to Sparta in historical truth. Only gradually, above all through the dialogue exchanged with Phorcyas-Mephisto, does she become aware that she is only a spirit from the underworld, an ideal (however powerful her role as ideal), an *Idol* (line 8879; here translated as "myth"). Faust experiences less difficulty in accommodating himself to Helena in the central section of the act; yet it is clear from the example of courtly devotion set for him toward his lady and queen by Lynceus (in his two songs, lines 9218–45 and 9273–332) that Faust, too, must learn the language of love in terms appropriate to the role imposed on him by literary tradition. He thus courts Helena and wins her by teaching her to rhyme (lines 9372–84). Euphorion alone seems incapable of understanding himself in terms of the literary-cultural tradition through which he has come into being; though such lack of reflectivity seems appropriate to the idyllic and operatic medium of his performance, as it also indicates the cause of his tragic fall. The offspring of this poetic union between classical beauty and Romantic love destroys itself because it cannot comprehend and understand what it is. Equally important for the success of the *Helena* is the implied response imposed upon the audience by this performance. This is indicated, for instance, by the role of Phorcyas-Mephisto as stage manager or master of ceremonies. His presence in the *Helena* provides a constant reminder—or it should do so—that the entire sequence is no more than a poetic or theatrical event, a phantasmagoria upon a stage, constructed and directed by the devil and populated with spirits. Our task as audience is to maintain a conscious awareness that this vast panoramic spectacle is no more than that. We submit to the illusions of this theater only at the peril of our understanding. What it means for us as it unfolds and advances is essentially the same, so Goethe implies, as the meaning of our cultural tradition itself, insofar as it is accessible to us through the experience of art. Such experience above all is what the *Helena* is intended to convey, and our response will determine the success of our understanding in regard to what happens to Faust. The result for him, as always, in this greatest instance of striving for the moment of ideal fulfillment, is error and failure. The meaning of all this for us, who only observe it as audience, need not constitute perhaps a corresponding error and failure. That question is left open, however, by the silence of Mephistopheles at the end (after line 10038), when he removes his mask and costume as if "to provide in an epilogue such comment on the play as might be necessary."

"Before the Palace of Menelaos at Sparta" (lines 8488–9126)

Goethe's imitation of Greek tragedy in the first section of the *Helena* commands respect as a tour de force of poetic form. Totally alien conventions and structures of drama are achieved with sufficient authority to deceive even the spirit heroine and her Chorus into believing, at least for a time, they have truly returned to ancient Sparta. The basic structure of the sequence corresponds closely to conventions of Euripidean drama familiar to Goethe from the original sources. A number of purposeful variations are also imposed on this structure, however, which provide an eminently Goethean (or is it Mephistophelean?) sense of artifice, to the point where even the characters on the stage recognize they are participants in an elaborate deception. The basic principle Goethe follows is an alternation between units of dialogue in spoken verse (iambic trimeter) and formal lyrical odes sung by the Chorus. The long opening speech by Helena (lines 8488–809) corresponds closely to conventions of the *Prologos* in Euripides, in which the main character presents herself and establishes a sense of the dramatic situation. Helena's speech is indeed very long and rhetorically elaborate, including the formal celebration of the house to which she returns (lines 8502 ff.) and a direct quotation of the speech of instructions that Menelaus supposedly spoke to her (lines 8541–59 and 8568–78). Goethe interrupts her prologue several times, presumably to avoid monotony, by having the Chorus speak separate stanzas in metrical responsion (lines 8516–23 correspond to lines 8560–7 as strophe and antistrophe, lines 8591–603 are a variation on that unit as epode). It is contrary to the conventions of Attic drama, of course, for the Chorus to enter the theater with the actor who speaks the prologue. The Chorus does not notice this, but presumably Goethe intends to indicate that they have arrived here with Helena, as spirits released from the underworld, in a manner that is alien to the conventions of their role. What follows is a sequence of three formal odes (lines 8610–37, 8697–753, 8882–908) interspersed with three episodes, as follows: Panthalis, the Chorus leader, with Helena when she returns in haste from the palace to report on her meeting inside with Phorcyas; Phorcyas and Helena in a formal agon (or dramatic conflict), in which one half of the Chorus also participates as separate Choretids in stychomythia; all the characters, finally, in an elaborate exchange, which leads to a breakdown in the form of the drama itself. Everything in this sequence pertains to the confrontation of the Grecian spirits with the devil in his disguise, involving both an elaborate exposé of their insubstantiality (which causes Helena to collapse in a faint, line 8881) and a complex manipulation of emotion by Phorcyas, which gradually persuades the Chorus and even Helena to submit to his power (lines 9071 ff.). All three choral odes are concerned with the identity of the Chorus in relation to their situation in the drama, both as regards their journey from the underworld (which they confuse in the second ode with the burning of Troy) and the threat of evil that they sense in Phorcyas. The formal agon of the second episode involves both a sequence of mythological invective between the Chorus and Phorcyas (where Mephistopheles is clearly in his element) and a formal review of the traditional legends of Helena in a double stychomythia between Phorcyas and the heroine (lines 8848–81), resulting in her final recognition that she is only a "myth." In the final, extended episode, Phorcyas, who himself introduces the archaic verse form of trochaic tetrameter (lines 8909–29), which is associated with heightened emotion, purposefully imposes a panic upon both Helena and the Chorus when he insists that they are to be the victims of the supposed sacrifice planned by Menelaus. He calls out a gang of lesser devils disguised as muffled dwarfs (see stage direction after line 8936), and he stages sound effects of trumpets in the distance, leading the Chorus to believe the army of Menelaus is approaching (stage direction after line 9062).

Along with all this, Phorcyas-Mephisto also begins the elaborate transformation of the classical medium into the medieval German world through the lengthy description he provides of the castle of Faust and his attendants (lines 8984–9049). Clearly, both the Chorus and Helena are intrigued by more than the prospect of rescue; the exotic picture painted by Mephistopheles of Gothic splendor with more than a hint of erotic attraction, both in Faust as lord of the house (lines 9006 ff.) and in his youthful attendants, who offer new dances to the Chorus (lines 9044 ff.), gradually captivates even Helena. Goethe introduces to this final episode two dramatic devices in particular that are totally alien to the technique of Greek tragedy: first, the Chorus, speaking apparently in unison, interrupts the dialogue several times out of sheer emotional intensity (see lines 8925 and 8927, 8973, 9029, 9044, and 9050–51; these lines are quite distinct from the units of trochaic tetrameter assigned to the Chorus: 8957–61, 8966–70, 9122–6, and also with Phorcyas: 9063–70); second, the moment of crisis and reversal upon which the entire sequence hinges, the moment of decision for Helena is indicated by a stage direction of one word: "Pause" (after line 9070). The dynamics of development and dramatic interaction in Goethe's Greek tragedy are thus anything but Greek in origin, reflecting strategies and devices eminently suited to Mephistopheles in his role as attendant and surreptitious manager-director of the entire show. Also note, finally, that the spectacular set change that seems to involve a dislocation in space from Sparta to the medieval fortress northward in the Peloponnesus is in fact an elaborate theatrical deception caused by the mists and smoke that Phorcyas-Mephisto conjures forth (see stage direction after line 9087, followed by a detailed descriptive response of the Chorus, lines 9088–126). And when the smoke clears to reveal the courtyard of the Gothic fortress, Phorcyas-Mephisto has disappeared, surrendering the stage to Faust.

"Inner Courtyard of a Castle" (lines 9127–573)

The central section of the *Helena* constitutes Goethe's poetic tribute to the Germanic Middle Ages. Faust appears to Helena within the walls of a Gothic fortress, dressed in the ceremonial attire of a medieval knight, not as the historical Faustus of the sixteenth century but as the representative of what Goethe, along with other historians of literature at that time, called the Romantic age, the era of Christian knighthood and Gothic art, the era of courtly love, *Minnesang* (the medieval German love lyric), and chivalric romances. In thus associating the hero of his drama with the cultural milieu of the Middle Ages, Goethe implicitly acknowledges the affinity of his *Faust* to the enthusiasm for Germanic antiquities that had emerged during the era of the Napoleonic wars, particularly among such Romantic critics as the brothers Schlegel, in the form of a militant nationalism. The history of Goethe's reluctant and rather skeptical response to this movement is complex and often ambivalent. At the instigation of his friend Boisserée, for instance, he had been persuaded to lend his name in support of the proposal to complete construction of the famous Cologne Cathedral, and he became a genuine admirer of the collection of medieval German and Flemish paintings that Boisserée had assembled in the Rhineland. At the same time, however, he maintained his commitment to the norms of classical art, even though he tempered his earlier defense of these norms (particularly in the program for the visual arts that he developed around 1800 with a group of friends at Weimar, which became known as "the Weimar friends of art") with an implicit historical relativism, which acknowledged the style and technique of Christian medieval art as appropriate for the culture of that era. Goethe resisted, however, often in open opposition to the temper of his time, all aspects of cultural nationalism. The central section of his *Helena* provides eloquent demonstration of this cosmopolitan relativism, whereby the era of German medieval art is located in a developmental sequence between classical antiquity and the modern period. Faust may represent this middle age, by virtue of the popular legend of the sixteenth-century conjurer and the reputation that Goethe's own *Faust*, Part One, had quickly achieved among the Romantic nationalists in Germany as the greatest German poem, but the meeting of Faust with Helena, where classical beauty is wooed and won by the medieval Romantic spirit, results in a radical transformation of both parents in their impetuous and ultimately tragic offspring, Euphorion, the spirit of modern poetry.

Particularly interesting are the various forms of imitation and allusion that Goethe provides in his theatrical re-creation of medieval art and poetry. The courtyard of the castle clearly suggests aspects of Gothic architecture, especially as described to the Chorus and Helena by Phorcyas-Mephisto (see lines 9017–30), decorated with colorful heraldic emblems, shields, and banners. The procession of youths that accompanies Faust when he first enters (described by the Chorus, lines 9148–81) provides a sense of high ceremony, which Faust's appearance and behavior also sustain. The elaborate throne with its carpets and canopy, constructed on the stage by the pages and squires, also establishes an appropriate setting for Helena as the judge and ruler (line 9214), lady and queen, of this court of love. Indeed, it is only with Helena's arrival that the civilizing and transforming power of chivalric love is established in this court, in accord with the highest ethical ideals of medieval poetry and art. Such transformation is apparent both in the songs of celebration offered to her by the watchman Lynceus (lines 9218–45 and 9273–332) and in the mercy Helena displays in response to his praise, freeing him of all fault despite Faust's initial condemnation for failing to announce her arrival (lines 9192–212). The songs of Lynceus, it has been claimed, imitate the style and form of the so-called *Minnesang*, especially the poems of Heinrich von Morungen (d. 1222) that had been included in Ludwig Tieck's anthology *Love Songs from the Swabian Epoch* (1803). Helena's beauty is compared by the watchman to the light of the rising sun, which surprised him in approaching from the south and blinded him (recalling a corresponding effect of the rising sun on Faust himself in "Charming Landscape" at the beginning of Part Two). In the second song by Lynceus, which surveys the triumphant military conquests of the Germanic tribes, Helena is offered the booty of war as tribute to her beauty and her power as the lady of this court. The treasure chest (which must come from Mephistopheles, as did the chests with which Gretchen was tempted in Part One) contains jewels that enhance Helena's natural beauty: emeralds (line 9307), pearls (line 9310), and rubies (line 9311), associated with her breasts, her ears and lips, and her cheeks. Through such poetic service to the lady, the military attributes of Faust's Germanic fortress—"wisdom, opulence, and power" (line 9323)—are made subservient to classical beauty. Property is denied, concern for the self is denied, in the complete submission of "I" and "mine" to "thou" and "thine" (lines 9325 ff.).

The high point of Goethe's thematic application of medieval poetics to the meeting between Faust and Helena occurs through the introduction of rhyme (lines 9372–84). She is attracted by the pleasant sound of Lynceus's songs, the accommodation of one word to another, like a caress in the ear of the hearer. Faust then asserts that rhyme is also accompanied by a correspondence of sense, where separate elements of language and meaning are brought into harmonious interaction. This model of romantic medieval poetry defines the nature of the love that Faust offers Helena, and by learning to rhyme in exchange with him, she also learns to love him. Indeed, the sequence of couplets following a brief choral ode (lines 9411–8) achieves the consummation of their love as a poetic climax. Rhyming is doubled in each couplet, as the lovers seek to express the full meaning of their union. For Helena, the spirit from the underworld, a sense of reality is achieved within the present moment; whereas for Faust language fails, and time and space dissolve into a dream. In their second couplets, each of the lovers expresses an appropriate sense of paradox: Helena, the classical beauty in the Romantic domain, feels "bereft" of life and yet renewed, and Faust, seeming to fulfill the conditions of his wager with Mephistopheles, asserts a complete satisfaction with the present moment (*Augenblick* in the German). It is thus a supreme irony that Mephistopheles immediately intervenes, appearing for the first time in Faust's Gothic fortress, to disrupt the poetic union of the lovers through an intentional parody of their rhyming. This interruption indicates how fragile and insubstantial this moment of synthesis actually is, constituting for Faust no more than a vision, a dream, a poetic fiction within the phantasmagoric medium of a theatrical show.

Faust's Survey of Pastoral (lines 9506–73)

Goethe here indicates the significance of the final transformation of scene in the *Helena*. Faust's speech provides a complex résumé of the European pastoral tradition, looking especially to Virgil's use of Arcadia as idealized landscape in his *Eclogues*. Arcadia is spoken of as the "last redoubt" (line 9513) of Europe, connected by a "branch" of mountains across the isthmus to mainland Greece, an "un-island," and also as the center of the Peloponnesus itself, the middle that will be surrounded, like the fortress of warriors mentioned by the Chorus (line 9505), by the protection of Faust's Germanic chieftains, sheltering the pastoral retreat within. To this is added the emphasis of association with Helena's own birthplace; Sparta and Arcadia are confused by the connecting link of the Eurotas (line 9518), the river that flows south from Arcadia to Sparta, where Leda was confronted by Zeus in his guise as swan—a reference that recalls both the earlier visions of the encounter by Faust (see lines 6903–20 and 7277–94). Faust thus asserts that the landscape of their retreat is also the place of Helena's birth, the origin of her primal and ideal beauty, where she broke out of her egg (line 9519)—a mythical analogue to the emergence of Aphrodite from the sea—to the wonderment of the nymphs of Eurotas's reeds (see lines 7263–70) and her mother and sister, Leda and Clytemnestra. In effect, Faust is proposing that he retreat with Helena into the center and the origin of her own native place, where she shall truly reign as a spirit of place (genius loci), reaffirming the authenticity of her ideal beauty within the primal, pastoral, ideal landscape. The intricacy and precision of this accommodation of a European poetic tradition to the particular thematic situation of Goethe's drama is astonishing and entirely unique.

The central section of the poem (lines 9526–61), almost formulaic in quality, provides a measured survey of the various aspects of landscape that nearly became clichés within the post-Virgilian pastoral tradition. What should be noted here above all is the exercise in abstraction that Goethe has employed, removing these various elements of landscape from their context in the dialogue and action of Virgil's *Eclogues*, where landscape is always part of the background, never depicted as significant in itself alone, since the pastoral mode depends always on a sophisticated sense of situation, involving human relationships between the various idealized shepherd figures. It seems an eminently Romantic shift of emphasis, which Goethe certainly introduced by intention, to represent the landscape itself as the embodiment of the ideal, quite without explicit reference to the human habitation it provides. The landscape is also populated with its appropriate nature spirits—Pan, the goat-god who traditionally dwells as lord within the woods and groves of the pastoral landscape, and his nymphs (lines 9538 ff.), who are presumably no different from those mentioned in connection with the Eurotas (and who will later be joined by the Chorus, when they are all transformed into natural spirits at the very end of the *Helena*; see lines 9992 ff.). Also striking, and without parallel in classical pastoral, is the stanza describing the tall trees, the "hoar forests," of oak and maple (lines 9542 ff.). Emphasis is placed especially on the vertical thrust of their growth, as an urge to reach "higher regions" and an interlacing of their branches as they arch toward the sky. The distinction between oak and maple also seems to assume symbolic implications with reference to this vertical desire: the one "looms defiant," while the other "rises in purity," glutted with its sweet sap. One is tempted to interpret this peculiar element of Goethe's pastoral with reference to Faustian desire, perhaps in specific association with the Gothic forms of his native German tradition, especially in the use of the columns and arches that so strikingly imitate the rising trunks and branches of a forest, striving to reach the divine—a view of Gothic architecture that Goethe had come to share with his friend Boisserée. The final important focus in this central section of the poem is the child, an element of the pastoral that may derive from Virgil's famous fourth eclogue, where the expectation of the child's birth brings also the promise that the golden age will be reestablished. "The enchanting child" (line 9554) must be Euphorion, whether or not Faust himself here alludes to the as yet unborn offspring of his union with Helena. In accord with the semblance of immortality within the Arcadian realm (lines 9550 ff. and 9556–7), he will seem to be divine, in fact resembling Apollo (lines 9558–9), god of music and poetry, as Apollo had also once joined the shepherds (an allusion to his year's service to King Admetus as shepherd), an indication of the perfect coherence and totality of the pastoral realm. The central part of the poem thus concludes by affirming an ideal of unity that would unite mortal and divine in the expected offspring of this marriage. That such union also has significance for a concept of poetry is suggested by the office of Apollo himself.

A problematic aspect of this poetic recital by Faust is the nature of his authority and the validity of what he says. Goethe makes no concessions to dramatic plausibility, since Faust himself can have no direct experience of what he describes. Yet he speaks with the confidence that the pastoral tradition in poetry itself provides. This confidence also extends to a sense of setting that the poem establishes for the drama, whereby the ideal of harmony and communion that Faust associates with Arcadia in terms of his love for Helena becomes perfectly fused with the reality of place. In a sense, the language of the poem creates the place, as perhaps has always been true of pastoral poetry. It represents a landscape of the mind, projected upon an imagined remoteness—Sicily for Theocritus, Arcadia for Virgil—that is primal, even original: the Golden World before time began, as Hesiod (Works and Days 109) and Ovid (Metamorphoses 1.89) call it and Goethe here alludes to it (line 9565); yet this is also timeless, even out of time, in an eternal spring, where past and future have no meaning. In this sense, Helena, as a spirit returned from the underworld and as the embodiment of the ideal of beauty, belongs to Arcadia as the appropriate landscape for that spirit and that ideal. Goethe also alludes to the myth of Helena's marriage with Achilles after death, when they were located—in a manner analogous to Faust and Helena here—upon "blessed ground" (auf sel'gem Grund, line 9570; here "smiling harbors"), where their offspring Euphorion was born.

Arcadia, the ideal pastoral landscape, which constitutes the setting for the conclusion of the Helena act, is created by and through Faust's poetic depiction of it. The mechanical change of scene, which appears to happen instantaneously and automatically at the end of the poem (see the stage direction before line 9574), is merely a visual acknowledgment within the theater of what has already been achieved in poetry for the loving pair. Faust also knows that this is so, in a manner quite appropriate to the self-conscious, self-reflective aspect of the pastoral tradition, and he expresses this awareness emphatically in a manner the reader should not ignore. The last stanza also applies this sense of poetic fulfillment to Helena in terms of her journey from Hades, fully in accord with the myth of her marriage upon the blessed isle: "tempted to dwell upon blessed ground, you fled into the happiest destiny!" (9570 f.; in Arndt's translation, "For refuge lured to smiling harbors, / You fled to fortune's blithest kiss!"). And at the very end, commanding the change of scene and the establishment of its appropriate condition, with the authority of Adam giving names to paradise, Faust asserts his absolute expectation that "our bliss" shall be "Arcadian-free" (line 9573).

Phorcyas's Fairytale about Euphorion (lines 9596–628)

Euphorion, whose name Goethe borrowed from the legend of Helena's posthumous marriage to Achilles (see also lines 7435 and 8876), was born (according to the legend) with wings. His name derived from the fertility of the land. Jupiter fell in love with him, and since he could not possess him he destroyed him with a thunderbolt on the island of Melos, as Euphorion was fleeing from him. As we know from a conversation with Eckermann (December 20, 1829; see below), Goethe intended Euphorion to personify the spirit of poetry; such is also indicated by the Chorus when they address him as "poesy pure" (*Heilige Poesie*, line 9863). Phorcyas's tale, however, chiefly owing to its ironic tone, resists such allegorical reduction. What emerges instead, somewhat in the manner of a fairy tale, is a sense of who Euphorion is from what he does. He is born with "a peal of laughter" (line 9598) and immediately tumbles and springs about, as if full-blown, in spontaneous and exuberant manner: "tender frolic, fond caresses, / Teasing love's inane endearments, playful shouts and gay exulting" (lines 9600–1). Phorcyas-Mephisto calls him a naked genius without wings (though he suddenly claims to have wings just before his final, fatal leap; see lines 9897–8), a faun without any bestial qualities. His jumps and leaps indicate both a boundless desire, which manifests itself in upward motion, and a power derived from the Earth, which Faust associates with the mythological figure of Antaeus (line 9611), the son of Earth, whose strength never diminished so long as he touched his parent. Both Helena and Faust, who are quoted by Phorcyas-Mephisto (lines 9607–11), emphasize the peril as well as the strength of this quality. We may surmise that, unlike pure spirits, Euphorion may not achieve free flight—so Helena warns him—but like creatures of nature (which grow out of the Earth) he enjoys resilience and strength—so Faust assures him. In this regard, the child appears to exhibit a mixture of attributes derived from his parents, who contrast so radically with each other. Goethe's conception of Euphorion as a naked genius without wings suggests an intentional variation on an iconographical source. It seems likely that he had in mind a painting by Annibale Carracci (1560–1609)—one of the Italian Baroque painters whom Goethe often mentioned, alongside Raphael, as a master of the medium—entitled *The Genius of Fame* (*Der Genius des Ruhms*, originally *L'onore*), which since 1746 has been in the Johanneum in Dresden, in the same hall as Raphael's *Sistine Madonna*. The painting depicts the naked body of a youth with wings, soaring toward the heavens. Likelihood of such influence is increased by the climactic assertion of Euphorion just before his abortive attempt to fly that the path to fame (*Ruhm*) is opening before him (line 9876).

The Euphorion Opera *(lines 9679–938)*

The meaning of this operatic sequence depends in large measure upon the implicit musical form, which can be surmised at best from a careful analysis of the structure as potential song. Without some effort to reconstruct the music that the text demands, the entire sequence will appear superficial and banal. In order to appreciate what Goethe here attempted to achieve, some sense of his expectations for the Euphorion drama as opera must be provided. It is necessary to differentiate the formal units of statement that would have manifested themselves in discrete set pieces both as music and as ballet. This can be done only through careful attention to meter, since everything else in the language, including the substance of what is said and the voice that says it, is made to depend on this implicit musical form. The following meters can be distinguished: 1) trochaic, usually in a ballad stanza (as in the opening section), where it serves as a kind of neutral norm, presumably representing song without dance; 2) dactylic, usually in short two-stressed lines, which suggest a three-four waltz meter for both music and dance; 3) a short iambic line, which begins with three neutral syllables followed by a strong-stressed feminine ending (x x x x́ x), indicating a kind of folk-dance measure, perhaps the traditional *Ländler*; 4) a slow, four-stressed line with first- and second-stressed syllables juxtaposed (x́ x́ x x x́ x x́), which suggests a stately, martial tempo for heroic, military, ceremonial music; 5) some use of iambic four-stressed lines just before the fall of Euphorion, which suggests a kind of lyrical interlude before the dramatic climax; and 6) a double stanza in trochaic meter—eight lines, four-stressed, alternating rhyme—for the choral dirge at the very end. Everything in this operatic sequence is made subordinate to the actions of Euphorion as the central heroic figure. Both Helena and Faust, along with the Chorus, are reduced to roles in response, observing, reacting, and following the lead of Euphorion. The role of Euphorion is essentially divided into two parts, the first predominantly erotic (proceeding from a solo of pure self-expression through an exchange with the Chorus to an aggressive chase sequence involving motifs of seduction, rape, violence, and destruction) and the second predominantly militant (where the triumphant heroic stance of the martial meter is offset by the tragic leap and fall at the end).

All this may be regarded as an elaborate allegory for the workings of the spirit of poetry; yet Goethe seems to have more than that in mind thematically, especially insofar as there may be an ironic, even a parodistic relationship implied between Euphorion and his father. His flamboyant operatic and balletic tragedy is a kind of *Faust* in miniature, involving the same fundamental forces of will and impulse, of Faustian striving, and the same inevitable error and failure, in accord with the universal principle of human action expressed by the Lord in the "Prologue in Heaven" (line 317). The progression of concern from love to war, including acts of violence in both instances, also seems to reflect Faust's own progress from his love affairs with Gretchen and (now) Helena toward his involvement in the affairs of the empire, leading in Act V to his attempt to establish a new society liberated by Mephistophelian technology. Faust's failure in each instance is no less categorical, even if less flamboyant and spectacular than Euphorion's fall. We certainly are meant to recognize this parallel, just as Faust himself appears to (as indicated by his conspicuous silence). There is hardly a line in the entire opera where Faust may be considered to speak or sing his own mind, and he is completely silent from Euphorion's death (his last words are with Helena and the Chorus, then with Helena, lines 9891–2, 9895–6, 9903–4) until his monologue at the outset of Act IV (lines 10039 ff.)

Byron and Euphorion (stage direction following line 9902)

The figure we are meant to recognize in the body of Euphorion is, of course, George Gordon, Lord Byron (1788–1824). Goethe made the identification unambiguously in his conversation with Eckermann of July 5, 1827 (see below). What does the association here imply? The authenticity of Byron's genius was beyond question for Goethe; the younger English man represented, indeed embodied, the spirit of poetry that he identified with the modern, postrevolutionary era, the period we now call Romanticism. Goethe said of him (to Eckermann, July 5, 1827): "He was the greatest talent of the century, . . . neither ancient nor romantic but like the present day itself." Euphorion represents precisely the same spirit, especially within the structure of the Helena act as it surveys the entire tradition of Western literature. The death of Euphorion-Byron is the fall of modernism, if not the final collapse of the European poetic tradition. And this fall is inherent in the spirit that is destroyed, as Goethe often emphasized about Byron. His genius was magnificent but destructive, directly in opposition to the moral order of the society in which he lived and even in conflict with the spirit of his age. A magnificent description of the "daemonic" force that Goethe associated with Byron and intended to demonstrate in Euphorion is provided in the final pages of Goethe's autobiography, *Poetry and Truth*, Book 4, chapter 20 (written probably in 1831 and published only after the poet's death), which has often been quoted and deserves consideration here:

. . . the daemonic element appears in its most terrifying aspect when it manifests itself predominantly in a human being. During the course of my life I have been able to observe several such men, sometimes closely, sometimes from afar. They are not always the most admirable persons, not necessarily the most intelligent nor the most gifted, and rarely are they remarkable for their goodness of heart; but an extraordinary force goes out from them, and they have an incredible power over all creatures, yes, even over the elements; and who can say how far such an effect may not extend? All the moral forces banded together are powerless against them; in vain do the more enlightened among mankind strive to render them suspect either as deceivers or as deceived; they attract the masses, and they can only be vanquished by the universe itself with which they are in conflict. It is from observations of this nature that the strange and terrifying saying probably arose: *Nemo contra deum nisi deus ipse* ("No one contrary to God, unless God himself ").

Metamorphosis of the Chorus *(lines 9992–10038)*

The concluding choral song, where each of the four sections is taken by a separate group, departs from all sources and models, both classical and modern. Goethe establishes once again in *Faust* a mode of poetic discourse that is unique and yet perfectly suited to what he wishes to convey. The meter ostensibly is trochaic tetrameter, which offsets and balances the lengthy account by Phorcyas-Mephisto of Euphorion's birth at the outset of the Arcadian sequence. Here, as in the earlier speech, however, Goethe adapts and transforms the classical verse to fit the kind of experience he wishes to convey. These lines are saturated with bewildering activity. Active verbs in every conceivable grammatical form, especially as participial adjectives and substantives, fill almost every foot of each line in a seemingly endless rolling rhythm that rarely subsides at the end of the line. The effect is to dissolve all sense of separate verses into the illusion of continuous, uninterrupted movement. The closest analogue to this sequence would be the spirit song of the first study scene in Part One (lines 1447–505). Few parallels can be found anywhere in literature to the emotional, near-hypnotic effect of this choral sequence, where the ear itself can participate in the natural metamorphoses that are described. The dramatic intention of the poem, of course, is to conclude and resolve the visionary, mythical sequence of *Faust* that began with the "Classical Walpurgis Night" and has come to fill fully one fourth of the drama. The manner of resolution, totally without the participation of the central characters, finds an exact parallel in the withdrawal of the spirits at the end of the earlier phantasmagoric interlude, when the amateur theatricals of the "Walpurgis Night's Dream" blended into the rising dawn as Ariel led the troupe of spirits off to the hill of roses. Similarly, in the scene "Charming Landscape" at the outset of Part Two—a scene composed very soon after the Helena act was finished—the elfin chorus that sang the night song of renewal to Faust also retreats at Ariel's command in response to the emerging day. That retreat of spirits into the protection of the natural realm provides a thematic clarification of the effect intended here. Spirits from the underworld who have assumed the guise of a Greek chorus willingly abandon themselves to a process of ecstatic dissolution in which they blend into and become identical with the various activities of nature. Their voices in song begin to speak with the sounds of nature, thus providing yet a further instance of that mode of poetic language in *Faust* where the processes of nature are expressed directly in words. An implicit irony is also included here in that the seeming loss of personality by the Chorus also achieves a degree of fusion between spirit and substance that offsets Faust's own failure to do the same with Helena in some kind of permanent form. Where his own phantasmagoria concluded by dissipating into mists and silence, the Chorus merge with nature so perfectly that the spirit of antiquity is renewed and fulfilled within the everyday realm of natural activity. The highest and ultimately impossible goal of human striving is thus juxtaposed with a triumphant alternative as familiar as the here and now of nature. Goethe also indicates the extent to which such irony is intended by having each part of the Chorus interpret in terms of classical myth the natural process in which they lose themselves. The radical dichotomy that earlier seemed apparent between the Chorus's response to the account of Euphorion's birth, where they interposed the ancient myth of Hermes (lines 9629–78), and the cult of feeling introduced by Phorcyas-Mephisto in response to the musical form of the Euphorion opera (lines 9679–94), is thus resolved here in the perfect blending of myth and nature and the representation of both in the language of the final choral ode.

Act IV (lines 10039–1042)

Act IV, written during the first half of 1831, was the very last section of the drama to be completed. It has rarely claimed the interest of readers, primarily because the action and events depicted seem only indirectly and incidentally related to Faust's career. It has often been assumed that Goethe was simply filling a gap in the plot, completing the action involving the Emperor, which had been established in Act I, and preparing for the more central action of Act V, where Faust's great land reclamation project is put into effect. Act IV is also the shortest in Part Two and easily gives the impression that it is no more than filler. Such a view is mistaken, however, as recent commentaries have begun to recognize.

One source of difficulty for a reader of Act IV is the abrupt and radical transition that here occurs in the drama after the rich, bold, and often fantastic symbolic and mythical excursions that have occurred during the preceding two acts of Part Two. The return to a sense of material reality in the high mountains of the Alps, as indicated by the initial stage direction, "Sheer, jagged pinnacles," necessarily brings a feeling of reduction and loss for the drama after the radical dislocations of the action in Acts II and III: to the mythical realm of Greece in the "Classical Walpurgis Night" and to the poetic-theatrical spaces of the Helena act. That feeling of abrupt contrast is intended, of course, as Faust's own response in his opening monologue makes clear. We also are shortly to return to the political sphere of the Emperor, which was left behind at the end of

Act I, though even here there is a radical shift of emphasis. Much that had transpired in the earlier scenes at court, above all in the Carnival Masque and in the staging of the spirit show of Paris and Helena, shifted the burden of dramatic action away from issues of politics and economics toward seemingly arbitrary and frivolous entertainments of theatrical show and the artifice or illusion appropriate to that medium. The drama was diverted almost from the outset of Part Two into the regions of art and imaginative performance in ways that also reflect at several levels the medium of drama and theater as such. Both Faust and Mephistopheles participate in forms of activity that make them simultaneously the creators or producers of theatrical shows and also actors participating centrally in the shows thus staged. All this has now been removed from the stage, dissipated like a dream vision after waking into the reality of a new day. In this regard, the opening monologue by Faust in Act IV resembles the monologue in "Charming Landscape" that introduces Part Two, when Faust awakens at dawn on a grassy meadow, following the catastrophe of Gretchen's execution at the end of Part One. The burden of reflective discourse in this later monologue, however, is the exact opposite of the earlier soliloquy, as the symbolism of clouds viewed from the summit of this high mountain peak (on which see below) replaces the vision of the rainbow created by the mist thrown up from the waterfall in the earlier scene. The differences between these two monologues are important for the radical shift of direction that the drama is now to pursue.

Yet one further fundamental shift in attitude and perspective should be noted here. Faust's striving to satisfy his desire has been directed, since his rejuvenation in the Witch's kitchen and his encounter with the magic mirror there, toward union with the Feminine as object of his desire, first in the seemingly arbitrary seduction of Gretchen and second in the quest for Helen of Troy. In the course of the drama both have been gained and lost, as Faust indicates in his response to the two cloud formations that he views and interprets in his monologue. The theme of love or erotic desire, however, which has manifested itself in Faust's responses to the Feminine with apparent negative results, now disappears categorically from the drama. Not until the very last scene of Act V, "Mountain Gorges," does the Feminine reenter the drama to reestablish the theme of erotic desire at a level beyond the limits of the hero's mortal existence. Despite the occasional presence of minor female characters, such as the allegorical figure of the sutler Grab-swag (*Eilebeute*) in the final scenes of Act IV and the aged figure of Baucis in the opening scenes of Act V, the realm of action for Faust after his return to Germany, his involvement in the politics and conflicts of the Empire, and his subsequent technological-industrial endeavors is curiously void of the Feminine and its effects. It may even be argued that the role of nature itself is now transformed, so that the productive and creative forces that emanate from the natural processes of life, as indicated even at the very outset of the drama by the hymn of the Archangels in "Prologue in Heaven" and by the rising of the sun on Easter morning at the end of "Night," accompanied by the return of spring to the land with its creative and redemptive powers, are now replaced by forces that emanate from strictly human motives, defined by reductive politics and warfare in Act IV and by Faust's land reclamation project in Act V. The action of the drama from here to the end may be described as unnatural—even antithetical to nature—in the fullest sense, where the processes of nature are systematically perverted and circumvented into forms of destruction, deception, and corruption of all human values.

It is, in short, a world in which the demonic powers of Mephistopheles quickly assume control in a manner that must be regarded as radically evil. Despite the motives and designs of Faust, it is the devil who provides the means and measures for action within this world. Readers of Goethe's drama should not be deceived by any sense of familiarity and trust that the roles played by Mephisto with such diversity and flair—indeed, with wit and occasional charm—may have achieved. There is a message in the final acts of Part Two concerning developments in the real world of politics and technology to which Faust returns that can be judged only in terms of Mephisto's strategies of deception, perversion, and demonic control. At a conscious level of allegorical significance, the world of the drama clearly depicts conditions that Goethe witnessed in Europe as they developed during the years following the upheavals of the French Revolution and the Napoleonic wars and that he regarded as pernicious and perverse. Acts IV and V offer the poet's ultimate legacy for the future, composed from the perspective of his wisdom during the last years of his life. Goethe looked forward to the development of modern Western industrial society, in terms that can be understood only in categorically negative terms. The events that take place in these final acts of the drama, in the world inhabited by Faust but controlled by Mephistopheles, are sinister indeed. Efforts by critics to extract positive lessons from all this or to define progressive policies for the future of humankind based on what happens here are not persuasive. In Acts IV and V, more than ever, a sense of *Faust* as a tragedy—indeed, as the tragedy of humankind in general—needs to be acknowledged.

Particularly ironic is the fact that in the history of reception for Goethe's *Faust* claims have often been made by radical ideologies and extremist political regimes that the figure of Faust should be regarded as a norm for human behavior, despite the fact that the drama in its final acts offers a powerful indictment against such claims. This is particularly true with regard to that which Oswald Spengler, in his comprehensive critique of Western civilization published after World War I, *The Decline of the West*, labeled "Faustian man." In retrospect, such norms, wherever they have been proclaimed in the real world, produce inhuman, tyrannical, and destructive behavior, such as was perpetrated against humanity by the Nazi regime in Germany after 1933. Similarly, claims made with reference to Faust by the East German Communist regime during the 1950s and later—above all, in speeches by Walter Ulbricht—now seem grotesquely askew, namely that the form of socialism achieved by that regime should be regarded as the fulfillment of Faust's utopian view of a future society consisting of "a free people in a free land" (*Auf freiem Grund mit freiem*

Volke stehn, 11580). In addition, in the mid-nineteenth century, interpretations of Goethe's *Faust* were offered in the United States arguing that the protagonist should be considered a model for the pioneers settling the American West. From a Marxist perspective, Faust has been regarded as a negative model for the high capitalism of the nineteenth century, or from another technological perspective, as a precursor, at least in Act V, of the kind of industrial development that has devastated the natural environment and threatens the future habitability of the planet. The point to bear in mind with regard to all such readings is that *Faust* and Faust —both the drama and the central character—lend themselves to a great variety of political and ideological interpretations, none of them explicit and perhaps none of them fully valid within Goethe's text; but the events of the drama suggest that whatever developments may occur in the world Faust leaves behind at his death, the future will be in the hands of the devil and his demonic forces, and the outcome will affirm Mephisto's role in the latter part of the drama as the agent of radical evil within the world. This is not in any way a positive or an optimistic point of view.

Faust's Opening Monologue and the Symbolism of Clouds *(lines 10039–66)*

The transition to a new stage in Faust's career comes about once again through a monologue. This follows the pattern established at the earliest stage of composition in "Night," subsequently developed further in "Forest and Cave," and carried to its most sophisticated and programmatic level in "Charming Landscape." But Faust has not appeared alone on stage since the very beginning of Part Two. In this monologue, spoken on a high rocky summit of the Alps, Faust takes final leave of Helena and juxtaposes and contrasts her form with that of Gretchen from Part One. The Feminine in its complex role as stimulus and as object of Faust's desire is identified symbolically with the cloud formations that Faust (and presumably the audience along with him) observes in the sky. From an outline sketch for Act IV (Paralipomena 179) we may be certain that these clouds are intended to signify the legacy of Helena and Gretchen for Faust. The cloud formations also retreat to the distance, in the one case toward the horizon and in the other upward toward the heavens, so that Faust in his reflective mode of thought is left in solitude as the Feminine departs from his life for good. The apotheosis of Gretchen will return in the very last scene of the drama, "Mountain Gorges," in the company of the Mater Gloriosa. But for now, this sense of departure is central to the events still to take place. This shift is also signaled by the role of Mephistopheles, who is shortly to arrive after playing a subordinate role in both the "Classical Walpurgis Night" and in the Helena act. (Also note that Goethe had already composed the final scene of the drama in early December, 1830, in close temporal proximity to the final scene of the "Classical Walpurgis Night" with the epiphany of Galatea.)

Goethe's use of cloud symbolism is quite precise, based on years of scientific study and careful observation. In purposeful correlation with the manifestation of mist and rainbow thrown up by the waterfall in "Charming Landscape," these cloud formations constitute a suspension of water as droplets in the air, the creative element of life made visible, as demonstrated in the concluding festival of the "Classical Walpurgis Night." Such suspension in air and ether also makes visually manifest the forms of beauty attributed to the Feminine from its first appearance in the magic mirror of the Witch's kitchen. These clouds thus symbolize the embodiment of this ideal as the highest norm of art and also the most exalted object of Faustian desire. To understand the implications of this symbolism, a reader should consult Goethe's essay "On Cloud Formations" (1817, "*Wolkengestalt, nach Howard*," Weimar edition, II, 12, 5–58; first published in Goethe's journal *Zur Naturwissenschaft überhaupt*, 1820). As Goethe openly acknowledged, he was indebted to the work of the English meteorologist Luke Howard, whose study "On the Modifications of Clouds" (1803) introduced the names still used to distinguish different forms of clouds: stratus, cumulus, cirrus, and nimbus. In a poem that Goethe composed in honor of Howard, "*Howards Ehrengedächtnis*," first published in both German and English in *Gold's London Magazine* (1821), these different cloud formations are described in brief poetic stanzas. The two that pertain to Faust's monologue, cumulus and cirrus, are described as follows:

Cumulus

Still soaring, as if some celestial call
Impell'd it to yon heaven's sublimest hall;
High as the clouds, in pomp and power arrayed,
Enshrined in strength, in majesty displayed;
All the soul's secret thoughts it seems to move,
Beneath it trembles, while it frowns above.

Cirrus

And higher, higher yet the vapours roll:
Triumph is the noblest impulse of the soul;
Then like a lamb whose silvery robes are shed,
The fleecy piles dissolv'd in dew-drops spread;
Or gently wafted to the realms of rest,
Finds a sweet welcome in the Father's breast.

In Faust's monologue, the cloud formation that carries him back to Germany from Greece, formed from the veil Helena left behind when she returned to the underworld, corresponds to the cumulus. After it deposits him on the rocky mountain summit, the cloud withdraws toward the eastern horizon, where it hovers far off in a shape that constitutes a sublime parody of the Feminine, resembling a huge supine female body—"Juno, Leda, Helena" (10050). This vision of "a godlike female form" (10049) provides one last glimpse of the object of desire that first appeared to Faust in the magic mirror of the Witch's kitchen and that here recalls to mind everything Helena has signified for the drama since Faust's quest for her began in Act I. As distant cloud formation, of course, it is both inaccessible and lifeless, like ice-capped mountains, "a distant arctic range" (10053), yet it still may serve as the visual embodiment of symbolic meaning, reflecting as in a mirror the "deep sense of fleeting days" (10054). Insofar as this vision is a kind of reflection (*Wiederspiegelung*), it stands in precise analogy to the rainbow invoked by Faust at the end of his monologue in "Charming Landscape": "This mirrors all aspiring human action" (4725). Both these naturalistic symbolic forms—cloud formation and rainbow—stand in complex relation to everything that art has come to signify in Part Two of *Faust*. Both achieve a paradoxical sense of permanence—like the moment (*Augenblick*) that is made to tarry—in the midst of temporal flux and transience, achieved only through the process of mirroring, in the manner of painted image in relation to the reality it represents. The contrast between these two symbols, however, stands as a measure for the path the drama has pursued. The rainbow is beautiful above all for its color, whereby the blinding light of the sun—symbolizing the overwhelming power of divinity, like the Earth Spirit conjured at the outset in "Night" —is refracted into the varying hues of life, which may be seen and comprehended: *Am farbigen Abglanz haben wir das Leben* (4727). The gigantic female form of the distant cloud, by contrast, resembles more the cold and lifeless shape of a statue, such as the representations of the gods of antiquity in marble, which had constituted for Goethe and many others in his time, following the aesthetic teachings of J. J. Winckelmann, the highest norm of classical beauty in art. Yet the shape remains no less remote and lifeless, despite the brief union in a spiritual marriage achieved between Faust and Helena in Act III. It signifies neither the unity of aesthetic experience nor the vivid immediacy of the living form itself, but the vision of the Feminine as distant cloud nonetheless reflects in blinding ways—as Faust's eloquent statement puts it—"deep sense of fleeting days" (*spiegelt blendend flüchtger Tage großen Sinn*, 10054).

The second cloud formation, the cirrus, is perhaps less clearly delineated in Faust's description during the remaining lines of the monologue. That this more ethereal and ascendent form symbolizes Gretchen would perhaps not be fully recognized by a reader without the explicit indication provided by Goethe's outline sketch for Act IV. Yet the language offers unique praise for the value of this "enchanting shape" to the speaker. It recalls the "long-lost, most cherished boon of earliest youth" (10059). Also of importance is the extent to which Faust's response to this alternative vision of cloud as Feminine anticipates the final redemption of his soul in the concluding scene of the drama. Readers should bear in mind that Goethe composed Act IV in the months just following the completion of that scene, "Mountain Gorges," in December, 1830. This image of the Feminine—which should not be identified literally with the character of Gretchen as she lived, loved, and died but rather with the ideal that she represented—may also be understood with reference to theories of beauty in "Romantic" art, specifically in Christian painting from the Middle Ages and the Renaissance, as they were developed during Goethe's own time and to which he also responded in his later writings on art. In contrast to the perfected form of classical sculpture, the figures in Romantic painting (as it was called), characteristically the figures of Christ and the Virgin Mary, were defined by an ineffable "beauty of the soul" (10064), an inwardness of spirit that shines through the visible figure like a transcendent and immortal essence from beyond the limitations of substance and shape. The suitable aesthetic response to such beauty is likewise a spiritual, intuitive empathy, as of soul to soul. Precisely such a response is indicated in Faust's final lines in the monologue, describing the effect this ascending cloud formation has upon him: "the lovely image is enhanced / And, undissolving, wafts aloft into the ether, / Drawing away with it the best my soul contains" (10064–6).

Faust's Dialogue with Mephistopheles in "High Mountains" (lines 10067–344)

In this scene, we are reminded that the relationship between Faust and the devil has been constituted from the outset through verbal exchange in witty, often ironic responses by Mephisto to Faust's wishes and assertions. We are also reminded, however, that such a dialogue between them has not occurred at all in Part Two, at least since their discussion about the Mothers in "Dark Gallery" of Act I. Nor will there be again such a sustained and intimate conversation between them during the remainder of the drama. For this reason, what is said here warrants careful attention. The arrival of Mephisto seems intentionally comic, as he rides like some demonic hitchhiker on the seven-league boots of fairy tale, which march through time and across the disparate media of the drama like a parody of progress. The scene of his dialogue with Faust emerges, however, as indicated by the reference to the Gospel of Matthew (ch. 4; after 10131), as a highly serious reworking by Goethe of the temptation of Christ by Satan in the wilderness, when he is shown all the kingdoms of the world in an attempt to corrupt his mission by the prospect of power and rule. Unlike Christ in his resistance, Faust responds to the devil's temptation with his last great request in the drama, even though the project he has in mind goes quite contrary to what Mephisto expects of him.

The polarity between fire and water also reenters the discussion, with Vulcanism opposed to Neptunism as competing models for geological creation, such as earlier encountered in the exchange between Anaxagoras and Thales in the "Classical Walpurgis Night." Mephisto describes in vivid detail how the surface of the Earth, including the high mountain ranges (such as the one they here stand on), was formed by the devils in hell after they had been banished from Heaven as fallen angels. In response to the eternal fires burning below, the devils—so Mephisto explains—began to cough, belch, and fart, and thus produced such a pressure of gas that it broke through the thick crust of the Earth to form the inversion of the surface from lowest to highest. Such a parody of the kind of mythical explosion—volcanic earthquake—that earlier brought the giant Seismos above ground suggests (as the final lines of the speech indicate) that

Goethe once again is using Mephisto to subject current scientific theory to ridicule, though the allusion to the Epistle to the Ephesians in the New Testament (6.12; after 10094) and the use of one of Goethe's later favorite oxymorons—"an open secret" (*ein offenbar Geheimnis*; 10093)—suggest that more is at stake here than merely slapstick parody of creation by demonic fire. Faust's own description of such creation (10095–104) is far more neutral and accurate as scientific analysis, suggesting that for once he perhaps speaks for the author. Mephisto does not relent, insisting upon the demonic aspect of these natural processes and indicating that "the artless common people" (10116) share the superstition that the devil was responsible for distinctive geological formations. Not only the names assigned to nature's distinctive monuments—"Devil's Rock," "Devil's Bridge," 10121—but also the phenomena themselves serve as signs (*Zeichen*, 10127) of his handiwork. Mephisto will shortly act upon such superstition when he intrudes with his magic in the Emperor's war.

The remainder of the conversation between Faust and Mephisto turns to the question of a new project for the ambitions of their shared career. The respective proposals appear to be in radical opposition: Mephisto assumes that they shall become involved in the life and affairs of the modern city, exploiting the excesses and the energies of urban development for Faust's profit and satisfaction (10136–76); Faust by contrast describes the ebb and flow of the tides along the coast of the realm, introducing his idea of taming the force of the ocean with dikes and dams in order to secure new space for the construction of his own urban realm (10181–233). The irony in this apparent opposition is the convergence of both proposals upon the technology and political power of the modern metropolis. Mephisto focuses on the corruption and decadence of the city as it already exists— Faust associates the activity he describes with Sardanapalus (10176), synonymous by reputation with all the excesses of such a world; Faust is challenged instead by the prospect of taming the forces of nature—pushing back the ocean and thus creating the space for the construction of a brave new world that will be the product of his will and over which he will have absolute power. We are here provided with the only explanation the drama offers for the great project of the final act in Part Two, where Faust becomes identified with the development of modern technology and the effort to tame the forces of nature and control the urban world, in which human beings dwell. Mephisto prefers the cities that have already come to be (one thinks of Paris or London in the context of the Industrial Revolution), whereas Faust wants to begin from nothing, imposing human culture on nature by defeating it through the power of his will (perhaps on the model of cities created from the wilderness in the new world of the Americas: New York or Washington). Note the military language in his demand: "There dares my spirit soar past all it knew; / Here I would struggle [*kämpfen*], this I would subdue" (*besiegen*, 10221). Readers will recall the role of water and its elemental evolutionary powers in the "Classical Walpurgis Night." What Faust proposes, even if it seems all too familiar to the world of modern urban technology and development, will involve a fundamentally unnatural act, imposing the demonic and volcanic forces that Mephisto provides against the creative processes of life that are symbolized by neptunic creation in the sea. Act V will demonstrate the outcome of this last Faustian project in terms that indicate where the poet stands in regard to this plan.

The remainder of this scene focuses on the Emperor, the chaotic conditions that have emerged in his realm, and the war of rebellion that has broken out against him. Mephisto surveys the developments that have occurred during the intervening time since Act I (how much time has passed while the drama moved out of time cannot even be estimated), resulting directly from the fiscal reform proposed by him and the introduction of paper money. A state of general anarchy and open rebellion, as described by Mephisto in vivid detail (10234–96), suggests that Goethe intends these developments in the political sphere of the drama to reflect on larger issues in the public conflicts of post-Napoleonic nineteenth-century Europe. The legitimacy of monarchic rule is called into question here, though the behavior of the general population in abusing the fraudulent medium of exchange is no less distinctive than the self-indulgence of the Emperor. Literary sources, above all the historical drama of Shakespeare (mentioned earlier with regard to the characterization of the Emperor in general), are also important for the dramatic technique of the scene. Of interest also is the use of music, presumably in the manner of an orchestra for grand opera, to accompany the action of the military campaign. The initial stage direction (before 10234) indicates that the music should be heard at first from behind the audience in the theater. Subsequently (stage direction before 10297), "drums and warlike music resounds from below." Such stage directions are also repeated at several junctures throughout the next scene, when the actual battle takes place. The challenge of staging this scene will also be apparent, since the opening location at the top of a high mountain summit is followed abruptly by the indication that Faust and Mephisto climb down to the middle space of the mountain range to observe the armies drawn up for battle (after 10296). This shift suggests that Goethe intended no semblance of realistic stage setting, perhaps in anticipation of panoramic techniques in the modern theater, developed only in the twentieth century. Also note that the plan put forward by Mephisto that they intercede in support of the Emperor, so that Faust can perform the role of Generalissimo (10310; we recall the figure ridiculed in the battle of the Pygmies and the Cranes during the "Classical Walpurgis Night," 7644–53), is immediately recognized by Faust to involve fraud and deception through magic tricks and illusion ("It's fraud! Vain magic, sleight of hand!," 10300). Mephisto, by contrast, acknowledges that he plans to release the primal powers of the mountains themselves: "From primal mountains, primal human force" (*Aus Urgebirgs Urmenschenkraft*, 10317).

These primal powers are embodied in the three allegorical figures who suddenly appear at the very end of the scene, called the "Mighty Men" (*Gewaltigen*; borrowed from the Second Book of Samuel, 23.8). They remain as the agents of Mephisto's demonic will through to the completion of the urban development in Act V. Their names—Pugnacious, Rapacious, and Tenacious—assigned by age and attitude and including contrasting costumes (10331–44), also associate them with the mythological figures from the "Classical Walpurgis Night" who were involved with the digging out and hoarding of natural wealth from below ground: the Griffins, the giant Ants, the Arimaspians (7093–111). Each of the three describes himself in brief statements that emphasize the sequential and coordinated relation of their modes of violence: Pugnacious, the youth, is concerned with grabbing (*Fassen*, 10334); Rapacious, a mature warrior, is defined by taking (*Nehmen*, 10337); and Tenacious, an old warrior, completes the process by holding and hoarding (*Behalten*, 10342). The extent to which warfare by magical deception and brute violence in Act IV recapitulates the more symbolic action presented in conjunction with the earthquake of Seismos in Act II deserves to be further explored. In this case, by contrast with the "Classical Walpurgis Night," it is the power of the devil to work his magic that holds sway. Faust's strategy of intervention in the affairs of state through the demonic tricks of Mephistopheles does not suggest that the rescue operation for the Emperor will have any more legitimacy than the economic plan for paper money introduced by Mephisto in Act I.

Winning the Emperor's War: "In the Foothills" (lines 10345–782)

Readers are likely to become impatient with this scene, unless they happen to be devoted to accounts of battles and military campaigns. Why should Goethe include such an extended and detailed account of this engagement by the Emperor's forces with his opponents? More is clearly at stake than the action in itself as part of the plot for Faust's involvement with affairs of state. There seems to be an excessive pride in presenting the details of an imagined battle. This fact has led some commentators to suggest that Goethe is responding to accounts of actual battles from the history of warfare in Europe, extending from the late Middle Ages through the era of Frederick the Great in Prussia to the wars of the French Revolution and the campaigns of Napoleon. Goethe had himself participated in the military campaign against France in 1792 and in the Siege of Mainz in the following year, detailed accounts of which he had published as part of his autobiography in 1822. He also lived in Weimar at the time of the crucial defeat of Prussia at the hand of Napoleon in the Battle of Jena-Auerstadt in October, 1806. Much closer to hand and possibly the immediate occasion for the strategy of battle in Act IV was the July, 1830, revolution in Paris, to which Goethe responded as negatively as he had done to the French Revolution forty years earlier. All these experiences of war and political upheaval contributed to the complex and unexpected direction taken by this scene of conflict and reversal when Goethe composed it during the early summer of 1831. Thematically, this battle scene may also be connected to several earlier episodes in the drama that include a sense of warfare and public conflict, such as the battle of the Pygmies and the Cranes in the "Classical Walpurgis Night" and the imagined or fictional warfare that seemingly threatens to intrude at several points during the Helena act. Even the disguise of the Emperor as Pan in the Carnival Masque, along with the several mythological groups that accompany him, should be considered with regard to the Emperor's role in this scene. The presence of these groups—the Fauns, the Satyrs, the Gnomes, and the Giants, all of whom make up "the savage host" (*das wilde Heer*, 8001)— evokes the behavior of troops in warfare. The war of the Emperor in Act IV is, of course, the direct consequence of the inflation resulting from the introduction of paper money by Mephisto, so that the intrusion of Faust and Mephisto into this military campaign may be regarded as a further stage in their involvement with the affairs of the realm. The motive for their intrusion, furthermore, as made clear during the conversation between Faust and Mephisto in the preceding scene, is to secure for Faust as reward for victory the use of the tidal lands along the shore, where he plans to build his new city. All this happens indeed according to the plan.

The battle as staged in this scene includes a strong sense of theater, despite the difficulty that performing the scene would no doubt involve. The location of the entire episode, of course, is at a distance from the battle itself, in front of the Emperor's tent on a height of land, from which the field may be observed offstage, the action described and interpreted by those who appear and speak. This technique of observation and description is usually called "teichoscopia" (*Mauerschau* in German, from the Greek meaning "observation from a wall"), as in Homer's *Iliad* (Book 3), when the old men of Troy observe, describe, and respond to the action on the field of battle in ways that enable the reader to share in the events. So also in this scene the audience would learn what is happening only from the description provided by the characters. Nonetheless, that description provides a vivid sense of a collective action, a vast spectacle unfolding as if on some imagined stage beyond our view. The progress of the battle is also marked by the sound of military music, presumably performed offstage as well, yet fully audible to the audience, as indicated by several stage directions: "Drums and martial music from below" (before 10345), "Fearful flourish of trumpets from above" (before 10571), "Sounds of warlike tumult in the orchestra" (after 10782). Of interest also is the fact that the perspective established for the entire scene is defined by the position of the Emperor with his Commander-in-chief and aides. We never actually see his opponents, in particular the Rival Emperor who leads his armies against the Emperor. It is also to this place that Faust comes, dressed in armor and accompanied by the three Mighty Men, to be followed somewhat later by Mephistopheles. Initially, the Emperor and his Commander-in-chief are in charge of strategy for the battle, but by the end both have retreated into the tent and Faust has assumed command alongside Mephisto. During the conclusion of the scene, only these two are on stage as the forces of the Rival Emperor are routed by the devil's magic.

The progress of the battle is defined by three distinct stages: 1) the consultation between the Emperor and the Commander-in-chief about their plan of battle (10345–422); 2) the arrival of Faust with the three Mighty Men to intercede with supernatural force (10423–546), followed by the speech of Mephisto concerning his strategy of fraud (10547–70); 3) the application of magic by Faust and Mephisto while the Emperor rather skeptically looks on (10571–706), followed by the conclusion with its rather dubious triumph when Faust and Mephisto have been left alone on stage (10707–82). In the opening section, the Commander-in-chief describes to the Emperor (and to us) how the three components of their forces are arrayed, respectively, on the right flank, on the central plain, and along the cliffs to the left, in accord with an advantageous lay of the land. The battle plan clearly follows traditional wisdom for the use of troops in warfare, presumably as Goethe was familiar with such strategy from various published sources. The Emperor also responds to the plan, significantly, by recalling the circumstances of his earlier irresponsible masquerade in court, in particular when he was confronted by the false fire at the end of the Carnival Masque (see 10417–22). When Faust subsequently proposes to intercede, these traditional tactics for battle are replaced by the use of magic. An obscure allusion is made to the Necromancer of Norcia (10439–54), a figure mentioned in a Florentine chronicle of 1581, a certain Maestro Cecco of Ascoli, who was burned for sorcery in 1327, known to Goethe from the autobiography of Benvenuto Cellini (where the story is mentioned), which Goethe earlier translated from the Italian and published in German in 1803. We may surmise that this sorcerer is here mentioned by Faust as a quasi-historical pseudonym for Mephistopheles, who is shortly to secure victory for the Emperor through the use of magic and illusion. Initially, this magic involves the assigning of the three Mighty Men, allegorical embodiments (as we know) of the secret forces of the mountains, to join the fighting in each of the three areas of the battle: Audacious on the right flank (10503–18); Rapacious to the center, joined by the sutler woman Grab-swag, who appears from nowhere with looting of the Rival Emperor's tent in mind—as shall be apparent in the next scene (10519–36); and Tenacious on the left, where the fighting involves holding a narrow pass through the rocky heights (10537–46).

Mephistopheles appears at precisely the auspicious moment (*Augenblick*; cf. 10463–5 and 10500) when the battle commences. As indicated in his initial speech, with a lengthy aside of explanation to the audience, Mephisto has brought illusory backup troops to the fighting, consisting of empty armor borrowed from antiquarian collections, which are animated by spirits to produce a loud noise and thus to panic the troops of the Rival Emperor. The Emperor realizes that supernatural forces are being imposed on him and initially resists this assistance. He asks Mephisto to explain to whom he would be indebted for this aid, to which the answer is given rather cryptically: "the lofty master" (*dem Meister, jenem hohen*, 10603–11). Although this response implies that the sorcerer of Norcia is meant, we are inclined to interpret the answer to mean the devil himself. The end of the battle, which follows the action resulting from the initial arrangement of the Emperor's forces, demonstrates the effects of Mephisto's magic in decisive ways. The right flank holds, due to the effects of Audacious's brute violence, though Faust compares the sight to the mists of the fata morgana along the Sicilian shores (10577–92). The center also holds, as the Emperor observes with reference to the flashing lance tips held by the phalanx, from which "flickering flamelets" are dancing, associated by Faust with St. Elmo's fire (10593–602).

The left side proves more critical and requires more drastic intervention. When an eagle in flight is attacked by a griffin, Faust and the Emperor perceive the event as an omen in the manner of those that occur in Homeric epic. They interpret the two birds as signifying the two opposing leaders in this war, so that the defeat of the griffin ("a beast of fable," 10627) signifies the coming victory by the Emperor over his rival. Mephisto and the Emperor then exchange speeches (in which trochaic meter briefly replaces the normal iambic lines used in the scene, 10640–63), which describe the ebb and flow of the battle in terms of natural forces, lightning and floods. The Emperor begrudgingly grants to Mephisto the right to command the action, though he refuses to give him the staff of the Commander-in-chief, and then retreats into his tent (10703–6). As the struggle to secure the narrow pass on the left becomes critical, Mephisto sends his ravens—birds of omen, according to Germanic mythology—to bring the elements of fire and water magically into play. First, with the assistance of water sprites, the Undines, in a mountain lake above the high cliffs, streams of water appear to flow down over the forces of the Rival Emperor, forcing them back (10710–41). Then, with volcanic force that is said to derive from the mountain dwellers, "dwarf-folk" (10746)—though we surmise that the cause is a demonic "summer lightning" (Wetterleuchten, 10750 and 10753)—fire rains upon the army, adding to the illusionary elemental magic that secures this fraudulent victory. The final device, an overwhelming noise produced from the empty armor as in an echo chamber, described in Mephisto's last speech (10768–82), brings a general "Panic"—the term associated intentionally with the legendary scream of the great god Pan—identified, through the convenience of rhyme, as "shrill and stridently satanic." The forces of water and of fire are thus summoned to serve the military ends unleashed by Mephisto's magic, providing a thematic recapitulation of corresponding destructive moments earlier in the drama. We think of the meteor that descended and crashed upon the mountain Seismos in the "Classical Walpurgis Night," as also the illusion of fire that threatened to burn the Emperor in his disguise as Pan at the Carnival Masque. Also related symbolically is Euphorion's fall to death, when in his gaudy armor and in view of the warring armies from the top of a cliff in Arcadia, he throws himself off in a vain attempt to fly like a bird, only to descend to the Earth, sputtering and flashing like a meteor. The violence of volcanic revolution thus consistently brings death and destruction in Goethe's Faust; yet here at the end of the battle in Act IV these powers serve to save and secure the Emperor in his inauthentic though legitimate position of political power. The consequences of this elaborate military campaign with the intrusion of the devil's magic are not reassuring for a political reading of Faust, despite the efforts of so many scholars to affirm the career of the central character in its final phase.

"The Rival Emperor's Tent" (lines 10783–1042)

Once again, Goethe surprises the reader by displacing the expected scene and substituting a scene that seems to have little or nothing to do with the central plot of his drama. Draft sketches preserved in manuscript outlining the plan for Act IV indicate that Goethe initially intended to conclude the act with the Emperor's official dispensation to Faust of stewardship over the tidal shores of the realm, where Faust plans to push back the sea and build his new community. Goethe abandoned this plan in the process of composing the final sequence for the drama, with this last scene written during the month of July, 1831, less than eight months before he died. Few readers are likely to regard this brief final scene for Act IV as anything other than a letdown. What is its significance for an understanding of the drama as a whole, and how should it be interpreted?

Neither Faust nor Mephisto is present during this scene, and only once near the very end (11035–42) is mention made of the Emperor's having granted control of the coastline to "that most ill-famed man." The scene is located, curiously, in the tent of the now-defeated Rival Emperor, where treasure, presumably seized from the Emperor himself (as indicated by the aide who refers to it as "the imperial hoard," 10818), is heaped all around. The brief opening section shows us the attempt of one of the Mighty Men, Rapacious, in company with his female companion, Grab-swag, to loot as much of the treasure as possible. They are surprised by the aides of the Emperor, who chase them away before they secure the treasure. This event is followed by a longer sequence in which the Emperor meets with four of his princes, those who appeared with him in the opening of Act I as his ministers, all of them now promoted (to Arch-Marshal, Arch-Chamberlain, Arch-Steward, and Arch-Cupbearer), each of whom receives appropriate awards and favors for rendering support. At the very end of the scene, the Arch-Chancellor, also now entitled the Archbishop, confronts the Emperor with regard to the demands of the church. How do these two sections of the scene relate to each other, and how do both relate to the concerns and strategies of Faust and Mephisto? The issue throughout, positively or negatively, is payoff for service rendered. Faust secures his fiefdom as a grant from a guilty sovereign, whose victory in war was achieved by the use of the devil's deception and magic. The ministers are rewarded, in effect, for their loyalty, though none of them—so far as we can tell—participated directly in the war, yet all benefited in questionable ways from the devil's scheme for fiscal reform by the introduction of paper money. Only the Archbishop, representing the complex and rather dubious motives of the church, calls the Emperor to task for allowing the devil to rescue his rule, exacting a high price for his guilty conscience. The speedy looters, by contrast, who try to make off with as much of the treasure as they can carry, are thwarted by the Emperor's aides from achieving their aim, which of course is criminal and violent. All these actions have political implications that are important for an understanding of the drama, and not one of the characters involved in these payoffs emerges without some guilt and responsibility for events that stand as reprehensible, if not indeed criminal. Goethe thus establishes a broad context in which Faust may be judged alongside the Emperor and his ministers, not to mention the looters, as guilty of such negative acts. The means are corrupt and pernicious, regardless of the ends.

The brief opening sequence with Rapacious and Grab-swag belongs among the most sardonic of the satirical scenes in the entire drama. It may be helpful to recall the examples in Part One of the drunken students in Auerbach's Tavern and the marmosets in the Witch's kitchen. Needless to say, Rapacious and Grab-swag are intended to be unsavory characters, thugs or ruffians, who command no respect whatsoever. They speak in couplets of a curiously singsong quality, so that their exchange loses all sense of realistic dialogue. Their attempt to loot the treasure also includes a double fiasco, since the chest of gold proves too heavy for Grab-swag to carry, so that it falls to the ground and breaks apart, and the subsequent attempt to fill Grab-swag's skirt with loot fails because of a hole in it. We seem here to achieve a sense of slapstick worthy even of the most debased episodes in the Nordic "Walpurgis Night." There may well be a political allegory intended here, as much as in the earlier scenes of satire just referred to, but in a sense Goethe is also writing a strong instance of theatrical violence. This scene of looting may possibly comment allegorically on the looting of artworks and treasure from all over Europe by the armies of Napoleon, with so much of the spoils having been removed to Paris until after the final defeat of the emperor at the battle of Waterloo in 1815. Correspondingly, the aides who discover the looters speak in their own form of chant, in couplets, after the looters flee, until the fourth and last of the aides brings the episode to a conclusion with a remarkable evocation of the experience of the battle as a whole in its dreamlike quality: "Your eyes were hung about with mist, / Your hearing hummed and buzzed and hissed" (10845 f.). This reads like a reliable summary of the effect of the entire conflict on a neutral observer, with which the audience in the theater might well concur.

The concluding portion of the scene, employing the old-fashioned six-stress Alexandrine line from neoclassical French drama, focuses on the Emperor's negotiations with his ministers and the Archbishop. The main concern here is the institutionalizing of a new agreement for determining the succession to the throne through the collective decision by these ministers (10953–60). This arrangement as described by the Emperor derives from the so-called Golden Bull of Emperor Charles IV in 1356, which Goethe knew from a study by Johann Daniel von Olenschlager (a friend of Goethe's family in Frankfurt) published in 1766 and which he consulted again in July, 1831. Of thematic importance to the drama is the emphasis on the official parchment with the Emperor's signature that will formally secure this arrangement (10971–4). Such an agreement, derived from historical tradition, appears to establish a legitimacy that offsets the earlier use of the Emperor's signature on the certificates of paper currency in Act I. The effects of the victory just achieved on the battlefield, however, raise several serious questions concerning this claim to legitimacy. The language of the Emperor's two formal speeches—one to his ministers (10849–72) and one to the Archbishop after he enters (10931–50)—is rhetorically overelaborate and self-important. The response by each of the four ministers to their promotion indicates an exclusive concern with feasting and carousing, presumably on the model of the revelry for Carnival and the theatrical spirit show sponsored by the court in Act I. The Emperor also acquiesces in this plan for festival celebration (10909–14) in terms that suggest he may have learned nothing from his involvement with Faust and Mephisto. Finally, in his exchange with the Archbishop after the ministers leave, he is made to confront his guilt for collusion with the powers of Satan (10981–1002). The Archbishop then outlines his conditions for an expensive penance, including the construction of an elaborate cathedral. He also demands a formal written agreement, a "deed of transfer" (11021), which the Emperor must sign, that serves as a counterdocument to the arrangement for the succession of power. Finally, as an afterthought, the Archbishop demands payment of "booty-gold" from the state's coffers: "All land appurtenances, impost, tithe and rent / Forever" (11024 f.). Such a price from an empire in financial chaos makes the loot of treasure from the Rival Emperor's tent, earlier attempted by Rapacious and Grab-swag, seem like petty thievery. The outcome of the Emperor's dubious triumph in battle thus appears to be a subordination of his rule to the apparent greed of the church. This arrangement, which may include an oblique allusion by Goethe to the so-called Holy Alliance among the European powers after the fall of Napoleon, needs to be kept in mind as the political and ethical background for the new society built by Faust in Act V, which by a subsequent demand from the Archbishop must also pay "tithe and rent and bounties" (11038).

Act V (lines 11043–2111)

Goethe indicated in the prose summary of Part Two, which he dictated in 1816 (see below), that the ending of Faust had already been written and that the action he was summarizing would finally establish a connection with that ending. In a conversation with his friend Boisserée in the preceding year, he indicated satisfaction with his conclusion for the drama, a product of what he termed "the best time," that is, the years around 1800, when he completed Part One of Faust, in close association with such friends as Schiller and the philosophers at Jena. Goethe expressed similar confidence in the earlier material at various points in later conversations with Eckermann, where he addressed his labors at closing the gap, which he finally did by composing Act IV, during the first half of 1831. Scholars, meanwhile, have provided further documentation on the composition of Act V, demonstrating that one of the crucial manuscripts for this section (the so-called H2), which contains in fair copy the scenes "Midnight," "Great Outer Precinct of the Palace," and "Entombment" (11384–843), was prepared in 1825–26, when Goethe began work again on Part Two. This manuscript may be regarded as the final text for these scenes, which were based on drafts, now lost to us, that probably had been written a quarter century earlier. Thus the core of Act V, including Faust's meeting with Care, followed by his death and Mephistopheles' struggle to seize his soul, reflects Goethe's perspective on the drama from the time when he composed the so-called great lacuna of Part One, extending from the latter half of "Night" through the pact and wager in "Study [II]." The significance of this dating for the interpretation of Faust's end cannot be overemphasized, even though the continuity of Act V with the rest of Part Two is achieved with complete authority. In addition, the opening scenes of this act—the Philemon and Baucis episode in "Open Country" and the two scenes with Faust that follow, "Palace" and "Deep Night" (i.e., 11043–383)—were composed very late, most probably during April and May, 1831. The final scene of the drama, "Mountain Gorges" (11844–2111), composed during the final weeks of 1830, constitutes a separate epilogue that establishes a conceptual frame for *Faust* as a whole, balancing and intentionally offseting the "Prologue in Heaven" that precedes Part One. The question of Faust's final redemption after his death thus raises problems of interpretation quite separate from the incidents that take place in Act V itself. The reader of Act V must suspend the cosmic perspective of Part Two, though without any sense of contradiction, in order to view the events at the end of Faust's life from the ethical perspective of Part One, in particular the scene in which Faust makes the original wager with Mephistopheles. At the end, the drama again focuses quite appropriately on the actions of the central character, even if the world of Act V is totally different in every way from the world of Part One. Many readers have felt, quite correctly, that Faust is responsible for the deaths of Philemon and Baucis, along with that of the totally innocent Wayfarer, to the same degree that he is responsible for Gretchen's death. The issue of moral judgment in both cases should not be diminished, as it cannot be ignored. When completing Part One, around 1800, Goethe intentionally transformed the traditional Faust legend into a universal human tragedy, and the concluding section of Part Two, despite the more cosmic, mythical, and symbolic actions that occur during the quest for Helena, returns to address the broader ethical issues relating to this human tragedy. For this reason, along with the apparent dramatic power of the writing as such, Act V has always commanded greater interest than the rest of Part Two among readers concerned primarily with the question of Faust's moral responsibility for his actions.

Goethe intentionally expands the dramatic perspective of Act V beyond the subjective limits of Faust's fall. It is important to see such figures as the Wayfarer in "Open Country" and Lynceus in "Palace" and "Deep Night" as offering viable alternatives for human existence in contradistinction to Faust's absolutist program of self. The same also may be said for the couple Baucis and Philemon, who have endured to old age in rustic simplicity and natural piety, even though they prove incapable of accommodating themselves to the new society created by the infernal technology of Faust's industrial revolution. The old couple are merely his victims, a vestige of the old order that has been swept aside. Nor are the Wayfarer and the Keeper of the Tower any more effective in surviving or resisting Faust's economic and social project, though we feel nonetheless that they stand apart from his ethos and represent valid alternatives for human existence. In the final lines spoken by the Wayfarer (11075–8), as he approaches the place where the shore used to be, he indicates that he has gathered in his lifetime of travel a fullness of experience, a sense of "the boundless ocean," which sustains his "prayerful devotion" in the face of nature and of life itself. Lynceus, by contrast to the man of travels who has traversed the open spaces of the world, surveys these spaces with his all-perceiving eyes from a fixed center in the tower, gathering to himself a corresponding sense of life's fullness and also providing in his song of praise (11288–303) an affirmation of nature in all its diversity. This stance of affirmation resembles, ironically, that which Faust himself expressed in his monologue at the outset of Part Two, in response to the rainbow in "Charming Landscape." But Faust long since abandoned such an affirmative stance and has become obsessed by his land-development project and the illusion of absolute power.

A corresponding contrast of values and attitudes may be perceived between Faust's situation in Act V, a situation that demands consideration in relation to the wager with Mephistopheles and the question of victory or defeat at the hands of the devil, and the setting of Faust's salvation in "Mountain Gorges," where his "immortal essence" (stage direction before 11934) receives the beneficence of a grace that is totally alien to his newly built society and completely separate from any causal relation to his fall and death. Readers who look to the events of Act V for any hint whatsoever concerning the cause of Faust's salvation will be disappointed. The most that can be argued—as has often been done—is that Faust's final speech, his monologue at the edge of his grave (11559–86), outlines a projected ideal of society, a utopian prefiguration, that represents the highest impulse of the Faustian spirit. But critics have also neglected the ironic contrast between Faust's vision and the agency of a perverse and inhuman power that now controls his city. Mephistopheles has summoned forth the Lemures, who sing grotesque ditties as they dig Faust's grave. Nor is there any reason to doubt that they will inherit the realm Faust leaves behind at his death. Faust's spirit is saved by the intervention of a transcendent redemptive power, identified with the Feminine in its response to authentic love; but the worldly city built by Mephistopheles and his henchmen at Faust's instigation, which represents a new world for the future of humankind— the world in which all readers of *Faust* must locate themselves—is abandoned to the control of demonic powers. This sense of loss for the world as a whole, which is not diminished or mitigated at all by Faust's subsequent salvation, is a central aspect of the tragic fall that Act V represents. No reader of Goethe's *Faust* should take lightly the implications of its generic subtitle: A *Tragedy*.

Characteristically, Goethe prevents any single response from dominating the final act of *Faust*. The mood of the scene in which Faust dies—poised between the utopian vision of his final speech and his collapse into the hands of the Lemures—is immediately replaced by infernal slapstick. The popular tradition of the devil as comic relief, particularly as the butt of a cosmic joke, is allowed to take possession of Mephistopheles, regardless of the complexity and versatility he has achieved as a character in the course of the drama. The scene "Entombment" provides a parody of medieval morality plays, as the traditional hell-mouth opens on the stage, belching forth grotesque devils, who serve as Mephistopheles' troops in opposition to the host of angels that suddenly descends without warning to claim Faust's soul. The pitched battle that concludes the scene brings ignominious defeat for Mephistopheles, as he allows himself to be aroused sexually by the sight of the naked male cherubs, apparently conceived by Goethe on the model of the putti and amoretti of Renaissance paintings. Many questions remain unanswered within the scene itself. Like Shakespeare's Shylock when he is hooted out of court, Mephistopheles appeals to some sense of justice, receiving no satisfaction from a system of transcendence that, from the very outset in "Prologue in Heaven," has little sympathy for the devil's point of view. Faust's salvation is at best a spontaneous aftereffect of his death, for which the angels offer here no word of explanation. Nor do they feel any need to explain the heavenly grace they represent, if in fact they are consciously aware that they do so. All such explanation, not through any rational argument but through the dramatic representation of transcendence itself as an ultimate mystery, is provided in the scene "Mountain Gorges," which concludes the drama.

Baucis and Philemon with the Wayfarer in "Open Country" (lines 11043–142)

It would be difficult to imagine a more striking contrast than that which occurs in the transition from the end of Act IV to the beginning of Act V. This contrast is already apparent in the verse forms Goethe uses. The conclusion of Act IV is written in six-stress Alexandrines, the traditional verse form of neoclassical drama, imported from France. The opening scene of Act V, "Open Landscape," is written in four-stress trochaic meter, which Goethe no doubt borrowed from Spanish Baroque drama, above all the plays of Calderón, which he admired. Yet the contrast of tone and mood is equally great. Where the confrontation between the Emperor and the Archbishop following the fraudulent victory in battle conveys a sense of political corruption and compromise for the affairs of state, the opening scene of Act V transports us into the traditional realm of pastoral, where all aspects of life are defined by simplicity and humanity. This is also the world of ancient virtues, defined by the mythological background to the figures who appear and the events from the past to which they refer. Theirs is a world of poverty and piety, defined by their simple hut and the small chapel in which they worship their "God of ancient days" (11142; translated by Arndt as "trusting God as heretofore"). The Wayfarer is also a figure of virtue, who returns to this shore, where he had been shipwrecked in a storm many years earlier and rescued from death by the aged couple who live here. All three figures derive from ancient legend, and their world suggests at most the sense of mythological remove that the scene in Arcadia at the end of the Helena act evoked, however briefly and unsuccessfully.

Initially, there appears to be no trace of either Faust or the Emperor. The world of Acts I and IV seems as remote as the mythological setting of the "Classical Walpurgis Night" and the poetic events of the Helena act. Yet Faust's great project of land reclamation has gone forward, and the lives of this ancient Ovidian couple have been directly affected by the events that have transpired since the end of Act IV, when Faust received permission to attempt his project. We are meant to assume—as Goethe indicated to Eckermann (conversation of June 6, 1831, below)—that many years have passed, perhaps a full half century, and that Faust is now an extremely old man, himself a full century old. We are provided with no reliable information about what has transpired, except through the description by Philemon to the Wayfarer (11083–106) and subsequently by Baucis as well (11123–34). Where earlier—also, presumably, before Faust began his project so many years before—the Wayfarer had been washed up on shore as victim of a storm at sea, now the coast has been pushed back to the horizon; and on the land secured by thus taming the force of the sea, Faust has erected a modern city, complete with the magnificent palace, where he dwells, at its center. This setting indicates a successful outcome to the land-reclamation project he introduced as a plan during the conversation with Mephisto in the opening scene of Act IV. What Goethe achieves, however, by having the aged couple who dwelt in this place prior to Faust's arrival describe what has happened, is the superimposition of an earlier, simpler, and more authentic human perspective upon Faust's achievement of his modernist urban-development project. The language of the scene in its stately simplicity conveys as much, as does also the lifestyle of the characters, with their simple supper served in the small garden of their cottage and the service of evening prayer that they conduct in their chapel as the sun goes down, ringing the bell and kneeling in worship (11139–42). The sound of the chapel bell, which Faust hears in the next scene and which causes him such distress (see 11151), should be compared to the sound of the Easter Chorus overheard by Faust at the end of "Night," in Part One, and the effect of the chapel bell here contrasted with the power of spiritual renewal in response to the Chorus there. As Baucis says of Faust's role in general from her perspective, "Something wrong was all about it / That I cannot fathom yet" (11113–4).

The pushing back of the sea by building dikes and dams, the clearing of the land and its preparation, as also the construction of the city itself, have all occurred through the forces of technology, which should be associated with the devil and his henchmen, the three Mighty Men from Act IV, who will appear in the next scene as they return home by ship from a pirate raid upon the open sea. In her description, Baucis makes clear that the work was done primarily by night, involving the forces of fire and accompanied by screams of agony and the loss of many lives (11123–30). Readers of *Faust*, Part Two, will see that volcanic forces of fire and subterranean energy, the unnatural instruments of Mephisto, have been at work here, taming the more natural and productive neptunic force of the sea. The successful completion of Faust's project in constructing this brave new urban world is just as questionable as the victory he achieved through the use of Mephisto's magic in the war between the Emperor and his rival. And since Goethe introduces the final act of the drama from the perspective of these virtuous survivors from a simpler, more authentic era of existence, the reader can only concur with the negative judgment passed by the aged couple on the work of Faust and his technology. We are thus introduced to the world of Faust the Developer through the eyes of those who predated it and who are shortly to become its victims.

Goethe's choice of names necessarily invites comparison of the situation here with that described by Ovid in his *Metamorphoses* with regard to the pious yet poor old couple Philemon and Baucis (8, 611–724). It is a familiar legend. The gods Jupiter and Mercury come to Earth in disguise, seeking to find virtuous human beings and to judge the lives being led there. Only this aged couple in their poverty, living in a simple hut, receive the gods in their home and provide basic hospitality. The result is a categorical negative judgment against humankind by the gods, who bring down a flood in which all drown, excepting only these two. Philemon and Baucis thus become the priests in a new temple constructed where their hut had formerly been, and they serve in piety toward the gods for the rest of their days, being transformed upon their deaths into two trees, an oak and a linden, which grow over the temple, uniting their branches and providing shade. In *Faust*, Goethe reverses this myth of hospitality and genuine devotion in striking ways. Instead of the gods in disguise, the Wayfarer arrives, having once been rescued by the couple from a storm at sea and now receiving their hospitality as he did then. The power of the sea before Faust arrived had been, apparently, similar to the power of the flood that drowned the inhabitants of the city in Ovid. Faust's new city is built only after the shipwreck and after the Wayfarer originally went on his way, and the construction is achieved, ironically, by taming the power of the sea and pushing it back to the horizon. The Wayfarer's return at this time provides a kind of closure and affirmation for the lives of the aged couple, who will not die natural deaths and will not become symbols of a natural blessing for a new temple of worship in honor of the gods whom they served. Instead, Faust will send Mephisto and the three henchmen to root them out by force, resulting in the violent deaths of all three — Philemon, Baucis, and the Wayfarer—along with the burning of their chapel as well as their hut. The legend of Baucis and Philemon is thus transformed into the very opposite of the original myth of natural piety and simple humanity in Ovid. Goethe must have known full well what the implications of this reversal must be, since he has Mephisto refer explicitly to the story of Naboth's vineyard at the end of the following scene, after Faust has ordered him to remove the old couple from their home and their land (see 11287). In the biblical story, King Ahab covets the vineyard of his neighbor Naboth, who refuses to sell the land he has inherited from his forefathers. As a result, Queen Jezebel has Naboth falsely accused of heresy and killed by stoning. This example from literary tradition, like the one from classical antiquity, provides a context in which the moral judgment of Faust's actions cannot be in any doubt.

Lynceus, the Keeper of the Watchtower
("*Palace*" *and* "*Deep Night," lines 11143–66 and 11288–337*)

No explanation is given for the appearance of this remarkable observer at the center of Faust's new world. There is no reason, however, to think that he is any different from the watchman with the same name in the central section of the Helena act, who was assigned to keep the lookout for Helena's arrival at Faust's medieval castle (9218–355). That figure in turn derived from classical legend, specifically from the Lynceus, the "lynx-eyed," mentioned during Faust's encounter with Chiron in the "Classical Walpurgis Night," the watchman for the Argonauts in their quest for the Golden Fleece (7377). In Act V, the watchman serves as the vehicle of description for the violent deaths of Baucis and Philemon, which he observes at the outset of "Deep Night." Yet he also signifies more in his fundamental stance as the lookout, whose position is at the highest point of the palace in the center of Faust's city. He is even provided with perhaps the last lyric poem written by Goethe, the song at the outset of that scene (11288–303), a sequence of short two-stressed iambic lines with alternating rhyme that constitute what may be regarded as four distinct stanzas (though the text as printed in the scene is not divided, each of the four-line units makes up a single complete sentence). This lyric has often been taken to be a kind of legacy by Goethe to the value of sight and vision for his own life and work. Lynceus observes the world around him, above all the natural world, in all its diversity, and that which he sees, he also affirms and celebrates in song. The "ever-comely design" (11297) provides him with pleasure and, in doing so, affirms also his own sense of self (*Gefall ich auch mir,* 11299; translated by Arndt as "I take pleasure in mine"). This turn of the lyric of descriptive praise to the subject that sings such praise is characteristic of Goethe's lyric poetry in general. The final stanza affirms everything seen because it is all beautiful: *Ihr glücklichen Augen, / Was je ihr gesehn, / Es sei wie es wolle / Es war doch so schön!* (11300–3). Readers will recall the terms that Faust set in his original wager with Mephistopheles: "If the swift moment I entreat: / Tarry a while! you are so fair!" (*Werd' ich zum Augenblicke sagen: / Verweile doch! Du bist so schön!,* 1699 f.) If the tragic dilemma of Faustian humanity in its boundless striving is never to secure the moment that is genuinely beautiful, the contrary condition appears to be that of the watchman-singer, who merely stands and observes the natural world as it lives and goes, affirming everything as beautiful and, through his song, affirming the continuing and constantly varied beauty of life itself. In his two appearances in Act V, Lynceus thus serves as an effective counterfigure to Faust. It is appropriate that his final two lines, as indicated by the stage direction, are sung and not spoken, providing a kind of mournful epitaph for the old couple and their guest: "To dead centuries assembling / What throughout them pleased the gaze" (*Was sich sonst dem Blick empfohlen, / Mit Jahrhunderten ist hin,* 11336 f.)

Mephisto as the Agent of Faust's Urban Project

Apart from his role as overseer in the scenes surrounding Faust's death ("Great Outer Precinct of the Palace" and "Entombment"), Mephisto is defined in Act V as the agent of Faust's will in achieving his urban project. This has presumably been the case from the time when the land along the coast was first reclaimed, so that his relationship with Faust as the absolute ruler of this new domain has become habitual. We may therefore assume that his report to Faust after he sails into harbor with the Mighty Men on the ship filled with booty from the high seas defines his attitude toward this enterprise in reliable terms. His is a litany of ever-expanding and arbitrary violence (11171–88). Having departed with only two ships, he has returned with twenty: "Free ocean makes you scruple-free, / Cobwebs of caution swept to sea" (*Das freie Meer befreit den Geist, / Wer weiß da, was Besinnen heißt!*, 11177 f.). A principle of freedom for the spirit is here invoked that knows neither limits nor scruples. The devil has no conscience on the high seas, and presumably in behaving so he merely puts the will of his master into effect. Above all, he asserts that might makes right, that the ends justify the means; only the What matters, not the How (11184 f.). His philosophy of action assumes a quasi-secular theological status in the final couplet of his speech, where he parodies the traditional Christian trinity: "For commerce, war, and piracy, / They form a seamless trinity" (*Krieg, Handel und Piraterie, / Dreieinig sind sie, nicht zu trennen*, 11187 f.). The rationale for expanding power and possession is thus definitively articulated, and Faust does not in any way object. Mephisto, indeed, merely defines the political and economic basis on which Faust's empire is built. The application of such policy to the problem of removing Baucis and Philemon is thus automatic. "Have you not colonized long since?" asks Mephisto (11274), and so the removal of this native remnant is a simple matter. Faust intends that the old couple be relocated—he claims to have in mind a housing project somewhere (a "handsome little farm," 11276)—but for Mephisto it is all merely a matter of force (*Gewalt*, 11280).

Critics have not always been willing to place full blame for Mephisto's actions on Faust, but have instead assumed that the relocation of Baucis and Philemon is in principle justified in the name of progress. Yet the old couple was dwelling here first, and by legal right they are the legitimate owners of their home and property. But Faust insists on absolute control of this land and the city that has been constructed on it. In this regard, he may be interpreted as more than just a developer and a colonizer, more than a capitalist and an imperialist; he is an absolutist of the self, who seeks to impose his will on the world without compromise and without tolerance for anything less than complete control. When Faust complains that he wanted exchange, not robbery (11371), his agents—Mephisto with the three Mighty Men—answer in chorus to mock his false naïveté: "Give way to force, for might is right; / And would you boldly offer strife, / Then risk your house, estate, and—life" (11375–7). If this sounds familiar and characteristic of modern Western society, then the role of Mephisto should also be recognized as no more than a technological means to an end imposed upon it; the devil is merely the instrument for the Faustian will. Whatever the outcome may be, whether from piracy on the high seas or from the violent murder of the original inhabitants on the land, the full blame and responsibility must fall on the one who originated the action, not the one who carried it out.

Faust's Encounter with Care in "Midnight" (lines 11384–510)

The figure of Care has always caused difficulty for readers of *Faust*, Part Two, especially because her appearance is so unexpected and her attitude toward Faust so enigmatic, despite the precise dramatic and ethical motivation offered by the murder of Philemon and Baucis. The Four Gray Crones of "Midnight"—Want, Debt, Care, and Need—describe themselves as sisters of Death, who is expected shortly. They materialize out of the smoke from the burning wreckage of the cottage and chapel, as indicated by Faust's speech at the end of "Deep Night" (11378–83). Yet the Crones themselves are totally alien to the mood and manner of even the most supernatural figures in Part Two. They are refugees from popular superstition, from the spirit world of ghosts and demons, witches and wraiths, such as were represented in Part One in such scenes as "Witch's Kitchen" and "Walpurgis Night." A close parallel may be surmised with the Witches in Shakespeare's *Macbeth*, the hags who inhabit the blasted heath of Scotland. Goethe may have been influenced by Schiller's adaptation of that play for production at the Weimar Theater in 1800 (a time that coincides with the presumed date of the initial draft for this scene). The supernatural quality of Care's appearance is further heightened, ironically, by Faust's opening speech in the scene (11398–419), in which he expresses an abhorrence for the oppressive atmosphere that permeates his own chamber. Such an attitude of apprehension provides a significant contrast to Faust's accommodation of demonic powers in the two study scenes of Part One. The role of Care, however, must be defined within a frame of reference quite separate from the pact with the devil, especially since we have no reason to believe that Mephistopheles is himself responsible for Care's appearance or is even aware of her presence. In this regard, Faust's comments concerning Care in the latter part of the opening scene of the drama may help clarify her nature (634–51). Care is there defined as an alien counterforce to the power of the spirit in its dynamic, creative activity. This conflict of concerns indicates an irresolvable dilemma for the human condition, represented in the drama by Faust himself.

The confrontation between Faust and Care results in Faust's blinding and indicates a complete failure of his purpose in creating his own new world. The encounter does not constitute an exchange in the normal sense of a conversation. Care speaks in trochaic meter, in what can be described only as a chant or a mystical reverie. In her three speeches (11424–31, 11453–66, and 11471–86), she describes herself and her powers, surveying the effect she has on her victim, whom she refers to repeatedly but only with a third-person pronoun. Faust systematically resists this spectral figure, refusing to acknowledge her and her power over him. His initial speech to her (11433–52) surveys his entire career as a questing for satisfaction, which yet fails in every moment (*Augenblick*) to achieve such satisfaction. At the end of their exchange, he asserts that he will never recognize her power: *Ich werde deine Macht nicht anerkennen* (11494). In response to such defiance, Care simply breathes on him, and with that he is blind. Care then disappears as mysteriously as she came, leaving Faust to his imminent death. This encounter signals a categorical failure for Faust in ethical terms, since Care approaches as a direct consequence of his arrogant self-centeredness and his demand for absolute power, which have caused the death of Philemon and Baucis and the Wayfarer. The significance of this failure, however, goes beyond the limits of good and evil, implicating the hero of Goethe's drama in what may be regarded as an existential tragic fall. Nor is this failure diminished at all by Faust's subsequent salvation, which proceeds from a totally independent act of grace, instigated by agents of Heaven, in particular by the spirit of Gretchen as one of the penitent women who attend the Mater Gloriosa. Care thus functions as a contrast-figure to the Feminine, a negative ground to the projected female objects of Faustian desire. Accordingly, Faust's fall from his encounter with Care serves as an analogue to Gretchen's tragic fall, in Part One. The sense of tragedy in both instances, however different their cause, is complete and uncompromising. Care also resembles, more than any other figure in *Faust*, the Evil Spirit that overwhelms Gretchen's guilty conscience in "Cathedral." Both these spirits affect their respective victims as destructive powers of conscience in ways that contrast significantly with Mephistopheles' role in his relationship to Faust.

Faust's Apparent Renunciation (lines 11403–7)

Faust's few lines at the beginning of "Midnight," just after Care has slipped in through the keyhole but before he becomes aware of her presence, have played an important yet ultimately misleading role in *Faust* scholarship, because several critics have argued that he here rejects magic and thus, by implication, his relationship to Mephistopheles. The statement, however, is formulated in the subjunctive as a condition contrary to fact: If I were only able to remove magic (*Magie*) from my path and unlearn all my magic spells (*Zaubersprüche*), then indeed, oh Nature, I would stand before you as a man alone (i.e., just as a man), then it would be worth the effort to be a man. Faust introduces this statement with the assertion that he has not yet fought his way to freedom: *Noch hab' ich mich ins Freie nicht gekämpft* (11403). The several scholars who have insisted that Faust somehow earns his salvation through his actions in the fifth act look to these lines as the signal of a categorical reversal in his attitude. The cause would be his remorse at the news from Mephisto that Philemon and Baucis were killed, and the outcome would be the utopian vision of his final speech (11559–86), after he has been blinded by Care and just before he falls dead at the edge of the grave being dug for him by the Lemures. It is crucial that these lines just prior to the encounter with Care be taken in context. It should also be noted that Mephisto is not present when Faust speaks them and that there is no indication at any point that Faust has the ability to change anything about his relations with the devil, nor is there any indication that he is prepared to renounce his absolute control over the world he has built, including the death of the old couple as a consequence. Readers should also recall that in the traditional Faust legend the doomed doctor suffers remorse at the last hour, just before the devil comes to drag him off to hell. In Goethe's drama, the last hour has come, and Faust is surrounded by an oppressive sense of hostile "spook and elf" (11410), which is shortly to manifest itself as Care. There is no turning back, there is no reversal of attitude or change of heart; at best there is a momentary reflection about what might be the case if things were different. The spectral figure of Care is shortly to make very clear that nothing has changed or can change in Faust.

Faust's Final Speech and Death and Mephisto's Response ("Great Outer Precinct of the Palace," lines 11511–603)

The end of Faust's mortal existence is fraught with ambivalence, presumably so intended by Goethe. The focus of this ambivalence is, appropriately, Faust's crucial last speech (11559–86), since death follows swiftly upon his encounter with Care. The heading for the scene just preceding, "Midnight," indicates a sense of moment at the turning point from night toward new day, but in this case, as indicated by Faust's blinding, there will be no new day. It is the midnight of his life, the time at which, according to the original chapbook about the damnation of Faustus, the devil came to fetch him to hell. Here, instead, in his blindness, Faust emerges cautiously from his chambers into the outer precinct of the palace, where Mephisto has summoned the Lemures, skeleton creatures from the underworld, who are instructed to dig Faust's grave. Faust, however, is possessed of one overriding idea: to impose his will upon those who serve him in order to fulfill his utopian plan for urban development. The brief speech with which the preceding scene concludes articulates this obsession in terms of his absolute authority: "To bring to fruit the most exalted plans, / One mind is ample for a thousand hands" (11509 f.). As he emerges from the palace, the sound of digging delights his ears, since he assumes that his will is being put into action by willing workers under the direction of his overseer, Mephisto. It is in such a situation of total misconception that Faust then speaks his final words.

Critics have long been divided with regard to the validity of Faust's last vision. He projects upon the future the completion of his project, imagining how his brave new world would be under such conditions, and in the pleasure of such imagined fulfillment he declares that he might then enjoy the moment he wishes would tarry, thus fulfilling also the terms of his wager with Mephisto. Readers who have been committed to a justification for Faust's salvation based on his actions in the final act of his life have always insisted that this vision of a utopian future should be accepted as valid, thus affirming also the human value of his urban project. As has also been mentioned, various extremist political regimes—notably in Germany under the Nazis and in the former East Germany under the Communists—have proclaimed that they were the actual fulfillment of Faust's utopian dream. History has thus far given the lie to all such claims, making it today more difficult than ever to affirm Faust's dream. A more cautionary reading would suggest that Goethe intended the reader to respond with skepticism. Particularly instructive is the fact that Faust's speech—first drafted (so far as can be determined) after Part One had been completed, that is, around 1800—had originally been much shorter and more straightforward in its claims for an optimistic future. At that time, the projected affirmation of the beautiful moment was formulated in the indicative mood. In the manuscript prepared from these drafts in fair copy in 1826 (H2), the speech is only nine lines long:

> From the ditch, which crawls through swamps
> And finally reaches the sea.
> I win a place for many millions
> There will I also dwell among them,
> Stand truly upon my own ground and earth.
> I may say to the moment:
> Oh, tarry yet, thou art so fair!
> The trace of my earthly days can
> Never in eons disappear.

Goethe may thus originally have intended Faust's optimism about the future to be taken at face value. By the time he completed the drama thirty years later, however, the human and environmental implications of Faust's development project had become much more complex and more sinister. This shift may reflect a change in Goethe's outlook on the world as he approached his own death, or it may indicate a more nuanced formulation of Faust's final situation, whether or not the character is fully aware of what is happening. The much-expanded version of the last speech is more oblique in formulating even the possibility that the moment might be affirmed. Faust's utopian vision still includes an Edenic space for millions of inhabitants, though he now also acknowledges that this space depends upon constant vigilance against the natural force of the sea, which is held back by the dikes and where any breach must instantly be secured by "communal spirit" (11572). Faust's ultimate wisdom is now also formulated in terms of labor, rather than the fruits of labor, in one of the most well-known aphorisms in the drama: "He only earns both freedom and existence / Who must reconquer them each day" (11575 f.). Only in the final lines does Faust reaffirm the utopian quality of the life he envisions as future goal for humankind: "Such teeming would I see upon this land, / On acres free among free people stand." To elaborate by paraphrase the implicit logic to the fulfillment of the wager with Mephistopheles: If such a condition were ever to be achieved, I might be allowed to entreat the moment, "Oh tarry yet, thou art so fair!" (11582). On the basis of such a vision, Faust can still assert (as in the earlier, shorter draft) that the trace of his mortal existence will never in eons be impaired. Finally, from all these conditions and qualifications, he can say that in the foretaste of such happiness to come (*Im Vorgefühl von solchem hohen Glück*, 11584), he now enjoys the highest moment (*Genieß ich jetzt den höchsten Augenblick*, 11585).

The greatly expanded version of Faust's final speech establishes crucial resonances back through the drama, not only to the terms of the wager made with Mephisto in the second study scene but also to the monologue in "Forest and Cave," with its thematic formulation about the impossibility of achieving complete satisfaction of desire. Even the terms of the original encounter with the Earth Spirit in "Night," which resulted in such a categorical failure of Faust's assertion of equality, may here be translated into the terms of a collective human history with the utopian social goals defined by Faust as the creator and ruler of this new urban domain. The outcome has not changed, even if the attitude of the protagonist is more cautiously formulated in terms of future possibility. The present is controlled by forces that are far more sinister and completely indifferent to Faust's vision of fulfillment. What is offered instead is the mere fact of death, immediate and uncompromising, where the question of a future possibility simply does not arise, because it is unknown and unknowable. The devil is concerned with the here and now, and Mephisto simply doesn't mention the question of the wager. The terms with which he responds to Faust's death deserve just as careful study as does Faust's last speech. To the devil, that last moment, even if it brought Faust the foretaste of an imagined fulfillment, is merely "the final moment, worthless, stale, and void" (11589). The moment of death is simply that: a moment, which brings quite arbitrarily the sense of an ending, in which time alone triumphs, like the tick of the clock that stops (precisely in the terms that Faust had used at the time of his wager; see 1705). It is the Lemures, curiously, who assert that time has stopped (11593 f.) and who insist that all is simply "over" (*vorbei*), not "fulfilled" (*vollbracht*), as Mephisto stated. This exchange over Faust's corpse leads to Mephisto's brief concluding speech, which is one of his most programmatic statements as spirit of negation (11597–603). It is all over and thus pure nothing-at-all (*reines Nicht*), totally meaningless (*vollkommnes Einerlei!*). What does such constant striving—as in Faust's entire career—such eternal creating (*das ew'ge Schaffen*), achieve other than what can be swept away to nothingness? Mephisto becomes even more categorical: "All over is as good as never was, / And yet it whirls about as if it were" (*Es ist so gut, als wär' es nicht gewesen, / Und treibt sich doch im Kreis, als wenn es wäre*, 11601 f.). The key to understanding Mephistopheles' ultimate stance, the categorical and uncompromising stance of negation and denial, occurs in the unique coinage of his final exclamation: *Ich liebte mir dafür das Ewig-Leere* (11603). The double-adjectival abstract noun *das Ewig-Leere* ("the Eternal-Empty") signifies a principle of universal meaninglessness, according to which everything Faust lived for, however futile his striving may have been with regard to his various objects of desire (including his final project of urban development), collapses into nothingness. Nowhere in the entire drama, with the single exception perhaps of the monologue spoken by Mephisto just after the pact and wager have been contracted (1851–67), does the devil reveal his fundamental, unwavering nihilism in such categorical terms. Readers should keep this phrase, *das Ewig-Leere*, in mind as a uniquely Goethean neologism with which to confront the very opposite, positive principle of life and art expressed in the penultimate line of the drama by the Chorus Mysticus: *das Ewig-Weibliche* ("the Eternal-Feminine," 12110).

The Battle between the Devils and the Angels in "Entombment" (lines 11604–843)

Critics have often seemed embarrassed by Goethe's sudden shift of dramatic mode in the scene following Faust's death, where a kind of medieval theatrical slapstick is introduced that transforms Mephistopheles, in the last view we have of him, into a figure of ridicule and even disgust. Readers must ask why Goethe wrote such a scene. It helps somewhat to be reminded that the original conception and draft for "Entombment" dates from around 1800, even if our earliest manuscript for the scene (H2) was written out in 1826. The proximity of the slapstick battle of devils and angels thus belongs in fairly close proximity to the "Walpurgis Night" of Part One, where the confused procession of witches and warlocks on their way to the summit of the Brocken takes place. The obeisance to Satan as goat and the sexual orgies of the May Day rites offer the closest parallel in all of *Faust* to what transpires in this penultimate scene of Part Two. There is also an appealing quality of theatrical bravado involved in the staging of this battle scene. We should perhaps keep in mind that previous battles—such as the war between the Pygmies and the Cranes on the slopes of Seismos in the "Classical Walpurgis Night," the staged hostilities along with the military bravado and self-destruction of Euphorion in the Helena act, and the war between the Emperor and the Rival Emperor in Act IV —are also eminently theatrical events, whether they are actually performed on stage or merely reported by eyewitnesses. "Entombment" also brings with it a curious kind of satire directed against the traditional notion of damnation for Faustus.

Mephistopheles believes with some justification that he has won his wager with Faust, and even if he has not clearly done so, the pact signed by Faust in blood still offers evidence that the devil should have power over his soul after death. Yet Mephisto perceives that he may lose Faust's soul if it is allowed to escape through one of the orifices of the corpse and the devils summoned to assistance are not closely attentive. "Catch the fluttering flibbet as it flies," says Mephisto to his troops (11673). The use of the great hell-mouth on stage, through which the varied comic devils, some fat, some lean, emerge from sulfurous flames, also indicates the manner of demonic slapstick that Goethe here intends from the tradition of the medieval theater. The same holds true for the arrival of the angels from above, accompanied by a heavenly "aureole" (stage direction before 11676). In contrast to Mephisto, who speaks in broad, bombastic rhetorical tones, "with fantastic gestures of conjuration, fugelman-fashion" (stage direction before 11636), the angels sing as a chorus, employing brief lyrical outbursts in the short two-stressed lines familiar from the spirit chorus that lulled Faust to sleep in the first study scene of Part One (1447–505). The angels also use a singularly amusing, though appropriate, weapon against the devils: they strew roses, which upon contact turn into flames. We are here reminded also of earlier tactics used by Mephisto—as in "Auerbach's Tavern" or in the Carnival Masque—where either the fraudulent wine or the fake gold turned to demonic fire when dropped.

The high point of the action occurs when Mephisto is distracted by the naked bodies of the Angels in the form of the small plump boys familiar from paintings and sculpture of the European Rococo (from which Goethe no doubt borrowed them). The scandal of the scene is found in the blatant homosexual desire elicited by these "pretty children" (11769). When one of them in particular catches the devil's fancy, Mephisto tries to flirt, suggesting that the Angel remove his robe and turn around to offer "a backward view" (11799). Mephisto even speculates that he is here feeling for the first time the pangs of erotic desire—"Is this love's essence that appeared?" (11784)—such as those that motivated Faust through so much of his career in response to the several female figures he encountered. We are reminded also of Euphorion's attempt to seize and ravish one of the chorus girls, who then also turned into fire. The result of Mephisto's distraction is all too predictable within the slapstick of the scene: the Angels appear in such superior numbers that they fill the stage, drive the devils back to hell, and push Mephisto to the edge of the proscenium (stage direction before 11780), so that he forgets to keep close watch on Faust's corpse. The Angels then "soar up, carrying off Faust's immortal essence" (stage direction before 11825), leaving Mephisto in solitude and remorse, gnashing his teeth, shaking his fist and in a general rage and bluster, very much in the manner of the traditional comic devil from the medieval morality plays. The first step in the salvation of Faust's immortal soul thus takes place as farce, and Mephisto—perhaps recalling his role as jester or rogue in the court of the Lord during the "Prologue in Heaven"—is driven off the stage and out of the drama as the butt of a transcendent joke.

"Mountain Gorges, Forest, Cliffs, Wilderness" (lines 11844–2111)

Two closely related aspects of the final scene have caused difficulty for readers: first, the question of Faust's salvation and its cause within the context of the drama as a whole; second, the apparent Christian vision of the scene, which many have viewed as Goethe's surrender to some kind of theological doctrine, even if the entire scene remains only a symbol for a mystical experience of transcendence. A thematic continuity for this scene with the drama may nonetheless be established, especially in light of the close proximity of the dates of composition for "Mountain Gorges" and the festive conclusion of the "Classical Walpurgis Night." Goethe completed both scenes at virtually the same time during December, 1830. Both scenes offer a celebration of the highest manifestations of the Feminine, and both demonstrate a mode of activity in response to this principle by the human spirit—call that mode erotic desire or Faustian striving—that is free of any limitation, as it is also, in these two instances alone, free of any control imposed by demonic or infernal power. Mephistopheles is absent from both the festival at the Aegean Sea and from the heavenly ascent in "Mountain Gorges." To be honest, of course, so also is Faust the human character absent from both. In the former case, Homunculus's response to Galatea includes the climactic act of self-sacrifice and primal procreation that affirms the cosmic power of Eros. In "Mountain Gorges," the soul, or immortal essence, of Faust, which remains silent throughout and is apparently passive as recipient of divine grace, also enjoys the privilege of a spiritual rebirth, culminating in its response to the penitent spirit of Gretchen, which draws it upward toward higher regions in pursuit of the Glorious Mother. The possibility of a union between the Faustian spirit of desire and the Feminine establishes an ideal norm of creation against which everything else in *Faust* may be measured.

The attainment of such an ideal union between the questing spirit and the Feminine lies beyond human limits, as demonstrated by Faust's entire career with all the error and suffering it causes. No interpretation of Goethe's drama should consider the final scene as some kind of reward or fulfillment for Faustian striving in its own terms. Death is the prerequisite of Faust's salvation, and the cause for this dispensation of undeserved grace lies beyond anything Faust achieved in life, apart from remaining true to his constant striving. In this regard, the speech of the Angels who bear Faust's immortal remains toward Heaven should be taken seriously. Goethe himself considered this the key to Faust's salvation (as he remarked in his conversation with Eckermann on June 6, 1831; see below). The Angels assert that they are able to rescue a spirit only if it has been ceaseless in its active striving, but they intercede to save such a soul only if instructed to do so by the power of a "transfigured love" from above (11934–41). These Angels have been sent to rescue Faust, we thus surmise, by the Mater Gloriosa, presumably in response to the intercession of Gretchen's spirit, which is subsequently dramatized at the end of the scene. The orthography of this speech by the Angels, as printed in all editions of the drama and as contained in the complete manuscript for Act V in the Goethe Archive in Weimar (H1), complicates the grammatical structure of what is said. The two crucial lines referred to by virtually every study of *Faust*—"Whoever strives in ceaseless toil / Him we may grant redemption" (11936 f.)—are contained within quotation marks, though no actual quotation is being made. Similarly, a period occurs at the end of this two-line formulation, as if it were a complete sentence; yet the following line begins with the coordinating conjunction "And," in such a way that a sequence of conditions is implied within a continuous sentence. This statement would best be schematized as follows: if A, then B, and if C, then D. The necessary condition for salvation must include the entire statement as a single, coherent unit. In effect, this condition reaffirms the inherently paradoxical statements by the Lord back in the "Prologue in Heaven," namely, that "man ever errs the while he strives" (317) and "a worthy soul through the dark urge within it / Is well aware of the appointed course" (328 f.). All that is missing in the "Prologue" is mention of the redemptive power of love and the role of the Feminine as object of desire. A splendid irony is thus contained in the conclusion of Goethe's drama, considering the earlier tragic consequences of Gretchen's love for Faust—for her as well as for him—and the subsequent perambulations of his career in Part Two, above all in his urban development project at the end. Nor should this intercession from above on Faust's behalf be interpreted as an act of moral forgiveness, which could only make a travesty of Gretchen's death. Salvation occurs here within the realm of pure spirit as a strictly gratuitous act by the Feminine.

The Christian iconography of the ascension in "Mountain Gorges" claims no more authority as religious doctrine than did the feudal court of the Lord in "Prologue in Heaven." In both cases, Goethe dramatizes a spiritual event within a conventional theatrical setting. Scholars have devoted considerable effort to tracing specific sources for the action and the figures who appear in the final scene. Visual analogues have been cited, as in the frescoes of the Campo Santo, in Pisa, portraying anchorites in the wilderness of Thebes; or the painting by Titian depicting St. Jerome in the wilderness; or the description of the sacred mountain of Montserrat (near Barcelona, in Spain), contained in a study of the Basques written by Wilhelm von Humboldt in 1800. The most important literary tradition used by Goethe in this scene has, however, largely been neglected by scholars. It seems unquestionable that Dante's mystical ascent in the final cantos of the *Paradiso* served as the central model for the dramatization of Faust's salvation. This is apparent, above all, due to the role played by the Virgin Mary, here called Mater Gloriosa, with her train of female attendants. In the final cantos of the *Paradiso*, the Virgin serves as focal point for the poet Dante's power of mystical vision, a power developed by him through his love for Beatrice and her intercession on his behalf. She is his companion in the ascent through the heavens toward the Virgin, with whom she finds her appropriate place—like Gretchen in "Mountain Gorges" at the side of the Mater Gloriosa, among the other devotees of the Madonna, female penitents who, like herself, were also guilty in their lives of misplaced love. Another analogue to Dante's final mystical vision is the use Goethe makes of the Holy Anchorites, who do homage to the Glorious Mother in a complex hierarchy of devotion and celebration. These figures recall the various saints and mystics encountered in the final section of Dante's poem.

The role of Doctor Marianus is particularly crucial in this regard, insofar as his final appeal to the Mother (12096–103) is adapted directly from the prayer addressed to the Virgin by St. Bernard of Clairvaux in the very last canto of the *Divine Comedy*. The most exalted of the Glorious Mother's devotees, positioned in his cell at the summit of the mountain, this Marianic Doctor serves as an extreme counterfigure to Faust as we first encountered him in his academic study at the outset of the drama. Doctor Marianus also resembles Nereus, father of the nymph Galatea in the "Classical Walpurgis Night," in that both represent an extreme of selfless devotion to the respective embodiments of the Feminine. Our final view of Doctor Marianus, just prior to the Chorus Mysticus that concludes the scene and the drama, shows him "prostrate in adoration," celebrating the Madonna, thanking her as "Holy Virgin, Mother, Queen [and] / Goddess" (12102 f.) for her sustaining grace, and praying that she ever remain so: *bleibe gnädig!* Of interest thematically is that the prayer of Doctor Marianus begins with a call to "all who are contrite and tender" (*Alle reuig Zarten*, 12097) to glance or gaze upward toward the glance or gaze of rescue (*Blicket auf zum Retterblick*, 12096). This call establishes a reciprocity of the glance or gaze between those who are truly penitent and the Glorious Mother, who forgives and rescues all who are so, using the term (*Blicken*) that is familiar from Faust's wager with Mephistopheles concerning the ideal moment (*Augenblick*), which through such a plea as the one is here uttered as prayer may be caused to tarry for its beauty. The character of Faust, who failed again and again in life to achieve such a moment, now in spiritual apotheosis beyond death and his mortal body, suspended in silence until his soul responds to the appeal of Gretchen's spirit, is thus offset by this mystical devotee of the Virgin, who celebrates in his prayer and hymn the highest object of love's penitence and devotion as the true means to salvation.

Chorus and Echo (lines 11844–53)

Particularly close attention should be given to the opening passage in the scene, ten lines of what seem to be two-stress dactyls, assigned rather cryptically to "Chorus and Echo." We have no way of knowing who participates in this utterance, presumably sung to an otherwise indeterminate mystical musical accompaniment. (Gustav Mahler's choral setting for these verses, in his Eighth Symphony, is in many ways exemplary.) The anchorite fathers may sing together as chorus, but that would seem too pedestrian for the evocation of natural processes and the scenery or setting appropriate to it. More suitable would be Goethe's once again giving voice to nature itself, as powers of the spirit express the activity that gives them identity in a language that perfectly fuses sign and signified. Description and incantation here become identical, as was earlier the case, for instance, in the hymn of the Archangels, in the Earth Spirit's self-presentation, in the spirit chorus that hypnotizes Faust in the first study scene, and in the chorus of nature spirits that accompanies Ariel in "Charming Landscape." Certain parallels in the songs of the Sirens during the "Classical Walpurgis Night" might also be important. The rhythm and syntax of these ten lines are also peculiar and distinctive, in ways that, alas, defy translation. In the original, each of the first three lines begins with a single bisyllabic noun signifying generically a natural object, followed by a comma and a phrase consisting of a pronoun of apposition and a predicate defining the activity of the particular object named at the outset. The rhythm of the line is thus broken by a caesura after the second syllable, so that all sense of the dactylic meter is lost: *Waldung, sie schwankt heran, / Steine, sie lasten dran, / Wurzeln, sie klammern an / Stamm dicht an Stamm hinan* (in Arndt's translation: "Wild-forest swaying near, / Ponderous boulders here, / Tree roots entwine and close, / Tree trunks in serried rows"). The last word in each of the first four lines consists of an adverb designating a sense of direction or destination for the activity described: *heran, dran, an, hinan,* where the fourfold rhyme is essentially of the repetition and variation of the identical sound. The distinction between the several natural objects or agents named—"forestation," "rocks" or "cliffs," "roots" and "trunks" of trees—seems less important than the differentiated activity of "swaying," "weighing," and "entwining." A network of dynamic, organic interrelationships is thus established, evoking a sense, once again, of great creating nature as cosmic symbolic power.

The remaining lines of the passage elaborate on the implications of the opening. The pattern of bisyllabic nouns at the outset of every line continues with *Woge* ("waves"), *Höhle* ("caves"), and *Löwen* ("lions"). The use of a pronoun in apposition (*sie*) occurs only for the lions, and the activities described become more varied: the waves "gush up" and the caves "shelter," with the monosyllabic verbs *spritzt* and *schützt* in position at the ends of consecutive lines to rhyme with each other. The description of the lions is complicated by a bold enjambment of a double-adverbial form: *stumm- / Freundlich* ("silent-friendly"). The predicate of the statement about the lions, however, introduces an interesting variant on the sequence of directional adverbs (*herum,* "around," instead of the several terms with *-an*) and adds a prepositional phrase with the first-person plural pronoun *um uns* ("around us," not translated by Arndt). Precisely who is to be included in this plurality of those surrounded by these friendly and quiet lions is difficult to say, although the several father figures in the scene to follow no doubt participate in this congenial relationship. Finally, as concluding couplet to this mystical chorus, a remarkable formulation of blessing, consecration, and love occurs, all attributed (so it seems) to these lions, employing a twofold accusative as direct object for the verb "to honor": *Ehren geweihten Ort / Heiligen Liebeshort.* (i.e., "[They] honor [the] consecrated place, [the] sacred space of love"; translated by Arndt as "Honor the hallowed grove, / Refuge of sacred love"). This Chorus and Echo, with which Goethe opens the final scene of *Faust,* has not received much attention from critics; yet in truth the formulation is just as remarkable—indeed, astonishing—a poetic achievement as the concluding Chorus Mysticus. What there constitutes a kind of metacommentary in universal terms (see below) is here an unmediated evocation of natural process itself in affirmation of a mystical, pastoral ideal space. When has a scene in drama ever been introduced by such a musical-poetic prelude in words?

The Four Fathers: Ecstaticus, Profundus, Seraphicus, and Doctor Marianus

The perspective of the entire scene "Mountain Gorges," from the opening Chorus and its Echo to the final Chorus Mysticus, is firmly grounded in lyrical-meditative statements from the several devotional father figures: Pater Ecstaticus, Pater Seraphicus, Pater Profundus, and Doctor Marianus. The first of these, "Ecstatic," who levitates about in the air, chants or sings a single twelve-line stanza (11854–65), using the same rhythmic two-stressed lines employed by the Chorus and Echo with which the scene opens. In a sense, the speech by Pater Ecstaticus could thus be regarded as the Echo of the opening Chorus. The second figure, "Profound," located in the depths, also has only one speech, also presumably sung, which consists of three stanzas of eight lines each, using four-stressed iambic meter with alternating feminine and masculine rhymes. This verse form exactly recapitulates the form of the hymn sung by the Archangels at the outset of the "Prologue in Heaven" and thus suggests an intentional reciprocity between the two passages, located respectively at the start of the prologue and the epilogue to the drama. The third father figure, "Seraphic," located in the central region of the mountain, has a somewhat more complex role. He exchanges speeches in four-stress trochaic lines (the meter derived from Spanish drama) with the chorus of "Blessed Boys," spirits of infants born at midnight who died instantly and thus have no knowledge of life. They hail Pater Seraphicus as their spiritual father, and they subsequently join the other groups of angels, the victorious troops from the battle with the devils in the preceding scene, who are carrying the immortal remains of Faust upward toward Heaven. The spirits of the Blessed Boys, curiously, enter into a sympathetic relation to Faust's soul, which they describe as in its "pupal stage" (11982), though in their last speech, very near the end of the scene (12076–83), they indicate that Faust's soul—perhaps in analogy to Homunculus after he has fused with the sea and come into existence—is growing at a pace that exceeds the ascent of the Blessed Boys, so that they hope to learn from him as from a teacher of life. All four father figures, in a hierarchy of ascent toward Heaven from Ecstaticus to Profundus and on to Seraphicus, ending finally with Doctor Marianus, thematize levels of selfless devotion, thus affirming the centrality of love for the act of forgiveness and redemption that the Mater Gloriosa represents and performs, an act that extends to Gretchen's penitent soul and even to Faust's immortal remains.

Mater Gloriosa and the Group of Penitent Women

The appearance of the Mater Gloriosa with her train of devotees provides yet another surprise. Insofar as the final scene may legitimately be regarded as an epilogue to the drama, set over against the "Prologue in Heaven" as part of a frame, we would expect the figure of the Lord in his heavenly court to reappear. The Glorious Mother serves as a substitute for the traditional patriarchal deity instead. No doubt, the central importance of the Feminine throughout most of *Faust* is partly responsible for her appearance, just as the return of Gretchen's spirit—already anticipated in Faust's monologue at the outset of Act IV, where he watched the ascent of the cirrus cloud toward Heaven—reintroduces the theme of love for Faust as a redemptive power. Yet even more striking is the emphasis placed here on penitence, not only for Gretchen, who is called "the One Penitent" (in Latin, *Una Poenitentium*), but also with regard to the three otherwise unfamiliar female figures who appear along with her. Each of the three has a title in Latin, followed by a reference to the respective source (which may have been added to the fair copy of the manuscript by Riemer, yet no doubt on Goethe's instructions).

1. Magna Peccatrix is perhaps most likely to be known from the Gospel of Luke, where she washes Jesus' feet with her tears in the house of Simon the Pharisee, then kisses them and wipes them dry with her hair. The central theme of penitence and forgiveness for sins is indicated by Jesus' words in response: "Her sins, which are many, are forgiven, for she loved much" (Luke 7.47).

2. Mulier Samaritana is known from the Gospel of John, where Jesus visits the well of Jacob and, tired from his journey and the heat of the day, asks her to give him water from the well to drink. She is a sinner, according to the account, because she has had five husbands and the man with whom she curently lives is not her husband. In response to the request from Jesus, however, the woman of Samaria recognizes him as the true Messiah.

3. The third woman, Maria Aegyptiaca, is the most obscure of all. In the *Acts of the Saints*, a seventeenth-century Jesuitical collection of stories about Catholic saints, Goethe found an account of her conversion. After living for seventeen years as a prostitute, she was prevented by an invisible force from entering the Church of the Holy Sepulchre in Jerusalem. She prayed to the Blessed Virgin for forgiveness and was miraculously transported into the church, where she heard a voice instructing her to dwell beyond the Jordan River. Subsequently, Mary of Egypt lived for forty-eight years as a strict penitent in the desert and at her death was buried in the sand as holy ground by the monk Socinius.

All three women may be compared to Gretchen in their guilt for carnal sins, for which all three were forgiven when they truly repented. They set an example for Gretchen's forgiveness as well. Indeed, all three together, following their separate speeches in the scene, pray directly to the Glorious Mother on Gretchen's behalf, urging that her one act of sin be forgiven. Gretchen speaks immediately after this appeal (12069–75), adapting the prayer of the Stabat Mater, which she once spoke to the statue of the Virgin as Mater Dolorosa in the niche outside the city wall, after Faust had made her pregnant out of wedlock (see 3587–619). Her appeal now to the Mater Gloriosa is not for herself but for the soul of Faust, following the example of Beatrice in Dante's *Divine Comedy*, who intercedes with the Virgin on the poet's behalf. Gretchen's soul wishes to lead Faust's soul into the bright light of a new morning (12092 f.). In response to this prayer as well as the appeal of three repentent sinners, the Glorious Mother grants the request in her two-line speech, the only words she utters in the scene: Gretchen will soar upward to higher spheres (presumably along with the Mother) and Faust, when he becomes aware of her presence, will also ascend. Goethe may here once again be following the example of a painting, in this case a work by the obscure artist Benedetto Caliari, dating from around 1595, showing the Virgin Mary holding the Christ child, hovering in the air, while three figures of female penitents kneel before her in prayer. Goethe knew this painting, which is now in the Museo Betrario di Murano, from his visits to Venice, either in 1786 or 1790, when it hung over the altar in the Chiesa del Soccorso.

Chorus Mysticus (lines 12104–11)

Among the many difficult and obscure passages in *Faust* that have caused much misunderstanding and debate, none may be so challenging as the final poetic passage of eight short two-stressed lines assigned to an otherwise unexplained Chorus Mysticus. Much of this difficulty derives from controversy concerning the final two lines, where the Eternal-Feminine is named for the only time in the drama. Yet the language of the entire passage is curiously abstract and general, so that the question of reference and context needs to be raised for all of it. Who is speaking (or singing)? And what is being stated?

In manuscript drafts for the final section of "Mountain Gorges" (HgII and Hn), the attribution for the final passage is "Chorus in Excelsis" (though in the later of these manuscripts, the term "mysticus" is written in Goethe's hand after "in Excelsis" is crossed out). The point seems to be that no specific individual character or even collective group of characters is speaking or singing here. There is no referent for the final words of the drama, nor even any context that defines how this utterance occurs. The only comparable instance to such openness and indeterminacy of statement is found at the very end of the festival that concludes the "Classical Walpurgis Night," when Eros is celebrated as cosmic creative force by "All in Unison" (*All-Alle!*, 8484–7). At these moments, Goethe intends the scope of his drama to transcend all particularity of representation. With the Chorus Mysticus, however, there is also an apparent sense of an ending, of completion and of fulfillment, that is to be memorialized. For this reason, the question of reference and reflection must extend beyond anything in the last scene or even in the last act of Part Two. In fact, in the manner of a transcendent postlude, the Chorus opens a universal perspective, which gathers the full complexity of the entire drama into itself. Only as such an all-inclusiveness do the verb forms in the present tense — "is" and "becomes"—have any validity, as also do the repeated adverbial terms of immediate place: "Here." Each of the four statements, each filling two lines, implicates the others, almost as if the same thing were being stated in four different ways. The use of general adjectival substantives in all four also adds to a sense of repetition and variation. A few comments with paraphrase on each statement may help to clarify the implications of what the Chorus proclaims.

1. Everything that is transient (*Alles Vergängliche*), that is, that which is subject to time and change, to the processes of life, nature, thought, and art—these are arbitrary instances for such an all-inclusive claim—is only a simile, or a figure, or an "equation" (*Gleichnis*). This idea implies that everything temporal and transient merely stands for something else, eternal

and immutable, perhaps unspoken and unknown, that is, not known and presumably unknowable.

2. That which is insufficient or inadequate, which fails to reach its goal —*das Unzulängliche*, not a term that evokes any familiar verbal usage, is constructed from a verb form (*zulangen*) that implies reaching toward or attaining something—here (wherever that may be) becomes an event (*Ereignis*, a term suggesting in its original sense of *er-äugnen*, "something that comes into view").

3. That which cannot be described (*das Unbeschreibliche*), or perhaps, in closer alignment to the verb "to write" (*schreiben*), that which cannot be put into language, here (again without a clear sense of "where," except that it implies the same place as the preceding assertion) it is, or has been, done (*ist . . . getan*). The verb "to do" (*tun*) evokes, of course, the primal deed that Faust introduces to his translation of *Logos* in the opening line of the Gospel of John (1237).

4. In apparent departure from the minimalist formulations preceding, the final couplet asserts that the Eternal-Feminine (*das Ewig-Weibliche*) "draws us onward" (*zieht uns hinan*). The first three statements, however oblique in their formulation, appear very similar to each other in affirming a state of being or a happening, whereas the fourth appears at first to resist any sense of such a universal or generic activity. Who is meant here by "us," and what does it mean to be "drawn onward"? More detailed comment is necessary here.

One possible response—though by no means the only viable one—to the entire Chorus would be to consider the four statements as a kind of meta-commentary on the drama that is now and here completed, that is, as a suitable reference to the work as a whole. There would thus also be intended an intuition of closure, extending back to the metatheatrical comments of the "Prelude in the Theater," even though the links would be no more than implicit. The drama as a whole thus functions as a *Gleichnis*, a figure or symbol, where everything that happens in this temporal and transient process stands for something else, signifies or presents that which is not temporal or transient. Similarly, with an oblique allusion perhaps to the central force of desire and will in the drama, that is, to Faustian striving, that which cannot be achieved or reached by such effort in any definitive or tangible way, here (in and through the work as a whole) has come into view and is now an *event*. Third, in terms that may intentionally recall Faust's effort to translate the *Logos* from the opening of the Gospel of John as "Deed" (*Tat*; see 1237), that which cannot be adequately described, or represented, or even just written into language, has here and now been done, or en-acted. All three statements thus may serve in productive ways as a meta-reflective commentary on what the drama has achieved as a whole.

May we not argue the same for the final couplet with regard to the effect of the Eternal-Feminine *upon ourselves* (insofar as we serve as the readers of or audience for the drama itself)? Thus, however we interpret the term "Eternal-Feminine," its effect *on us* is correctly formulated as a "drawing onward" (*hinan-ziehen*). Our experience as recipients of Goethe's work would also thus be characterized in a quasi-Faustian manner, in response to that power or agency within the work that affects us in such a Faustian way, as a *drawing onward* by the Eternal-Feminine. And perhaps we may also achieve an intuition of what the Eternal-Feminine may signify for us by contrasting it with the only legitimate counterterm in the entire work, a neologism with precisely the same form as double-generic-adjectival noun, namely the term with which Mephistopheles brought Faust's death scene to a close: *das Ewig-Leere* (11603). Note that the abstract term "Eternal-Feminine" does not pertain at all to the difference between male and female readers of *Faust*.

How appropriate that the final term of the Chorus Mysticus may designate a positive, creative principle as it affects us in the theater or on the page, in a manner that is the exact opposite of the negative, even nihilistic denial of any meaning that Mephisto applies to Faust's entire lifetime. Thus, as for the devil everything was then over and done, without any substance or value, content or meaning, so for us, by contrast, everything in the drama that may legitimately be described through the term "Eternal-Feminine" affects us, and continues to do so, as a *drawing onward*. In this unique manner, through his Chorus Mysticus, Goethe at the very end of his long and productive life as a writer brought *Faust* to a close, signaling perhaps to his reader that not only the work but also everything he had lived and thought was now complete and fulfilled or accomplished (*vollbracht*, 11594). To indicate this, he wrote, for the only time in his career, on the last page of the fair copy in manuscript for this work, which would be published only after his death: FINIS.

CONTEXTS

Goethe's own drawing for Faust's encounter with the Earth Spirit
in the scene "Night."

Lithograph by the French Romantic artist Eugène Delacroix,
published in the 1820s, of Faust in his study.

Faust offering his arm to Gretchen (Margarete) as she leaves confession in church, illustrated by the German Romantic artist Peter Cornelius.

Faust and Mephistopheles ascending the Brocken in the Harz
Mountains to attend the revels of the Walpurgis Night, as illustrated
by Cornelius.

Faust and Mephistopheles riding past the gibbet on magic horses to the dungeon where Gretchen awaits execution, as illustrated by Delacroix.

The end of the scene "Dungeon," as illustrated by Cornelius.

Faust and Mephistopheles with Gretchen in the scene
"Dungeon," as illustrated by Delacroix.

Giorgione, *Venus Sleeping in a Landscape*, located in the Gallery of Paintings in Dresden, which Goethe visited. This image may have been the source of the vision in the magic mirror of the Witch's kitchen.

Correggio, *Leda and the Swan*, now in the Gallery of Paintings in Berlin. Goethe owned an engraving of this painting, which presumably served as an influence for Faust's dream in Act II of Part Two.

Raphael, *Triumph of Galatea*, in the Villa Farnesina in Rome, which Goethe visited. The epiphany at the end of the "Classical Walpurgis Night" derives from this image.

The Composition of *Faust*

The following table provides a schematic overview of the entire work in terms of its formal structure. At the simplest level, this structure may be defined according to the titles of individual scenes (most of them given by the poet), here listed with the appropriate line numbers. Beyond this, the table provides a summary of the metrical forms that appear in the various scenes (sometimes in astonishing complexity even within single scenes), and also the dates of composition scene by scene, insofar as these can be definitely or approximately fixed.

Metrical Form

The range and variety of verse forms in *Faust* is more complex than in any other work of literature. Goethe undertook to imitate and adapt forms from the entire tradition of Western poetry. The variety of verse forms is especially great in Part Two, which contains several scenes depending sometimes on a sense of earlier poetic structures, sometimes on quasi-musical effects; examples are the Carnival Masque in Act I, the "Classical Walpurgis Night" in Act II, the entire Helena act, and the closing scene of the tragedy. But the flexibility and the dramatic effectiveness of much of *Faust* depends on the use of what is often called the "*Faust* verse" (sometimes referred to in Germany as "madrigal verse"). In German poetic drama, it had become customary by the end of the eighteenth century to use Shakespearian blank verse (unrhymed iambic pentameter). Goethe had begun work on *Faust*, however, using an adaptation of the traditional and popular poetic form from sixteenth-century German literature (the era of the historical Faustus) called *Knittelvers*. This is a very free poetic line, often iambic with four stresses, but often varying the number of stressed syllables and the pattern of unstressed syllables and using a varying rhyme scheme with both masculine and feminine endings. For Goethe, this verse form had from the start a quaint, archaic, somewhat rough-hewn quality, like the style of old woodcuts. As his work on *Faust* proceeded, however, especially in the Gretchen tragedy and, later, in the section written around 1800 for Part One, Goethe developed this archaic and crude verse form into a highly sophisticated and subtle instrument of stylistic and poetic variation.

Dates of Composition

Goethe worked on *Faust* for more than sixty years from its conception around 1770, when he was a young man in his twenties, to its completion in 1831, a year before his death. The documentary evidence for reconstructing his labors is enormous, including Goethe's own comments in his diaries and correspondence and the many manuscripts of Faust that have been preserved (especially of Part Two). Any outline of the dates of composition scene by scene must acknowledge that individual scenes may have a complex evolution, extending over many years (consider the scenes "Midnight," "Great Outer Precinct of the Palace," and "Entombment" in Act V), so that the final text results from a process of development that is no longer visible in the text; and also that dates of composition for individual scenes, and even for sections of individual scenes and single lines, can often be given by approximation only, even where the evidence from documents is fairly precise. Reconstructing the process of composition remains a highly artificial and abstract venture; even if we know from a particular manuscript that Goethe worked on a particular scene on a particular day, this does not necessarily tell us anything about how the scene was written or why.

In general, the history of composition for Faust falls into six periods, each of which ended when Goethe set the project aside for several years or decided to publish some newly completed part of it.

a. The *Urfaust*, or "original *Faust*" (c. 1772–5). We know very little about when Goethe first began writing *Faust*, though there is evidence to suggest that the earliest scenes (which in the text of the *Urfaust* as we have it may already have been the result of considerable revision; and who can tell how many scenes were thrown away or completely lost?) were probably written in the last three years before Goethe moved to Weimar late in 1775. It is generally acknowledged that the composition of the Gretchen tragedy was a more or less coherent creative endeavor, perhaps done fairly quickly and perhaps one of the later parts of the *Urfaust* to be written. (Our text of the *Urfaust* derives from a transcription by Luise von Göchhausen, a lady of the court at Weimar; it was prepared from Goethe's manuscript, soon after he settled in Weimar, and rediscovered in 1887.)

b. *Faust. A Fragment* (1788–90). In March and April, 1788, when Goethe was in Rome, he undertook to prepare *Faust* for publication in an edition of his *Collected Works*. The scenes "Witch's Kitchen" and "Forest and Cave" were composed at that time in the form in which we know them. Further work occurred after Goethe returned to Weimar in late 1789, involving the recasting into verse of prose scenes from the original (e.g., "Auerbach's Tavern").

c. *The Tragedy*, Part One (1797–1806). Work on *Faust*, Part One, began again in June, 1797, in response to repeated urging from Schiller (see below). At that time (June 24) Goethe wrote the "Dedication," organized the materials in his manuscript, and outlined his plans for work to be done. By the end of 1797, the "Walpurgis Night's Dream" was complete (though not originally intended for *Faust* at all), and a draft for most of the Walpurgis Night as we have it was written in the following year or so, along with a numbered sequence and sketch of scenes for the play. "Dungeon" appears to have been recast from prose to verse in April and May, 1798. The "Prelude in the Theater" was probably composed in conjunction with Goethe's work on the renovation of the Weimar Theater in the

summer and fall of 1798. The "Prologue in Heaven" was presumably
written soon after Goethe's study of Milton's *Paradise Lost* in the summer
of 1799. Sustained work on the "great lacuna" (lines 606–1769), a crucial
part of the drama that Goethe had put off writing for twenty-five years,
appears to have occurred during 1800–1, along with further work on the
"Walpurgis Night." Nothing further was done on Part One until early
1806, when Goethe prepared his final manuscript for publication in
vol. 8 of the new edition of his *Collected Works*.

   d. *Helena. Classical-Romantic Phantasmagoria. Interlude to "Faust"*
(1825–6). Goethe began work again on *Faust* in March, 1825, by turning
to the first draft of the *Helena* (lines 8488–802), which had been written
in September, 1800. He continued composing Act III until early June,
1826. After minor revisions, it was sent to the publisher that autumn to be
included in vol. 4 of the final edition of the *Collected Works* (*Ausgabe
letzter Hand*).

   e. In February and March, 1825, Goethe revised earlier drafts of three
scenes for Act V ("Midnight," "Great Outer Precinct of the Palace," and
"Entombment"), which had been written in 1800–1. Goethe's scribe prepared a manuscript fair copy of these scenes in March and April, 1826.

   Act I of Part Two (lines 4613–6036) was published separately in vol. 12
of the final edition of the *Collected Works*, which appeared in 1828. The
scenes in the Emperor's court (Imperial Residence) were composed in
sequence during the latter half of 1826 and most of 1827. The opening
scene of Part Two, "Charming Landscape," was composed in two sections:
Faust's monologue in terza rima (lines 4679–727) in the spring of 1826;
Ariel's song and the elfin chorus (4613–78) in the summer of 1827.

   f. The concluding scenes of Act I ("Pleasance," "Dark Gallery,"
"Brightly Lit Ballrooms," and "Hall of Chivalry") and the opening scenes
of Act II ("Narrow, High-Vaulted Gothic Chamber" and "Laboratory")
were composed during the latter part of 1829. The "Classical Walpurgis
Night" was begun during the first half of 1830 and completed in December of that year, at the same time that the final scene of Act V, "Mountain
Gorges," was written. Act IV and the opening scenes of Act V ("Open
Country," "Palace," and "Deep Night") were written during the first half
of 1831. Goethe sealed up the completed manuscript of Part Two in July,
1831, for publication after his death. It appeared in 1832 as the first volume of his *Posthumous Works*.

Analytical Table

Scene (with Line Numbers)	Metrical Form	Date of Composition[1]
Dedication (1–32)	ottava rima	June 24, 1797 (C)
Prelude in the Theater (33–242)	Faust verse	late 1798 (C)
Prologue in Heaven (243–353)	Faust verse, with hymn in four-stress iambics, eight-line stanzas	late 1799 (C)
THE TRAGEDY'S FIRST PART		
Night (354–807)		
a) 354–605, excluding 598–601	Knittelvers and Faust verse, with free rhythm	ca. 1772–3 (A)
b) 598–601 and 606–807	Faust verse, with choral hymn in two-stress dactylics	probably 1799–1800 (C)
Outside the City Gate (808–1177)	Faust verse, with songs	1800–1 (C)
Study (I) (1178–529)	Faust verse, with eight-line stanzas, four-stress iambics, free verse (Spirits), short line incantations, and song in two-stress short line	1800–1 (C)
Study (II) (1530–2072)		
a) 1530–769	Faust verse, with spirit chorus in free verse	1800–1 (C)
b) 1770–867 and 2051–72	Faust verse	1788–9 (B)
c) 1868–2050	Faust verse	before 1775 (A); revised 1789 (B)
Auerbach's Tavern in Leipzig (2073–336)	Faust verse, with songs and chants	before late 1775 in prose (A); revised as verse 1789 (B)
Witch's Kitchen (2337–604)	Faust verse, with chants and spells	March–April, 1788 (B)
[Gretchen tragedy] (2605–3834)	Faust verse (with exceptions as noted)	1774–5 (A); revised 1789 (B)

Street (2605–77)		
Evening (2678–804)		
On a Walk (2805–64)		
The Neighbor's House (2865–3024)	(with ballad)	
Street (3025–72)		
Garden (3073–204)		
A Garden Pavilion (3205–16)		
Forest and Cave (3217–373)		
a) 3217–341	(with monologue in blank verse)	1788–9 (B; after "At the Well") before late 1775 (A; part of Valentine scene, after "Cathedral")
b) 3342–69		
Gretchen's Chamber (3374–413)	four-line stanzas in two-stress loose iambics	
Marthe's Garden (3414–543)	(with "credo" in short-line free verse)	
At the Well (3544–85)		
By the City Wall (3586–619)	prayer, with varying line and stanza	
Night ("Valentine scene") (3620–775)		
a) 3620–45 and 3650–9	(with song)	1775 (A) (see "Forest and Cave")
b) 3646–9 and 3660–995	free verse, with choral hymn in Latin	March, 1806 (C)
Cathedral (3776–834)	*Faust* verse, with songs and chants	1775 (A)
Walpurgis Night (3835–4222)		1798–9 and 1800–1; completed early 1806 (C)
Walpurgis Night's Dream or the Golden Wedding of Oberon and Titania. Intermezzo (4223–398)	trochaic ballad stanza	1797; revised December (C)
lines 4335–42		added 1826 for *Collected Works*

1. First publication (including the copy by Luise von Göchhausen) is indicated following date of composition by a letter in parenthesis, as follows: (A) *Urfaust*; (B) *Fragment*; (C) Part One; (D) *Helena*; (E) Act I, Part Two (to line 6036); (F) Part Two.

509

Analytical Table (cont)

Scene (with Line Numbers)	Metrical Form	Date of Composition[1]
Dreary Day. Field	prose	perhaps 1772–3 (A)
Night. Open Field (4399–404)	free verse	before late 1775 (A)
Dungeon (4405–612)	*Faust* verse, with song and irregular short lines	before late 1775 in prose (A); revised as verse April–May, 1798 (C)
THE TRAGEDY'S PART TWO IN FIVE ACTS		
Act One (4613–6565)		
Charming Landscape (4613–727)		
a) 4613–78	song (four-stress trochaics in eight-line stanzas), with *Faust* verse	summer, 1827
b) 4678–727	terza rima	spring, 1826
Imperial Residence[2] (4728–6565)		
Throne Room (4728–5064)	*Faust* verse	summer, 1827 (E)
Spacious Hall ("Carnival Masque," 5065–5986)		autumn and winter, 1827 (E)
a) Procession with Herald (5065–456)	*Faust* verse (Herald); varying four-stress trochaics and iambics, often in four-line stanzas	
b) Allegory of Plutus (5457–800)	*Faust* verse (with brief sequence of four-stress trochaics)	
c) Pan and his train (5801–986)	*Faust* verse; two-stress iambics; four-stress trochaics in four-line stanzas; four-stress trochaics	

510

Scene	Verse	Date
Pleasance (5988–6172) a) 5988–6036 b) 6037–172	*Faust* verse	early 1826 (E)
Dark Gallery (6173–306)	*Faust* verse	late 1829 (F)
Brightly Lit Ballrooms (6307–76)	*Faust* verse	late 1829 (F)
Hall of Chivalry (6377–565)	*Faust* verse	late 1829 (F)
Act Two (6566–8487)		
[Faust's Study] (6566–7004)		
Narrow, High-Vaulted Gothic Chamber (6566–818)	*Faust* verse, with chorus and four-stress trochaic six-line stanzas	late 1829 (F)
Laboratory (6819–7004)	*Faust* verse	late 1829 (F)
Classical Walpurgis Night (7005–8487)		January to June, 1830; completed December, 1830 (F)
Pharsalian Fields (7005–79)	iambic trimeter; four-stress trochaics	
On the Upper Peneios (7080–248)	*Faust* verse; four-stress trochaics	
On the Lower Peneios (7240–494)	*Faust* verse, with four-stress trochaics, dactylic chant, and free rhythm	
On the Upper Peneios, as before (7495–8033)	four-stress trochaics; *Faust* verse; songs; free rhythm	
Rocky Inlets of the Aegean Sea (8034–487)	dialogue in *Faust* verse, with alternating episodes in four-stress trochaics, irregular three-stress line, anapestic choral verse, iambic and dactylic systems, with variants of all these	

1. First publication (including the copy by Luise von Göchhausen) is indicated following date of composition by a letter in parenthesis, as follows: (A) *Urfaust*; (B) *Fragment*; (C) Part One; (D) *Helena*; (E) Act I, Part Two (to line 6036); (F) Part Two.
2. The first act of Part Two may be properly said to commence after "Charming Landscape," which serves as a symbolic prelude to the entire second part of *Faust*. The stage direction for the opening scene in the Emperor's court, "Imperial Residence," applies to the entire first act.

Analytical Table (cont)

Scene (with Line Numbers)	Metrical Form	Date of Composition[1]
Act Three (8488–10038) [Helena. Classical-Romantic Phantasmagoria. Interlude to Faust] (8488–10038) Before the Palace of Menelaos in Sparta (8488–9126)	imitation Greek tragedy: dialogue in iambic trimeter and occasional trochaic tetrameter, with choral odes in responding stanzas	March, 1825 to June, 1826; final revisions to early 1827 (D)
Inner Courtyard of a Fortress (9127–573)	gradual shift from iambic trimeter to blank verse, with interludes of choral odes and songs in ballad stanza, concluding with pastoral lyric in four-line iambic stanzas	
Arcadia (9574–10038) *Parabasis* [Prelude] (9574–673) Euphorion opera (9674–938)	trochaic tetrameter; choral ode sequence of musical forms: prelude in trochaic stanzas; dance sequence with solos, choruses, and ensemble in a variety of short lines, leading to a climax in ceremonial measure (six-syllable line with varying stress pattern), followed by couplets and choral dirge	

Scene (lines)	Verse	Date
[Postlude] (9939–10038)	sequence of speeches in iambic trimeter, blank verse, and *Faust* verse, with free verse and trochaic tetrameter	early February to late July, 1831 (F)
Act Four (10039–11042)		
High Mountains (10039–344)	iambic trimeter; *Faust* verse	
In the Foothills (10345–782)	*Faust* verse, with four-stress trochaics	
The Rival Emperor's Tent (10783–11042)	*Faust* verse; Alexandrines	
Act Five (11043–142)		
Open Country (11043–142)	four-stress trochaics	April–May, 1831 (F)
Palace (11143–287)	*Faust* verse, with iambic short lines	April–May, 1831 (F)
Deep Night (11288–383)	song in two-stress short lines; four-stress trochaics; *Faust* verse	April–May, 1831 (F)
Midnight (11384–510)	four-stress anapestic chant; alternating *Faust* verse and four-stress trochaics	draft ca. 1800–1; fair copy February–March, 1825 (F)
Great Outer Precinct of the Palace (11511–603)	song; *Faust* verse	draft ca. 1800–1; fair copy February–March, 1825 (F)
Entombment (11604–843)	song: *Faust* verse, alternating with two-stress irregular dactylics	draft ca. 1800–1; fair copy February–March, 1825 (F)
Mountain Gorges (11844–12111)	profusion of varying lyric and choral forms (dactylic and iambic systems with varying lengths of line)	December, 1830 (F)

513

1. First publication (including the copy by Luise von Göchhausen) is indicated following date of composition by a letter in parenthesis, as follows: (A) *Urfaust*; (B) *Fragment*; (C) Part One; (D) *Helena*; (E) Act I, Part Two (to line 6036); (F) Part Two.

Goethe on *Faust*

Various documents, both public and private, have been preserved from many stages in Goethe's work on *Faust*, which offer valuable indications of his own purpose and attitude concerning his work. The following selections, many of which are here translated into English for the first time, provide a chronological survey of Goethe's views.

From Goethe's Autobiography, *From My Life, Poetry and Truth*, vol. 4 (1812)†

[From the account of his first meeting with Herder in Strassburg, 1771 (Book 10)]

I took great care to conceal from him [Herder] my interest in certain subjects which had rooted themselves in me and seemed to be developing gradually into poetic form. These were Götz von Berlichingen and Faust. The former's account of his life had gripped my inmost being. The image of this rough, well-intentioned, independent man living at a time of wild anarchy aroused my deepest interest. As to the other, the significant puppet play about him resounded and hummed within me in many tonal variations. I too had dabbled in all knowledge and had quite soon discovered the futility of this. I too had tried all sorts of things in life only to abandon them in ever greater discontent and torment. These and many other matters I now had constantly in mind, and took delight in them in lonely hours, without, however, writing anything down. But most of all I concealed my mystic-cabalistic chemistry, and everything connected with it, from Herder, although I still liked to study it in secret and develop it more logically than it had been transmitted to me.

[Goethe recalls the impact of Faust on his circle of friends in Darmstadt after he returned to Frankfurt from Strassburg (1772), in the context of his interest in fifteenth- and sixteenth-century culture and architecture (e.g., the cathedral at Strassburg, which he celebrated in his essay "On German Architecture") (Book 12).]

It would be impossible to state how much this circle stimulated and benefited me. They willingly listened when I read my finished or unfinished works aloud, they encouraged me when I told them candidly and in detail what I was planning to do, and they scolded me when, for the

---

† Vol. 4 of *Collected Works in Twelve Volumes*, ed. Thomas P. Saine and Jeffrey L. Sammons, trans. Robert R. Heitner (New York: Suhrkamp Publishers, 1989), 306 and 376.

sake of a new project, I neglected something already begun. *Faust* was already well along, *Götz von Berlichingen* was gradually taking shape in my mind, I was occupied with my study of the fifteenth and sixteenth centuries, and the cathedral edifice in Strassburg had left me with a very grave impression of itself that made a suitable background for such literary works.

From *Italian Journey*, vol. 3: *Second Sojourn in Rome* (1829)†

[*Writing from Rome near the end of his Italian journey (March 1, 1788) to Duke Carl August in Weimar, Goethe describes his experience in returning to the manuscript drafts for* Faust, *which he had not touched for more than a decade, as he prepares the* Fragment *for publication in his collected works* (Schriften, *vol. 7, 1790).*]

I have had the courage to think over my last three volumes all at the same time, and now I know exactly what I want to do; may Heaven give me the disposition and good fortune to do it.

It was a full week, seeming to me in retrospect like a month.

First, I made the plan for *Faust*, and I hope that it has been a successful undertaking. Of course, finishing the play now is different from finishing it fifteen years ago, but I do not think it will suffer on that account, especially since I believe I have found the thread again. I also feel confident about the tone of the whole; I have already written a new scene, and if I were to discolor the paper with smoke, I doubt that anyone would be able to distinguish it from the old ones. My long rest and isolation have brought me back entirely to the level of my own existence, and it is remarkable how much I have remained the same, and how little my inner self has been affected by the years and events. The old manuscript sometimes puts me in a reverie when I see it lying before me. It is still the original one, in fact, just the main scenes, written down spontaneously and without plan; now it is so yellow with age, so worn (the quires were never bound), so brittle, and crumpled at the edges, that it really does look like an old codex. And just as I then, by meditation and surmise, put myself back into an earlier world, I must now put myself back into my own olden times.

Faust Plan of 1800††

Ideal striving to achieve an influence upon and a feeling for the whole of Nature.

† Vol. 6 of *Collected Works in Twelve Volumes*, ed. Thomas P. Saine and Jeffrey L. Sammons, trans. Robert R. Heitner (New York: Suhrkamp Publishers, 1989), 424.
†† The precise date of the writing of this plan (translated by Cyrus Hamlin) is not known, but it clearly reflects Goethe's general view of the drama at the time when he returned to the composition of Part One (c. 1797–1800). Mention of the division of the drama into two parts indicates that the plan must have been written after that decision was made (probably in 1800).

The appearance of the Spirit as Ge-
         nius of the World and of Action.

Conflict between Form and the Formless.
Preference for formless content
over empty form.
Content provides form
Form is never without content.
Such contradictions, instead of uniting them,
         make them more disparate.
Bright, clear scientific striving Wagner
Dull, warm —— —— Student
~~Life's Deeds Essence~~
                                 viewed from without
Enjoyment of Life by the person   Part I   in a stupor
                                                  Passion
              directed outwards and Enjoyment with Consciousness.
Enjoyment of Deeds second   ——   Beauty.
              from within.
Enjoyment of Creation   Epilogue in Chaos on the way
                                                  to Hell.

From Goethe's Correspondence with Schiller, 1794–1801†

Schiller to Goethe

JENA, NOVEMBER 29, 1794

No less great is my desire to read those parts of your *Faust* which are as yet unpublished; for I can honestly say that what I have read of it is to me like the torso of an Hercules.[1] There reigns in those scenes the power and the fulness of genius which unmistakably reveals the first master, and I should like as far as possible to follow the great and bold spirit that breathes in them.

---

† Goethe's close friendship with Friedrich Schiller (1759–1805) from 1794 until the latter's death was important for the development of thought and work for both writers. The almost daily exchange of letters between Jena, where Schiller lived until 1800 when he moved to Weimar, and the nearby Duchy of Weimar, where Goethe had resided since 1775, allows us to follow this development of ideas in detail. The excerpts included here reveal the extent to which Schiller took an active role in persuading the older poet to return to *Faust* during the years from 1797 to 1801, leading to the eventual publication of Part One soon after Schiller's death. The letters are reprinted from *Correspondence Between Schiller and Goethe from 1794 to 1805*, trans. L. Dora Schmitz (London: George Bell and Sons, 1890).
1. Schiller refers to the *Fragment* of 1790, included by Goethe in his collected works (see August Wilheim Schlegel's review, below), which Schiller must have read in its published form.

Goethe to Schiller

WEIMAR, DECEMBER 2, 1794

Of *Faust* I cannot as yet let you have anything. I cannot make up my mind to untie the packet in which it is imprisoned. I could not copy without working it out, and I have no courage for that. If anything could induce me to do this at some future time it would certainly be your interest in it.

Goethe to Schiller

WEIMAR, JUNE 22, 1797

As it is extremely necessary that in my present restless state I should set myself something to do, I have determined to take up my *Faust* and, if not to finish it, at all events to bring it a good deal further, by breaking up what has been printed and arranging it in large masses with what is already finished or invented, and of thus further preparing the development of the play, which is in reality as yet only an idea.[2] I have merely taken up this idea and its representation again, and have pretty well made up my mind about it. I only wish, however, that you would be so good as to think the matter over on one of your sleepless nights, and to tell me the demands which you would require of the whole, and in this manner to narrate and to interpret to me my own dreams like a true prophet.

As the different parts of this poem—in what relates to mood—might be treated differently, provided only that they be kept subordinate to the spirit and tone of the whole, and as, moreover, the whole work is subjective, I can work at it at odd moments, and am therefore at present able to do something to it.

Schiller to Goethe

JENA, JUNE 23, 1797

Your resolution to set to work at your *Faust* was indeed a surprise to me, especially just now, when you are thinking of a trip to Italy. But I have at once and for all given up the idea of measuring you by the usual standard of logic, and am therefore convinced beforehand that your genius will see you well through the task.

The request you make that I should tell you of my requirements and *desideria*, is not so easily fulfilled; but as far as I can I will try to discover your thread, and if that cannot be managed, will do so as if I had accidentally found the fragments of *Faust* and had myself to work them out. This much only I will here remark, that *Faust*—the piece itself I mean— in spite of all its poetic individuality, cannot quite ward off the demand for a symbolical treatment, as probably is the case with your own idea.

2. From Goethe's diary we know that the poem "Dedication," which speaks of the experience of returning to *Faust* after decades of neglect, was composed on June 24, 1797, two days after this letter was written.

The duality of human nature and the unsuccessful endeavour to unite in man the godlike and the physical, is never lost sight of; and as the story runs and must run into what is fantastic and formless, people will not consent to remain by the subject, but will be led from it to ideas. In short, the demands on *Faust* are both philosophical and poetical, and you may turn in whichever direction you please, the nature of the subject will force you to treat it philosophically, and the imagination will have to accommodate itself to serve a rational idea.

But I can scarcely be telling you anything new by saying this, for you have already, in a great measure, begun to satisfy this demand in what you have already, accomplished.

Goethe to Schiller

WEIMAR, JUNE 24, 1797

Thank you for your first words on my reawakening *Faust*. We shall probably not differ in our views of this work, and yet quite a different kind of courage comes over one when one sees one's thoughts and projects characterised by another; and your sympathy is fruitful in more than one sense.

I shall now first of all endeavour to finish the large masses that are already invented and half wrought out, put them into some connection with what has been printed, and go on in this way till the circle is exhausted.

Schiller to Goethe

JENA, JUNE 26, 1797

Your *Faust* I have now again read through, and I feel actually giddy from the *dénouement*.[3] This, however, is very natural, for the matter is based upon some special conception, and so long as this is not grasped, a subject much less rich than the present one would put reason into a state of dilemma. What I am anxious about in regard to it is that, in accordance with its character, *Faust* appears to require a totality of material if, at the end, the idea is to appear completely carried out; and I know of no poetic framework for holding together a mass that springs up to such a height. However, you will know what you have to do.

For instance, it was, as I think, appropriate that *Faust* should be led into active life, and whatever sphere you may select from this mass, it nevertheless seems to me that his nature will demand too great an amount of circumstantiality and breadth.

As regards the treatment, I find the greatest difficulty to be that of proceeding happily between what is jest and earnest. Reason and common sense seem to me in this subject to be struggling as if for life and death.

---

3. Schiller presumably is referring to the conclusion of the drama (i.e., the traditional damnation of Faust), which had not yet been written at the time. Whether he had any notion that Goethe would ultimately have his hero saved, or whether Goethe himself so intended at that time, is uncertain.

In the present fragmentary state of *Faust* this is felt very much, but expectation is led to look to the fully-developed whole. The devil gains his point in face of common sense by his realism and *Faust* his in the face of the heart. At times, however, they seem to exchange their parts, and the devil takes reason under his protection against *Faust*.

One difficulty I also find in the fact that the devil annuls his existence, which is idealistic, by his character, which is realistic. Reason alone can believe in him, and it is only common sense that can allow and comprehend his existence as he is.

I am in fact very anxious to see how the popular tale will link itself to the philosophical portion of the whole.

Goethe to Schiller

WEIMAR, JUNE 27, 1797

Your remarks about *Faust* gave me great pleasure, naturally they coincide very well with my own projects and plans, only that I shall make this barbarous composition accommodate itself more to my wishes, and I propose rather to touch upon than to fufil the highest demands. In this manner, reason and common sense will probably beat each other about like two boxers, and afterwards sit down amicably together. I will take care that the parts are pleasing and entertaining, and that they offer subjects for thought; in the poem itself, which will ever remain a fragment, I may apply our new theory of the epic poem.[4]

Goethe to Schiller

WEIMAR, MAY 5, 1798

My *Faust* I have brought a good bit further. The old and very confused manuscript still on hand has been copied, and the parts arranged in separate boxes and numbered according to a detailed scheme; hence I shall now be able to make use of every moment when I feel in the humour for it, work out the various parts, and sooner or later have them put together.

A very curious thing struck me while doing this: some tragic scenes I had written in prose, and owing to their naturalness and power, as compared with the rest, are quite unbearable.

Schiller to Goethe

JENA, MAY 8, 1798

I congratulate you upon your progress with *Faust*. As soon as you definitely know what has still to be done to the subject, it may be said to be all but finished, for to me the most difficult part about it seems to be its *limitlessness*. A remark you made lately that on account of some of your

---

4. This alludes to the short essay "On Epic and Dramatic Poetry," which had been written jointly by Goethe and Schiller through their correspondence during 1797 and which Goethe subsequently published in his journal *Ueber Kunst und Alterthum* in 1827.

tragic scenes having been written in prose, they proved powerfully affecting, confirms an earlier experience of yours in the case of Marianne in your *Meister*,[5] in which case likewise pure realism violently affects a pathetic situation and produces a seriousness which is not poetical: for according to my idea, it belongs to the nature of poetry that it should ever unite within itself seriousness and play.

Schiller to Goethe

WEIMAR, SEPTEMBER 13, 1800

I congratulate you upon the advance you have made in your *Faust*. But be sure not to allow yourself to be disturbed by the thought that it would be a pity to barbarise beautiful figures and situations, should such be met with. A similar case might often present itself to you in the second part of *Faust*, and I should be glad, once and for all, to silence your poetic conscience on this point. The barbarous element in the treatment which is imposed upon you by the spirit of the whole, cannot destroy its higher character or do away with what is beautiful in it; it can only modify it and prepare it for some other faculty of soul.[6] Just that which is higher and more elevated in the motives, gives a peculiar charm to the work, and Helena here stands as a symbol of all the beautiful forms which will stray into it. It is a very great merit to proceed consciously from what is pure to what is impure, in place of soaring up from what is impure to what is pure, as is the case with us other barbarians.[7]

Goethe to Schiller

JENA, SEPTEMBER 16, 1800

The consolation you give me in your letter that the union of what is pure with what is adventurous cannot give rise to a poetic monstrosity altogether objectionable, I have already found confirmed by experience, inasmuch as this amalgamation gives rise to strange results in which I myself take some interest.

Schiller to Goethe

WEIMAR, SEPTEMBER 23, 1800

The recital, the other day, made a great and significant impression upon me; one feels the noble, sublime spirit of ancient tragedy come wafting

5. The character of Marianne in Goethe's novel *Wilhelm Meister's Apprenticeship*, is the hero's first love, who bears his child and subsequently dies rejected because of a misunderstanding.
6. Schiller refers to the medieval milieu of *Faust* as "barbaric" in accord with the normative classical aesthetics that he shared with Goethe during the latter 1790s. There is no question that Goethe agreed with him at that time, feeling generally estranged from the legend of Faust.
7. As Goethe wrote to Schiller on September 12 (the letter is not included here), he had begun to work on the Helena episode for *Faust*. Several hundred lines written at that time for the opening of Act III in Part Two survive in manuscript. Goethe emphasizes that the heroine attracts his attention because of her ideal classical beauty, but that he finds no way of reconciling this to the medieval ("barbarous") setting of *Faust*. He did not find the way until twenty-five years later.

towards one from the monologue, and its effect is the right one, for it excites what is deepest, in a calm and yet powerful manner.[8] If you were not to bring back anything poetical from Jena but this and what you have already settled in your own mind about the further course of this tragic part, your stay in Jena would have met with its reward. If you succeed with this synthesis of what is noble and barbarous, as I have no doubt will be the case, you will have found the key to the remaining portion of the whole, and it will then not be difficult for you—as it were—analytically to determine and dispute the meaning and spirit of the other portions from this point; for the summit, as you yourself call it, must be seen from, and look towards all the various points of the whole.

Goethe to Schiller

OBER-ROSSLA, APRIL 6, 1801

Faust also has meanwhile had something done to it. I hope that soon the only thing wanting in the great gap will be the disputation,[9] that, it is true, will have to be looked upon as a distinct piece of work, and one which will not be accomplished at a moment's notice.

Outline of the Contents for Part Two (1816)†

At the beginning of the second part Faust is discovered sleeping. He is surrounded by choruses of spirits who conjure up for him in visible symbols and charming songs the joys of honor, fame, power and sovereignty. In flattering words and melodies they disguise what are actually derisive propositions. He awakens feeling strengthened, all previous dependence upon sensuality and passion cast off, his mind, purified and fresh, striving towards the highest.

Mephistopheles appears to him and gives him an amusing and stimulating description of the Imperial Parliament at Augsburg, which has been summoned by the Emperor Maximilian; he pretends that it is all taking place down on the square beneath the window, where Faust, however, can see nothing. Finally, Mephistopheles claims to see the Emperor

---

8. Schiller visited Goethe on September 21, when the latter was in Jena, and Goethe read to him Helena's monologue from the draft for that sequence of *Faust*.

9. Here Goethe refers to the uncompleted lacuna in the drama between the opening scene (after Wagner leaves) and the end of the pact scene (before the student comes in), lines 605–1770, as the "great gap," which he managed to fill only at the time of this letter. The "disputation," a scene subsequently abandoned, was to have occurred between the two study scenes (see the interpretive note to the pact scene, above).

† The following text was dictated by Goethe in December, 1816, for inclusion in the fourth volume of his autobiography, *Poetry and Truth*. After discussing the early stages of composition for *Faust*, he intended to outline the unwritten Part Two, since he did not believe at that time that he would ever complete the drama. Goethe was subsequently persuaded by Eckermann to delete the outline from the published version of his autobiography, in hopes that the drama would indeed be finished eventually. The text of the outline was published only in 1888 in the critical apparatus to the Weimar edition of *Faust*, Part Two (Paralipomenon 63). Of particular interest here is how straightforward Goethe's view of Part Two still was in 1816. What he describes is not essentially different in its dramatic mode (like an echo from medieval romance) from Part One. (The translation is by Dolores Signori and Cyrus Hamlin.)

speaking with a prince at a window of the town hall and assures Faust that the Emperor is asking about him, his whereabouts, and whether by any chance he could be brought to the court. Faust lets himself be persuaded, and his magic cloak makes the journey swifter. In Augsburg they land before an empty hall, and Mephistopheles goes out to spy. Faust meanwhile lapses into his earlier abstruse speculations and his demands upon himself, and, when the former returns, Faust sets the remarkable condition that Mephistopheles not enter the assembly hall but remain at the door; further, that in the Emperor's presence no kind of magic or deception shall occur. Mephistopheles consents. The scene shifts to a large hall where the Emperor, just finished with a banquet, goes to a window with a prince and acknowledges that he desires Faust's cloak in order to hunt in the Tyrol and be back again for tomorrow's session. Faust is announced and graciously received. The Emperor's questions all concern earthly dilemmas and how magic could solve them. Faust's replies suggest higher demands and higher means. The Emperor does not understand him, the courtier even less. The conversation becomes confused, falters, and Faust, bewildered, looks round for Mephistopheles, who immediately steps behind him and answers in his name. Now the conversation becomes animated, several people move closer, and everyone is pleased with the extraordinary guest. The Emperor demands to see apparitions, and they are promised. Faust leaves to make preparations. At that moment Mephistopheles assumes Faust's guise to entertain women and young ladies and eventually is considered to be quite invaluable, since by lightly touching a wart on the hand or somewhat more smartly kicking a corn with his disguised hoof he effects a cure; and a blond young lady even allows him to dab her face with his lean and pointed fingers, since her pocket-mirror immediately gives her the comforting assurance that one freckle after another is disappearing. Evening approaches, a magical theater builds itself. The figure of Helena appears. Observations by the ladies about this beauty of beauties enliven the otherwise awesome scene. Paris enters and is subjected by the men to the same treatment which Helena received from the women. Faust, in disguise, agrees with both sides and this leads to a very amusing scene.

They cannot reach an agreement concerning the choice of the third apparition, and the summoned spirits become restless; several important ones appear together. Strange relationships develop, until at last the theater and the phantoms disappear simultaneously. The real Faust, illuminated by three lamps, lies unconscious in the background. Mephistopheles takes to his heels, something of the duality involved is suspected, no one feels at ease about the matter.

When Mephistopheles encounters Faust again, he finds the latter consumed by an intense passion. He has fallen in love with Helena and now demands that the conjurer procure and deliver her into his arms. Difficulties are perceived. Helena belongs to Orcus, and, though she can be conjured forth by magic, she cannot be held fast. Faust will not give up, and Mephistopheles undertakes the task. Infinite longing by Faust for highest beauty once it has been glimpsed. An old castle, whose lord is off to wars in Palestine, but whose steward is a magician, serves as dwelling for the new Paris. Helena appears; corporeality is restored to her by a magic ring. She believes she has just come from Troy and is arriving in Sparta. She finds everything bleak, desires company, especially masculine, which throughout her life she was never able to do without. Faust enters and, as a German knight, appears wondrous strange at the side of the heroic figure from antiquity. She finds him loathsome, but because he knows how to flatter, she gradually submits to him, and he becomes the successor of so many heroes and demi-gods. A son results from this union, who, as soon as he comes into the world, dances, sings, and cleaves the air with a fencer's thrusts. Now, one must understand that the castle is surrounded by a magical boundary, within which alone these half-realities can come to be. The ever-growing boy is a source of much joy to his mother. He is allowed everything but to cross a certain brook. One holiday, however, he hears music from beyond and sees the countryfolk and soldiers dancing. He crosses the boundary, mingles with them and gets into a quarrel, injures many but at last is killed by a sacred sword. The magician-steward saves the corpse. The mother is inconsolable; and as Helena wrings her hands in despair, she brushes off the ring and falls into Faust's arms; he, however, embraces only her empty garment. Mother and son have disappeared. Mephistopheles, who up to this point has witnessed everything in the guise of an old housekeeper, tries to comfort his friend and infuse a desire for property into him. The lord of the castle has been killed in Palestine, monks want to seize his lands, and their benedictions destroy the magic circle. Mephistopheles advises physical force and provides Faust with three henchmen named Raufebold, Habebald, Haltefest. Faust now believes himself sufficiently equipped and dismisses Mephistopheles and the steward, wages war with the monks, avenges the death of his son, and wins extensive lands. Meanwhile he grows old, and how things go from there will be demonstrated when we eventually assemble the fragments, or rather the discontinuously produced passages already composed for this second part, thereby salvaging some things which will be of interest to readers.

Second Sketch for the Announcement of the *Helena* (1826)†

HELENA. CLASSICAL-ROMANTIC PHANTASMAGORIA. INTERLUDE TO *Faust*

The character of Faust, at the exalted level to which our new version has raised him out of the old rough-hewn folktale, represents a man who, feeling impatient and uncomfortable within the general limits of earthly

† In 1826, Goethe decided to publish the newly completed text of the third act of *Faust*, Part Two, as an independent unit within his final collected works (*Ausgabe letzter Hand*). The act thus appeared under the independent title given here. In order to clarify the context of this strange piece within the still unpublished and largely unwritten second part of his drama, Goethe drafted several descriptive prose summaries during the latter months of the same year. The text, here translated for the first time into English by Cyrus Hamlin and Dolores Signori, is the longest of these, though only the first six paragraphs were actually published (in the Journal *Ueber Kunst und Alterthum*, which Goethe edited).

life, regards the possession of highest knowledge and the enjoyment of richest goods as inadequate to satisfy his longing in the very least, a mind which, turning in every direction, always returns in a more unhappy state.

Such a disposition is so similar to the modern one that a number of clever heads have felt impelled to attempt to solve the problem. The way in which I have come to terms with it has won approval; excellent minds have thought about it and commented on my text, which I have acknowledged with gratitude.[1] I was astonished, however, that those who undertook to continue and complete my fragment did not arrive at the obvious thought, that in composing a second part one must necessarily transcend completely the melancholy sphere of the drama thus far [i.e., Part One] and lead such a man into higher regions through more dignified circumstances.

How I had begun to do this for my part lay at hand for me in private, leading me occasionally to attempt at least part of the sequel, but I carefully concealed my secret from one and all, always in the hope of advancing the work toward a desired conclusion. But now I must no longer hold back and, with the publication of my collected endeavors, keep no more secrets from my readers; indeed I feel obliged to offer gradually all my efforts—even in fragmentary form.

Therefore I have decided to communicate at once, in the very next printer's lot, the above minor drama, complete in itself, which is to be fitted into the Second Part of *Faust*.[2]

But in order to bridge somewhat the large gulf between the well-known pathetic conclusion of *Part I* and the entrance of a Grecian heroine, for the moment I offer for kind acceptance first a summary of what occurs in between and hope it will suffice for the present.[3]

It is related in the old legend, we must know, and the puppet play of *Faust* does not fail to show this scene, that Faust in his peremptory arrogance demands from Mephistopheles possession of the beautiful Helen of Greece, and that after initial resistance Mephistopheles complies. We felt it our duty not to omit such a significant motif from our version. What follows, we hope, will clarify for the moment how we have tried to meet this need and what approach seemed suitable to us.

At a great banquet at the German Emperor's court Faust and Mephistopheles are requested to conjure up apparitions. Unwilling, yet under pressure, they call forth the desired idols of Helena and Paris.[4] Paris ap-

---

1. Among the comments on *Faust* by Goethe's contemporaries included in this edition, which Goethe may here have had in mind, would certainly be the correspondence with Schiller, the review by A. W. Schlegel, and perhaps the more perceptive discussions by Friedrich Schlegel and by Schelling (assuming that they were known to Goethe). Other published comments by younger friends and admirers of *Faust*, which are now of historical interest only, must also have been in Goethe's mind.
2. The *Helena* was actually published in vol. 4 of Goethe's collected works in the year 1827. At that time, none of the "Classical Walpurgis Night," which is here described in such detail, had yet been composed.
3. Goethe was here dictating a draft for a prose summary that was not in fact published during his lifetime. Much of the obscurity in the paragraphs that follow derives (as Goethe himself must have sensed) from the nature of the mythical drama itself, which could be clarified in poetic terms only through the actual process of composition. This subsequently occurred four years later, during 1830.
4. Goethe here outlines the scenes that were finally included at the end of Act I in Part Two.

pears, the women's rapture knows no bounds; the men try to cool this enthusiasm with specific critical comments, but in vain. Helena appears, the men are beside themselves; the women observe her attentively and manage to point out mockingly that her heroic feet are too large and her ivory-colored complexion is probably painted on, but especially they contrive, through obloquy all too well founded in her actual history, to throw a dubious light on her magnificent person. Carried away by this sublime and beautiful figure, Faust is emboldened to push Paris away as he leans to her embrace; a thunderbolt strikes him down, the apparitions disappear, and the festival ends in turmoil.

Faust comes to his senses again out of a long catatonic sleep, during which his dreams have been visibly and circumstantially enacted before the eyes of the audience.[5] He appears in an exalted mood and, completely absorbed by his supreme vision, insists vehemently that Mephistopheles enable him to possess Helena. Not wishing to admit that he has no say in the Classical Hades, indeed that he is not even welcome there, Mephistopheles resorts to his former, well-proven method of making his master jump about in all directions. This leads us to quite a variety of things which deserve attention. Finally, to assuage the growing impatience of Faust, he advises him to visit, merely in passing on the way to their destination, the recently appointed Professor and Doctor Wagner, whom they find in his laboratory, greatly rejoicing at the creation of a little chemical man.[6]

Suddenly this creature bursts out of his glowing glass container and steps forth as a nimble, well-formed little dwarf. The formula for his creation is hinted at in a mystic way. He offers a demonstration of his abilities; in particular, it turns out that he embodies a universal historical world calendar—that is, he can tell at any moment at those times when sun, moon, earth, and planets have been in the same position what has occurred among men since the creation of Adam. As a sample of this he announces on the spot that the present night coincides precisely with that hour when the Battle of Pharsalia was prepared for, and which both Caesar and Pompey passed sleeplessly. On this point he gets into an argument with Mephistopheles, who, on the basis of Benedictine reckoning, will not believe that that great epochal event occurred at this hour, but claims that it took place several days later. The point is made that the devil should not use monks as his authority. Since he stubbornly insists upon this right, however, their dispute is in danger of lapsing into an interminable chronological controversy, when the little chemical man offers further proof of his profound historical-mythical skill by drawing attention to the fact that this was also the moment when the festival of the Classical Walpurgis Night began, which had been held in Thessaly ever since the beginning of the mythical world and, in accord with the complete coherence of world

5. In the final version of the drama, Faust reawakens only when he touches the ground of Greece (at the beginning of the "Classical Walpurgis Night"). His dream of Helena's conception, when Leda was ravished by Zeus in the guise of a swan, is described by Homunculus in Wagner's laboratory (lines 6904–20).
6. Goethe does not yet speak here of Homunculus, though he offers a vivid sense of Wagner's fantastic chemical experiment (how close to Mary Shelley's *Frankenstein*!).

history as determined by its epochs, was the actual cause of that disastrous event.[7] All four decide to travel there [i.e., to Pharsalia]. Despite their haste, Wagner does not forget to take along a clean phial, to collect here and there, if he can, the necessary elements for making a little chemical woman. He puts the glass container into his left breast-pocket, the little chemical man into his right one; and thus they entrust themselves to Mephistopheles' magic cloak.[8] A boundless swarming profusion of geographical-historical remarks from the mouth of the little man in the pocket, concerning the regions they drift over, allows them no chance to compose themselves, what with the arrow-like speed of their flight, until finally they reach the plain of Thessaly by the light of a clear though waning moon. Here on the heath they first encounter Erichto [*sic*], who is eagerly inhaling the inextirpable reek of decay which clings to these fields. Erichtonius joins her, and their kinship, which was unknown to antiquity, is proved etymologically. Unfortunately she must often carry him on her arm, since he is not good at walking, and indeed, when this infant prodigy evinces a strange passion for the little chemical man, must take the latter on her other arm, a situation by no means calculated to restrain Mephistopheles from making malicious comments.[9]

Faust has entered into a conversation with a crouching Sphinx, in which the most abstruse questions are foiled *ad infinitum* by equally puzzling answers. In a similar pose close by, a watchful Griffin, one of the guardians of gold, interjects without producing any enlightenment. A colossal Ant, another hoarder of gold, joins them and makes the conversation even more confusing.

But now that reason in conflict with itself must despair, trust in the senses is to be undermined too. Empusa appears, wearing a donkey's head in honor of the present festival. By constantly changing her form she stimulates the other, well-defined figures, not, to be sure, to metamorphosis, but to continual impatience.[1]

Now there appear Sphinxes, Griffins, and Ants, in numbers multiplied past counting, developing as it were out of themselves.[2] Back and forth, what is more, swarms and runs the entire plethora of monsters from antiquity, Chimeras, Tragelaphs, Crickets, and, in their midst, many-headed serpents in vast number. Harpies flutter and sway in vague circles like bats; the dragon Python itself appears in multiple form, and the Stymphalian

---

7. Much of the information concerning the battle of Pharsalus was derived from the Latin poet Lucan, who wrote an epic on the event. The whole idea of the "Classical Walpurgis Night," however, is Goethe's own, one of the most incredible poetic conceptions in the history of literature.
8. In the final drama the trip to Greece is also made on Mephistopheles' magic cloak. Goethe subsequently decided, presumably for practical reasons of dramatic execution, not to have Wagner go along. The whole motif of a little chemical woman was subsequently dropped, to be replaced by the festival of Galatea and Homunculus's spiritual fusion with the sea.
9. Erichtho speaks the prologue to the final "Classical Walpurgis Night." The role of Erichtonius was abandoned in the final drama.
1. Empusa with the donkey's head appears quite late in the text of the "Classical Walpurgis Night" (lines 7732–55).
2. This scene of general confusion was subsequently included in abbreviated form near the beginning of the "Classical Walpurgis Night" (lines 7214–48). The various creatures are explained in the footnotes to that passage.

vultures, sharp-beaked, with webbed feet, whip past one by one, swift as arrows. But suddenly, with tuneful song, a flock of Sirens hovers over them all like a cloud. They plunge into the Peneus [*sic!*] to bathe amid splashing and piping, then they perch on trees in the glade next to the river and sing their loveliest songs.³ First comes an apology by the Nereids and Tritons, who, in spite of the sea's proximity, are prevented by their physique from participating in this festival. Then they urgently invite the entire party to enjoy themselves, one and all, in the various waters and gulfs, and also on the islands and coasts, of the area; part of the crowd accepts this enticing invitation and plunges seaward.

Our travelers, more or less accustomed to such spirit pranks, hardly take notice of all that is buzzing around them. The little chemical man, crawling along on the earth, gleans from the humus a great many phosphorescent atoms, some radiating a blue, others a purple fire. He conscientiously consigns them to Wagner's phial, though he doubts the possibility of creating a little chemical woman from them. But when Wagner shakes them hard in order to observe them more closely, followers of Pompey and Caesar appear ranked in cohorts in a boisterous effort to reclaim these components of their individuality needed for legitimate resurrection. They almost succeed in possessing themselves of these despiritualized bits of matter; but the four winds, whose courses this night are in continual collision, take the present owner into their protection, and the spirits must resign themselves to being told by all that the components of their Roman grandeur have long ago been scattered to the four winds, absorbed and transformed by a million phases of evolution.⁴

This does not reduce the tumult but appeases it for a moment in that attention is turned to the center of the vast plain.⁵ There the earth quakes, then swells up to form a mountain chain, north to Scotusa and south to the Peneus, which even threatens to block the river. The head and shoulders of Enceladus come writhing forth; he has made a point of working his way here beneath land and sea in celebration of this important hour. Flickering flames leap out of various chasms; and the natural philosophers, Thales and Anaxagoras,⁶ who would not miss this occasion for anything, start a violent quarrel concerning this event, the one attributing it all to water and moisture, the other viewing everything in terms of molten, melting masses; each declaims his solo over the roar of the general chorus; both quote from Homer and each cites the past and present as proof. Thales in vain offers as evidence spring floods and deluges, speaking with pompous, didactic complacency; Anaxagoras, as fiery as the element which possesses him, speaks a more impassioned language and prophesies a rain

3. In the final drama, the Sirens play an even greater role than Goethe here envisions for them, due to the addition of the festival at the Aegean, for which they constitute a kind of chorus.
4. All the events here described with reference to Wagner's intended role in the "Classical Walpurgis Night" were subsequently omitted.
5. The volcanic explosion that produces the mountain Seismos (instead of Enceladus) occurs on the upper Peneios in the "Classical Walpurgis Night" (lines 7495–675).
6. The argument between the two pre-Socratic philosophers, Thales (who is popularly believed to have derived all life from water) and Anaxagoras (who supposed that fire was the origin of life), occurs in the presence of Homunculus in the final drama (lines 7851–950).

of stones, which, to be sure, at the next moment falls down from the moon. The crowd extols him as a demi-god, and his opponent is forced to retreat to the seashore.

As yet the peaks and gorges of the mountain are not firm or fixed when, swarming out of gaping crevices on all sides, armies of Pygmies occupy the upper arm and shoulders of the still-crouching giant, and use these as a dance floor and playground; meanwhile armies of croaking Cranes beyond number circle the summit of the giant's head and his hair as if it were an impenetrable forest, and announce an entertaining battle before the general festival concludes.[7]

All this and more is to be imagined, if it can be, as taking place simultaneously. Mephistopheles meanwhile has made the acquaintance of Enyo [one of the Phorcyads], whose grandiose ugliness comes close to unnerving him and startling him into making impolite and insulting remarks.[8] But he pulls himself together and, in consideration of her exalted ancestors and her considerable influence, he tries to win her favor. He comes to an understanding with her and forms an alliance, of which the public terms do not promise much, but the secret ones are all the more remarkable and fraught with consequences. As for Faust, he has approached Chiron, the centaur, who as a neighboring mountain-dweller is making his usual rounds.[9] A serious pedagogical conversation with this prototypical private tutor is, if not interrupted, at least disturbed by a circle of Lamiae, who intrude incessantly between Faust and Chiron; they are charming creatures of every kind, fair, dark, large, small, delicate or strong of limb; each speaks or sings, strides about or dances, hurries past or gesticulates, so that, if Faust had not absorbed the highest image of beauty within himself, he would necessarily be seduced.[1] But Chiron himself, ancient and imperturbable, wishes to clarify for his thoughtful new acquaintance the principles by which he educated his distinguished heroes, whereupon the Argonauts and finally Achilles are described.[2] But when the pedagogue considers the outcome of his efforts, little that is gratifying emerges; for the heroes live and act as if they had never been educated.

When Chiron now hears of Faust's desire and intention, he rejoices to meet again at long last a man who demands the impossible, since he always used to approve the same in his pupils. At the same time he offers assistance and direction to the modern hero, carries him back and forth on his broad back across all the fords and gravel-banks of the Peneus, passes Larissa on the right, and shows his rider here and there the places where Perseus, the unfortunate King of Macedonia, stopped for a few

---

7. The battle between the Pygmies and the Cranes occurs soon after the appearance of Seismos in the "Classical Walpurgis Night" (lines 7606–75), though its repercussions are also described in the scene with the philosophers.
8. In the final drama Mephistopheles visits all three of the Phorcyads, none of whom is actually named (lines 7951–8033).
9. The meeting between Faust and Chiron at the banks of the Peneios was placed fairly early in the final text (lines 7319–488). The encounter with the river nymphs, which immediately precedes this meeting in the drama, was apparently not yet conceived.
1. The temptation by the Lamiae occurs in the "Classical Walpurgis Night" quite independent of Faust, and Mephistopheles, quite appropriately, is their dupe (lines 7676–800).
2. The pedagogical speeches by Chiron occur in lines 7365–462, though the emphasis finally falls much more upon Faust's fascination with Helena.

minutes to catch his breath during his most terrifying flight.[3] Thus they make their way downstream to the foot of Olympus; here they encounter a long procession of sibyls,[4] many more than twelve in number. Chiron describes the first who pass as old acquaintances and then commends his charge to the judicious, kindly daughter of Tiresias, Manto.[5]

The latter informs him that the entrance to Orcus is about to open, since the hour is approaching when formerly the mountain had to split open to allow so many great souls to descend. This indeed happens, and, the horoscope of the moment being favorable, they all climb down together in silence.[6] Suddenly Manto covers her charge with her veil and pushes him away from the path against the rock wall, so that he is afraid of being smothered to death. Soon, when he is released, she explains this precaution: the Gorgon's head which for centuries has been growing ever larger, was advancing up the chasm towards them;[7] Proserpina likes to keep it away from the level of the festival because the assembled ghosts and monsters, losing all composure at the sight of the head, would scatter immediately. Manto herself, highly endowed being though she is, dare not gaze at it; had Faust glimpsed it, he would have been destroyed immediately, so that nothing of either his body or his spirit would ever again have been found in the universe. They finally arrive at the vast court of Proserpina, crowded with many shapes; here there is opportunity for an infinitude of incidents, until Faust, when he is presented, is favorably received as a second Orpheus,[8] though his request is considered to be somewhat strange. The speech of Manto as his representative must be impressive; she first invokes the power of precedent and recounts in detail the favor received by Protesilaus, Alcestis, and Euridice.[9] Did not Helena herself once before receive permission to return to life in order to ally herself to Achilles, whom she had earlier loved?[1] Of the further course and current of her speech we may divulge nothing here, least of all the peroration which causes the Queen, moved to tears, to give her consent, and refer the petitioners to the three judges, in whose memory of bronze all is

---

3. Such a geographical survey, including any allusion to Perseus, was subsequently omitted from the final drama.
4. See the footnote to *Faust*, line 7455.
5. The scene with Manto, brief and yet astonishingly effective, occurs in lines 7465–94.
6. The entire sequence of the descent to Hades as here envisioned was subsequently abandoned, apparently only at the very last stage of composition, in 1830. Perhaps Goethe saw the scene at the Aegean Sea that concludes the "Classical Walpurgis Night" as an adequate symbolic substitute for Faust's visit to the underworld.
7. According to ancient myth, the head of the Gorgon (some sources speak of three Gorgons) would turn to stone anyone who looked at it. Goethe appears to have had some specific allegorical intention for introducing this figure here. He subsequently abandoned the plan when he composed the final text.
8. Orpheus, the mythical singer, descended into Hades to request the return to life of his dead wife, Eurydice. This request was granted by Persephone (or Proserpina) on the condition that he not turn back to look at his wife until they had returned to the upper world. Orpheus turned at the last minute before they emerged and Eurydice was lost to him. The parallel between Faust and Orpheus is mentioned by Manto in line 7493.
9. All three of those here named were released from Hades under certain conditions for the sake of those in life who loved them: 1) Protesilaus, first of the Greeks killed at Troy, was allowed to return to his wife, Laodamia, for three hours; 2) Alcestis, wife of Admetus (see Euripides' play), was brought back from death by Hercules; 3) Euridice was the wife of Orpheus (see the previous note).
1. This obscure legend of Helena's return to life to marry Achilles is mentioned in *Faust*; see lines 7435 ff. and note.

engraved which seems to disappear in Lethe's stream as it flows past their feet.

It now turns out that previously Helena had been allowed to return to life on condition that she restrict herself to the island of Leuce. Now she may return under the same conditions to the land of Sparta, to appear there, as if truly alive, in a house modeled on that of Menelaus. There it would be up to the new suitor how far he might influence her volatile spirit and impressionable mind, and win her favor.[2]

At this point, the announced Interlude of *Helena* begins, which is adequately related to the main course of the drama yet, for reasons which will become apparent, is offered separately for the time being.

This brief sketch should, of course, have been executed and embellished with all the advantages of the poetic and rhetorical arts and then presented to the public; as it stands, however, it may serve for the moment to clarify the events which need to be fully known and carefully considered as antecedents to the announced *Helena*, the Classical-Romantic Phantasmagoric Interlude to *Faust*.

W[EIMAR], 17 DECBR, 1826

From Goethe's Letters and His Conversations with Eckermann†

Conversation, Monday, January 10, 1825
[*Goethe responds to an English visitor who reports that he has been reading* Faust, Part One, *and finds it hard going.*]

"Really," said * * * [Goethe], "I would not have advised you to undertake *Faust*. It is mad stuff, and goes quite beyond all ordinary feeling. But since you have done it of your own accord, without asking my advice, you will see how you will get through. Faust is so strange an individual, that only few can sympathize with his internal condition. Then the character of Mephistopheles is, on account of his irony, and also because he is a living result of an extensive acquaintance with the world, also very difficult. But you will see what lights open upon you. * * * "

2. Goethe here indicates a condition for Helena's existence for Faust in Act III that is only indirectly apparent in the final text. The reason she is ultimately lost to Faust at the end of the act is not adequately explained by this statement.

† Johann Peter Eckermann (1792–1854) was a close associate of Goethe during the last years of his life, being in almost daily contact. He served as coeditor of the unpublished literary remains (including *Faust*, Part Two), and he also published his *Conversations with Goethe*, in 1836–48 (here taken from the translation by John Oxenford, 1850). Regarding himself as an intimate biographer (somewhat on the model of Boswell for Samuel Johnson), Eckermann offers very detailed, often word-for-word accounts of his meetings with the elder poet. Whether or not he is strictly accurate in what is reported, the work remains an invaluable source of information, especially with regard to Goethe's thought and opinions on every conceivable subject, including *Faust*. To a large extent (if we may trust what Eckermann says), it was he who first persuaded Goethe to think seriously during the early 1820s of trying to complete the second part of his drama.

The letters to Boisserée and Zelter and the letter of March 17, 1832, to Wilhelm von Humboldt are taken from Goethe, *Selected Letters*, trans by M. von Herzfeld and C. Melvil Sym, 1957. Reprinted by permission of the Edinburgh University Press.

Conversation, Tuesday, January 18, 1825
[*Goethe discusses the creative use of poetic sources by poets.*]

"The world," said Goethe, "remains always the same; situations are repeated; one people lives, loves, and feels like another; why should not one poet write like another? The situations of life are alike, why then should those of poems be unlike?"

*   *   *

"Lord Byron, * * * " said I, "is no wiser, when he takes *Faust* to pieces, and thinks you found one thing here, the other there."

"The greater part of those fine things cited by Lord Byron," said Goethe, "I have never even read; much less did I think of them when I was writing *Faust*. But Lord Byron is only great as a poet; as soon as he reflects, he is a child. He knows not how to help himself against stupid attacks of the same kind made upon him by his own countrymen. He ought to have expressed himself more strongly against them. 'What is there is mine,' he should have said; 'and whether I got it from a book or from life, is of no consequence; the only point is whether I have made a right use of it.' Walter Scott used a scene from my *Egmont*, and he had a right to do so; and because he did it well, he deserves praise. He has also copied the character of my Mignon in one of his romances; but whether with equal judgment, is another question. Lord Byron's transformed Devil[1] is a continuation of Mephistopheles, and quite right too. If, from the whim of originality, he had departed from the model, he would certainly have fared worse. Thus, my Mephistopheles sings a song from Shakespeare [see lines 3682–97], and why should he not? Why should I give myself the trouble of inventing one of my own, when this said just what was wanted? Also, if the prologue to my *Faust* is something like the beginning of Job, that is again quite right, and I am rather to be praised than censured."

To Sulpiz Boisserée,[2] October 22, 1826
[*On the* Helena]

Helena is one of my oldest conceptions, as old as that of *Faust* itself, and though I have changed its form again and again, the idea has always been the same. I showed Schiller as much of it as I had done at the beginning of the century; our correspondence tells how he kept encouraging me to go on with it. I did so; but nothing but the fullness of time could round off this work that now covers a good three thousand years from the Sack of Troy to the destruction of Missolonghi. The whole thing is a kind of phantasmagoria, of course, but with real unity of place and action.

That is enough about it. Is it not perhaps worse than if I had said

---

1. A reference to Byron's play *The Deformed Transformed* (1824).
2. Enthusiast for medieval art and architecture (1783–1853), who first met Goethe in 1811, when he solicited support from the older poet for a project to publish engravings of the uncompleted cathedral of Cologne. Goethe visited Boisserée in the Rhineland in 1814 and 1815 in order to study his collection of medieval German and Flemish painting. The younger collector and art historian became a devoted correspondent until Goethe's death, and he followed the progress on *Faust*, Part Two, a work of particular interest to medieval enthusiasts, with eager expectation.

nothing? Whatever value is to be put on the work, I have never written anything like it, so it can count as the very latest.

Conversation, Wednesday, November 29, 1826
[*Goethe's response to the engravings for* Faust *by the French painter Eugène Delacroix (1798–1863).*]

"Since we are talking of Mephistopheles," continued Goethe, "I will show you something Coudray has brought me from Paris. What do you think of it?"

He laid before me a lithograph, representing the scene where Faust and Mephistopheles, on their way to free Margaret from prison, are rushing by the gallows at night on two horses. Faust rides a black horse; which gallops with all its might, and seems, like its rider, afraid of the spectres under the gallows. They ride so fast that Faust can scarcely keep his seat; the wind has blown off his cap, which, fastened by straps about his neck, flies far behind him. He has turned his fearful inquiring face to Mephistopheles, to whom he listens. Mephistopheles, on the contrary, sits undisturbed, like a being of a higher order: he rides no living horse, for he loves not what is living; indeed, he does not need it, for his will moves him with the swiftness he requires. He has a horse merely because he must look as if he were riding, and it has been quite enough for him to take a beast that is a mere bag of bones, from the first field he came to. It is of a bright colour, and seems to be phosphorescent in the darkness of night. It is neither bridled nor saddled. The supernatural rider sits easily and negligently, with his face turned towards Faust in conversation. The opposing element of air does not exist for him; neither he nor his horse feels anything of it. Not a hair of either is stirred.

We expressed much pleasure at this ingenious composition. "I confess," said Goethe, "I myself did not think it out so perfectly. Here is another. What say you to this?"

I saw a representation of the wild drinking scene in Auerbach's cellar, at the all-important moment when the wine sparkles up into flames and the brutality of the drinkers is shown in the most varied ways. All is passion and movement; Mephistopheles alone maintains his usual composure. The wild cursing and screaming, and the drawn knife of the man who stands next him, are to him nothing. He has seated himself on a corner of the table, dangling his legs. His upraised finger is enough to subdue flame and passion.

The longer this excellent design was looked at, the greater seemed the intelligence of the artist; who made no figure like another, but in each one expressed some different part of the action.

"M. Delacroix," said Goethe, "is a man of great talent, who found in *Faust* his proper aliment. The French censure his wildness, but it suits him well here. He will, I hope, go through all *Faust*, and I anticipate a special pleasure from the witches' kitchen and the scenes on the Brocken. We can see he has a good knowledge of life, for which a city like Paris has given him the best opportunity.

I observed that these designs greatly conduce to the comprehension of a poem.

"Undoubtedly," said Goethe; "for the more perfect imagination of such an artist constrains us to think the situations as beautiful as he conceived them himself. And if I must confess that M. Delacroix has in some scenes surpassed my own notions, how much more will the reader find all in full life and surpassing his imagination!"

Conversation, Monday evening, January 15, 1827
[Goethe comments on the difficulties of composition with regard to the
as yet unwritten "Classical Walpurgis Night."]

I turned the conversation to the second part of Faust; especially the "Classical Walpurgis Night," which existed as yet only as a sketch, and which Goethe had told me he meant to print in that form.[3] I had ventured to advise him not to do so; for if it were once printed it would be always left in this unfinished state. Goethe must have thought that over in the meantime, for he now told me that he had resolved not to print the sketch.

*   *   *

"Why," he replied, "one goes on, and must go on; but it is difficult."

" 'Tis well," said I, "that your outline is so complete."

"The outline is indeed complete," said Goethe; "but the most difficult part is yet to be done; and, in the execution of parts, everything depends too much on luck. The 'Classical Walpurgis Night' must be written in rhyme, and yet the whole must have an antique character. It is not easy to find a suitable sort of verse;—and then the dialogue!"

"Is not that also in the plan?" said I.

"The what is there," replied Goethe, "but not the how. Then, only think what is to be said on that mad night! Faust's speech to Proserpina, when he would move her to give him Helena—what a speech should that be, when Proserpina herself is moved to tears! All this is not easy to do, and depends much on good luck; nay, almost entirely on the mood and strength at the moment."

Conversation, Thursday evening, January 25, 1827
[Goethe comments on the Helena as he prepares to send off the man-
uscript for independent publication.]

A sealed packet lay upon the table. Goethe laid his hand upon it. "This," said he, "is Helena, which is going to Cotta to be printed."

I felt the importance of the moment. For, as it is with a newly-built vessel on its first going to sea, whose destiny is hid from us, so is it with the intellectual creation of a great master, going forth into the world.

"I have till now," said Goethe, "been always finding little things to add

3. Here Eckermann refers to the prose summary of the "Classical Walpurgis Night," which is contained in the "Second Sketch for the Announcement of the Helena," above. According to what Eckermann says here, it was he who persuaded Goethe not to publish the sketch in hopes that the work itself would ultimately be written.

or to touch up; but I must finish, and I am glad it is going to the post, so that I can turn to something else. Let it meet its fate. My comfort is, the general culture of Germany stands at an incredibly high point; so I need not fear such a production will long remain misunderstood and without effect."

"There is a whole antiquity in it," said I.

"Yes," said Goethe, "the philologists will find work."

"I have no fear," said I, "about the antique part; for there we have the most minute detail, the most thorough development of individuals, and each personage says just what he should. But the modern romantic part is very difficult, for half the history of the world lies behind it; the material is so rich that it can only be lightly indicated, and heavy demands are made upon the reader."

"Yet," said Goethe, "it all appeals to the senses, and on the stage would satisfy the eye: more I did not intend. Let the crowd of spectators take pleasure in the spectacle; the higher import will not escape the initiated —as with the *Magic Flute* and other things."[4]

"It will produce a most unusual effect on the stage," said I, "that a piece should begin as a tragedy and end as an opera. But something is required to represent the grandeur of these persons, and to speak the sublime language and verse."

"The first part," said Goethe, "requires the first tragic artists; and the operatic part must be sustained by the first vocalists, male and female. That of Helena ought to be played, not by one, but by two great female artists; for we seldom find that a fine vocalist has sufficient talent as a tragic actress."

"The whole," said I, "will furnish an occasion for great splendour of scenery and costume. I look forward to its representation. If we could only get a good composer."

"It should be one," said Goethe, "who, like Meyerbeer, has lived long in Italy, so that he combines his German nature with the Italian style and manner.[5] However, that will be found somehow or other; I only rejoice that I am rid of it. Of the notion that the chorus does not descend into the lower world, but rather disperses itself among the elements on the cheerful surface of the earth, I am not a little proud."

"It is a new sort of immortality," said I.

Conversation, Sunday, May 6, 1827
[*Goethe responds to the inquiries of a German reader concerning the central "idea" of* Faust.]

"The Germans are, certainly, strange people. By their deep thoughts and ideas, which they seek in everything and fix upon everything, they

---

4. Goethe regarded Mozart's *Magic Flute* (1791) as the norm for the opera of fancy that he imitated in the text of his *Helena*, especially the last third of the act, in which he explicitly insists upon a musical-operatic accompaniment. Goethe's interest in Mozart's opera was sufficient to persuade him to write a sequel, for which he hoped a corresponding musical genius might be found as composer.
5. Giacomo Meyerbeer (1791–1864), whose work in grand opera achieved international acclaim during the second decade of the nineteenth century, apparently seemed the most suitable alternative to the dead Mozart as a possible composer for the operatic sections of *Faust*, Part Two.

make life much more burdensome than is necessary. Only have the courage to give yourself up to your impressions: allow yourself to be delighted, moved, elevated; nay, instructed and inspired for something great: but do not imagine all is vanity, if it is not abstract thought and idea.

"They come and ask what idea I meant to embody in my *Faust*; as if I knew myself, and could inform them. 'From heaven, through the world, to hell,' would indeed be something;[6] but this is no idea, only a course of action. And further: that the devil loses the wager, and that a man continually struggling from difficult errors towards something better, should be redeemed, is an effective—and, to many, a good enlightening—thought; but it is no idea at the foundation of the whole, and of every individual scene. It would have been a fine thing indeed if I had strung so rich, varied, and highly diversified a life as I have brought to view in *Faust* upon the slender string of one pervading idea.

"It was, in short," continued Goethe, "not in my line, as a poet, to strive to embody anything *abstract*. I received in my mind impressions, and those of a sensuous, animated, charming, varied, hundredfold kind—just as a lively imagination presented them; and I had, as a poet, nothing more to do than to round off and elaborate artistically such views and impressions, and by means of a lively representation so to bring them forward that others might receive the same impression in hearing or reading my representation of them.

"If I still wished, as a poet, to represent any idea, I would do it in short poems, where a decided unity could prevail, and where a complete survey would be easy; * * * I am rather of the opinion, that the more incommensurable, and the more incomprehensible to the understanding, a poetic production is, so much the better it is."

To Karl Friedrich Zelter,[7] May 24, 1827
[On the beginning of Act IV]

And now let me tell you in confidence that helpful good spirits have led me back to *Faust* just where descending from the cloud [that brought him from ancient Greece] he meets his evil genius once more. Don't tell anyone about this; but I should like you to know that I think I shall go forward boldly from this point and fill in the gap between it and the ending that has been ready for a long time.

To Christian Gottfried Nees von Esenbeck,[8] May 25, 1827
[On the Helena]

Patiently and secretly I am making progress [with *Faust*], as will be apparent to you from the three thousand years of *Helena*. For sixty years now I have been tracking it down, in order to force at least something from it. * * * There are various things in it which I value because they

---

6. Goethe quotes from Faust, Part One, line 242.
7. Carl Friedrich Zelter (1758–1832), composer and musician in Berlin, was one of Goethe's most intimate correspondents during the period from 1796 until the poet's death.
8. Christian Gottfried Nees von Esenbeck (1776–1858), a physician and botanist, corresponded with Goethe especially on matters of natural science during the last two decades or so of Goethe's life.

have been on my mind for so many long years, for they derive from a time which will never come again and require only a bit of ingenious editing: complete plans, drafted schematically, with certain details already worked out. And it takes only a pure and inspired decisiveness on my part, hence the work has a validity as a kind of whole and will surely please many readers. Thus with an all-out effort last year I finally brought my *Helena* to harmonious life. How many times this piece had been shaped and reshaped over the vast reach of years. Now finally it will abide in a fixed form within its moment of time.

Conversation, Thursday, July 5, 1827
[*Goethe comments on the* Helena.]

Goethe spoke further of *Helena*, now it had again become a subject of discourse. "I at first intended a very different close," said he. "I modified it in various ways, and once very well, but I will not tell you how. Then this conclusion with Lord Byron and Missolonghi was suggested to me by the events of the day, and I gave up all the rest.[9] You have observed the character of the chorus is quite destroyed by the mourning song: until this time it has never belied its girlish nature; but here of a sudden it becomes nobly reflecting, and says things such as it has never thought or could think."

* * *

"I wonder," said Goethe, laughing, "what the German critics will say? Will they have freedom and boldness enough to get over this? Understanding will be attempted in the manner of the French; they will not consider that the imagination has its own laws, to which the understanding cannot and should not penetrate.

"If imagination did not originate things that must ever be problems to the understanding, there would be but little for the imagination to do. It is this which separates poetry from prose—in which understanding always is, and always should be, at home."

To Karl Jakob Ludwig Iken,[1] September 23, 1827
[*On the* Helena]

Let me first express my pleasure that you communicate your interest in my *Helena*. Considering the high level of culture among the best minds of our homeland, I indeed expected such a favorable response; yet the fulfillment of such hopes and desires is always most enjoyable and necessary. I had this in mind when I at last completed this work, so long intended and prepared for, and even as I worked I balanced the cost in time and energy and in strict perseverance against such a profit. I never

---

9. An allusion to the final chorus of the Arcadian sequence in the *Helena*, lines 9907–38, where the death of Euphorion is lamented in terms that include an allusion to the death of Lord Byron, from fever, at the battle of Missolonghi in Greece in 1824.
1. Karl Jakob Ludwig Iken (1789–1841), scholar and editor of a newspaper in Bremen, interested particularly in matters relating to Greece, corresponded occasionally with Goethe during the 1820s.

doubted that those readers for whom I was really writing would quickly grasp the main point of this composition. It is high time that the vehement opposition of Classicists and Romantics be resolved. The essential thing is that we develop our minds; from what point we do so would be insignificant, were it not for the danger of being misled by false models. We are grateful to richer and purer insights into Greek and Roman literature for liberating us from monastic barbarism during the fifteenth and sixteenth centuries. From such a lofty vantage point can we not learn to appreciate everything in its true physical and aesthetic worth, both what is ancient and what is modern?

In hopes of such a sympathetic response I let myself go completely while composing my *Helena*, without worrying at all about its public or even any individual reader, convinced that whoever could grasp and comprehend the whole would gradually assimilate the details with affectionate patience. On one hand, nothing will remain a secret to the philologist, who will indeed take pleasure in the re-creation of the antiquity which he already knows; on the other hand, a sensitive reader will penetrate what is playfully concealed here and there; *"Eleusis servat, quod ostendat revisentibus."*[2] And in this instance I would be delighted if the mysterious provides the occasion for friends to return to it again and again.

With regard to other obscure passages in both my earlier and my recent poems I offer the following for consideration: Since many of our experiences cannot be expressed plainly and directly, I long ago chose the following means for revealing my secret meaning to attentive readers, by using images which are set against each other and which simultaneously mirror themselves in each other. Since everything which I have expressed is based upon my experience of life, may I perhaps suggest and hope that my readers will want to experience my poems again and will do so. And certainly each of my readers will discover for himself that from time to time something new appears pleasurably in particular aspects of things which are already familiar to him in general, something which truly pertains to us, since it indicates mental development and thereby leads us on to fresh growth. But this happens to us with everything that presents or contains something of substance.

Conversation, Monday, October 1, 1827
[*Goethe discusses the scene "Imperial Residence. Throne Room."*]

* * * Went to Goethe, who read to me the second scene of his new *Faust.*

"In the emperor," said he, "I have endeavoured to represent a prince who has all the necessary qualities for losing his land, and at last succeeds in so doing. He does not concern himself about the welfare of his kingdom and his subjects; he only thinks of himself and how he can amuse himself with something new. The land is without law and justice; the judge is on the side of the criminals; atrocious crimes are committed with impunity. The army is without pay, without discipline, and roams about plundering

---

2. "Eleusis keeps what it only shows to those who revisit it" (Seneca, *Natural Questions*, 7.31.6).

to help itself as it can. The state treasury is empty, and without hope of replenishment. In the emperor's own household, there is scarcity in both kitchen and cellar. The marshal, who cannot devise means to get on from day to day, is already in the hands of the Jews, to whom everything is pawned, so that bread already eaten comes to the emperor's table.

"The counsellor of state wishes to remonstrate with his Majesty upon all these evils, and advises as to their remedy; but the gracious sovereign is very unwilling to lend his sublime ear to anything so disagreeable. Here now is the true element for Mephisto, who quickly supplants the former fool, and is at once at the side of the emperor as fool and counsellor."

Goethe read the scene and the interspersed murmuring of the crowd excellently, and I had a very pleasant evening.

Conversation, Thursday, February 12, 1829
[Concerning the music that Goethe envisioned for Faust]

"Yet I do not give up hope," said I, "of seeing suitable music composed for *Faust*."

"Quite impossible!" said Goethe. "The awful and repulsive passages that must occasionally occur are not in the style of the time. The music should be like that of *Don Juan*. Mozart should have composed for *Faust*.[3] Meyerbeer would pehaps be capable; but he would not touch anything of the kind; he is too much engaged with the Italian theatres."

Conversation, Sunday, December 6, 1829
[Concerning the length of time between planning and composing Faust]

To-day after dinner, Goethe read me the first scene of the second act of *Faust*. The effect was great. We are once more transported into Faust's study, where Mephistopheles finds all as he had left it. He takes from the hook Faust's old study-gown, and a thousand moths and insects flutter out from it. By the directions of Mephistopheles as to where these are to settle down, the locality is brought very clearly before our eyes. He puts on the gown, intending to play the master once more, while Faust lies behind a curtain in a state of paralysis. He pulls the bell, which gives such an awful tone among the old solitary convent-halls that the doors spring open and the walls tremble. The servant rushes in, and finds in Faust's seat Mephistopheles, whom he does not recognize but for whom he has respect. In answer to inquiries he gives news of Wagner, who has now become a celebrated man, and is hoping for the return of his master—he is, we hear, at this moment very busy in his laboratory, trying to make a Homunculus. The servant retires, and the Bachelor enters—the same whom we knew some years before as a shy young student when Mephistopheles (in Faust's gown) made game of him. He is now a man, and so full of conceit that

---

3. A reference to Mozart's opera *Don Giovanni* (1787). It is significant that Goethe does not mention Beethoven as an appropriate composer for *Faust*, though Goethe had met Beethoven in the early years of the century. Beethoven, of course, had died by this time, and *Faust* would not find its appropriate musical setting until Berlioz composed the *Damnation of Faust* from the French translation by Gérard de Nerval (consisting mainly of Part One).

even Mephistopheles can do nothing with him, but moves his chair farther
and farther and at last addresses the pit.

Goethe read the scene to the end. I was pleased with his youthful productive strength, and with the closeness of the whole. "As the conception,"
said Goethe, "is so old—for I have had it in my mind for fifty years—the
materials have accumulated to such a degree that the difficulty is to separate and reject. The invention of the second part is really as old as I say;
but it may be an advantage that I have not written it down till now when
my knowledge of the world is so much clearer. I am like one who in his
youth has a great deal of small silver and copper money; which in the
course of his life he constantly changes for the better, so that at last the
property of his youth stands before him in pieces of pure gold."

We spoke about the character of the Bachelor. "Is he not meant," said
I, "to represent a certain class of ideal philosophers?"

"No," said Goethe, "the arrogance peculiar to youth, of which we had
such striking examples after our war for freedom, is personified in him.
Indeed, everyone believes in his youth that the world really began with
him, and that all merely exists for his sake.

"Thus, in the East, there was a man who every morning collected his
people about him, and would not go to work till he had commanded the
sun to rise. But he was wise enough not to command till the sun of its
own accord was on the point of appearing."

Conversation, Wednesday, December 16, 1829
[Goethe comments on Homunculus's relation to Mephistopheles.]

To-day, after dinner, Goethe read me the second scene of the second
act of *Faust*, where Mephistopheles visits Wagner, who is on the point of
making a human being by chemical means. The work succeeds; the Homunculus appears in the phial, as a shining being, and is at once active.
He repels Wagner's questions upon incomprehensible subjects; reasoning
is not his business; he wishes to *act,* and begins with our hero, Faust, who,
in his paralysed condition, needs a higher aid. As a being to whom the
present is perfectly clear and transparent, the Homunculus sees into the
soul of the sleeping Faust; who, enraptured by a lovely dream, beholds
Leda visited by swans, while she is bathing in a pleasant spot. The Homunculus, by describing this dream, brings a most charming picture before our eyes. Mephistopheles sees nothing of it, and the Homunculus
taunts him with his northern nature.

"Generally," said Goethe, "you will perceive that Mephistopheles appears to disadvantage beside the Homunculus,[4] who is like him in clearness of intellect, and so much superior in his tendency to the beautiful
and to a useful activity. He styles him cousin; for such spiritual beings as
this Homunculus, not saddened and limited by a thorough assumption of
humanity, were classed with the dæmons, and thus there is a sort of relationship between the two."

"Certainly," said I, "Mephistopheles here appears a subordinate: yet I

---

4. Goethe presumably here alludes only to the scene in Wagner's laboratory, which he was working
   on at the time.

cannot help thinking he has had a secret influence on the production of the Homunculus. We have known him in this way before; and, indeed, in the *Helena* he always appears as secretly working. Thus he again elevates himself with regard to the whole, and in his lofty repose he can well afford to put up with a little in particulars."

"Your feeling of the position is very correct," said Goethe; "indeed, I have doubted whether I ought not to put some verses into the mouth of Mephistopheles when he goes to Wagner and when the Homunculus is still in a state of formation, so that his co-operation may be expressed."

"It would do no harm," said I. "Yet this is intimated by the words with which Mephistopheles closes the scene:

> At last we after all depend
> Upon dependents we created. [lines 7003–4]

"True," said Goethe, "that would be almost enough for the attentive; but I will think about some additional verses."

"But those concluding words are very great, and will not easily be penetrated to their full extent."

"I think," said Goethe, "I have given them a bone to pick. A father who has six sons is a lost man, let him do what he may. Kings and ministers, too, who have raised many persons to high places, may have something to think about from their own experience."

Faust's dream about Leda again came into my head, and I regarded this as a most important feature.

"It is wonderful to me," said I, "how the several parts of such a work bear upon, perfect, and sustain one another! By this dream of Leda, *Helena* gains its proper foundation. There we have a constant allusion to swans and the child of a swan; but here we have the act itself, and when we come afterwards to *Helena*, with the sensible impression of such a situation, how much more clear and perfect does all appear!"

Goethe said I was right.

"You will see," said he, "that in these earlier acts the chords of the classic and romantic are constantly struck; so that, as on a rising ground, where both forms of poetry are brought out and in some sort balance one another, we may ascend to *Helena*.

"The French," continued Goethe, "now begin to think aright on these matters. Classic and Romantic, say they, are equally good: the only point is to use these forms with judgment, and to be capable of excellence— you can be absurd in both, and then one is as worthless as the other. This, I think, is rational enough, and may content us for a while."

Conversation, Sunday, December 20, 1829
[*Goethe comments on Euphorion and the Boy Charioteer (from the Carnival in Act I).*]

Meanwhile, *Faust* came once more into my head, and I talked of the way to render the Homunculus clear on the stage. "If we do not see the little man himself," said I, "we must see the light in the bottle, and his important words must be uttered in a way that would surpass the capacity of a child."

"Wagner," said Goethe, "must not let the bottle go out of his hands, and the voice must sound as if it came from the bottle. It would be a part for a ventriloquist such as I have heard. A man of that kind would solve the difficulty."

We then talked of the Grand Carnival, and the possibility of representing it upon the stage. "It would be a little more than the market-place at Naples," said I.

"It would require a very large theatre," said Goethe, "and is hardly to be imagined."

"I hope to see it some day," was my answer. "I look forward especially to the elephant, led by Prudence, and surmounted by Victory, with Hope and Fear in chains on each side. This is an allegory that could not easily be surpassed."

"The elephant would not be the first on the stage," said Goethe. "At Paris there is one, which forms an entire character. He belongs to a popular party, and takes the crown from one king and places it on another, which must indeed have an imposing effect. Then, when he is called at the end of the piece, he appears quite alone, makes his bow, and retires. So you see we might reckon on an elephant for our carnival. But the whole scene is much too large, and requires an uncommon kind of manager."

"Still, it is so brilliant and effective that a stage will scarcely allow it to escape. Then how it builds itself up, and becomes more and more striking! First, there are the beautiful gardeners, male and female; who decorate the stage, and at the same time form a mass, so that the various objects as they increase in importance are never without spectators and a background. Then, after the elephant, there is the team of dragons, coming from the background, through the air, and soaring overhead. Then the appearance of the great Pan; and how at last all seems afire, until put out by the wet clouds that roll to the spot. With all this carried out as you have conceived, the public will, in its amazement, confess that it has not senses and intellect enough to appreciate such spectacular riches."

"Pray, no more about the public," said Goethe; "I wish to hear nothing about it. The chief point is, that the piece is written; the world may now do with it as it pleases and use it as far as it can."

We then talked of the Boy Charioteer.[5]

"That Faust is concealed under the mask of Plutus, and Mephistopheles under that of Avarice, you will have already perceived. But who is the Boy Charioteer?"

I hesitated, and could not answer.

"It is Euphorion," said Goethe.

"But how can he appear in the carnival here, when he is not born till the third act?"

5. The Boy Charioteer is a central allegorical character in the Carnival Masque of Act I. Euphorion, of course, is the offspring of Faust and Helena in Act III, which was composed first (and may thus justify the inverse sequence in Goethe's thinking here) but comes later in Part Two of *Faust*.

"Euphorion," replied Goethe, "is not a human, but an allegorical being. In him is personified poetry; which is bound to neither time, place, nor person. The same spirit who afterwards chooses to be Euphorion appears here as the Boy Charioteer, and is so far like a spectre that he can be present everywhere and at all times."

Conversation, Wednesday, December 30, 1829
[*Goethe discusses the paper-money scene and the spirit show of Paris and Helena in Act I.*]

To-day, after dinner, Goethe read me the next scene.

"Now they have got money at the imperial court," said he, "they want to be amused. The Emperor wishes to see Paris and Helen; and through magical art they are to appear in person. However, since Mephistopheles has nothing to do with Greek antiquity, and has no power over such personages, this task is assigned to Faust, who succeeds in it perfectly. The scene showing the means Faust must adopt to render the apparition possible is not complete yet, but I will read it to you next time. The actual appearance of Paris and Helen you shall hear to-day."

Conversation, Sunday, January 3, 1830
[*General remarks on* Faust]

* * * [Goethe] had taken up the latest French translation of his *Faust*, by Gérard; which he turned over, and seemed occasionally to read.

"Some singular thoughts pass through my head," said he. "This book is now read in a language over which Voltaire ruled fifty years ago. You cannot understand my thoughts upon this subject, and have no idea of the influence Voltaire and his great contemporaries had in my youth, and how they governed the whole civilized world. My biography does not clearly show the influence of these men in my youth, and what pains it cost me to defend myself against them and to maintain my own ground in a true relation to nature."

* * *

He praised Gérard's translation as very successful, although mostly in prose.

"I do not like," he said, "to read my *Faust* any more in German; but in this French translation all seems again fresh, new, and spirited. *Faust* is, however, quite incommensurable, and all attempts to bring it nearer to the understanding are vain. Also, the first part is the product of a rather dark state in the individual. However, this very darkness has a charm for men's minds; and they work upon it till they are tired, as upon all insoluble problems."

Conversation, Sunday, January 10, 1830
[*Goethe discusses the Mothers scene in Act I ("Dark Gallery").*]

This afternoon, Goethe afforded me great pleasure by reading the scene in which Faust visits the Mothers.

The novelty and unexpectedness of the subject, and Goethe's manner of reading the scene, struck me so forcibly that I felt myself wholly transported into the situation of Faust when he shudders at the communication from Mephistopheles.

Although I had heard and felt the whole, yet so much remained an enigma to me that I asked Goethe for some explanation. But he, as usual, wrapped himself up in mystery, as he looked on me with wide open eyes and repeated the words:

The Mothers! Why, it strikes a singular chord. [line 6217]

"I can reveal to you no more," said he, "except that I found in Plutarch that in ancient Greece mention was made of the Mothers as divinities. This is all that I owe to others, the rest is my own invention. Take the manuscript home with you, study it carefully, and see what you can make of it."

Conversation, Sunday January 24, 1830
[Goethe comments on the "Classical Walpurgis Night."]

We then talked about the "Classical Walpurgis Night," the beginning of which Goethe had lately read me.

"The mythological figures that crowd upon me," said he, "are innumerable; but I restrain myself, and select those that produce the proper pictorial effect. Faust has now met Chiron, and I hope I shall be successful with the scene.[6] If I work hard I shall have done the 'Walpurgis Night' in a couple of months. Nothing more shall take me off Faust; for it will be odd enough if I live to finish it, and yet it is possible. The fifth act is as good as done, and the fourth will almost write itself."

Conversation, Sunday, February 13, 1831
[Concerning the final stage of composition]

* * * Goethe * * * told me he was going on with the fourth act of Faust, and had satisfied himself with the beginning.

"I had," said he, "long since the what, as you know, but was not quite satisfied about the how; hence it is the more pleasant that good thoughts have come to me.

"I will now go on inventing, to supply the whole gap, from the Helena to the fifth act, which is finished, and will write down a detailed plan, that I may work with comfort and security on those parts that first attract me.

"This act acquires quite a peculiar character, so that, like an independent little world, it does not touch the rest, and is only connected with the whole by a slight reference to what precedes and follows."

"It will then," said I, "be perfectly in character with the rest; for, in fact, 'Auerbach's Tavern,' 'Witch's Kitchen,' the Blocksberg, the Imperial Diet, the masquerade, the paper money, the laboratory, the 'Classical Walpurgis Night,' the Helena are all of them little independent worlds, which, each

---

6. An allusion to Faust's meeting with the centaur Chiron in the "Classical Walpurgis Night" (lines 7331–488).

being complete in itself, do indeed work upon each other, yet come but little in contact. The great point with the poet is to express a manifold world, and he uses the story of a celebrated hero merely as a sort of thread on which he may string what he pleases. * * * "

"You are perfectly right," said Goethe; "and the only matter of importance is, that the single masses should be clear and significant, while the whole always remains incommensurable—and even on that account, like an unsolved problem, constantly lures mankind to study it again and again."

Conversation, Thursday, February 17, 1831
[*General comments on* Faust]

I asked about *Faust*, and what progress he had made with it.

"That," said Goethe, "will not again let me loose. I daily think and invent more and more of it. I have now had the whole manuscript of the second part stitched together, that it may lie a palpable mass before me. The place of the yet-lacking fourth act I have filled with white paper; and undoubtedly what is finished will allure and urge me to complete what has yet to be done. There is more than people think in these matters of sense, and we must aid the spirit by all manner of devices."

He sent for the stitched *Faust*, and I was surprised to see how much he had written; for a good folio volume was before me.

"And all," said I, "has been done in the six years that I have been here; and yet, amid so many other occupations, you could have devoted but little time to it. We see how much a work grows, even if we add something only now and then!"

"That is a conviction that strengthens with age," said Goethe; "while youth believes all must be done in a single day. If fortune favour, and I continue in good health, I hope in the next spring months to get a great way on with the fourth act. It was, as you know, invented long since; but the other parts have, in course of execution, grown so much, that I can now use only the outline of my first invention, and must fill out this introduced portion so as to make it of a piece with the rest."

"A far richer world is displayed," said I, "in this second part than in the first."

"I should think so," said Goethe. "The first part is almost entirely subjective; it proceeded entirely from a perplexed impassioned individual, and his semi-darkness is probably highly pleasing to mankind. But in the second part there is scarcely anything of the subjective; here is seen a higher, broader, clearer, more passionless world, and he who has not looked about him and had some experience will not know what to make of it."

"There will be found exercise for thought," said I; "some learning may also be needful. I am glad that I have read Schelling's little book on the Cabiri, and that I now know the drift of that famous passage in the 'Walpurgis Night.' "[7]

7. See footnote to line 8074.

"I have always found," said Goethe laughing, "that it is well to know something."

Conversation, Monday, February 21, 1831
[Goethe discusses the two "Walpurgis Night"s.]

"The old 'Walpurgis Night,' " said Goethe, "is monarchical, since the devil is there respected throughout as a decided chief. But the 'Classical Walpurgis Night' is thoroughly republican; since all stand on a plain near one another, so that each is as prominent as his associates, and nobody is subordinate or troubled about the rest."

"Moreover," said I, "in the Classical assembly all are sharply-outlined individualities; while, on the German Blocksberg, each individuality is lost in the general witch-mass."

"Therefore," said Goethe, "Mephistopheles knows what is meant when the Homunculus speaks to him of *Thessalian* witches.[8] A connoisseur of antiquity will have something suggested by these words, while to the unlearned it remains a mere name."

"Antiquity," said I, "must be very living to you, else you could not make all these figures step so freshly into life, and treat them with such freedom as you do."

"Without a lifelong occupation with plastic art," said Goethe, "it would not have been possible to me. The difficulty was in observing due moderation amid such plenty, and avoiding all figures that did not perfectly fit into my plan. I made, for instance, no use of the Minotaur, the Harpies, and certain other monsters."

"But what you have exhibited in that night," said I, "is so grouped, and fits so well together, that it can be easily recalled by the imagination and made into a picture. The painters will certainly not allow such good subjects to escape them; and I especially hope to see Mephistopheles among the Phorcyades, when he tries the famous mask in profile."

"There are a few pleasantries there," said Goethe, "which will more or less occupy the world. Suppose the French are the first to perceive *Helena*, and to see what can be done with it for the stage. They will spoil the piece as it is; but they will make a wise use of it for their own purpose, and that is all we can expect or desire. To Phorcyas they will certainly add a chorus of monsters, as is indeed already indicated in one passage."

"It would be a great matter," said I, "if a clever poet of the Romantic school treated the piece as an opera throughout, and Rossini collected all his great talent for a grand composition, to produce an effect with the *Helena*. It affords opportunities for magnificent scenes, surprising transformations, brilliant costumes, and charming ballets, which are not easily to be found elsewhere; not to mention that this abundance of sensible material rests on the foundation of an ingenious fable that could scarcely be excelled."

"We will wait for what the gods bring us," said Goethe; "such things

---

8. See line 6977.

are not to be hurried. The great matter is for people to enter into it, and for managers, poets, and composers to see their advantage in it."

Conversation, Monday, June 6, 1831
[*Goethe discusses Philemon and Baucis and the Angels' song about Faust's salvation (lines 11934–41).*]

Goethe showed me to-day the beginning of the fifth act of *Faust*, hitherto wanting. I read to the place where the cottage of Philemon and Baucis is burned, and Faust, standing by night on the balcony of his palace, smells the smoke, which is borne to him by a light breeze.

"These names, Philemon and Baucis," said I, "transport me to the Phrygian coast, reminding me of the famous couple of antiquity. But our scene belongs to modern days, and a Christian landscape."

"My Philemon and Baucis," said Goethe, "have nothing to do with that renowned ancient couple or the tradition connected with them. I gave this couple the names merely to elevate the characters. The persons and relations are similar, and hence the use of the names has a good effect."

We then spoke of Faust, whom the hereditary portion of his character —discontent—has not left even in his old age, and who, amid all the treasures of the world, and in a new dominion of his own making, is annoyed by a couple of lindens, a cottage, and a bell, which are not his. He is therein not unlike Ahab, King of Israel, who fancied he possessed nothing, unless he could also make the vineyard of Naboth his own.

"Faust," said Goethe, "when he appears in the fifth act, should, according to my design, be exactly a hundred years old, and I rather think it would be well expressly to say so in some passage."

We then spoke of the conclusion, and Goethe directed my attention to the passage:

> Pure spirits' peer, from evil coil
> He was vouchsafed exemption;
> "Whoever strives in ceaseless toil,
> Him we may grant redemption."
> And when on high, transfigured love
> Has added intercession,
> The blest will throng to him above
> With welcoming compassion. [lines 11934–41]

"In these lines," said he, "is contained the key to Faust's salvation. In Faust himself there is an activity that becomes constantly higher and purer to the end, and from above there is eternal love coming to his aid. This harmonizes perfectly with our religious views; according to which we can obtain heavenly bliss, not through our own strength alone, but with the assistance of divine grace.

To Heinrich Meyer,[9] July 20, 1831
[On Faust, Part Two]

It is always surprising to me how egoism, which is isolated from everything, revolutionary in part and secluded in part, permeates all kinds of
lively activities. Let me only acknowledge that I have withdrawn my own
into the innermost aspect of my work and have been organizing the second
part of my *Faust*, which I began serious work on again four years ago,
filling in the important gaps and joining the existing material together from
the perspective of the conclusion and from the beginning toward the conclusion. I hope I have succeeded in eliminating all discontinuity between
the earlier and the later material.

For a long time I knew what I wanted, indeed even how I wanted it,
and I carried it around within me for many years like a fairy tale, only
composing particular passages which attracted my attention from time to
time. But this second part was not to be, and could not be, as fragmentary
as the first. Common sense plays a greater role in it, as will have been
apparent from that part of it which has already been printed. It finally
required, to be sure, really strong resolution to work it into a whole, so
that it would stand up to the scrutiny of an educated mind. For that reason
I firmly resolved that it must be completed before my birthday. And so it
will be. The whole thing now lies before me and I have only incidentals
to correct. Then I will seal it up, and then, whatever happens, it will
increase the specific substance of those volumes of my work still to appear.
Though it still contains problems enough, since—like world history and
human history—each problem solved creates a new one to be solved, it is
certain to provide pleasure for those who can respond to a gesture, a hint
or a delicate intimation. Such a reader will even find more in it than I
could give. And thus a great stone has been pushed over the mountaintop
and rolled down the other side. But immediately there are others lying
behind me which also need to be dealt with, in order that what is written
may be fulfilled: "Such labor has God given to man."

To Wilhelm von Humboldt,[1] December 1, 1831
[On Faust generally]

Concerning my *Faust* there is much to say and there is little to say. In
a happy moment the following passage came to mind:

> Call yourselves poets by vocation?
> Then order up your poetry. [lines 220–1]

9. Johann Heinrich Meyer (1760–1832), art historian and active member of the so-called friends of
   art in Weimar (*Weimarer Kunstfreunde*), who strongly supported Goethe's classical taste in art
   during the period following the poet's Italian journey in 1786–8, remained a close friend, collaborator, and correspondent of the poet until Goethe's death.
1. Wilhelm von Humboldt (1767–1835), statesman, historian, linguist, and general man of letters,
   became a close associate of both Goethe and Schiller during the mid-1790s, especially on matters
   pertaining to literature and aesthetics. His later correspondence with Goethe constitutes one of
   the most important documents for German nineteenth-century as well as for Goethe's later
   thought.

And by means of a mysterious psychological tranformation, which perhaps deserves to be studied, I believe that I have elevated my mind to a kind of productivity which brought all this forth in a full state of consciousness and which pleases me still, even though perhaps I could never swim again in such a river, a productivity which Aristotle and other prosaic minds would ascribe to a kind of madness. The difficulty in achieving this consisted in the fact that the second part of *Faust*, the published sections of which have perhaps attracted your attention, has been thought through for fifty years in all its aims and motifs and has been worked through in fragments—according to my pleasure with one or another incident— though the whole of it remained full of gaps.

Now common sense will make greater demands of the second part than the first and for this reason it was necessary to work more in anticipation of the needs of an intelligent reader, even though there is enough left over by way of transitions to be supplied for him. It was necessary to fill in certain gaps for both historical and aesthetic continuity; and I kept this up until finally it seemed advisable to cry out: "Close the irrigation canal, the fields have had enough."

And then I had to find the courage to seal up my bound copy of the play, which contains a mixture of printed and unprinted material, so that I would not be tempted to add still further here and there; whereby indeed I regret not being able to share this with my most valued friends—something a poet does so gladly.

To Wilhelm von Humboldt,[2] March 17, 1832
[Last words on Faust]

After a long involuntary pause I am beginning like this, and yet simply impromptu. The Ancients said that the animals are taught through their organs; let me add to this, so are men, but they have the advantage of teaching their organs in return.

Every action, and so every talent, needs some inborn faculty which acts naturally, and unconsciously carries with it the necessary aptitude, and which, therefore, continues to act in such a way that though its law is implicit in it, its course in the end may be aimless and purposeless.

The earlier man becomes aware that there exists some craft, some art that can help him towards a controlled heightening of his natural abilities, the happier he is; whatever he may receive from without does not harm his innate individuality. The best genius is that which absorbs everything within itself, knows how to appropriate everything, without this in the least impairing its fundamental dispositions, called its character, but rather enhancing and furthering them throughout as much as possible.

Here begin the manifold relations between the conscious and the unconscious. Take for instance a talented musician, composing an important score; consciousness and unconsciousness will be like warp and weft, a simile I am fond of using.

---

2. This is the last letter Goethe wrote. Final changes in the manuscript of *Faust* had been made (according to Goethe's diary notations) during January, 1832. He became ill on March 16 and died on March 22.

Through practice, teaching, reflection, success, failure, furtherance and resistance, and again and again reflection, man's organs unconsciously and in a free activity link what he acquires with his innate gifts, so that a unity results which leaves the world amazed.

These general remarks may serve as a rapid answer to your question, and as an explanation to the note I return herewith.

For more than sixty years the conception of *Faust* has lain here before my mind with the clearness of youth, though the sequence with less fulness. I have let the idea go quietly along with me through life and have only worked out the scenes that interested me most from time to time. So in the second part gaps remained, waiting for this kind of interest before they could be joined to the rest. It was difficult to do through conscious effort and strength of personality something that really should have been the spontaneous work of active nature. But it surely would not be right if this were not possible after my long life of thought and action, and I am not afraid of people being able to pick out the new from the old, the later from the earlier work. We can leave that to future readers.

It would naturally be an infinite joy to me if during my lifetime, too, I could dedicate these serious jests to my valued friends everywhere. I have always been grateful for their interest and should like to hear their response. But the present age is so senseless and confused that I know I should only be poorly rewarded for my many years of sincere effort at erecting this strange building. It would be driven like a wrack on the shore and lie there, getting gradually covered by the sands of time. The world is ruled to-day by bewildering wrong counsel, urging bewildered wrong action. My most important task is to go on developing as much as possible whatever is and remains in me, distilling my own particular abilities again and again. You, my friend, are doing the same up there in your castle.

Tell me about your work, too; as you know, Riemer[3] is still busy on the same sort of studies as we are, and our evening conversations often touch on these subjects. Forgive this long delayed letter. In spite of my retirement, there is seldom a time when I am in the mood to remind myself of those mysteries of life.

---

3. Friedrich Wilhelm Riemer (1774–1845), Goethe's longtime coworker on questions of classical antiquity.

Comments by Contemporaries

WILHELM VON HUMBOLDT

[Response to the Newly Published *Fragment* of *Faust*]†

Indeed Gretchen in Goethe's *Faust* is an entirely new [kind of] character. This naïveté and pious innocence! And in her expression such nature and truth. The manner in which she declares herself to him, the way she returns his kiss, is masterfully [portrayed] beyond all description. And on the other side is Faust. His greatness, all encompassing, his ability to weave the whole of nature into his feelings, is only portrayed in such strength and beauty by Goethe. His eternally active drive for truth and knowledge, his enthusiastic feeling for moral nobility, the unceasing presence of unattainable beautiful ideals, the fullness and blessedness on one side which springs forth from it and the sense of his own poverty on the other, are so truly drawn in Faust. Everywhere one can see in him the exalted spirit which strives beyond the limits of the human, which gathers to itself every spark from mankind which is more than human and ascends upwards from such heights. Gretchen's character is charming in every way and her expression is often so moving; the way she cannot comprehend at all what Faust sees in her, the way she tells of her work at home, the exactness of her mother, the tending of her little sister, and then the passage:

> Now I myself am bared to sin!
> Yet all of it that drove me here,
> God! Was so innocent, was so dear! [3584–6]

If only the whole of it were not so patchwork [*buntscheckicht*]. Right from the start there are fatal scenes, some of them beautiful of course, but so indelicate and raw. The tender scene of the first meeting between Gretchen and Faust is forever ruined by Frau Marthe. Goethe should not have had them walking [in the garden scene] in juxtaposition. For as often as I read what Gretchen says, I see always in my mind this intolerable Marthe coming towards her. In such a way the whole thing shifts peri-

† Letter to his fiancée, Caroline von Dacheroden, Berlin or Tegel, May 21, 1790; in his published correspondence with Caroline, vol. 1, Nr. 52, 150–1; trans. Cyrus Hamlin. This effusion in the context of a love letter, by a reader who was later to become one of Goethe's closest friends and the leading humanist of the age, indicates—within a few short weeks of the publication of the *Fragment*—how powerful an impact *Faust* had on those who were responsive to its poetic and dramatic power.

odically. "Your" song—"My peace is gone"—I have now memorized. Oh!, it is sung as if from my own soul.

HENRIK STEFFENS

[First Impression of *Faust*]†

Among the books which I received from the library was a small volume entitled Goethe's *Complete Works*, vol. VII. I call it this way because Goethe's name was completely unknown to me and the title hardly attractive. As I began to read, I could not stop. The volume as is known contains Goethe's *Faust*, specifically the Fragment, which ends with the scene where Gretchen, plagued by the whisperings of the evil spirit, kneels in the cathedral. * * * This work captivated me in a way that was hitherto unknown to me. The language itself seemed to me to have a sound which to this day I have never heard [elsewhere], to possess a secret power, a magic, which I did not know. Admittedly the deeper pain of unmeasured knowledge was still foreign to me, but each day brought me something new, and this was appropriated and enjoyed with pleasure, and the unease with which I tried to bring some order to this growing mass had nothing in common with that inner devouring agony. All the same it was as if I intuited the pain which cannot remain for long unfamiliar to a mentally active disposition. * * * Much, indeed everything [in *Faust*], had for me a wondrous, mysterious attraction. I was drawn ever anew to its strange language, which sounded to me like a wonderful spiritual music from the inmost and hidden reaches of the soul. The secret pain which is barely sensed in the joy of knowledge became a goad that heightened, rather than hindered my desire. Many passages were involuntarily preserved in my memory, they could not be displaced. The worry and lament of Gretchen seemed to me to be the deepest of human existence. A mysterious horror joined with an infinite desire. This inner activity was concealed from everyone. A new ground tone for my entire being had been sounded and resonated quietly with powerful echoes in my inner soul. Even now there are still passages in *Faust* which, when they are encountered unexpectedly, overpower me and seize me with the power of an entire life. This was the inmost, first and deepest devastation of my youthful mind, which was struck with manifold variations and which could be heard ever anew from the inmost depths as the mysterious lamentation of an innocent existence. That Goethe's *Faust* gave my whole religious disposition a turn that was very different from its hitherto innocent stance, can easily be perceived. In earlier times all poetry grew from an innocent,

---

† From *Was ich erlebte* (10 vols., 1840–3); trans. Cyrus Hamlin. Steffens (1773–1845), a Norwegian whose entire academic career was pursued in Germany, became one of the leading Romantic philosophers of nature (*Naturphilosophen*). In his autobiography, published at the end of his life, he recalls the experience of discovering Goethe's *Faust: Ein Fragment* in Copenhagen, soon after it was published, when he was only a teenager. His account offers a vivid picture of the powerful impact that Goethe's fragment had upon its initial readers, at least among those who belonged to the generation of Romantics, then just coming into maturity.

childlike, naïve belief; it developed as a secular blossom of worship, it was the fragrance of flowers, in which the sensuous glory of color faded away and died with the consciousness of bliss. I could pray, indeed prayer was for me a need. Now prayer had already become alien to me, only an inner anxiety forced it out in transient moments of regret, which became ever more seldom, and an inclination developed to grasp religion out of poetry, indeed to conceive it anew as a deep poetry of human existence, once it had disappeared in its original form. This intention was admittedly not clear to me at the time, but it was all too certain that all religious sensibility had become insecure, indeterminately dark and was suspended strangely between truth and poetry.

AUGUST WILHELM SCHLEGEL

[Review of the *Fragment* of 1790]†

"Faust, a Fragment." The meaning of this dramatic poem lies too deep, is too far-reaching, and, since the piece is only a fragment, too little developed not to run the risk that a large proportion of readers will overlook it and dwell instead upon lesser works. Faust, as Goethe has heightened and expanded the folk legend for his purposes, is a man for whose understanding science and for whose stormy heart ethically moderate enjoyment are too confining; whose feelings carry within themselves the mark of inborn nobility and genuine love of nature; and whose actions are uncertain, aimless, and corruptible; a man who, at one moment, pushes himself beyond the limits of mortality in order to establish alliances with higher spirits and, at the next, surrenders himself to the devil for unrestrained sensual gratification; noble enough not to be infected by the insensitive mockery of the demon who serves him in the satisfaction of his desires, and not strong enough to master the passions which make such a guide necessary to him. Equally removed from comfortable, inactive repose and from the joy of successful activity, Faust has squandered his life in endless research. At last he tears himself free, rejects all science as the dead skeleton of nature, and hurries to embrace living nature herself. Bold enthusiasm carries him upwards into the world of spirits. New youth is given him. A girl who lives alone in modest seclusion and childish contentment attracts him and falls victim to his passion. He destroys her domestic peace: this good, weak creature perishes from love and remorse. All this is presented overpoweringly and, in Goethe's manner, tossed off with a degree of carelessness and yet with the utmost truth. But the poet takes us no further. In certain respects, to be sure, Faust's fate has long since been decided: his path, once he has taken it, leads unavoidably to ruin. But will this apply only to his external condition or will it also affect

---

† Schlegel (1767–1845), who subsequently emerged as the leading practical critic of European Romanticism, here offers an immediate response to the first public appearance of Goethe's drama, the *Fragment* of 1790. (From *Göttingische Anzeige von gelehrten Sachen* [1790], Stück 154; in *Collected Works*, ed. Böcking [Leipzig, 1846], vol. 10, 16 ff.; trans. Dolores Signorl and Cyrus Hamlin.)

the inner man? Will he remain true to himself and, even in the final instance, still deserve human compassion because he falls as a human being with great abilities? Or will the depraved spirit to whom he has surrendered himself bring him to the point where he becomes himself the creator of evil, himself a devil?—This question still remains unanswered.

Just as the design of this play is unique (for it cannot in any way be compared with any of Goethe's own works, nor with those of any other dramatic poet), so also is its treatment. No single tone, or style, or general norm holds sway, to which the particular ideas must adapt and arrange themselves. The poet has set only one law for himself: to follow the freest ranging of his mind. Hence the sudden transitions from popular simplicity to philosophical profundity, from mysterious, magical oracles to expressions of general common sense, from the sublime to the burlesque. In the versification, too, one finds just as diverse an alternation: here the meter of Hans Sachs,[1] there rhymed lines of all measures and lengths; here and there also irregular lyrical rhythms. In many places one misses that polish of versification which is the work of mechanical diligence; nowhere is there a lack of energy or expression. Here too a superior mind reveals itself, which can afford to ignore discretion and yet never miss its mark.

FRIEDRICH SCHLEGEL

[On *Hamlet* and *Faust* as Philosophical Tragedies]†

* * * True philosophical poetry interests not only the understanding but also the intellect. Poetry which is "characteristic" develops and advances naturally to philosophical tragedy which is the complete antithesis of aesthetic tragedy. The latter is the consummation of beautiful poetry, consisting of purely lyrical elements whose ultimate effect is the highest harmony. The former is the highest artistic form of didactic poetry, consisting of purely characteristic elements, whose ultimate effect is the highest disharmony. Its catastrophe is tragic, but not its entire substance: for the prevailing purity of the tragic element (an essential condition of aesthetic tragedy) would impair the truth of characteristic and philosophical art.

This is not the place to develop in detail the as yet completely unknown theory of philosophical tragedy. Yet let me illustrate the concept of this poetic form as I conceive it with a single example, which is a very interesting phenomenon in itself and, in addition, one of the most important

1. German poet (1494–1576) and leading *Meistersinger* of the Nuremberg School, renowned for his use of the *Knittelvers*, or doggerel rhyme.
† Friedrich Schlegel (1772–1829; younger brother of August Wilhelm), in his essay "On the Study of Greek Poesy" (1795), from which the passage here included is taken (*Prosaische Jugendschriften*, ed. Jacob Minor [Vienna 1906], vol. 1, 106–8, 114; here trans. by Cyrus Hamlin), first elaborated the basic polarity between classical and Romantic poetry, which subsequently achieved European notoriety. Within this polarity Schlegel argued for a fundamental distinction between aesthetic tragedy, exemplified by the drama of Sophocles, and philosophical tragedy, here discussed with specific reference to Shakespeare's *Hamlet* as norm. Mention of *Faust*, which remains no more than that here, indicates how Goethe's play came to replace Shakespeare as the model for Romantic philosophical tragedy.

documents for the "characteristic" quality of modern poetry and which for content and perfect coherence is so far the most admirable of its kind.— *Hamlet* is often misunderstood when it is praised for particular passages. A rather inconsistent tolerance, if the whole is really so disjointed, so senseless as is often silently assumed! In reality the coherence of Shakespeare's dramas is so simple and lucid that it should be comprehended in its own right by open and unbiased minds. The basis of this coherence, however, often lies so deeply hidden—the invisible ties, the connections are so delicate—that even the most ingenious critical analysis will fail if it lacks tact, if false expectations or false principles are applied. In *Hamlet* all the individual parts develop necessarily from a common center and relate back to it again. Nothing is extraneous, superfluous, or accidental in this masterpiece of artistic wisdom. The center of the whole is found in the character of the hero. Because of his unique situation all the power of his noble nature is concentrated in his reason, and his power to act is completely destroyed. His spirit is divided, as if torn apart in opposite directions on the rack; it collapses and perishes from an excess of idle reason, which oppresses him more painfully than do all those with whom he comes into contact. There exists perhaps no more perfect representation of irresolvable discord, which is the true subject of philosophical tragedy, than such an utter disparity between the reflective and the active power as in the character of Hamlet. The total effect of this tragedy is one of maximum despair. All the impressions it makes, which individually seem large and important, become trivial and disappear in the face of what here appears as the final, unique result of all being and thought: the eternal, colossal dissonance which infinitely separates mankind and fate.

In the entire realm of modern poetry this drama is one of the most important documents for the aesthetic historian. In it the mind of its creator is most visible; what appears sporadically throughout the other works of the poet is here perfectly united. Shakespeare among all artists is the one who most completely and most strikingly embodies the spirit of modern poetry. He unites the most charming blossoms of romantic fantasy and the gigantic dimension of the Gothic heroic age with the subtlest strains of modern social life and the most profound and extensive poetic philosophy. With regard to these last two (i.e., social life and philosophy), it might appear at times that he had anticipated the developments of our own age. Who has surpassed him in the inexhaustible supply of what is interesting? in intensity of all passions? in the inimitable truth of the "characteristic"? in unique originality? He spans to the fullest extent the particular aesthetic advantages of every kind of modern writer, highest excellence and, with regard to the singularity of the moderns, even the eccentric peculiarities and errors which they carry with them. Without exaggeration he may be called the peak of modern poetry. How rich he is in individual beauties of every kind! How often he so nearly achieves the highest which can be attained! * * *

The character of the aesthetic development of our age and our nation betrays itself in a remarkable and magnificent phenomenon. Goethe's poetry is the dawn of genuine art and pure beauty.—The sensual power which sustains our age and our people was only the smallest of the advantages with which he first appeared as a young man. The philosophical content, the "characteristic" truth of his later works can be compared with the inexhaustible wealth of Shakespeare. Indeed, if *Faust* were to be completed, it would probably far surpass *Hamlet*, the English poet's masterpiece, with which it seems to share a common purpose. What in *Hamlet* is only fate, event—weakness, is in *Faust* disposition, action—strength. Hamlet's mood and his inclination are the result of his external situation; Faust's corresponding inclination is his natural character. * * *

FRIEDRICH WILHELM JOSEPH SCHELLING

[On *Faust* as Tragicomedy]†

In moving from tragedy to comedy [in this discussion of contemporary drama] it is without doubt most appropriate to mention the greatest German poem, Goethe's *Faust*. But it is difficult to offer a sufficiently convincing judgment concerning the spirit of the whole based on what we possess of it thus far. So my claim that this poem is by intention far more Aristophanic than tragic may seem striking, in face of the usual view.

Therefore I shall content myself with offering a very general view of this poem, so far as I think I understand it.

Not only is there a sense of fate in the plot; here the "In-Itself" of the universe and of nature confronts as an insurmountable necessity the knowledge of the individual as an individual. The subject as subject cannot enjoy the infinite as infinite, which is nonetheless a necessary inclination of the subject. Here, therefore, is an eternal contradiction. At the same time, the power of fate, which here stands in opposition to and in conflict with the subject, is more ideal, as also holds no less true for the plot. A suspended harmony could here be established in two directions, and the conflict could seek a twofold solution. The point of departure is the insatiable thirst to behold and, as subject, to enjoy the inner essence of things; and its initial direction is to satisfy ecstatically this insatiable desire beyond the aims and limits of reason, as expressed in this passage from *Faust*:

> Go, spurn intelligence and science,
> Man's lodestar and supreme reliance,
> Be furthered by the liar-in-chief

† F. W. J. Schelling (1775–1854) delivered his lecture course *Philosophy of Art* (reprinted from the *Collected Works* [1859], vol. 1.5, 731 ff.; trans. by Cyrus Hamlin) a number of times over a period of years from 1799 to 1804. Schelling's discussion of Goethe's *Faust* is brief and very general, based entirely on the published text of the *Fragment* of 1790, though even on the basis of this incomplete text Schelling asserts that *Faust* is the greatest German poem and the prototype of philosophical tragedy. Also important is Schelling's emphasis on the unique blending of the tragic and the comic in *Faust*, by which he means the imposition of Mephistophelean irony (which is very close to what came to be called Romantic irony) upon a tragic conflict of existential proportions. Schelling addresses himself to the new philosophical theory of tragedy by shifting his attention away from "plot" (the traditional focus of Aristotelian theory) to the interaction of opposing forces: the individual or subject (that is, Faust himself) and necessity or fate, here called "the 'In-Itself' of the universe and of nature." Schelling is also the first critic of Goethe's drama to intuit the eventual salvation of the hero, and he is the first reader of the drama to identify Faust with the human condition, associating the popular legend with a basic tendency in what he refers to as the "German temper."

> In works of fraud and make-believe,
> And I shall have you dead to rights. [lines 1851–4]

The other way out for the mind's unsatisfied striving is that of plunging into the world, to experience earth's sorrow and happiness. In this direction as well the result is decisive; here, too, it is eternally impossible for the finite to participate in the infinite; which is expressed in these words:

> Fate has endowed him with a forward-driving
> Impetuousness that reaches past all sights,
> And which, precipitately striving,
> Would overleap the earth's delights.
> Through dissipation I will drag him,
> Through shallow insignificance,
> I'll have him sticking, writhing, flagging,
> And for his parched incontinence
> Have food and drink suspended at lip level;
> In vain will he be yearning for relief. [lines 1856–65]

In Goethe's *Faust* both these tendencies are represented or, rather, immediately united, so that the one proceeds directly from the other.

For dramatic reasons greater weight had to be placed on the second tendency, the encounter of such a mind with the world. So far as we can tell from the *Fragment*, we clearly recognize that *Faust* is intended to advance in this direction to the heights of tragedy.

Yet the cheerful quality of the whole, even in the first draft, the truth of its misguided striving, the authenticity of a demand for the highest life, already allows us to expect that the conflict will be resolved at a higher level and that Faust will attain fulfillment by being raised up to higher spheres.

In this regard, strange as it may seem, this poem has a significance which is truly comparable to Dante, though it is more of a comedy and divine more in a poetic sense than Dante's *Divine Comedy*.

The wild life into which Faust throws himself becomes by a necessary consequence a Hell for him. His initial purification from the pangs of knowledge and false imagination, in accord with the playful intention of the work as a whole, will have to consist in an initiation into the basic principles of devilry, as the appropriate basis for an enlightened perspective on the world—just as his fulfillment will consist in rising above himself, by which he may perceive and learn to enjoy what is essential.

Even so little concerning the nature of this poem, which in part must be intuited more than known, shows how completely original it is in every aspect, a work comparable only to itself and completely self-contained. The kind of fate [it demonstrates] is unique and would deserve to be called a new discovery, were it not to an extent already present in the German temper and thus represented in its essential form in the mythological person of Faust.

Through this singular conflict, which begins in knowledge, the poem has assumed an epistemological aspect, so that if any poem may be called philosophical, then Goethe's *Faust* above all deserves this distinction. A magnificent spirit, which here unites the power of this exceptional poet with the profundity of a philosopher, has opened in this poem an eternally fresh source of knowledge, which would itself suffice to renew science (*Wissenschaft*) in our time and to infuse into it the freshness of a new life. Whoever seeks to penetrate the true sanctuary of nature, let him be nourished by these tones from a higher world and let him drink in its power in early youth, a power which emanates from this poem, as if in dense rays of light, and which thus moves the inner heart of the world.

GEORG WILHELM FRIEDRICH HEGEL

[Paraphrase of *Faust*, from *The Phenomenology of Mind*]†

In so far as [self-consciousness] has risen from out of the substance of ethical life and the quiescent state of thought, and attained its conscious independence, it has left behind the law of custom and of substantial existence, the kinds of knowledge acquired through observation, and the sphere of theory; these lie behind it as a gray shadow that is just vanishing. For this latter is rather a knowledge of something, the independent existence (*Fürsichseyn*) and actuality of which are other than those of self-consciousness. It is not the seemingly divine spirit of universality in knowledge and action, wherein (all individual) feeling and enjoyment are stilled, that has passed into and fills this new level of self-consciousness; but the spirit of the earth, a spirit which holds that being alone as true reality which is the reality of individual consciousness.

> It repudiates sense and science
> The highest gifts possessed by men—
> It has gone over to the devil,
> And must be o'erthrown.[1]

It plunges thus into life, and carries to its completion the pure individuality in which it appears. It does not so much make its own happiness as take it directly and enjoy it. The grey shades of science, laws and principles,

---

† Hegel (1770–1831), *Phenomenology of Mind* (1807), from the section "Desire and Necessity"; trans. Sir James Black Baillie. Readers of this most difficult and abstruse philosophical work have long acknowledged Hegel's argument to include here an intentional allusion to Goethe's *Faust*, if only because of the four lines quoted in modified form from the *Fragment* of 1790. What Hegel provides in fact is a kind of paraphrase through abstraction, whereby the situation of Faust, as represented dramatically by Goethe in the *Fragment*, is translated into the conceptual dynamics of the developing Spirit that constitutes the argument of Hegel's *Phenomenology*. This provides at best an abstract analogue for Goethe's drama that cannot in any sense serve as a commentary on it. The importance of this passage for assessing the impact of Goethe's *Faust*, even in the very limited scope of the first published *Fragment*, on the development of idealist philosophy justifies its inclusion here, even though the language is bound to remain obscure to any reader unfamiliar with the vocabulary of the *Phenomenology of Mind*.

1. Hegel cites the first two and the last two lines of Mephistopheles' soliloquy, without indicating the omission of the middle section. He also intentionally transforms the rhetorical-dramatic form of the original, where Mephistopheles addresses the absent Faust in the imperative. Even more significant is the inversion of the next to last line in the speech. Where Mephistopheles asserts that Faust would "needs come to grief" even if he had not surrendered himself to the devil, Hegel states that self-consciousness will come to grief precisely *because* it *has* surrendered itself to the devil.

which alone stand between it and its own reality, vanish like a lifeless mist that cannot contend against the living certainty of its reality. It takes to itself life much as a ripe fruit is plucked, which comes to meet the hand that takes it.

MADAME DE STAËL

"Faustus"†

Among the pieces written for the performance of puppets, there is one entitled "Dr. Faustus, or Fatal Science," which has always had great success in Germany. Lessing took up this subject before Goethe. This wondrous history is a tradition very generally known. Several English authors have written the life of this same Dr. Faustus, and some of them have even attributed to him the art of printing—his profound knowledge did not preserve him from being weary of life, and in order to escape from it, he tried to enter into a compact with the devil, who concludes the whole by carrying him off. From these slender materials Goethe has furnished the astonishing work, of which I will now try to give some idea.

Certainly, we must not expect to find in it either taste, or measure, or the art that selects and terminates; but if the imagination could figure to itself an intellectual chaos, such as the material chaos has often been painted, the "Faustus" of Goethe should have been composed at that epoch. It cannot be exceeded in boldness of conception, and the recollection of this production is always attended with a sensation of giddiness: The Devil is the hero of the piece; the author has not conceived him like a hideous phantom, such as he is usually represented to children; he has made him, if we may so express ourselves, the evil Being *par excellence*, before whom all others * * * are only novices, scarcely worthy to be the servants of Mephistopheles (this is the name of the dæmon who has made himself the friend of Faustus). Goethe wished to display in this character, at once real and fanciful, the bitterest pleasantry that contempt can inspire, and at the same time an audacious gaiety that amuses. There is an infernal irony in the discourses of Mephistopheles, which extends itself to the whole creation, and criticizes the universe like a bad book of which the Devil has made himself the censor.

Mephistopheles makes sport with genius itself, as with the most ridiculous of all absurdities, when it leads men to take a serious interest in any thing that exists in the world, and above all when it gives them confidence in their own individual strength. It is singular that, supreme wickedness and divine wisdom coincide in this respect; that they equally recognize the vanity and weakness of all earthly things: but the one proclaims this

† The book by Mme. Anne-Louise-Germaine de Staël (1766–1817) *On Germany*—the excerpt given here is from the original English edition, published by John Murray (London, 1814), vol. 2, 181–5—became the single most important source for the dissemination of German Romantic ideas throughout Europe. Mme. de Staël's comments indicate the kind of impact that Goethe's *Faust*, Part One, had on the sensibility of the reading public in the later Romantic era.

truth only to disgust men with what is good, the other only to elevate them above what is evil.

If the play of "Faustus" contained only a lively and philosophical pleasantry, an analogous spirit may be found in many of Voltaire's writings; but we perceive in this piece an imagination of a very different nature. It is not only that it displays to us the moral world, such as it is, annihilated, but that Hell itself is substituted in the room of it. There is a potency of sorcery, a poetry belonging to the principle of evil, a delirium of wickedness, a distraction of thought, which make us shudder, laugh, and cry, in a breath. It seems as if the government of the world were, for a moment, entrusted to the hands of the Dæmon. You tremble because he is pitiless, you laugh because he humbles the satisfaction of self-love, you weep, because human nature, thus contemplated from the depths of hell, inspires a painful compassion.

Milton has drawn his Satan larger than man; Michael Angelo and Dante have given him the hideous figure of the brute combined with the human shape. The Mephistopheles of Goethe is a civilized Devil. He handles with dexterity that ridicule, so trifling in appearance, which is nevertheless often found to consist with a profundity of malice; he treats all sensibility as silliness or affectation; his figure is ugly, low, and crooked; he is awkward without timidity, disdainful without pride; he affects something of tenderness with the women, because it is only in their company that he needs to deceive, in order to seduce; and what he understands by seduction, is to minister to the passions of others; for he cannot even imitate love. This is the only dissimulation that is impossible to him.

The character of Mephistopheles supposes an inexhaustible knowledge of social life, of nature, and of the marvellous. This play of "Faustus," is the night-mare of the imagination, but it is a night-mare that redoubles its strength. It discovers the diabolical revelation of incredulity,—of that incredulity which attaches itself to everything that can ever exist of good in this world; and perhaps this might be a dangerous revelation, if the circumstances produced by the perfidious intentions of Mephistopheles did not inspire horror of his arrogant language, and make known the wickedness which it covers.

In the character of Faustus, all the weaknesses of humanity are concentrated: desire of knowledge, and fatigue of labour; wish of success and satiety of pleasure. It presents a perfect model of the changeful and versatile being whose sentiments are yet more ephemeral than the short existence of which he complains. Faustus has more ambition than strength; and this inward agitation produces his revolt against nature, and makes him have recourse to all manner of sorceries, in order to escape from the hard but necessary conditions imposed upon mortality. * * *

[THOMAS CARLYLE]

[First Notice of *Faust* in English]†

Goethe is likely to figure in after ages, as one of the most remarkable characters of his time; and posterity will derive from this tragedy their most lively impressions, both of his peculiar excellencies and defects. *Faust* was conceived while its author was passing from youth to settled manhood,— a period of inquietude in every life,—frequently, as in his case, of a darkness and despondency but too well suited to furnish ideas for such a work. It was executed when long culture and varied experience had ripened his powers; and under a splendour of reputation, which admitted the most confident, even careless exertion of them: its object is to delineate whatever is wildest and most mysterious in the heart and the intellect of man; and its chief materials are drawn from the heart and the intellect of the writer. In perusing it, accordingly, we seem to behold the troubled chaos of his own early woes, and doubts, and wanderings,—illuminated in part, and reduced to form, by succeeding speculations of a calmer nature,—and portrayed by a finished master, in all its original vividness, without its original disorder. In studying the scenes of *Faust*, we incessantly discover marks of that singular union of enthusiasm with derision; of volatility * * * with strength and fervour; of impetuous passion, now breaking out in fiery indignation, now in melting tenderness, now in withering sarcasm, with an overflowing gaiety, not only sportive and full of the richest humour, but grotesque to the very borders of absurdity, or beyond them, —which appears to belong exclusively to Goethe. In *Faust* too, we trace the subtle and restless understanding, which, at one period or another of its history, has penetrated into almost every subject of human thought; the sparkling fancy, and, as a necessary consequence, the boundless command of language and allusion—to clothe and illustrate, as if by enchantment, all the conceptions of a most capricious, though lofty and powerful imagination.

Except the character of Faust himself, that of his new associate is by far the most striking and original in the whole of this wonderful drama. Mephistophiles is not the common devil of poetry, but one much more adapted to his functions. It is evident that he was a devil from the first and can be nothing else. He is emphatically "the Denyer." he fears nothing, complains of nothing, hopes for nothing. Magnanimity, devotion, affection, all that can sweeten or embellish existence, he looks upon as childish mummery. His powerful intellect enables him to understand all those sentiments and their modes of acting upon men: but the idea of them

† Published anonymously in *The New Edinburgh Review* (January–April, 1822). This essay may be the most important critical discussion of *Faust* published in English during Goethe's lifetime. It was intended as a polemical response to an edition of the twenty-six engravings to *Faust* by Moritz Retsch, which were reprinted in London in 1820 with accompanying descriptive statements in English. Carlyle never openly revealed his authorship of the essay—one of his earliest—and it is to this day not included in the collected works. The earliest reprint (from which the excerpts here are taken) was in a German publication by Richard Schröder, a librarian in Berlin, *Thomas Carlyles Abhandlung über Goethes* Faust (Braunschweig, 1896).

excites no pleasure in his mind; and he regards all their manifestations as
the most weak and ridiculous anility. Pride would be a thing too noble for
him; yet his servile conduct proceeds less from natural sycophancy, than
from an utter contempt of moral distinctions. He feels it no more disgrace-
ful to cringe and fawn, that he may avoid the trouble of asserting and
commanding, than it would be to go round the base of a mountain, that
he might avoid the trouble of going over its summit; it is the easiest mode
of accomplishing his purpose in both cases, and nothing more. He might
be accused of inordinate vanity, but his unfeigned disregard for the appro-
bation of others gives to his self-esteem a character more sinister than that
of ordinary vanity. He cares for the suffrage of no one—irony is the only
tone in which he speaks of all things; and the universe itself appears in
his eyes little better than a huge puppet-show, and its whole history a paltry
farce, in which there is nothing to excite any feeling but derision from a
rational thinker. He does not even appear to hate any one very deeply. His
aim with Faust seems rather that of an *amateur*, than of a regular demon:
he tempts him chiefly as an intellectual recreation. No doubt, his motives,
like all motives, are mixed; but he seems in the course of his operations
to display, not so much the rancour and envy natural to his profession as
a desire purely scientific—a curiosity to see how ridiculous the empty
dreamer, with all his elevations and refinements, his imaginary woes and
still more imaginary joys, will look at last. In many respects Mephistophiles
resembles some French *philosophe* of the last century. There is the perfection of the intellectual faculties with a total absence of the moral; the
extreme of fanciful pleasantry and acute thought, with the extreme of arid
selfishness and contemptuous apathy. Upon all those passions and emotions which * * * men are ennobled by experiencing, he reasons with
the keen sagacity and easy disdain of the most accomplished cynic. The
sciences fare still worse with him. Logic, medicine, law, theology, as they
pass in review before him, are ridiculed till they seem hardly even worth
despising. His wit, and knowledge, and gaiety, and humour, are boundless;
but in his hands they do not illuminate—they consume. "It is written on
his front that he never loved a living soul." He cannot pity, or admire, or
worship—he can only mock. His presence is like a moral Harmattan, the
"mortifying wind" of the desert, under which every green thing is parched
and dies.

*   *   *

Goethe's conception, both of Faust and Mephistophiles, bears not only
far more relation to the habits of a refined and intellectual age, but is also
far more ingenious and poetical in itself. The introduction of magic is but
accessory to the main result: it is intended merely to serve as the means
of illustrating certain feelings, and unfolding certain propensities, which
exist in the mind, independently of magic; and the belief we are required
to give it is of the most loose and transient nature. Indeed, if we can only
conceive that an assemblage like his *dramatis personæ*, so discordant, and
so strangely related to each other, has been formed by any means, the
author appears to care little whether we believe in it at all; and throughout
the play, glimmering indications frequently become visible of the ridicule

with which the characters themselves, whatever they profess in public, inwardly regard the whole subject of *diablerie* in all its branches. Nor does Faust's misery, at any period of his history, spring from so common a source as the dread of his future doom; "this sun shines on all his sorrows," and it would hardly alleviate them perceptibly, if the hereafter were to be for him an everlasting blank. Mephistophiles, too, is a much more curious personage than formerly. "The progress of improvement," as he himself observes, "has been so considerable of late, that is has extended even to the devil—the northern phantom with horns, and tail, and claws, being no longer visible upon earth." He is a moral, not a physical devil; and the attributes of his character harmonize with the rest of the intellectual machinery by which Goethe undertakes to work upon our feelings. It is machinery of a much finer and more complex sort than that employed by Marlow [*sic*]; the management of it is infinitely more difficult; but the effect which he makes it produce is also much more ennobling, and reaches much farther into the mysteries of our nature.

*   *   *

The work, of which we have traced this brief and imperfect sketch, is undoubtedly one of the most singular that have ever appeared in Europe. We scarcely know under what class to arrange it, or how to mark out its rank in the scale of literary dignity. As a mere drama, its faults are many; and its beauties, though of a high order, are not of the highest. There is not * * * plot sufficient to create dramatic interest; and though many scenes are of great power, and many situations of high tragical effect, they hang too loosely together to constitute a perfect work of this class. Perhaps the most striking peculiarity of the whole performance is the wonderful versatility of talent which it implies. To group together the wicked scornful malignity of Mephistophiles with the pastoral innocence of Margaret, the chaotic gaiety of the Brocken, and the impetuous enthusiasm of Faust, was a task which few could have meditated, and none but Goethe could have accomplished. It presupposes a union of poetical and philosophical powers, such as have rarely met together in the history of mind.

It is to the character of Faust, however, as displayed in the opening scenes of the play, that we turn for the highest proof of Goethe's genius. They give us the most vivid picture we have ever seen of a species of mental convulsion, at once in the extreme degree moving and difficult to paint. It is the destruction of a noble spirit by the force of its own thoughts; a suicide of the mind, far more tragical than that of the body. Faust interests us deeply at first; he is at the utmost pitch of misery, and has no feeling of self-accusation; he possesses all the grandest attributes of our nature, and has meant to use them well. His fault seems but the want of worldly wisdom, and the lofty, though unhappy constitution of his mind; he has been born with the head of a sceptic and the heart of a devotee; in grasping at the sublime, he has lost even the useful; when his earthly hopes are all blasted, no moral consolation is in store for him; "he has not an object, and yet he has not rest." The sleepless agitation, the arid tearless wretchedness, natural to a human being so situated, have been delineated by Goethe with a beauty and verisimilitude, to which there are

few parallels, even in easier subjects. An unlimited supply of the finest
metaphors and most expressive language, combines with the melody of
the verse to make the earlier part of Faust one of the richest spots in the
whole circle of modern poetry.

Faust and Mephistophiles personify the two propensities, as implanted
by nature, and modified by education—to admire and to despise, to look
at the world on its poetical or on its prosaic side—which by their combination, in different proportions, give rise to so many varieties of moral
disposition among men. It is not without reluctance, that in the play before
us, we behold the inferior principle triumphant in the end. Faust's crimes
are many, but his will seems to have had little share in them; even after
his connection with the fiend, he feels virtuously, even nobly, though he
acts ill; and, when we see Mephistophiles at * * * length succeed in
ruining a being so greatly his superior in all respects, it seems as if the
spirit of evil were made victorious over that of good, the lower part of
man's nature over the higher. But if such be our feeling, it is not with the
poet that we must quarrel. "The soul that sinneth, it shall die" is the law
of nature as well as of revelation; and acts of desperate rashness, though
without any purpose morally bad in the author of them, as they produce
fatal consequences to the individual or to others, must be punished accordingly. Faust's criminality existed long before he forsook his retirement,
or addicted himself to the converse of spirits; it began when he allowed
his desires to reach beyond the boundaries wherewith nature had circumscribed them, when he allowed his mind to wander—even in the search
of truth—till it doubted the existence of a Providence, and the foundation
of moral distinctions.

HEINRICH HEINE

[Faust] †

I would not be a German if at the mention of Faust I were not to
express some interpretive thoughts on it. For everyone from the greatest
thinker to the most insignificant literary scorekeeper, from the philosopher
down to the doctor of philosophy whets his wits on this book. For that
matter, it is really as spacious as the Bible and, like it, embraces heaven
and earth, together with man and his exegesis. Here again, the subject
matter is the main reason for the popularity of Faust; however, that he
searched out his material in folk legends is proof of Goethe's unconscious
profundity, his genius, which always contrived to grasp what was closest at
hand and appropriate. I can assume the content of Faust to be familiar;
for the book has recently become famous even in France. However I do

† From The Romantic School by Heine (1797–1856), German poet and critic. Trans. Dolores
Signori, with the assistance of Walter Arndt; from Heine's Collected Works, ed. H. Kaufmann
(Berlin; Aufbau Verlag, 1961), vol. 5, 55 ff. This work was published in France in 1833 as a reply
to the views of Madame de Staël (see p. 558). Heine is concerned with the public reputation of
the Faust legend beyond the confines of Germany, especially with reference to the subliterary,
popular mode in which this legend had been transmitted.

not know whether the old folk legend itself is known *here*, whether in this country, too, at annual fairs a grey book, poorly printed on blotting paper and decorated with rough woodcuts, is sold, in which you may read in great detail how the arch-magician Johannes Faustus, a learned doctor who had studied all sciences, in the end threw away his books and formed an alliance with the devil, whereby he was able to enjoy all sensual pleasures on earth, but in exchange had to give his soul over to infernal perdition. Whenever the people of the Middle Ages saw great intellectual potency anywhere they ascribed it to a dæmonic pact; Albert Magnus, Raimund Lullus, Theophrastus Paracelsus, Agrippa von Nettesheim, even Roger Bacon[1] in England were considered sorcerers, necromancers, exorcists. But legend and song report far stranger things of Doctor Faustus, who demanded not only knowledge of all things but also the most tangible of pleasures from the devil; and this, significantly enough, is the Faust who invented the printing-press and lived at the time when sermons began to be preached against strict Church authority, and independent research started; hence with Faust ends the medieval religious era, and there begins the modern, critical era of science. It is indeed very significant that at precisely the time when by public belief Faust lived, the Reformation began, and that he himself is supposed to have founded the art which secures for knowledge a victory over faith, namely the printing press; an art, however, which also robbed us of the Catholic peace of mind and plunged us into doubt and revolutions—or, as someone else would put it, finally delivered us into the power of the devil. But no, knowledge, the understanding of things through the intellect, science gives us at last the pleasures of which religious faith, Catholic Christianity, has cheated us for so long; we apprehend that men are called not only to a heavenly but also to an earthly equality; the political brotherhood preached to us by philosophy is more beneficial to us than the purely spiritual brotherhood which Christianity has procured for us; and knowledge becomes word, and the word becomes deed, and we can attain the Kingdom of God during our life on this earth; if on top of it we may still partake of that heavenly bliss after death which Christianity so specifically promises us, we shall be all the better pleased.

The German people in its profundity long ago intuitively surmised this: for the German people is itself that learned Doctor Faustus, that spiritualist who finally through his intellect has grasped the inadequacy of the intellect and demands material pleasures and restores to the flesh its rights; yet, still caught up in the symbolism of Catholic poetry where God is considered the representative of the spirit and the devil representative of the flesh, they characterized that reinstatement of the flesh as a fall from God, as an alliance with the devil.

It will still be some time, though, before what was prophesied with such

---

1. English scholastic philosopher (c. 1214–1292), who had a keen interest in natural science and in controlled experiments; Albertus Magnus (1200–1280), German scholastic philsopher, whose interest in natural science led him to study combinations of metals; Raimund Lullus (1235–1316), Catalan mystic and poet, who used his great learning to propagate the Christian faith throughout the Islamic world; Theophrastus Paracelsus (1493–1541), Swiss physician and alchemist; Agrippa von Nettesheim (1486–1535), German physician and philosopher, who wrote a defense of magic, *De occulta philosophia.*

profound meaning in that poem materializes among the German people, before it understands, by the intellect itself, the usurpations of the intellect, and vindicates the rights of the flesh. That, then, will be the revolution, the great daughter of the Reformation.

MARGARET FULLER

"Goethe"†

Faust contains the great idea of [Goethe's] life, as indeed there is but one great poetic idea possible to man, the progress of a soul through the various forms of existence. All his other works, whatever their miraculous beauty of execution, are mere chapters to this poem, illustrative of particular points. *Faust*, had it been completed in the spirit in which it was begun, would have been the *Divina Commedia* of its age.

But nothing can better show the difference of result between a stern and earnest life, and one of partial accommodation, than a comparison between the *Paradiso* and that of the second part of *Faust*. In both a soul, gradually educated and led back to God, is received at last not through merit, but grace. But O the difference between the grandly humble reliance of old Catholicism, and the loop-hole redemption of modern sagacity. Dante was a *man*, of vehement passions, many prejudices, bitter as much as sweet. His knowledge was scanty, his sphere of observation narrow, the objects of his active life petty, compared with those of Goethe. But, constantly retiring on his deepest self, clearsighted to the limitations of man, but no less so to the illimitable energy of the soul, the sharpest details in his work convey a largest sense, as his strongest and steadiest flights only direct the eye to heavens yet beyond.

Yet perhaps he had not so hard a battle to wage, as this other great Poet. The fiercest passions are not so dangerous foes to the soul as the cold skepticism of the understanding. The Jewish demon assailed the man of Uz[1] with physical ills, the Lucifer of the middle ages tempted his passions, but the Mephistopheles of the eighteenth century bade the finite strive to compass the infinite, and the intellect attempt to solve all the problems of the soul.

This path Faust had taken: it is that of modern necromancy. Not willing to grow into God by the steady worship of a life, man would enforce his presence by a spell; not willing to learn his existence by the slow processes of their own, they strive to bind it in a word, that they may wear it about the neck as a talisman.

Faust, bent upon reaching the centre of the universe through the intel-

---

† Fuller (1810–1850), a friend of Ralph Waldo Emerson (see p. 567), a leader of the Transcendentalist movement in New England, and editor of *The Dial*, the literary journal produced by that movement, taught herself German in the early 1830s and quickly became an enthusiastic reader of Goethe. She translated the play *Torquato Tasso* (unpublished during her lifetime) and, subsequently, Eckermann's *Conversations with Goethe*. The essay from which this excerpt is taken was published in an early issue of *The Dial* (1841).
1. A reference to Job in the Bible.

lect alone, naturally, after a length of trial, which has prevented the harmonious unfolding of his nature falls into despair. He has striven for one object, and that object eludes him. Returning upon himself, he finds large tracts of his nature lying waste and cheerless. He is too noble for apathy, too wise for vulgar content with the animal enjoyments of life. Yet the thirst he has been so many years increasing is not to be borne. Give me, he cries, but a drop of water to cool my burning tongue. Yet, in casting himself with a wild recklessness upon the impulses of his nature yet untried, there is a disbelief that anything short of the All can satisfy the immortal spirit. His first attempt was noble, though mistaken, and under the saving influence of it, he makes the compact, whose condition cheats the fiend at last.

*   *   *

> Canst thou by falsehood or by flattery
> Make me one moment with myself at peace,
>   Cheat me into tranquility? Come then
> And welcome, life's last day.
>   Make me but to the moment say,
> Oh fly not yet, thou art so fair,
>   Then let me perish, &c.[2]

But this condition is never fulfilled. Faust cannot be content with sensuality, with the charlatanry of ambition, nor with riches. His heart never becomes callous, nor his moral and intellectual perceptions obtuse. He is saved at last.

With the progress of an individual soul is shadowed forth that of the soul of the age, beginning in intellectual skepticism, sinking into license, cheating itself with dreams of perfect bliss, to be at once attained by means no surer than a spurious paper currency, longing itself back from conflict between the spirit and the flesh, induced by Christianity to the Greek era with its harmonious development of body and mind, striving to reëmbody the loved phantom of classical beauty in the heroism of the middle age, flying from the Byron despair of those, who die because they cannot soar without wings, to schemes, however narrow, of practical utility,—redeemed at last through mercy alone.

The second part of Faust is full of meaning, resplendent with beauty; but it is rather an appendix to the first part than a fulfilment of its promise. The world, remembering the powerful stamp of individual feeling, universal indeed in its application, but individual in its life, which had conquered all its scruples in the first part, was vexed to find, instead of the man Faust, the spirit of the age,—discontended with the shadowy manifestation of truths it longed to embrace, and, above all, disappointed that the author no longer met us face to face, or riveted the ear by his deep tones of grief and resolve.

When the world shall have got rid of the still overpowering influence of the first part, it will be seen that the fundamental ideal is never lost

---

2. Adapted by Fuller from lines 1692–706.

sight of in the second. The change is that Goethe, though the same thinker, is no longer the same person.

RALPH WALDO EMERSON

[General Remarks on Goethe]†

But of all men he, who has united in himself and that in the most extraordinary degree the tendencies of the era, is the German poet, naturalist, and philosopher, Goethe. Whatever the age inherited or invented, he made his own. He has owed to Commerce and to the victories of the Understanding, all their spoils. Such was his capacity, that the magazines of the world's ancient or modern wealth, which arts and intercourse and skepticism could command—he wanted them all. Had there been twice so much, he could have used it as well. Geologist, mechanic, merchant, chemist, king, radical, painter, composer,—all worked for him, and a thousand men seemed to look through his eyes. He learned as readily as other men breathe. Of all the men of this time, not one has seemed so much at home in it as he. He was not afraid to live. And in him this encyclopædia of facts, which it has been the boast of the age to compile, wrought an equal effect. He was knowing; he was brave; he was clean from all narrowness; he has a perfect propriety and taste,—a quality by no means common to the German writers. Nay, since the earth * * * had become a reading-room, the new opportunities seem to have aided him to be that resolute realist he is, and seconded his sturdy determination to see things for what they are. To look at him, one would say, there was never an observer before. What sagacity, what industry of observation! to read his record is a frugality of time, for you shall find no word that does not stand for a thing, and he is of that comprehension, which can see the value of truth. His love of nature has seemed to give a new meaning to that word. There was never man more domesticated in this world than he. And he is an apology for the analytic spirit of the period, because, of his analysis, always wholes were the result. All conventions, all traditions he rejected. And yet he felt his entire right and duty to stand before and try and judge every fact in nature. He thought it necessary to dot round with his own pen the entire sphere of knowables; and for many of his stories, this seems the only reason: Here is a piece of humanity I had hitherto omitted to sketch;—take this. He does not say so in syllables,—yet a sort of conscientious feeling he had to be *up* to the universe, is the best account and apology for many of them. He shared also the subjectiveness of the age, and that too in both the senses I have discriminated. With the sharpest eye for form, color, botany, engraving, medals, persons, and manners, he

---

† Emerson (1803–1882) was the leading intellectual of the Transcendentalist movement in New England, and his *Essays* (First Series, 1841; Second Series, 1844) established a philosophical basis for American culture. He was a devoted reader of Goethe and included a chapter on him as "The Poet" in *Representative Men* (1850). In "Thoughts on Modern Literature," a less well-known essay published in *The Dial* in 1840, and from which this excerpt is taken, Emerson discusses Goethe as the most important writer in modern literature.

never stopped at surface, but pierced the purpose of a thing, and studied to reconcile that purpose with his own being. What he could so reconcile was good; what he could not, was false. Hence a certain greatness encircles every fact he treats; for to him it has a soul, an eternal reason why it was so, and not otherwise. This is the secret of that deep realism, which went about among all objects he beheld, to find the cause why they must be what they are. It was with him a favorite task to find a theory of every institution, custom, art, work of art, which he observes. * * *

* * *

If we try Goethe by the ordinary canons of criticism, we should say that his thinking is of great altitude, and all level;—not a succession of summits, but a high Asiatic table land. Dramatic power, the rarest talent in literature, he has very little. He has an eye constant to the fact of life, and that never pauses in its advance. But the great felicities, the miracles of poetry, he has never. It is all design with him, just thought and instructed expression analogies, allusion, illustration, which knowledge and correct thinking supply; but of Shakespeare and the transcendant muse, no syllable. Yet in the court and law to which we ordinarily speak, and without adverting to absolute standards, we claim for him the praise of truth, of fidelity to his intellectual nature. He is the king of all scholars. In these days and in this country, where the scholars are few and idle, where men read easy books and sleep after dinner, it seems as if no book could so safely be put in the hands of young men as the letters of Goethe, which attest the incessant activity of this man to eighty years, in an endless variety of studies with uniform cheerfulness and greatness of mind. They cannot be read without shaming us into an emulating industry. Let him have the praise of the love of truth. We think, when we contemplate the stupendous glory of the world, that it were life enough for one man merely to lift his hands and cry with St. Augustine, "Wrangle who pleases, I will wonder." Well, this he did. Here was a man, who, in the feeling that the thing itself was so admirable as to leave all comment behind, went up and down from object to object, lifting the veil from everyone, and did no more. * * * His are the bright and terrible eyes, which meet the modern student in every sacred chapel of thought, in every public enclosure.

But now, that we may not seem to dodge the question which all men ask, nor pay a great man so ill a compliment as to praise him only in the conventional and comparative speech, let us honestly record our thought upon the total worth and influence of this genius. Does he represent not only the achievement of that age in which he lived, but that which it would be and is now becoming? And what shall we think of that absence of the moral sentiment, that singular equivalence to him of good and evil in action, which discredits his compositions to the pure? The spirit of his biography, of his poems, of his tales, is identical. * * *

All great men have written proudly, nor cared to explain. They knew that the intelligent reader would come at last, and would thank them. * * * We can fancy him saying to himself;—There are poets enough of the ideal; let me paint the Actual, as, after years of dreams, it will still appear and reappear to wise men. That all shall right itself in the long Morrow, I may well allow, and my novel may easily wait for the same regeneration. The age, that can damn it as false and falsifying, will see that it is deeply one with the genius and history of all the centuries. I have given my characters a bias to error. Men have the same. I have let mischances befall instead of good fortune. They do so daily. And out of many vices and misfortunes, I have let a great success grow, as I had known in my own and many other examples. Fierce churchmen and effeminate aspirants will chide and hate my name, but every keen beholder of life will justify my truth, and will acquit me of prejudging the cause of humanity by painting it with this morose fidelity. To a profound soul is not austere truth the sweetest flattery?

Yes, O Goethe! but the ideal is truer than the actual. That is ephemeral, but this changes not. Moreover, because nature is moral, that mind only can see, in which the same order entirely obtains. An interchangeable Truth, Beauty, and Goodness, each wholly interfused in the other, must make the humors of that eye, which would see causes reaching to their last effect and reproducing the world forever. The least inequality of mixture, the excess of one element over the other, in that degree diminishes the transparency of things, makes the world opaque to the observer, and destroys so far the value of his experience. No particular gifts can countervail this defect. * * *

Goethe, then, must be set down as the poet of the Actual, not of the Ideal; the poet of limitation, not of possibility; of this world, and not of religion and hope; in short, if I may say so, the poet of prose, and not of poetry. He accepts the base doctrine of Fate, and gleans what straggling joys may yet remain out of its ban. He is like a banker or a weaver with a passion for the country, he steals out of the hot streets before sunrise, or after sunset, or on a rare holiday, to get a draught of sweet air, and a gaze at the magnificence of summer, but dares not break from his slavery and lead a man's life in a man's relation to nature. In that which should be his own place, he feels like a truant, and is scourged back presently to his task and his cell. Poetry is with Goethe thus external, the gilding of the chain, the mitigation of his fate; but the muse never essays those thundertones, which cause to vibrate the sun and the moon, which dissipate by dreadful melody all this iron network of circumstance, and abolish the old heavens and the old earth before the free-will or Godhead of man. That Goethe had not a moral perception proportionate to his other powers, is not then merely a circumstance, as we might relate of a man that he had or had not the sense of tune or an eye for colors; but it is the cardinal fact of health or disease; since, lacking this, he failed in the high sense to be a creator, and with divine endowments drops by irreversible decree into the common history of genius. He was content to fall into the track of vulgar poets, and spend on common aims his splendid endowments, and has declined the office proffered to now and then a man in many centuries in the power of his genius—of a Redeemer of the human mind. He has written better than other poets, only as his talent was subtler, but the ambition of creation he refused. Life for him is prettier, easier, wiser, decenter, has a gem or two more on its robe, but its old eternal burden is not relieved; no drop of healthier blood flows yet in its veins. Let him pass. Humanity must wait for its physician still at the side of the road, and confess as this man goes out that they have served it better, who assured it out of the innocent hope in their hearts that a Physician will come, than this majestic Artist, with all the treasuries of wit, of science, and of power at his command.

MODERN CRITICISM

STUART ATKINS

[Survey of the Faust Theme]†

I. The Historical Figure

Various documents of the first decades of the sixteenth century mention a contemporary necromancer calling himself Faust. In 1507 the abbot J. Tritheim wrote in reply to an inquiry:

> Georg Sabellicus . . . is a worthless fellow . . . who should be castigated to stop his proclaiming of abominable and sacrilegious doctrines. . . . He has chosen to call himself *Magister Georgius Sabellicus, Faustus junior, fons necromanticorum, astrologus, magus secundus, chiromanticus, aëromanticus, pyromanticus, in hydra arte secundus* ([*Epistolae*] *ad diversos*, Hagen [1538]. p. 312; see A. Tille, *Faustsplitter*, Berlin [1900], no. 1).

"Sabellicus" and "Faustus" may be humanist latinizations of a German place name and a German family name (or of two family names), but both "the Sabine"—for ancient Rome the Sabine Hills were the country of witchcraft—and "the Fortunate" are traditional epithets of magicians.

Tritheim reports having been in Gelnhausen the year before at the same time as Faust and hearing from clerics there Faust's boast that, "if all the works of Plato and Aristotle . . . had been lost, he through his genius would, like a second Esra, restore them entire and better than before." In Würzburg, Tritheim continues, Faust even claimed that he could perform all the miracles of Christ; subsequently he was appointed schoolmaster at Kreuznach because of his vaunted alchemical learning, but had to flee when his debauchery of his pupils was discovered.

In 1509 a Johann Faust from Simmern (a principality incorporated into Württemberg in 1504) received the A.B. at Heidelberg; if he was Tritheim's Faust, later tradition was right in claiming that the astrologer was born at Knittlingen (the chief town of Simmern) in the early 1480's. In 1513 Conrad Mudt (Mutianus Rufus, supporter of Reuchlin and friend of Melanchthon) saw and heard Georg Faust at Erfurt; he wrote to a fellow humanist that this "immoderate and Foolish braggart," calling himself the "demigod from Heidelberg," before astonished listeners "talked nonsense at the inn." The accounts of the bishopric of Bamberg record a payment in 1520 to "Doctor Faustus" for casting the Prince-Bishop's horoscope; in 1528 the town council of Ingolstadt forbade the soothsayer Jörg (i.e., Georg) Faust to remain in their city; and in 1532 the junior burgomaster of Nuremberg recorded denial of entry to "Dr. Faust, the great sodomite and necromancer." From 1532 to 1536 the same "philosophus" practiced medical alchemy and soothsaying in the Rhineland and Lower Franconia

† From "Motif in Literature: The Faust Theme," *Dictionary of the History of Ideas: Studies of Selected Pivotal Ideas*, Philip P. Weiner, Editor in Chief (New York: Charles Scribner's Sons, 1973), vol. 3, 244–53.

with some success; he is reported to have died in 1540 or 1541 at a village in Württemberg.

II. The Legend and Its Sources

During Faust's earlier years, i.e., before the Reformation, humanists and theologians gave little or no credence to the pretensions of the shabby exploiter of contemporary interest in magic. In the course of time, however, some successes—and, obviously, unflagging self-advertisement—established his reputation as a soothsayer and necromancer, and various Protestant theologians, among them Luther and Melanchthon, alluded seriously to his diabolical powers. Soon after his death it was said that he had been destroyed by the Devil, with whose demons he claimed to have consorted, and many traditional tales of the supernatural became attached to his name. Some were collected, ca. 1575, by Christoph Rosshirt in an illustrated manuscript still preserved, by which time there was possibly in circulation a Latin or German manuscript account of his life. From this hypothetical work may derive the story-line of the earliest published work exclusively devoted to the Faust legend:

> *Historia con D. Johann Fausten . . . Gedruckt su Franckfurt am Mayn, durch Johann Spies, M.D.L.XXXVII* (The History of Dr. Johann Faust, the notorious magus and nigromancer: how he indentured himself to the Devil for a stated period, what strange things be therein saw and himself instigated and performed, until he finally received his just deserts. Chiefly compiled from his own posthumous writings and published as a horrid example, frightful instance and well-meant warning to all arrogant, cocksure and godless men. [Motto:] James 4:[7.] "Submit yourselves to God. Resist the devil, and he will flee from you." Printed at Frankfurt by Johann Spies. 1587).

This first Faust-book, the work of an anonymous Protestant with theological training, immediately became a best seller. There were several printings of it, including an unauthorized edition with additional material, in 1587; by 1600 it existed in English, Danish, French, and Dutch translations, as well as in further modified and augmented German versions. The last lengthy Faust-book (1674) was reprinted as late as 1726, only to be replaced in popular favor by a shorter chapbook (1725) whose anonymous author (*ein Christlich Meynender,* "a man of Christian principles") interpreted the legend as a demonstration of the harmful consequences of pre-Lutheran superstition.

Popular interest in Faust thus coincided almost exactly with the heyday of general belief in witchcraft as a punishable heresy. The story of the Renaissance charlatan (or self-deluding magus) became a conflation of folkloristic motifs of greater and lesser antiquity, all now attached to a recently contemporary exemplar of man damned for using forbidden powers. In many societies tales have been told of sorcerers and magi who, if not deified, came to terrible ends because they failed to control the natural forces they unleashed (legend of Pope Sylvester II; Frankenstein motif), or because they insufficiently propitiated the supernatural beings who enabled them to control these forces. Fear and envy of a successful elite well explain the universal fondness for myths of this type, although conservative piety and a deepfelt human need of religious mystery may also underlie them.

Faust's vagrant life made him an elusive and mysterious figure whose supernatural attainments could neither be verified nor disproved, and he quickly became the protagonist of a modern magus myth—its hero insofar as he represented the thirst of an age of geographical and scientific discovery for new knowledge and power, its villain insofar as these threatened accepted religious and theological assumptions. For although some men thought of magic as applied science (H. C. Agrippa, *De occulta philosophia* [1531], Ch. 42: "Natural magic is . . . nothing but the chief power of all the natural sciences . . .—perfection of Natural Philosophy and . . . the active part of the same"; Giordano Bruno: *Magus significat hominem sapientem cum virtute agendi*, "A magician signifies a man of wisdom with the power to act"), science itself seemed frightening for many more, so that even the most reputable alchemist or other scientist could arouse ambivalent feelings.

Magic, though widely practiced in later antiquity, had been regarded by intellectuals as vulgar superstition (cf. Theocritus' and Vergil's Thessalian eclogues, and Lucian's *Philopseudos*, §14) and was used as a serious literary motif chiefly to heighten the depiction of mythical and historical horrors (plays of Seneca; Lucanus' *Pharsalia*). As oriental religions permeated the Greco-Roman world, however, and their exponents vied for influence, a literature of theological propaganda developed in which rival magics occupied a central place. The most important of these religions was Christianity, which claimed exclusive rightness for its own magic, labeling all other "illicit" (Augustine, *De civitate Dei* xii, 14).

Like the theologians of Faust's century, that of the Reformation and Counter-Reformation, the early Church Fathers used great learning and subtlety to demonstrate either the illusory or the evil nature of alien divinities, and there were soon many stories vividly illustrating the greater efficacy of the true faith. The New Testament tells how the newly converted Simon Magus vainly attempted to buy from Peter the gift of the Holy Spirit and then immediately repented his error (Acts 8:9–24), but soon an apocryphal gospel (and Clement of Alexandria) reported Simon's ignominious failure to demonstrate his boasted power of flight. This new story presumably reflects confusion of the earlier Simon with Simon the Gnostic, in his turn denigrated by an account of putative sexual relations with Helen of Troy, who was credited with the birth of his child. Gnosticism, moreover, introduced forms of dualistic thought that continued into Manichaeism, a still greater threat to Christian orthodoxy, and various Saints' legends illustrate the dangers of regarding any power of darkness as the equal of the one God. A fourth-century story tells how, despite recourse to demons, including the Prince of Hell himself, a magician named Cyprian fails to win for a pagan lover the pious Justina, a simple girl with many counterparts in the Apocryphal Acts of Apostles and Saints, and how he is subsequently converted to Christianity. There were also legends of another Cyprian (of Antioch—later confused with the Carthaginian martyr) who repents his vain use of illicit magic to achieve knowledge and love and later dies a bishop-martyr. (The version of this story in which the demon who has promised the Christian girl's love is constrained to offer a quickly unmasked demon-substitute ["Egyptian Helen" motif] is the ultimate plot-source of Calderón's martyr drama *El mágico prodigioso*.)

Toward the end of the fifth century a new motif appears: the pact with a single demon or devil. The "Life of Basil of Caesarea" tells how he redeems a slave who through the services of a magus had assigned his soul to a devil in order to marry his master's pious daughter. As his wife, she notices his avoidance of church and seeks Basil's conversive help; discovering the truth, the saint prescribes effective penance and after some effort routs the devil and his minions. (The struggle between good and evil forces for a soul, later so important in art and literature, is here subordinate to the theme of the need of atonement and the power of grace; the urgency of countering Manichaeism explains the new stature of the single devil-figure.) In later legends still higher intercession is required: Theophilus of Cilicia, repenting of his recourse to magic, is saved only by the Virgin Mary. Until after the Reformation, however, the repentant mortal regularly found redemption through contrition, penance, and good works even if he had signed away his soul in blood (a motif introduced in the thirteenth century) and even though, from Saint Thomas Aquinas on, witchcraft was more and more often officially considered heresy.

If Faust was less fortunate than his precursors, the blame must be placed not on him but on the religious schism that began with Luther. For those who obdurately clung to "false" doctrine there was now no alternative to eternal damnation. Copernican astronomy cast doubts on a traditional cosmogony, humanism glorified pagan moral philosophers and much morally dubious pagan literature, Neo-Platonic and Pansophic mysticisms taught "natural" revelation and even the possibility of man's unaided achievement of salvation, Trinitarianism was openly repudiated—leaders of the Unitarian movement were Laelius Socinus and his nephew Faustus (1539–1604)—and advocates of libertinism and atheism were beginning to be less cautious than in the late Middle Ages. With so many rival beliefs urging irreconcilable claims, witchcraft could exert a more powerful spell than ever before over the minds of persons of all social and intellectual classes. The Council of Trent might reaffirm 'Saint Thomas' doctrine that neither charms nor conjuring can have effect on the free will, but Protestants accepted Luther's denial of absolute human freedom at the very time they were deprived of all effective external intercession with their God. For them, Faust's eternal damnation was only too real a possibility: significantly, sixteenth-century legend associated Faust with Wittenberg, where Luther had taught the reality of the Devil and where Giordano Bruno was allowed to lecture (1586ff.) after having been denied that privilege at the theologically stricter university of Marburg. Faust represented many things that were anathema to good Christians, but above all a new and challenging secular intellectualism. (The long identification of Faust with Johann Fust, Gutenberg's collaborator, first found in a Dutch chronicle of 1531, was an unconscious euhemeristic recognition of printing's revolutionary importance for the dissemination of new ideas.)

In the *Historia*, although he is an "Epicurean" or sensual materialist, Faust's greatest fault is "speculation"—scientific theorizing and skeptical philosophizing that make him intellectually and spiritually incapable of faith; he may fear Hell (Catholic-theological *attritio*) but will prove incapable of contrition as preached by Luther. His story falls into three large sections. The first tells how, having studied theology, he turns to magic and medicine (cf. Paracelsus). Soon, however, magic completely engrosses him, and through his conjurings he makes contact with emissaries of Hell. After various quasi-theological disputations he abjures Christianity, signing a blood pact that barters his soul for twenty-four years of magical powers and the services of the devil Mephostophiles [*sic*], who provides both high living and copious lore about Hell and its torments. The second section describes Faust's successes as astrologer and soothsayer, a visionary visit to Hell, and magical flights to various parts of the earth. (At Rome he plays pranks on the Pope, from the Caucasus he surveys paradise and its four rivers—the large place occupied by travel motifs reflects an important interest of the Age of Discovery and, perhaps the unsettling effect that glimpses of dissimilar civilizations had on sixteenth-century man.) It concludes with accounts of astronomical, meteorological, and spirit lore.

The final and longest section recounts Faust's last eight years. He performs many feats formerly attributed to earlier magicians, especially during a stay at the court of the emperor Charles V: he conjures up Alexander the Great and one of his wives, causes horns to grow out of a courtier's head, makes a haywain and its horse vanish, furnishes aerial transportation, builds a castle in an inaccessible place, and shows a group of students Helen of Troy. Defying the warning of a mysterious old man to turn again to God, he renews his pact with Hell. His life now becomes more profligate than ever. When but two years remain to him, he takes as paramour Helen of Troy; she bears him a son with precocious prophetic gifts who vanishes with his mother at Faust's death. In his final days Faust vainly laments his evil ways and the imminent torments of Hell; in the last hours before he is horribly killed by supernatural powers he urges student companions from Wittenberg to resist the Devil and lead godly lives with faith in Christ.

III. The Morality Figure

The *Historia* is a prose morality largely compiled from sixteenth-century books of travel description, magic, demonology, theological discussion, religious-moral edification, proverb lore, and humorous anecdote. Its central action, more concentrated on a single protagonist (and a single antagonist) than earlier magus stories, had dramatic possibilities that Christopher Marlowe and others immediately recognized and exploited. (A late fifteenth-century Faust play performed at Liège is mentioned in the article "Jesuit Drama," *Oxford Companion to the Theatre*, ed. P. Hartnoll, p. 416; the account of a Nuremberg carnival procession of 1588 reports that Venus was attended by the girl "whom Doctor Faust in the play abducted.") In his *Tragical History of Doctor Faustus* (ca. 1590; 1st ed., 1604; 2nd ed, with important textual variants, 1616), Marlowe largely follows the morality-play tradition, though treating his hero, who is certainly a glorious, at times gloriously lyrical, Renaissance malefactor, with an empathy lacking in the Faust-book. (V. Errante has suggested that Faustus has traits of Giordano Bruno, who was well received in London in the early 1580's.)

More wilfully wicked than his German model, Marlowe's Faustus rebels with obviously youthful arrogance against conventional modes of thought and feeling. Sated with traditional learning and having turned to necromancy as the potential source "Of power, of honor, of omnipotence," he offers his soul through Mephistophilis [sic]—appearing at his summons only because it has involved blasphemy—to Lucifer "So he will spare him four and twenty years. / Letting him live in all voluptuousness." Mephistophilis is thus the agent of the sin of Luciferian pride that, together with insufficient faith in divine mercy, will ensure Faustus' ultimate damnation, despite repeated warnings from Mephistophilis and the morality figures of his Good and Evil Angels, and despite a repulsive masque-like parade of the Seven Deadly Sins shown him as a "pastime" by Lucifer, Belzebub [sic], Mephistophilis. Unlike the protagonist of the Historia, Faustus shows no intellectual curiosity once he has signed his blood-pact, chiefly occupying himself with demonstrations of his magical powers (largely pranks) that culminate in the showing of Helen of Troy to student admirers. A last warning to repent momentarily reduces him to the thought of suicide, but despairing of mercy he reaffirms the blood-pact on condition he have Helen as paramour, and soon he is borne off by Devils through the hellmouth of medieval art and stage. (In the 1616—perhaps partly earlier—text, his mangled limbs are returned to his chambers so that they may be discovered, as in the Historia, by the horrified students.)

Through traveling actors Marlowe's play soon reached Germany and became the source of a long series of sensational dramas (including, with the eighteenth century, puppet shows). It thus directly or indirectly inspired both English and German popular stage spectacles (harlequinades, operettas, ballets) until well into the later eighteenth century. Broadsides from the seventeenth and eighteenth centuries (including English sheet music) generously testify to the continuing familiarity of the story of the heretic or villain who is damned because he has preferred evil to good.

In the age of Enlightenment, however, damnation was no longer a matter of wide vital concern. Evil, for Luther the instrument of God, had become an obscuring of truth by passion (Descartes) or even, with Leibniz, a sensed deprival of perfection grounded in awareness of a discrepancy between any part and the whole. (Ugliness and incongruity were to be integral to the visual and literary arts in G. E. Lessing's aesthetics, and the essential function of dissonance had long been recognized by musical theorists.) To relativistic and materialistic thinkers, evil was but a necessary concomitant of the good; an obdurate sinner like the traditional Faust no longer seemed to have serious human significance.

In the 1750's Lessing, seeking indigenous themes that might aid the liberation of German drama from a stifling French neo-classicism, began a "Faust"—its central action apparently was to be a dream—whose hero gains redemption because a genuine thirst for knowledge and truth cancel out ambition and self-seeking. Lessing later repudiated the conception of drama as a moral-didactic medium, and the play was never completed.

IV. Goethe

The transmutation of morality play into symbolic drama was Goethe's achievement. He began *Faust*, in the spirit of Storm-and-Stress primitivism, as a loosely constructed play in what was in his youth considered the Shakespearean manner (numerous short scenes in verse and prose). It was to be "popular" in tone, although the theme of an intellectual hero's full self-realization demanded representation of levels of thought and experience irreconcilable with this intention. The so-called *Urfaust* (a manuscript comprising parts and groups of scenes written in the 1770's) briefly introduces Faust as he turns to magic in the hope of transcending sterile intellectuality through intuitive understanding, then shows him in the company of Mephistopheles as he woos, wins, and causes the death of Margarete (Gretchen) even as through love he begins to intuit the full complexity of life.

In subsequent decades Goethe completed *The First Part of the Tragedy* (false title in 1808 ed.), reconciling the obligatory folkloristic elements of the legend with his conception of Faust as the symbol of man seeking the meaning of life and the maximal realization of its possibilities. He replaced the traditional—and theologically unsound—pact with Hell by a challenge: if Faust, who regards himself as representative of all men, is ever satisfied by shallow pleasures or by a sense of having achieved all he would and could, he will gladly renounce this life, the only meaningful existence he can conceive of. Mephistopheles, now defined in a prologue in heaven as the spirit of negation, embodies all inner and outer forces hostile to human aspiration and achievement, and functions as the machinery allowing Faust a wide variety of representative human experiences. The Lord (God, the Good) is also anticipatorily defined—in terms that reflect the historical-genetic interests of the Enlightenment and the increasing importance of evolutionary biology in the later eighteenth century (Buffon; Lamarck; Goethe's own theories of metamorphosis)—as creativity, becoming (*Werden*), and love, the potentialities of self-realization on every level of being to which man has access by virtue of his innate impulse to strive and aspire. The dramatic action has become Faust's achievement of a symbolic totality of experience, and the poem as a whole shows his ever increasing understanding of the order of Nature and of Man as immanently meaningful.

By 1800 Goethe had begun the second and final part of *Faust*, most of which was written 1825–31. Like Part I, it is loosely structured and composed in a variety of dramatic and poetic styles. Ideologically, its function is to show Faust's involvement in less narrowly private or personal spheres of human concern than those of Part I. Faust interests himself in the German Emperor's state affairs (finance in Act I, war in Act IV), but like his legendary prototype he is constrained to provide court entertainments. These include magical feats, but they are primarily important as attempts at artistic self-expression and artistic communication. In Act I he stages first an allegorical masque, the chief theme of which is prudent distinction between tangible and intangible wealth or values, then a stately dumbshow of the Rape of Helen at which he himself confuses illusion with reality; his attempt to "rescue" Helen—or Beauty—from Paris produces an explosion that volatilizes the two figures and paralyzes him for an indeterminate period. The central action of Part II thus takes place outside the normal world of time and successively represents—possibly as two dream plays of Faust in a trancelike state—the realms of myth and history.

Myth—in the Classical Walpurgisnight of Act II—includes not only the legends of gods and heroes, of animal and human creatures symbolic of hostile or friendly natural forces, but also (early) philosophy, science, and art as modes of expressing man's intuition of a meaningful cosmic order. Faust, the would-be winner of Helen, is the spokesman of the heroic, but he plays a minor role in this Aristophanic comedy. Mephistopheles is also of secondary importance, being chiefly the dupe of his own lusts and of illusion and superstition. The main interest shifts to a mythopoeic symbol of potential life, their companion Homunculus (an artificial synthesis of organic substances achieved by the successor to Faust's professorship), and to the eager aspiration of this miniature Faust for normal physical existence and constructive activity.

History—in Act III, "Helen"—is represented with radical syncopation as the unbroken continuum of Western culture from the Greek heroic age to the Greek Wars of Independence. Helen, to escape the vengeance of Menelaus, takes refuge with northern invaders (the Migration of the Peoples merges into the medieval establishment of Near Eastern kingdoms) whose leader Faust, ceding her suzerainty over Greece—and, as Beauty, over all the world—woos and wins her. When military threats presage far-reaching political changes (the rise of national states, but also the restructuring of Europe in the Napoleonic era), Faust and Helen withdraw to a timeless Arcadia where a son is born to them. Faust briefly enjoys family happiness, but his son Euphorion, a Byron-like poet-hero, escapes into life to fight and die for his country's freedom. The idyll ends abruptly, Helen vanishes, and Faust returns to Germany (to historical reality) again attended by Mephistopheles.

The episode of Helen has been an "aesthetic education" in Schiller's sense, has revitalized Faust's resolve, made after Margarete's death, to seek a worthy outlet for his energies. Envisioning a state or society unfettered by the past, with Mephistopheles' assistance he crushes a rebellion against the Emperor in return for the privilege of winning from the sea new land that he can colonize. (The past is inescapable, however, for the Church immediately secures its right to traditional levies—Goethe was less optimistic than many of his contemporaries about the realizability of socialistic utopias.) The final act shows Faust outwardly successful and prosperous, but inwardly dissatisfied with an achievement that cannot be entirely credited to his own finite powers. His irritation is momentarily directed against pious Christian neighbors, whose destruction he causes by his impatient eagerness to resettle them elsewhere; although not directly guilty of their death—the agents of his will are Mephistopheles and (men of) violence

—he now abjures further recourse to supernatural assistance and again accepts human mortality. Faust, suddenly a blind and dying old man, still hopes to complete his grandiose reclamation project, but he dies even as he envisions its benefits enjoyed by future generations of self-reliant men, like himself free from subservience to a purely speculative-transcendental or a merely primitive-magical system of belief. His formulation of a social-religious humanistic faith is his supreme insight, but the conclusion of the drama insists that it be recognized as an expression of *faith* (rooted in the feeling that men can know the divine only as immanence). After Mephistopheles has logically pointed out that all achievement is transitory and death the empty end of any life, Faust's "immortal part" is snatched away from eagerly expectant devils, and we are granted a final vision (Faust's?) of a world of saints and angels, of Margarete and the Virgin Mother, in which Faust is vouchsafed further striving, activity, and spiritual growth.

In its cautious optimism Goethe's *Faust* is still a work of the late Enlightenment, but in its communication of the sense of the unfathomable complexity of human experience it is also an expression of European romanticism. Goethe was not, however, consciously a romantic, and so he sought to represent a totality of critical, emotional, aesthetic, and ethical experiences not as a romantic infinitude, but as a symbolically comprehensive finitude (German Classicism). He imbued the Faust legend with broad mythical significance: magic is no longer mere wish-fulfillment or make-believe, nor simply a convenient poetic device serving to create atmosphere or to further a plot, but the legitimate though paradoxical symbol both of man's religious intuitions and of his ever limited freedom. If Goethe presents Faust sympathetically as an aspiring idealist, he also makes clear that idealism and aspiration can be the expressions of dangerous subjectivity, of alienation from reality: only Faust's insight into his own finiteness, his recognition that lofty intentions do not guarantee the avoidance of error, seems to be represented without dramatic—or other ironical—ambivalence. Man is redeemed by insight, not by achievement, and only through consciously directed activity, wise or foolish, successful or unsuccessful, can this insight be gained.

Faust is thus a tragedy of being—and hence perhaps of "divine discontent"—but not of the will to power or knowledge, or of mere aspiration and romantic longing. Its parts may be loosely connected and some even potentially discrete, but all illustrate facets of this central theme, which as the paradoxical failure of high aspiration appears in every important action or subaction of the poem. Faust's will—or that of some analogous figure (Homunculus, Euphorion, even Mephistopheles)—is repeatedly frustrated. Not success, however, but the power of self-regeneration that he shares with all life (a point more than once made explicit) is his salvation. If this was not clear to Goethe as he began *Faust*, he nevertheless knew it intuitively, for the larger part of the "Urfaust" concerns itself with the tragedy of Margarete, a motif for which the Faust legend to all intents and purposes offered no source: a destructive seduction by love is a more universal experience than seduction by learning or magic, by wealth or power, and Gretchen, whose Christian faith is transparently naive, through instinct rather than reason finally achieves full moral autonomy when she refuses to evade her responsibility, her atonement of guilt, by fleeing with Faust. In the end, Faust heroically accepts finitude too.

V. The Nineteenth-Century Hero

Surveying subsequent treatments of the Faust theme, in 1910 W. A. Phillips declared:

> . . . [Goethe's] Faust remains for the modern world the final form of the legend out of which it grew, the magnificent expression of the broad humanism which, even in spheres accounted orthodox, has tended to replace the peculiar studium theologicum which inspired the early Faust-books (Encyclopaedia Britannica, 11th ed., art. "Faust").

Other "Fausts" appeared during the composition and publication of Goethe's drama or shortly thereafter, notably dramatic works by Friedrich Müller (1778), J. H. von Soden (1797), J. F. Schink (1804). C. D. Grabbe (1829), a novel by F. M. Klinger (1791), a lyric scene by Pushkin (1826), and a verse story by Nikolaus Lenau (1835f.), but none can be said to add important new dimensions to the legend.

Publication in 1790 of Faust, ein Fragment—somewhat less than half the text of Part I—established the preeminence of Goethe's poem, which the speculative philosopher F. W. von Schelling immediately hailed as Germany's "characteristic poetic work," as an expression of the ambivalent feelings arising from a peculiarly German Begier nach Erkenntnis der Dinge ("thirst for cognition"). (In Faust II Goethe satirized the hunger for spiritual infinitude attributed to his protagonist in Schelling's Philosophie der Kunst [1802].) Thanks to romantic philosophy, by its very nature "mythic" (glorification of the Absolute without any strict theological frame of reference; speculative indifference to the evidence of empirical science), Goethe's Faust was soon to become itself a myth. Mme de Staël's response to Faust I (De l'Allemagne, Part 2, Ch. 23 [see p. 558]) is cooler than that of the German romantics and her mentor A. W. Schlegel, but despite an obviously neo-classical literary bias she concludes her influential discussion of the work and its author with the words:

> . . . when a genius such as Goethe's rids itself of all trammels, its host of thoughts is so great that on every side they go beyond and subvert the limits of art.

Goethe's Faust, regarded as a work both uniquely German and sui generis, was thus long admired (as by Shelley and Byron) or condemned (chiefly by Christian moralists) according to the worth attached to secular German thought and culture. The Faust of Grabbe's Don Juan und Faust is not only a "profound" thinker, but also a German nationalist and a scientific positivist, and even Nikolaus Lenau's romantic-philosophical hero derives his stature in the first instance from his preeminence in research (Forschen). As Germany, especially after the establishment of the Second Empire, ceased to be "the land of poets and thinkers" only, Goethe's poem was read ever more frequently as a glorification of action, which alone could permit full realization of individual and social values; if Faust still symbolized all mankind, mankind's best interests were facilely equated with those of Germany. Elsewhere Faust still stood for German romanticism's "mystical faith in will and action" (the formulation is that of Santayana, frankly hostile to idealistic and vitalistic systems of German philosophy from Fichte on, in *Three Philosophical Poets*, 1900).

Faust was also to stand for the power of modern science and technology to create a better world (Elie Metchnikoff, *Goethe et Faust*, 1907), or—this was closest to the spirit of Goethe, except when equated with the cult of the Superman (*Übermensch* is used in Goethe's text only with pejorative irony)—for a fruitful religious or ethical liberalism. German artists depicted Faust as a Teutonic hero, while in France—and for musicians—he chiefly remained a symbol of human frailty or spirituality.

VI. Faustian Ambivalences in the Twentieth Century

Few nineteenth-century interpreters of Goethe's work shared Kierkegaard's view that Faust's (to him: also Goethe's) unqualified glorification of activity was compensation for a sickness of the soul. In the twentieth century, however, both the positive values long attached to the "Faust myth" (Jakob Burkhardt, 1855) and the propriety of regarding Goethe's *Faust* as its supreme artistic expression have been seriously questioned. Adulation of Faust's ruthlessness as an empire builder was condemned even when not recognized as contrary to the tenor of Goethe's text. The benefits of science and technology that Faust long symbolized—G. W. Hertz even interpreted the work as natural-scientific myth (*Goethes Naturphilosophie im Faust*, 1912)—began to seem ever more uncertain. And a theological resurgence made doubtful even the heroic stature of so self-concerned, or at least so strong-willed, a figure. (Only esoteric and theosophic interpretations, notably those offered by the anthroposophist Rudolf Steiner from 1902 on, now minimized the theme of ethical choice in Goethe's drama.) "Faustian" could thus variously mean "Promethean," "superhuman" (Hermann Hesse lectured on "Faust and Zarathustra" in 1909), "dualistically torn between (or simultaneously impelled by) pleasure principle and cognitive desire," "mystically monistic," "socialistically progressive" (cf. A. V. Lunacharsky's play *Faust i gorod* [*Faust and the City*], 1918), as well as "German in its best—or, at the height of World War I, worst—sense."

With the publication of Oswald Spengler's *The Decline of the West* (1918 and 1922) "Faustian" acquired a new meaning. In his morphology of civilizations (*Kulturen*) Spengler opposed the Faustian culture-soul of the West to the Apollonian (or Euclidian) and Magical souls of Greco-Roman and Arabian culture. His Faustian soul knows the lure of infinitude and transcendence, has an ethic of instinct or voluntarism rather than of reason, and its heroes are men of action with Nietzsche's morality of masters. (If Goethe's Faust translates *logos* as *Tat* ["deed," "action"] rather than, say *Ordnung* ["order"—for Goethe a highest value], he does not do so in a moment of supreme insight!) Although the importance that Spengler's concept of the Faustian attributes to practical achievement is that of later historicism and scientism, romantic elements predominate in his thought, which is thus more German than Western (Dabezies, p. 152). For H. Trevor-Roper (*Historical Essays*, London, 1957), Burckhardt is a "Faustian historian."

Simultaneous with the explanation of history in symbolic and mythic terms was an ever more frequent reading—and even creating (Thomas Mann)—of literary works as forms of symbolic and mythic expression. Beginning with his *Psychologische Typen* (1921), C. G. Jung encouraged the interpretation of Goethe's *Faust* as a visionary work, i.e., not as mere poetic invention, but as the expression of archetypal truths (Faust variously as hysteric, as magus-magician, as savior-sage, and—after World War II—as subhumanly ignorant of ethical emotion, the protagonist of a work revealing a characteristically "German" alienation from all concrete realities). Following both Freud and the earlier Jung, Maud Bodkin (*Archetypal Patterns in Poetry: Psychological Studies of Imagination*, Oxford, 1934) could still recognize that Goethe's poem "is not wholly removed in spirit from such tragedy as that of Shakespeare," deriving its strength from such archetypal figures—"expressions of the sense of self in relation to forces that appear under the names of God, or Fate, and of the devil"—as Margarete (woman as symbol of a transmutation of sentiment or feeling into spiritual values) and Mephistopheles ("an apt embodiment of forces that threaten the ideals of the more concrete persons of the drama"). Her interpretation of Faust's final "ascension" as the archetype of human "feigning for individual lives, after bodily death, the renewal that we know [to be] true of the life-force within them" is particularly apt, since this was the meaning Goethe seems *consciously* to have attached to it.

Under National Socialism Faust could conveniently symbolize service to the state and humanity (Alfred Rosenberg), the supreme value of action (Hitler), and of course the German genius and Führer-principle. The irony of this did not go unappreciated abroad, and in Dorothy Sayers' morality *The Devil to Pay* (premiere: 1939) Faust's worst crime is having tried to play god, Paul Valéry's *Mon Faust* (1941; 1944f.), comprising *Lust, ou la Demoiselle de Cristal* and *Le Solitaire, féerie dramatique* (both uncompleted), transposes Goethe's "chief figures"—for Valéry these are Faust and Mephistopheles, the extremes of the human-humane and the inhuman—into a modern world. In *Lust* (the name is that of Faust's attractive secretary) the uncreative impotence of reason (science? rationalization?) is accepted as bitter reality, although Faust—poet, thinker, and "member of the Academy of Dead Sciences"—brilliantly displays reason's power in his discussions with Mephistopheles, who contracts not to serve him, but to receive his services. Mephistopheles cannot even tempt one of Faust's young admirers ("the Disciple," whom Faust has cautioned against emotionalism) with offers of knowledge and power, or of love. Yet Faust himself seems capable of something like love or affection, although Valéry chooses—this is clearly a corrective to vitalistic interpretations of the Faust figure—to emphasize the centrality of thought and memory to human awareness, even to that of immediate experience.

In *Le Solitaire*—the figure is a nihilistic philosopher who, scorning Faust's, and any, intellectualism; consistently destroys himself—the central

theme is even more Goethean: awareness of the potentiality of regeneration (although its Faust is too wise to accept the chance to relive life). The
dispute for Faust's soul which was to conclude this play was never written,
but what exists of *Mon Faust* is a timeless challenge—there is no mention
of purely contemporary events—to perversely irrational and pretentious
interpretations of the Faust myth.

In contrast to Valéry's "Faust," that of Thomas Mann concerns itself
directly with the ideological and political forces that, producing Nazism
and the cultural debasement of Germany, culminated in the catastrophe
of World War II. Mann's title, *Doctor Faustus: The Life of the German
Composer Adrian Leverkühn as Told by a Friend* (1943–46, published
1947), refers to the *Historia* of 1587, which is the inspiration of his protagonist's German style and final musical composition, and from which
derive the main "traditional" motifs that structure his novel. (Goethe's
Faust was insufficiently apocalyptic to serve Mann's thematic needs; a
writer long devoted to interpreting mythic archetypes, Mann may have
shared the regret—occasionally expressed earlier, as by Heine in notes to
his Faust ballet [1851]—at Goethe's failure to adhere closely to the original
Faust legend.) Leverkühn's pack with the devil is his fantasy that syphilitic
infection is the price of heightened creative powers. (Mann had long
thought to discern a connection between disease and artistic creativity, and
had first conceived in 1901 the idea of portraying a syphilitic artist as a
Faust figure.) *Doctor Faustus* repudiates nationalistic and nihilistic interpretations of Faust and the Faustian; parallels in it to recent developments
in historical, philosophical, theological, psychological, and scientific speculation insist that the cultivation of musical abstraction by its coldly intellectual hero also symbolizes a general alienation from humane values that
only a spiritual breakthrough may possibly overcome.

Mann's return to the Faust-book form of the legend coincides with a
widespread trend to doubt the exemplary significance of Goethe's *Faust*.
Some theologically-minded critics, still reading it as a glorification of ruth-
less activity, condemned it as an expression of humanistic amoralism,
while others interpreted it as a morality play warning against the destructive
consequences of human effort unredeemed by theological grace. Although
Marxists largely continued to see in it a paean to progress and secular
human values, and although there seems to be a positive connotation in
F. R. Stannard's use of "faustian" to characterize a mirror- or reverse-time
universe (*Nature* [August 13, 1966], 693ff.), pessimistic interpretations of
the poem prevailed immediately after World War II—hence the frequently
expressed subjective preference (e.g., E. M. Butler, A. Dabezies) for pre-
Goethean forms of the legend in which the "existential" distinction between good and evil is made with (naive) clarity. Goethe, however,
interpreted the Faust story in a tragedy, not in a morality play, and the
lasting significance of the Faust legend will surely again be recognized as
deriving not from the theme of existential despair (which it shares with
many other tales and myths), but from the paradox of self-limiting and
even self-destroying aspiration which, as Goethe knew, the legend symbolizes with apparently unique distinction.

JAROSLAV PELIKAN

Faust as Doctor of Theology†

At least four monumental dramas in the spiritual and literary history of the West are situated in the framework of the days of Holy Week: Palm Sunday was, according to the custom in Leipzig, the day for the performance of Johann Sebastian Bach's *Passion of Our Lord According to Saint Matthew*; the morning of Good Friday was the setting for the opening of Dante Alighieri's *Divine Comedy*; that day is also, in the Good Friday Spell, the time of the climax, both dramatically and musically, of Richard Wagner's *Parsifal*, when "every creature gives thanks, everything that blooms and soon perishes, as today a Nature freed from sin reaches the day in which its innocence is restored"; and the night of Holy Saturday, with the choir of angels intoning, "Christ is risen!" (737), and the unbelieving scholar explaining, "I hear the message all right, but what I lack is the faith" (765), begins the action of Johann Wolfgang von Goethe's *Faust*.

As the history of its reception over the past century and a half has demonstrated, it is possible to read Goethe's *Faust* in many ways. Being a reworking, or rather a recasting, of a Faust legend that goes back to the Middle Ages or perhaps even earlier, it has led comparativists and historians of literature to continue to analyze its connections with that legend. There is a long tradition of interpreters who have seen it as a vast allegory, or perhaps better a series of allegories, about the human condition in the modern age. Because, as a recent biography of Goethe suggests, "more must be known, or at any rate there must be more to know, about Goethe than about almost any other human being" on account of the massive amount of source material, it is almost inevitable that this, his most comprehensive work, should have become for many scholars a *roman à clef*, or an *autobiographie à clef*. Each incident, and sometimes it seems each phrase, finds a counterpart in that source material about his life and thought * * *—he did, after all, call his writings "fragments of a great confession." Early in the twentieth century, one of the most far-reaching interpretations of *Faust*, Oswald Spengler's *Decline of the West*, saw in the figure of Goethe's hero "the *Faustian* soul, whose prime-symbol is pure and limitless space. . . . Here infinite solitude is felt as the home of the Faustian soul." Part One, at any rate, has easily lent itself to Marxist interpreters as a bourgeois tragedy about the exploitation of a proletarian Margarete by a member of the élite. The relation between technology and society represented by Faust's effort to tame the sea, late in Part Two, has raised for some readers, notably the distinguished physicist Werner Heisenberg, many of the problems of that relation played out on a dramatic scale. Freudian readings of *Faust*—of the closing scene, for example—have sought to relate it to various experiences of the poet's childhood and earlier

† From *Faust the Theologian* (New Haven: Yale UP, 1995), 1–24. The author's footnotes have been omitted. All quotations from *Faust* are the author's prose translations.

life. To the disciples of Carl Jung, in contrast, *Faust* has provided a host of opportunities to penetrate the tale's symbolism in search of a deeper meaning. The ideologues of National Socialism, and those literary scholars who became their willing followers, saw the drama as a glorification of the qualities of Aryan culture; conversely, the collapse of that ideology brought with it the deepening conviction that it would never be possible to read *Faust* in quite the same way again. And it is not necessary to be a feminist to agree with the criticism that as a drama written by a poet who freely admitted that he found the charms of young women irresistible and who went on pursuing them when he was well into his seventies, *Faust* is also the account of a protagonist whose eventual fulfillment is made possible only by the immolation of two women—Gretchen the innocent, and then Helen the beautiful—and who is said to achieve eventual salvation through being drawn upward by the Eternal Feminine of the final line.

[My] reading of *Faust* * * * , without involving itself in an ongoing debate with any of these and other interpretations, is an effort to look at the character of Faust as, in one critic's delightful phrase, "an ungovernable theological problem-child," and thus to relate it to theology, theology as an account of religious faith but also theology as an academic discipline among other academic disciplines. Despite the several nineteenth-century efforts to make him into one, Goethe was not an orthodox Christian theologian, nor did he want to be seen as one. But he did want to be seen as standing, in some sense, within the Christian tradition—*and* within the Classical tradition *and* within the humanistic tradition *and* within the scientific tradition! A justification for taking this approach to *Faust* in relation to theology may also be found in the ever-deepening unawareness of the Christian tradition among Goethe's present-day readers, including sometimes even the scholarly ones. Their puzzled references (to remain for now only within Part One) to Margarete's church attendance at the beginning of the Gretchen tragedy (2621–6), or to her prayer before the Virgin Mary as Mater Dolorosa (3588–3619) and her attendance at a Requiem Mass with the singing of the *Dies irae* (3776–3834) near the end of it, often seem to treat these like the exotic rituals of some distant tribe, interesting and intelligible only to cultural anthropologists; Goethe, by contrast, regardless of what he may or may not have believed, knew and understood such things quite well. * * * For despite Goethe's frequently quoted words about "fragments of a great confession," both Goethe's beliefs and Faust's beliefs are too complicated for any simple identification of the one with the other. Readers of *Faust*, including scholarly ones, would be well advised to heed the recent warning that it is in the "closeness of relationship between the writer and the play, rather than between the writer and the play's principal character, that the special status of *Faust* among Goethe's works is grounded." * * *

Heinrich Faust (the name Heinrich, the closing word of Part One [4612], was apparently one of Goethe's additions to the traditional Faust story, in which the man's name had been Johann) is a man of great learning, especially if, despite the language of Mephistopheles about restoring his lost youth to him (2348–50), he is only thirty years old, as modern interpreters seems to have agreed. He is, as the old peasant calls him, "a man of enormous erudition" (984). Employing no more sarcasm than usual, Mephistopheles also greets him that way when they first meet: "I salute the learned gentleman!" (1325). Later, Mephistopheles does seem to be speaking also for Faust, and for the entire community of learned men, when, wearing Faust's doctoral garb, he exclaims: "I know it well, to be far along in years and still a student, in fact an old mossback! Even a man of learning goes on studying because there is nothing else he can do. One builds a modest house of cards, but even the greatest mind never completes it" (6637–41).

Although there seems to be no direct mention in *Faust* of a university or other institution of higher learning to whose faculty he belongs, in *Urfaust* Faust does refer to himself as a "professor" (7); also in *Urfaust*, Mephistopheles disguised as Faust speaks in a "professorial tone" (403). It would surely be forcing the interpretation to take the removal of those references in the definitive version as implying that for that version he is no longer a professor; for he continues to have students, whom he has been "leading by the nose, back and forth, for the past ten years" (361–63). New students, moreover, come to him for advice about how to become as learned as he is, and in as many fields; as one says, "I would like to become really learned and to comprehend everything in Earth and Heaven, all of science and all of Nature" (1898–1901). Those two terms, "all of science and all of Nature," cover the spectrum of scholarship and science, as do the words "everything in Earth and Heaven." Surrounded by his library, Faust speaks of himself as "hemmed in all the way to the lofty ceiling by this stack of books—worm-eaten and dust-covered, with sooty paper stuck over them" (402–5). And in that setting he asks, "Should I perhaps read in a thousand books?" (661). Those thousands of books, moreover, come "out of a hundred scholarly disciplines" (657).

In at least some of these scholarly disciplines Faust has taken advanced university degrees. On their visit to the Witch's Kitchen, Mephistopheles introduces Faust to one witch as "a man who holds many degrees" (2581), and Faust says of himself at the beginning of the drama: "I carry the title of Master, and even of Doctor" (360). It is as "Doctor" that he is known throughout Part One. That form of reference and address seems to be a customary way for the common people to speak about a scholar, for it is also as "Doctor Luther" that the German Reformer is identified in the tavern song that Brander, one of the Merry Companions, sings in Auerbach's Cellar in Leipzig (2129). "Herr Doktor" is used as a term of authentic, if fawning, respect when it comes from Wagner, Faust's *famulus*, or academic assistant (941), or from the old peasant (981). It is a considerably more mocking title when Mephistopheles uses it (in conjunction with the polite third-person plural form of address in the verb) in speaking about Margarete's interrogation of Faust concerning his religious faith (or lack of it), "I followed it very closely: the Doctor was being catechized" (3522–23) or about Valentin's attack on him (3704). Mephistopheles calls Faust "Doctor" even on Walpurgis Night while he is running interference for him through the "mob" (4024). Yet the title seems to be employed only rarely for Faust in Part Two (cf. 6663), for reasons that are not ob-

vious. Perhaps it is that, beginning already with the pact and then especially with the death of Gretchen, Faust is seen as having put behind him
the entire apparatus and nomenclature of the dry-as-dust scholar. The academic titles that do appear in Part Two, including "Doctor," are applied
to others rather than to Faust himself, as when Wagner, the sometime
academic assistant, is identified ironically as Faust's unlikely successor,
"the distinguished Doctor Wagner, who now holds first place in the world
of learning" (6643–44), or when Mephistopheles disguises himself as a
docent (6588), or when, in that disguise, he has an interview with the
Bachelor of Arts (6689–6806), whom he had met earlier as a prospective
student (1868–2048).

But if Faust can say, "I carry the title of Master, and even of Doctor"
(360), it does not seem out of place to ask him, following the form of
inquiry in which Mephistopheles puts the question in his discussion with
the student, "You must declare yourself: Which faculty do you choose?"
(1896–97). And again a bit later Mephistopheles asks: "But make your
choice of a faculty!" (1968). Among the "hundred scholarly disciplines"
(657) represented in his library, then, which are the ones of which Doctor
Faust is a "Master" or a "Doctor," and which "faculty" (or faculties) had
he himself selected when he was only a student? His own opening sigh,
"With strain and sweat I have studied my way all through philosophy,
jurisprudence, and medicine—and, alas, theology, too" (354–57), is a list
not of scholarly disciplines but of entire faculties, all four of the faculties
at the German university (in Goethe's day, if not in Faust's). In his claims
to have "studied his way all through" the curriculum of each, he does not
specify whether this represents the chronological order in which he has
studied them, with theology coming last, or whether this is a traditional
arrangement; in either event it could be taken as an ironic acknowledgment of theology as "queen of the sciences" in the medieval schema. In
Urfaust, there is yet another sequence—"I have studied and sweated my
way through philosophy, medicine, and jurisprudence—and, alas, theology, too" (1–4), with the positions of law and medicine reversed at the
middle of the cursus studiorum, but with philosophy still first and theology
still last. And in the Faustbuch of 1587 and other early versions of the
Faust legend it is explicitly stated that Faust became "a Doctor of Theology" but that then he "did not want to call himself a theologian any
more, became a secular man, and called himself Doctor of Medicine."

It is, however, certainly amusing, and perhaps important as well for the
irony of what has with condign irony been labeled this "subversive classic,"
to note that by far the most comprehensive and systematic review of these
four faculties does not come from Doctor Faust at all, whichever may be
his own academic home base, but from his surrogate, Mephistopheles,
dressed, as the stage directions specify, "in Faust's academic garb" (at
1851) and affecting a properly professorial "dry tone" (2009). After intoning the ominous theme, "If you will only despise reason and science"
(1851–67) * * * Mephistopheles-as-Faust proceeds, in response to the
questions of a prospective student, to review the faculties of the university,
though in a somewhat different sequence from the one in the opening
words either here in Faust or in Urfaust: the first two are, as in Faust,

philosophy and law, but the second pair are reversed, theology and then medicine. (Thus the only constant element in all three catalogs is that philosophy always comes first.)

Each of the four faculties receives the benefit of a sarcastic analysis by Mephistopheles, with at least the suggestion that the order, or at any rate the assignment of first position to philosophy, may be significant: "Make good use of time, which flies by so quickly. But a sense of proper order will teach you to save time. Therefore, my dear friend, I advise you to begin with the course in logic" (1908–11), as the proper foundation for any of the others. This advice is followed by a hilarious review of the various Classical syllogisms and fallacies from Aristotle's *Organon*, until the student exclaims, "I do not completely understand you" (1942), and, more desperately, "It all makes me feel so stupid, as if I had a mill-wheel going around in my head" (1946–47). After logic, Mephistopheles recommends, "above everything else," the study of metaphysics, and at the crushing rate of five hours of lectures per day. For those five hours a day, the student should be prepared to listen to the professor, in accordance with the pedagogical method of the universities, "in such a way that afterwards you will be able to recognize better that he is not saying anything except what is already in the book. But you must be busy with writing it down, as though the Holy Spirit himself were dictating it to you!" (1948–63).

Turning now to the second faculty, the student admits an aversion to the study of law: "I cannot bring myself to study jurisprudence." The mentor agrees, concluding that in the curriculum of the law faculties "there is never any reference to the law that is inborn within us" (1969–79), because they concentrate on positive, written law rather than on natural law. In spite of his own aversion to jurisprudence, however, Faust does find it possible, from time to time in the course of the drama, to put his study of the law to good advantage. Thus when Mephistopheles explains to him at their first meeting that, as the devil, he is obliged to leave a room by the same door through which he has entered it as a poodle, Faust can ask him mockingly, "So even hell has its laws?" (1413). The third faculty is theology (of which more in a moment), while the fourth and last is medicine, which, in *Urfaust* (335) but not in *Faust*, the student declares as his (or perhaps his family's) choice of major field: "I am to study medicine." Here in *Faust* the student asks, "Would you please say a relevant word or two also about medicine?" (2003–4). Mephistopheles obliges with a "relevant word" all right, and with a counsel of despair also about the preparation of the physician, who at best can do the patients no good and at worst can do them much harm (2011–36).

After the devil's brief parody of the study of law, the student sighs (though without an "alas"): "By now I would almost be ready to study theology!" Mephistopheles prefaces his response with a disclaimer, which is couched in typically devilish double entendre and which conflates Faust's bitter words about his father the physician, "This was the remedy, the patients died" (1048), with his immediately following words about himself the accomplice, "I myself administered the poison to thousands" (1053). "I would not want to lead you astray about this science," the guidance counselor says to the neophyte. "It is so difficult here to avoid going the wrong way. There is so much poison hidden in it that it is hard to tell the poison from the cure" (1982–87). Then follows a description of the two principal skills of the theologian, as the devil in his cynicism sees them. The first is what Horace called "swearing by the master's words * * *," a phrase that Mephistopheles, possessing a good Classical education, quotes verbatim in German translation: "Here again the best way is to listen to only one [lecturer] and to swear by the master's words." The other indispensable skill for the theologian to cultivate is logomachy, the high art of quarreling about mere words. After the student has the temerity to express an interest in theological "concepts," he is told that these are not necessary; "for even when concepts are lacking, a word can come in at just the right time. You can battle mightily with words, construct a system out of words, believe strongly in words—and you must not diminish a single word by a single iota" (1982–2000). Faust's own lack of respect for "the word"—as he says of himself, "It is impossible for me to put such a high valuation on the word" (1226)—suggests that Mephistopheles is speaking here for Faust, or at any rate for one of the "two souls dwelling, alas, within [his] breast" (1112).

In spite of some indications that "Doctor" Faust is Doctor of Medicine, therefore, it does appear plausible that he may be Doctor of Theology, too, not only in earlier versions but in Goethe's. In favor of this hypothesis there are several hints, which singly may be of varying importance but which taken together carry considerable force: the share of attention given to theology here in the Baccalaureus scene; Faust's lumping together of "doctors and masters and scribblers and clerics" (367); the conjunction of the Doctor title with the subject matter of theology in the devil's sneer, "The Doctor was being catechized" (3523), which appears already in *Urfaust* (1215); the singling out of theology, among the four faculties enumerated in Faust's opening soliloquy, as the only one to receive from him the additional editorial comment of an "alas" (356); and the continuing "critique of theology" throughout. Although it has been suggested that Faust's scholarly past, including therefore the academic study of theology, is forgotten after the opening scene, Doctor Faust does in fact remain well informed about theological and ecclesiastical matters and takes a considerable interest in them, which suggests to one scholar that "Goethe's Faust has studied 'alas, theology, too'; and if he has also turned away from it, he has not allowed it to drop completely from his memory." Or, as that same scholar has said elsewhere, commenting on Faust's credo (3432–58), "Faust's own mind is far from being untutored in the hidden subtleties of such apparently simple questions. He is versed to the point of satiety in the centuries-old debates about their logical and theological status, and indicates as much when he again seems to evade the answer by putting a counter-question."

Throughout the drama, moreover, Faust attracts the attention of various theological types. Several in fact put in an appearance, rather incongruously, even in the Walpurgis Night's Dream. The first is the Orthodox Theologian, with his typically orthodox (but well-grounded) suspicions regarding the identity of Mephistopheles: "There are no claws, no tail, but it is indubitable that he is a devil, as are the gods of Greece" (4271–74). Then there are the Pietists, who provoke the following comment from the Crane: "I enjoy fishing in clear water or in muddy water: that is why you see a pious gentleman keeping company with devils." To this the Child of the World (presumably Goethe) replies: "Yes, believe me, for such pious folk anything can become a vehicle. Even here on the Blocksberg they hold their conventicles" (4323–30), suggesting that Pietists seem to be everywhere. Following immediately thereafter is the Dogmatician, whose argument is a textbook case of the logical fallacy of reasoning in a circle, also with regard to the identity of Mephistopheles: "I will not allow myself to be diverted by either criticism or doubt. The devil must be something real, for otherwise how could there be a devil?" (4343–46). A little later, there is the Chancellor, who belongs to the same camp, reacting to unconventional theological formulas with the warning: "That is no way to speak to Christians. Atheists are burned at the stake for that, because such talk is extremely dangerous. . . . the heretics and the witchmasters—they bring ruin on both the city and the country!" (4897–99, 4911–12). Each is a tellingly accurate caricature of the *odium theologicum* with which Faust, if he is a Doctor of Theology, is only too well acquainted on the basis of his theological studies and from which he takes refuge in his own unconventional theologies.

In the light of Goethe's belief that "Christ has been demythified and secularized into a very human Jesus while institutional Christianity is regarded with a suspicious hostility," it cannot be a coincidence that so many of the references to theology and religion, here and throughout *Faust*, are spoken in such tones of caricature, satire, irony, and ridicule. Nor is this true only of the remarks that are put into the mouth of Mephistopheles. One exchange at the beginning of the drama seems to anticipate such a tone. Wagner observes, "I have often heard it said that a comedian could have something to teach a parson," to which Faust replies, "Yes, if the parson is a comedian, which might be the case from time to time" (526–29). Even though Mephistopheles suggests sardonically that God himself seems to have lost his sense of humor—"The pathos of my lot ought to make you laugh," he declares, "if, that is, you had not forgotten how to" (277–78)—comedy and humor are a medium for theology. In a letter written five days before his death to Wilhelm von Humboldt, founder of the University of Berlin, Goethe said of *Faust*: "There is no question that it would give me infinite joy if even during my lifetime I could send *these very serious jests* * * * to my worthy, gratefully acknowledged, and widely scattered friends with my compliments, share them with them, and get their response." Four months earlier he had said the same thing in greater detail, writing to Sulpiz Boisserée: "When I had placed the seal on my completed *Faust*, I still did not feel good about it. For I could not avoid the feeling that my worthiest friends, who are in general agreement with me, would not soon have the pleasure of enjoying *these seriously intended jests* * * * for a few hours, and thus of becoming aware of what had been running around in my head and mind before it finally took on this form." * * *

But this * * * should not be used, as it sometimes is, to trivialize these "jokes" by failing to note that they are "very serious" and that they were "seriously intended." This applies in special measure to the theology: it is Mephistopheles, not God, who has the last word in the Prologue in Heaven (350–53), but it is God's own Chorus Mysticus who have the last word in the drama (12104–11). And He who laughs last does laugh best —regardless of what Mephistopheles may think of the Lord's sense of humor (277–78). The treatment in the drama of what has been called "the devouring materialism of the Church," aptly illustrates the special quality of the theological irony. Mephistopheles quotes the words of Margarete's parish priest upon being shown the jewel box: "That was the right thing to do, for there is great gain in overcoming [temptation]. The church has a strong stomach, and it has swallowed entire countries without ever overeating. Only the church, my dear ladies, can digest ill-gotten gains" (2834–40). The motif resurfaces in the confrontation of the Archbishop and the Emperor at the end of Part Two, Act IV, over the dangers of being in league with the devil, a scene that is filled with ironic references to the penance by which the Emperor is to pay up "by giving back to the sanctuary a pittance from [his] tainted fortune" (10991–92), thereby making everything right with the church and with God. Nevertheless the irony makes a serious and valid point. For all his greed and hypocrisy, the Archbishop has identified the precise evil that Faust must shake off if he is ever to recover his freedom and humanity, as Faust himself acknowledges at the beginning of the next act: "If I could only put magic far out of my path, utterly unlearn the formulas of sorcery, and stand in thy presence, O Nature, just as a man, that would make it worthwhile to be a human being" (11404–7). Similarly, an earlier confrontation over theology, the pious but naive "catechizing" (3523) of Faust by Margarete, is at one level certainly "a jest." That is, moreover, how Faust treats it, with his cavalier declaration of tolerance, "I have no intention of robbing people of their feelings and their church" (3420), and his no less cavalier declaration of anticlerical intolerance, "If you ask such questions of the priests or sages, their answer seems to make fun of the questioner" (3428–30). But at another level it is, in Margarete's eyes, "seriously intended," as she sighs, "One has to believe in this," and "Oh, if I only could make an impression on you!" (3421–22). And once again it is, in the event, her seriousness that prevails over the cynicism of both Faust and Mephistopheles, in the eschatological denouement of the drama. Therefore, even with due attention to all of the ironies that have so preoccupied recent readers, it would appear to be, at the very least, one legitimate reading of that denouement to ask what it was that the genius of Gustav Mahler found so exalted in it and that he celebrated so sublimely by juxtaposing it with the medieval hymn *Veni Creator Spiritus* in his Eighth Symphony. Of this "full-scale musical context [of] the *Veni Creator Spiritus* and [of] the belief in immortality voiced by Goethe in the final scene of *Faust*," Bruno Walter declared, on the basis of a profound knowledge of Mahler both personal and musical coupled with a profound knowledge of Goethe's works, "No other work [by Mahler] expresses so fully the impassioned 'Yes' to life."

In the theodicy that pervades Goethe's *Faust* one scholar has found "in accordance with Goethe's intention, an intersection between the religious element of a predestined justification of Faust before God and the dramatic element of the alternatives of damnation or salvation, an intersection that has not yet been resolved." The eschatology represented by the outcome of that tension between predestination and free will is the ultimate irony of Faust's victory over a power "that constantly intends to do evil and constantly does good" (1335–36). In this respect as in many others, Goethe's *Faust* seems to resemble an earlier "seriously intended jest" in the grand style, and one that was explicitly identified as a "comedy," Dante's *Divine Comedy*. There is, however, at least one significant difference, pointed out long ago by one of the earliest and most discerning readers of *Faust*, Carl Gustav Carus, in a letter dated 26 December 1834: "And have you not often in spirit drawn the parallels between the great work of Dante and this work of Goethe? Except that in the former the most painful and the most blessed conditions of the soul pass by the viewer (which is why it is called a 'spectacle,' *Divine Comedy*), whereas in the latter the protagonist is constantly being moved and must restlessly pass through all the anguish and joy of life."

A Dantean story line is adumbrated more than once in the two prologues to the drama. At the conclusion of the Prelude on the Stage, the Director, authorizing the use of elaborate stage props and machines, prescribes the following for the drama: "So within the confines of this house of boards you can stride through the whole circle of creation, and with deliberate speed you can wander from heaven through the world to hell" (239–42). It seems unlikely that, as some interpreters maintain, the sequence in this final line, "from heaven through the world to hell," represents Goethe's original intention about Faust's eternal destiny. * * * Yet this line does suggest "an illuminating relationship with the end of Part Two." For in fact, of course, Faust does "stride" (albeit with something less than "deliberate speed") not, as the Director imagines, "from heaven through the world to hell," but "from the world through hell to heaven"—the very path traversed by Dante the pilgrim. The course of that "wandering" constitutes the plot of *Faust*, which is therefore a narrative of development and growth, a theme that is important for Goethe's understanding both of the individual and of history. Thus *Faust* is, to allude yet again to Dante, a narrative of pilgrimage. The leitmotif of pilgrimage, development, and growth reappears in the Prologue in Heaven, where the verbs employed are not "wandering * * * " but "straying * * * " and "striving * * * ." "Man will stray, as long as he goes on striving" is the Lord's own formulation of the leitmotif (317). Already in this passage, Mephistopheles, as becomes his wont throughout Part One, calls Faust "Doctor." But the Lord God identifies Faust instead as his "servant * * * " (299), which is what Faust remains through all the changes and chances of his "straying" and "striving." As the Lord God says of him, in anticipation of the teleology many thousands of lines later, "Even though he serves me now in a confused manner, I shall soon lead him into the light. When the tree is in leaf, the gardener knows that there will be flower and fruit to adorn the years to come" (308–11)—the "soon" in those words being meant no more literally than the "with deliberate speed" in the Director's.

Therefore, despite all the "confusion," the sorcery and witchcraft and downright blasphemy (1583–1606) into which he "strays" in the course of his "wandering" and "striving," Faust is being led "into the light" and retains at his core a deep sense of reverence, a sense that Mephistopheles finds incomprehensible but that Faust continues to affirm: "The capacity for awe is the best feature of humanity. The world may extract a heavy payment for such feelings, but someone who has been stirred feels the Numinous profoundly" (6272–74). It is a capacity for awe in the presence of the Numinous from which, "when he is most powerfully touched at the very depths of his existence," Faust is never altogether alienated. The numinous objects of Faust's sense of awe and reverence, however, do not remain the same. One permissible way to read the drama, therefore, would seem to be to watch the development, the "wandering," the "straying," and the "striving," in relation to these objects of reverence. * * *

Goethe himself provided a typological framework within which to chart Faust's theological *Bildungstrieb*, in an aphorism that has been my long-time favorite among the epigrams collected in the *Maxims and Reflections* compiled from various of his writings, letters, and other fragments: "When we do natural science, we are pantheists; when we do poetry, we are poly-theists; when we moralize, we are monotheists." The epigram actually derives from a letter Goethe originally wrote to Fritz Jacobi dated 6 January 1813: "For my part, I cannot be satisfied, amid the manifold directions of my being, with only one way of thinking. As a poet and an artist, I am a polytheist; on the other hand, I am a pantheist as a natural scientist—and one of these as decisively as the other. And if I have need for one God for my personality as a moral man, that, too, is provided for."

It deserves to be noted that within the range of the three "ways of thinking" distinguished by Goethe there is no mention of the fourth pos-sibility, atheism. And the same appears to be true of Faust, who falls into despair and who even seems to contemplate suicide (720–36, 1579–80), but who does not appear to consider the atheist alternative. This is because "in reality, Goethe's Faust has not in any way renounced God. . . . There-fore Faust is a God-seeker, not a God-denier." As Faust says to Margarete in his credo, "Who can perceive God and then presume to say: 'I do not believe in him'? The All-comprehending, the All-preserving, does he not sustain and embrace you and me and himself?" (3435–41). The debate over which was preferable, atheism or superstition, had been raging up to Goethe's time. Yet, in the face of all the superstition swirling around him and sometimes within him, Faust does not seem to consider atheism; when it appears at all in the text, atheism is seen as a polemical device rather than as an existential option (4898). Goethe's contemporaries and critics may have equated his "pantheism" and "Spinozism" with "atheism," but he did not. At one place in *Dichtung und Wahrheit*, reacting to the mys-tical theology of his Swiss contemporary, Johann Caspar Lavater, and echoing the words of a letter he had written to Lavater already in 1782, he did exclaim: "All unsuccessful attempts at conversion leave him who has been selected for a proselyte stubborn and obdurate; and this was especially the case with me when Lavater at last came out with the hard dilemma,—'Either Christian or atheist!' Upon this I declared that, if he would not leave me my own Christianity as I had hitherto cherished it, I could readily decide for Atheism, particularly as I saw that nobody knew precisely what either meant."

But that polemical comment is still a long way from placing atheism as an option on the same level alongside pantheism, polytheism, and monotheism, as is clear also from his comment earlier in Book Three of *Dichtung und Wahrheit* about French atheism: "How hollow and empty did we feel in this melancholy, atheistic half-night, in which Earth vanished with all its images, Heaven with all its stars."

There is another, not inconsiderable reason for "privileging" * * * this typology of pantheist, polytheist, monotheist: it comes from Goethe himself, rather than from Marx or Freud or, for that matter, the Bible or the Christian theological tradition; and there would seem to be some degree of prima facie plausibility to any schematism that is the author's own. Although he was not applying it explicitly to his treatment of the legend and character of Faust, he evidently did see in it a kind of theological taxonomy, according to which there was a correlation evident between the particular activity and task in which his own mind and spirit were engaged and the one or another particular view of the Divine to which he was just then committed. In the letter to Jacobi of 1813, Goethe invoked this taxonomy for a highly personal credo about his own view of the Divine (or, rather, views of the Divine) and about how each of the major tasks of his lifework—as poet and artist, as natural scientist, and as moral man (and in that order)—was correlated with an appropriate "Denkweise." But when the section "From the Literary Remains" was anthologized from his letters and other works for the *Maxims and Reflections*, not only was the order changed—from polytheism/pantheism/monotheism to pantheism/polytheism/monotheism—but the pronoun was also changed from the first person singular to the first person plural, thus raising it from the status of a personal confession (which it obviously is, and remains) to that of a philosophical and theological generalization; as their editor says of the saying collected in the *Maxims and Reflections*, "the sense is generalized, refined, deepened." And if this maxim is a valid generalization for Goethe and not a casual or purely idiosyncratic notion, to whom should it apply more fittingly than the character of Faust? There is, moreover, a genetic case to be made for its application to Faust. For the three periods of his development in the drama correspond to the sequence of Goethe's writing, beginning with the early "pantheistic" sections belonging to the author's original conception, continuing with the "polytheism" of Walpurgis Night and Classical Walpurgis Night as written in the first quarter of the 1800s, and closing with the "monotheism" of the sections written near the end of Goethe's life. Quoting the words of Goethe's letter to Jacobi, one critic has urged that "the close of *Faust* is the best evidence of how these words are meant," a judgment that the following exposition shares, despite its sharp differences from the interpretation that he has given.

There is, of course, a great danger that in the application of any such typology, even one of Goethe's minting, to so multifaceted a work as Goethe's *Faust* its categories will do violence to the complexity of the drama and its characters. The director in the Prelude at the Theater speaks about the drama as "a sort of ragout" (100), and Faust uses the same word in the opening scene (539): a ragout cannot have only one ingredient. There is an even greater danger: to forget that in Goethe's formulation, both in the letter to Jacobi and in the *Maxims and Reflections*, these three categories of "ways of thinking" are not distinguished from one another chronologically, and that they are not meant to be mutually exclusive; any such schematism would do violence to what have been called "the varying modes of Goethe's thought." Rather, the categories are distinguished from one another, so to speak, vocationally and psychologically. As Faust moves from one vocation to another, he seems to manifest many of the features of the way of thinking and theological worldview with which that vocation is associated in Goethe's maxim. Precisely because the distinction is not meant to be chronological, some features of one of these vocations will manifest themselves also within the context of another: Faust the poetic artist retains the natural scientist's interest in Nature, in geology and optics, and especially in applied physics and marine engineering, until just before the end of the drama, and Faust the moral philosopher has at least somewhat intimated this concern from the beginning of the drama. As this is true of these three vocations of natural scientist, poetic artist, and moral philosopher, so it also applies to the theological worldviews of "natural scientist as pantheist" and of "poetic artist as polytheist," together with that of "moral philosopher as monotheist."

Nor is this merely because Faust, like Goethe, cannot be content with one way but must come to terms with "the manifold directions of [his] being." Rather, the species of morality, and thus the definition of monotheism, through which Faust finds salvation, though it transcends both his scientific pantheism and his poetic polytheism, does so not by negating either of them but by fulfilling both of them and making them sublime. What Goethe said in his diary on 30 June 1830, while studying the literary fragments of his youth, would also apply to the person of Faust: "The truth, but undeveloped, so that it can be regarded as error." Every effort to make Goethe's *Faust* into a "Christian" drama in any orthodox or traditional sense has found itself blocked by that conjunction. As two of the prayers in the closing scene put it, both of them addressed by the Doctor Marianus to the Virgin Mary: "Let every nobler intent be placed at thy service!" (12100–12101); and "Grant approval to that which moves this man's breast, so earnestly and tenderly, and which it now bears before thy presence with the holy desire of love" (12001–4). These nobler intents, higher aspirations, and earnest yearnings are the expressions of an intellectual and spiritual "Eros, which started everything" (8479) and which finds fulfillment in God. Goethe's younger contemporary, the Danish philosopher Søren Kierkegaard, likewise distinguished three categories or, as they are sometimes translated into English, "existence-spheres": the aesthetic, the ethical, and the religious. Because the title of the work in which Kierkegaard most fully developed that distinction is translated into English as *Stages on Life's Way*, these three are usually called "stages." Kierkegaard's stages are not strictly chronological either, but in his philosophy of religion and his theology they are, ultimately, mutually opposed. If Goethe's "ways of thinking" are to be employed in any analogous way as "stages * * *" or, in a term he sometimes used, as "stages of development * * *," on the contrary, they must be seen as developmental but dialectical, and therefore as interpenetrating one another; and that is how they are being employed here to interpret Goethe's *Faust*.

BENJAMIN BENNETT

Interrupted Tragedy as a Structural Principle in *Faust*†

Probably the most vexed question in traditional *Faust* scholarship is the question of "unity." At a certain level of generality, the attempt to answer this question, to assert that *Faust* (or for that matter any text) is or is not a unified artistic work, necessarily involves *petitio principii*. One's choice of criterion determines one's conclusion, and equally reasonable criteria are available on both sides of the issue. In order to be discussed at all, therefore, the question must be limited; and in the present chapter, accordingly, I will set forth one particular way of seeing *Faust* as a unified construct, but without claiming to have discovered "the" organically complete and hence true structure of the work, as if it were a plant or the shell of a chambered nautilus. My only claim is that arguments that assert some sort of structural unity tend by nature to be more ambitious, rather than dismissive, and so contribute more energy to the discussion, provided they are properly relativized. * * * The relativization of * * * such argument thus follows automatically, and the crucial question becomes not whether the work is unified, but why it apparently presents its own unity as a particular kind of problem.

1

On the basis of Goethe's own utterances we can draw any number of conclusions about the unity of *Faust*, so that Goethe's utterances are of little practical use in dealing with the question. Nor may we take too seriously, as an argument against artistic unity, the differences among the various "periods" when Goethe added material to the work; our idea of these periods, after all, depends on specific interpretations of Goethe's writings (among them *Faust* itself) and so can be shaken by any new interpretive insight. A plausible genetic hypothesis would perhaps strengthen the case for artistic unity, but genetic arguments are by nature tentative; the interplay of influence, tradition, and convention, or of the poet's systematic thought and his direct response to experience, can never be fully understood. Nor is it necessary that the idea of a work's ultimate unity precede its composition; it will become evident below that Goethe is not likely to have had a clear idea of where *Faust* was leading him until at least quite close to the completion of Part One. And in any case, the

† From *Goethe's Theory of Poetry*: Faust *and the Regeneration of Language* (Ithaca: Cornell UP, 1986), 19–39. The author's footnotes and his quotations from the German have been omitted. In some places, quotations from Arndt's translation have been substituted. Other quotations are the author's prose translations.

unifying structural idea I will attempt to identify is an extremely simple one, so that there are no grounds for denying out of hand the possibility that Goethe retained it and returned to it repeatedly over a long period.

I will not argue that *Faust* is homogeneous, or even that it is complete in the sense of being symmetrical or closed off. Even the Romantic open-endedness of *Faust* (if the work has this quality) does not interfere with structural unity of the sort I will attempt to demonstrate, which is a unity similar to that of theme and variations in music, arising from the rhythmic repetition, on various levels and scales and in various guises, of a single master pattern. Or perhaps the analogy of rhythm in architecture is more exact, that rhythm of shape and proportion by which the dimensions of a clerestory window, for example, are related to the dimensions of the cathedral's floor plan. My point is that a master pattern in *Faust* is the pattern of interrupted tragedy.

The first occurrence of this structural theme is the opening scene of the drama proper, "Night." This scene, in its entirety, including the appearance of the *Erdgeist* and Wagner, is essentially nothing but a monologue. Its basic philosophical duality, even in the *Urfaust* version, is represented not by the signs of Macrocosm and Earth Spirit, but rather by the two actual figures who appear, the Earth Spirit and Wagner; and they in turn only mark a duality within Faust, as is later made clear in his speech about the "two souls" in his breast. When the Earth Spirit informs Faust, "You resemble the spirit you comprehend, not me!" and Faust then asks, "Not you? Whom then? I, God's own image, and I come up not even to you?" (512–17), it is no accident that this question is answered by Wagner's knock. * * * The immediate goal Faust has set himself, an escape from dead learning into an intimate, active contact with living nature, corresponds to the *Erdgeist*, but his approach to this goal by way of learning, even magical learning, bears an inescapable resemblance to the mere intellectuality of Wagner. * * * "Flee! away! out into the natural countryside!" (418) cries Faust, but he is using a *book* to guide him, not his own supposedly natural feelings; and when he complains later, referring to Wagner, "That this abundance of visions must be interrupted by that dried-up plodder!" (520–21), he is actually railing against an insidious intellectual tendency in himself. Wagner does not arrive until the vision has *already* been disrupted by Faust's own improper attitude toward it, the attitude of supposed intellectual superiority that is betrayed especially in the words "not even you!"

The Earth Spirit and Wagner, then, both represent aspects of Faust, and the whole scene is the dramatization of an inner tension. That Faust despises Wagner only corroborates this point, since he obviously also despises himself as an intellectual; and that in *Urfaust* the Earth Spirit appears "in a revolting form" (*Urfaust*, after 129) corresponds to the recognition that Faust, despite his boasts, is also not truly in sympathy with that "genius of the world and of deeds." Precisely his desire to view the Earth Spirit and his raising the question of whether he and the spirit are "similar" (500) indicate his imperfect grasp of the situation, for the only way to establish real contact with the "spirit of activity" is simply to act, not to observe and seek enjoyment in observing. Two tendencies in Faust's nature appear: the

desire to realize his existence as vigorous activity (*Erdgeist*) and the ineradicable habit of critical intellect (Wagner) that thwarts this desire in
the very process of generating it. Faust is repelled by *both* tendencies for
the simple reason that both exist and each repels the other.

Neither is it insignificant that Wagner approaches Faust with the words
"I take it you were reading a Greek tragedy" (523), for the inner duality
dramatized in "Night" possesses a fundamentally tragic character that is
already wholly prefigured in the vision of the Macrocosm. Man's perceiving and thinking mind provides him with an idea of "how everything
weaves itself into the whole, how each thing is operative and alive in the
other" (447–48) as well as with an idea of his own central position in this
universal harmony, his quasi-divine nature as microcosm to the macrocosm. It is our nature as thinking beings, the nature of the perceiving and
thinking mind as a reflected image of the universe, that constitutes our
quasi-divinity in the first place. God himself has charged his angels, "And
that which is suspended in wavering appearance, fasten it down with enduring thoughts" (348–49); and Faust, in the grip of the macrocosmic
vision, is moved to ask, "Am I a god?" (439). But at the same time, the
very act of thinking, of envisioning this macrocosmic harmony, also alienates us by placing us in the distanced position of mere knowers or viewers,
no longer *within* what we envision, and the vision itself is thus reduced to
a mere object of knowledge, "but a show" (454), no longer the actual
world that surrounds and includes us. The trouble with man is that his
nature *is* quasi-divine, that he *is* "an image of the godhead" (516, 614),
but that the immediate experience of his own divinity eludes him like
Tantalus's fruit. To the extent that he knows of it * * *, he is also alienated from it and fails to experience it directly. Like Faust, he then becomes
"resentful" (after 459), and desires to cast aside his knowledge in favor of
an utterly passionate involvement in natural existence. But this is impossible, since what he seeks can have significance for him as an achievement
(in other words, can be *found*, as the thing sought for) only in relation to
a continuing of the knowledge that must supposedly be obliterated. Hence
the incongruous image of Faust's seeking nature with a book in his hand.
Hence, once again, the falseness of Faust's relation to the Earth Spirit,
which is already clear in his evoking the spirit *as* a vision. Hence his "not
even thee?" (517), which reveals that he has not actually relinquished his
sense of intellectual superiority.

Man's tragic dilemma is that he is in truth a kind of god yet can achieve
in experience no direct contact with his own divinity. * * * The two
distinct states in which we exist, physical and spiritual, do not remain mere
states but are transformed by the tension between them into opposed
drives.

Dr. Jckyll & Mr. Hyde

You are by just a single urge possessed:
Oh may you never know the other!
Two souls, alas, are dwelling in my breast,
And either would be severed from its brother;
The one holds fast with joyous earthy lust
Onto the world of man with organs clinging:

The other soars impassioned from the dust,
To realms of lofty forebears winging. (1110–17)

Our quasi-divine, potentially infinite consciousness, by detaching us from
natural existence, presents us with nature as an object of nostalgic yearning, while on the other hand the actual experience of our narrow physical
existence generates a need for spiritual self-development. Our condition is
thus hopelessly in conflict with itself, for both nature and spirit are objects
of yearning yet at the same time forms of confinement that we seek to
escape as soon as we experience them. "Thus I career from desire to
enjoyment, and in enjoyment I pine for desire" (3249–50).

The tragic hopelessness of this self-divided condition also determines
the relation between the two scenes that follow "Night," "Outside the City
Gate" and the first "Study," in which Faust's interlocutors are Wagner and
Mephistopheles respectively. To understand the symmetry here, we must
understand that Mephistopheles not only is related to the Earth Spirit (this
much is clear from the reference in "Forest and Cave" [3217–46]), but at
least in one aspect of his nature is a form of the Earth Spirit, and in fact,
from Faust's point of view, the only accessible form. Again, we cannot
achieve a total submergence in unreflecting experience by way of the
conscious desire for it, since the desire itself already constitutes an intellectual detachment from our experience. Such total submergence can occur only in spite of conscious will, which is why "the spirit who always
negates" (1338) is the only conceivable vehicle for appeasing the urge that
prompts Faust to invoke the Earth Spirit. Unreflecting experience must
come unbidden, as Mephistopheles does, and must come not as an intellectual vision but as an incalculable force that constantly thwarts our expectations and desires; otherwise it does not submerge us at all but merely
justifies and reinforces the superior attitude of Faust's "not even thee?"
(517).

The succession here, therefore, a scene with Wagner followed by a
scene with Mephistopheles, refigures exactly the central polarity of the
"Night" monologue, for though the Easter morning chorus has prevented
Faust's suicide, the tragic dilemma itself is not resolved. Faust's demands,
to be sure, are now more moderate. On the Easter walk he seeks not utter
immersion in nature but merely the normal enjoyment of nature in human society ("Here I am Man, am free to be!" [940]), and in his study
he does not seek knowledge of himself as divine but is now content to
contemplate the divine conventionally, through Scripture. Even these
moderated desires, however, are unfulfillable: when we seek relaxation in
contact with nature ("Outside the City Gate"), our inescapable companion
is the drive to know (Wagner), which alienates us; and when we then
enter the precinct of knowledge ("Study"), we are accompanied by Mephistopheles, the Earth Spirit in a more accessible and so more dangerous
form, the nagging sense that our knowledge is futile and the corresponding
drive for overwhelming experience. There is no way to alleviate the tragic
division in our nature, our necessary and unceasing dissatisfaction with
ourselves, and at the crucial point in "Outside the City Gate" at the
moment when the poodle first appears, the idea of the tragic is called to

mind * * * in Wagner's warning about spirits that attack from all four points of the compass (1126–37).

The beginning of *Faust* thus strongly emphasizes the idea of the tragedy of self-consciousness, tragedy rooted in an internal division of the self. Our self-consciousness, by separating us from ourselves, denies us satisfaction even from what we actually possess; we may know about the divine aspect of our nature, but we must receive this knowledge as torment, not joy. And the purest possible form of this particular tragic vision is monologue tragedy, as in "Night." External action would only confuse the issue, since the tragic is based entirely upon a situation within the individual; instead, the hero simply steps forth, does nothing but conduct an essentially internal dialogue with himself, and 383 lines later is ready to commit suicide. It is this maximally condensed or refined tragedy that is interrupted by the Easter morning chorus. But the interruption does not solve the problem. What the angels actually do is raise a question: Can the man-god (Faust as Christ) really somehow manage to arise from the deadly despair into which his human divinity must lead him?

2

Once we understand the sense of the tragic in "Night" and in the two scenes following, the tragic aspect of the work as a whole is not difficult to grasp; for its other tragic actions, though more externally conceived, are also referable to the hopeless self-conflict of self-consciousness. Gretchen has already in effect lost her innocence when her conversations with Faust open for her an unaccustomed perspective upon her own person, so that her thinking is divided against itself ("zerstückt" [3385]); the Helen-Euphorion tragedy is the disintegration of an ideal synthesis of the intellectual-Nordic with the physical-Hellenic; and the Emperor's trouble is that he cannot renounce the desire to combine "ruling and at the same time enjoying" (10251), which is parallel to Faust's desire for an unreflecting immersion in experience without renunciation of his intellectual mastery of it. Moreover, once we recognize the arbitrariness with which the original monologue tragedy is interrupted, numerous other instances of interrupted tragedy suggest themselves throughout the work, especially in Part Two: the Helen tragedy, interrupted by the change to "Inner Courtyard of a Castle"; the intervention of magic to save the Emperor in act 4; and if the requisite symbolic connections are admitted, the lengthy tragic development, more interrupted than not, of the force or configuration embodied successively by the Boy Charioteer, Homunculus, and Euphorion. But what principle underlies this thematic repetition of a structural unit? Why should these tragedies be interrupted in the first place?

Let us consider Gretchen's tragedy. First there is a more or less cohesive dramatic action leading to a form of guilt that, while not objectively unambiguous, is subjectively unquestioned ("Cathedral"); then this action is sharply interrupted by the excursion into a practically actionless realm of symbolism ("Walpurgis Night," "Walpurgis Night's Dream"); and only after this interruption does the tragic action proceed to its inevitable conclusion (Gretchen's death), which is alleviated, however, by a hint of ultimate salvation, "Redeemed!" (4611). The significant point about this sequence is that the structure of *Faust* as a whole, considered as Faust's tragedy, repeats it exactly on a larger scale. First, in the whole of Part One there is a relatively cohesive dramatic action leading to a state of guilt on Faust's part, which is to a certain extent mitigated; then follows a lengthy excursion into the symbolic (acts 1–3 of Part Two) during which Faust practically vanishes as the well-delineated character of Part One and appears mainly in allegorical guise; and only after this interruption, in acts 4–5, does the dramatic action resume, when Faust (quite literally, at the beginning of act 4) descends from the clouds of imagination, places his feet on the ground once more, and after taking a moment to establish the connection with Part One by thinking about Gretchen, sets himself a relatively practicable task that will occupy the rest of his life—as he had set himself a humane task in the scene "Dreary Day," after the "Walpurgis Night's Dream." The sequence, as I say, is the same as that in the Gretchen tragedy: dramatic action leading to guilt, symbolic interruption, then resumption of the action leading to a catastrophe that is modified by a vision of ultimate salvation.

In absolute terms, Part One as a whole is less cohesive dramatically than the first part of the Gretchen action by itself. But the relative cohesion of Part One (considered as a Faust action), by comparison with acts 1–3 of Part Two, corresponds to the relative cohesion of the Gretchen action up to "Cathedral" by comparison with the "Walpurgis Night"; and this parallel of relative cohesion and interruption (with respect to Faust in one case, Gretchen in the other) is what makes the structural parallel. The window is not as big as the cathedral, but its proportions are the same. Moreover, the Gretchen action, though interrupted, is by no means forgotten in the "Walpurgis Night"; not only the appearance of Medusa as Gretchen (4183–4209) and the dance with the young and old witches (4128–75), which recalls the scene "Garden," are important, but also such touches as the "Peddling Witch" (4104–9) with evil implements that have actually been used earlier, and the appearance of Baubo (3962–67), the woman who comforts Demeter by displaying her genitals and so reminding the goddess of the power of generation—we think of pregnant Gretchen. And this phantom presence of Gretchen in the "Walpurgis Night" strengthens the parallel I am drawing; for Faust—as Plutus, as court magus, as Antaeus or as Orpheus in search of a "mythological woman" (7428), as medieval nobleman, as Arcadian lover and father—leads the same sort of symbolic existence in acts 1–3 of Part Two. We are, so to speak, constantly reminded of Faust; but apart from the brief conversation in the "Dark Gallery," we do not actually see the dramatic personality we know from Part One until the beginning of act 4. In fact, the typically Faustian character, unreasonable self-dissatisfaction coupled with absurd impatience ("A curse on patience, above all!" [1606]), is not fully reestablished until we hear the old man ranting in act 5 about the "damned ringing" (11151) from the nearby chapel, whereby we are also reminded of the work's first tragic pulse, the "Night" monologue, which had been interrupted by church bells. Only in act 5 do we again receive in fully developed form what we immediately recognize as a characteristic Faust-Mephistopheles action, Mephistopheles exploiting Faust's impatience in order to saddle him with the murder of yet another inoffensive family, as Gretchen's family had been destroyed earlier.

The overall pattern of the Gretchen tragedy is thus repeated exactly in the whole of the Faust tragedy: action leading to guilt, a symbolic-mythical interruption, resumption of tragic action leading to an alleviated catastrophe. And I contend that the source of those two symbolic interruptions is the same as what we are taught by the "Night" monologue to recognize as the source of the tragic itself, namely human self-consciousness— except that in the "Walpurgis Night," and in the first three acts of Part Two, not the fictional self-consciousness of a character but the *actual* self-consciousness of a spectator or reader must be imagined as operating. It is this suggestion that is conveyed by the comic topical allusions and the depiction of various typical spectator attitudes with which the "Walpurgis Night" and the "Walpurgis Night's Dream" are largely taken up. The outside world in general, and in particular the consciousness of spectator or reader, intrudes directly into what would otherwise be, by convention, the self-contained fiction of the stage. We are reminded of the Director's complaint about audiences in the "Prelude in the Theater":

> While they are not accustomed to the best,
> Still they are frightfully well-read and clever. (45–46)

This pretentiously erudite audience is a principal object of satire in the "Walpurgis Night" and the intermezzo that follows it, and I contend that the invitation to laugh at an aspect of our own situation, as spectators or readers, is calculated to distract us (precisely by showing us an image of our distraction) from our otherwise presumed aesthetic involvement in the fiction as an illusion of reality. What interrupts the Gretchen tragedy, in other words, is both an image and an immediate instance of our own distracted consciousness, our awareness of an actual and a literary world beyond the imaginary reality on stage. The work adopts an ironic perspective relative to itself as a symbolic illusion; it becomes self-reflexive, no longer wholly involved in itself as a cohesive, psychologically plausible experience. And essentially the same thing happens in the first three acts of Part Two (interruption of the Faust action), which are composed of a series of allegorical ceremonies with mere interludes of something closer to dramatic action. Perhaps it is more accurate to speak of the interruption in Part Two as reflecting the intrusion of a creating rather than a perceiving consciousness, a poet's rather than a spectator's. But for practical purposes the distinction between poet and spectator disappears here anyway. If the author appears in the work as a consciousness clearly outside the normal limits of the fiction, then his perspective is essentially the same as a spectator's; and if the spectator's detachment is an effective force in the fiction, then the state of being a spectator has become part of the process of poetic creation or invention.

Especially the "Walpurgis Night," therefore, teaches us to think of the interruptions of tragedy as a repeated mirroring within the fiction itself of the audience's necessary and natural detachment from the fiction. A spectator or reader (or author) is not immediately involved in the tragic quality of the action that unfolds before him. Observation (like creation) implies distance; an audience responds to the tragic anguish of the character on stage with a species of pleasure. In *Faust*, however, the audience's detached perspective is permitted to interrupt the tragic movement, to have a specific and visible effect on what happens in the drama. Thus a curiously direct relationship is created not only between spectator and poet, but also between the audience and Faust; for the two main interruptions in the Faust action, after the "Night" monologue and after the whole of Part One, are referable not only to the audience's detached consciousness with respect to the fiction, but also to Faust's own detached consciousness with respect to himself. Faust is held back from suicide not by the actual message of the angelic chorus but by the *memory*, the complication of self-consciousness, that it awakens in him (781–82); and in the scene "Charming Landscape" the emphasis is specifically upon the renewed perspective, relative to himself, afforded Faust after his repose. The audience's consciousness, in the interruptions, thus functions in the same way as Faust's own; actual consciousness (the audience's) and fictional consciousness (Faust's) merge. By an ingenious dialectical twist—which belongs, incidentally, to the inventory of literary devices employed by Goethe's contemporaries as well—our very detachment from the fiction is made to generate a kind of identification with a character in the fiction.

3

The important point, however, is that the source of the interruptions of tragedy in *Faust* is the same as the source of the tragic itself. (Thus, by extension, the situation of the audience, as an audience, is tragic in the same way as Faust's situation.) The "Night" monologue provides an anticipatory instance of this state of affairs, for the chorus of angels that closes it, like the Earth Spirit and Wagner, is essentially an aspect of Faust's own mentality, in precisely the sense that that mentality is tragic. Faust is driven to despair, to the brink of nonexistence, by the dialectical operation of the inescapable self-consciousness that alienates us mentally from ourselves in every instant of existence, so that we never truly experience our ideal knowledge of ourselves and are never intellectually in command of our experience; no sooner do we begin to experience our being as a significant whole than our knowledge of this experience separates us from it, and our being is thus no longer whole after all. This natural law of self-consciousness, however, applies not only to Faust's conventional knowledge and to his visions of Macrocosm and Earth Spirit, but also to his despair; no sooner is he wholly committed to death, no sooner does he wholly experience the truth that "manly dignity" (713) requires suicide, than he is also self-consciously detached from this truth and finds himself now with a new perspective on his situation and condition. The Easter chorus is but an image of the final dialectical twist, within Faust's mind, by which the tragic brings about its own interruption. This dialectic of self-consciousness, which, in the very process of bringing us constantly to the brink of nonexistence, also maintains us in existence, is part of what Goethe is thinking about in *Poetry and Truth*, at the end of book 8, when he recalls his youthful ideas on the "pulse" of being; and it is significant that the idea of the pulse also figures prominently at the beginning of the second major interruption in the Faust action, in Faust's first speech of Part Two, "life's pulse is throbbing fresh and heady" (4679).

The tragic aspect of self-consciousness is that in the process of revealing to us our eternal or divine nature it also entails our repeated self-separation, thus constant mental change, so that we can never actually grasp or utilize the ideal truth about ourselves, but must learn "that nothing perfect or complete is ever granted a human" (3240). And yet just this endlessly mutable, thus renewable perspective relative to ourselves is also always available as a *relief* from the tragic; it is always possible for us to assume a point of view from which the tragic no longer appears tragic after all, no longer an occasion for despair. This is the principle that operates in *Faust* through the repeated interruption of a tragic process by some reminder of the work's own ironic, self-aware illusoriness; we think not only of the Gretchen tragedy and the whole Faust action, but also of the Helen tragedy, which is interrupted by the change to a medieval setting that presumably reflects the European Christian cultural identity of the audience actually watching.

Or we think of the action of act 4, where Goethe sketches with remarkable economy the Emperor's character and situation:

> A rival Emperor profits me—I feel
> My sovereignty's never been more real.
> The armor, first but as a soldier borne,
> With more exalted purpose now is worn.
> At every feast, as brilliant as it was,
> Danger I missed, for lack of other flaws. (10407–12)

A life of mere appearances is no longer sufficient for the Emperor, as for Faust earlier the life of the envisioning intellect had been no longer sufficient; like Faust, the Emperor now desires to realize himself fully as an individual by immersing himself in overwhelming experience, even if it means his destruction * * *:

> Man trust but self! Who craves for throne and crown,
> Let him in person merit such renown. (10467–68)

The groundwork is thus laid for a heroic action, and even after the Rival Emperor refuses single combat the situation is still pregnant with a potential tragic development. The Emperor is about to be trapped in a net of circumstances; his culpability is compensated by his heroic resolve, which * * * is the more pathetic for being denied the opportunity to realize itself in a vigorous open fight, even if defeated. The Emperor is a hero in a world where heroism no longer counts; or at least he could be such a hero, and his futility itself could give him a certain stature.

But this is not the way act 4 actually develops. Faust arrives, talking virtual nonsense about mountain spirits, and Mephistopheles wins the battle with a trick. The Emperor is saved, but he is also denied the chance to experience his own apparent destiny; and this interruption of tragedy is again referable to our detached perspective as an audience, for it represents the intrusion of a larger symbolic action, which we have been following for over ten thousand lines, into a circumscribed fictional reality where it does not belong. Especially interesting in this connection is Mephistopheles' description of the rout of the hostile army:

> I can see nothing of these watery lies,
> The spell bewilders only human eyes,
> I am amused by the bizarre affair.
> In masses, whole platoons, away they bound,
> The fools think they are being drowned,
> They pant and snort while walking safe and sound,
> And ludicrously paddle on dry ground. (10734–40)

This speech is significant not only with respect to the poetic theme of shadow and substance, but also as the grotesquely exaggerated expression of an audience's situation relative to dramatic action upon a stage. What we would actually see at a performance of *Faust* is exactly what Mephistopheles describes; even the highly developed stage machinery of the nineteenth century could not produce the optically convincing illusion of a flood. But it is more important to recognize that what we see in a theater is *always* essentially what Mephistopheles sees: people (the actors) responding passionately to a state of affairs that we, from our extrafictional perspective, know to be mere illusion. No audience is ever really swept up in a stage illusion; we are always detached at least to the extent of knowing who we are and what we are doing in reality. The Director in the *Faust* "Prelude" makes a point of this fact, and Mephistopheles, to the extent that we recognize the relevance of his words to our situation, now reminds us of it at the decisive point in the interruption of the Emperor's tragedy, thus reminding us that this interruption also has to do with our own consciousness as spectators.

4

I have argued that self-consciousness is the source both of the tragic itself and of the interruptions of tragic movements in *Faust*, and I have argued that the audience's self-conscious detachment from the fiction thus forms the basis for a developed form of more than emotional identification with the central fictional figure. But the audience's self-consciousness appears to be directly operative only in the interruptions, in the movements of relief from the tragic. In what sense, if any, is the audience, as an audience, also involved in the specifically tragic aspect of self-consciousness?

The interruptions of tragedy in *Faust*, first of all, do not constitute an "avoidance of tragedy." Faust and Gretchen are saved, but only after the tragic futility of their situations has been presented with great clarity and force; the interrupted Helen tragedy, by contrast with what the uninterrupted tragedy would have been, tends toward the elegiac but still represents the nonaccomplishment of an important ideal; the Emperor, though saved, finds himself at the end laying the foundations for a recurrence of the disorder of act 1—and he does this, significantly, in "The Rival Emperor's Tent," for he is now acting as his own worst enemy—which gives rise to a sense of futile cyclicity; and the career of the figure last manifested in Euphorion is actually culminated as a tragedy.

What is avoided is not the tragic itself, but rather tragic catharsis. By experiencing, via a fictional action, the force of the inherent tragic quality of the human condition, but without undergoing its real consequences, the audience gains perspective upon the tragic, hence at least a temporary relief or pleasure. I suggest, however, that it is the intellectual *anticipation* of this relief that is reflected structurally in the interruptions of tragedy in *Faust*. If we know in advance that the tragic action on stage is meant to overpower us with its force, in order finally to provide us with relief or pleasure, then this anticipatory knowledge interferes with the tragic effect from which pleasure is meant to flow; the trouble with audiences, again, is that "they are frightfully well-read and clever," or as the Director also says:

> With eyebrows raised they sit in the enclosure
> And long to be amazed, with due composure. (41–2)

A theater audience, like Faust with the Earth Spirit or the Macrocosm, desires consciously to be overwhelmed by an intense experience, and this conscious desire interferes with its own object. In *Faust* this interference is permitted to influence the stage action itself, as an interruption or premature relief from the tragic. The structural anticipation of catharsis, however, has the effect of denying us any actual catharsis by denying us the "reconciling closure" in form that catharsis depends on. The anticipation of catharsis in structure deforms or dedramatizes the tragic process and so prevents catharsis. And this idea of an intellectual anticipation of experience, which modifies the experience itself, is of course also central in the makeup and unfolding of Faust's own character, from the "Night" monologue down to his very last words, "In the anticipatory feeling of such lofty happiness I now enjoy the supreme moment (11585–86).

But then, why are the tragic actions in *Faust* allowed to complete themselves even after their interruption? Why is tragedy not simply "avoided"? The answer to this question is contained in the argument above concerning the manifestation on the stage itself of the intellectual detachment of a real or imaginary audience; for it follows from this argument that our very detachment has the effect, paradoxically, of *involving* us in the complex stage action, of creating a *real* sympathy between ourselves and the stage, not the precarious sympathy of a supposed emotional susceptibility to illusion. We do inevitably enjoy a certain amount of detached perspective relative to the dramatic fiction; but if the fiction in turn incorporates a direct reflection of our detachment, then the net result is a kind of ironic involvement. Or to look at it differently, our detachment as an audience is reflected, within the fiction, as a temporary relief from the tragic; but this temporary relief within the fiction, as it affects us, interferes with the climactic or cathartic form of relief from the tragic that is otherwise proper to our situation as an audience. We, as an audience, are therefore denied any real relief from the tragic, and our involvement in the fictional action is by consequence an involvement, specifically, in the unrelieved experience of its tragic quality. An avoidance of tragedy is entirely out of the question. The tragic in *Faust* is not a particular pattern of actions or events that might conceivably be either finished or replaced by an alternative pattern. It is, rather, an atmospheric quality that pervades every imaginable human situation, including that of the audience.

The complex form of identification with Faust that our sense of conscious detachment itself procures for us is thus an identification with Faust's tragedy. Again, the two main interruptions in the Faust action, the Easter chorus and the first three acts of Part Two, are referable not only to our detachment as an audience, but also to Faust's intellectual detachment from himself; and if Faust is detached from his own destiny in the same way we are, if indeed his inevitable repeated detachment is itself the tragic quality of that destiny, then we for our part are involved in his destiny in the same way he is. The source of the interruptions of tragedy, again, is the same that the "Night" monologue teaches us to recognize as the source of the tragic itself; and insofar as we are made aware, by the interruptions, of the intellectual complexity of our own situation as spectators or readers, we are therefore also placed in precisely the situation by which the tragic is generated. Tragedy, once interrupted, returns to itself not by way of an imaginary fatal mechanism within the fiction but by way of an ironic mechanism built into the relationship between fiction and audience. That the tragic movement, moreover, after being interrupted, in each case arrives at only an alleviated or attenuated conclusion is entirely appropriate; a strong tragic climax would require, as a response, precisely the sort of cathartic satisfaction that is excluded by the nature of the tragic in *Faust*. The tragic, again, is a pervasive atmosphere in this work, not a blinding truth waiting for its revelatory catastrophe. * * *

It is the ironic aspect of *Faust*, paradoxically, that reflects the tragedy of the human condition at its deepest, the truth that in real life there is no real or lasting catharsis, no cleansing, the truth that our existence, by virtue of self-consciousness, is ineluctably tragic, but that precisely because of our self-consciousness we are always as it were one step ahead of ourselves and so never undergo our own tragic destiny in a definitive, knowable, cathartically satisfying form, that we never actually experience the wild joy of the "shipwreck" Faust longs for. Human nature requires, but never satisfactorily receives, a violent tragic destiny as a test or proof of itself. * * * The same perspectival flexibility that always relieves human anguish * * * also always entangles us in it again, but never quite deeply enough, just as the original threat to the Emperor's court is eventually made more serious by the trick (paper money, in act 1) that relieves it, but still not serious enough to test the Emperor as a hero (in act 4). The "very serious jokes" Goethe plays in structure are also the very substance of the tragic vision.

That the question of catharsis was a consideration for Goethe in composing *Faust* also emerges from the essay "Nachlese zu Aristoteles Poetik," which was written toward the beginning of the final phase of work on the poem. We read there:

> If the poet, for his part, has done his duty, if he has created a signif-
> icant plot-problem and resolved it in a worthy manner, then the same
> process will take place in the spectator's mind. The intrigue will con-
> fuse him, and the resolution enlighten him, whereupon he will go
> home none the better for his experience. In fact, given enough ascetic
> self-attentiveness, he would be puzzled at himself, puzzled to find
> himself, at home, every bit as frivolous or stubborn, every bit as im-
> petuous or weak, every bit as loving or loveless, as he had been before
> going to the theater. (WA, 41/2:251)

The trouble with theatrical catharsis, with the satisfying enlightenment
produced by a conclusive tragic ending, is that it uplifts us only to put us
down again in the place we started, "none the better"; and I contend that
catharsis is avoided in *Faust* for just this reason. By not carrying out the
poet's supposed "duty," Goethe in *Faust* is attempting to do more, to create
a tragedy beyond tragedy, a work that will leave us in a sense *dissatisfied*
and so make a difference in our real life—a work that will convey the
tragic dimension of our existence not in a climactic revelatory flash, but
as an unrelenting atmospheric quality that follows us even when we leave
the theater.

Perhaps, therefore, the answer to the question posed by the Easter morning chorus (Can the man-god survive the despair into which his own
human divinity drives him?) is contained in the mere fact that when *Faust*
is over we resume our normal daily pursuits, not "better" morally, but in
a new atmosphere, with a deepened philosophical sense of the significance
of these pursuits. Perhaps even our act of leaving the theater, or the book,
has a place in the meaning of *Faust*. Shortly before the arrival of a second
chorus of angels, Mephistopheles says:

> Over! Stupid name.
> Why over?
> All over and pure nothing—just the same!
> What has this constant doing ever brought
> But what is done to rake away to naught?
> So it is over! How to read this clause?
> All over is as good as never was,
> And yet it whirls about as if it were.
> The Ever-empty is what I prefer. (11595–603)

But we, in the process of watching or reading, have found ourselves involved in an experience of the truth that the pervasive transience and
futility, hence ultimately the nonentity of all things human, is a necessary
consequence of our self-conscious, self-detached mode of being. The mere
fact that we nevertheless continue to exist, therefore, constitutes an arbitrary rejection of Mephistopheles' otherwise irrefutable argument, a kind
of resurrection from the deadly despair in which his logic * * * must
otherwise entrap us. What Faust says of the townspeople earlier can now
be said of us in a somewhat different sense: "They celebrate the resurrection of the Lord, for they themselves are resurrected" (921–22). The ironic
involvement of the audience with the fiction has the effect, ultimately, of
transforming even our daily existence beyond the limits of the work into

a kind of *imitatio Christi*, a constant resurrection from the constant tendency toward nonexistence that is generated by our inevitable self-conscious condition. Catharsis is denied us; we do not leave behind the tragedy of *Faust*; rather, the work compels us to continue living in the atmosphere of the tragic. And that we continue living at all, therefore, takes on the quality of a moral achievement.

Or to look at it somewhat differently, tragic anguish and tragic pleasure are traditionally separate, the former enacted on the stage and the latter experienced in the audience. But Goethe attempts a synthesis of the two in a single polyphonic complex of activity that is realized not only within the envisioned fiction, but also in the magnetic field of conscious tensions that arises between work and audience, in that our own detached perspective is made to function as a structural determinant and a source of the tragic. This complex of activity is totally tragic in the sense that tragic anguish and tragic pleasure are fused in it, in the sense that it contains the whole anguish of human existence but builds this anguish out of jokes, always ironic but never in such a way as to become merely a joke, thus ultimately continuous with the infinitely problematic quality of real life. And yet this opening of the work's structure into the real world is also itself incorporated into the structure (in the interruptions) as a governing theme, so that in the final analysis we can perhaps speak of *Faust* as "a tragedy" after all, a cohesive poetic work with tragic force.

* * *

FRANCO MORETTI

[Goethe's *Faust* as Modern Epic]†

"In the Beginning Was the Deed"

Action is the clearest revelation of the individual, of his temperament as well as his aims: what a man is at bottom and in his inmost being comes into actuality only by his action.

Hegel's words. * * * Without action, in short, no hero. Hence, no epic. This is the right background against which to read one of the great monologues in *Faust*:

> "In the beginning was the Word"—thus runs the text.
> Who helps me on? Already I'm perplexed!
> I cannot grant the word such sovereign merit,
> I must translate it in a different way
> If I'm indeed illumined by the Spirit.
> "In the beginning was the Sense." But stay!

---

† From "Faust and the Nineteenth Century," *Modern Epic: The World System from Goethe to García Márquez*, trans. Quintin Hoare (London and New York: Verso, 1997), 11–98. Reprinted by permission of Verso UK. The author's footnotes have been omitted. His quotations from *Faust* have been replaced with Arndt's translation.

Reflect on this first sentence well and truly
Lest the light pen be hurrying unduly!
Is sense in fact all action's spur and source?
It should read: "In the beginning was the Force!"
Yet as I write it down, some warning sense
Alerts me that it, too, will give offense.
The spirit speaks! And lo, the way is freed,
I calmly write: "In the beginning was the Deed!"

                                                        1224–37

"Im Anfang war die Tat": this is undoubtedly the idea defended by Faust in the "Study" scene that follows shortly afterwards and that Goethe, in the plan he drafted in about 1800, made the basis for the entire poem. But the principle so proudly proclaimed never finds much correspondence in the actual work. Before the first part of *Faust* was even finished, Schiller was already communicating his own doubts to Goethe in this respect: "In my opinion," he wrote on 26 June 1797, "Faust should be led into active life . . ." With the publication of Part Two, the disappointment increased. Heine criticized Goethe's "indifference" to action, while Vischer hoped for a Faust caught up in the Peasants' War. Finally, at a juncture decisive for the destiny of the "grand world"—1938—this is what Thomas Mann wrote:

> Goethe did not do much to represent poetically those "depths of sweet and sensual sin" [*Faust*, 1751], or that life of action alternating between success and chagrin, to which he would have liked his hero to sacrifice himself [. . .] A long time had to go by before Faust, after so many bizarre magical adventures, turned to undertakings that might truly be termed tests of indefatigable human activity.

Well, then: Goethe wants an active hero, he gives him marvellous and fitting words to pronounce, he lends him the aid of the infernal powers, and yet—nothing. For scene after scene—the long promenade in "Outside the City Gate"; the silence in "Auerbach's Tavern" and "Witch's Kitchen"; the sleep and dreams scattered almost everywhere; the mere walk-on part in the two "Walpurgis Night" scenes and in the civil war—Faust remains ever more enmired in a kind of idle contemplation. Here, the contrast with the ancient epic is really very strong. In Homer, even the hero's *inactivity*—Achilles in his tent—produces practical consequences of great importance; it is, in its own way, action. In *Faust*, on the contrary, the hero's presence seems always to leave things as they were, in a kind of gigantic spectacle. In the words of Mephistopheles:

> . . . these days you are to witness
> Examples of my pleasing arts galore.
> I'll give you what no man has seen before.
>   1672–4

We were seeking a hero, and have found a spectator. What is to be done?

Perhaps, to begin with, we can reverse the argument and see in Faust's inertia the only chance for the modern epic totality. If Hegel is actually right, and in the modern world "the vitality of the individual appears as transcended," then nothing is left but to seek "the universal individual of mankind" *in passivity.* In this new scenario, the grand world of the epic no longer takes shape in transformative action, but in imagination, in dream, in magic. It is a shift clearly perceptible in the passage from Marlowe to Goethe. This is how Faust speaks in the last years of the sixteenth century:

> Having thee ever to attend on me,
> To give me whatsoever I shall ask,
> To tell me whatsoever I demand
> *Doctor Faustus*, I, 3, 93–5

Here, everything still depends upon Faustus's will. The first person pronoun grips the passage, appearing twice in each line, as origin and aim of every action ("To give *me* whatsoever *I* shall ask"); as for Mephistopheles, he is a mere executor, devoid of creativity or autonomy. But since everything depends on Faust, the hero's subjectivity is also the *limit* of the work: whatever is not "inside" him does not belong in his world—which consequently cannot amount to much. Ultimately, Faustus sells his soul in exchange for a few fairground tricks, while the high ambitions of those "whatsoevers" (apart from the vision of Helen) remain a dead letter. If the strong-willed hero does make Faust's *tragedy* extraordinarily vivid, the legend's *epic* potential, on the other hand, is totally thwarted by him.

Very well. And here is Goethe's Faust:

> And what to all of mankind is apportioned
> I mean to savor in my own self's core,
> Grasp with my mind both highest and most low,
> 1770–73

Here, the dramatic will has almost turned back upon itself. Basically, Faust wills not to will: to share the destiny of his species, rather than intervene in it. With respect to Marlowe, the situation is reversed; the tragic potential of the plot is weaker, and its epic potential more powerful. For Faust's words allude precisely to what was of no interest to Marlowe's hero: the genuinely epic immensity—the experience allotted to the whole of mankind—of a universe to be "embraced in one's inner self." We are speaking, of course, of a totality cut in half, unidimensional, where passivity threatens to transform the hero into his exact opposite. But it is nevertheless a totality rediscovered—and at a moment, as we shall see, in which Europe has a great need for breadth of vision. Moreover, this passive hero has a great virtue: remaining extraneous to action, he also remains extraneous *to guilt.* A brief parenthesis, and I shall have more to say about this.

Literary Evolution

An epic with no hero. A *Faust* without Faust, or at any rate with a non-Faustian Faust. But if that were the case, why the compact with the Devil? Is it not precisely Faust's will to act that makes it necessary? And does

Mephistopheles not make his appearance at the very moment in which Faust translates St John's *"logos"* by the word "Deed?"

All true. But the genesis of a figure does not always coincide with its effective function, and there is nothing to prevent us surmising that Mephistopheles—albeit initially created to be Faust's servant, as in Marlowe—actually performs a very different role. Some confirmation of this already comes, in fact, from the first great episode in which Mephistopheles is involved: the seduction of Margarete. Here, when Faust is quite clear about what he wants, no assistance is of any use to him: if he just had a little time, he exclaims soon after meeting the girl.

> If I were granted seven hours,
> I should not need the devil's powers
> To lure a fledgling to my bed.
> 2642–44

When Faust is ready to act, in other words, Mephistopheles is very little use. To be sure, he collects a few jewels and helps Faust to fence: but it is not he who drives the action forward, and Part One could easily do without him. Part One: the "tragic" part. But not Part Two—the "epic" part—in which Mephistopheles moves decidedly to the foreground: he invents paper money, sets the Empire on fire, brings the legends of antiquity back to life, fights a civil war, constructs Holland, flies from one witches' sabbath to another . . .

So let us linger for a moment on this discontinuity between genesis and function. Mephistopheles, as I have just said, was devised for the initial tragic nucleus of *Faust*, but there serves practically no purpose. On the other hand, he fulfils a decisive function in the poem's epic expansion, which did not form part of Goethe's initial plans: the "Prologue in Heaven," "Walpurgis Night" and gradually all the great phantasmagorias of Part Two. Without Mephistopheles, there would be nothing of all this. In other words, there would be no *Faust*, Part Two, and perhaps not the modern epic either. At all events, not *this* modern epic, which started off from *Faust*. So, an entire literary genre became possible (became, finally, imaginable) because Goethe found the character capable of supporting its construction. Yet, *that character had not been created to fulfil that function at all.* What is more, Goethe had him there, ready and available, from the first scenes of the Margarete tragedy. Yet, *it took him a quarter of a century to realize what he could do with him.*

Faust, Part Two, as the result of chance, in other words. And a delayed-action chance, what is more. Strange? Yes. Indeed absurd, if you think that literature is the product of a conscious project. * * * Despite all his plans of work and well-ordered days, the author of *Faust* was not an engineer but a *bricoleur*. Rather than planning an epic poem and rationally preparing the means to achieve it, he chanced to find in his hands—right in the middle of a tragedy—a character with a strong epic potential. And so, after decades of hesitation, he eventually put together an epic poem. With respect to the dominant historiographical models, the relationship between means and ends is precisely reversed: the tools, the concrete technical possibilities, are everything; the project, the ideology, the poetics—nothing. And this, let it be clear, is not a defect. Quite the contrary. Because plans and poetics function (perhaps) when inside a stable formal paradigm: in times of "normal" literature, so to speak. But if paradigms are shifting they are a waste of time, because change is not planned: it is the fruit of the most irresponsible and free—the blindest—rhetorical experimentation. Poetics plod along behind this, often far behind. They certainly do not guide it, and usually do not even really understand it. The most famous invention of the twentieth century—the stream of consciousness—will provide us with a splendid example.

Bricolage as the motor of literary evolution. Mephistopheles as the key to epic *bricolage*. Yet Mephistopheles is there by chance, since Goethe decides without any real dramatic necessity to abandon the familiar wicked counsellor of seduction tragedies * * * and replaces him with the Devil. For years and years, the difference between the two figures seems negligible. Then, all of a sudden, it emerges. Unlike the counsellor, Mephistopheles can do more than one thing: in other words, he is capable of *changing function*. And this is a decisive quality. For literary evolution does not normally proceed by inventing new themes or new methods out of the blue, but precisely by discovering *a new function for those that already exist.* * * *

* * *

Bricolage, then. And refunctionalization. The former is a *macro*-structural concept: it describes how a text functions as a whole. The latter is a *micro*-structural concept: it describes what happens to the elementary components of a work. Yet, in this case, there is a profound need for agreement between micro and macro. Refunctionalization can occur only in an elastic structure, able to absorb novelty without disintegrating. *Bricolage*, for its part, requires versatile "bits," able to add a new function to the original one. It is a circle, in which the parts and the whole presuppose one another and mutually support one another. * * *

* * * And this imperfection, I repeat, is entirely logical: for between *bricolage* and refunctionalization there may well be an admirable agreement—but certainly, by definition, no preordained harmony. If then, as I hope, these two concepts will make literary history more comprehensible and more interesting, they will nevertheless introduce into it also the very concrete possibility of *failure*. Which again makes it more comprehensible, and far more interesting.

Rhetoric of Innocence

Let us return to Faust. And to his first victim: Margarete. Seduced; driven to poison her mother and drown her son; then herself slain, as her brother had already been. Object of an extreme affective ambivalence, wherein love conflicts with impatience at the narrow world's fetters (so that Faust introduces himself to her under the name "Heinrich," which will also—in a stroke of intuitive genius—be her very last word). So there would be nothing strange if Margarete were the "phantasm" par excellence of the Faust story, and returned to haunt him. * * * But although Margarete does indeed return, she does so in the guise of an angel ("Una Poenitentium, once known as Gretchen") and in order to intercede for Faust's salvation. And more generally, although *Faust* is a work literally invaded by phantasms and ghosts, the uncanny, sinister element plays almost no role in it. This is a singular feature, and deserves further examination.

Among the many peculiarities of the composition of *Faust*, there is one that leaps to the eye. The tragedy of Margarete is written straight off, indeed is already complete in 1775. It could and should be the end of the work. But no, the thing seems to condemn Goethe to forced labour— additions, plans, rewritings, alterations—for over half a century, until the very last months of his life. Why on earth such tenacity? Is it perhaps because that very early *Faust* has not been much of a success?

On the contrary. It has turned out only too well, and Goethe wishes precisely to exculpate his hero from the burden of that bygone sin. This is the "de-tragicization of Faust's tragedy." * * * It is a process that begins as early as the "Prologue in Heaven" added in 1799, where Faust's name echoes for the first time when the Lord challenges Mephistopheles to lead him astray: as if to demonstrate that Faust is not master of his own existence, since higher powers contend over—and even bet upon—it. And when we get to the evocation of Mephistopheles, likewise composed in 1799 . . . evocation?—not at all! Faust is piously translating the sacred words of the Gospel "Into the German tongue I hold so dear" (1223), when he finds the Devil in his room—and eventually accepts his company only after two very heated scenes, in which Mephistopheles resorts to wheedling, promises, dazzling quips, professions of humility . . .

In short: Faust makes his compact with the Devil because he is seduced by him. Like Margarete, before Margarete—and actually more than Margarete, since it is the Lord himself who has incited Mephistopheles to tempt him. And can he who has been seduced ever be guilty of seduction?

But that's not all there is, in those two scenes entitled "Study" in which the compact is sealed. To start with, there is another oddity of composition. In the many variants of the Faust legend, one fact always remains constant: the compact with the Devil is the main thing, so it precedes everything else. The first scene with Mephistopheles to be written by Goethe, however, is the one entitled "Dreary Day. A Field" (probably dating from 1772–3), in which Faust curses his companion, blames him for Margarete's fate, and swears to be rid of him: almost as though Goethe wanted first and foremost to emphasize in his own mind the *hostility* between Faust and Mephistopheles, rather than their agreement. The latter is indeed for him the hardest moment in the entire poem: he will succeed in tackling it only after *thirty years* of hesitation, thus finally filling the "great lacuna" of which he writes to Schiller on 6 April 1801. And it takes some doing, even then: for hundreds and hundreds of lines * * * the moment of the compact is curiously delayed by false starts, digressions, postponements and duplications.

Compact? Not even that, but a wager—half agreement, half challenge. Hence, impossible to decide whether Mephistopheles is Faust's ally or his worst adversary: a constitutive duplicity of the work, which allows Faust to unload ultimate responsibility for his own actions on to his wicked companion. This is what Mephistopheles is needed for in *Faust*, Part One. Not to help Faust seduce Margarete, but for the opposite reason: because Faust could actually do everything on his own—and Goethe wants to *avoid* that. Just as he parries Valentine's blows in the nocturnal duel, Mephistopheles shields Faust from the violence of the seduction and, in effect, from all violence. Thanks to him, a strategy is born that will be fundamental for the modern epos, indeed for the whole of Western culture: a strategy of denial and disavowal—a projection of violence outside oneself. Goethe's brilliant and terrible discovery: the rhetoric of innocence.

The mechanism of projection, activated as early as the "Evening" scene—when Faust would like to go, but Mephistopheles makes him leave the jewels in Margarete's room—becomes intensified, of course, once the seduction has occurred. It is the "disgust" for Mephistopheles of "Forest and Cave," the hatred of "Dreary Day. A Field." But Mephistopheles, unruffled, illuminates with well-mannered cynicism the reality of projection: "There, there, I will not grudge you on occasion / The luxuries of innocent evasion" (3297–8). Deep down, the true compact is precisely this: not to "the modest ear blurt out / What modest heart yet cannot do without" (3295–6); to keep well separated the heaven of values and the earth of desires—unsullied ends and unscrupulous means. After the murder of Philemon and Baucis:

> So you have turned deaf ears to me!
> I meant exchange, not robbery.
> This thoughtless violent affair,
> My curse on it, for you to share!
> 11370–73

But Mephistopheles was not deaf: it is just that, in the places and times of *Faust*, "war and trade and piracy" form an "undivided trinity" (11187–8). *Faust* is the poem of primary accumulation, Lukács writes in *Goethe and his Age*: it tells us of "capital running with blood." Quite true, and Mephistopheles is there to take upon himself the curse of that blood. In the counterpoint between him and Faust, there is thus established that blend of truth and lie * * * typical of a West that is proud of its own world dominion, but prefers to overlook the violence sustaining it. * * *

We have seen how Goethe exculpates Faust from the violence exercised upon Margareta. Let us now turn to the female figure at the centre of *Faust*, Part Two. At the start of Act III:

Exalted much and much disparaged, Helena,
I leave behind the strand where first we came ashore
8488–9

Admired, censured: Helena is defined by the judgements of others, closed
upon themselves in the form of a chiasmus. Her present reality is relegated
to the second line * * *. Even her name is detached from the living
person, enclosed between two commas, like something alien: and all this
from Helena's own lips. This really is not a woman, but a thing—of which
Faust will easily take possession. But how will he manage to justify his
conquest, and transform force into right?

In the first place, thanks to a laborious preceding history ("Before the
Palace of Menelaus in Sparta"), in which the Greek king seeks to make
Helen a sacrificial victim. Against this background, the arrival of Faust
takes on a wholly different value. It is no longer an act of conquest, but a
liberation from barbarism: an ideologically very effective reversal, that for
good reason appears in one way or another in all the masterpieces of
colonial imagination. * * *

And there is something else as well. Here is Faust, upon the arrival of
Helena:

In wonderment, o Queen, I see at once
Unerring markswoman, and here her prey;
I see the bow from which the arrow sped
And this one drooping. Arrow follows arrow,
Striking myself. All over and athwart
I sense their wingèd whir in space and keep.
What am I now? You render all at once
Rebellious my most faithful, insecure
My battlements. I come to fear my army
Obeys already her who wins unarmed.
What choice have I but to consign myself,
And all I owned in fancy, unto thee?
9258–69

Here, according to the commentaries, Christian-mediaeval love and pagan-
classical beauty meet. Certainly true * * *. But the courtly love of Faust
serves also to reverse, and thus mask, the real relation of power: to declare
the booty of war, prisoner in the conqueror's castle, a "conquering unconquered lady." The mechanism of projection is now flanked by that of
reversal.

So, an innocent compact. Then, innocent behaviour. Finally, an innocent *desire*. Given that concrete action is Mephistopheles's business,
Faust's wishes take on a quite specific form. "Have it according to your
bent! / Confide to me your crochets' full extent," declares Mephistopheles
in Act IV (10196–7). And Faust: "my eye was lately dwelling . . ."
The * * * construction at once invests his vision with something involuntary. And then:

On the high sea my eye was lately dwelling,
It surged, in towers self upon self upwelling.
[. . .]
Forward it steals, and in a myriad starts,
Sterile itself, sterility imparts;
It swells and grows and rolls, and spans
The noisome vacancy of dismal strands.
There wave on wave imbued with power has heaved,
But to withdraw—and nothing is achieved;
Which drives me near to desperate distress!
Such elemental might unharnessed, purposeless!
There dares my spirit soar past all it knew;
Here I would struggle, this I would subdue.
                              10198–99; 10212–21

A vast, untamable expanse, full of strange creatures and infinite riches, at the disposal of whomsoever can exploit them . . . Beyond its literal meaning, Goethe's sea cannot but remind us of the world outside Europe: its energy incapable of progress relates it to the Hegelian "peoples without history," and justifies conquest of it as a process bestowing meaning. Yet all this still remains in the form *of a metaphor*: present in Faust's words— but also masked by them. To battle the waves, and even consign them to exile (10229 ff.), is certainly no crime. More than a concrete act of conquest, moreover, this is just a seashore reverie: once again, the activity of a "passive" hero. And what harm can it ever do to dream? * * * No, to dream is no crime. It is a wholly innocent activity. Or, perhaps, it is a wholly innocent way of preparing oneself for something else, which is not innocent at all.

"He Sees Visions of Giant Undertakings . . ."

Another of Faust's visions:

> I wish a scaffold to be woven
> From branch to branch, for vistas deep
> Of my achievement's fullest sweep,
> With all-embracing gaze to scan
> The masterpiece of sapient man,
> As he ordains with thoughtful mind
> New homestead for his teeming kind.
>   11244–50

These inspired lines give no hint of it, but within a few moments Faust will command Mephistopheles to "clear from my path" the old couple (Philemon and Baucis) ruining the masterpiece. This is the "splitting" characteristic of bad faith, as I said earlier: and it has been a productive splitting, in which Faust's vision has acquired an extraordinary force and intensity. "With all-embracing gaze to scan / The masterpiece of sapient man": who would not wish to be there at his side? And again:

> To drain this stagnant pool of ills
> Would be the crowning, last achievement.
> [. . .]
> Lush fallow then to man and cattle yields
> Swift crops and comforts from the maiden fields,
> New homesteads near the trusty buttress-face
> Walled by a bold and horny-handed race.
> A land of Eden sheltered here within,
> [. . .]
> Yes—this I hold to with devout insistence.
>
>   11561–73

An inland paradise. Careful, though. This is not a seducer who has repented and whose only thought is now of work. Faust has not repented at all: he has merely shifted his field of action, transforming himself into an *economic* seducer. * * *

To separate work from capitalism, in short: to hide the alien, violent forms work is assuming, and thus save it. This is a true constant of Goethe's work. * * *

The outcome * * * is the very particular form assumed in these works by the notion of "totality": a term which we had encountered in the *Aesthetics*, in Faust's monologue, and in a number of commentaries, but which I then left aside to speak of devils and phantasms, reveries and innocence. Yet I was not changing the subject. For those metaphors are the pillars, and the masks, of the modern totality: they embody its violence—and *hide* its violence. And something similar happens also to the hero. "Universal individual of mankind," Faust has been called: true, and false. False, if this is taken to mean that his person combines within it all that is significant in modern humankind. True, if it means that Goethe put Faust in a position to desire, and obtain, the advantages of an entire world. * * *

                              *   *   *

* * * *Faust* is a kind of Europe in verse, full of ruined castles and pointless conflicts, and literally invaded by the past: characters, places, metres, stories, allegories, phantasms . . .

The present invaded by the past: but is the burden an overwhelming one? And is Goethe's attitude really the "reverent" one of a "descendant"? Certainly not. If anything, *Faust* is an epoch-making work for the opposite reason: because it *lightens* antiquity, and so neutralizes what might threaten the spiritual wellbeing of the modern world. Hardly an unchangeable past:

> In the Classical Walpurgis Night, all the forms of ancient history and myth are released from their traditional positions and transformed in their very essence. It is the de-functionalization of myth . . . the emancipation of the past from the fetters of necessity.

And again:

> If the past must be allowed a form of existence in the present [. . .] then it must abandon the mode of Reality for that of Possibility.

The past as "Archive of the ages, * * * a storehouse of poetical and historical memories" to be manipulated as you please. * * * "Proctophantasmiac"—the parody Enlightenment man of "Walpurgis Night"—is left
to suffer beneath the weight of bygone centuries and assail the "despotism
of spirits." But Faust by no means anathematizes the *altes Volk* of mediaeval illusions: instead, he takes it into his service, and makes it conquer
the land where his industrial empire will arise—just as, at other moments,
he uses the figures of antiquity to entertain the imperial court. Vampires
in reverse, the living feed off the dead, and force the shades of the past to
recite for them. * * * Creation of the new from the past . . . As in
bricolage: old materials, and new treatment. The result is an ambiguous
register, halfway between Fair and archaeology; between satirical reduction
and scholarly seriousness. What is more important here: the "objective"
meaning of the classical figures, fixed by tradition—or their "subjective"
reinterpretation, mediated through the modern hero? "Are these now
dreams," Faust wonders beside the Peneus, "or memories?" (7275).

Dreams or memories? Goethe does not reply, because they are both;
and the first consequence of such interweaving is a drastic devaluation of
the historical sense, culminating in the notorious pastiche of the third act,
when Faust, in the guise of a crusader knight, teaches Helen of Greece
to speak rhymed verse. Freed from their historical positions, figures and
styles from different epochs coexist here, as on the Pharsalian plain, "outside time" (7436). * * * It is the passage * * * from an irreversible sequence emphasizing the "after" to a synchronic arrangement highlight-
ing the "alongside." And thereby it is also an excellent example of that
paradoxical state of affairs * * * called "non-contemporaneity": the fact
that many individuals, albeit living in the same period, from the cultural
or political viewpoint belong to different epochs. "Not all people exist in
the same Now * * * They do so only externally, through the fact that
they can be seen today. But that does not mean they are living at the same
time as each other." * * *
    * * * The man of the future, Homunculus, ends by shattering against
Galatea's mythical shell; the son of Helen and Faust repeats the flight of
Icarus, and plunges to earth with the face of Byron. Economic crises in
the first and fourth acts of Part Two; wars in the third and fourth; fires in
the first, second and fifth; an earthquake during the "Classical Walpurgis
Night," which moreover commemorates the most celebrated civil war of
Antiquity . . .

Criticism has so insisted on the "serenity" of *Faust* Part Two that one
scarcely gives it a second thought: but this is actually the poem of the
"state of exception." And Faust, for his part, finds himself perfectly at ease
in the radical crisis of every established order. Powerful, but not hampered
by the weight of landed estates; always ready to move and to shift his own
interests; remote, yet at the same time close to us. * * * In his very person he embodies the imbalance of non-contemporaneity and exploits it
ruthlessly. He always arrives with Mephistopheles from another epoch,
bearing with him some brilliant invention with which he upsets the normal

course of things, so that he is then needed once again to re-establish order. It is his way of penetrating every place and effectively taking control of it. * * * It is a way of constituting a totality and turning it to his own advantage. * * *

And yet, after first destroying then saving an empire, Faust asks for a ridiculous reward: a strip of salt water, where "the land's not there" (11039). "The most resourceful rose with one accord / And said: He who can give us peace is lord" (10278–9): and the one to make peace is Faust. But Faust renounces the empire. Why?

"So Many Little Independent Worlds"

*   *   *

* * * It is not that the advent of the capitalist world-system makes the Faustian aspiration to world dominance null and void. If anything, the opposite is true: it gives it extra sustenance and scope—and even extra wickedness. But such dominance is no longer conceivable as military conquest pure and simple, and the * * * figure of the "emperor of the world" no longer has any real meaning. That is where the new Faust comes in. One who has nothing of the warrior about him, * * * and who, instead of laying waste the world, prefers to "incorporate it": to insert here and there such limited but highly effective devices as banknotes or a feudal castle, which will tilt the reality of things to his own advantage. Just like the great hegemonic powers of the modern world, moreover, Faust is interested not in a uniform subjection, but in dominance of the sea and the sky, in order to move speedily from one end to the other of this composite system (Greek periphery in Act III, imperial semi-periphery in Act IV, "Dutch" core in Act V).

In this light, the well-known dispute about the unity of Goethe's poem may perhaps be viewed with fresh eyes. All the main scenes of *Faust*, says Eckermann on 13 February 1831,

> are so many little independent worlds, each complete in itself; and although they do impinge upon one another, they scarcely come into any contact. The poet's principal object is to represent a multiform world, and he uses the story of a famous hero merely as a sort of connecting thread upon which to string together whatsoever he pleases.—"You are perfectly correct," Goethe replied . . .

No, perhaps not quite perfectly. The famous hero is something more than a mere thread: and *Faust*, for its part, is the story of how the independence of those "little worlds" is lost. To be sure, the "grand world" is by no means uniform, here. However, it is always *one*. A question of narrative technique will help clarify the matter.

*   *   *

So far I have spoken about the first half of the epic world: the "independent worlds" of Eckermann, the "autonomous parts" of Schiller and Goethe. And the second half? The incorporated, unified world of Faust and Mephistopheles? Perhaps we may turn here to a different theory of the epic form. * * *

* * *

* * * Does this mean that the modern epic remains an ensemble devoid of unity, an archipelago of "independent worlds" like that of Eckermann? No, not necessarily. It merely means that the unity of this form does not lie in a *definitive conclusion*, but in its perennial *ability to begin again*. A unified world is not necessarily a *closed* world: and if *Faust* is made up almost entirely of digressions, that does not mean that it lacks any unitary Action—but that *the digressions have themselves become the main purpose of the epic Action.*

Digressions—indeed, their very proliferation—as substance and purpose of the Action. And why not? Digression * * * is the technique that seeks "to fit the whole world inside a single text": just what is needed for the modern epic. Faust's movement from world to world is *a sign of his power*: it indicates the freedom of movement, the spiritual mobility, the cynicism even, that are necessary in the new world-system. After all, the closed ending * * * was the appropriate conclusion for a territorial empire: for the rectilinear Action of the military campaign, which aims precisely to eradicate any alternative development. But in the case of the world-system, the teleology of this premodern plot is replaced by the perpetual digression of *exploration*: an activity that by no means excludes violence, but that operates in a system with too many variables to obtain definitive results.

There remains a very solid link between epic and power, then—but it no longer takes the form of a goal to be reached, because every goal is now felt as a fetter: a *limitation* of power, rather than a confirmation of it. We can glimpse here what will be the most typical ideology of the twentieth century: ideology as an opening of possibilities, rather than their repression. * * *

World Texts

* * *

The construction of national identity—henceforth required of the novel—is thus replaced, for the epic, by a far larger geographical ambition: a global ambition, of which *Faust* is the unchallenged archetype. The takeoff of the world-system has occurred—and a *symbolic form* has also been found for this new reality. But what technique is to be used to represent the world?

We arrived at non-contemporaneity through a discussion of history: it was necessary to explain the smashing of linear time in *Faust*, Part Two. * * * History has become intertwined with geography. * * * So this is what constitutes "the fundamental experience of progress": transforming synchrony into diachrony; taking geographical facts, neutral in themselves (social forms of a different kind), and arranging them according to an ascending teleology—which will then end by legitimizing the dominion of the "advanced" West over the "backward" periphery. For world texts, which likewise work upon non-contemporaneous phenomena, nothing would be more logical than to share this finalism. * * * But *Faust* is quite another matter. * * * The fact is that, if it is read in teleological terms, it becomes quite incomprehensible. It starts off from the Renaissance of the Imperial Court, then moves from there to the Mothers who exist before and outside time; it goes back to the Renaissance, where French Revolution *assignats* crop up; then it goes back to the Classical Walpurgis Night, on the anniversary of Pharsalus; farther back—between Homer and the tragedians—with the "Helena" Act; forward to the Crusades; back to Arcadia; two millennia forward in the vision of Byron, then again to the Renaissance; the ghosts of mediaeval wars are evoked; it moves forward to Holland, and then to the industrial visions of the dying Faust; and ends in a Marian-Catholic atmosphere, between Middle Ages and Counter-Reformation.

This is a sequence which—as a sequence—has no meaning. Rather than a teleological development, Goethe has constructed a zigzag that leaps from one epoch to another without any consistency; and as for the destination of the whole, the "Mountain Gorges" scene still awaits a defender adequate to the task. In Part Two, history cannot be taken literally, as history: for it to have any meaning, it must be interpreted as a great rhetorical figure. It must stand for something else. * * *

The ideology of progress, as we have seen, privileges *non-contemporaneity* of the contemporaneous: the "Alongside" becomes a "Before-and-After," and geography is rewritten as history. Well, for the modern epic the opposite is true: *contemporaneity* of the non-contemporaneous moves into the foreground: the "Before-and-After" is transformed into an "Alongside"—and history thus becomes a gigantic *metaphor for geography*. The treasures with which Mephistopheles sets the great machine of Part Two in motion * * * are "a German substitute for colonial resources: derived not from the distance of adventure, but from the depths of the past"; in the early nineteenth century, * * * "the ancient, the distant and the popular were all equated." In this metaphorical field, which seems to unite more or less the whole of European culture, the shifting back and forth in time of Faust and Mephistopheles loses its senselessness: if we replace the "ancient" by the "distant," the zigzag then turns into a series of geographical expeditions, where arrival in far-off epochs recounts (and masks) landing on distant shores. And as for Goethe's games with the past, or those legendary personages who end up "working" for Faust—they too are metaphors: for playing with the world, and for a concrete power over real persons in the present. And since every metaphor always involves an emotive aspect, a value judgement, let us add: once again, they are metaphors *of innocence*, which present the power of the West as something fundamentally innocuous. Doing violence to the past, when all is said and done, is of no importance. You cannot harm a phantasm.

* * *

Rhetoric of innocence: history as metaphor for geography. I have spoken of these constructions stressing their social utility: their ideological function. But what kind of ideologies are these? Who has ever heard of them? No one, I think, *and that is why they are interesting*. For, in the great concert of ideology, literature has *its own* arias: fresh, unrepeatable—not "foreseen" by the surrounding ideologies. The epic form comes close, for example, to the ideology of progress, and even works with the same ingredients; yet it does not give us an "epic of progress": * * * a society does not normally have any need for duplicates. Once a thing has been said in one language, there is no interest in repeating it wholesale in another language (even supposing—which I do not admit, incidentally—that this would be possible).

"Unforeseen" ideologies, then. And unforeseen for a very simple reason: because they are born not as *ideologies*, but as *rhetorical experiments*. Mephistopheles permits symbolic moves of immense importance: yet, as we have seen, his own origin is accidental, and it is only by manoeuvring his figure more or less at random that the rhetoric of innocence takes shape, without any conscious project. And the same thing is repeated with non-contemporaneity. In a first moment, Goethe is merely coming to grips with the epic form: hence, as its conventions require, he makes Faust advance into the great world of the past. Here a second stage begins (likewise fundamentally rhetorical), in which Goethe starts to play with the relationship between past, present and future, thus creating those strange scenes in which different epochs meet and mingle. And finally there is a third stage, in which this work of *bricolage* shows that it can confront (and camouflage) a historical experience of immense importance: the new world dominance of the West. The form has constructed its own ideology—and a very effective one. But all this is the result of a purely formal dynamic. It was not the primary object of Goethe's work, and rhetoric met history only at the end of the process.

But does it really make much difference whether ideology precedes rhetoric or follows it? It makes an enormous difference. For, in the former case, ideology might guide form to the desired end; not so in the latter, since it comes up against the rigidity of ready-made rhetorical choices. This is why literary ideology is always somewhat askew in relation to others: because it rests upon a jumble of fortuitous experiments, rhetorical fetters and unpredictable turns. Sometimes this way of doing things actually functions better than conscious discourse: it produces Mephistopheles, and the perverse, unsurpassed intelligence of Goethean innocence. At other times, however, the chain of formal choices imposes trappings that are perhaps too cumbersome. To stay with *Faust*, this is what happens with non-contemporaneity—where classical mythology involves perhaps too many scholastic ingredients to have a really widespread effectiveness. * * *

"An Incredible Musical Pandemonium"

* * *

* * * The polyphonic form of the modern West is not the novel, but if anything precisely the epic: which specializes in the heterogeneous space of the world-system, and must learn to provide a stage for its many different voices. Already in *Faust*, in fact, polyphony is the style of the "grand" world, whose otherness it signals vis-à-vis the "little" one (though "narrow" would perhaps be more accurate) in which Margarete lives. Here, as the girl's first words suggest—"I'm neither fair nor lady" (2607)—the purest monologism holds sway: things and persons have a single, immutable name. But along comes Faust, and the semantic rigidity of the narrow world is undermined: for his seduction consists largely in persuading Margarete to listen to "the turn of phrase . . . different" from that of the priest, and to accept that "it's what all hearts proclaim, / All places in the light of heaven's day, / Each in its language" ("Gretchen's Chamber," 3462–4). It is a coaxing, artful polyphony, which becomes wholly sinister in the "Cathedral" scene, where the Evil Spirit's laughter mingles with the grim Latin chorus of the *Dies Irae* and with the desperate prayer of Margarete herself. The time is past when her thoughts were all bound up in a "little worn prayer-book" (*Büchelchen*, 3779: the diminutive of a diminutive, for a tiny, little world). Faust has taught her many other words, and many thoughts. But it is a poisoned gift:

> Oh! Oh!
> Would I were rid of thoughts
> That course my mind along, athwart,
> To spite me!   3794–7

* * * The "Dungeon" scene, when madness multiplies Margarete's "voices" and takes her to the gallows, is the fitting complement for this black-magic polyphony. And yet, Goethe suggests, that very same power that acts with devastating violence in a confined world can play quite another role in a wider space. In the crowd scenes in *Faust*, Part Two, polyphony no longer has anything sinister about it: it is an index of creativity, of euphoria. Each new voice is a new presence: autonomous, self-aware, clearly delineated. Voices of today, and of antiquity; real, and imaginary; sacred, and profane; alone, in groups, in chorus. . . .

But where are all these voices to be put? And even before that, indeed, how is their sudden appearance to be explained? The poem's chronology gives the answer: by the "Walpurgis Night." The first polyphonic scene to be composed by Goethe—and fortuitously so, no doubt, because of its obvious links with the Faust story. A fortuitous choice. Indeed, a dubious digression ("vulgar diversions", in Faust's own words) from the tremendous crescendo of Margarete's tragedy. But the digression works, and chance is transformed into necessity. The "Walpurgis Night" is *selected*, and becomes the model for all the polyphonic scenes in Part Two. * * *

Voices that talk and talk without paying any attention to one another, as almost everywhere in *Faust*, Part Two. * * *

In short, polyphony as cacophony. A defect? No. For, as I have already said, the choice of the witches' sabbath *works*: it is repeated from one work to another, because it resolves—albeit in a rather odd way—a decisive problem for the modern epic form. The fact is that Goethe and the others, needing to represent the take-off of the capitalist world-system, are in search of what we might call * * * "world effects": devices that give the reader the impression of being truly in the presence of the world; that make the *text* look like the world—open, heterogeneous, incomplete. The Babel of the witches' sabbath is not, of course, the only possible solution to the problem. In the modernist epoch, for example, many others will emerge—from collage to free verse, from the emancipation of dissonance to metonymic drift. But meanwhile the witches' sabbath was there, and it worked, because a tumult of discordant voices always suggests a large, crowded space. Never mind if the scene appears chaotic and maybe a bit incomprehensible. In the expanding universe of modernity, many things are as yet unclear; and it is necessary to learn to live with noise: to represent it—and, indeed, hear it—without too many embellishments.

So, then: thirty-odd different voices in the first "Walpurgis Night"; another thirty in the "Dream"; and forty in the "Classical Night." Polyphony, to be sure: a world effect. But *where* to put them, all these voices? On Sunday, 20 December 1829, talking to Eckermann about the allegorical masquerade (forty-odd different voices here too), Goethe observes that you would need "a theatre so large as to be almost unimaginable." * * * And indeed, among all the reasons why *Faust*, Part Two is "unperformable," there is certainly also the fact that the confined space of the stage is incompatible with the expansive movement of an action seeking to give voice to an entire world. * * *

* * * Goethe finds himself confronted by a completely new world order, and he tries to grapple with it by constructing a symbolic form capable of representing its essence. If the technical means at his disposal reach only so far, fine!—it will be a partial solution, imperfect as usual. And the polyphony of the witches' sabbath is precisely that. A great discovery, but a far from definitive one. So long as you read it, it works. But if you try to stage it, * * * then it becomes a "museum curiosity": "all the harder," moreover, "if imaginary forms are to be represented which have a voice but no body [. . .] What will happen in the case of the spirits?"

* * * Eckermann and Goethe had been on the wrong track: the masquerade did not require immense stages crammed full of yelling extras. It did not need *more* space, but a parallel space. Like that of radio, in fact —or even * * * that of the stream of consciousness. But in the meantime? Between the prophetic magic of *Faust* and twentieth-century technology, how to imagine a space for polyphony? And where to locate it?

First and foremost, far away from the nation-states situated in the core of the world-system, which are becoming ever more homogeneous, hence ever less polyphonic. * * *

*   *   *

"With All the Certainty of a Mechanical Process"

There is a short exchange near the beginning of *Faust*, whose thrust and counterthrust sum up the difficulties of the encyclopaedic ambition in the modern world. To Faust, who would like to "savor in my own self's core, / what to all of mankind is apportioned," Mephistopheles replies, with a sneer, that between the individual and the species there now exists an unbridgable gulf. Better drop it, dear " 'Sir Microcosm' ": "the whole / Is made but for a god's delight!" (1771, 1770, 1802, 1780–1). A god, a superman, a being above ordinary mankind? Quite the contrary, * * * to recover a relation to totality, superficiality is the answer—credulity, silliness. Encyclopaedic rhymes with idiotic.

*   *   *

Allegory and Modernity

"Anyone who has not looked about a bit, and had a few experiences, will get nothing out of *Faust*, Part Two": thus Goethe to Eckermann on 17 February 1831—and, to judge by the misunderstandings that accompanied the poem's reception, it was a truly prophetic comment. But it was also something of a self-fulfilling prophecy, since the difficulties of *Faust* depend only to a small degree upon the reader's experiences, and to a much greater extent upon Goethe himself, who opted here for a decidedly allegorical structure.

Now, allegory is a specific rhetorical figure, which poses a problem of comprehension quite similar to that of the linguistic sign as such. For, in both cases, we have a two-sided linguistic entity (for the sign, signifier/ signified; for allegory, literal meaning/allegorical meaning), and a wholly conventional relation between the two levels. * * *

* * * And it is precisely this conventional nature of the allegorical sign that provides the point of departure for one of the most celebrated controversies of modern aesthetics: the clash—particularly sharp precisely in Goethe's day—between allegory and symbol. Being conventional, allegory gradually acquires a whole series of pejorative connotations. It is an artificial figure, mechanical, dead. Its instrumental use of the literal meaning (reduced to a mere signifier of the second level of meaning) is seen as a humiliation of sensuous reality—and thus of the aesthetic sphere itself— to the benefit of a somewhat pedantic abstraction. And finally (an offence that effectively says it all) allegory is a tendentially denotative, or univocal, form: reducing the semantic plurality of literature, it leaves us with the poverty of a single authorized meaning.

* * * The twentieth century has decisively revoked the condemnation of allegory, and indeed seen in this figure the sign of a particular self-awareness of modern literature. * * * Not only is allegory manifestly the keystone of *Faust*, Part Two—it is rightly so. The fact that Goethe renounced his own theoretical convictions (favouring the symbol) is a sign

of his historical intelligence: of his having understood that allegory is *the poetic figure of modernity*. And, more precisely, of *capitalist* modernity.

At the end of the first Act, * * * the paper money episode underlines the semiotic nature (conventional: allegorical) that the new form of wealth will have. * * * Between the inner form of allegory and Marx's analysis of the commodity * * * there is a clear structural parallelism. Like the commodity, allegory humanizes things (making them move and speak), and it reifies human beings. In both cases, furthermore, an abstract reality (exchange value, allegorical meaning) subordinates and almost hides the concrete reality of use value and literal meaning. And then, of course, there are the "ghosts" and "social hieroglyphics" of the first volume of *Capital*; the "secrets," the "magic," the "fetishes," the "sensuous things transcending sensuousness" . . .

* * *

* * * The image of an economist brought up on Goethe (and on Hegel, who in the matter of allegory sees things exactly like Goethe), just getting ready to draft the preliminary exposition of his theory: a philosophical and also somewhat literary exposition, in which he wishes to highlight the enigmatic and inhuman features of the new social relations. Nothing odd, then, about his search for a guiding image to express his position effectively. Nor anything odd about his finding it in the semantic field "overturning of the sensuous world," which—for German aesthetics—characterizes allegory: a field that is "available" * * * and that is already oriented in a polemical direction.

* * * The construction of an aesthetic form consonant with new social relations is a long and rocky process, where cultural heritages of all kinds come into play and the most absurd attempts gain a footing. That Goethe should find—immediately—the form *perfectly* appropriate for capitalist reality is something so odd as to appear frankly unbelievable. Perfection ill becomes history—and it becomes materialism even less well. If we value both, then whenever we meet something resembling perfection, it is more reasonable to think of an *imitation* (conscious or otherwise) than of an autonomous process of duplication in different spheres.

If this is true, then * * * allegory becomes the *explicans* of an *explicandum* that, of course, is not the existence of commodities, but the polemical and paradoxical formulations of the early chapters of *Capital*. * * * For Marx, for example, commodities can be exchanged because they are qualitatively different, and quantitatively equal: in the semantic field, however, there is no way of reproducing the distinction between quantity and quality. Again, for Marx, the equivalence between commodities rests upon the equal quantities of labour embodied in them: but, once more, the idea of embodied labour has no meaning in the realm of allegory. And if this falls, the labour theory of value falls too, as does that of the fetishism of commodities. In other words, the whole of Marx's theory (whether right or wrong) collapses, and only analogies of formulation remain.

To find a link between allegory and modernity, therefore, we shall have to change course. And we may as well confront the main difficulty of the undertaking at once.

"You, I Think, Should Know Us All"

* * * The same thing happens with allegory as with any linguistic sign—and, more precisely, as with the words of a foreign language. At first, they are utterly incomprehensible; then, once the code is found, they become perfectly clear. * * *

A clear counterposition, therefore, between ignorance and certainty. Whether this is then seen as the death of art, or as a lucid acknowledgement of its conventional nature, it is how things are for allegory. But is it how they are for *Faust*, too? Hardly. Instead of presenting us with the clear alternative of darkness or clarity, the poem is situated in a kind of no-man's-land, where figurative meanings pile up on one another with no further control. There occurs here, on a large scale, what happens in concentrated form in the allegorical masquerade of the "Spacious Hall" scene. In principle, as the various figures successively make their entrances, a Herald explains their meaning. Indeed, he is there to re-emphasize that allegory requires an official explanation, from the person who knows the code: "Who now approach, you will not recognize" (5345); "A mystery—but I reveal its sense" (5398).

Everything seems to be proceeding as it ought. At a certain point, however, the Herald's explanatory abilities fail:

> Yet I fear that ghostly raiders
> Through the windows might invade us,
> And from spooks and spells that bait you
> I could never liberate you.
> If the dwarf was suspect-seeming,
> Yonder, look! a mighty streaming.
> Of the figures there, my station
> Calls for due interpretation.
> But what passes comprehension,
> Explanation also passes,
> Help you all my good intention!—
> 5500–5509

* * * The person responsible for such perplexity, the Boy Charioteer, challenges the Herald:

> Herald, up, as you are bound,
> And before afar we flee,
> Name us here, describe and show us;
> We are allegories, see,
> And as such you ought to know us.
> 5528–32

Yet—nothing. The Herald tries to follow an indirect route ("I could not tell your name by sight; / But to describe you—that I might": 5533–4), but it is completely useless: between literal meaning and allegorical meaning, as we know, there is a purely conventional connection, and the description of the one offers no indication as to the content of the other. In the Boy Charioteer's scornful conclusion:

> How to announce the masks, you know, I gather,
> Their inwardness to fathom, though, is rather
> Beyond the herald's courtly sphere;
> Acuter sight is needed here.
>
> 5606–9

* * * The most programmatically allegorical scene in *Faust* opens in a climate of total faith in the univocal interpretation—and ends in the most total perplexity. And indeed, what happens when an allegory fails to be understood?

*   *   *

A chain reaction of subjective interpretations. * * *

A varying allegory: not univocal at all, but *polysemous*. It is a paradoxical situation in which allegory seems, as it were, to have betrayed its own mission. And if there are some who decide to drop hermeneutics and abandon themselves contentedly "to the pictorial moment of poetry [. . .] this ineffably rich, many-coloured and sensuous ornament," the most widespread reaction nevertheless is different. In a mixture of bewilderment and admiration, it is recognized that the polysemy of *Faust* will end up generating * * * an ever more endless army of exegetes. * * * And yet, how shall I put it, *misunderstandings suit Faust:* instead of weakening its effectiveness, they have surrounded it with a vast semantic aura, making it into a truly unique work in Western literature. For this is precisely Goethe's great invention: to have constructed, in *Faust*, Part Two, *a mechanism that allows readers to make mistakes.* * * *

The Sign Run Amok

In *Faust*, allegory is a message coming from antiquity; from the world of shadows. * * *

*   *   *

* * * In Goethe, indeed, the old allegorical decoding of the Herald breaks down precisely when it comes to Pluto, god of wealth. Spectacular wealth, at first: necklaces, jewels, precious stones. Then wealth as gold. Finally—though the transitions are all very swift—wealth as paper money. It is a whirl of signs and metamorphoses, which the Herald does not understand; and which in the late-feudal world of the Empire, as is to be expected, produces conflict and disintegration. But in the central thread of the plot, wealth waiting to be invested becomes instead a creative power: it drives "fancy" to "its highest flight," Faust explains to the Emperor, and places "trust unbounded in this boundlessness" (6115, 6118). And shortly afterwards, turning to Mephistopheles:

You failed, my friend, to see the hitch
In all the hoaxes you were using.
First we arranged to make him rich,
Now we're expected to amuse him.

6189–92

* * * Is it the whim of a sovereign, who has at last a bit of money to spend? Yes, but the whim is called Helen of Greece—and will take Faust to the Mothers, to the "Classical Walpurgis Night," to Helena, to Euphorion . . . Would the boundless machinery of *Faust*, Part Two, ever have started, without those first banknotes?

"But Infinite Forms Do Not Exist . . ."

So, the more redundant literature was, for the purposes of social cohesion, the freer its form, and its interpretation, became. The sacred text declined: the book that had to keep society united, and that therefore demanded a univocal interpretation. The world text was born: which had no "political" responsibilities, and which therefore allowed multiple readings. To be sure, literature had for some time been sliding towards the periphery of the cultural system. But the *Wirkungsgeschichte* of *Faust*—in which the work's exceptional prestige has been accompanied by the most improbable elucubrations—gives the change a flavour of inevitability. * * * Everyone will find a different truth in the poem—*and they will all be valid*. And this pulverization of the world text's audience will be my point of departure for a few provisional conclusions.

The first scene of *Faust*, Part One, the "Prelude on the Stage," is almost entirely devoted to a discussion between the Poet and the Director on the nature of the modern audience. "Invoke me not the motley crowd unsteady," the Poet exclaims, "Whose very aspect puts the mind to flight!" (59–60). The mass audience, pushing and shoving in front of the box-office in an "unruly flood," is the exact opposite of his art: a jumble of casual impulses, whereas the latter is unity—a "harmonious whole" that "engulfs the world and draws it back into his soul." The Director listens, but then tries to play it all down:

You give the audience a solid eyeful,
So they can gasp and marvel all the time,
You'll grip them by sheer quantity of trifle,
Your popularity will climb.
Mass calls for mass in order to be won,
Each ends up choosing something for his own;
Who brings a lot, brings bits for everyone,
And they will all be happy going home.
You stage a piece—serve it in pieces, do!
Why, it's a snap to make this kind of stew;
It's served as fast as cooked up in your head.
What use is it to bring your whole instead,
The public shreds it anyway for you.

91–103

The Poet, of course, cannot accept such advice. And in this, as in his general attitude towards the mob, he is quite close to the voice that speaks in the "Dedication" to *Faust*—hence, people usually add, to Goethe himself. No doubt. However, the Goethe who writes *Faust* is in agreement with the Director. Read those suggestions again: many things, and amazing ones; varied registers for differing tastes; an episodic structure, where everyone will find something for themselves; a work that cannot be an organic whole, and that even the most scrupulous of directors is indeed obliged to break into pieces . . .

Was it an ironic way of preparing us for Part Two, to have it announced by a small capitalist of letters? A delightful, but implausible, hypothesis. In 1798, when he is drafting the "Prelude on the Stage", Goethe has no inkling of what is going to happen to *Faust*. So it is far more likely that the Director is there to give expression to that tendency towards social atomization which, from the French Revolution on, has constituted one of Goethe's major preoccupations. Yet the fact remains that the author of *Faust*, Part Two, does follow this seemingly contemptible advice. So what has happened?

What has happened is what we have now encountered more than once in the course of our analysis: the basic components of the modern epic do not emerge as *desirable innovations*, but as *problems to be solved*. The all-encompassing hero makes his appearance as an idle chatterer; polyphony as an infernal din; the episodic plot as a collapse of action; allegory as an incomprehensible legacy of the past. And now the overall structure of *Faust* is heralded in a poetics of mercantile inspiration, which emphasizes its mechanical nature. As I have said more than once, these are the visible traces of literary evolution: the signs of a constrained historical process, which must accept such materials as come to hand, and try to turn them to the best possible advantage. And there is also the evil star of an inherited form, which clings to an existence at variance with its times, and finds itself working in singularly adverse conditions. The entire structure of the world text, indeed, is an excellent example of a difficulty that two centuries of work have not yet managed wholly to overcome.

Let us return for a moment to the "Prelude in the Theatre." On one side, the Poet: spokesman of the work as *"ein Ganzes,"* a unitary whole. On the other, the Director: advocate of the work *"in Stücken,"* in pieces. Organic form against mechanical construction, as people begin to say between the eighteenth and nineteenth centuries. And *Faust* * * *, as it proceeds, tilts ever more clearly towards the mechanical. The initial impulse withers and dies; the new parts are added without being connected to one another. At the thematic level, the natural element fades away, and the stage is thronged with dead, artificial, museum forms. Figures * * * of Civilization. * * *

* * *

A form that may be cut at will. Above all, one that may be *added to* at will. To which may be added a section experimenting with polyphony;

then another about money and allegory; and yet another on the growth of the world-system . . . . "Give them more—give them excess," said the Director in the "Prelude." * * * "The principle of composition most truly epic in character is that of simple addition. On a small as well as on a large scale, epic brings independent elements together." * * * A form in continuous growth: one "that wouldn't exclude something merely because it didn't fit." * * * A form "distending itself for centuries, like pythons swallowing sheep," * * * and thus becoming the "incommensurable whole" of which Goethe speaks a year before his death. All definitions dictated by pride in a form that dares to contend in breadth with the entire world. * * *

FRIEDRICH A. KITTLER

[Faust and Discourse Networks]†

German Poetry begins with a sigh.

> I have pursued, alas, philosophy,
> Jurisprudence, and medicine,
> And, help me God, theology,
> With fervent zeal through thick and thin.
>   (354–7)

If this is not the sigh of a nameless self—no self appears in the sentence —it is certainly not the sigh of any known author. What moves through the cadence of old German *Knittel*-verse is a pure soul. The verses of the other German Classical Poet confirm this: the sigh "oh!" [*ach!*] is the sign of the unique entity (the soul) that, if it were to utter another signifier or (because signifiers exist only in the plural) any signifier whatsoever, would immediately become its own sigh of self-lament; for then it would have ceased to be soul and would have become "Language" instead. * * * Where speaking takes place, there the Other of the soul begins: academic titles and pedagogical deceit.

> And, here, poor fool, I stand once more,
> No wiser than I was before.
> They call me Magister, Doctor, no less,
> And for some ten years, I would guess,
> Through ups and downs and tos and fros
> I have led my pupils by the nose—
>   (358–63)

Thus the university discourse of all four faculties brings forth the sigh —in the historical formation known as the *res publica litteraria*. The Republic of Scholars systematically prevents the fortunate occurrence that a living Spirit could manifest itself to another Spirit. It unilaterally instructs

† From "The Scholar's Tragedy: Prelude in the Theater," *Discourse Networks 1800/1900*, trans. Michael Metteer, with Chris Cullens (Stanford: Stanford UP, 1990), 3–24. The author's footnotes have been omitted. His quotations from *Faust* have been replaced with Arndt's translation.

all its members—these "doctors, and teachers, and scribes, and Christers" (or, more exactly, physicians, philosophers, jurists, and theologians) to go "rummaging in phrases," for as long as life or reading lasts, in a heap of books "gnawed by worms, covered with dust" ("Doktoren, Magister, Schreiber und Pfaffen," 367; "in Worten kramen," 385; "Den Würme nagen, Staub bedeckt," 403). Faust, M.A.—indeed, Ph.D. to boot—sits in a library without new acquisitions, reads, makes extracts, and writes commentaries, in order then to dictate to his students in lecture what old books have dictated to him. The Republic of Scholars is endless circulation, a discourse network without producers or consumers, which simply heaves words around. Faust's raid on his stacks locates no one who could be the writer, creator, or author of a book—no one, then, who could understand, digest, or process any of these books. In a word: the old Republic of Scholars cheats Man of Man.

German Poetry thus begins with the Faustian experiment of trying to insert Man into the empty slots of an obsolete discourse network.

The first test in the series introduces into the anonymous junk heap of books the product of an author with a name.

> Full-armed with that mysterious script
> Which Nostradamus' wisdom yields,
> Why ask for more companionship?
> In Nature's proper school enrolled,
> You learn the course of stars and moons,
> Then will your power of soul unfold
> How spirit with its like communes.
> In vain to hope reflection dry
> Could make the sacred tokens clear—
> You spirits, you who float nearby,
> Give me an answer, if you hear!
> (419–29)

To take a book by an author—his autograph manuscript, moreover—out of the dusty pile is to put a stop to the endless circulation of words. Among the copies of copies that fill the libraries of scholars, the author Nostradamus (who, not accidentally, is also a magician) manifests himself in the inimitable character of his manuscript. His imaginary presence makes scholarly brooding on signs as superfluous as the voice does writing. Everything takes its course as if his book were no longer a book. Described or designated signs are supposed to be able to hear the reader, and thus a virtual orality emerges. [The] impossible happens: a Spirit manifests itself to another * * * or (as Faust says) speaks. Insofar as impossibility never ceases not to write itself, this invocation of Nostradamus, through which something ceases not to write itself in order to assume instead the name of Spirit or Soul, is the contingency that since then has been called German classical literature.

If only the author Nostradamus had not written. "Was it a god that fashioned this design?" ("War es ein Gott, der diese Zeichen schrieb," 434) is Faust's first ecstatic question as he glimpses the symbol of the macrocosmos among the magic ideograms. But this supposed god—a magnified image of the authorship—manifests himself only for an instant, in the apprehension of his act of writing. Once what has been written has been seen and is known, authors withdraw behind their signs like God behind his Creation. The signs lead the reader, to whom they designate pure "creative Nature" ("Die wirkende Natur," 441) away from the producer to the product. Consequently, the macrocosmos ideogram represents how "all one common weft contrives" ("Wie alles sich zum Ganzen webt," 447) and thus how the designated cosmos has the texture of the sign that designates it. In this "continuum of representation and being," this "being as expressed in the presence of representation," there is no absence and no gap except that the divine act of writing and creating is lacking. Hence Faust the interpreter of signs is once more robbed of what his experiment meant to introduce into the configuration of early modern knowledge: Man standing behind and above all bookish rubbish. With a return of the primordial sigh, a failed experiment breaks off. "What glorious show! Yet but a show, alas!" ("Welch Schauspiel! Aber, ach, ein Schauspiel nur!" 454).

The second test takes the opposite path: the consuming reader, rather than a productive author, is introduced as Man into the heap of books. For once, Faust does not just glimpse and gaze at signs. The first unperformable stage direction in European theatrical history declares that "he seizes the book and mysteriously pronounces the sign of the spirit" (at 481). "Mysteriously" indeed. This event, speaking out loud, is possible for books composed of letters, but not for a collection of magic ideograms, especially when the ideograms combine unsayable figures and equally unsayable Hebrew letters. Magical signs exist to be copied under the midnight moon, not to be spoken out loud. But the Faustian experiment consists in turning the semiological treasury of signifiers into the oral reserves of a reader.

Therefore the designated Earth Spirit becomes a voice, which calls both itself and Faust voices as well:

> With bated breath you yearn to meet me,
> To hear my voice, to gaze upon my face;
> [. . .]
> Where is the Faust whose voice rang out to me [. . .]?
> (486–87, 494)

One who has become a vocalizing reader, and hence breath, also experiences written signs as the breath of a mouth. Where the Republic of Scholars knew only pre-given externalities, a virtual and supplementary sensuality emerges. Faust no longer transforms the sign of a sign into the representation of an absent author (as in the case of the macrocosmos) but into its effect on him, the reader.

> Not so this sign affects my soul, not so!
> You, Spirit of the Earth, are nigher,
> I sense my powers rising higher,

Already with new wine I am aglow,
[. . .]
I feel you float about me, spirit I adjured.
(460–63, 475)

It is no longer a question of the author's sacred power to create signs, but rather of the magic power of signs to liberate sensual and intoxicating powers in the reader once the signs have disappeared into the fluid medium of their signified—a voice. The chain of these forces climaxes in a moment of consumption: the reader Faust, whose mouth can drink signs-become-oral like young wine, replaces the author Nostradamus. This fulfills his wish no longer to experience mere spectacles but rather by an act of reading to suck on "breasts" or "all life's sources twain" ("Quellen alles Lebens," 456)—an elementary and infantile form of consumption.

But one cannot invoke the Mother by her metaphors with impunity. Faust's drinking of signs is an ecstasy and production that exceeds his powers. Instead of remaining master of the conjured sign, the reader disappears into the weave or textum of the signified. The Earth Spirit, who weaves "at Time's scurrying loom" ("am sausenden Webstuhl der Zeit," 508) literally on the text of history, reduces Faust again to nothingness.

These two failed experiments delimit the borders within which the third takes place. The third test concerns neither the production of a foreign author, who disappears behind the representative signs, nor the consumption of signs to the point of intoxication, then drowning in the inexhaustible text. Faust gives up wanting to liquefy archaic ideograms with his alphabetical orality. First, he opens a book composed of quite ordinary Greek letters, which has always been there to be read. The book has authors with names, but Faust does not name them. Furthermore, the book has a reader, Faust himself, but this reader remains forgotten and is bypassed because he is involved only as Man. The third test puts in the place of the productive author and the consuming reader a single authority, which thus represents the enthroning of Man. A new return of the primordial sign finally leads to success.

But oh! though my resolve grows even stronger,
I feel contentment welling from my soul no longer.
Yet why must the flood so soon run dry,
And we be left again in thirst to lie?
I have had proof of it in such full measure.
Still, for this lack there's compensation:
The supernatural we learn to treasure,
We come to long for revelation,
Which nowhere burns so finely, so unflawed,
As in the Gospel of our Lord.
I feel an urge to reach
For the original, the sacred text, appealing
To simple honesty of feeling
To render it in my dear German speech.
(1210–23)

This feasible job is the continuation and translation of an unquenchable longing. Faust opens the Bible in order to overcome a shortcoming, which always drove him "Alas—[to know] life's springs" ("Ach, nach des Lebens Quelle," 1201) in order to slake a thirst—and which after two failed tests makes even the poisonous brown juice of the phiole look good. But in the meantime he has grown more modest. Gratification no longer needs to stream into that lack from the unique Source but rather from a text, which substitutes for it. Instead of the absolute and fatal consumption of the Earth Spirit, which is the essence of life itself, or of the phiole, which is termed the essence of all blissfully intoxicating juices, he consumes a surrogate. In its verbal form, to be sure, the surrogate has the value of an original, its opposite; but it remains a surrogate, because even the Primary Text is a text like all others in the heap of books. For once, Faust seems not to transgress the limits and restrictions of the university discourse; he translates "the source of life" in good humanistic fashion as bibliophile *ad fontes* and takes a book as a voice of nature. But this limitation assures that the third test will be successful. German Poetry does not begin with the magic testing of unalphabetical signs, nor does it renounce the themes and texts that were stored in the great archive of the Republic of Scholars; it merely gives up the manner of dealing with texts prescribed in that Republic. Faust translates, like innumerable scholars before and after him, from papers handed down from antiquity. The fact that he does not write Latin does not yet speak against "the proper guild-scholarly character of his historical world." What turns the ex-M.A. into an anachronism and hence into the founding hero of an incipient, a transcendental Knowledge, is something else. Translation becomes hermeneutics.

> "In the beginning was the Word"—thus runs the text.
> Who helps me on? Already I'm perplexed!
> I cannot grant the word such sovereign merit,
> I must translate it in a different way
> If I'm indeed illumined by the Spirit.
> "In the beginning was the Sense." But stay!
> Reflect on this first sentence well and truly
> Lest the light pen be hurrying unduly!
> Is sense in fact all action's spur and source?
> It should read: "In the beginning was the Force!"
> Yet as I write it down, some warning sense
> Alerts me that it, too, will give offense.
> The spirit speaks! And lo, the way is freed,
> I calmly write: "In the beginning was the Deed!"
>   (1224–37)

Saying (in words) that he cannot possibly value words or even (as the secret eavesdropper of this private conversation will paraphrase it) "one so down on the word" (1327; "das Wort so sehr verachtet," 1328) Faust takes his exit from the Republic of Scholars. The rules decreed by Humanism and the Reformation for dealing with books were becoming obsolete. Humanism proceeded as philological activity, and philology means love of the word. Luther's belief in and translation of the Bible were obedient to the rule of *sola scriptura* and meant in a quite practical sense that students in the catechumenical schools that arose along with the Reformation had to be able to learn sacred texts by heart and "recount" them "word for word." If the Primary Text were, for example, the Decalogue, then the *Little Catechism* (in contradistinction to the later *Analytical*) programmed a learning by heart not only of that law but also—although with the question "What is that?" it was supposed to mediate between law and persons—of Luther's explanations. Incontrovertible word sounds as reduplication of an incontrovertible wording—that was true scriptural faith.

"Someone has been found who all day long speaks only the words: 'The Bible is in my head, my head is in the Bible.'" No words could better express the early modern order of words. But in 1778, the year they were recorded, their speaker was in an insane asylum. Two hundred years of inscribed faithfulness to Scripture suddenly sounded pathological to the new sciences of man. There was now every reason to exchange the wording for what should have been written if the translator had had his way. Faust's Germanicization of a sacred original solely on the basis of sincere feeling is an epistemological break. "The slightest alteration in the relation between man and the signifier, in this case in the procedures of exegesis, changes the whole course of history by modifying the moorings that anchor his being."

The beginning of the Gospel according to Saint John is a unique weave or textum of words, which with complete autonymity calls the Word the Beginning. The beginning with the word *word*, this beginning in its unspeakable replication—which all discourses, because they are themselves composed of words, cannot overtake—gave rise, until the early modern period in Europe, to the form of the commentary. * * *

In the new space of the scholar's tragedy, such industrious humility does credit only to the famulus Wagner, this bookworm with his critical zeal, his learned hunt for sources, and his dream of rhetorical persuasion. Faust, by contrast, ostracizes rhetoric and rhetoricians with the same rhetorical question:

> Of parchment then is made the sacred spring,
> A draught of which forever slakes all thirst?
> From naught can you refreshment wring
> Unless from your own inmost soul it burst.
> (566–69)

He wants, not to leave thirst and desire open, as do philologists and rhetoricians, but to quench them so thoroughly that they are extinguished. The name of the death of desire, however, is soul. Therefore the new refreshment, when applied to the Gospels, consists in translating from one's own soul and honest feeling. Certainly, feeling and soul are also only translations, a nominalizing paraphrase of the sigh *oh!* as the unique signifier that is not a signifier. But they make possible another beginning and alter the function of all rhetoric. One who no longer wants to know about parchments and the letters on them does not simply give up reading and explicating, rhetorical variations and mutations. Even the lonely scholar works with paper, which he fills up, like the teachers and students of old-

European universities and Latin schools when they imitated classic or sacred texts, that is, wrote paraphrases. On Faust's writing paper, too, "word" is paraphrased and replaced successively by "mind," "force," "act." But in the speeches that comment on this writing, the transcription is not described as a rhetorical procedure. The paraphrases are no longer understood as drawn from a treasury of tropes and figures; they are assigned the inverse function of denoting the true and authentic meaning of a word. This word turns out to be the word *word*. It is not one word or signified among others; it is the word as signifier submitted to the primacy of the signified. By means of rhetorical variation Faust undertakes a semantic quest for the transcendental signified.

The transcendental signified, however remote from language it may seem, arises technically or grammatologically from a sequence of reiterated crossings-out. As soon as Faust writes down a word (*niederschreibe*, 1234), a strange Something pulls him and his pen up short. This Other, though called "Spirit," is not too supersensory to have eyes. A gaze reads along with what the hand writes down and by so doing makes sure that the pen does not run away with itself ("Feder sich nicht übereile!," 1231). Indeed it is characteristic of manual writing under normal circumstances—in sun or lamplight, and given eyesight—that one can watch one's hand in the present moment of writing and, where necessary, make corrections. * * * By contrast, the eyes of theatergoers cannot look over the shoulders of the heroes of Scholarly Tragedies. We must resort to a hypothetical reconstruction. The sheet of paper on which Faust wrote must have looked something like this:

the Act.

the ~~Force~~.

In the Beginning was

the ~~Mind~~.

the ~~Word~~.

These crossings-out distinguish hermeneutical translation from rhetorical paraphrase. With the revocation of the first and absolute Word disappears the free play of the many varying and verbose words that can represent each other in one and the same syntactical position. The logic of signifiers is a logic of substitution; the logic of signifieds, a fantasy according to which one irreplaceable signified replaces all replaceable signifiers. If three of them were not crossed out, the words on Faust's page would form a paradigm of signifiers in Saussure's sense. They do not because in his freedom the translator does not perceive their coherence (what indeed is called a system). Faust hesitates, but not because no one can pronounce simultaneously all the exclusive elements of a paradigm. He hesitates because he seeks the one and only meaning lying outside all differentiality and therefore no longer sees words that have already been crossed out.

If he had seen them, it would have been readily apparent that all his trial runs are the vain efforts of a German to exhaust the polysemy of the Greek word for "word." Had Faust consulted his Greek dictionaries, he would have noticed that he, Faust of the honest feeling, does not undertake the substitutions, but rather that already speaking in advance of him is the entire tradition that successively translated the *logos* as scholastic *sensus*, Leibnitzean force, and transcendental philosophical act, in so many epochs in the history of being. But this Occidental "series of substitutions of center for center" in which "successively, and in a regulated fashion, the center receives different forms or names" and hence becomes endlessly further inscribed and denied, is already a matter of no consequence for the translator, because he himself is stepping out to found a new and irrevocable center. Faust characterizes in the "history of the sign" the moment without "paradigmatic consciousness."

Faust's syntagmatic consciousness isn't much better. For sheer love of semantics the word sequences of the primary text are left unchanged or simply ignored. Faust is far from orienting his search for signifieds along the contextual lines of John. He does not hunt around in his heap of books for a commentary on parallel passages. His pen already balks at the first line; no glance falls on the following lines or on the text as a whole, which would illuminate the mysterious word via its concordances. The barking and howling of a dog is enough to prevent Faust on that day and forever from reading further.

Signs are found in three formal relations. If the two outer relations of the sign—to its immediate neighbors in what precedes and what follows in the discourse and to its virtual substitutes in the treasury of language— are both excluded, then there remains only the inner or imaginary relation between signifier and signified. This relation is what, particularly since Goethe's aesthetics, is "commonly called a symbol." For a century the Faustian coup suspended the attribution of the sign to the group of which it is an element. This loss has very pragmatic grounds, for the relation to the signified is the sole one that does not attend to the discourse of the Other. To observe textual recurrences would mean to submit the translation to a superior author or work worthy of imitation. To observe paradigmatic columns, as Faust's pen inconsequentially piles them up, means to submit translation not to honest feelings but to the rules of a language.

But Faust is alone. He writes without consulting books, outside any discursive network. No one ordered a Bible translation from him, no one is going to get one dedicated to him or receive it as due—not his nearest colleague and not the nearest publisher. They, however, are the control mechanisms of scholarship, and they alone hold scholars to the observance of the formal relations of the sign. In dictionaries dwell the paradigms, in grammars the syntagms. As a student of philology, Nietzsche described how his guild would have had to scrutinize or rap the knuckles of this ex-M.A.:

> Whenever such types deign to practice philology, we are in our rights to raise our eyebrows a little and scrutinize attentively these strange workers. How they are accustomed to do things in philological matters Goethe told us in the mirror of his Faust. We recall the hair-raising methods by which Faust treats the beginning of the John Prologue and confess the feeling worthy of a Wagner that for us Faust is utterly ruined, as a philologist at any rate.

Faust's deed is a free translation. Not only semantically, in that the word *word* is not repeated in the wording of the text, but above all pragmatically: because it does not attend to any external discursive controls. A hair-raising discursive practice only fills in what the many negations of the introductory monologue have already sketched out:

> No doubt can plague me or conscience cavil,
> I stand not in fear of hell or devil—
> But then, all delight for me is shattered;
> I do not pretend to worthwhile knowledge,
> Don't flatter myself I can teach in college
> How men might be converted or bettered.
> (368–73)

The renunciation of impossible teaching made possible a free writing, which exceeds philological or indeed theological scruples. Free writing has no definite function for definite addressees and therefore does not lead students about by the nose. It finds no place in the discourse network from which Faust derives, because it itself begins a new discourse network. Having reached the zero point, Faust rejects along with traditional knowledge Knowledge itself, without (like his many successors) proclaiming free writing as the new science that more than any other would harbor the conceit of bettering and converting human beings, indeed, of making them for the first time into human beings.

Knowledge and ignorance, new doctrine and free act: in the zero hour of transcendental knowledge, these still lie side by side. "The explication that Faust attempts, the opposition of word and meaning, of deed and force, is—despite the reference to Fichte—neither philosophically clear nor purely poetic; it is, therefore, one of those places where philosophy and poetry are disinclined to join together in a complete unity." This nonclosure characterizes the new beginning. In free translation poetic and philosophic discourse conspire in a fashion that henceforth will be called German Classicism. Schiller reads Kant for three years in order to be read himself for a century from the standpoint of Kant. Hegel reads and interprets poetry until his philosophy of art enters into relationship with poetic imagination. Thus an oscillation comes into being between poetry and thought, which do not join together in complete unity because the two discourses are not even close to being able to write down the points where they cross one another.

Faust's *Act* is the fleeting act of writing itself. To write "In the Beginning was the *Act*" truly marks the end. First, the translation comes to an end because it has at last found the beginning itself. Second, the translation comes to the conclusion that the sought-after transcendental signified of *logos* lies in the search itself. Faust's crossings-out and substitutions receive a name, which gives a brand name as well to the authentic meaning of what has been crossed out, in Greek as well as in German. The translator, who so despises words, nonetheless does nothing but make words. No acts other than that of writing are seen in the quiet study in which the poodle no longer barks and has yet to bark again. Consequently the free translation ends as anonymously as the Gospels had begun. On the one hand there is the Word, from which all words stem, even those of the Gospel writers— on the other is the act, which is all that writing is, even the writing of the translator. A writer who writes around the sentence "I am writing," however, fulfills the modern conception of authorship. Free writing has brought Faust back to his first test. The author Nostradamus, whose manuscript momentarily guarantees his presence for the reader, is replaced by the author Faust, whose handwriting is the act of his own self-presence. Other translations of *logos* could justify themselves by counting out an average of common connotations between the primary text and the translation; translation as "act" is itself the act of writing off the wording (or casting it to the winds) instead of further copying it (or passing it down to posterity).

An act, in actuality, neither philosophical nor poetic. Before the Faustian revolution, poetry had a lot to do with the written and nothing with the strange, fugitive act of writing. The order of representations excluded the representability of the act of production. What philosophy had to say in the classical age, when it explicated Holy Scripture, is in accord with the outcome of Faust's gesture, but not with the gesture itself. Spinoza's *Tractatus Logico-Politicus*, which was certainly before the eyes of the author of the Scholar's Tragedy, justified Faust's high-handed treatment of the Bible by anticipating his contempt of words, but did not go so far as to make a new and free translation of those incriminated written words.

> I only maintain that the meaning by which alone an utterance is entitled to be called Divine, has come down to us uncorrupted, even though the original wording may have been more often changed than we suppose. Such alterations . . . detract nothing from the Divinity of the Bible, for the Bible would have been no less Divine had it been written in different words or a different language. That the Divine law has in this sense come down to us uncorrupted, is an assertion which admits of no dispute.

The difference between German Poetry and classical philosophy is produced by the words of the philosopher themselves. They are and remain commentaries, no longer upon the text but upon its pragmatic and semantic aspects. Therefore they dare to voice the scandalous suspicion that others could have changed or falsified the text of the Bible, but they keep silent about their own systematic falsification. Faust, by contrast, does not say whether or that he falsifies; when he does something, he does it. Hence the philosopher replaces "discourse" and "word" semantically with "meaning," the poet pragmatically with "act." That it is an intrusion and a falsification to understand the words of the Apostle "and I think also that I have the Spirit of God" as "by the Spirit of God the Apostle here refers to his mind, as we may see from the context," Spinoza had prudently not mentioned. Only poetry, a century later, first lifted the veil and publicly translated the spirit of God as its own.

In the classical period representations or (to put it plainly) deceit and masquerade went that far. Earlier, the *Tractatus* had insisted that no one could doubt the divinity of scripture, while its own "scripture" did nothing else; but this was done, for reasons of security, to deceive readers and students. Faust's farewell to his M.A. status, which only led students around by the nose, announces to this strategy and this art of writing, which arise from within and against persecution, that he is quitting. Poetic free writing exits from the discourse of the Other. At the precise place where the name MAster turns into "empty sound and smoke," Faust's authorship begins. And as always, when someone tries not to deceive others, only self-deception remains.

Faust lays claim to the beginning as an act this side of all representations, an act that is first of all his own. And yet he does not write with complete freedom. In the quest for the signified of a Something that [*logos*] means, without its yet being the verbal meaning, hence like "the symbol which is the thing, without being the thing, and yet the thing"—Faust has a method. Words, which could not possibly mean [*logos*], no matter in what language game or in what professional jargon, are excluded. German Poetry in its foundational act is not so free as to write in place of [*En arché ēn ho logos*], let us say:

In the beginning was blabla

There are grounds for the omission. No discourse, not even the freest possible translation, can manage without authorized controls. In no culture is the dice throw of discourse not steered and curbed, checked and organized. For the ex-M.A., it is true that all controls that circumscribed the traditional European universities by means of estates and guilds fall by the wayside. But even in his lonely study Faust does not remain alone. For one thing, there is the poodle, whose barking triggers the translation attempt and later puts a stop to it. That Faust orders the poodle (in vain, incidentally) to "stop your barking" (1238; "Pudel so laß das Heulen," 1239) so he can search in peace for the Word instead of the word already betrays an authorized control, which is to some extent universal. It orders human beings to distinguish between human language, animal howling, and inhuman blabla. And at the other end there is "the Spirit," whose counsel enables the translation attempt to be completed. The fact that Faust twice justifies his unheard-of Germanizing as the input of "the Spirit" points to a second authorized control, whose emergence in turn can be precisely dated.

An anonymous Spirit, which has little to do with the Biblical [*logos*] but bears a close relation to Spinoza's bold conjecture about the passage from Paul, curbs his freedom. Faust translates according to the spirit and not the letter, but he does translate. A privately-shouldered obligation has replaced the professional one vis-à-vis the proper academic addressees and overseers. That does not alter the fact of discourse control. The Spirit does just what the good and evil spirits of the Republic of Scholars did: it can "illuminate" and "warn"; it brakes the quick tempo of writing. Its "reservations" help ensure that German Poetry does not start out with howling or blabla.

The lonely study, too, is therefore a scenario and therefore always already destined for the stage. "The 'subject' of writing does not exist if we mean by that some sovereign solitude of the author." Aside from the mysterious poodle, a writer and a speaker act together in the playlet. "The Spirit" does not write but rather speaks. The translator writes, but when he reflects on what has been written, "the Spirit" is the agent. At times it becomes unclear which of the two speaks: whether, for example, in the command of "I" to his pen as "your [*deine*]" pen (1231) Faust has the floor or whether it is "the Spirit" who uses the familiar form of address.

As so often in dialogues, the name of "the Spirit" remains unstated. Instead, something simply happens on stage. Out of the poodle comes, aroused by vexatious biblical words, a Spirit. The mask drops—Mephisto was seconding the entire scene of writing. Indeed, there cannot be more than one Spirit in the same room. The scene of the Logos has never been read literally enough: it describes the birth of German Poetry out of the Spirit of Hell.

Faust's first question to the Spirit after its unmasking reads: "What are you called?" ("Wie nennst du dich?" 1327). That is a hard question to answer when posed of someone who "so remote from everything external, / Past all appearance seeks the inmost kernel" (1328–9; "weit entfernt von allem Schein, / Nur in der Wesen Tiefe trachtet," 1329–30), of someone, that is, who embodies sheer contempt of language. Thus Mephisto can continue to conceal his name. But there are indices, nonetheless. A Spirit who, like the contemporary directors of the *Gymnasien*, becomes restless and displeased when someone still practices reading and translating the Bible; a Spirit who can offer all earthly joys and in exchange wants only the soul; a Spirit, too, whose royal self in the *Tragedy: Part Two* invents paper money—that can only be the "new idol," which Nietzsche finally called by its true name. The lectures "On the Future of Our Educational Institutions" describe with an outlaw's keen sight a lecturing procedure that corresponds point by point with Faust's writing procedure, at the end of which the idol removes his mask.

> The student listens to lectures. When he speaks, when he sees, when he is being social, when he is practicing the arts, in short, when he lives, he is independent, that is to say, independent of the educational institution. Very often the student writes at the same time he listens to lectures. These are the moments when he dangles from the umbilical cord of the university. He can choose what lectures he wants to listen to, he does not have to believe what he hears, he can close his ears when he is not in the mood to listen. This is the "acroamatic" theory of teaching.
>
> The teacher, however, speaks to the students who attend his lectures. Whatever else he thinks and does is cut off by a monumental divide from the consciousness of his students. Often the professor reads while he lectures. In general, he wants as many students as possible; if need be, he is satisfied with a few, almost never with just

one. A speaking mouth and many, many ears, with half as many writing hands: that is the external apparatus of the academy; set in motion, that is the educational machinery of the university. Moreover, the possessor of this mouth is cut off and independent from the possessors of the many ears: and this double independence is celebrated with lofty pathos as "academic freedom." Moreover, the individual— to raise this freedom a notch higher—can say more or less what he wants, the others can hear more or less what they want: only, standing at a modest distance behind both groups, with a certain tense, supervisory mien, is the state, there in order to make clear from time to time that *it* is the purpose, goal, and essence of this odd speaking and listening procedure.

Faust's free translation is clearly a special instance of state-permitted academic freedom. The two licenses—for the student to hear more or less what he wants and for the professor to say more or less what he wants— come together to produce the Faustian scene of writing. As students do not have to believe what they hear, so Faust can hear the message of the Easter bells without conviction and translate the Prologue to Saint John without mentioning the words the *Word* or the *Son*. As professors say more or less what they want, so Faust does not read what is written but what should be written. As students write while they are listening, so the translation follows the dictates of the Spirit, who does not write but speaks. And finally, as professors read while they speak, so the Faustian new beginning rests on a read text. Accordingly, within the poetic freedom that is Faust's act appears, as its precondition, the academic freedom of the new state universities. But Faust, whose first words already announce to the old university system that he is quitting, does not yet know this and cannot know yet how well a professorship in the new system would suit him. Of course, he does not plan a "reform of the universities," but he triggers one. After 1800, professors, especially in chairs of philosophy, made a career of free translation—of *Faust* in particular. In the course offerings of nineteenth-century universities (in the words of their best specialist), "the old expression *tradere* continued to be used, but even the youngest of lecturers—indeed perhaps he the most—would have seen in this an insult were it to be taken at face value."

Academic freedom and poetic freedom (not to be confused with poetic license) are both guaranteed by the state. To pose the act in place of the word is above all a political act. In enlightened Prussia in 1794, one and the same code, the *Allgemeines Landrecht*, granted a copyright to books (which made the act of their authors inalienable) and a new statute to institutions of learning, which "separated them from the organs of churchly administration dependent on tradition": "Schools and universities are institutions of the state."

In their alliance the two legal acts founded the "alliance between the state and the educated," which not only led to the "transformation of the form of rule and government" but for a century bore along German Poetry. The Spirit in Faust's study is no solitary. Everywhere reformers, appointed and protected by the articles of the *Landrecht*, visited the studies and educational institutions of the Republic of Scholars, in order to write down everything about them that required reform. * * *

Such school visitors were all the rage circa 1800. Jean Paul Richter called it "one of the greatest pedagogical errors" that "religious books are turned into reading machines"; the *Journal of Empirical Psychology* relaxed its customary discretion to castigate by name a living teacher whose "literal method" (as the word already indicates) in New Testament instruction required students to begin by "noting" "the name," then to write on the blackboard names and other curious features as abbreviated initial letters, and finally to learn them by heart. For the empirical psychologist, an alarming question was raised: "To what extent would such a dreadfully one-sided development of so subordinate an intellectual power as memory derange human reason?"

Thus one and the same Spirit growls at the reading of the Bible like the poodle and furnishes inspired readings of the Bible like "the Spirit." * * * The discourse network of 1800 revokes Luther's commandment to "recount from word to word." This is replaced by the new commandment to have only that read which students and teachers "understand." It is formulated clearly enough and, as the "only" indicates, enforces a selection and control of discourse like all others, even if hermeneutics owes its victory to having initially masqueraded as the opposite of that control. But people did not fall for it right from the start. Like Faust's thesis—namely, that his translation into his beloved German was at the same time a revelation of the sacred original—the project of the reformers, of replacing the Bible with primers simply to preserve its sanctity, was a transparent strategy. "The question was put as follows: Is it not sacrilege toward the books of religion to use them to teach children to read? Whereupon a general Yes! resounded. Really the question was meant as follows: Isn't it time to do away with or limit the old instructional materials?" And "Understanding" was meant as it was understood. * * *

Doing away with old instructional materials, even in literal ABC wars, marks the birth of the new. Instead of the word, the act enters, and instead of the Bible, Poetry: from the primer to the National Classic * * *; from the sigh "oh!," which "the creative child breathes out in artless song" to "the greatest system of art, itself containing several systems more." * * *

Poetry is at once the means and goal of understanding, as demanded by the reformers in office, hence the correlative (and not the object) of the new human science: hermeneutics. Its distinction lies in linking together all the information channels participating in understanding. First, poetry itself functions as understanding, that is, as the transmission of words into pure meanings; second, it allows understanding. * * * Finally, it can understand others and other things *and* be understood by others—otherwise. The discourse network of 1800 has in essence been accounted for once this three-part schema is filled in with appropriate names and terms.

First, however, we must emphasize that power stands over the entire relation. The discursive net called understanding has to be knotted. There is such a thing as understanding and being understood only once a new type of discourse control has learned to practice its "modest distance" in order merely to point out from time to time that the state is the "purpose, goal, and essence of this odd speaking and listening procedure." Over the free space of hermeneutics there stands, as above every language game, an "order-word." This command is the unique knot that itself will not and cannot be understood. The state remains closed off to every hermeneutic. Because understanding, despite its claim to universality, is one speech act among others, it cannot get behind the speech act that instituted it. Texts that are part of the hermeneutic net allow the power that governs them to come to light only in a masked fashion. The translator Faust is watched over by a devil in poodle's garb.

The only texts that are unmasked are those that exist not to be read and understood. In the drama, Faust's academic freedom remains as mysterious as it does in its innumerable interpretations; no one can say whether the free writing has addresses or who they are. The *Code Napoléon*, by contrast, names naked necessity as the origin of the desire to understand; it is the first law book that punishes judges if they refuse hermeneutics: "The judge who shall refuse to judge, under the pretext of silence, obscurity, or the inadequacy of the law, can be pursued as guilty of the denial of justice." Words of power, and only they, are what make necessary—that is, make a matter of life and death—the search for a transcendental signified even where (according to judges) there is no empirical signified or where (according to Faust) there is only a word. A new law decrees hermeneutics and with it readers/writers who apply it in all its senselessness, and in so doing surround it with a cloud of meaning. The judge must apply the law because otherwise he would fall outside it. The poet must apply interpretations because otherwise—Faust's translation in the presence of that poodle being in the last resort an apotropaic act—he'd go to the devil. The cloud of meaning legitimating the judge's activity is the illusion that, despite its incomprehensible nature, the law nevertheless validly applies to a referent, a punishable body. The nebulous legitimation of literature is that texts appear to be hermeneutically intelligible and not, rather, a matter of what has been programmed and programs in turn.

There is evidence of this in the Scholar's Tragedy. Only its hero can believe that texts and signs are all designed to be understood and to correspond to understanding (in the way he reproaches the junkpile of books for making understanding impossible, attributes understanding to the signs of Nostradamus and the Word of John, and finally puts understanding into practice in his own translating). This belief in meaning—with which the Scholar's Tragedy ends—encounters its truth. The devil is merely Faust's confrontation with a text that cannot understand nor be understood but is power itself. Mephisto demands Faust's signature.

Signatures, like law books, program people without taking the detour of understanding. The pact scene is therefore the opposite of free translation. In the latter we have the poetic or academic freedom of paraphrase; in the former, the bureaucratic act of signing one's name, which henceforth founds between the devil and the ex-M.A. "not a mere contractual relation based on deed and reciprocal deed but rather a unique relation of service and power and at the same time a relation of trust. . . . It is, if not indissoluble, nonetheless on principle and in fact of life-long duration." This relation—as will not be hard to guess—is that between civil servants and the state.

When Goethe was named privy minister of the Duchy of Saxony-Weimar, obligations to which he was bound until death were "read out loud and put before" the author of the Scholar's Tragedy. So too ought Faust's "spoken word" be "enough" to commit his days "into eternal peonage" ("Ist's nicht genug, daß mein gesprochenes Wort / Auf ewig soll mit meinen Tagen schalten?" 1718–19). Among the young duke's overtures to reform were "suggestions for simplifying the forms and flourishes on decrees—for example the full array of titles and offices cited on even the simplest documents." But this paper campaign foundered on the resistance of his minister Goethe, whose memorandum concludes: "A Chancellory does not have anything to do with material things; for him who is concerned only with observing and drawing up formalities, a little pedantry is necessary. Indeed, even if the 'By God's Grace' should be retained only as an exercise in official script by the chancellors, there would be some sense in it." In the Tragedy, the same word, *pedant*, characterizes the devil, who, as if there were no such thing as spoken words, demands from Faust "for living or for dying . . . a line or two" ("Um Lebens oder Sterbens willen . . . ein paar Zeilen," 1714–15). In this perverse world where privy ministers are more bureaucratic than their duke, Mephisto figures as the official and Faust as the poet. This doubling, for its part, simply duplicates the double life with which German Poetry begins. "In contrast to his poetic style, Goethe's files are marked by their elaborate, stilted bureaucratic style. With justice he could say in this respect: 'two souls dwell, oh! in my breast'—the bureaucrat and the poet."

The object of exchange in the devil's pact is the soul. A stroke of the pen transfers ownership to the devil for life and thereafter. Thus the soul, instead of merely forming "the reactivated remnants of an ideology," is "the present correlative of a certain technology of power," as central Europe conceives of it circa 1800. * * * It is no wonder that Faust shrinks back from the demand for a signature as from a spook. The facility of the kind of writing that understands gives way to a symbolic bonding—poetry gives way to power. In signatures there is nothing to interpret or to quibble about. The "Act" that took place in free translating could play about or paraphrase the naked fact of writing: the "Act" was and remained "in the beginning," or in the past tense. The act of signing, by contrast, knows only the pure present and the precise future of its fatality. In his striving Faust attains a status that is certainly the loftiest of all but that, in its ever-binding fatality, is also the most burdensome. * * *

The "pact" that educational bureaucrats concluded with the state circa 1800 was to this extent "extravagantly extensive" in its "substantial and formal content." Faust, because he cares little for the beyond promised to him by the Bible, signs in this world and for this world so as to assure it and his contractual opposite "[that] my utmost striving's fullest use / Is just the part I have bespoken" ("Das Streben meiner ganzen Kraft / Ist grade das, was ich verspreche"; 1742–43). Transcendental knowledge sets up a new beginning, which bursts open solitary studies. Faust, the man who

writes, vanishes in order to become the myth of German educational bureaucrats and of literary criticism; Faust, the man who is consigned to the
devil, steps onto the stage.

Henceforth there is no further mention in *The Tragedy, Part One* of
writing and reading. "Faust's writing skills attested to in literature aren't
worth much": they are "exhausted in the five words of the Bible translation" and the "signing of the pact." He who from a limited academic has
become Universal Man, after a brief detour into the cellar of academic
freedom, takes a path that his interpreters call the way to nature. But it is
much more plainly a way of speaking and listening. After the last writing
scene, the devil's pact (which is never mentioned again), only voices are
heard. Power remains modestly in the background in order to make room
for the impossible: a "natural" discourse. In higher education, M.A.'s con-
versed with their assistants; devils disguised as Ph.D.'s, with their pupils—
it was a matter of males and only males. Whoever is fed up with this art
of deceit has to go back beyond writing and reading. Genuine nature can
only be conveyed through channels that are fundamentally excluded from
the discourse of the university. Taking one step back, the ex-M.A. Faust
discovers the Other, the female Other who in the discourse network of
1800 calls forth Poetry.

NEIL M. FLAX

The Presence of the Sign in Goethe's *Faust*†

In a helpful development current literary studies are becoming more
aware that the "modern" preoccupation with the question of language is
part of a coherent semiological tradition rooted in the eighteenth century.
If "the being of language continues to shine ever brighter upon our horizon" * * * or if we are experiencing a "crisis of language," part of the
credit certainly goes to Saussure or Mallarmé. But the same concerns had
already attracted the attention of writers of the Enlightenment and the
Romantic period. The project of uncovering the early history of semiotics
in the eighteenth century has not yet touched Goethe to any great extent. * * * A move in this direction might, however, prove useful.
Goethe's well-known definitions of "symbol" and "allegory" helped crystallize a new, Romantic conception of the arts as "symbolic." They also
ensured that the new aesthetic theories would continue to take a semiological perspective. As the vocabulary of aesthetics developed in the mid-
eighteenth century, "allegory" and "symbol" gradually came to designate
two alternative semiotic modes, the former abstract, arbitrary, artificial, and
essentially verbal, the latter sensory, motivated, natural, and essentially
visual (or visualizing). In basing theories of art on the symbol-allegory

† *PMLA* 98 (1983): 183–203. The author's footnotes and his quotations from the German have
been omitted. His quotations from *Faust* have been replaced with Arndt's translation.

distinction, Romantic writers reaffirmed the seminal recognition of Enlightenment philosophy that aesthetic and semiological concerns are inseparable. * * *

In contrast to many of the other German writers who helped to formulate the Romantic idea of the aesthetic symbol—Herder, Kant, Schelling, Hegel—Goethe was able to invoke his notion of the symbol in a broad range of important literary works. At once poet and theorist, he presents a useful test case for the complex relations between the idea and the practice of the Romantic symbol. Most Goethe studies have assumed that these relations are unproblematic; the traditional approach cites the Goethean definitions of the symbol, whether drawn from his aesthetic or his scientific writings, and then demonstrates that the literary works exemplify and fulfill the symbolist ideal. * * *

* * * In the symbol, the many dichotomies posed and lamented by Romantic thought—particular and universal, material and ideal, natural and supernatural, subjective and objective, internal and external, individual and transcendental, temporal and eternal—all miraculously, if momentarily, dissolve. As a reconciler of all oppositions, the symbol serves a redemptive function. Not merely a representation, the symbol in some mysterious manner participates in and realizes the sacred. In effacing the conflict between matter and spirit, the symbol necessarily speaks at once to the mind and to the senses. The revelation is always linguistically mediated (whether by pictorial or by verbal signs), but somehow the aesthetic symbol—and this is its essential and miraculous difference from ordinary language—manages to turn the mediation of signs into an unmediated vision of divinity or ultimate truth. * * *

* * * Most traditional Goethe scholarship has accepted the doctrine of the revelatory symbol uncritically, as an article of faith, and has assumed that the author's literary works simply put the theory of the symbol into direct and entirely successful poetic practice. * * * I want * * * to focus on *Faust* specifically in its status as the established model of Goethean symbolism. I suggest that this paradigm of symbolist doctrine not only shares the perplexities of Romantic aesthetics in general; it also reveals how these perplexities are historically embedded in a theory of signs. I do not mean to convert the play into a theoretical treatise. *Faust* is a thoroughly dramatic work, but it consistently presents the problems and conflicts of its protagonist as semiotic issues. It thus belongs to that larger body of Romantic literature whose hallmark is an overt concern with the problem of language.

In fact, from its opening moments *Faust* seems positively to call out for a reading sensitized to the question of the sign. The word "Zeichen" 'sign' appears no fewer than seven times in the opening pages of the text (four times in the stage directions and three times spoken by Faust), and the phenomenon of the sign plays a pivotal role, * * * not only in the first scene but repeatedly during the ensuing action. The question of language is already prominent in Faust's well-known opening monologue. Recalling the various academic disciplines he has mastered, Faust deplores their failure to provide true knowledge:

> So I perceive the inmost force
> That bonds the very universe,
> View all enactment's seed and spring,
> And quit my verbiage-mongering.
> (382–85)

After identifying "words" as the chief obstacle to a vision of essential reality, Faust complains of his long years of confinement among books and papers ("Büchern und Papier") and library shelves ("Entombed within this book-lined tower" [402]). The lament climaxes with the familiar line "Flee! Up! Escape to open fields!" (418). But a curious twist immediately follows Faust's cry. The one thing that he proposes to take with him on his flight from the world of books is a book:

> Full-armed with that mysterious script
> Which Nostradamus' wisdom yields,
> Why ask for more companionship?
> (419–21)

And as soon as he mentions the "companion" book of Nostradamus, he forgets about his flight into nature and starts leafing through the book for some "sacred sign" [427] that will reveal the inner workings of nature.

The irrepressible bibliotropism in the midst of a renunciation of books, the expectation that a written sign could yield a more immediate contact with nature than could a trip into nature itself—these will prove to be essential Faustian gestures. Repeatedly during the drama Faust will interpose the book (or the picture) between himself and the unmediated presence he craves. He will alternately denounce the futility of words and affirm their revelatory power. Yet instead of being mere contradictions or vacillations, these paradoxical turns reflect a dualistic conception of language that had great currency in the age of philosophical aesthetics and that derived from an ancient hermeneutic tradition. According to this long-lived and still flourishing belief, "ordinary" language is mechanical, clichéd, empty, lifeless, while "mystical" language (which becomes "poetic" language for the Romantics) is organic, vital, radiant, germinal, revelatory. Following this theory, Faust renounces his academic library and turns to the mysterious signs in the Nostradamus book. The crucial irony here is that Faust's turn to magical or sacred signs, far from liberating him from the constraints of "empty" language only thrusts him deeper and deeper into the discontents of the semiotic condition. Precisely in the attempt to transcend language by means of the revelatory sign, Faust reinforces the linguistic limits he hoped to escape. Wherever he has recourse to a transcendental signifier, he rediscovers the non-convergence of signifier and signified. As he repeatedly confronts this basic precondition of any sign use, he finds that revelatory language is finally indistinguishable from the ordinary language in his pile of scholarly books. Neither language can provide the direct access to absolute being that he craves. The sacred symbol does not merely come to stand in questionable opposition to conventional language. The opposition itself generates discrepancies that end in undoing the very idea of transcendence to which it first gave meaning.

These, in any case, are the conclusions that a close examination of the openly "semiotic" episodes in the play suggests.

The insistence of the term "Zeichen" in the opening moments of the drama indicates that the two signs Faust contemplates in the Nostradamus book may be worth scrutinizing, not only for what they represent or how they affect Faust but strictly as signs from a semiotic perspective. Viewed in this manner, the two signs reveal a fundamental and far-reaching dichotomy. The macrocosm sign * * * , a map of the universe according to the traditional Ptolemaic-Christian model, is a visualizing diagram of a cross section of the concentric spheres that were held to constitute the creation. In the terminology of traditional semiotics, the macrocosm sign is a "natural" or "analogous" or "motivated" or "iconic" sign. It resembles in some perceptible way what it represents. By contrast, the conjuring sign of the type used by Faust to invoke the Erdgeist * * * makes no attempt to visualize or resemble its referent, although many pictures of spirits and demons existed in the Renaissance. Instead, it uses words to refer to and invoke a spirit. It is what semiotics terms an "artificial" or "conventional" or "arbitrary" or "immotivated" sign, relating to its referent through a self-contained system of differential tokens.

The dichotomy of pictorial and verbal, or "motivated" and "arbitrary," signs is a fundamental tenet of modern semiotics. The dualism, however, was already a commonplace of semiological and aesthetic discourse in the eighteenth century. Lessing gave the distinction special prominence in his *Laokoon* (1766). And recent studies have argued that the opposition of verbal and visual representations was the starting point of the entire newly developing philosophy of aesthetics. The Romantics, in turn, often saw the distinction between "allegory" and "symbol" as the difference between arbitrary and motivated representation. The discovery of the semiotic dichotomy in the first scene of *Faust* cannot be viewed then as an anachronism. By emphasizing the two opposing types of sign use at the outset, the play establishes its concern with the most urgent issue confronting philosophy and literature in the age of Kant: the ability of the representations that mediate all human cognition to deliver some knowledge of ultimate, unmediated, extralinguistic reality.

These are the terms in which Faust contemplates the two signs in the Nostradamus book. He sees the sign of the macrocosm as a type of divine writing ("Was it a god that fashioned this design" [434]) that inspires a sense of codivinity in its beholder ("Am I a god? I feel such light in me!" [439]). The Erdgeist sign, while displaying a number of important differences from the macrocosm sign, has a similarly redemptive effect. It infuses its beholder with a feeling of participation in the divinity it represents:

> Not so this sign affects my soul, not so!
> You, Spirit of the Earth, are nigher,
> I sense my powers rising higher,
> Already with new wine I am aglow,
> (460–63)

Both signs, then, although not in themselves aesthetic objects, exemplify the sacral, revelatory, transcendental function of the symbol that is at the heart of Romantic aesthetics and epistemology.

To understand Faust's turn from the first, pictorial sign to the second, verbal sign, we need to refer briefly to the Enlightenment debate that supplied Romantic writers with the basic terms of their theory of art. To put it most simply, the aesthetic debate in the eighteenth century hinged on the question whether "natural" pictorial signs or "arbitrary" verbal signs are better suited to convey real knowledge of the world they represent. Pictorial signs have the virtues of sensory immediacy, clarity, and universality but the limitation of having to resemble slavishly the mere physical aspect of their referents. Verbal signs can deal with abstract ideas and concepts and can freely combine and disconnect the data of the physical world. But they suffer in their lack of sensate, material presence and in their consecutiveness. Since words must occur one at a time in sequence and cannot enter the consciousness all at once, they do not provide that instantaneous, global, all-encompassing cognition that truth needs to convey. Nevertheless, Enlightenment aesthetics, culminating in Lessing's *Laokoon*, seems to reach a qualified decision in favor of verbal over pictorial semiosis. The superiority of language is that it supposedly affords greater freedom to the creative and productive powers of the human imagination. Moreover, it contains the means to overcome its inherent immateriality and sequentiality.

Faust's reasons for rejecting the macrocosm sign in favor of the Erdgeist sign directly echo the terms of the Enlightenment debate. The pictorial macrocosm sign, while filling him with awe at the revealed forces at work in the universe, reduces Faust to the role of pacified spectator: "What glorious show! Yet but a show, alas!" (454). The verbal Erdgeist sign, by contrast, liberates his powers of imagination and participation: "I feel emboldened now to venture forth / To bear the bliss, the sorrow of this earth" (464–65). Faust's turn from the immobilizing macrocosm sign to the activating Erdgeist sign thus traces a movement that is clearly marked by the semiotic debates of Enlightenment philosophy. The opening scene of the play defines the fundamental issue as transcendence, specifically transcendence of the constraints of language (exemplified by Faust's "narrow" study). Faust's fascination with the two Nostradamus signs and his rationale for favoring one over the other suggest that from this moment his metaphysical quest will be inseparable from the problem of the revelatory sign.

The acute irony of Faust's turn to the Erdgeist sign lies in the effectiveness of the magical symbol, which succeeds in evoking the Erdgeist. But the epiphany serves only to remind Faust that for him there is to be no transcendence, since the Erdgeist scornfully rebuffs his attempt to place himself among the gods. The encounter dramatizes the governing paradox of the entire play. The epiphanic symbol, precisely when it is most effective, ultimately reaffirms the impossibility of transcendence.

Once we recognize the importance of semiological issues in *Faust*, it also becomes easier to account for the many literary and pictorial citations that pervade the text and that continue to provide a rich lode for Goethe scholarship. * * * The superabundant allusions are not merely expressions of the author's "universal" or "electic" spirit or of his advocacy of "Weltliteratur." They are underwriting a new ideology of the aesthetic artifact, which provocatively claims to be the paradigm of all sign making and the sole medium of any redemptive cognition. The numerous references to the Bible, Greek mythology, Dante, Shakespeare, Raphael, Correggio, Rembrandt, and others are citations of a thoroughly citational literary and pictorial tradition that the Romantics suddenly, and paradoxically, transformed into a religion of aesthetic primacy.

Faust's struggles with the intractable citationality of the sign also provide an element of comedy that has not always been sufficiently appreciated. The hero is perpetually fleeing the library while bringing along a book, and the fine absurdity of that quintessential gesture resounds throughout the play. Of course the recurrent gesture is not merely absurd. It is also deadly serious. It represents the most demanding challenges of the high Romantic condition: the quest for unmediated presence in the mediation of signs, the risky wager that language can be at once the obstacle and the means to transcendence. But for Faust, as for many other quest heroes in the literary tradition, a trace of idiocy is never entirely absent from the relentless pursuit of an ideal.

If *Faust* addresses the question of the sign, the issue assumes special prominence in the Bible-translation scene. The very act of translation immediately raises a host of perplexing problems about the authority and truth value of language. And to focus the problem even more sharply, the passage Faust "happens" to choose for translation is the opening line of the Gospel of John, "In the beginning was the Word," a locus classicus of that "logocentric" tradition in Western thought according to which divine presence is identified with spoken language.

As the episode opens, Faust has just returned from his Easter Sunday stroll with Wagner. He is feeling unusually content, but his mood quickly gives way to a sense of unease. With his characteristic bibliotropism, Faust reaches for the Bible, where he hopes to find the comforting "revelation" that Holy Scripture can best provide: "revelation, / which nowhere burns so finely, so unflawed, / as in the Gospel of our Lord" (1217–19). The episode hinges then on an orthodox statement of faith in the revelatory power of sacred language. But from the moment that Faust begins to translate the "original" Greek into German, the simple credo becomes more and more precarious. Faust first questions the traditional translation of "Logos" as "Word" and starts to look for a better translation: "I cannot grant the word such sovereign merit / I must translate it in a different way" (1226–27). He considers and writes down three alternative translations— "Sense," "Force," "Deed." He finally identifies the third translation as the true one, claiming the help of divine inspiration: "The spirit speaks" (1236).

In denying the divine status of "the Word" and proposing a truer translation of "Logos," Faust plunges into a number of insoluble paradoxes. He repeats the same contradictory gesture that launched the action in the opening scene of the play. He dismisses the "Word" as mediator of transcendent truth but immediately turns to written language to recover that

lost truth. Then he asserts that his own word for "Logos" has divine au-
thorization. But "der Geist," the term he spontaneously uses to invoke the
divine authority, is merely another conventional German translation—
through the Latin "Spiritus"—for "Logos," the very term whose correct
translation he is supposedly first discovering. "Tat" emerges as the authentic rendering of "Logos" because of the writer's—that is, Faust's—direct
access to extralinguistic truth, but the "direct" access to higher truth is
already mediated by a prior translation. And the prior translation is evidently unsatisfactory since Faust continues to search for a better one. The
double circularity of Faust's actions—resorting to language to supply the
truth language is said to lack and invoking by name the deity whose proper
name Faust is trying to discover—indicates that he has once again en-
trapped himself in the aporias of revelatory writing.

Faust's invocation of "der Geist" is not an incidental or dispensable
element in the scene. The truth of his translation relies on the ancient
vatic and odic convention according to which authentic speech or authentic writing is divinely "inspired" ("begeistert"). By a complex chain of
metaphoric associations, the trope of "inspiration" identifies a true utterance with physical arousal, divine presence, and breath. This is not the
place to disentangle the dense web of metaphors. My point is simply that
the overt tautologies of Faust's translation begin to raise questions even
about the reliability of divine "inspiration." The more the linguistic status
of the series "Logos-Wort-Geist" is foregrounded by Faust, the more unavoidably the concept "Begeisterung" itself starts to confess its implication
within the same chain of metaphors. In the context of Faust's translation,
"inspiration" exposes its dependence on the system of tropes it pretends to
support. Ultimately Faust adds a link to the chain of metaphoric substitutions, but in doing so he confirms the obstacles to passing beyond the
chain.

These are still somewhat theoretical aberrations. Faust's faith in sacred
signs becomes interesting dramatically when it results in practical actions
that have highly equivocal consequences. Such is the outcome of the
conjuring of Mephistopheles, which begins at the moment Faust completes his translation of John 1.1. In the flush of success as an inspired
writer Faust finally manages to evoke the spirit who will help him to escape
from the sterility of the scholar's study. Faust's exorcism of the demon in
the poodle is in fact a direct continuation of his work with sacred writings.
First he recites a series of four spells from the *Clavicula Salomonis*, a
pseudobiblical Renaissance magic book. When that strategy fails, he confronts the poodle with a hallowed sign of Christ, the letters "INRI" inscribed on the crucifix: "Then see this sign" (1300). Finally he holds up
a mystical emblem of the Trinity, a triangle with the eye of God in the
center. In obvious parody of the Erdgeist encounter, the magic sign works.
It compels the demon to appear. But here again the outcome of this
"successful" conjuring with magical signs is another defeat. Faust finds in
his long association with the devil that even with supernatural help transcendence still eludes him.

That Mephistopheles, the great Adversary, should display the same credulous awe of sacred symbols as Faust does is a particularly engaging and

humorous aspect of the devil's early appearances in the play. His first scene
dwells at some length on the power of the symbol above Faust's door—a
pentagram, whose five points correspond to the five letters in the holy
name "Jesus"—to keep him imprisoned in Faust's study. The next time
Mephistopheles appears, he pedantically insists that he cannot let himself
in until Faust calls out "Enter" three times. The magical signs that Faust
uses to conjure the demon—the set of four spells (1272) and the sacred
triangle—are also strongly identified with numerological symbolism. That
these associations with numerology are hinting at semiotic issues finally
becomes clear in the Witch's Kitchen scene, where both Faust and
Mephisto sharply ridicule the Witch's numerological incantation ("your
witch-arithmetic" [2540–52]). As Mephisto sardonically remarks: "It has
at all times been the custom / By Three in One and One threefold / To
propagate not truth but fustian" (2560–62). The reference to Trinitarian
theology exposes the question implicit in all the examples of numerological faith: How can the synthetic, conventional code of numbers also be
the direct emanation of divine power? The import of the episode goes
beyond the initial comedy of having Faust and Mephisto denounce as
"error" and "nonsense" the same numerology they have just been practic-
ing. Faust could, after all, maintain that *his* numerology is authentically
theological, while the Witch's is vulgar hocus-pocus. But the potential use
of numbers for both revelation and obfuscation unsettles the entire basis
of numerology as a true symbolism. The uncertainties that emerge as soon
as a semiotic system is converted into an agency of revelation afflict not
only verbal language but numerical language as well. Here too, it proves
impossible in practice to maintain that opposition between "ordinary" and
"revelatory" uses of language on which all symbolist theories depend.

Nevertheless, even as the numerological symbolism is being questioned,
it is made to work. Mephisto may ridicule the Witch's hocus-pocus, but
he insists that without it her magic potion will fail to restore Faust's youth.
And in fact the potion and the incantation do succeed, as effectively as
did Faust's Erdgeist sign and his mystical triangle. The text never denies
that magical symbols can work; rather, it shows that when they do work,
they only forestall the promised epiphany.

This is the lesson the Gretchen tragedy spells out in detail. The
Gretchen story begins in the Witch's kitchen, when Faust first glimpses
the image of ideal feminine beauty (possibly Helena) in the magic mirror
and Mephisto remarks: "You'll soon see Helen of Troy in every skirt!"
(2603–04). In effect, the romance that has long stood as a model of pure,
spontaneous, artless love is mediated at its outset by the intervention of a
picture. Moreover, Faust describes the image in the same terms that idealist aesthetics uses to define the revelatory symbol: "A form from heaven
above . . . The loveliest woman in existence! . . . quintessence of all
heaven's rays! / Or could its like on earth be found?" (2429–40). Yet the
symbolic icon that first prompts the romance ultimately prevents its fulfillment. In the one passage where Faust tries to account for his rapid loss
of interest in Gretchen, he blames the "beautiful image" (3248). He complains that Mephisto has used the image to arouse Faust's carnal desires
and to distract him from the true quest for the deity, which nature alone

can satisfy (3220–42). Whether the "beautiful image" refers here to the picture in the magic mirror or to the image of Gretchen in his mind, the meaning is the same. A representation that originally seemed to promise contact with a "heavenly" being ends in impeding that contact.

The paradoxical structure of the sign as the mechanism that at once proffers and defers presence regulates Faust's relation to Gretchen from the start. Faust never feels the "essence" of Gretchen more intensely than in the scene soon after their first meeting when he visits her bedroom and in her absence worships the magically evocative traces of her presence. The episode enacts the semiotic condition. Faust falls in love with the eloquent imprints and vestiges of Gretchen's existence, left behind on the surfaces of her room. From that emblematic moment, the romance is fated to recapitulate what Faust first experienced with the Erdgeist apparition. When revelatory signs work, it is only to reestablish the difference between representation and presence.

Episodes openly concerned with the question of the transcendental signifier are prominent throughout the Gretchen drama. Faust is already declaring "eternal" love for Gretchen when he has barely met the girl, and indeed the hoped-for access to eternity is his love's raison d'être. But the difficulty of ensuring that the word "ewig" can have any reliable meaning continues to plague Faust. As the inveterate despiser of verbal language (1328), Faust would ideally like to communicate his eternal love for Gretchen without the mediation of the falsifying word. When Gretchen plucks the petals of a fortune-telling daisy and has the good luck to end on "he loves me," Faust seizes on the sign as an irrefutable token of his feelings, since a flower bypasses conventional human language and speaks the honest speech of nature, which is at once the speech of God: "Yes, my child! Yes, let this flower-word / Be godly oracle to you. He loves you!" (3184–85). He further develops his antiverbal position by appealing to the language of gestures to express his ineffable emotion: "Let this gaze, / This pressure of my hands express to you / What is ineffable" (3188–90).

Faust's statements are immediately anomalous in that the transparent languages of nature and gesture nevertheless require a running verbal commentary to clarify their meaning. Gretchen's recital of the conventional binary formula "he loves me, he loves me not" first turns the daisy into a revelatory sign. Even more damaging to Faust's position, the "divinity" of the blossom-word lures him into another treasonous attempt at translating the holy word of God. Faust apparently feels that he can now speak with the authority of revealed truth to sanction his speech. But in iterating the blossom-word in his own words, he immediately falls into a speech act of radical self-alienation, by declaring his love for Gretchen in the third person: "Er liebt dich!" With his very first attempt to speak his love to Gretchen, he infects his feelings with that chronic self-division that the romance was supposed to heal. The irreducible gap between signifier and signified comes into play even between "divine" speech (the infallible daisy) and its referent (the equivocal emotions that will doom the affair).

Finally Faust gives up the struggle to speak his love without words, as he confronts the fact that no natural sign conveys love's most essential trait, its "eternality." He falls back on the verbal mediation he was intent on avoiding: "To give one's whole self, and to feel / An ecstasy that must endure forever! / Forever!" (3191–93). He cannot assure Gretchen—or himself—that his love is eternal without recourse to conventional words, but his dependence on fallible language to establish the immortality of his love presents Faust with the same linguistic barriers to transcendence that faced him in his library.

During the romance with Gretchen Faust discusses the validity of language with a curious insistence, as if the problem of speaking one's love were indispensable to the emotion. Faust's statements on the subject fluctuate extremely. When he first confesses his love for Gretchen to Mephistopheles, he passionately insists that "ewig" is the one true word to name his feeling (3059–66). In his last conversation with Gretchen before the final catastrophe, he insists that his inner feelings are forever beyond the reach of falsifying language: "I have no name for it! / Feeling is all; / Name is but sound and fume" (3455–57). A close analysis of these passages would reveal not only that they directly contradict one another but also that each undermines its premises with its own rhetoric. Where Faust claims that language is the authentic expression of a primal inner truth, it turns out that the originating truth was itself established as the effect of a prior linguistic operation, naming. Where Faust claims that inner truth is forever inaccessible to language, it turns out that the untainted truth is nevertheless wholly structured by the most basic linguistic operation, binary opposition (3440–52).

The internal and reciprocal contradictions summarize the impasses of Faust's quest for transcendence of the semiotic condition. Whether he affirms or denies the truth of language, he still comes back to the intractable refusal of language to yield to an immediate presence beyond it. The destruction of Gretchen in the course of that circular itinerary suggests that the issue is of more than merely academic interest. The nonconvergence of representation and reality, that is, the failure of Gretchen to be "the quintessence of all the heavens" depicted and promised by the image in the magic mirror, can be fatal.

It might be expected that the destruction of Gretchen would move Faust to reconsider the implications of his quest for transcendence. But the catastrophe only prompts a change in the chosen medium. The magical, theological, and primarily verbal signs that were the vehicles of revelation in Part One give way to pictorial and overtly aesthetic signs in Part Two. Faust signals the shift to a visual and aesthetic mode of mediation in his opening monologue. Acknowledging the impossibility of directly contemplating the sun, he turns to the rainbow as the emblem of the irreducibly mediated nature of all human cognition: "Life is ours by colorful refraction" (4727).

Many have taken the monologue as Faust's renunciation of transcendence, an admission that through suffering he has learned to accept the limits to human ambition. But the reading disregards the dialectic of idealist thought, which insists that only through the mediation of the sensuous symbol (the rainbow, for example) can a vision of ultimate truths take place. As a symbol provided by a divinely ordered nature for the essential share of mediation in any redemptive cognition, the rainbow is not at all a token of renunciation for Faust. It is, rather, a reaffirmation of his role as the Quixote of epiphanic signs, only now in the mode of visual instead of verbal revelation. The terminology "farbigen Abglanz" that Faust uses to describe the rainbow is borrowed from a long Neoplatonist tradition that views "symbolic images," whether discovered in nature or created by the pictorial artist, as the visible "colored reflection" of an ineffable divinity. Faust's homage to the rainbow thus opens the way for the classical works of pictorial art that will now become his primary medium of sacred revelation.

The emergence of the work of pictorial art, or symbolic image, as the model of redemptive semiosis in Part Two exposes issues that remained latent in Part One. It was easy enough to distance Faust's faith in magical signs as long as it was associated with necromantic superstition. With the turn to an explicitly aesthetic mode of revelation, matters become more complicated, since the drama now deals with an article of faith that not only is widely shared by its audience but also informs the creation of the work itself. The various works of art that Faust now uses to further his pursuit of a sacred vision are the same works that served as models for the emerging theory of aesthetic symbolism: classical Greek art, Greek mythology, and Italian Renaissance painting.

Goethe's commitment to that theory is not in question. I am not arguing that the play overtly condemns symbolist doctrine. On the contrary, the anomalies of the symbol that the work conveys arise precisely because Goethe presents the symbol with conviction. This conception of the symbol is critically opposed to Faust's idea of the revelatory sign, and it is helpful now to define the difference. Faust's relation to magical signs is credulous and uncritical, and the work gets its ironic energy by systematically exposing the consequences of that naiveté from a position of higher wisdom. The play satirizes Faust's chronic refusal to understand that the symbol, as a semiotic phenomenon, can never provide a release from the realm of representations. In contrast, the symbolist text maintains that the proper function of the aesthetic symbol is to announce its semiotic nature, to reveal itself as a sign and declare its fictitiousness, and thereby to affirm the primacy and the verity of the semiotic condition. It is an extreme Johannine faith, revised to equate the human sign-making capacity with the divine act of writing that inscribed the universe. The ideal is no longer the surpassing of language but the ultimacy and divinity of language. By a slight but decisive shift, the sign itself has come to occupy the position of metaphysical truth to which it formerly served as the accessory.

Yet this Romantic doctrine of "the literary Absolute," which can be taken as the paradoxical governing concept of *Faust*, repeats the same fantasy of going beyond language that the work satirizes in the figure of Faust. The ironic detachment of the text does not keep it exempt from the impasses it exposes, and symbolist theory eventually smuggles transcendence back into the symbol. The aesthetic sign achieves its power of revelation by referring to its own semiotic nature. The condition of its success is to be overtly autotelic. But at the same time, the self-reflexive sign, as undisguised writing, evokes the idea of a prior signatory. Its truth is to bear witness both to its own autonomy and to the activity of the divine writer who first inscribed it. From the outset then, divine writing is burdened with the contradictory functions of being self-sufficient and dependent, essential and supplementary. Another impasse is generated in the ideal realm where all contraries were to be resolved.

In effect, the Romantic symbol is an attempt to rescue divinity from the depredations of semiotics by deifying the sign. But as soon as the theory of the symbol reestablishes the complementary couple of writer and writing on a cosmic scale, all the uncertainties of representation and presence that Faust confronts in his earthly semiotic condition reemerge in the realm of metaphysical truth. The same problem persists: How can the subject of writing, whether human or divine, overcome the contingency of the writing that constitutes its humanity or divinity?

With a certain inevitability, the figure who forms the complement to the autonomous symbol makes an appearance in the play. The Lord appears in the Prologue in Heaven in his status as the Supreme Creator, and his position at the threshold of the action frames the entire drama. Everything that acts as a gospel of aesthetic symbolism in Part Two and that culminates in the presentation of Helena as the ideal symbol is bracketed by the prior appearance of the Lord as the first artist. Yet at the same time, his explicitly theatrical appearance, with its elaborate machinery of baroque illusionist drama, works to reappropriate the Lord himself for the category of the self-referential aesthetic artifact. But the divine figure who appears as a self-declared fiction then evokes the activity of a prior "maker"—the Poet and the Theater Director who plan the cosmic play in the preceding Prelude in the Theater. These "creators," however, are promptly converted to the status of fictions, as they in turn are framed by the ostensible author of the play, who speaks the preceding Dedication and introduces the characters who are about to appear on stage. This infinite regress of autonomous signs and transcendental writers struggling endlessly for the position of priority creates the conditions for the inherent instability of the symbol in the exemplary symbolist text.

Dozens of pictorial allusions have been identified in *Faust II*. * * * Obviously it is not possible to discuss the entire series, but a few pictorial citations directly involved in Faust's quest for a sacramental vision help to focus the issue of the revelatory sign. These are pictures of deities that regularly appear at moments of impending theophany and thus perform the same equivocal intervention of the sign that was seen with the various magical and sacred inscriptions in Part One. The works to be considered are, first, a painting of Endymion and Luna that is recreated on stage when the pantomime figures of Helena and Paris appear before the audience at the Kaiser's court; next, Faust's dream of Leda and the swan at the beginning of Act 2, which, as described by Homunculus, evokes any number of well-known paintings on the subject; and, finally, the triumph of Galatea at the close of Act 2, a favorite theme of Renaissance painting, perhaps most familiar in the version by Raphael at the Villa Farnese in Rome.

The critical question about the picture of Endymion and Luna is why

Goethe introduces this particular allusion into the action at all. It is by no means self-evident that Helena and Paris should appear in the dumb show in a manner that immediately reminds the audience at the Kaiser's court of familiar pictures of another pair of mythological lovers. Nor to my knowledge does the literary or the iconographic tradition contain a precedent for the encounter of a sleeping Paris with a waking Helena. The image, an invention of the Faust drama, is presented specifically to motivate the Endymion and Luna citation.

The task set for Mephistopheles and Faust is to show the Kaiser the ideal model of human beauty. As Faust puts it, "Ideals female and male, ideally mated, / He would inspect distinctly corporated" (6185–86). Helena and Paris are to appear as the archetypes of perfect human beauty, of which all other human beings are more or less imperfect copies. Such are the connotations of the term "Musterbild." The word predicates a quality of priority or primacy for Helena and Paris, against which all other embodiments will seem secondary and derivative. But once the quasi-Platonic expectation has been aroused, what transpires in the dumb show proves quite paradoxical. The dramatic high point of the Helena and Paris pantomime is a tableau vivant in which the two lovers appear in the stereotyped poses of familiar Endymion and Luna paintings, a pictorial quotation that the audience at court is able to identify at once: "Endymion and Luna! A tableau!" (6509). The supposed "model forms" of human beauty appear in the role of copies. What was heralded as a Platonic paradigm materializes as a self-declared reproduction and, moreover, a reproduction of a painting of an entirely different couple in classical mythology.

The event illustrates and allegorizes a fundamental principle of semiotics: signs derive their meaning not from any necessary connection to the thing they denote but only from their relation to other signs within the same semiotic system. Helena and Paris can stand for "ideal beauty" only in relation to another couple who already carry the same predicate. Without the intrasemiotic reference, there is no guarantee that their appearance will signify "ideal beauty"—as opposed to some other idea, such as "adultery" or "warfare." And the other couple in turn carries the predicate "ideal beauty" only by reference to yet another signifier within the code, another representative of the same idea. Semiotic systems are infinitely circular and irreducibly metaphoric. There can never be a "Musterbild," an archetype, an origin within a code, because the correlation of the individual with the idea always depends on a detour through a prior token of the same idea.

On the dramatic level, the irony of the recognition is devastating. Faust volunteers, with extravagant heroism, to penetrate to the realm of "the Mothers," the supposed source of all phenomena, and to bring back the archetypes of human beauty. But the prize of his colossal quest for origins appears as a citation and thus sacrifices the archetypal primacy that motivated its appearance. In effect, the parousia can occur only as a quotation, but to the extent that it is a quotation, it cannot be a parousia.

The inherent anomalies of Faust's position are underscored by his and Mephisto's consistent references to the realm of the Mothers as a realm of "images" or "pictures": "to forms' unbounded swarming!"; "Enswathed in likenesses of manifold entity"; "Life's images are floating, live, yet lifeless too" (6277, 6289, 6430). The origin of all existence is conceived as iconocentric, a direct counterpart to the logocentric doctrines that appear in Part One. And yet Faust imagines that he can discover in this realm of icons the transcendent essence of perfect beauty. When the divine "essence" finally appears as a quotation of a surrogate motif taken from the storehouse of routine iconography, Faust's quest for a revelatory image is seen to be as contradictory as the verbal version in Part One. The pattern is set for the inadvertent demystification of the symbolic icon that will be Faust's fate in Part Two.

The same gesture is soon repeated. Faust is discovered lying unconscious in his laboratory, immobilized by the explosion that took place when he tried to seize the pantomime image of Helena. In the words of Mephistopheles, Faust is "stupefied" by desire for Helena (6568). But once again a reproduction of a picture interposes itself between the desiring subject and the object of his desire. Faust wants Helena, but his dream vision, as described by Homunculus, reproduces the familiar image of Leda and the swan as stereotyped by countless works in the iconographic tradition. The double displacement enacted in the Helena-Paris pantomime recurs. Faust's desire is deflected to a metaphoric or metonymic substitute (Leda for Helena) appearing as a pictorial citation.

The encounter of Leda and Zeus as swan is, of course, the moment of Helena's conception, and Goethe scholarship has traditionally taken the episode in Faust's dream as a homage to the "morphological laws" that require genetic, organic, and incremental preparation for Helena's eventual appearance. * * * But the naive literalism of the reading duplicates the Faustian credulity that the text is engaged in satirizing. The fragmentation and discontinuity of the action render Helena's eventual appearance inexplicable in any terms of organic causation. Instead, Faust's evocation of the Leda picture reemphasizes that any appearance of Helena is necessarily embedded in a vast, encoded, literary-iconographic system and as such will never be the experience of pure, noncontingent presence that Faust expects it to be. The allusion's occurrence in a dream lends the episode of the Leda citation its ironic bite. Even in dreams—the medium of consciousness that one might (innocently) expect to be least constrained by linguistic rules—the iron laws of semiosis prevail, and the dreamer sees his beloved through a coded metonymy.

With our third pictorial citation, the triumph of Galatea at the climax of the Aegean festival, the advent of the divinity is again anticipated. But the arrival of the goddess—or rather the ghost of the goddess—takes place as a tableau vivant reproducing one of the most familiar images in Renaissance art. What accounts for the surprising and somewhat arbitrary prominence of the Galatea motif at this climactic moment in the action is Galatea's irreducibly pictorial identity. Galatea enters the Renaissance classical tradition as a painting, described in the *Imagines* of Philostratus (c. A.D. 250; first Italian trans., Venice, 1503) and subsequently reconstructed by dozens of Renaissance painters and engravers. If not for the frequent reproduction of the image, Galatea would remain an obscure reference in the poetry of Theocritus. A distinctly minor sea spirit assumes preeminence in the Aegean festival only by virtue of a long history of pictorial transmission and precisely in order to evoke that antecedence. Galatea epitomizes the divinity whose manifestation is inseparable from its iconography, whose "live" appearance reenacts prior representation in pictures, and who thereby confirms the semiotic contingency of all revelation.

The occurrence of an overtly pictorial epiphany at this moment carries with it a corrosive irony, for the audience expecting the epiphany is it-self an audience of gods. These are no mere ordinary mortals caught in the prison house of language but fellow divinities awaiting the parousia. Yet even here, in the realm of divine cognition, the advent can occur only through the mechanism of a pictorial citation. The background of eighteenth-century semiotic philosophy is especially pertinent. We recall that according to that earlier phase of idealist aesthetics, the work of art enables humanity to break through the limits of its sign-bound conscious-ness and achieve something like divine intuition, a global, instantaneous, direct cognition of ultimate reality as it is known to God himself. The lacerating and thoroughly Mephistophelian response of the Galatea epi-sode to that idealist dream is to say in effect: When the gods have to stage an epiphany, they borrow a picture from Raphael. For deities no less than for mortals, ours is inescapably a universe of mediating representations. Nowhere is there unmediated vision or uncoded revelation.

The many aesthetic artifacts in *Faust* that Goethe called the "antece-dents" to Helena might justify their role as revelatory images if the figure whose advent they prepare, Helena, did in fact provide an experience of absolute presence. But the Helena who finally appears is even more overtly compounded out of citational materials than were her prefigurations. She arrives parodying classical Greek trimeters, identifies herself as the subject of ancient legend and fable, and faints when others remind her of less flattering versions of her myth. She then seals her union with Faust by learning how to imitate medieval poetry—that is, by rhyming her speech —and she bears a son who is a reincarnation of Byron. A complete account of Helena's essential citationality would carry us beyond the scope of this discussion, but her aesthetic, literary, and fictive status is evident. The figure whom Faust takes to be a primal reality persistently exposes herself as a reproduction. Undeniably, there is a revelatory quality in Faust's en-counter with Helena. The vast system of artistic "antecedents" does finally produce a manifestation. Symbols do work. But the effect of the manifes-tation is merely to reassert the impossibility of the transcendence that was promised by the antecedent symbols. The referent of the revelatory icons turns out to be not a primal reality but another symbol, a collage of texts, a multilayered, self-proclaimed fiction. Helena is, in short, the paragon of aesthetic symbolism. Her mission is to confirm that the ultimate truth of revelatory signs is the truth of unlimited representation.

It is the one lesson that Faust is unwilling to learn, and the encounter ends in cruel disappointment for him. He is forced to conclude that even when he is married to the incarnation of ideal beauty, transcendence still escapes, him. Once again, "Must agony overwhelm / Delight so soon?"

(9903–04). (Not that the disappointment brings him to renounce his meta-physical quest; he resumes the pursuit immediately.) Yet the equivocal structure of the revelatory sign requires that Helena is not to have the final word. The autonomous symbol must in turn submit to the higher agency of the anthropomorphic maker of symbols, personified here by Mephisto. As a sort of stage manager or master of ceremonies, he rises up in front of the curtain that closes the Helena act, to unmask the proceedings as theater and illusion and to reassert the primacy of the artist over the aes-thetic sign. At the moment the text is most effectively exposing the illu-soriness of Faust's quest, it nevertheless reiterates the same dream of a living presence outside the realm of representations. (Of course Mephisto, even in front of the curtain, does not cease to be a theatrical fiction, but as such he points in turn to his living creators "outside" the fiction: the Poet and the Theater Director who set the whole play going in the Pro-logue. Romantic symbolism repeatedly finds itself evoking the same infi-nite series of the writer and the written vying for priority.)

The ever-optimistic reader might expect that Faust's eventual departure for heaven would at last break the recurrent pattern and overcome the quandaries of the epiphanic sign. The expectation is doomed to disap-pointment. The citation of familiar pictures actually increases as Faust comes closer to "eternity." The way to heaven is lined with pictorial quo-tations, including Luca Signorelli's fresco *Rose-Strewing Angels*, in the ca-thedral at Orvieto; the frescoes in the Camposanto at Pisa depicting anchorites in the Theban wilderness; a painting attributed to Titian, *Saint Jerome in the Wilderness*; and Titian's *Ascension of Mary*, at Santa Maria dei Frari in Venice. That the same Faust who began with a cry of an-guished protest against his prison house of books and his obfuscating painted-glass windows should end up in a heaven filled with Renaissance religious painting and echoing with citations from Dante and the New Testament is an irony that must be termed supremely malicious. The logocentric and iconocentric myths fulfill themselves with a vengeance. Divine presence is revealed to be the repetition of citations and the repro-duction of representations carried out to infinity. Even the concluding Chorus Mysticus reaffirms the principle of transcendental surrogation by invoking as its deity the Holy Virgin, whose official epithet in Christian theology is "Mediatrix."

The ironic conclusion is of course entirely consistent with the doctrine of Romantic symbolism, according to which divinity and signifying are identical. But it is not clear that the symbolist text has thereby escaped the Faustian dilemmas it satirizes. To address the issue, I turn to the postponed question whether Faust, in conjuring the Erdgeist, did not experience at least a momentary glimpse of an absolute being. Did not the Erdgeist scene offer some minimal warrant of a revelatory semiosis? If so, what was the nature of the deity? From the final perspective of Faust in his intertextual, picture-gallery heaven, it begins to appear that even the rev-elation in the opening scene of the drama was another reproduction of a picture. I refer to the famous Rembrandt etching, the so-called *Dr. Faus-tus*, that Goethe used as the frontispiece to the first edition of *Faust* in

1790 * * * . The frontispiece in eighteenth-century editions of novels and plays normally illustrates a dramatic high point of the text. The choice of the picture by Rembrandt instead of the customary original engraving suggests that the Erdgeist scene is destined from the beginning to present itself to the reader in the quality of a tableau vivant. There is evidence that Rembrandt's etching was sufficiently well-known in the eighteenth century for readers of the play to be reminded of it merely by Faust's actions in the first scene. But the frontispiece makes the connection unavoidable. The recurrent pattern of Part Two in which a theophany can occur only as the quotation of a familiar picture, is already established from the earliest moments of Part One.

But apart from indicating the citationality of Faust's vision, the Rembrandt etching, in the way it depicts the spirit, describes an even more fundamental aspect of the Faustian predicament. In a single stroke that prefigures the entire semiotic argument of the play, the spirit appears to Dr. Faustus with a visage that is nothing other than its own conjuring sign. The divine reality sought by the magus turns out to be a replica of its own inscribed, linguistic representation, presumably seen by the magus in the book before him. The referent of the revelational sign is another sign and, moreover, a sign that stresses its semiotic (that is, repeatable) status by pointing to its reflection in a mirror. With an admonishing finger, the spirit refers once again to the inexorable law of universal semiosis: Revelation is always the reproduction of a repeated representation.

Yet at the same time the ineluctable sign declares its absolute truth (in symbolist terms) by finally achieving what is unattainable in ordinary language and what Lessing defined as the ideal goal of aesthetic practice: the complete congruence of arbitrary and motivated representation. The conjuring sign in Dr. Faustus' book turns out to be not only the verbal emblem of the deity in the window but its portrait as well. Icon and writing reach a perfect unification. And the synthesis achieved by the sign in the book is matched by a no less momentous fusion by the spirit in the window, which accomplishes the long-sought, impossible convergence of a transcendental signifier with its transcendental signified. The deity that appears to Dr. Faustus *is* its own sign. Its presence and its representation coincide. The high Romantic dream of a condition in which being and signifying would be one and the same is at last fulfilled.

The glimpse of a motivated and plenitudinous writing, however, provides for a rather unstable moment of redemption. The divine spirit appears not simply as an autonomous text but as a text embedded in a human figure. And with good reason. Were the radiant sign to appear without the support of a human frame, there would be no guarantee that its appearance is indeed a living presence and not just another representation. The embeddedness in a human figure enables the sign to shift from the state of mere referring to one of vital being. Moreover, to offer an isolated piece of writing as the ultimate ground of existence would also imply that human beings were the product rather than the producer of writing—an implication that would seriously affront human dignity (unlike Johannine doctrine, which ensures the subordination of the originating Word to a creating God).

For a variety of reasons then, it is critically important that divine writing not be deprived of its base in a conscious subject. The anthropomorphic figure reinstates subjectivity by pointing, with a "universal" prelinguistic gesture, to his written visage. The figure thereby becomes an ideal Romantic symbol, by literally pointing to its semiotic nature as its truth. But the existence of a conscious subject outside the sign, able to point to its reflected verbal image with a finger, immediately begins to undermine the symbolist claims for the plenitude of language. Writing reverts to that supplementary, exterior, detachable status that first prompted the quest for transcendence of the semiotic condition. The human frame that establishes the divinity of the sign at the same time displaces the sign from its position of primacy. And yet conversely, as soon as the mark of unique selfhood, the face, appears as a reproducible sign, the individuality of the divine self begins to waver and semiotic replication regains the upper hand. The final effect of the Romantic deification of the sign is that the inseparable figures of writer and writing resume their perpetual struggle for dominance at the core of absolute Being.

At its inception then, *Faust* presents an image that not only establishes the importance of semiotic issues in the play but also anticipates the equivocations that these issues implacably generate. All the revelatory signs in the work exhibit the same reversibility, arguing either for the Romantic myth of the divinity of the sign or for the Faustian myth of the eternal displacement of divinity beyond the sign. In providing an illustration for the Romantic deification of the written word, the Rembrandt etching also projects the later predicaments of the symbolist faith. The picture contains the two conflicting views of language that developed out of the Romantic movement and that, under the names of structuralism and phenomenology, still contend with each other today: language as the autonomous master structure that generates itself, stands above the individual subject, and marks the outer limit of human understanding, and language as the medium with which a transcendental human subject evokes and masters reality for itself. In attempting to reconcile theology and semiotics, Romantic symbolism sets in motion a contradictory system of ideas about language that nevertheless continues to exert exceptional power. It is precisely "the being of language" in its impassable ambivalence that begins "to shine ever brighter" in Dr. Faustus' window.

To a considerable extent the nineteenth-century, Biedermeier image of Goethe as the apostle of triumphant humanism still prevails. Not only in literary journalism, where a "Goethean sense of harmony and well-being" passes as proverbial, but also in serious criticism, his work is usually accepted as edifying and affirmational. The profound insecurities of the semiotic condition conveyed by *Faust* suggest that the inherited model may tend to leave some aspects of Goethe's work unaccounted for. The role of the sign in *Faust* should also suggest that Goethe's celebrated antagonisms with other German Romantics are less important than his shared involvement in producing the Romantic religion of writing. On this view, the specter that is currently haunting our intellectual life—the specter of an incurable indeterminacy of discourse—could perhaps be recognized as the same spirit that Faust unwittingly conjured forth with his book of magical signs.

MARC SHELL

The Economics of Translation in Goethe's *Faust*†

In Goethe's *Faust*, * * * contracts in which one party leaves a conditional deposit with another provide the ground for the dramatic generation of the plot. In Part One, for example, Faust deposits his soul in order to transfer to himself special powers, and in Part Two the Emperor deposits his subterranean estate in an attempt to save the empire from ruin. Faust's contract with Mephistopheles elucidates his attempt to translate linguistically the "Word" of the Bible (*Grundtext*) into action, and the Emperor's contract elucidates an attempt to translate, by the medium of paper money, real estate (*Grundbesitz*) into gold. In *Faust*, as we shall see, translational contracts connect the intellectual possession of an idea, which concerns language, with the possession as property of a commodity like gold, which concerns economics. The way in which linguistic and economic translations are identified with and opposed to each other in *Faust* suggests an economy significant to the study of literature and of philosophical dialectic in general.

Translation

When he first appears on stage, Faust is intellectually and financially bankrupt (364, 374). He would overcome this dual dilemma by mining the meaning of verbal and pictorial symbols. He seems to say: "In order to make mine the hidden treasures of the symbolic world and of myself, I must give myself over to magic." His first attempt to interpret or translate to himself the meaning of a sign (*Zeichen*; 427, 434) results in his learning that he is not a god (439). His second attempt results in his learning that he is not a superman (*Übermensch*; 490). Faust, who believed himself to be the image of God, is like (*gleichen*) only the spirit he can conceive (*begreifen*; 512). Who is this spirit?

Before Faust and we learn the answer to this question, Faust's search is interrupted, ironically, by his famulus, Wagner. Wagner has overheard Faust's monologues (as have we). He mistakenly believes that Faust was merely reciting an antique play (as *Faust* appears to some modern readers), and assures Faust that such recitation is profitable (524). Faust agrees with Wagner's apprehension that his words were playful, but only because they cannot yield active results (556). He wonders whether it is ever necessary to juggle words (553). Wagner believes that language is the means (*Mittel*) by which to translate (*übertragen*) to oneself the source (*Quelle*) that all men seek (562–63); Faust distrusts bibliolatrous researchers because they obscure the meaning he seeks. For Faust one's own soul (*eigne Seele*) is the holy source. He pities Wagner for his fruitless philological search to acquire intellectual treasure (*Schatz*) and alludes to Heraclitus' fragment

† From *Money, Language and Thought: Literary and Philosophical Economies from the Medieval to the Modern Era* (Berkeley: U of California P, 1982), 84–130. The author's footnotes have been omitted. His quotations from *Faust* have been replaced with Arndt's translation.

about those who seek to translate to themselves, or to mine, gold and cannot discover it (604–5, compare 6766–67).

Throughout *Faust*, as we shall see, the general problem of acquisition is expressed in terms of translation. In this work of literature, * * * such words as *Übertragung* mean both "economic transference of property" and "linguistic transfer of meaning." Translation in *Faust* thus includes the inheritance of intellectual property from previous generations. On the one hand, Faust seems to have wanted to carry on the medical tradition bequeathed to him by his father. "What you received but as your father's heir, / Make it your own to gain possession of it!" (682–83). On the other hand, Faust now knows the difficulties of appropriating knowledge, and he knows that his father did not practice true medicine. On Easter Day, when the people sing the praises of Faust the doctor's son (1007), for example, he insists that he served his father only as a steward who distributed a dangerous drug (*Gift*; 1053). He argues that the people should praise only the divine Father and/or Son, who made a pact with the people on the first Easter Day. Wagner is unable to understand Faust's dissatisfaction with himself. "Come, does an honest man do ill / Pursuing with good faith and will / The art with which he was entrusted?" (1057–59). Wagner cannot understand that Faust, in his dissatisfaction, is living up to the standards that God expects from him. In the Prologue to *Faust*, God the Father insists that Faust, who refuses merely to carry on the medical knowledge of his father, is not so much a *Doktor* (which is what Mephistopheles calls him [941]) as the knight of God (299).

Although the servant of God, Faust needs the devil, or at least a devilish agent. "Outside the City Gate" of the human city, Faust recognizes that he is a mere *Mensch* (940), but soon he wishes to become or to form an alliance with a sub- or nonhuman *Unmensch* (compare 3349). He wishes for a magic mantle that can carry (*tragen*) him to alien (*fremde*) lands (1123). Almost immediately there appears on stage an inhuman being, a poodle, that will soon become, by means of an act of linguistic translation, an agent of translation in general.

Wagner believes that when one opens up an ancient parchment the very heavens will descend on one (1108–9). Faust, however, does not share Wagner's reverence for the written word. He seeks to translate (*übertragen*) into his own medium the alien source that is the holy Original or sacred *Grundtext* (1220–23). Martin Luther, Protestant contemporary of the historical Faustus, translated the apostle John's sentence about the universal origin, "En archē ēn ho logos," as "Im Anfang war das Wort" ("In the beginning was the Word"; compare 1224). Faust protests, however, that he cannot treasure the Word as much as the *logos* (1226, compare 1216). (Perhaps, too, he holds that in the beginning there was something other than the *logos*.) He translates John's *logos* into his own terms as Act (*Tat*; 1237). "In mining the meaning from words," Faust seems to say, "I must change it in order to make it mine."

For Faust's active translation of the divine Word, most traditional scholars would excommunicate him from the university on such grounds as bad Greek and religious heresy. Here in Faust's study that translation makes for the transformation of the poodle into the devilish *Unmensch* (nonhuman being) Mephistopheles (1238–321). (I shall suggest later why the translation should precipitate the appearance of the infernal beast.) Faust's translation, or perhaps his inscription of it with a feather pen (*Feder*; 1231), thus prepares the way for (or is itself an architectonic part of) the motive spring (*Triebfeder*) of the tragedy: the deal that Mephistopheles strikes with Faust.

Unlike the other spirits with whom Faust communicated, Mephistopheles likes and is like Faust (1646). Faust and Mephistopheles conclude a pact (*Pakt*; 1414) or bond (*Bündnis*; 1741) apparently different from Jesus's bond (*Bünde*; 748) of the first Easter Day, the mere symbol of which frightens Mephistopheles (1300–2). Mephistopheles proposes that he serve Faust, in return for which Faust shall do the like (*das gleiche*) for him when they meet in the beyond (1658–59). Faust counterproposes a bet and states the terms: "If the swift moment I entreat: / Tarry a while! You are so fair! / Then forge the shackles to my feet" (1699–1701). By this wager, which brings to earth the bet in heaven between God and Mephistopheles (compare 315–17), Faust makes a hypothec, or hypothetical deposit, of his soul in return for a still undefined power, and Mephistopheles gambles that he can give Faust the (Rousseauian) rest for which, it seems to Mephistopheles, Faust yearns. * * * The motive spring of Goethe's *Faust* is this pact in which Faust risks losing his soul. The plot (*hupothēsis*) of *Faust* contains many such conditional deposits—hypothetical hypothecs—which seem to move the plot forward. Its moving force is the prompter (*hupothētēs*) Mephistopheles, who enables Faust to progress by a kind of spiritual or intellectual hypothesization.

Before he begins to serve Faust, Mephistopheles demands that their oral agreement be written down (1714–15). Faust mocks Mephistopheles' Wagnerian demand, and uses the language of the mint to criticize written documents. "A square of parchment, though, all writ and stamped [*beschrieben und beprägt*], becomes a specter [*Gespenst*] that repels all men" (1726–27). Faust puts no credence in written documents: "The word is cramped" (1728). But Mephistopheles is insistent. Although he does not care what kind of paper is used, he demands that Faust sign (*unterzeichen*) in blood (1731–37). To humor the vampyric devil, Faust writes his signature in blood. The signed pact is a "letter of hypothecation," which * * * grounds the subsequent action of the drama. Mephistopheles, as we shall see, treats the writing that certifies the hypothetical hypothecation of Faust's soul as a credit note, brandishing it during the drama as a deed entitling him to Faust's soul (11613, compare 6576).

*   *   *

* * * In *Faust* Part Two, * * * the relationship between symbol and thing, which is presented in Part One primarily as the difference between word and concept, is represented as the tension between coined or paper money and commodity. The seemingly appropriative power of money, which Mephistopheles here offers to Faust, is actually a powerful logic of symbolization, a money of the mind, with which the devil, as Luther has him, plans to abuse unthinking men in order to damn them.

Just after Mephistopheles' famous statement about Faust's going over (*sich übergeben*; 1866) to the devil, Goethe shows how Mephistopheles is planning to damn Faust by showing how he damns his foil, the Student who interrupts Faust's conversation with Mephistopheles. Pretending to be Faust, Mephistopheles disorients the Student by confusing his understanding of the relation of words to things and concepts. His method is to disjoin words and things, to urge the Student to attend only to the written word (1952–53). He praises the "possessibility" of written knowledge, which, as the Student comes to believe, one can carry (*tragen*; 1967) about in black and white. The gate to the temple of certainty is to hold "fast" to the words of the master (1990–92). No need, it seems, to work to understand concepts. At first the Student is loath to accept Mephistopheles' advice, and argues that there must be a concept for each word (1993). But Mephistopheles argues that even where concepts fail the proper word can be found (1995–96). The Student is duped by Mephistopheles' argument that one should credit or believe in (*glauben*; 1999) mere words and that nothing, not even an iota, can be robbed or misappropriated (*rauben*) from a word. A word, like an intellectual possession, is secure from robbery. (At the end of *Faust* there is some suggestion that Mephistopheles, who believes in the power of the note he has asked Faust to sign, himself believes that nothing can be taken from its written words.) Mephistopheles neglected to sign his agreement with Faust, and he is pleased to sign the notebook of Faust's foil, the Student who came to see Faust with money and fresh blood (2045, 1877). Slightly altering the words of Eve to the serpent, he makes his sign (*Zeichen*; 2046). When next we see this foil to Faust, he is an easily damned Baccalaureus (6790).

It is not so easy to damn Faust. In Part One Goethe begins to explain Faust's eventual salvation in terms of Faust's intuition of nameless concepts (*Begriffen*). Faust, for example, conceives (*greifen*) a feeling of love for which he knows no name or word (3059–66): he seems to believe in the ineffability of the divine symbol (1307). Mephistopheles tries to take advantage of Faust's intuition of the ineffable by arguing that Faust's feeling for Gretchen is mere animal desire, and Gretchen herself is displeased that Faust does not name the divine. Throughout the drama, however, Faust continues to stand by the ineffability of feelings and concepts. Words, he argues, bring a false sense of certainty. Faust's refusal to be misled by crediting signs that have no meaning is a characteristic that enables him, though allied with a horsepowerful *Unmensch*, to become a true *Mensch*.

Wealth and Poetry

Faust, Part Two, begins with an empire that is in hock (*verpfändet*; 4874), just as Part One began with the bankruptcy of an individual who lacked money. In Part Two, as we shall see, the Emperor makes a social bond that recapitulates at the political level the bond Faust made with Mephistopheles.

Mephistopheles insinuates himself into the court of the economically pressed empire and cleverly directs the courtiers' attention away from their thesaural problem, the lack of goods and specie to pay off their debts, to a fiduciary solution, a dependency on a new kind of credit. He argues that the Emperor can pay off his creditors (*Gläubiger*) merely by being believed. "Could confidence be bruised [*mangelten*] / Where sovereignty brooks no insolence" (4878–79). Mephistopheles insinuates that lack of money (*Geld*; 4890), not treasure, is the problem plaguing the empire. If men only believed in the empire, then the Emperor would not need to mine the land for gold. Mephistopheles pretends to be interested in mining, in bringing goods and specie that are deep under the ground up to the light of day (4892); he seems to be a social vampire that would bleed the veins of the mountains and discover "gold . . . minted and, unminted" (4893–94), both medium of exchange and commodity. In fact, however, his interest is only in the medium, and in using the effects of the mint on the minds of men.

Mephistopheles' stated plan is to employ man's natural and spiritual power (*Natur- und Geisteskraft*; 4896) to produce (perhaps to represent) subterranean treasure. The Chancellor argues correctly that this plan is inimical to feudalism and Christianity, but Mephistopheles counters with a critical credo of his own: "What you don't coin you think does not avail [*gelte nicht*]" (4922). And prompting, or speaking ventriloquistically through a dummylike astrologer, he argues that gold can be a cornucopia like the sun. The Emperor cares more for satisfying his desires than for scrutinizing the actual source of the promised means to do so (cf. 4945–46). Believing that Mephistopheles intends to use the underground, rather than the crediting minds of gullible men, as his source of treasure, the convinced Emperor grants to Mephistopheles the shadowy obscurity of the underground. He hopes that whatever therein is valuable will come to the light of day (5034; a hope that, ironically, echoes God's statement in the "Prologue in Heaven" that a good man will eventually see the light).

By whom or what will the promised gold be discovered? In Part Two Mephistopheles suggests that the members of the court might take up hoes in order to mine the treasures of the earth (5039), as he suggested in Part One that Faust might hoe in the fields in order to regain youth (2354). In Part Two the Emperor seems to accept this type of work as a means of raising a herd of golden cattle (5040–41). (Faust rejected the hoe as a suitable means [*Mittel*; 2360–64].) The desire of the Emperor for the things of which Mephistopheles has told him, however, becomes so great that it must be restrained. Mephistopheles therefore diverts the Emperor's attention to what will seem, like goods and specie, to satisfy his desire: the deceptive but credited productions of magical art. * * *

Mephistopheles arranges for subtle changes in the aesthetic production, the masque that was to have been the court's pleasant diversion from the problem of thesaural scarcity in the empire. The Herald of the masque, a proctophantasmiac (4158–60), suspects rightly that ghosts (*Gespenster*; 5501) are disrupting the show. He notes, for example, that Zoilo-Thersites (played by Mephistopheles) interrupts the goddess of all activities (*Tätigkeiten*; 5449–60). Although he claims to be able to "make the high low" and vice versa (5467), the Herald is unable to interpret, or mine below the surface meaning of, three allegorical figures that appear on stage: Boy

Charioteer; Plutus, or Wealth (played by Faust); and Starveling (played by Mephistopheles). Boy Charioteer introduces Plutus to the courtiers as the answer to the desire for gold (5569–71), and in a riddling poem he calls himself "Poetry" and describes his relationship to Plutus in terms of dispensation:

> I am profusion, I am poetry;
> The poet who fulfills himself
> By squandering his inmost wealth.
> I, too, am rich beyond all measure,
> Count myself Plutus-like in treasure,
> I quicken and adorn his feast,
> By lavishing what he has least.
> (5573–79)

In *Faust,* * * * poetry is identified with cornucopian dispensation. This association is as old as Aristotle and Alcidamus, and was common among many eighteenth-century thinkers, such as Alexander Gottlieb Baumgarten. Goethe's Boy Charioteer seems to refer to the Longinian theory in which sublimity or dispensation is the polar opposite of orderly disposition. The effect of sublime language is irresistible transport, while the effect of disposition is persuasion. "Sublimity flashes forth at the right moment, scatters everything before it like a thunderbolt, and displays the power of the orator in all its plenitude." The sublime precipitates a sense of production by the reader. "Our soul is naturally uplifted by the truly [sublime]; we receive it as a joyous offering; we are filled with delight and pride as if we had ourselves created what we heard." Longinus' polar opposition of economy to sublimity, moreover, involves a corresponding opposition of work or resistance to beauty. The audience, like the writer, may be inventive and skillful, and may work hard at understanding the events that it sees or reads. The audience, however, cannot control its reaction to the sublime. As in the philosophy of Immanuel Kant, the beautiful is that which can, indeed must, be comprehended without work, so the sublime here is that which we in the audience believe, however erroneously, that we ourselves have created or produced effortlessly. It is the sublime that Goethe depicts in many productions (compare 236) and that, finally, Goethe shows to be unworthy of credit. Without work there is no production; without resistance there is no justifiable feeling of liberation from resistance. In *Faust* the opposition between disposition (Longinus' "body") and dispensation (Longinus' "soul") creates a tension between creditable, real activity and uncreditable, unreal activity. As we shall see, such figures as Homunculus (a soul without a body), Boy Charioteer (who calls himself "Dispensation"), and the poet Euphorion end in a sublime manner.

Boy Charioteer's attempt to explain the relationship of Poetic Dispensation to wealth (Plutus) is not successful. The courtiers do not understand his riddle about aesthetic and economic production, and they are enraged when Boy Charioteer's apparently valuable gifts are metamorphosed into insects (5699, compare 6592–603, 1516–17). The annoyed Herald exclaims: "The scamp, for rich rewards foretold / He offers but the gleam of gold!" (5604–5). But, as Boy Charioteer argues, the Herald fails properly to interpret the transformation (5609). The Boy must appeal to Plutus, who thus upholds the credentials of Poetry.

> I gladly say: You're spirit of my spirit.
> Your deeds enact my mind alone,
> Your wealth is greater than my own.
> This twig of green, your service to redeem,
> Above all crowns and circlets I esteem;
> Hear all this truthful eulogy:
> My cherished son, I take delight in thee.
> (5623–29)

Plutus calls the boy his son, but the latter soon raises questions about this supposed kinship. The "father" and "son" differ along the lines that defined the wager between Faust and Mephistopheles (the opposition between rest and activity). Boy Charioteer asks Plutus:

> Should they devote themselves to you? to me?
> While idleness rewards your devotees.
> My followers can never rest at ease.
> (5702–4)

In *Faust*, Goethe thus considers the kinship between wealth and poetic dispensation. * * *

Plutus dismisses Boy Charioteer after the Boy has brought a casket from the chariot to the appropriate area on stage. Like other caskets in the works of Goethe, the one carried by the Boy in *Faust* is full of dangers. The courtiers believe they see in it all things, including rolls of coins and ducats that jump as if stamped (*geprägt*; 5715–26). They see the answer to all desire. The Herald is disturbed that the audience takes the seeming for the real. He argues that what they see is mere seeming (*Schein*) or play (*Spiel*), that the contents of the casket are *Goldschein*. "You think they'd give you gold or worth?" (5730). His warning goes unheeded.

The finale of the masque is signaled by the arrival of Pan (played by the Emperor). Accompanying him are gnomes who mine, or bring to the light of day, gold, "what they use to pimp [*kuppeln*] and steal" (5857). Seeming to do the work required to satisfy desire, they would bleed the veins of the mountains for golden blood (5850–51). Instead of actually digging, however, the gnomes flatter Pan as a potential source of all things:

> Here we now discover bubbling
> Wondrous fountain ready-breached,
> Promising to yield, untroubling,
> What before could scarce be reached.
> (5906–9)

The gnomes promise that the Emperor can introduce, or himself become, a cornucopian source of wealth. "Speak the word only," they implore Pan. One of the gnomes (later to be identified as the Chancellor) makes a plea for the Emperor to do something (later to be identified as certifying a credit note) that will profit all the world. Whatever else the Emperor does, he is taken with and in by the fiery source (*Feuerquelle*) in the casket. His close approach to this source precipitates an explosion that ends the masque. This explosion becomes an important focus in the remaining scenes of Part Two, in which Mephistopheles will seem to establish a fiduciary economy that reveals the secrets of nature. * * * The masque is an allegorical exploration of a lack of aesthetic and economic funds.

In the following episode, generally called the "Paper Money Scene," what was presented in the *Schein* of the masque as plenty of *Gold* issues as paper money or *Geldscheine*. When the scene opens we learn that the creditors of the Emperor are somehow paid; the army is rehired, and there is fresh blood in the soldiers' ranks (6047). The Chancellor explains what has happened when he reads aloud a text inscribed on a leaf of paper:

> "To All it may Concern upon Our Earth:
> This paper is a thousand guilders worth.
> There lies, sure warrant of it and full measure,
> Beneath Our earth a wealth of buried treasure.
> As for this wealth, the means are now in train
> To raise it and redeem the scrip again."
> (6057–62)

During the masque the Emperor set his signature to this negotiable paper with a feather pen (*Federzügen*; 6064–70), just as Faust in Part One set his signature to the contract with Mephistopheles with a feather (*Feder*). (Faust's words mocking Mephistopheles' demand in Part One that their contract be a written one—"A square of parchment, though, all writ and stamped, / Becomes a specter that repels all men" [1726–27]—make us leery of this "ghost money" in Part Two.) The monetary bargain, which promises delivery of assigned underground goods, is thus the foil to the contract between Mephistopheles and Faust, which seemed to promise delivery of a soul. As a "magic cape" (1122) seemed to redeem Faust's situation in Part One, so the "magic leaves" (*Zauberblätter*; 6157) of money seem to redeem the political economy of the empire in Part Two. They are "gilded leaves" that, like the "leaf" on which Faust wrote his pact, seem able to transform all that is bad into good. The "poem" on the paper seems to turn it into a "golden leaf."

Unlike the contract in Part One, this signed document promising delivery is reproduced thousandsfold with a stamp (6074). The wonderful technology brings to mind mechanical reproduction by the coin maker's anvil die and the printer's press; Mephistopheles' amazing technique recalls achievements like those of the medieval printer and moneylender Fust. Printing in Fust's medieval world surpassed the old alphabet, but the new monetary sign (*Zeichen*) that is paper money does more: it makes all other symbols supernumerary and at the same time elicits belief in the greatest treasure (6081–82). * * * In this part of *Faust* the new and ideologically subversive mode of symbolization is linked with the historical advent of paper money.

Paper Money and Language

Understanding the significance of paper money in *Faust* requires both consideration of historical and literary antecedents and exploration of the theoretical problems of aesthetic and philosophical—as well as economic —inflation that the Paper Money Scene poses.

In the Paper Money Scene, Goethe imitates Marco Polo's brilliant description of paper money in China, in which Polo tries to explain Chinese financial institutions, which his European audience did not believe to exist, in terms of alchemy and flight. Goethe himself disliked and distrusted paper money. In *Faust* he recalls such disastrous European monetary experiments as the issuing of *notes de confiance* by John Law * * * , the "Don Quixote of finance." * * * He alludes to the hypothecal and land-secured *assignats* issued during the French Revolution * * * and to the Austrian redemption notes (called "Scheingeld"). And he takes into consideration Shakespeare's account of how Richard II, more "Landlord of England" than its king, issued "blank charters" and "rotten parchment bonds."

The theoretical relationship between aesthetic and monetary theory was explored by several European and American writers during the first part of the nineteenth century, but only Goethe seriously considered the connection between economic symbolization in paper money and aesthetic symbolization in poetry. In *Faust* this connection involves the inflation that follows from the Emperor's allowing the printed papers to pass for gold.

> It circulates like gold of true assay?
> The Court, the Army take it in full pay?
> I scarce believe it, though you say I ought.
> (6083–85)

His own Marshall reassures the astonished Emperor by describing the widespread circulation of the "flying moneys":

> The fugitives could never now be caught:
> The stuff was scattered broadside in a wink.
> The money-changers' benches groan, and clink,
> Each single sheet is honored in their court
> In gold and silver, though a trifle short.
> (6086–90)

Although the Emperor seems not to notice, the Marshall's words imply that inflation is already affecting the economy of the empire. Just as verbal inflation serves to damn the Student from Part One, so the monetary "kites" * * * lead the empire toward political disaster in Part Two. * * * If the amount of gold is unmeasurable in the same way that Boy Charioteer's gifts are supposed to be, then the inflationary discount must increase infinitely. All moneys, including crowns, will become worthless, as will the crown itself.

Mephistopheles, who had argued earlier in Part Two that belief was all that the court needed to obtain golden wealth, now allies aesthetic with monetary symbolization. Through the medium of the dummylike Faust, he suggests that the *Kaiserland* is a poetical reserve and that the treasure in the land is, like the fantastical goods parceled out by Poetic Dispensation or Boy Charioteer (5576–79), infinite and unquantifiable. Faust himself compares mining with imagining:

> The plethora of treasure which, congealed,
> The depths of Your dominions hold concealed
> Lies unexploited. Concept most immense
> Is to such wealth a negligible fence
> (6111–14)

Thought cannot measure buried wealth. The winged bills, he says with some irony, fly higher than fantasy can imagine.

> Imagination in its loftiest flight
> Will not encompass it, strain as it might.
> Yet spirits gifted with profoundest sense
> Place in the boundless . . . boundless confidence.
> (6115–18; cf. 640–51)

To Faust's apparent advocacy of credit, Mephistopheles adds reminders of the ability of paper money to take the place of gold and to help one know exactly what one possesses (6119–20), just as writing, which he praised to the Student in Part One, helps one know what one knows. Mephistopheles and Faust thus formulate a false and inflationary economics of thought. The inadequacy of that economics is later revealed in a flight of fantasy by Euphorion, the son of Faust and Helen, akin to the Boy Charioteer. In Act I, however, only the fool (whose role in the foolish court Mephistopheles until now has usurped) openly questions the insubstantiality of the paper money notes. He asks that he be allowed to translate the papers given to him by the Emperor into real estate (*Grundbesitz*; 6171), what Kant calls *Substanz*. As the fool suspects, it will turn out that the *Pfand*, or pledge, that the banknote represents is an idealist *Pfänderspiel* (5194), or play of forfeits.

The Paper Money Scene is part of a critique of the idealist philosophy that operates without material guarantees or substantial securities. * * *

In *Faust* the tension between promise and delivery is presented as an opposition between the ideal and the real. What seems to guarantee a promise—Faust's conditional promise to deliver his soul, for example, and the Emperor's promise to deliver underground treasure—is a creditable deposit, a *sumbolon* or hypothec. As Kant argues in a discussion of money and contractual transference of ownership (*translatio/Übertragung*), some contracts require an immediate cash transfer that connects purchase with sale and thus serves as a secure guarantee. In other contracts, alienation of property depends on an exchange of a cautionary pledge or of collateral. Money that changes hands in cash transfers should not be confused with caution money: caution money is not part of the purchase price. * * * In *Faust* Mephistopheles hopes that paper money—which is insubstantial in the sense that real estate is substantial—will entirely replace both cash transfer and real collateral. His conceptual conflation of monetary *sumbola* with their linguistic counterparts leads toward a devilishly insidious confusion between monetary hypothecs in economic transactions and dialectical hypotheses in idealist philosophy.

In *Faust*, moreover, the word of the Emperor on the banknote seems to substantiate credit and exchange just as the word of God in some English idealist philosophies substantiates the credibility of human discourse. * * * In *Faust*, Mephistopheles teaches a monetary as well as a linguistic immaterialism. The "absolute" (6736) in many German idealist philosophies—one of which the damnable Student, who disdains empirical knowledge (6758), has adopted as his own—is associated by Mephistopheles not only with a lack of substance but also with an *ab*sence of monetary solvency or of *solida* (Roman coins of "solid" gold).

Why is paper money more to Mephistopheles' liking than coin? During its historical metamorphosis from commodity (a lump of gold) to coin (a commodity impressed with the stamp of the state) to paper money (a mere impression), *solid* metal undergoes and participates in culturally and philosophically subversive changes. The widespread use of coins, which are both symbols and commodities, may precipitate some conceptual misunderstanding of the relationship between signs and things, but it does not encourage its users to believe that symbol and commodity, or word and concept, are entirely separable. * * * Paper money, on the other hand, does appear to be a symbol entirely disassociated from the commodity that it symbolizes.

A theory of coin and paper money that treats them both as kinds of inscriptions may shed further light on the difference between their modes of symbolization, a difference that Mephistopheles uses to his own ends. On the one hand, it is clear that a coin is a composition of a numismatic inscription and a metallic ingot into which the inscription is impressed and to which the inscription refers as a valuable commodity. On the other hand, it is unclear whether paper money should be conceived as a composition of an inscription and an inscribed paper (*Zettel*), whose reference to an untold, unmined, and perhaps nonexistent commodity is ultimately irrelevant to its validity, or whether it should be conceived as a composition of an inscription, an inscribed thing, and a commodity for which the inscription and the inscribed thing, taken together, are an ersatz. Thus the paper money, or *Ersatz* gold (6057–62), in *Faust* raises questions crucial to understanding not only symbolization, but also the epigram, which [has been] defined as a genre in which the inscription and the inscribed thing are to be thought of as two theoretically inseparable parts of the same whole.

Goethe's analysis of the relationship between language and money had a remarkable influence on social theorists from Wilhelm von Schütz to Oswald Spengler. The theorist for whom *Faust* was a dominant influence throughout his life, however, was Karl Marx. In his ideological analyses of the alienation that obtains in linguistic and monetary appropriation, Marx returns again and again to *Faust*; and many works by Marx can be understood as attempts to interpret and develop Goethe's concern with the relationship between linguistic and monetary alienation and with Hegelian idealism (which Marx calls "mind's coin of the realm"). * * *

* * *

The Evocation of Helen

At a magic mirror before which he stands in Part One, Faust sees the image (*Bild*) of a beautiful woman (2429–30, 2436, 2600). Images, like words, may be deceptive. Mephistopheles, who remarks that "people by and large, just given a word, / Believe [*glaubt*] there needs must be some sense behind it" (2565–66), hopes that Faust will soon be deceived into seeing a beautiful Helen (in general) in every woman (in particular; 2603–4). The heart of Faust, indeed, is soon impressed (*geprägt*) by the image of Gretchen. (Similarly, in Part Two the courtiers are stamped by the sight of the things in the casket [5719].) Mephistopheles, hoping to use the magic image (*Zauberbild*; 4190) for his own ends, decides to mediate between Faust and the woman he believes that Faust seeks. Acting the pimp (*Kuppler*; 3030, 3338), he argues that the value of a woman's love is measurable by gold (3156, 3314), just as he argued earlier that love, the feeling that for Faust was ineffable, "measures up to" a word. If Mephistopheles could convince Faust of this theory of measurement or payment as he convinced the Student of his linguistic theory, then the love of Gretchen would no longer seem to Faust to be immeasurable or inexpressible in words.

The problem of translation is thus linked with that of prostitution. Mephistopheles, whose metamorphosis from poodle to devil accompanied Faust's linguistic translation of word to act, plays the intermediary. * * *
Part One of *Faust*, then, depicts Mephistopheles' attempt to convince Faust that Gretchen is a whore, which is what Valentine calls her (3730, compare 3767), and that Faust and he are an inseparable duo: "I am the broker here and you [Faust] the suitor" (4071). * * *

The motif of pimping continues into Part Two. During the masque, for example, Mephistopheles, who plays the role of Avarice, breaks through a redeemable security or hypothecary pledge of order (*Ordnung Unterpfand*; 5761), erected by Plutus, and delivers a propagandistic speech in favor of paper money, which is supposed to represent, even to produce, gold. He promises the members of the court the golden treasures of the bowels of the earth and the sexually satisfying treasures of an erotic find. * * *
Mephistopheles forms the "gold" contained in the casket into a phallus, a quintessential symbol of male desire. Gold, like sexual desire, is omnimorphous; it can be metamorphosed or translated into anything (5781–82, compare 4977–92). The phallus, like money, is architectonic. "That stuff complies with any shape you mold" (5782).

In his praise of paper moneys, moreover, Mephistopheles associates banknotes with love letters. Seeming to recall his praise of the possessibility and portability of written words delivered to the Student in Part One (1966–67), he suggests that both letters and moneys are mediators between whore and client:

> One is no longer plagued by purse or package,
> A note borne next the heart is easy baggage,
> It aptly couples there with love epistles.
> In priestly breviaries it chastely nestles,
> The soldier, too, for ease of hips and loins
> May now discard the ponderous belt of coins.
> Your Highness pardon if this stately matter
> I seem to slander by such lowly chatter.
>
> (6103–10)

The lofty work to which Mephistopheles here refers is the printing of paper money in Part Two. The other productions called works in *Faust* are the creation of the world, to which reference is made in the "Prologue in Heaven," and the creation of Helen herself in Part Two. Throughout Part Two we ponder the status of Hellenic beauty. Is Helen a prostitute like the one that Mephistopheles and Valentine wrongly assume Gretchen to be? Is she a mere ghost like paper money? Or is she somehow real?

In Part Two Helen appears twice, first as a ghost and then, apparently, in reality. These appearances recapitulate the Gretchen and paper money episodes.

Helen's first appearance follows the Emperor's request that Faust bring forth Paris and Helen, the prototypic images (*Musterbilder*) of man and woman (6185). In the masque, as we have seen, Faust and Mephistopheles produced the *Schein*, or appearance, of gold. (What was presented artfully in the masque as plenty of gold was represented in the Paper Money Scene as the cornucopia of monetary *Geldscheine*.) The Emperor's present request for ideals makes Faust remark: "First we arranged to make him rich, / Now we're expected to amuse him" (6191–92). The production of aesthetic ideals, he suggests, is part of the same structure as that of monetary wealth. Mephistopheles, however, insists that to produce Helen (a love "treasure"; 6315, 6323) is not so easy as to produce paper money. Helen, he insists, is not so easy "[to] magic . . . up as cheaply / as now the guilders' paper phantom" * * * (6197–98). Mephistopheles pretends that the machines of the devil are not able to pass (*gelten*; 6202) for heroines, but proposes nevertheless to translate Helen from Greece to Germany if Faust visits the Mothers (6216), who * * * seem to confer rights of subscription. Faust, who remarked, "For every trick you ask an added fee" (6206), agrees to the contract.

The artful production of Helen does not require extra magic. The Herald notes that the room is already inhabited by spirits (6378). The astrologer introduces the playlet, but he is interrupted by Mephistopheles, who rises from the prompter's box and reminds us that prompting is "Old Nick's rhetoric forte" (6400). Mephistopheles presents an Aristotelian theory of probability and possibility, and, arguing "ventriloquistically" through the astrologer, suggests that the tension between probability and possibility is resolvable by credit: "Lay eyes upon your bold desire-in-chief, / It is impossible, and hence deserves belief." If one were to restrain reason with a magical word, then daring fantasy could make the impossible appear probable (*glaubenswert*; 6415–20).

In the following playlet, Helen in particular is supposed to be credited as the Beautiful (*Schönheit*) in general. The allegory is a kind of cornucopian dispensation. "The others but the bold magician traces; / He confidently shows, a lavish host, / To each the wondrous, what he craves the most" (6436–38). As it turns out, Faust is more taken by the image of Helen than other members of the court. To him she seems a blessed boon, the source of beauty (*der Schönheit Quelle*; 6488). The image he saw in the magic mirror, he now says, was a mere smoke image (*Schaumbild*; 6497) of Hellenic beauty.

Faust is so enraptured that Mephistopheles must prompt him to keep to his part (6501). He reminds Faust that Paris, whose seizure of Helen Faust would now repeat, is a mere ghost; that Faust himself is the author of the phantasmagoria entitled "Der Raub der Helena" ("The Rape/ Robbery of Helen"; 6546–48). The German Faust, however, still wants to appropriate to himself the Greek Helen. Like the Emperor at the end of the masque, he oversteps the bounds of art, and, holding the key brought from the Mothers, tries to seize Helen.

> What rape! Is it for nothing here I stand?
> Does this key count for nothing in my hand?
> It led through wave and swell and awesome strand
> Of desolation back here to firm land.
> (6549–53)

The German Faust would appropriate the Greek Helen from the Trojans and thus hold fast to reality. * * * Like the Emperor at the end of the masque, Faust grabs for the ideal as though it were real. "Der Raub der Helena" ends, like the masque, in an explosion.

Faust, however, does not cease to attempt to appropriate, or translate, Helen to himself. Classical Walpurgisnacht (Act II) depicts his dreamlike search for her, and the Helena Act (Act III) depicts its apparent success. In Act III Goethe makes what is impossible appear probable to Faust and to us. (We replace the courtly audience from Act I.) The German man acquires the Greek woman; the German devil Mephistopheles travels with this man from Germany to Greece, to which the devil is alien, and the devil is translated (*übertragen*; 8013) into the Greek Phorcyas; and Helen, speaking German in Greek syntax, is united with Faust in a kind of matrimony. Faust, it seems, accomplishes in a medieval castle, perched amid ancient Troy/Greece and Goethe's Germany, the kind of appropriation of the Hellenic that he sought. It appears that Faust accomplishes in the central act of Part Two what Goethe sets forth as two complementary maxims for translators: with the help of a middleman Faust brings himself to an alien (*fremde*) nation and also brings that alien nation to himself in such a way as to find its property (*Eigenheit*) in himself.

Helen sings of the marvelous union between herself, Faust, and their child Euphorion as a bond (*Bund*); Faust sings of their being bound together (9705); and the chorus, too, sings to their union (*Verein*; 9710, 9736). For a while everyone credits the union as a treasured possession and boon (*Schatz, Hochgewinn, Besitz,* and *Pfand*). But they are ultimately deceived. Although the aim of some translation is to make familiar what was strange, no middleman (*Vermittler*) can translate or appropriate the Hellenic treasure (*Schatz*) to Germany in such a way that the alien Helen can become homely fare (*Hausmannskost*). In *Faust*, the apparent union of the German and the Greek falls apart. Its product and sign, Euphorion, is too much an outburst of divine spirit, which, as Longinus noted, is difficult to bring under control. Prefigured in the masque as Boy Chari-oteer, or Poetic Dispensation, Euphorion is as little at home in Germanic Greece as was the Boy in the masque. His end, like that of the child of Faust and Gretchen in Part One, is swift. Euphorion flies too high (9821), as does paper money, and, like Homunculus, he ends in the sea. The bond between Helen and Faust is shattered. Poetry, it turns out, is illusive and inflationary. Whatever necessity impelled Euphorion to break the law-ful but dreamy bond (9883), his leave-taking precipitates that of Helen herself.

Helen may represent "reality" in Faust. * * * Once Helen learns to speak German, however, Mephistopheles has some control over her. Mephistopheles, Goethe says, is a director of the Hellenic ghosts in Act III; he can stop the action. (See stage directions at 8929–30 and 8936–37.) He knows that Helen is a ghost as "congealed" (8930) as the golden treasure in the underground to which Faust elsewhere refers (6111). Goethe himself wrote of Byron, on whom Euphorion is modeled, that he was "much money and no authority." Like the *Schein* of the masque, in which gold appears to be discovered, Helen is a paper model.

The Law of the Fist (Faustrecht)

Faust, Part Two, * * * depicts allegorically the downfall of a society typified by feudal dueling and the rise of a society typified by modern war-ring. The political allegory begins with the spiritual dueling between Faust and Mephistopheles in Part One, and occupies many scenes of Part Two. War informs *Faust*, Part Two, from "Der Raub der Helena" to the politically significant conflations of such concepts as robbery and contribution (*Raub* and *Kontribution*) or deceit and exchange (*Täuschung* and *Tausch*).

In Classical Walpurgisnacht, a Hellenic version of the Germanic Wal-purgisnacht of Part One, insectiform animals and pygmies mine golden treasure from an island mountain that seismic forces have raised above sea level. The griffon (*Greif*), a political tyrant, supervises the mining and guarding of the treasure, and, like Faust, he tries to grasp (*greifen*) "maidens, gold, or crowns" (7102 * * *). The griffon speaks of gold in leaves as Mephistopheles spoke of paper money (7582, 6104). He implores his pygmy miners not to allow their enemies to rob them (7584), and encourages them to "Hurry in the gold!" (7600). Similarly, he expounds a theory of etymology, or digging for verbal sources (7094–98). But as the Centaur Chiron, who carries Faust through classical antiquity, tells Faust, who is seeking the Hellenic ideal of woman, it is erroneous to seek literal sources. Helen's age, for example, Chiron compares to a fact that philol-ogists would unearth but that is unimportant to Helen's timeless form, which poets alone can bring to show (*Schau*; 7429).

Two philosophers, Anaxagoras and Thales, watch the geographic and political events on the island mountain. Anaxagoras makes an offer to a foil to Faust, the chrysaloid Homunculus: "If you can take to governing [*Herrschaft*], I plan to have you crowned as king" (7879–80). The clever Thales, who better understands the workings of symbolic appropriation, urges Homunculus to reject the devilish offer. Thales' advice is prudent, for the island mountain is destroyed in the night of its birth. This destruction suggests to the spectator a possible end to a Faustian attempt to make all things one's own property (*Eigentum*) and to establish over it the kind of mastery that Hegel calls "law of the fist" (*Faustrecht*).

At the beginning of Act IV we know that Faust wants mastery, which he associates with property. "Sway I would gain, a sovereign's thrall! / Renown is naught, the deed is all" (10187–88). Mephistopheles does not understand the human desire that impels Faust, and offers him "the kingdoms of this world and all their riches" (10131). Jesus refused the same offer in Matthew 4:8–10, and Homunculus refused Anaxagoras' similar offer in Classical Walpurgisnacht. Here Faust, who in Part One expressed his disinterest in amounts of wealth, eschews the devil's offer. Faust wants neither to dig in the earth nor to raise earthen islands from the sea, but to appropriate to himself a new shore between the land and the sea. He wishes to harness the force of the sea itself: "There dares my spirit soar past all it knew; / Here I would struggle, this I would subdue" (10220–21). In formulating this plan for subduing the ocean and making new real estate, Faust recalls the terms of the original wager with Mephistopheles: "This is my wish, in this dare further me!" (10233).

Mephistopheles too assuredly concludes that the expedition of Faust's command will be easy for him (10234). From the conditions of war he believes he can win shore rights for Faust. As it happens, the Emperor (*Kaiser*) is warring against a counter-emperor (*Gegenkaiser*). Mephistopheles and Faust plan to form an alliance with the Emperor in order to gain land rights, seize booty, and otherwise gain their own ends. * * * Faust, who earlier conspired with Mephistopheles in the showing of false wealth and in the subsequent conflation of government and pleasure (10245, 10251), knows that the victory that he and Mephistopheles plan to promise the Emperor is deceit, magic delusion, or hollow *Schein* (10300).

When the besieged Emperor appears on stage, he expresses fear that he acted wrongly in making paper money (10422), and again describes his experience at the end of the masque. In the casket, he says, he saw a mirrorlike source (*Quelle*) that revealed to him a counter-emperor. Somehow his own breast was sealed, "I felt my spirit sealed [*besiegelt*] with hardihood / When mirrored [*bespiegelt*] in that realm of fire I stood" (10417–18). In the forms in which they are used, *Spiegel* ("mirror") and *Siegel* ("seal") rhyme with each other, and with *Geld* ("money"). (The description of the sealing of Faust's breast by the image of Helen in Part One contains similar associations of *Spiegel* with *Siegel*.) A mirror, which produces a counterfeit image, is as much an agent of personal alienation, or translation out of oneself, as is money. The mirror, and the seal described by the Emperor, who now faces the counter-emperor, reveal to us, as did the Paper Money Scene, the material, spiritual, and aesthetic results of the Emperor's signing promissory notes.

Faust, appearing in court as a necromancer supposedly obligated to the
Emperor (10447), promises to supply military weapons and personnel. The
church berates such means, and the Emperor himself wonders to whom
he will be obligated for such help (10603). The General accuses the king
of making a union (*vereinigen*; 10693) with devilish forces, but even he
gives up command of the situation. Mephistopheles believes that he is
now in control. To Faust's "What shall we do now [*tun*]?" he gives an
answer that Faust hardly believes: "It's all done [*getan*]" (10710).

The true nature of Mephistopheles' "louts" (10329), with whose aid the
Emperor seems to win victory, is revealed allegorically when they rob the
tent of the counter-emperor. One seizes (*greifen*; 10788) the goods of
the counter-emperor; another is overly dispensative (*verschwenderisch*; 10816)
and loses his stolen treasure. To answer the followers of the Emperor, who
accuse them of robbery, the "louts" use Mephistophelian logic: their booty,
they say, is not illegal *Raub* but rather legal *Kontribution* (10828). * * *

In the following scenes the Emperor himself, while in the tent of the
apparently defeated counter-emperor, contributes the Empire legally to
those who seem to have helped him in battle. The treaties by which the
Emperor parcels out various rights—including the right to mint money—
depend on signs and signatures, as did Faust's contract with Mephistopheles and the Emperor's paper money:

> The Emperor's word is great and any gift ensures,
> Yet noble writ is needful for investitures,
> Needful his hand and seal.
> (10927–29, compare 10966)

The Arch-Chancellor refers to a holy signature or seal:

> I cheerfully confide this grant of gravest powers
> Forthwith to parchment, for the Empire's weal and ours;
> Our busy Chancery shall copy, seal, and date it,
> Your sacred signature, o Sire, corroborate it.
> (10971–74)

In private conference, the Archbishop accuses the Emperor of being in
league (*Bunde*) with Satan (10982, compare 10871). To redeem the sin
of the Emperor, he argues, it is necessary to erect an ecclesiastical monument and bell tower on the spot where the sin was perpetrated (11005–
16). The Emperor is willing to sign the documents: "A formal deed of
transfer [*eignen*] to the Church—design it, / Lay it before me and I shall
be pleased to sign [*unterzeichen*] it" (11021–22). The Archbishop also
demands "some requisitioned booty-gold" (11028) and the tithes, quit-
rents, and taxes from the Empire's shore (*des Reiches Strand*) that the
Emperor has granted to Faust. Although the land does not yet exist, the
Archbishop assumes that the church will eventually get everything that it
demands, and he cites scripture to his purpose (11040). At the end of
Act IV we hardly know to whom will belong the real estate yet to be
uncovered by Faust.

At the beginning of Act I, the Chancellor warned the Emperor that
"privation dealt, privation suffered, / Leave very Majesty bereft" (4810–

11). At the end of Act IV, the Emperor expresses his fear that this robbery or rape could well occur, as legitimate contribution, through the medium of signature: "Why not sign [*verschreiben*] over all the realm while we're about it!" (11042). The Emperor, victim of the designs of the devil, fears that he has written off, or translated to others, the empire that he once possessed.

The Dead Pledge (Faustpfand)

At the beginning of Act V, Faust seems to have transformed the old shoreline into his own real estate. A plot of land tenured by two old peasants, however, mars his proper self, or property (11151–55, compare 10187). He complains that his "lofty title [*Hochbesitz*] is impure" (11156). Some things are not his own (*eigen*), and the richer he becomes the more he understands how much he lacks (11241–52). Faust's goal is to translate all alien things into his own property. In the *Zueignung* (meaning both "dedication" and "appropriation") to *Faust*, however, we learn the ambiguity in all possession: "What I possess [*besitzen*] I see as from a distance, / And what has passed, to me becomes existence" (31–32). The difficulty of self-appropriation, which Goethe here expresses as he commences in 1797 the reworking of forms (*Gestalten*; 1) he first explored in the *Urfaust* of 1775, becomes for Faust in Act V, which Goethe composed as late as 1831, a fundamental problem of political alienation and appropriation.

As in Act I Poetic Dispensation (Boy Charioteer) claims to be able to provide Wealth (Plutus) with what he lacks, so in Act V Mephistopheles provides Faust with the peasants' land he wants. But Faust is displeased at the murderous means of the devilish appropriation: "So you have turned deaf ears to me! / I meant exchange [*Tausch*], not robbery [*Raub*]" (11370–71). Faust wanted *Tausch* ("exchange"); Mephistopheles translated this into his own discourse or way of acting as *Täuschung* ("deceit"). In *Faust*, however, exchange is the polar opposite of deceit, just as contribution is the polar opposite of robbery. In *Faust*, position is counterbalanced by negation in a dynamic union of mutual dependency. * * * Faust, then, may try to ignore the necessity of such an alliance, but Mephistopheles' agents defend their murderous actions by referring to laws, * * * which seem to legitimate the conceptual exchanges of *Kontribution* for *Raub* and *Täuschung* for *Tausch*.

Faust can no longer derive pleasure from the accumulation of things. Even the sight of merchant ships and of the caskets of booty that they carry does not delight him. * * * They serve only to remind him of what is behind * * * his merchant-mastership.

Finally, blinded by care, a declining Faust must depend on a hidden light within his individual self (11499–510). He believes that his imperial word is sufficient to handle a thousand hands: "The master's word alone imparts his might" (11502). But Faust is deceived. He imagines, for example, that servants of his are building a paradisiacal land (11569), but, as one of the peasants earlier predicted, servants of Mephistopheles are actually building a paradisiacal image (11086). Once again the informing tension in *Faust* is the difference between the symbol and the thing: the image and the land, the word and the concept, the ticket and the gold.

Faust's last monologue, perhaps, overcomes this difference. He imagines that servants are building a land where men will live "not safely [*sicher*], but in free resilience [*tätig-frei*]" (11564). The construction and maintenance of dikes ensures that the citizenry will work in ceaseless activity: "He only earns both freedom and existence / Who must reconquer them each day" (11575–76). He envisions in the future a free people that, significantly, will need neither mastery nor a master's word: "Such teeming would I see upon this land, / On acres [*Grund*] free among free people stand" (11579–80). Faust seems to fulfill the terms of the wager: "I might entreat the fleeting minute: / Oh tarry yet, thou art so fair!" (11581–82, compare 1706, 2710, 11600). With this statement Faust dies.

Mephistopheles and his servants believe that Faust mortgaged his soul in order to receive from them a short-term loan of power (11610). Although he pities Faust, Mephistopheles fully believes that Faust will now have to pay off his creditors, or believers (11611). On this account he takes the "bond with blood cemented" (11613) from his pocket and waves it before the audience as if it were a *mortuum vadium*, not on visible real estate, but on an invisible soul—as if it were a *gage morte*, or dead pledge.

In most earlier versions of the Faust legend, Faust is carried off to hell. In the "Prologue" to Goethe's *Faust*, however, God foretold a new role for the devil, who is the apparent marplot of the divine design, and hence predicted a new finale:

> Of all the spirits of negation
> The rogue has been least onerous to my mind.
> Man all too easily grows lax and mellow,
> He soon elects repose at any price;
> And so I like to pair him with a fellow
> To play the deuce, to stir, and to entice.
>   (338–43)

Mephistopheles, the unwilling agent of God, loses the hypothecated soul for which he struggled throughout *Faust*. He is about to seal the soul of Faust with his stamp (11662), when heavenly spirits translate to heaven the soul that he believed to be a treasure that was pledged (*verpfändet*) to him (11829–30).

Mephistopheles hardly understands losing his investment (11837), and many readers take his side. Some critics suggest that a gratuitous *deus ex machina* saves Faust. They suggest, in other words, that God is the mortmain of the mortgage, the security of which is the soul of Faust. This soul He redeems by raising it above the down-to-earth hypothecation in the pactual bond (*Pfand*), so that it becomes a heavenly chrysalis (*Unterpfand*; 11984) from which Faust is born a heavenly angel. Other readers suggest that the power of woman is the mortmain of the mortgage, and that Gretchen plays the major role in saving Faust (compare 12110). (If Gretchen is what saves Faust from bondage to Mephistopheles, then she has to have overcome her belief that everything and everyone is bound to gold: "For gold contend, / On gold depend / All things and men" (2802–4).

In an early version of *Faust*, Mephistopheles argues with God about the outcome of the bond. * * * Mephistopheles has wrought in the court a change no less than that of Hans Sachs' alchemist, but * * * he has victimized himself as well as the court. Mephistopheles, who throughout the drama stood by the bond, is, in the end, stood up by it. He it was who described to others the future amortization of paper money (6126), but as it turns out, Mephistopheles can receive the mortgaged soul of Faust no more than the people of the Empire, former believers (*Gläubige*) who have become creditors, could amortize their money.

Mephistopheles' failure to comprehend his loss involves a misunderstanding of monetary and contractual translation. In the *Nicomachean Ethics*, Aristotle defines money as "a guarantee of exchange in the future for something not given." In the *Grundrisse*, Marx shows how money can appear in the form of collateral (*Pfand*). Men place their faith in this collateral "because it is an objectified, mutual relation between their productive activity [*Tätigkeit*]. Every other collateral may serve the holder directly in the function of objectified exchange value. Money, however, serves him merely as 'the dead pledge or mort-gage [*Faustpfand*]' of society, but it serves as such only because of its social (symbolic) property; and it can have a social property only because individuals have alienated their own social relationship from themselves so that it takes the form of a thing." As *Faust* turns out, Faust, who sought what Hegel calls *Faustrecht* ("law of the fist"), is saved by Mephistopheles' misunderstanding of what Marx calls a *Faustpfand* ("dead pledge").

The Dialectical Plot

Goethe's *Faust*, as we have seen, exposes apparent similarities among linguistic, propertal, sexual, spiritual, and other kinds of translation. Translation not only is depicted by the plot of *Faust* as its content, but also is internalized in the plot as an informing element. *Faust* conflates its content, which includes the hypothecal contract depicted in the wager scene, with its form, which includes the series of apparently dialectical hypotheses that allow Faust to progress and that Faust finally seems to overcome. In Goethe's drama, as we have seen, Faust lays down his soul conditionally (hypothetically) as a deposit (hypothec) to Mephistopheles, a negative motive spring (*Triebfeder*) or prompter (*hupothētēs*) of subsequent action. The conflation of spiritual deposition, on which the making of the wager depends, and economic deposition, on which the movement of the plot (*hupothēsis*) depends, is the motor of progress in *Faust*.

* * * All the hypotheses of *Faust* are contracts of alienation, which tend both to ensnare by hypothecation and to offer the means by which to transcend hypothecation. In both the intellectual and economic aspects of *Faust*, man progresses or acts by setting forth (depositing) something, using it to translate himself over a spiritual or material barrier, and ultimately transcending what was originally set forth. Throughout *Faust*, spiritual and material deposition are comprehended in a single vision. * * *

* * *

Faust, who contracted with a devilish behind, is left behind in the de-velopment of the spirit. It is as though the whole plot of *Faust*—the in-terest, as it were, on the principal that is the original wager between Mephistopheles and Faust—can pass beyond the confrontation between Faust and his counterpart Mephistopheles neither logically nor dialecti-cally, but only by way of divine mechanics.

In an autobiographical remark Goethe seems to have recognized the lack of qualitative difference between the original hypothesis of *Faust* and its final result. He describes his own life in terms of making, as did Faust, the most of a single hypothec. "I am in the position of a man who in his youth has a great many silver and copper coins which in the course of his life he changes for ever larger denominations, until at last all his youthful possession lies before him in coins of pure gold." Gold counts more than silver and copper. As money rather than as metal, however, the gold coins are homogeneous with the coins of smaller denomination from which they are changed. Goethe admits no qualitative distinction between the wealth of his youth (Part One) and that of his age (Part Two). The changings of age merely repeat in greater denominations those of youth. Part Two, like Part One, delivers to the attentive reader no satisfactory sublation of the series of interrelated hypothecs and hypotheses that inform the plot of *Faust* and that it depicts.

Nor, perhaps, is *Faust* supposed by Goethe to satisfy such a reader. His contemporary Hegel argued that literature can depict dialectical struggle in some stages, but cannot work through the contradictions of partly neg-ative hypotheses and discover truth. Some readers of *Faust*, like the courtly spectators of the masque, may see in the masked ending of Goethe's work the pure gold—the true victory of Faustian Man—that they desired from the beginning. Others, like the fool at the end of the Paper Money Scene, are wise enough to cash in *Faust* for the search for wisdom that led Goethe to write it.

JANE K. BROWN

[The Spirit of Water: *Faust*, Part Two, Act II] †

If Act I was an effort to conjure Helen through the forces of fire, Act II is the attempt to conjure her from the water. At bottom it deals with the same problem as Act I, how to generate a graspable rainbow, how to bring up creative force or spirit from the depths to validate appearances. Now that we have moved into the realm of myth and art, now that we are in some sense inside the allegories created in Act I, this attempt will be more successful. Act I characterized the goal in terms of fire, gold, myth, imag-

† From "The Spirit of Water," *Goethe's Faust: The German Tragedy* (Ithaca: Cornell UP, 1986), 171–97. The author's footnotes have been omitted. Her quotations from *Faust* have been replaced with Arndt's translation.

ination, antiquity, and the beginnings of time. In Act II water imagery will predominate over fire; this represents a significant shift in focus. The emphasis will no longer be on the descent and the buried treasure, but on the ascent, on the continuity between lower and upper worlds, on how to go from spirit to concrete form. This is where both Faust and emperor/ Pan failed in Act I. The emphasis will appear to be less on creating art than on creating life; but we understand, of course, that the fundamental identity of art and Nature in the play makes the distinction spurious. Furthermore, both art and Nature have become, through the process of descent in Act I, projections of the seeking human mind. At least Acts II and III, if not IV and V as well, are continuations of the "show" begun with Faust's descent to the Mothers. It is a show created by Faust and stage-managed by that experienced director Mephistopheles.

The act begins with a series of "plunges," which indicate that it begins in the equivalent of the realm of the Mothers at the end of Faust's descent. The curtains open to reveal Faust in the state of unconsciousness into which he had plunged at the end of Act I. But he has also returned to his study, which the audience has not seen since Faust's departure into the world. He—and we—have thus plunged back into his past. Faust's old robe is still there; Wagner is still there; the student Mephisto led on is still there as well. As the travelers proceed to the "Classical Walpurgis Night" the act slips into a much deeper abyss. Erichtho's prologue takes us back to the origins of the Roman Empire in the battle of Pharsalus, fought between Caesar and Pompey in 48 B.C. Erichtho is the witch Pompey consulted before the battle; the poet of whom she complains is Lucan, who portrays her most dreadfully indeed in his epic, *Pharsalia*. Lucan is important here, because he identifies the Thessalian setting both as a land of witchcraft and as the cradle of history. Here Erichtho mediates the transformation of the historical world into a poetic or spirit world by reporting that the fires change color from red to blue (spirit fires burn blue). But this transformation plunges us even deeper into the abyss of time, into the prehistorical world of mythology. This is, in fact, mythology at its very oldest levels, for the sphinxes identify themselves as the oldest of mythological creatures, too old ever to have seen Helen.

The relative antiquity of the sphinxes may seem obvious to us, but it was a new idea in the eighteenth century. The first significant periodization of ancient art was made by Johann Joachim Winckelmann in his *History of Ancient Art* (1764). Previously, antiquity had been considered a permanent ideal, not a transient historical phenomenon. Winckelmann was widely admired, often revered, in mid-eighteenth-century art circles, and he profoundly influenced the historicist theories of the later part of the century and of the nineteenth century. Thus this apparently innocent reference signals a genuine historical beginning to the act and at the same time a genuinely historical pattern of organization for this re-creation of antiquity. But a historical view of antiquity is not only one from a modern perspective; it is also a view that recognized the existence of historical change and the impermanence of any single manifestation of the ideal.

As in Act I, this plunge into antiquity is mediated by the Renaissance, again in the form of Shakespeare. Any reader familiar with *Henry V* will immediately recognize the fundamental elements of Goethe's prologue— the hideous witch surveying the fires of the hostile armies by moonlight and the transformation into a spirit world—in the chorus at the beginning of Act IV. This eve of the battle of Agincourt might well have suggested the eve of the battle of Pharsalus to Goethe, because Fluellen, the pedantic captain who is fixated on military history, discusses Pompey and his camp within seventy lines of this chorus. Now, all the choruses in *Henry V* have as their main topic the need for the spectator to engage his imagination and supply what the stage can only hint at, "Minding true things by what their mock'ries be." * * * Indeed, *Henry V* is preoccupied with imaginative projection and the need for valid role-playing. Henry is a great and effective king, not because he is especially honest, but because he plays his role well. The Shakespearean echo is significant, then, on at least three levels. *Henry V* explores, like this part of *Faust*, the function and effectiveness of imagination. As a history play it is an especially appropriate source for a prologue to the most historically minded part of *Faust*. And finally, it provides once again a Renaissance gateway that opens up yet also frames our access to antiquity.

Homunculus, Wagner's curious creation (with a little help from Mephistopheles), identifies the significance of all these plunges into the past. The concept of the Homunculus comes from sixteenth- and seventeenth-century alchemy, which is a debased form of practical Neoplatonism. But even without the Neoplatonic background the language of fire and light that characterizes the creation of Homunculus connects him to earlier manifestations of spirit in the play. The way he first appears in the test tube as glowing coal then glorious jewel, and the way Mephisto presides over his emergence are strongly reminiscent of the vision of Mammon in the mountainside on the way to the Walpurgis Night in Part One (3916– 31). Wagner's pomposities—"Then man with his superior resource / Must henceforth have a higher, higher source" (6846–47)—identify the significant truth about Homunculus: he is a spark of divine spirit, who will spend the rest of the act in search of incarnation. Thus we have plunged, like Faust, into the realm from which the spark of pure spirit may be retrieved into the world.

The act begins, then, in the realm of the Mothers, at the bottom of the descent. Since the problem of the act is to incarnate spirit, the fundamental gesture of the act is generation, and this gesture is repeated over and over again. It begins in the re-creation of *Faust I* in the first scene. The repetition of the familiar set and the negative attitude toward it (it is moldy and dusty) set the tone. The parodistic tone continues with the new famulus, who is a parody of Wagner, and the Baccalaureus, who parodies himself as a student. But beyond the level of parody, the presence of a *new* famulus and the promotion of the student suggest an underlying tendency to generation and development even in this musty chamber. The chorus of insects that are born from Faust's old gown and greet Mephistopheles as their father emphasize this pattern. The exchange between the Baccalaureus and Mephisto also holds an important place here. It appears at first to be an inserted satire of the more extreme forms of German idealist thought, especially of Johann Gottlieb Fichte, whose system derived the world from the ego's initial postulation of itself. Nevertheless, creativity is the central theme, for the discussion turns on the Baccalaureus' arrogant faith in his own capacity to generate the world. Lines like

> Man's life is in his blood, and where, in truth,
> Is blood as lively ever as in youth?
> There is fresh blood that briskly circulates
> And out of very life new life creates.
> All is in motion, all astir with deeds,
> The weak succumbs, the vigorous succeeds.
>   [6776–81]

parodistically celebrate youth, vitality, and creation—the very theme of the act. Furthermore, if we ask where else have we seen such language, the obvious answer is from Faust himself in Part One. The circulating energy of nature in the macrocosm speech, the emphasis on power in the invocation of the earth spirit, the vitalism of Faust as waterfall in "Forest and Cave" all come to mind. This parodistic aspect of the scene establishes the essential ambiguity of the creation that takes place in Act II. On the one hand, it is natural, even vitalistic. But on the other hand, it is anachronistic and self-conscious (Mephisto even turns to the audience for help at 6772). Whatever is created in this act will not be real or natural but, like Homunculus, artificial.

In this respect Homunculus again illuminates the significance of the basic patterns of the act, for the imagery associated with his artificiality organizes much of the play. Because Homunculus is artificial, he is enclosed in a crystal vial (6884); he is, as Wagner suggests (6860), a crystallized man. But Homunculus is not the only flame enclosed in crystal. Immediately after his crystallization (he is not yet "born" because he lacks a body), Homunculus articulates and interprets Faust's dream of the conception of Helen, the myth of Leda and the swan. According to the myth, Zeus took on the form of a swan to rape Leda; Helen was the offspring of this union. In this vision Leda sets foot in the water, and, we are told, "The flawless body's graceful living flame / Is cooled in pliant crystalline caress" (6909–10). During the "Classical Walpurgis Night" the dream is repeated as a waking vision articulated by Faust himself. Leda is invisible but the water is once again crystal, this time a mirror (7284). Helen's mother is thus the equivalent of Homunculus, a spark of spirit protected in a crystal vial, the ideal not yet become embodied in reality. But Homunculus wants to become "real," to escape his crystal vial for a real body. In other words, he wants to proceed from artificial embodiment of the union of ideal and real (fire in crystal) to the living or natural embodiment of it (fire in water).

The image has already appeared once in Part One, in "Witch's Kitchen." It is not by chance that the fires, the fantastic apparatus and humming vessels of Wagner's laboratory recall the kitchen of Part One, nor that Homunculus recalls an important theme of "Witch's Kitchen" when he expects Mephisto to provide him shortcuts to activity in the world (6888–90). There, we remember, Faust saw the ideal embodied in the image of a beautiful woman in a magic mirror, spirit encased in crystal. After "Witch's Kitchen" Faust progresses from the mirror image to the

living Gretchen. In Part Two Homunculus will break his vial on the chariot of Galatea and pour his flame into the water. The next thing to follow
this union in the play will be the appearance of Helen. Similarly the
crystallized Leda will give way to her fluid (she will evaporate at the end
of Act III), but nonetheless embraceable "living" daughter.

In this regard it is particularly interesting that Goethe seems to have
based his descent/ascent structure on Aristophanes' *Frogs*. The wanderings
of the three northern travelers among the classical ghosts are presented
with broad Aristophanic humor. Especially when one takes account of the
loftiness of the classical ideal in Goethe's time, the irreverence of his
presentation must even have exceeded that of Aristophanes, who sends
Dionysos and his servant Xanthias wandering through the Greek hell. The
empusa Mephistopheles meets and the exchange of shape with the Phorcyads are both borrowed directly from *The Frogs*. But the strong parodistic
tendency of both plays is their most significant point of contact. As we
have just seen, the Baccalaureus scene parodies, in a sense, the concern
with creativity and generation in the act that is to follow. Similarly, the
first scene of *The Frogs* parodies the play's concern for the social value of
tragedy. In the first scene Dionysos' desire to recover Euripides appears
superficial in the extreme, but at the end the impending return of Aeschylus is presented as the salvation of the state. At its most serious moments
the play is comic, just as Act II is. The high point of the play, the dramatic
contest between Euripides and Aeschylus is a series of parodies of famous
or typical passages. In both plays parody serves the same function. It
mediates—indeed, makes possible—the recovery of the past and of the
spirit of poetry. In the first scene of the act Goethe parodies figures (Wagner, the student) who are themselves already parodies; in the larger structure of the act he parodies an author who is the arch-parodist of the
Western tradition. The emphasis on art and artificiality does not, then,
simply repeat what has come before. In Act II, Goethe specifies the kind
of art that is to represent spirit in the world. And once parody has been
identified as, in a sense, the highest art form for Goethe, the enormous
collection of allusions we have already identified in *Faust* takes on yet
another dimension of meaning. The allusions no longer simply identify or
generate positions on particular themes or issues, nor do they simply place
the play in contexts or traditions; now we see that allusiveness per se is
the defining quality of art for Goethe.

The "Classical Walpurgis Night" shows each of the three travelers engaged in the creative act, each in pursuit of form. Before considering their
quests in detail, it is worth reflecting briefly on the constellation. In the
"Walpurgis Night" of Part I, Faust also quested as a member of a trio; the
other two were Mephistopheles and the will-o'-the-wisp. Like Homunculus, the will-o'-the-wisp was a disembodied light; he followed, we remember, the zigzag pattern of the earth spirit. Although the will-o'-the-wisp
melts away, the parallel between the two Walpurgis Nights is nevertheless
significant, for the first one, like the second, is concerned with the
generative power of nature. The trio returns in Act I, this time as Boy-
charioteer–Plutus/Faust and Greed/Mephistopheles. Faust and Mephis-

topheles occupy their same places, while Boy-charioteer shares the element of fire with the two lights. Once again the third and most spiritual member is of a different, openly magical, order of being. In Part I, Faust needed to be turned away from too direct apprehension of spirit into the world; thus the will-o'-the-wisp evaporated and Faust never saw Satan. But in Act I the emphasis is entirely on the recovery of spirit, so that Boy-charioteer is the dominant member of the trio. Furthermore, * * * each of the trio in Act I shares characteristics with each of the others. Now in Act II this aspect becomes the most important. None of the three guides the others, but instead, each independently pursues the same goal—to locate his own appropriate form, to embody his own version of the Absolute. Faust, Mephistopheles, and Homunculus still occupy familiar positions in Goethe's dialectic; nevertheless, now that the Faustian quest has become the search for form in the temporal world instead of for the Absolute outside the world, all three are, in a sense, now genuine Fausts.

The "Classical Walpurgis Night" consists, then, of three parallel quests for the same thing. Goethe intertwines them to some extent, but basically they are arranged in three stages of increasing generality and illumination from dream to masque to ritual. The first quest is Faust's, and consists largely in the effort to realize a dream. This quest has already begun in the preceding scene when Homunculus described Faust's dream of the conception of Helen. Arrived in Greece, he first encounters the sphinxes, who, however, died out before the time of Helen. Now that he has gained entry, so to speak, to the history of Greek culture, Faust has no difficulty substituting spatial for temporal advance and can repeat the vision of Leda and the swan in his own words in "On the Lower Peneios." We have already seen the significance of water in this vision; that Faust has moved from the upper Peneios, where he originally landed, to the fertile flood plain of the river, closer to the sea and surrounded by water gods, is a measure of his approach to the realm of Helen. The second dream is, significantly, both less abrupt and more "real" than the first. This time Faust is conscious; the actual set on stage corresponds to what Faust describes in his vision; the mystic union is realistically hidden (Leda is in a bower), not abruptly veiled at the last minute by the poet. The supernatural act, the mating of swan and woman, is displaced by the more natural water play of Leda's maidens and the attendant swans. This convergence of dream and nature continues when Faust meets Chiron. The wise old centaur generates a context for the existence of Helen by telling Faust first about the greatest of Greek heroes, then about the childhood of the greatest of heroines. This historical contextualization proceeds so rapidly and so effectively that Chiron must finally remind Faust that as a mythical figure Helen exists independently of pedantic conceptions of time.

Nevertheless, we must not overlook the importance of what has occurred. Subjection to history prevented the sphinxes from providing information about Helen, and having a particular place in history allowed Chiron to know her. It is true, in order to approach any nearer to her it is necessary for Faust to escape from time. The exchange between Manto and Chiron identifies Chiron's restless motion with the flux of time.

Still roving ever, unabating?
You ever dwell in sheltered stillness pure,
While I delight in circulating.
Time circles me, while I endure.
[7478–81]

Manto's remark that she once smuggled Orpheus in through the same way
similarly identifies her with the eternal world of poetic imagination. Faust
himself has already made one such descent to the Mothers. There he
departed, we remember, from the spatial realm to fetch the shade (spirit)
of Helen; now he departs from the temporal flux to fetch a body for her.
The problem in Act I, however, turned out to be not the departure but
the return. For this reason, the path traced by Faust's quest is perhaps
more important than the ultimate arrival at Manto's temple, for this quest
establishes a particular, indeed unique, historical world to embody the
spirit he will fetch. This is the lesson of historicism. Although the ultimate
act of creation is a departure from time, nevertheless the substance of
Faust's quest is to generate a valid historical context or matrix to contain
his dream of the ideal.

As earlier in the first "Walpurgis Night" and in Act I, Faust's visit to the
Absolute—here Persephone—is elided. And as before, it is replaced by
Mephisto's burlesque of the same experience and, uniquely in this case,
by the more abstract and illuminating parallel quest of Homunculus.
Mephisto's burlesque quest reminds us, appropriately, more of the descent
of Dionysos in *The Frogs* than of Orpheus. As always, Mephisto is especially drawn to the grotesques—the sphinxes, griffons, ants, and arimasps.
The latter three, according to Herodotus (and indeed, according to the
most bizarre and fanciful sections, Books III and IV, of Herodotus' thoroughly Mephistophelean book), were collectors and guardians of gold.
Mephisto has in fact plunged here to the very realm of buried treasure he
himself promoted so vigorously in Act I. This is the role Mephisto has
played all along in *Faust*. As the reality principle he has led the way to
the Absolute.

Mephistopheles does, it is true, at first feel considerably out of his element. These classical monsters are rather too high-spirited for the poor
northern devil (7086–87). And yet this world that worries Mephisto actually replays the issues of Act I at a more intense level. Mephisto, who was
in his element in the world of empty appearances at court, cannot keep
up with the constantly shifting forms of the Lamiae or the empusa, much
less the appalling shifts from natural to artificial landscape brought about
by Seismos. The masque of Seismos—and it is a masque, for none of it
turns out to be real—presents once again the retrieval of gold from the
depths. As at the emperor's court the gold generates social inequity and
chaos. At the height of the disorder a meteor falls out of the moon and
destroys the whole appearance. We are reminded here, first, of the fire
that engulfs emperor/Pan and that Faust extinguishes by invoking the
power of water; second, we think of Helen in the dumb show, identified
with Luna, and of the explosion she sets off.

Mephisto does not, however, remain to witness the catastrophic end to this spirit masque, but sets off in the middle to pursue form, first in the shape of the Lamiae. When he fails to catch one, he rejects this mummery and masking (7795, 7797), as he significantly calls it. He turns then from the artificial mountain of the masque to Oreas, the living or natural rock. In this respect he repeats the pattern of Faust's quest, which moved from dream to historically grounded natural reality. The parallel continues when Mephisto approaches the cave of the Phorcyads. These three weird sisters, also known as the Graiae, were supposed to live off beyond the edge of the world, where neither sun nor moon shone; in this respect they embody the same kind of goal as the Mothers or, for that matter, Persephone. It is not surprising that they identify their cave as a temple, for Faust's way to the underworld led through Manto's temple. Furthermore, these three hags were the daughters of Ceto, a daughter of the primal sea, and Phorcis, the old man of the sea. Thus, like Faust and later Homunculus, even Mephisto arrives at the principle of water in this act. Nevertheless Mephisto makes one concession to his role as eternal negator: he does not descend to the Phorcyads but climbs. Once there he finds the burlesque version of what Faust seeks to give reality to his spark of the Absolute. Instead of the most beautiful woman who ever lived, Mephisto chooses for himself the ugliest hag. Yet there is still a subtle strand of identity between Helen and the Phorcyads. Helen is associated with swans by her heritage, but so are the Phorcyads; swan imagery will remain important in the play all through Act III. In the Phorcyads, Mephisto thus finds his own Helen. Faust has already donned his role as poet in Act I; as poet—a second Orpheus in this context—Faust creates a Helen apart from himself. Now Mephisto dons his garb for the play in which both are to perform in Act III.

Homunculus also seeks a role in the "Classical Walpurgis Night," but as has been typical of him thus far, his adventures illuminate the action at a more abstract level. Faust and Mephisto have sought specific, historical forms for the "sparks"; Homunculus seeks the general equivalent of this, a body to enclose his light and replace his crystal vial. Like Mephisto he briefly works through the problematics of Act I in that he watches the second part of the masque of Seismos. In his conversations with the two Greek philosophers, Anaxagoras (who believed the earth was created by the forces of fire) and Thales (who believed in the creative power of water), the masque is now explicitly interpreted as creation from fire. And like the others he turns from the fire to descend to the water, this time beyond the point Faust reached to the sea itself. There his flame attracts two old men of the sea, Nereus and Proteus—the first a prolific father, the second a god of transformation. These two embody the generative power and the form-giving capacity represented in the principle of water. But they also embody something more. When Thales approaches Nereus for advice, Nereus replies that neither Paris nor Ulysses took his advice and in the process gives a capsule summary of the history encompassed by the Homeric epics. In his next speech, where he explains that Galatea has replaced Venus, he opens up the later history of classical religion. Thus Thales completes the sense of historical context begun by the sphinxes' inability to talk about Helen. We have moved from the beginning to the end of the history of antiquity. Proteus offers the ultimate generalization of this theme. To become, he tells Homunculus, it is necessary to begin in the sea as the tiniest of living things and to evolve up the great chain of being. This is the historical flux enlarged to the cosmic scale of modern biology. And yet, like Faust, Homunculus is to gain a form from the great wealth of time only by the gesture of leaving time, of death. He breaks his vial on the chariot of Galatea, the historicized goddess of beauty and therefore the spiritual equivalent of Helen and embodiment of perfect form. In this moment we see on stage the merging of fire and water, of spirit and form. Crystal is exchanged for water; art paradoxically becomes life in the moment when Homunculus passes out of the world and through the looking glass. This epiphany of ultimate harmony is the moment of the creation of the rainbow, and it is properly hailed as the triumph of Eros. The epiphany that Faust expected in the embrace of Gretchen is now celebrated on stage for all of us to experience.

Like every other fulfilled moment in the play this triumphant epiphany can only take place in some kind of show. Nevertheless, it is a show that requires less interpretation than some of the previous ones, for Nereus explicitly tells us that the scene is the annual momentary epiphany of Galatea. It is thus a kind of ritual, the high point of which is explained for us. The other parts of the ritual are less clear at first glance. They do, however, all contribute to the epiphany of Galatea as the ultimate form in which life can be embodied. Before considering the series of figures we should note the importance of the moon in this scene. It remains, according to the stage direction, at the zenith throughout. The presence of the moon identifies the world of the "Classical Walpurgis Night" yet again as a mediating, artificial realm, especially since the sirens describe the Aegean inlets of the last scene as the place "where Luna doubly glistens" (7513), that is, where both moon and its reflection are present. That the moon remains at the zenith is especially important, though perhaps astonishing in view of the importance of history in the act and in view of the necessary transitoriness of Galatea's appearance at the end. If the moon stands still, this ritual is, like Faust's descent through Manto's temple, out of time. As a moment out of time the scene in some sense replaces Faust's scene in Hades, which Goethe attempted but never actually wrote. This final festival must thus be understood as the fulfillment of Faust's earlier dreams, as the creation of Helen. Homunculus as spirit is Zeus, the descending god, and Galatea is Leda, the woman in the water. The moment of union is ineffable; in the two earlier dreams it was veiled, here it passes in a rush. But this ineffability is associated, curiously and ineluctably, with the temporal flux. To keep the terms of Faust's old bet with Mephistopheles and to accept the transitoriness of the moment is no longer simply a matter of a disciplined imagination; that discipline is rendered profoundly necessary by the nature of human existence, which is poised between the historical rush of the world and the permanence of transcendence. The historical nature of the world requires that any manifestation of transcendence, because it must be in the world, be transitory. Only the affirmation of mutability enables anything approaching a truly fulfilled moment in time. And that affirmation takes place, we are shown, in the infinitely repeatable ritual of the act of love.

The succession of figures in this ritual would appear at first to be a philologist's dream (or perhaps nightmare). However, none of these figures really comes from any more arcane a source than Ovid's *Metamorphoses* or Herodotus' *Histories*, and both these texts would have been thoroughly familiar to any tolerably educated contemporary of Goethe. Even the allegorical harmonization of fire and water at the end was a cliché of the period. Metastasio's *Dido Forsaken* ends with the sea rising to douse the flames of Carthage, then a calming marine procession; an example closer to home would be the trials by fire and water in *The Magic Flute*. Furthermore, all of the speakers, in good masque tradition, tell the reader everything he needs to know about them. All it really takes to read this scene is self-confidence.

The larger shape of this progression of figures is the development of the representation of divinity (spirit in the world) from mixed human and animal form to the beauty of the pure human form. The sirens had first appeared among the sphinxes and griffons. Goethe follows classical and Renaissance tradition in conceiving them as women with the legs and wings of birds. Indeed, the sphinxes warn Faust about their hawklike claws among the twigs (7162–63). They embody the irresistible allure of the water, an allure that in this play it is proper not to resist, like Ulysses, but to follow, like Homunculus. Already at the beginning of the masque of Seismos they call upon all present to flee the earthquake for the safety of the sea, where Luna shines double; now they serve as the heralds to the final ritual masque.

First to appear, then, are the Nereids and Tritons—the latter explicitly identified as sea monsters (probably to be understood as humans with horses' bodies and fishes' tails). Their arrival identifies and starts to pull together the major themes of both the ritual and the play as a whole. They come in response to the song of the sirens. Their assertion "Tuneful singing draws us near" (8049) is echoed it turns out, in the very last lines of Part Two, "The Eternal-Feminine / Draws us on high" (12110–11). (Both predicates in German are *zieht uns hin/heran*.) The sirens, the water, Galatea are all what will be finally identified as the eternal feminine, the power of love. But the Nereids and Tritons have not come empty-handed, and their gifts are of great significance. They bring gold and treasure from the depths of the sea where it has lain in ships wrecked by the singing of the sirens. This is, of course, the gesture of Act I, the recovery of gold from the depths. Now it seems to be much easier to bring the gold back. But there is more. In Act I it was suggested that the gold in the depths had been buried at the fall of Rome, as the result of cataclysmic historical events. The mythical equivalent here, shipwreck, is less than cataclysmic. Indeed it is a repeated, common event for the sirens. Destruction, as well as generation, belongs then to the force of love. This is a perspective that readily embraces the Gretchen tragedy; indeed, from this point of view Mephisto's comment that Gretchen is "not the first" ("Dreary Day. A Field") appears rather less cynical. The power of love is the power of

nature, which encompasses death as well as birth. This is scarcely an original insight with Goethe, but it is one that *Faust* reinvests with profundity.
Finally, the Nereids introduce the theme of evolution; they go to fetch
the Cabiri to prove that they are more than fishes (8063, 8069), that the
direction of development lies toward their human half. The theme continues in the exchange between Nereus and Homunculus that follows.
Our attention is shifted to fully human forms, but more important, Nereus
defines humans as beings who ever strive to become like gods (8096),
though they consistently fail to transcend themselves. We are reminded of
Faust and the Earth Spirit. Once again a major theme of the play is placed
in a much larger context. Striving seen from the larger context of the
temporal flux becomes evolution, while the circular motions of the cosmos
become the cycles of repetition brought about by the complementary generative and destructive powers of love.

The discussion of the Cabiri confirms this reading. Goethe summarizes
with extraordinary virtuosity the various views as to the number and nature
of the Cabiri, a topic of some discussion in the period. The Cabiri seem
to have been the most primitive form of divinity, for they were worshiped
in the form of clay jugs (8220). However, our sources are unable to agree
upon either how many there were—three (8186), four (8187), perhaps
seven (8194) or eight (8198)—or whether they were indeed so primitive
as all that. Some were conceived as Olympian gods, therefore in human
form (8197), or even as fully transcendent (8199). They are seen as burlesque strivers—"Ever-famished perishers / For the out-of-reach" (8204–5).
But if the Cabiri comically represent striving as evolution, they also comically combine fire and water. On the one hand, they have a special relation to Neptune (8180–81); on the other, they are the equivalent of the
golden fleece (8212–15). The connection to gold is significant here, for
Herodotus identifies the Cabiri as the sons of Hephaestus, god of fire.
Small wonder, then, that the approach of the Cabiri precipitates a preliminary climax with double chorus that is exceeded only by the final
epiphany.

The Telchines focus both these concerns—the synthesis of fire and water, and history as evolution—onto the specifically human form. As the
smiths and temporary bearers of Neptune's trident, they enjoy a special
relationship to the water god. Similarly, they enjoy special protection from
Helios, god of the sun. As smiths they would also belong to Hephaestus.
All of these gods belong to the stage of Olympian religion in Greece,
which means they were consistently conceived in human form. And indeed, the Telchines emphasize at the end of their speech not only that
they have portrayed their god in hundreds of human versions but also that
they were the first people ever to do so. The burlesque of the Cabiri hints,
indeed, that one might transcend the conception of human form for the
gods, but everything else in the scene insists upon the superiority of human
form. This is the turn into the world of Part One, now focused into one
precise image that yet takes account of the subjective basis of artistic inspiration in Act I. The transcendent Absolute is to be sought not simply
in the world but in the beauty of the human form.

There can be no question that Galatea is one such manifestation of the

Absolute. Even before Homunculus empties his vial at her feet she is accompanied by the powers of spirit in the form of doves with wings "as dazzling-white as light" (8342). The scene abounds in traditional tags of Renaissance Neoplatonism, all of which identify Galatea as the ultimate *coincidentia oppositorum*, the embodiment of the harmony of all conceivable pairs of oppositions. The sirens, for example, call upon the Nereids to approach "in moderate haste" (8379; translated by Arndt as "gently pacing"). The phrase refers to the widely popular paradoxical motto *festina lente* (hasten slowly), a motto that was, probably not incidentally, often illustrated by dolphins. In the same speech the sirens describe Galatea:

> Grave she seems like godly faces,
> Shares immortals' earnest worth,
> Yet with all the luring graces
> Of the loveliest maid of earth.
> [8387–90]

She is thus the simultaneous embodiment of both divine and earthly love. At the sight of her, finally, Thales feels imbued with the beautiful and the true (8434), concepts central to ancient as well as Renaissance Platonism. Goethe's source for his final epiphany comes also from this same context; it is Raphael's *Triumph of Galatea*. Raphael's painting invests Galatea with all the attributes of Goethe's scene—the dolphins, the Nereids and Tritons, the scallop shell of Venus, the triple god of love above her head (replaced by Homunculus), the emblem of harmony (the bundle of arrows in the upper left-hand corner of the painting), the rapid motion past the observer and, above all, the intense excitement. From all of *Faust* this scene offers itself as the most openly Neoplatonic version and resolution of Goethe's dialectic.

Nevertheless, Galatea has her uniquely Goethean aspects as well. Working less from mythological sources than—apparently—from his own reading of the tradition in the visual arts, Goethe makes Galatea the historical successor to Venus. He was well aware of the tradition of representing Venus borne from the sea on a scallop shell. We are most familiar with this tradition from Botticelli's *Birth of Venus*, another monument of Renaissance Neoplatonizing. The exquisitely beautiful Galatea in her shell chariot described by Philostratus in the third century is easily conflatable with this Venus. The association is much easier to make when one realizes, as Goethe doubtless did, that the eighteenth century knew two Galateas. The first, the daughter of Doris and Nereus, is the sea nymph of classical mythology officially of concern here. The second is the statue created by Pygmalion and brought to life by Venus as a reward for the sculptor's devotion. Their son was Paphos (site of an important Venus cult), their great-grandson Adonis, later lover of Venus. Indeed, in some versions of the myth Venus herself marries Pygmalion in the guise of the beloved statue. Goethe's important innovation here is to shape these connections in historical terms, so that Galatea becomes the successor to Venus. Winckelmann had shown that classical art had a history, Goethe generalizes this insight to the entire classical ideal. Classical beauty per se is not recovered in Galatea; she is a version of it, a later evolution of what Venus once represented. Thus the paradox of the moon standing still but Galatea only flashing past is repeated; even in art there can be no permanent ideal. As in nature there can be only momentary manifestations and remanifestations of the ideal. And each of these manifestations will participate in the typicality of the eternal but will also have its own historical individuality.

Galatea is, then, a peculiarly historical manifestation of the ideal. Yet the connection of the name to the Pygmalion myth also ties Galatea to the other major precondition for all of Goethe's versions of the ideal, that they be artificial. For as the creation of Pygmalion, Galatea is the artificial come to life, nature outdone by art. In his *Italian Journey* (1817) Goethe uses the Pygmalion myth to clarify his own relationship to antiquity when he arrives in Rome:

> Wherever I go I find familiars in a new world; it is all as I anticipated and all new. I can say the same of my observations and my ideas. I have had no entirely new thought, have found nothing entirely foreign, but the old ones have become definite, so alive, so coherent, that they can count as new.
> When Pygmalion's Elise, whom he had shaped entirely according to his wishes and given as much reality and existence as an artist can, when she finally approached him and said, "It is I!" how different was the live woman from the worked stone.

The tension between the astonishing liveliness of his new mental world (compare also Mephisto's distress when he first arrives at the "Classical Walpurgis Night") and yet its familiarity reflects again the dynamic mediation between the transitory real and the eternal ideal. Goethe quickly progresses from what he sees to the tension within his own mind. Thus Elise/Galatea represents here what is projected from the poet's mind, not simply antiquity in human form. The ideal beauty in "Witch's Kitchen" appeared in a mirror frame; Gretchen, in a play within a play; Homunculus, in his crystal vial. The epiphany of Galatea leads this theme back, in a sense, to its mythological analogue and original.

In retrospect it is possible to see that the entire act consists of figures who are really projections of the sculptor's imagination. Sphinxes and griffons are typical monuments of ancient Egyptian and Near Eastern sculpture; the grouping of Peneios and his nymphs is typical of classical sculpture. Seismos is characterized as a colossal caryatid (7545); Goethe possessed a painting of the two-story caryatid from the temple of Zeus at Agrigento. The multitudes of Nereids, Tritons, hippocamps, and other sea creatures are not uncommon in Roman sculpture. The language of the act specifically calls attention to this underlying tendency. Chiron talks about the inadequacy of the sculptors' attempts to represent Hercules (7394); Mephistopheles spends ten lines expressing his amazement and regret that there has never been a statue of the Phorcyads. Not only does the act abound in well-known motifs of classical sculpture, but these motifs appear in roughly historical order from early (Egyptian) to late (Roman). Thus Galatea sums up the subliminal structuring principle of the act in both of her special aspects, as historicized and as "artificial" manifestation of the ideal.

And yet, if we consider this collection of sculptural motifs and the paths through which they would have been familiar to Goethe, a whole new dimension of significance emerges. It is obvious that Goethe knows that sphinxes belong to the oldest levels of ancient art and mythology, for they say as much (7197). Nevertheless, if we ask what sphinxes Goethe actually saw, the answer is not Egyptian sphinxes but the Renaissance grotesques that ornamented doorways, picture frames, ceilings, furniture, and who knows what else. The same is doubtless true of griffons, which were still a popular pattern on candlesticks, crockery, and table linen into the nineteenth century. Doubtless Goethe also knew the motifs from ancient carved gems, as did every connoisseur of classical art from the Renaissance on. But although such gems are rarely so fanciful and grotesque as the Roman wall ornaments on which the Renaissance grotesques are modeled, they are nevertheless closer to these paintings than to the major monuments of sculpture. Similarly, though Goethe doubtless saw Roman sculptures of sea creatures on visits to the Vatican, in Rome he would have passed innumerable examples of late Renaissance and baroque fountain sculptures every day. Nor are fanciful sea creatures confined to the fountains of Rome; Renaissance painting abounds with them as well. Goethe knew that paintings of the triumph of Galatea were not uncommon. In his first month in Rome he saw Raphael's *Triumph of Galatea* in the Villa Farnesina and, in the Palazzo Farnese, the Carracci frescoes that depicted—among a great multitude of Neoplatonist allegories surrounded by ornamental sphinxes and colossal caryatids—another Galatea (which owes much to Raphael's), as well as sirens sitting on the rocks. Goethe also knew and admired the tapestry by Raphael showing Saint Paul in prison (Sistine Chapel), in which the saint, a colossal bearded giant, bursts forth from underground with arms raised. In every instance, then, the implicit history of ancient sculpture is mediated by Renaissance images with which Goethe had had much more direct experience.

In the prologue to the "Classical Walpurgis Night" the mediation takes place, as we remember, through the Shakespeare references in Erichtho's speech. The finale also has a seventeenth-century literary mediator, this time Calderón, whose *Love, the Greatest Enchantment* Goethe admired in the translation of A. W. Schlegel. The play dramatizes the Circe episode from the *Odyssey* as an allegory of the soul deciding between virtue and pleasure, that is, between higher love and profane love. The latter is embodied in Circe, the witch who rules the elements in their aspect of deceptive and constantly metamorphosing appearances. She can raise volcanoes, storms at sea or in the air, and is served by a giant named Brutamonte (bestial mountain). Ulysses finally tears himself from her toils and escapes to the sea, but Circe intends to block his escape by raising a great storm. At this critical pass Galatea appears in her sea chariot, accompanied by the requisite Tritons and sirens. She protects Ulysses by her superior power to keep the sea calm, she explains, because Ulysses punished the cyclops Polyphemos, who had brutishly destroyed her lover Acis. Her constancy to her dead lover represents a higher love opposed to Circe's lust. Goethe does not, of course, share Calderón's counterreformation stance; nevertheless the glorification of love through the epiphany of Galatea clearly cites and builds on the triumphant conclusion of Calderón's masterpiece. Other parallels are also easy to find. The power of love as central theme, the structuring tension between fire and water, the consistent metaphor of water as crystal are all fundamental to Calderón's play. A crucial example of Circe's wickedness that appears twice in the play is the generation of fire from water. Goethe reverses this when Homunculus approaches Galatea to embody the wholesome blending of world and spirit (or, in Calderón's terms, profane and sacred love). When Circe is defeated by Galatea, her palace sinks and a volcano—Mount Aetna—rises in its place. This extraordinary occurrence and her comic servant Brutamonte surely have some connection to the masque of Seismos. And indeed, Brutamonte brings a chest onto the stage in which live a dwarf and a duenna who perform what can only be described as a kind of Punch and Judy show. The apparently bizarre and certainly peculiar combination of elements in Act II becomes more comprehensible, if *Love, the Greatest Enchantment* is understood as a subliminal, perhaps even subconscious, program for Goethe. But the greatest significance of this program is to show not simply that the act is framed by Renaissance gestures but that the "recovery of antiquity" in the act is at every moment self-consciously modern. Goethe's success in trapping his critics and explicators into reading his intensely Renaissance pastiche as a genuine recovery of antiquity is doubtless one of those "very serious jokes" in which the play abounds.

Nevertheless, the concern for history and historicity in the play is anything but a joke. We have already, in effect, observed two important functions of the concern with history. It has first of all been seen as a way to gain access to the best or most effective embodiment of the Absolute in the world, the culture of classical antiquity. It has also successfully temporalized art, which process in turn makes it possible to accept the transience of the moment on the theory that each age will have its own peculiarly appropriate moments of insight. In other words, art constitutes the intersection of myth and history. This formulation enables us, I think, to understand something more about Goethe's choice of materials for the act. I pointed out earlier that the figures in the final ritual of the act were not really very esoteric, and indeed this is true for the entire "Classical Walpurgis Night." There is virtually no mythological information in it that was not much more widely disseminated in the eighteenth century and that could not be gleaned from either Ovid or Herodotus. While *The Metamorphoses* and *The Histories* were indeed well-known sources of mythological information, Goethe certainly had other possibilities open to him that were equally well known, including Homer. Yet what Ovid and Herodotus have in common illuminates their importance for Goethe. For the most striking larger structural feature of both *The Metamorphoses* and *The Histories* is the way they proceed from mythology and legend to history. Ovid moves from the creation of the world to the Roman Empire; Herodotus, from the rape of Europa to the Persian War. And in Herodotus, the "father of history," there is further a persistent tension between mythological explanation and what might be termed rationalist or historical explanation. Herodotus is concerned, ultimately, to define and validate modes of knowledge. Ovid has somewhat different concerns; he seeks, like Virgil, to give the newly powerful Rome a cultural, historical, and spiritual context. Thus in their different ways both these works embody and are, I think, profoundly concerned with the intersection of mythology and history. If Herodotus tries to validate a mode of knowledge and Ovid to generate a cultural context, then Goethe surely attempts to do both. The advent of historicism requires that each age must interpret the past—antiquity, in particular—anew in order to "know" it. But this effort to know it is also an effort to validate it, to establish its importance for the present. Thus the "Classical Walpurgis Night" constitutes, ultimately, not a recovery of antiquity, but a validation (in the sense of establishing the value) of antiquity for Germany at the beginning of the nineteenth century. It is, ultimately, the validation of Goethe's own classicism.

But if the play constitutes the intersection of myth and history, it is also surely the intersection of meaning (or significance) and history. And indeed, history, as it is conceived in *Faust*, is of itself meaningless. This is already communicated by the setting, the battleground of Pharsalus. Erichtho reflects about it,

> How often has it not recurred! And will recur
> Eternally . . . Not one but grudges sovereign rule
> To others, most to him who seized it by his strength
> And strongly reigns.
> [7012–15]

History is meaningless violence, embodied later in the act in the restless circling of the centaur Chiron. The "historical background" in Act I, the state of the empire, was chaotic and dangerous; this pattern will persist in the rest of the play. And in retrospect, it was already true in Part One. "Outside the City Gate" showed us a world defined by love and war, and all Faust wanted from the pact was to cast himself into "time's on-rushing tide" (1754); in the "Prologue in Heaven" the archangels described the eternal circular motion of nature (compare Chiron!) and its violence. The temporal flux can only be given shape, history can only be fixed by an effort of the mind. * * *

Be that as it may, the need to shape history, to give it meaning from elsewhere, to marry the transient Galatea to Homunculus, illuminates the relation of the descents in *Faust* to perhaps the most important descent for European literature, the descent to hell in Book VI of Virgil's *Aeneid*. The parallel to *Faust* is inescapable since Aeneas is the only other seeker to be accompanied by a sibyl. Aeneas descends in search of his father, Faust in search of Helen; but in fact, both really seek the same thing, a meaningful past. Aeneas seeks his father to learn the future of his race, but the real issue for Virgil is not the future of the mythical Aeneas but the past of Rome. Similarly Faust seeks in Helen a historically validated vessel for the spirit he has recovered from the Mothers; what this search means for Goethe is a historically validated form for his own poetic insight, a past for the masterpiece of the new German literature. Aeneas returns to the world through the gates of ivory, the gates of false dreams. He thus becomes himself a kind of false dream, a fiction, who henceforth operates in a world in which every single action has significance for the future glory of Rome. Aeneas has become an allegory. But the case of Faust is no different. He will return to the world in the role of the medieval German invader of Greece, and will enter into a marriage with Helen that will be a manifest allegory of the relation of modern German culture to the classical past. The parallel to Virgil here is all the more striking because Faust's original confrontation with nature was cast in Virgilian terms. For it turns out that Faust's speech in response to the sign of the Earth Spirit is very similar to the description of the storm in Book III of the *Aeneid*. With Aeneas, then, Faust moves from the world as nature to the world as art. But the most profound sense of the parallel here must surely be that Virgil is the original "Western" poet, the greatest poet in our tradition who looks back to a classical past with longing and melancholy. What better model, then, for Goethe, when he attempts to assess his own relation to that identical yet of necessity profoundly different past?

However, we must never lose our Renaissance perspective. If Goethe argues with Virgil that history has meaning only when shaped by the mind, the imagery in which this argument is summarized is typically Renaissance. The ultimate embodiment of the multitudinous succession of forms that constitutes the temporal flux is Proteus, the god of transformations. In Act I the corresponding embodiment of the presence of spirit in the world was Pan. But the complementarity of Proteus and Pan, the many and the One, is yet another of the Renaissance Neoplatonist clichés that structure this part of *Faust*. Thus the marriage of Homunculus and Galatea has, once again, far more than natural or even cosmological significance. It is the marriage of fire and water, spirit and world, but also Pan and Proteus, meaning and history, the present and the past. And in this form it clearly adumbrates the coming marriage of the present and the past in the marriage of Faust and Helen.

HANS RUDOLF VAGET

[The Ethics of Faust's Last Actions] †

Act IV of Goethe's *Faust* consists of only three scenes precariously poised between the conclusion of Faust's classical-romantic dream journey and the beginning of his rule over the land by the sea. These scenes— "High Mountains," "In the Foothills," "The Rival Emperor's Tent"—have proven remarkably resistant to the exegetical labors of generations of *Faust* scholars. * * * Jane Brown was hardly exaggerating when she observed

---

† From "Act IV Revisited: A 'Post-Wall' Reading of Goethe's Faust," *Interpreting Goethe's Faust Today*, edited by Jane K. Brown, Meredith Lee, and Thomas P. Saine (Columbia, SC: Camden House, 1994), 43–58. The author's footnotes have been omitted. His quotations from *Faust* have been replaced with Arndt's translation.

in 1986 that Act IV has "traditionally been considered the least accessible part of a generally inaccessible work."

A considerable part of the interpretive difficulty vis à vis Act IV has been self-induced, arising from the persistent and apparently irresistible temptation on the part of progressive-minded interpreters in the East and West to enlist Goethe in the service of a truly epochal project, whose purport has been, ultimately, to legitimize socialist utopian thought. Indeed, this was widely held to be the politically "correct" task of the historical moment. Now that that moment has passed and socialism has begun rapidly to disappear from the historical agenda, it may be the appropriate time to revisit Act IV and take a fresh look at its peculiar political implications for *Faust* as a whole.

Let us no longer concern ourselves here with [the] famous dismissal of Act IV as poetically inferior. Lamentably, many commentators have taken [this] verdict as a welcome license to dodge the overtly political and ideologically messy issues posed by Faust's participation in the war and his support of the Emperor. Let us rather consider those commentators who have seriously reflected on Act IV precisely because it appears inaccessible: generally speaking, they have adopted two sharply differing interpretive strategies—strategies which * * * have dominated the entire history of *Faust* exegesis since the time of Goethe's death. One of these strategies is linked to the concept of nature; the other to the concept of history. It should be borne in mind, though, that for Goethe these were realms of a fundamentally different order. The realm of nature was governed by certain evolutionary laws comprehensible to man. History, on the other hand, was governed by no such laws and remained, in the last analysis, incomprehensible—a realm of "Tumult, Gewalt und Unsinn" (10127; "upheaval, chaos, violence!" in Arndt's translation) subject to demonic interventions. It should be obvious that our readings of *Faust* will differ greatly depending on whether we lean upon Goethe's concept of nature, or upon his concept of history. It seems to me that the special challenge of Act IV lies in its remarkable, if reluctant openness to the forces of history—incomprehensible and absurd though these forces may at first have appeared to Goethe.

Adherents of the "nature camp," so to speak, employ Goethe's philosophy of nature * * * to construct a coherent, perhaps all-too coherent, reading of *Faust*. The intention is almost always to demonstrate the hidden unity of the text and to affirm the essential identity of Goethe's poetic and scientific imagination. * * * Such a reduction of "Realgeschichte" to "Urgeschichte"—the most seductive and persistent siren call in Goethe scholarship—is still being practiced in many quarters. More than any other trend in the literature on Goethe it has contributed to the mummification of *Faust II* * * * This type of interpretive practice disengages Goethe's unusually charged text—charged with the energies of a troubled but acute historical sensibility—from its immediate historical nexus.

The other strategy has been to read *Faust* as a poetically encoded commentary, broadly speaking, on the history of the modern age. * * * The great temptation here is to make exaggerated claims for the prophetic and anticipatory powers of Goethe's poem, without first embedding it as firmly as possible in the historical moment of its creation. Even more common has been the tendency to make Goethe's text conform to certain preconceived notions about the course of history and the causes of historical change.

No school has been more thoroughly committed to the task of historical interpretation than the Marxists; and no one has had a higher stake in an ideologically coherent reading of *Faust* than *Faust* scholars of the former GDR. The importance of articulating a politically "correct" interpretation of Goethe's text, specifically of *Faust*'s final statement, becomes immediately apparent if we recall that the GDR defined its national identity with distinct reference to the progressive cultural heritage of German history; it prided itself on being not only the guardian but also the executor * * * of that heritage. * * * Alexander Abusch actually decreed in December, 1961 that the vision of the dying Faust anticipates the GDR's historical role of trying to drain the foul swamp of capitalism in Germany and to create the new land of the socialist state. Walter Ulbricht went even further and declared in March of 1962 that Faust's vision of a free people on liberated land was being realized by the people of the GDR; that the third part of Goethe's *Faust* was being written by the German Socialist state; and that the completion of "Part Three" would be achieved through the unification of all Germans in a socialist state.

Given such a broad historical agenda, it is understandable that the "correct" interpretation of *Faust* became a task of paramount importance—the secular equivalent of reading holy scripture in an ecclesiastical state. This required a more or less official reading—an orthodoxy; and it became the special assignment of a truly socialist *Faust* scholarship to produce it and to elaborate upon it. * * *

The linchpin of that orthodoxy—and this will take us back to Act IV— is the assertion that feudalism is overcome and destroyed by Faust. Other, more deviant voices in the Marxist camp were ignored or suppressed. * * * According to the official script, feudalism had to be overcome and succeeded by Faust's superior, forward-looking means of production as articulated in Act V. Without this crucial step, the fundamental assumption of all Marxist *Faust* interpretations would be untenable—the assumption of a historically inevitable progression from feudalism to capitalism and beyond to a vision of socialism. * * * There is indeed a long German tradition of reading ideas of progress and perfectibility into *Faust*, and of thereby adjusting Goethe's text, again and again, to the political agenda of the state—be it the Second or the Third Reich, or the "first socialist state on German soil."

The sudden disappearance from the historical scene of the state that claimed to be the heir and executor of Faust's utopian vision naturally casts a ghostly pall on the whole GDR project on behalf of Goethe's *Faust*. It is now, one would think, a closed chapter not only of German history but also of *Faust* exegesis. The once very vocal proponents of the Marxist reading of *Faust* in East and West are now faced with the sobering realization that they made an intellectual investment in a currency that was first depreciated and then withdrawn from circulation by the very power that was supposed to guarantee its value—history itself.

In what sense, then, can we speak of Act IV as the linchpin of the Marxist *Faust* orthodoxy? In essentially three regards, it seems to me. 1) Act IV, from the point of view of structure, provides the motivation for Faust's whole enterprise in Act V; it thereby reveals the moral and political underpinnings on which his rule is based. 2) Act IV—with its sequence of three scenes unfolding against the background of yet another crisis of the empire—decides the fate of feudalism. 3) Act IV, in a certain sense, represents Goethe's last word on *Faust*. It was written between January and July of 1831, that is to say, after Act V, with the exception of the Philemon and Baucis scenes, had been completed. Faust's death and salvation had long ago been settled. As soon as the final scenes were written, however, Goethe felt prompted to reconsider the question of how Faust acquired the land over which he rules. He decided to depart from his earlier plans for Act IV and to invent a set of three new scenes. * * * His sketches of 1816 called for Faust to acquire his land through a war of conquest fought in medieval Greece against the ["monks"], i.e. a religious authority. In 1831, Goethe decided to have Faust get involved in a civil war in the German empire and help the Emperor win it.

What we need to understand, then, is this: what might have motivated Goethe, at the last moment, so to speak, to change his mind about such a crucial point as Faust's acquisition of land and power? There is evidence—compelling evidence, in my view—to suggest that this final revision of the Faust material was triggered by the July Revolution of 1830. It led Goethe once more to contemplate the issues of revolution and restoration; it further led him critically to reconsider the doctrine and religion of Henri Saint-Simon (1760–1825) with its revolutionary program of social engineering, and to rethink the issue of land ownership, which he was reading about just then, in Niebuhr's *Roman History*.

If Act IV has remained a problem child for *Faust* scholarship, therefore, this may be attributed in no small measure to the fact that matters relating to its genesis and ideological climate have been largely ignored. This appears odd when one considers that the relevance of the July Revolution and of Saint-Simonianism was ably demonstrated as long as 60 years ago. * * * When in the early 1980s Nicholas Boyle and I, independently of each other, argued for a reconsideration of [these] findings and questioned anew the Marxist orthodoxy on *Faust*, the reaction ranged, predictably, from condescending rejection to benign neglect.

It is now high time to attempt to bring our reading of Act IV into line with what we know about its genesis. As soon as we do that, a different set of questions needs to be raised—different from the favorite preoccupation of so many *Faust* scholars with their clouds, volcanos, and waves. These questions must focus on plot and motivation as the basis for all moral and political considerations. Questions that need to be asked: Why at this late stage would Goethe want to change his plans and again address the issues of revolution and civil war? What motivation does Goethe provide for Faust's participation in the war? Are there any compelling reasons for Faust to support the Emperor, rather than his rival, the "Gegenkaiser?" What are the consequences of Faust's political involvement? And what light does Act IV throw on the question of Faust's salvation? ✦

There is no denying that the introduction of war and revolution into this part of *Faust* is surprising. So, too, is the laconic, almost offhand manner in which this whole episode is executed, to say nothing of its grim, satirical mood and its overtly operatic design. Many commentators have thus felt entitled to treat Act IV in a cursory manner and to move from the opening monologue directly to Act V. But the fact of the matter is that Act IV provides badly needed evidence regarding Faust's road to power—evidence crucial to the understanding of the whole text, despite the highly laconic manner of the octogenarian poet at this stage of the work.

When news of yet another revolution in Paris reached Weimar in the summer of 1830, Goethe was haunted by the thought that the French Revolution, *the* political trauma of his life, was rearing its head again. He viewed the events of July, 1830 as the greatest intellectual challenge * * * that he would have to encounter at the end of his life. As we have seen, Goethe's plans for the remaining scenes of *Faust* did until then not call for revolution and civil war. We are therefore on safe ground in concluding that he was moved to address these matters as a result of this "intellectual challenge" concerning the events in Paris. That Goethe used such an expression * * * can only be because he related the events in Paris to * * * *Faust.*

The manner in which Goethe finally confronted the issue of revolution reflects two crucial decisions made at the conceptual stage. Thus, in the introductory exchanges of "High Mountains" it is Mephistopheles who argues for the volcanic theory of the earth's origin. Given the well-known associations in Goethe's mind of "Vulkanismus" with revolution and, conversely, of "Neptunismus" with [a] theory of evolution, we can see that the political dice were loaded from the outset. In another strategic move, Faust was returned to German soil, there to be confronted again with an empire in turmoil and on the brink of chaos. We are led to realize that Faust's and Mephistopheles' fraudulent rescue action in Act I merely postponed the present crisis. Having returned Faust to the political arena, Goethe makes him face the consequences of his actions in Act I. In similar fashion, Goethe has the consequences of Faust's actions in Act IV become apparent only in Act V. There is a very high probability that Goethe was prompted to draw Faust's political profile more distinctly as a result of his reflection on the events of July 1830.

The chief function of the scene "High Mountains," then, is to reveal the motivation for Faust's participation in the war. From much of the older literature, however, one would not be able to draw this conclusion. Indeed, it would be difficult to gather that Faust is engaged in any political action at all. * * *

The underlying pattern of the scene is familiar from Part One: Mephistopheles tempts Faust; Faust rejects what is offered and demands something else instead. For the reader, everything depends on the realization that Faust's rejection of a life of leisure and his desire for land and power are perfectly consistent and all of a piece. At this crucial stage, Faust's inner motivation is laid out with great economy and precision. He has no intention of governing the multitudes of a modern metropolis, for fear of having to deal with insurrection—"And all one does is raising rebels" (10159). Nor is he attracted to the pleasure-seeking life-style of the aristocracy; this option he rejects as "Tawdry and up-to-date! Sardanapal!" (10176). The latter lacks the dimension of activity, the former that of complete, unchallenged domination.

Precisely these two conditions—meaningful activity and the exercise of power—are combined in what Faust now reveals to be his new goal. He has conceived the idea of claiming land from the sea and of controlling "such elemental might unharnessed, purposeless!" (10219). He desires nothing less than the domination of the sea and of nature. This project— in a certain sense representative of the ambition of Western man since the Renaissance—will offer him both creative activity and the delicious enjoyment of the exercise of power:

> Earn for yourself the choice, delicious boast,
> To lock the imperious ocean from the coast
> [10228–9]

Faust's high-minded desire to claim land from the sea has often been attributed to his encounter, in the previous act, with classical antiquity. However, no such recourse to a mythical source of inspiration is needed here, for the desire to dominate is deeply rooted in Faust's nature and represents the ultimate, most radical articulation of his ceaseless striving. Goethe makes the point by placing Faust's culminating project in a highly political context, and by revealing, step by step, the motivation of his desire for power. It can be grasped in Faust's statement to Mephistopheles:

> Sway I would gain, a sovereign's thrall!
> Renown is naught, the deed is all.
> [10187–8]

By "Eigentum" ["property"]—this is crucial for the understanding of Acts IV and V in their entirety—Faust means "Landeigentum," landed property, specifically that stretch of land by the sea that had caught his attention on his return to Germany. He needs that land for carrying out his project; in addition, by owning it he acquires feudal rights and power over the people living there. The desire for power thus stands revealed as Faust's deepest motivation. Landed property will give him the opportunity to control the vast, aimless forces of the sea and to claim additional territory over which he intends to rule with no resistance from any "rebels." All this is designed to maximize his enjoyment of power. Whether the people living on Faust's land derive any benefit from this seems to be of secondary importance. So many optimistic voices to the contrary notwithstanding, there is really no evidence that Faust's motivation is in any way generous, idealistic, or specifically "philanthropic."

And yet, at this juncture, there appears to be a certain contradiction in Faust's position, for his land reclamation project can be viewed as an audacious step; it points to the future and promises to improve the lives of the people. But this project cannot be realized without the acquisition of land. Eventually, Faust will obtain the land he desires, as Mephistopheles suggested, by rendering military service to the Emperor and receiving from him a fief as a reward. In other words, Faust chooses the classical feudal road to power, a road that leads not to the future but to the past. If so, the argument * * * that Faust's statement concerning "Herrschaft, Eigentum, Tat" [10186 f; "sway," "sovereign's thrall," "deed" in Arndt's translation] signals the advent of "the new world of capitalist civilization —progress through the action of the individual self, the continuously revolutionary process of bourgeois development," is hardly tenable.

In light of Faust's previous activities at the imperial court, it may seem self-evident and perfectly logical to some that he would choose to ally himself again with the Emperor. But is that decision—the most momentous political decision of his career—really self-evident? Goethe did see fit, though this is often overlooked, to present Faust with an alternative; he introduced a rival emperor and thereby indicated an alternative road to power. In Elizabethan drama, this is a familiar device. In *Doctor Faustus*, for instance, Marlowe introduces Bruno, a rival pope; Faustus sides with Bruno and thereby gains the favor of the emperor. And in *Richard II*, Shakespeare replaces the legitimate, but unfit king by Bolingbroke, the usurper, who, as Henry IV, will turn out to be an efficient and worthy ruler. It seems to me that Faust scholarship has not wondered enough about Faust's political choice vis à vis the "Kaiser" and "Gegenkaiser." Why, precisely, does Faust side with the Emperor and become the champion of restoration?

Faust clearly realizes that the Emperor is chiefly responsible for the present political anarchy and unfit to rule. The only reason given for his alliance is a personal one, and it sounds strangely insufficient: Faust feels sympathy for the Emperor in his present predicament—"I feel for him, he was so good and open" (10291). We already know, however, that Faust has a more compelling reason for acting the way he does: his power-driven desire to obtain land. Under normal circumstances, we would not question Faust's decision. He renders the Emperor a vital service by bailing him out militarily in the expectation of a reward in the form of territory. Under the feudal system, this was the sole legitimate way to acquire land. But these are not normal circumstances. The empire's very existence is threatened by insurrection. A rival emperor has been elected; the two parties are preparing for war. Faust could just as well support the "Gegenkaiser," who, beholden to him for victory, would probably not hesitate to offer him an appropriate reward. From a purely practical point of view Faust could obtain his land from either the Emperor or his rival. In fact, given the future-oriented, innovative aspects of his grand project, it would even make better sense to ally himself with the usurper, who at least promises reform.

Naturally, we would like to know more about the "Gegenkaiser" and his intentions. We do know that he is the chosen leader of a broadly based aristocratic opposition acting with the consent and blessing of certain clerics. No doubt is left as to the causes for their rebellion; the general state of anarchy has become intolerable:

Until at last the best had had enough.
The most resourceful rose with one accord
And said: He who can give us peace is lord.
The Emperor cannot, will not—let us choose,
Let a new Emperor new life infuse,
Make fresh the world and safe for men
So none will suffer, none abuse;
And peace and justice wed again.
[10277–84]

Clerics, we hear, "more than others took their side" (10287). Does this fact discredit the "Gegenkaiser's" cause, as orthodox Marxists would have us believe? I think not, given the constitutional role played by the Church in the Holy Roman Empire regardless of the person of the emperor. Furthermore, the Emperor's chancellor is also a cleric, an archbishop. After the restoration of the old empire he wields in effect even more power than the Emperor, as was the case during most of the history of the Holy Roman Empire. There would seem to be no point, therefore, in arguing that the "Gegenkaiser" would bring about an even more church-dominated, i.e. reactionary, regime. Nor will it do to discredit the "Gegenkaiser's" cause by arguing that we cannot believe that he really stands for peace, order, and justice because we hear about it only from Mephistopheles. This strikes me as a desperate and all too convenient argument. If we decided to discount everything Mephistopheles says, there would be no *Faust* at all.

Marxist commentators uniformly have discredited the rival emperor and his cause. They have been bound to do so by the premises of their historical master narrative; if they were to take the rival emperor for what he appears to be, they would be hard pressed to make sense of Faust's alliance with the Emperor. Our positive assessment of the "Gegenkaiser's" position is further supported by one of Goethe's sketches for Act IV. Here the political conflict is defined as one between a foolish emperor ("thöriger Kaiser") and a wise prince ("Weiser Fürst") [Paralipomenon No. 179, WA I, 15.2:237]. I can find no compelling evidence in the final text of a change in this basic design. Let us further recall in this context that *Faust* commentators have again and again associated the "Gegenkaiser" with Napoleon. Goethe's unpatriotic admiration for the upstart emperor of the French is well known. Napoleon may indeed be viewed as the great contemporary rival to the legitimate emperor of the old Holy Roman Empire.

An argument could be made that Faust sides with the Emperor for reasons of legitimacy. Nominally, of course, legitimacy rests with the Emperor. In reality, however, this Emperor has undermined and squandered his own legitimacy by failing to maintain order and guarantee justice. The centrality of this point is stressed in Act I by none other than the chancellor:

> The highest Good has like a halo shone
> About the Emperor's head, and he alone
> May validly accord it from above:

The equity of Law—What all men love,
What all demand, desire, can't do without,
His office must dispense it all about.
[4772–77]

The Emperor's failure in this crucial regard lends an aura of legitimacy to his rival. Under this Emperor, the empire has sunk into a pre-revolutionary situation. As always with Goethe, the responsibility for anarchy and revolution is traced back to the rulers and laid squarely at their feet. As for Faust, if legitimacy were indeed a serious concern, he would presumably hesitate to ally himself with the emperor. But given his comportment in Act V, it can hardly be argued that he considers justice the "höchste Tugend" ["highest virtue"]. As soon as he himself exerts power, he, too, quickly tires of trying to be just (11272). In his disregard for justice, Faust proves to be of the same ilk as his playboy Emperor.

It appears that the political configuration of Act IV is deliberately designed to contradict Faust's overtly non-political motivation and to plant questions in the reader's mind about the political and moral basis of his drive for power. Clearly, legitimacy and justice play no role here. If Goethe had wanted to display a Faust according to the GDR orthodoxy—a forward-looking man acting to overcome the injustices of feudalism—he would more likely have placed him on the side of the rival emperor. But Goethe seems to have had no interest in portraying Faust as the agent of progress and the grave-digger of the feudal system. The contrary is more likely the case: Faust enters into a pact with the Emperor; he and Mephistopheles offer military aid that turns out to be the decisive factor in winning the day for the Emperor and restoring the old, "legitimate" order. Goethe, it would appear, consciously departs from the Elizabethan model, and assigns Faust a place at the side of the old, legitimate, yet unworthy ruler. There is no indication that Faust acts reluctantly—as someone who sides with the Emperor only for lack of a better, more progressive alternative, for example, as some Marxist-oriented commentators like to suggest. Quite to the contrary, from his own point of view Faust's alliance with the Emperor makes perfectly good sense. He desires to rule and to exercise power, and thus orients his political will accordingly to the Emperor. And for good reason. There is a greater likelihood that Faust will be able to realize his will to power under a fully restored feudal system than under a reform-minded rival emperor. Faust will be able to carry out his plans for civil and social engineering more freely under the Emperor rather than under the rival emperor. His actions in Act V clearly bear out this assumption.

Act IV comes to a surprising conclusion. We are led to expect the ceremony of Faust's "Belehnung," his investiture with his new fief. As reward for his service to the Emperor, Faust would have had to be installed as the new lord over that coastal stretch of land that he requested. Goethe's notes call for such a scene. He omitted it, however, and wrote instead a rather sarcastic scene, "The Rival Emperor's Tent," in which the Emperor, in a satirical reenactment of the 1356 re-constitution of the German Empire, is forced to cede much of his power to the territorial princes. For the Emperor, this turns out to be a Pyrrhic victory.

Do the omission of Faust's investiture and the curtailment of the Emperor's powers signal the end of the feudal system? Can we therefore conclude with Marxist orthodoxy that the feudal system, at some unknown point between Act IV and Act V, was simply liquidated? As we have seen, Faust needs this particular political system to acquire land and power for himself. By no stretch of the imagination, therefore, can he be dressed up as the enemy of feudalism. Even though we do not witness the award of his fief, we hear of it on several occasions as a legal fact. It has been announced to the population by an official imperial herald. Nor is there any indication in Act IV that the feudal system is no longer functioning. The Emperor, ironically, may have suffered a loss of authority, but the feudal system endures, neither abolished nor weakened. What Act IV appears to evoke, then, is the transition, within feudalism, from an unchallenged central authority to a system of absolutism granting absolute power to the territorial princes, who recognize the Emperor only nominally as their sovereign. Faust must be viewed as such a territorial ruler in the absolutist mold. As such, * * * Faust may fairly be judged as a regressive figure, historically and politically speaking. In the last analysis, * * * Goethe's *Faust* arrives at the restoration of feudalism—hardly a forward-looking perspective in 1830!

Thus the Faust of Act V—far from occupying a post-feudal space—appears to be operating in an advanced stage of absolutism—a system that he himself helped bring about. The way in which he takes possession of his land in order to subject it to his will bears all the marks of a man who experiences heavenly bliss—"Seligkeit" ("bliss"; 10253)—when he commands and gives orders. Forced labor within the realm, and the inseparable triad of trade, war, and piracy (11187) in external relations, make this an evil empire by any civilized standards. What we are made to witness here is the inevitable outgrowth of a drive for power that appertains to Faust's striving from the beginning and that unmasks its pernicious propensity toward unchecked excess only now, in the last stage of Faust's career.

It is the function of the Philemon and Baucis episode—one of the very last additions to Goethe's 60-year-old Faust material—to demonstrate this point Faust has the old couple evicted from their inherited and tenaciously preserved land not for any justifiable reason, such as the common good, but simply because he cannot bear the thought of not owning and controlling everything. Without that plot of land, Faust finds himself unable to enjoy what he already possesses. And so he covets the old couple's small plot, deceiving himself into believing that this tiny addition to his property will be the last—the dot on the final "i." To a spirit like Faust's, however, there is always another undotted "i." He will discover new challenges and new frontiers until his dying moment. And indeed, in his last speech he envisages new ways to own and control more land. By that time, his crazed striving has gone completely out of control. Only a self-deluded *Faust* scholarship intoxicated by the heady dogma of the perfectibility and progress of the Faustian spirit could find anything admirable or elevating in Faust's dying vision.

To an unbiased mind, there is no way to morally justify the expropriation of their property and the death of Philemon and Baucis. On close inspection, however, such a justification of the unjustifiable turns out to be the *ultima ratio* of [the GDR] reading of Goethe's *Faust*. * * * The enforced expropriation of the old couple [is regarded] as a sacrifice necessary for the good of the collective. At this point, GDR orthodoxy fully reveals its moral insensitivity and political opportunism. Goethe's *Faust*, by means of some bizarre interpretive moves, is used to justify and make palatable the socialist policy of expropriation and collectivization.

Obviously, the striking prominence given to the question of landed property in the concluding parts of *Faust* cannot be tied to the socialist program of collectivization in our day. What weighed on Goethe's mind was a French forerunner of socialist collectivization, namely the "doctrine" of the Saint-Simonians. In the last years of his life, Goethe informed himself quite thoroughly about this latest ideology from France. His contemplation of its tenets formed part of that ["intellectual challenge"] of coping with the revolution of 1830. It was the Saint-Simonians who had called, among many other things, for a change in the laws governing land-ownership; they confidently declared this to be the last step to a new Golden Age. Here we find a remarkable parallel to Faust's behavior in Act V. Before he announces his own vision of a Golden Age—a liberated people on liberated land—he orders, chillingly and incongruously, the expropriation of Philemon and Baucis!

The longer we contemplate Faust's political profile in light of Goethe's negative reaction to the events of 1830 in general and to the Saint-Simonian utopia in particular, the more we see him as the irresponsible and dangerous social engineer that Goethe had come to see in the French reformer and his many disciples. The resemblance appears especially striking in Faust's last speech. When Faust arrogantly claims to know what is good for the masses and takes the lead on the road toward that goal—"To bring to fruit the most exalted plans, / One mind is ample for a thousand hands" (11509f.)—he essentially echoes the Saint-Simonians. Like the French reformers, Faust places the supposed concerns of the masses— variously referred to as "Menge," "Millionen," "Gewimmel," "Völkerschaft" and "Volk"—above the liberty and the dignity of the individual, whose existence is justified only to the extent that he/she contributes to the "improvement" of humanity. Very much in the spirit of the Saint-Simonians, Faust is bent on controlling land and on exploiting nature. The Saint-Simonian doctrine called for the abolition of hereditary title to land—a notion echoed in Faust's dying vision of a free people on a liberated land—liberated, above all, from the laws of inheritance. But Faust's inspired vision—the triumphant C-Major fanfare trumpeted by all Marxist readings of *Faust*—is about as trustworthy as the vow of sobriety of a derelict alcoholic. It is the vision of a blind man who is shown, most poignantly, to have deceived himself about such elementary matters as "Graben" and "Grab." Faust's last speech, all orthodox claims to the contrary, marks no conversion in a moral or political sense; it still bears the imprint of an authoritarian, power-hungry mind. * * *

The implications of reading *Faust* in the historical context of 1830 can only be described as sobering. They contradict the deep-rooted and apparently ineradicable desire to attribute to Goethe's Faust some sort of self-improvement in order to justify his eventual redemption. But there is absolutely no indication that Goethe, in the last years of his life, set much store in any program of social and political engineering. In his well-known last letter to Wilhelm von Humboldt—his final comment on *Faust*—Goethe refers to the misguided teachings and misguided actions of the day: "Verwirrende Lehre zu verwirrtem Handel waltet über die Welt" ["The world is ruled to-day by bewildering wrong counsel, urging bewildered wrong action"; Goethe's letter of March 17, 1832 (see above)]. It is time to recognize that Faust's last speech—the most politically exploited lines in all of German literature—is to be counted among those misguided teachings of the day.

In light of this we may begin to understand why in Marxist readings of *Faust* both the references to Saint-Simon and to the context of the 1830 revolution have been ignored, or played down. * * * Virtually all "perfectionist" readers avert their eyes from the most disturbing feature of Faust's political physiognomy—his affinity with feudalism—and they dodge the implications of Goethe's profound pessimism, his disavowal—in the very spirit and manner of Faust—of all social and political engineering.

* * *

MARSHALL BERMAN

[Faust as Developer]†

For as long as there has been a modern culture, the figure of Faust has been one of its culture heroes. In the four centuries since Johann Spiess's *Faustbuch* of 1587 and Christopher Marlowe's *Tragical History of Doctor Faustus* a year later, the story has been retold endlessly, in every modern language, in every known medium from operas to puppet plays and comic books, in every literary form from lyrical poetry to theologico-philosophical tragedy to vulgar farce; it has proven irresistible to every type of modern artist all over the world. Though the figure of Faust has taken many forms, he is virtually always a "long-haired boy"—an intellectual nonconformist, a marginal and suspicious character. In all versions, too, the tragedy or comedy comes when Faust "loses control" of the energies of his mind, which then proceed to take on a dynamic and highly explosive life of their own.

Almost four hundred years after his debut, Faust continues to grip the modern imagination. Thus *The New Yorker* magazine, in an anti-nuclear editorial just after the accident at Three Mile Island, indicts Faust as a symbol of scientific irresponsibility and indifference to life: "The Faustian proposal that the experts make to us is to let them lay their fallible human

---

† From "Goethe's *Faust*: The Tragedy of Development," *All That Is Solid Melts into Air: The Experience of Modernity* (New York: Penguin,1982), 38–40, 60–72. The author's footnotes have been omitted. His quotations from *Faust* have been replaced with Arndt's translation.

hands on eternity, and it is not acceptable." Meanwhile, at the other end of the cultural spectrum, a recent issue of *Captain America* comics features "the Deadly Designs of . . . DOCTOR FAUSTUS!" This villain, who strikingly resembles Orson Welles, soars over New York Harbor in a giant dirigible. "Even as we watch," he tells two bound and helpless victims, "those canisters containing my ingenious mind-gas are being affixed to special hookups within the dirigible's exhaust system. At my command, these loyal [robotized] National Force agents will begin flooding the city with it, bringing every man, woman and child in New York, under my absolute MENTAL CONTROL!" This means trouble: the last time Dr. Faustus passed through, he confused the minds of all Americans, leading them to paranoiacally suspect and denounce their neighbors, and generating McCarthyism. Who knows what he will be up to now? A reluctant Captain America comes out of retirement to confront this enemy. "And, unfashionable as it may sound," he tells his jaded 1970s readers, "I've got to do it for the nation. America could never be the land of the free once Faustus got it in his slimy grip!" When the Faustian villain is finally thwarted, the terrified Statue of Liberty feels free to smile again.

Goethe's *Faust* surpasses all others in the richness and depth of its historical perspective, in its moral imagination, its political intelligence, its psychological sensitivity and insight. It opens up new dimensions in the emerging modern self-awareness that the Faust myth has always explored. Its sheer immensity, not only in scope and ambition but in genuine vision, led Pushkin to call it "an Iliad of modern life." Goethe's work on the Faust theme began around 1770, when he was twenty-one, and continued intermittently for the next sixty years; he did not consider the work finished until 1831, a year before his death at the age of eighty-three, and it did not appear as a whole until after he was dead. Thus the work was in process all through one of the most turbulent and revolutionary eras in the history of the world. Much of its strength springs from this history: Goethe's hero and the characters around him experience, with great personal intensity, many of the world-historical dramas and traumas that Goethe and his contemporaries went through; the whole movement of the work enacts the larger movement of Western society.

Faust begins in an epoch whose thought and sensibility are modern in a way that twentieth-century readers can recognize at once, but whose material and social conditions are still medieval; the work ends in the midst of the spiritual and material upheavals of an industrial revolution. It starts in an intellectual's lonely room, in an abstracted and isolated realm of thought; it ends in the midst of a far-reaching realm of production and exchange, ruled by giant corporate bodies and complex organizations, which Faust's thought is helping to create, and which are enabling him to create more. In Goethe's version of the Faust theme, the subject and object of transformation is not merely the hero, but the whole world. Goethe's *Faust* expresses and dramatizes the process by which, at the end of the eighteenth century and the start of the nineteenth, a distinctively modern world-system comes into being.

The vital force that animates Goethe's *Faust*, that marks it off from its predecessors, and that generates much of its richness and dynamism, is an impulse that I will call the desire for *development*. Goethe's Faust tries to explain this desire to his devil; it isn't all that easy to explain. Earlier incarnations of Faust have sold their souls in exchange for certain clearly defined and universally desired good things of life: money, sex, power over others, fame and glory. Goethe's Faust tells Mephistopheles that, yes, he wants these things, but these things aren't in themselves what he wants.

> You heard me, there can be no thought of joy.
> Frenzy I choose, most agonizing lust,
> Enamored enmity, restorative disgust.
> Henceforth my soul, for knowledge sick no more,
> Against no kind of suffering shall be cautioned,
> And what to all of mankind is apportioned
> I mean to savor in my own self's core,
> Grasp with my mind both highest and most low,
> Weigh down my spirit with their weal and woe,
> And thus my selfhood to their own distend,
> And be, as they are, shattered in the end.
>   [1765–75]

What this Faust wants for himself is a dynamic process that will include every mode of human experience, joy and misery alike, and that will assimilate them all into his self's unending growth; even the self's destruction will be an integral part of its development.

One of the most original and fruitful ideas in Goethe's *Faust* is the idea of an affinity between the cultural ideal of *self*-development and the real social movement toward *economic* development. Goethe believes that these two modes of development must come together, must fuse into one, before either of these archetypally modern promises can be fulfilled. The only way for modern man to transform himself, Faust and we will find out, is by radically transforming the whole physical and social and moral world he lives in. Goethe's hero is heroic by virtue of liberating tremendous repressed human energies, not only in himself but in all those he touches, and eventually in the whole society around him. But the great developments he initiates—intellectual, moral, economic, social—turn out to exact great human costs. This is the meaning of Faust's relationship with the devil: human powers can be developed only through what Marx called "the powers of the underworld," dark and fearful energies that may erupt with a horrible force beyond all human control. Goethe's *Faust* is the first, and still the best, *tragedy of development*.

The Faust story can be traced through three metamorphoses: he first emerges as The Dreamer, then, through Mephisto's mediation, transforms himself into The Lover, and finally, long after the tragedy of love is over, he will reach his life's climax as The Developer.

※　※　※

Third Metamorphosis: The Developer

Most interpretations and adaptations of Goethe's *Faust* come to an end with the end of *Part One*. After Gretchen's condemnation and redemption, human interest tends to flag. *Part Two*, written between 1825 and 1831, contains much brilliant intellectual play, but its life is suffocated under ponderous allegorical weight. For more than 5000 lines very little happens. It is only in Acts Four and Five that dramatic and human energies revive: here Faust's story comes to its climax and its end. Now Faust takes on what I call his third and final metamorphosis. In his first phase, * * * he lived alone and dreamed. In his second period, he intertwined his life with the life of another person, and learned to love. Now, in his last incarnation, he connects his personal drives with the economic, political and social forces that drive the world; he learns to build and to destroy. He expands the horizon of his being from private to public life, from intimacy to activism, from communion to organization. He pits all his powers against nature and society; he strives to change not only his own life but everyone else's as well. Now he finds a way to act effectively against the feudal and patriarchal world: to construct a radically new social environment that will empty the old world out or break it down.

Faust's last metamorphosis begins at a point of deep impasse. He and Mephistopheles find themselves alone on a jagged mountain peak staring blankly into cloudy space, going nowhere. They have taken exhausting trips through all history and mythology, explored endless experiential possibilities, and now find themselves at point zero, or even behind that point, for they feel less energetic than they were at the story's start. Mephisto is even more dejected than Faust, for he seems to have run out of temptations; he makes a few desultory suggestions, but Faust only yawns. Gradually, however, Faust begins to stir. He contemplates the sea and evokes lyrically its surging majesty, its primal and implacable power, so impervious to the works of man.

So far this is a typical theme of romantic melancholy, and Mephisto hardly notices. It's nothing personal, he says; the elements have always been this way. But now, suddenly, Faust springs up enraged: Why should men let things go on being the way they have always been? Isn't it about time for mankind to assert itself against nature's tyrannical arrogance, to confront natural forces in the name of "the liberal mind which cherishes all rights"? (10202–05) Faust has begun to use post-1789 political language in a context that no one has ever thought of as political. He goes on: It is outrageous that, for all the vast energy expended by the sea, it merely surges endlessly back and forth—"and nothing is achieved." (10217) This seems natural enough to Mephisto, and no doubt to most of Goethe's audience, but not to Faust himself:

> Which drives me near to desperate distress!
> Such elemental might unharnessed, purposeless!
> There dares my spirit soar past all it knew;
> Here I would struggle, this I would subdue.
> [10218–21]

Faust's battle with the elements appears as grandiose as King Lear's, or, for that matter, as King Midas' whipping of the waves. But the Faustian enterprise will be less quixotic and more fruitful, because it will draw on nature's own energy and organize that energy into the fuel for new collective human purposes and projects of which the archaic kings could hardly have dreamt.

As Faust's new vision unfolds, we see him come to life again. Now, however, his visions take on a radically new form: no longer dreams and fantasies, or even theories, but concrete programs, operational plans for transforming earth and sea. "And it is possible! . . . Straight in my mind plan upon plan unfolds." (10222–27) Suddenly the landscape around him metamorphoses into a site. He outlines great reclamation projects to harness the sea for human purposes: man-made harbors and canals that can move ships full of goods and men; dams for large-scale irrigation; green fields and forests, pastures and gardens, a vast and intensive agriculture; *Spiritual Creation* waterpower to attract and support emerging industries; thriving settlements, new towns and cities to come—and all this to be created out of a barren wasteland where human beings have never dared to live. As Faust unfolds his plans, he notices that the devil is dazed, exhausted. For once he has nothing to say. Long ago, Mephisto called up the vision of a speeding coach as a paradigm of the way for a man to move through the world. Now, however, his protégé has outgrown him: Faust wants to move the world itself.

We suddenly, find ourselves at a nodal point in the history of modern self-awareness. We are witnessing the birth of a new social division of labor, a new vocation, a new relationship between ideas and practical life. Two radically different historical movements are converging and beginning to flow together. A great spiritual and cultural ideal is merging into an emerging material and social reality. The romantic quest for self-development, which has carried Faust so far, is working itself out through a new form of romance, through the titanic work of economic development. Faust is transforming himself into a new kind of man, to suit himself to a new occupation. In his new work, he will work out some of the most creative and some of the most destructive potentialities of modern life; he will be the consummate wrecker and creator, the dark and deeply ambiguous figure that our age has come to call "the developer."

Goethe is aware that the issue of development is necessarily a political issue. Faust's projects will require not only a great deal of capital but control over a vast extent of territory and a large number of people. Where can he get this power? The bulk of Act IV provides a solution. Goethe appears uncomfortable with this political interlude: his characters here are uncharacteristically pale and flaccid, and his language loses much of its normal force and intensity. He does not feel at home with any of the existing political options and wants to get through this part fast. The alternatives, as they are defined in Act IV, are: on one side, a crumbling multinational empire left over from the Middle Ages, ruled by an Emperor who is pleasant but venal and utterly inept; on the other side, challenging him, a gang of pseudo-revolutionaries out for nothing but power and plunder, and backed by the Church, which Goethe sees as the most voracious and cynical force of all. (The idea of the Church as a revolutionary vanguard has always struck readers as farfetched, but recent events in Iran suggest that Goethe may have been onto something.)

We should not belabor Goethe's travesty of modern revolution. Its main function is to give Faust and Mephisto an easy rationale for the political bargain they make: they lend their minds and their magic to the Emperor, to help him make his power newly solid and efficient. He, in exchange, will give them unlimited rights to develop the whole coastal region, including carte blanche to exploit whatever workers they need and displace whatever indigenous people are in their way. "Goethe could not seek the path of democratic revolution," [writes Georg Lukacs, the Hungarian Marxist critic]. The Faustian political bargain shows Goethe's vision of "another way" to progress: "Unrestricted and grandiose development of productive forces will render political revolution superfluous." Thus Faust and Mephisto help the Emperor prevail, Faust gets his concession, and, with great fanfare, the work of development begins.

Faust throws himself passionately into the task at hand. The pace is frenzied—and brutal. An old lady, whom we will meet again, stands at the edge of the construction site and tells the story:

> Vainly in the daytime labored
> Pick and shovel, clink and strike,
> Where at night the elf-lights wavered,
> By the dawn there stood a dike.
> Human victims bled and fevered,
> Anguish on the night-air borne,
> Fiery torrents pouring seaward
> Scored a channel by the morn.
> [11123–30]

The old lady feels that there is something miraculous and magical about all this, and some commentators think that Mephistopheles must be operating behind the scenes for so much to be accomplished so fast. In fact, however, Goethe assigns Mephisto only the most peripheral role in this project. The only "forces of the underworld" at work here are the forces of modern industrial organization. We should note, too, that Goethe's Faust—unlike some of his successors, especially in the twentieth century—makes no striking scientific or technological discoveries: his men seem to use the same picks and shovels that have been in use for thousands of years. The key to his achievement is a visionary, intensive and systematic organization of labor. He exhorts his foremen and overseers, led by Mephisto:

> From every source
> Find me more hands, recruit with vigor
> Spur them with blandishment and rigor,
> Spare neither pay nor lure nor force!
> [11552–54]

The crucial point is to spare nothing and no one, to overleap all boundaries: not only the boundary between land and sea, not only traditional
moral limits on the exploitation of labor, but even the primary human
dualism of day and night. All natural and human barriers fall before the
rush of production and construction.

Faust revels in his new power over people: it is, specifically, to use an
expression of Marx's, a power over labor-power.

> Up, workmen, man for man, arise anew!   *Faust as*
> Let blithely savor what I boldly drew.
> Seize spade and shovel, each take up his tool! *new "master"*
> Fulfill at once what was marked off by rule.   *"God"*

He has found, at last, a fulfilling purpose for his mind:

> I hasten to fulfill my thought's designing;
> The master's word alone imparts his might.
> [. . .]
> To bring to fruit the most exalted plans,
> One mind is ample for a thousand hands.
>   [11501–10]

But if he drives his workers hard, so he drives himself. If church bells
called him back to life long ago, it is the sound of shovels that vivifies him
now. Gradually, as the work comes together, we see Faust radiant with
real pride. He has finally achieved a synthesis of thought and action,
used his mind to transform the world. He has helped mankind assert its
rights over the anarchic elements, "render[ing] self-content the earth, /
Ordain[ing] a border to the waves, / The sea with rigid bonds en-
chain[ing]." (11541–43) And it is a collective victory that mankind will be
able to enjoy once Faust himself is gone. Standing on an artificial hill
created by human labor, he overlooks the whole new world that he has
brought into being, and it looks good. He knows he has made people suffer
("Human victims bled and fevered, / Anguish on the night-air borne . . ."
[11127f.]). But he is convinced that it is the common people, the mass of
workers and sufferers, who will benefit most from his great works. He has
replaced a barren, sterile economy with a dynamic new one that will "open
room to live for millions / Not safely, but in free resilience [*tätig-frei;*
11563f.]." It is a physical and natural space, but one that has been created
through social organization and action.

> Lush fallow then to man and cattle yields
> Swift crops and comforts from the maiden fields,
> New homesteads near the trusty buttress-face
> Walled by a bold and horny-handed race.
> A land of Eden sheltered here within,
> Let tempest rage outside unto the rim,
> And as it laps a breach in greedy riot,
> Communal spirit hastens to defy it.
> Yes—this I hold to with devout insistence,
> Wisdom's last verdict goes to say:
> He only earns both freedom and existence

Who must reconquer them each day.
And so, ringed all about by perils, here
Youth, manhood, age will spend their strenuous year.
Such teeming would I see upon this land,
On acres free among free people stand.
                                        [11565–80]

Walking the earth with the pioneers of his new settlement, Faust feels
far more at home than he ever felt with the friendly but narrow folk of his
home town. These are new men, as modern as Faust himself. Emigrants
and refugees from a hundred Gothic villages and towns—from the world
of *Faust, Part One*—they have moved here in search of action, adventure,
an environment in which they can be, like Faust himself, *tätig-frei*, free
to act, freely active. They have come together to form a new kind of
community: a community that thrives not on the repression of free individuality in order to maintain a closed social system, but on free constructive action in common to protect the collective resources that enable every
individual to become *tätig-frei*.

These new men feel at home in their community and proud of it: they
are eager to pit their communal will and spirit against the sea's own energy,
confident they will win. In the midst of such men—men whom he has
helped to come into their own—Faust can fulfill a hope he has cherished
ever since he has left his father's side: to belong to an authentic community, to work with and for people, to use his mind in action in the name
of a general will and welfare. Thus the process of economic and social
development generates new modes of self-development, ideal for men and
women who can grow into the emerging new world. Finally, too, it generates a home for the developer himself.

Thus Goethe sees the modernization of the material world as a sublime
spiritual achievement; Goethe's Faust, in his activity as "the developer"
who puts the world on its new path, is an archetypal modern hero. But
the developer, as Goethe conceives him, is tragic as well as heroic. In
order to understand the developer's tragedy, we must judge his vision of
the world not only by what it sees—by the immense new horizons it opens
up for mankind—but also by what it does not see: what human realities it
refuses to look at, what potentialities it cannot bear to face. Faust envisions,
and strives to create, a world where personal growth and social progress
can be had without significant human costs. Ironically, his tragedy will
stem precisely from his desire to eliminate tragedy from life.

As Faust surveys his work, the whole region around him has been renewed, and a whole new society created in his image. Only one small
piece of ground along the coast remains as it was before. This is occupied
by Philemon and Baucis, a sweet old couple who have been there from
time out of mind. They have a little cottage on the dunes, a chapel with
a little bell, a garden full of linden trees. They offer aid and hospitality to
shipwrecked sailors and wanderers. Over the years they have become beloved as the one source of life and joy in this wretched land. Goethe
borrows their name and situation from Ovid's *Metamorphoses*, in which
they alone offer hospitality to Jupiter and Mercury in disguise, and, ac-

cordingly, they alone are saved when the gods flood and destroy the whole land. Goethe gives them more individuality than they have in Ovid, and endows them with distinctively Christian virtues: innocent generosity, selfless devotion, humility, resignation. Goethe invests them, too, with a distinctively modern pathos. They are the first embodiments in literature of a category of people that is going to be very large in modern history: people who are in the way—in the way of history, of progress, of development; people who are classified, and disposed of, as obsolete.

Faust becomes obsessed with this old couple and their little piece of land:

> That aged couple must surrender,
> I want their linden for my throne,
> The unowned timber-margin slender
> Despoils for me the world I own.
> [. . .]
> Thus we are stretched on cruellest rack,
> In riches sensing what we lack.
> [11239–42, 11251f.]

old goes

They must go, to make room for what Faust comes to see as the culmination of his work: an observation tower from which he and his public can "gaze out into the infinite" at the new world they have made. He offers Philemon and Baucis a cash settlement, or else resettlement on a new estate. But what should they do with money at their age? And how, after living their whole long lives here, and approaching the end of life here, can they be expected to start new lives somewhere else? They refuse to move.

Traditional Society?

> That stubbornness, perverse and vain,
> So blights the most majestic gain
> That to one's agonized disgust
> One has to tire of being just.
> [11269–72]

At this point, Faust commits his first self-consciously evil act. He summons Mephisto and his "mighty men" and orders them to get the old people out of the way. He does not want to see it, or to know the details of how it is done. All that interests him is the end result: he wants to see the land cleared next morning, so the new construction can start. This is a characteristically modern style of evil: indirect, impersonal, mediated by complex organizations and institutional roles. Mephisto and his special unit return in "deep night" with the good news that all has been taken care of. Faust, suddenly concerned, asks where the old folks have been moved—and learns that their house has been burned to the ground and they have been killed. Faust is aghast and outraged, just as he was at Gretchen's fate. He protests that he didn't say anything about violence; he calls Mephisto a monster and sends him away. The prince of darkness departs gracefully, like the gentleman he is; but he laughs before he leaves. Faust has been pretending not only to others but to himself that he could create a new world with clean hands; he is still not ready to accept responsibility for the human suffering and death that clear the way. First he contracted out all the dirty work of development; now he washes his hands of the job, and disavows the jobber once the work is done. It appears that the very process of development, even as it transforms a wasteland into a thriving physical and social space, recreates the wasteland inside the developer himself. This is how the tragedy of development works.

But there is still an element of mystery about Faust's evil act. Why, finally, does he do it? Does he really need that land, those trees? Why is his observation tower so important? And why are those old people so threatening? Mephisto sees no mystery in it: "What passes here is far from new; / There once was Naboth's vineyard, too." (11286–87) Mephisto's point, in invoking King Ahab's sin in 1 Kings 21, is that there is nothing new about Faust's acquisition policy: the narcissistic will to power, most rampant in those who are most powerful, is the oldest story in the world. No doubt he is right; Faust does get increasingly carried away by the arrogance of power. But there is another motive for the murder that springs not merely from Faust's personality, but from a collective, impersonal drive that seems to be endemic to modernization: the drive to create a homogeneous environment, a totally modernized space, in which the look and feel of the old world have disappeared without a trace.

To point to this pervasive modern need, however, is only to widen the mystery. We are bound to be in sympathy with Faust's hatred for the closed, repressive, vicious Gothic world where he began—the world that destroyed Gretchen, and she was not the first. But at this point in time, the point where he becomes obsessed with Philemon and Baucis, he has already dealt the Gothic world a death blow: he has opened up a vibrant and dynamic new social system, a system oriented toward free activity, high productivity, long-distance trade and cosmopolitan commerce, abundance for all; he has cultivated a class of free and enterprising workers who love their new world, who will risk their lives for it, who are willing to pit their communal strength and spirit against any threat. It is clear, then, that there is no real danger of reaction. So why is Faust threatened by even the slightest traces of the old world? Goethe unravels, with extraordinary penetration, the developer's deepest fears. This old couple, like Gretchen, personify all the best that the old world has to give. They are too old, too stubborn, maybe even too stupid, to adapt and to move; but they are beautiful people, the salt of the earth where they are. It is their beauty and nobility that make Faust so uneasy. "Before my eyes my realm is boundless, / But at my back annoyance leers." [11153f.] He comes to feel that it is terrifying to look back, to look the old world in the face. "And should I seek my ease there—crawling / At alien shades my flesh would rear." [11159f.] If he were to stop, something dark in those shadows might catch up with him. "The bell but tinkles, and I seethe." [11258]

Those church bells, of course, are the sound of guilt and doom and all the social and psychic forces that destroyed the girl he loved: who could blame him for wanting to silence that sound forever? Yet church bells were also the sound that, when he was ready to die, called him back to life. There is more of him in those bells, and in that world, than he likes to think. The magical power of the bells on Easter morning was their power to put Faust in touch with his childhood. Without that vital bond with his past—the primary source of spontaneous energy and delight in life—he could never have developed the inner strength to transform the present and future. But now that he has staked his whole identity on the will to change, and on his power to fulfill that will, his bond with his past terrifies him.

> The tinkling chime, the linden bloom
> Close in like sanctuary and tomb
> [11253–4]

For the developer, to stop moving, to rest in the shadows, to let the old people enfold him, is death. And yet, to such a man, working under the explosive pressures of development, burdened by the guilt it brings him, the bells' promise of peace must sound like bliss. Precisely because Faust finds the bells so sweet, the woods so lovely, dark and deep, he drives himself to wipe them out.

Commentators on Goethe's *Faust* rarely grasp the dramatic and human resonance of this episode. In fact, it is central to Goethe's historical perspective. Faust's destruction of Philemon and Baucis turns out to be the ironic climax of his life. In killing the old couple, he turns out to be pronouncing a death sentence on himself. Once he has obliterated every trace of them and their world, there is nothing left for him to do. Now he is ready to pronounce the words that seal his life in fulfillment and deliver him over to death: *Verweile doch, du bist so schön!* Why should Faust die now? Goethe's reasons refer not only to the structure of *Faust*, Part Two, but to the whole structure of modern history. Ironically, once this developer has destroyed the pre-modern world, he has destroyed his whole reason for being in the world. In a totally modern society, the tragedy of modernization—including its tragic hero—comes naturally to an end. Once the developer has cleared all the obstacles away, he himself is in the way, and he must go. Faust turns out to have been speaking truer than he knew: Philemon and Baucis' bell was tolling for him after all. Goethe shows us how the category of obsolete persons, so central to modernity, swallows up the man who gave it life and power.

Faust almost grasps his own tragedy—almost, but not quite. As he stands on his balcony at midnight and contemplates the smoldering ruins that will be cleared for construction in the morning, the scene suddenly and jarringly shifts: from the concrete realism of the construction site, Goethe plunges us into the symbolist ambience of Faust's inner world. Suddenly four spectral women in gray hover toward him, and proclaim themselves: they are Need, Want, Debt, and Care. All these are forces that Faust's program of development has banished from the outer world; but they have crept back as specters inside his mind. Faust is disturbed but adamant, and he drives the first three specters away. But the fourth, the vaguest and deepest one, Care, continues to haunt him. Faust says, "I have not fought my way to freedom yet." [11403] He means by this that he is still beset by witchcraft, magic, ghosts in the night. Ironically, however, the threat to Faust's freedom springs not from the presence of these dark forces but from the absence that he soon forces on them. His problem is that he cannot look these forces in the face and live with them. He has striven mightily to create a world without want, need or guilt; he does not even feel guilty about Philemon and Baucis—though he does feel sad. But he cannot banish care from his mind. This might turn out to be a source of inner strength, if only he could face the fact. But he cannot bear to confront anything that might cast shadows on his brilliant life and works. Faust banishes Care from his mind, as he banished the devil not long before. But before she departs, she breathes on him—and with her breath strikes him blind. As she touches him, she tells him that he has been blind all along; it is out of inner darkness that all his visions and all his actions have grown. The Care he would not admit has stricken him to depths far past his understanding. He destroyed those old people and their little world—his own childhood world—so that his scope of vision and activity could be infinite; in the end, the infinite "Mother Night," whose power he refused to face, is all he sees.

Faust's sudden blindness gives him, in his last scene on earth, an archaic and mythical grandeur: he appears as a peer of Oedipus and Lear. But he is a distinctively modern hero, and his wound only drives him to drive himself and his workers harder, to finish the job fast:

> The night, it seems, turns deeper still—but shining,
> The light within continues ever bright,
> I hasten to fulfill my thought's designing;
> The master's word alone imparts his might.
> [11499–502]

And so it goes. It is at this point, amid the noise of construction, that he declares himself fully alive, and hence ready to die. Even in the dark his vision and energy go on thriving; he goes on striving, developing himself and the world around him to the very end.

Epilogue: The Faustian and Pseudo-Faustian Age

Whose tragedy is this? Where does it belong in the long-term history of modern times? If we try to place the particular type of modern environment Faust creates, we may at first be perplexed. The clearest analogue seems to be the tremendous surge of industrial expansion that England had been going through since the 1760s. Georg Lukacs makes this connection, and argues that the last act of *Faust* is a tragedy of "capitalist development" in its early industrial phase. The trouble with this scenario is that, if we pay attention to the text, Faust's motives and aims are clearly not capitalistic. Goethe's Mephisto, with his eye for the main chance, his celebration of selfishness and his genial lack of scruple, conforms pretty well to one type of capitalist entrepreneur; but Goethe's Faust is worlds away. Mephisto is constantly pointing out money-making opportunities in Faust's development schemes; but Faust himself couldn't care less. When he says that he means "[to] open room to live for millions / Not safely, but in free resilience" [11563f.], it's clear that he is not building for his own short-term profit but rather for the long-range future of mankind, for the sake of public freedom and happiness that will come to fruition only long after he is gone. If we try to cut the Faustian project to fit the capitalist bottom line, we will cut out what is noblest and most original in it and, moreover, what makes it genuinely tragic. Goethe's point is that the deepest horrors of Faustian development spring from its most honorable aims and its most authentic achievements.

If we want to locate Faustian visions and designs in the aged Goethe's time, the place to look is not in the economic and social realities of that age but in its radical and Utopian dreams; and, moreover, not in the capitalism of that age, but in its socialism. In the late 1820s, when the last sections of *Faust* were being composed, Goethe's favorite reading included the Parisian newspaper *Le Globe*, one of the organs of the Saint-Simonian movement, and the place where the word *socialism* was coined just before Goethe's death in 1832. The *Conversations with Eckermann* are full of admiring references to the young writers of *Le Globe*, who included many scientists and engineers, and who seem to have appreciated Goethe as much as he appreciated them. One of the standard features of *Le Globe*, as of all Saint-Simonian writings, was a constant stream of proposals for long-range development projects on an enormous scale. These projects were far beyond both the financial and the imaginative resources of early nineteenth-century capitalists, who—especially in England, where capitalism was then most dynamic—were oriented primarily toward the individual entrepreneur, the quick conquest of markets, the pursuit of immediate profits. Neither were those capitalists much interested in the social benefits that the Saint-Simonians claimed wholesale development would bring: steady jobs and decent incomes for "the most numerous and the poorest class," abundance and welfare for all, new modes of community that would synthesize medieval organicism with modern energy and rationality.

*   *   *

Goethe synthesizes these ideas and hopes into what I will call the "Faustian model" of development. This model gives top priority to gigantic energy and transportation projects on an international scale. It aims less for immediate profits than for long-range development of productive forces, which it believes will produce the best results for everyone in the end. Instead of letting entrepreneurs and workers waste themselves in piecemeal and fragmentary and competitive activities, it will strive to integrate them all. It will create a historically new synthesis of private and public power, symbolized by the union of Mephistopheles, the private freebooter and predator who executes much of the dirty work, and Faust, the public planner who conceives and directs the work as a whole. It will open up an exciting and ambiguous world-historical role for the modern intellectual—Saint-Simon called this figure "the organizer"; I have favored "the developer"—who can bring material, technical and spiritual resources together, and transform them into new structures of social life. Finally, the Faustian model will present a new mode of authority, authority that derives from the leader's capacity to satisfy modern people's persistent need for adventurous, open-ended, ever-renewed development.

*   *   *

Goethe presents a model of social action around which advanced and backward societies, capitalist and socialist ideologies, converge. But Goethe insists that it is a terrible and tragic convergence, sealed with victims' blood, undergirded with their bones, which come in the same forms and colors everywhere. The process of development that the creative spirits of the nineteenth century conceived as a great human adventure has become in our own era a life-and-death necessity for every nation and every social system in the world. As a result, development authorities everywhere have accumulated powers that are enormous, uncontrolled and all too often lethal.

* * *

Modern men and women in search of self-knowledge might well begin with Goethe, who gave us in *Faust* our first tragedy of development. It is a tragedy that nobody wants to confront—neither advanced nor backward countries, neither capitalist nor socialist ideologues—but that everybody continues to re-enact. Goethe's perspectives and visions can help us see how the fullest and deepest critique of modernity may come from those who most ardently embrace its adventure and romance. But if *Faust* is a critique, it is also a challenge—to our world even more than to Goethe's own—to imagine and to create new modes of modernity, in which man will not exist for the sake of development, but development for the sake of man. Faust's unfinished construction site is the vibrant but shaky ground on which we must all stake out and build up our lives.

JOHN HOLLANDER

What the Lovers in the Old Songs Thought†

Thinking "In the beginning was the—(What??)"
Faust tried, for openers, *Wort* . . . *Sinn* . . . *Kraft* . . . *Tat*
("Word"? Meaning? Power?—all these reeked of creed:
He finally settled simply on "the Deed".)
But none of these would do for true Beginning:
Our ghosts were there before all those, and not
Playing love's game in which there is no winning,
But doing love's work, continuous creation
Of all the celebrated lovers' tales,
Of all the letters, all the conversation,
All the strange fictions that plain fact entails
And all the silences that bridge the void
Of words exhausted. Let us take possession
Of Origin, then like some crafty Freud
Saying "In the beginning was Repression"
Or like some cabbalist "First was the Name"
What could we literary lovers claim?

† From *Figurehead and Other Poems* (New York: Alfred A. Knopf, 1999), 68. Copyright © 1999 by John Hollander. Reprinted by permission of Alfred A. Knopf, a Division of Random House Inc.

In the beginning was unlikeness? (*Good!*)
In the beginning was the opened door
Through which crept in the soul of all our sins?
In the beginning there was need for more?
In the beginning there was likelihood?—
The oldest gospel of our lives begins
"In the beginning there was metaphor."

Johann Wolfgang von Goethe: A Chronology

1749	Born on August 28 in Frankfurt am Main.
c. 1753–8	Becomes aware of the Faust legend, from public performances of the puppet play.
1765–8	Enrolled as student of law at the University of Leipzig. Frequent visitor at Auerbach's Cellar.
c. 1768–70	Plans a drama on the legend of Dr. Faustus.
1770–1	In Strassburg. Continues studies. Meets Johann Gottfried Herder, studies Shakespeare, and collects folksongs in the Alsace.
1772	On January 14, Susanna Margaretha Brandt is executed in Frankfurt for infanticide. She is thought to be the source for Gretchen (Margarete) in *Faust*.
1772	Goethe serves at the Imperial Court (*Reichskammergericht*) in Wetzlar, used later as setting for the novel *The Sorrows of Young Werther*.
c. 1772–5	Earliest version of *Faust* (*Urfaust*) composed.
1773–4	*Götz von Berlichingen* (historical drama) and *The Sorrows of Young Werther* (epistolary novel) published anonymously to great acclaim.
1775	In November, Goethe moves to Weimar to enter the service of Duke Karl August, in which he remains for the rest of his life.
c. 1776	Handwritten copy of *Urfaust* prepared by Luise von Göchhausen (first published in 1887).
1779	*Iphigenie in Tauris*, based on Euripides, composed and performed at Weimar, with Goethe in the role of Orestes.

731

c. 1780–6   First version of the novel *Wilhelm Meister (Theatrical Mission)* drafted, left incomplete; published in the Weimar Edition (1910).

1786–8   Journey to Italy.

1787–90   Collected *Writings* in eight vols. published with Göschen in Leipzig. *Faust. A Fragment* in vol. 7.

1788   New scenes for *Faust* ("Witch's Kitchen" and "Forest and Cave") composed in Rome for the *Fragment*.

1790   *Metamorphosis of Plants* published.

1791–817   Serves as director of the Weimar Theater.

1792–3   Participates in the military campaign against the Republic of France and the siege of Mainz.

1794–805   Friendship with Schiller. Frequent letters exchanged between Weimar and Jena.

1795–6   *Wilhelm Meister's Apprenticeship* published in four vols.

1797   *Hermann und Dorothea* (short epic) published.

1797–801   Composes new parts of *Faust. A Tragedy*: first (fragmentary) draft for the *Helena*, also several scenes for Act V of Part Two.

1798–800   Edits and publishes a journal on the visual arts (*Die Propyläen*).

1805   Schiller dies on May 9.

1808   *Faust, Part One* published in *Collected Works* with Cotta in Tübingen.

1809   *Elective Affinities* (novel) published.

1810   *Color Theory* published.

1811–4   Autobiography, *From My Life. Poetry and Truth*, published in three parts (a fourth part completed in 1832, just before his death).

1814–5   Visits the region of the Rhine and Main in two consecutive summers. Studies medieval painting in the collection of the brothers Boisserée.

1816–7   *Italian Journey*, vols. 1 and 2, published.

1816–32   Journal *On Art and Antiquity (Über Kunst und Alterthum)* published at intervals, containing most of his later writings on art and literature.

1817–24   Journal of science, *On Science in General, Especially Morphology*, published intermittently.

1819   The *West-Easterly Divan*, collection of poems modeled on the medieval Persian poet Hafiz, published.

1821   *Wilhelm Meister's Journeyman Years, or the Renunciants* (novel), first version, published.

1822   *Campaign in France* and *Siege of Mainz* published (supplements to his autobiography).

1823   Johann Peter Eckermann enters Goethe's service, primarily to assist with the editing of the *Collected Works*.

1825–31   *Faust, Part Two* composed (published posthumously in 1832).

1826–32   Contract with the publisher Cotta for the final *Collected Works (Ausgabe letzter Hand)*. Forty volumes appear by Goethe's death, followed by fifteen posthumous volumes (including *Faust, Part Two*).

1826–7   "Charming Landscape," the opening scene of *Faust, Part Two*, composed.

1827   *Helena. Classical-Romantic Phantasmagoria, An Interlude to Faust*, published in *Collected Works*, vol. 4.

1828   *Correspondence between Schiller and Goethe*, edited by Goethe in six parts, published.

1829   *Wilhelm Meister's Journeyman Years, or the Renunciants*, second expanded edition, published.

1829   On August 29, first performance of *Faust* (Part One) in Weimar, to celebrate Goethe's eightieth birthday. (He does not attend.)

1829   *Second Sojourn in Rome*, vol. 3 of *Italian Journey*, published in *Collected Works*, vol. 29.

1830   "Classical Walpurgis Night" for *Faust, Part Two* composed.

1831   February to July, final work on *Faust, Part Two* (mainly Act IV). The manuscript is sealed, to be published after his death.

1832   January 8 to 29, reads through the completed manuscript of *Faust, Part Two*, making minor corrections (in particular, expanding Faust's final speech).

1832   March 17, final letter, to Wilhelm von Humboldt concerning *Faust*.

1832   Dies on March 22, following a brief illness.

1832   *Faust, Part Two* published by Eckermann and Riemer as the first posthumous volume of *Collected Works*.

Selected Bibliography

Items are listed chronologically in all sections but the last two, which are alphabetical.

Editions of *Faust* Prepared by Goethe

Faust. Ein Fragment. In Goethe, *Schriften.* Vol. 7, pp. 1–168. Leipzig: Göschen, 1790.
Faust. Eine Tragödie [Part One]. In Goethe, *Werke.* Vol. 8, pp. 1–234. Tübingen: Cotta, 1808.
Helena. Klassisch-romantische Phantasmagorie. Zwischenspiel zu Faust [Part Two, Act III]. In Goethe, *Werke (Ausgabe letzter Hand).* Vol. 4, pp. 229–307. Stuttgart and Tübingen: Cotta, 1827.
Faust I and *Faust II,* lines 4613–6036. In Goethe, *Werke (Ausgabe letzter Hand).* Vol. 12, pp. 1–247 and 249–313. Stuttgart and Tübingen: Cotta, 1828.
Faust, der Tragödie zweiter Teil in fünf Akten. In Goethe, *Nachgelassene Werke.* Vol. 1 *(Ausgabe letzter Hand,* Vol. 41). Stuttgart and Tübingen: Cotta, 1832.

Scholarly-Critical Editions

Faust I, Faust II, and *Faust II, Lesarten.* In Goethe, *Werke (Weimarer Ausgabe).* Edited by Erich Schmidt. Sec. 1, vols. 14 and 15, pts. 1 and 2. Weimar, 1887–8.
Goethes Faust in usprünglicher Gesalt, nach der Göchhausenschen Abschrift [*Urfaust*]. Edited by Erich Schmidt. Weimar, 1887.
Faust. In Goethe, *Werke (Akademie Ausgabe).* Published by the German Academy of Sciences in Berlin [East]. Vol. 1, *Urfaust* and *Faust. Ein Fragment,* with a facsimile of the MS. of the *Urfaust.* Berlin, 1954. Vol. 2, *Der Tragödie 1. Teil.* Edited by Ernst Grumach and Inge Jensen. Berlin, 1958. Supplementary volume: *Urfaust, Faust. Ein Fragment* and *Faust I,* printed in parallel columns. Berlin, 1958.

Editions with Commentary

Faust. In Goethe, *Werke,* Vol. 12. Edited by Heinrich Düntzer. *Deutsche National Literatur,* edited by J. Kürschner. Vol. 93. Berlin, 1882.
Goethe's Faust. Edited by Calvin Thomas. Vol. 1: *The First Part.* Boston, 1892. Vol. 2: *The Second Part.* Boston, 1897.
Faust I and *II.* In *Goethes Sämtliche Werke (Jubiläums Ausgabe).* Edited by Erich Schmidt. Vols. 13 and 14. Stuttgart, 1903 and 1906.
Faust and *Urfaust.* Annotated by Ernst Beutler. *Sammlung Dietrich,* Vol. 25. Leipzig, 1939.
Faust. Eine Tragödie. In *Goethes Werke (Hamburger Ausgabe).* Vol. 3. Edited by Erich Trunz. Hamburg, 1949 (numerous reprintings to the present).
Die Faustdichtungen. In Goethe, *Artemis-Gedenkausgabe.* Vol. 5. Edited by Ernst Beutler. Zürich, 1950.
Goethe's Faust. Edited by R-M. S. Heffner, H. Rehder, and W. F. Twadell. Vol. 1: *Part I, Text and Notes.* Boston, 1954. Vol. 2: *Part II, Text and Notes.* Boston, 1955.
Faust. In Goethe, *Poetische Werke (Berliner Ausgabe).* Vol. 8. Edited by Gotthard Erler. Berlin (East), 1965.
Faust. In Goethe, *Sämtliche Werke (Bibliothek Deutscher Klassiker).* Vol. 7, pts. 1 and 2. Edited by Albrecht Schöne. Frankfurt, 1997.

735

Faust. Der Tragödie zweiter Teil. In Goethe, *Sämtliche Werke nach Epochen seines Schaffens (Hanser Ausgabe).* Vol. 18, pt. 1: *Letzte Jahre, 1827–1932.* Edited by Dorothea Hölscher-Lohmeyer. Munich, 1997.
Goethe. *Faust-Dichtungen.* Edited with commentary by Ulrich Gaier. Three vols. Stuttgart, 1999.

English Translations of *Faust*

Faust. A Tragedy [Part One]. Translated with notes by Charles T. Brooks. Boston, 1856.
Faust. A Tragedy. The First Part and *The Second Part.* Translated, in the original meters, by Bayard Taylor. Two vols. Boston, 1871.
Goethe's Faust in Two Parts. Translated by Anna Swanwick. London, 1878.
Faust. A Tragedy. The First Part. Translated by Alice Raphael. New York, 1930.
Faust, Parts I and II. Translated by George Madison Priest. New York, 1932.
Goethe's Faust [Part One]. Translated by Carlyle F. MacIntyre. Norfolk, CT, 1941.
Faust, Part One and Part Two. Translated by Philip Wayne. Two vols. (The Penguin Classics, Nrs. 12 and 93). Middlesex, England, 1949 and 1959.
Goethe's Faust. Parts I and II. An abridged version, translated by Louis MacNeice. London, 1951.
Goethe's Faust, Part One, and Sections from Part Two. The original German and a new translation by Walter Kaufmann. Garden City, NY, 1961.
Faust. Parts I and II. Translated, with an introduction and notes by Charles E. Passage. Indianapolis, IN, 1965.
Goethe's Faust. Translated by Barker Fairley. Toronto, 1970.
Faust I and II. In *Goethe's Collected Works (Suhrkamp Edition* [in English] *in Twelve Volumes).* Vol. 2. Edited and translated by Stuart Atkins. Boston, 1984.
Faust. Part One, Part Two. Translated with an introduction by David Luke. Oxford and New York, 1987 and 1994.
Faust, a Tragedy, Part One and Part Two. Translated by Martin Greenberg. New Haven, 1992 and 1998.

Bibliographies, Lexica, and Reference Materials on *Faust*

Atkins, Stuart. *Forschungsbericht: "Faustforschung und Faustdeutung seit* 1945," *Euphorion* 53 (1959): 422–40.
Atkins, Stuart. "The Interpretation of Goethe's *Faust* since 1958," *Orbis Litterarum* 20 (1965): 239–67.
Atkins, Stuart. *Essays on Goethe.* Edited by Jane K. Brown and Thomas P. Saine. Columbia, SC, 1995.
Bianquis, Geneviève. *Faust à travers quatre siecles.* Paris, 1955.
Butler, E.M. *The Myth of the Magus.* Cambridge, 1948.
Butler, E. M. *The Fortunes of Faust.* Cambridge, 1952.
Chisholm, David, and Steven P. Sondrup. *Verskonkordanz zu Goethes* Faust, *Erster Teil.* Tübingen, 1986.
Dabezies, André. *Visages de Faust au Xxe siècle: Littérature, idéologie et mythes.* Paris, 1967.
Dédéyan, Charles. *Le Thème de Faust dans la littérature européenne.* Four vols. in six parts. Paris, 1956–65.
Füssel, Stephan, and Hans Joachim Kreutzer, eds. *Historia von D. Johann Fausten. Kritische Ausgabe.* Stuttgart, 1988.
Henning, Hans, ed. with introduction. *Historia von D. Johann Fausten* (the *Faust-Book* of 1587). Halle, 1963.
Henning, Hans, ed. *Faust-Bibliographie.* Three parts in five vols. Halle, 1963. Berlin and Weimar, 1966–76.
Hohlfeld, A. R., Martin Joos, and W. F. Twadell, eds. *Wortindex zu Faust.* Madison, WI, 1940.
Hohlfeld, A. R. *Fifty Years with Goethe: Collected Studies.* Madison, WI, 1953.
Keller, Werner, ed. *Aufsätze zu Goethes* Faust I *(Wege der Forschung,* Bd. CXLV). Wissenschaftliche Buchgesellschaft Darmstadt, second ed.: 1984.
Keller, Werner, ed. *Aufsätze zu Goethes Faust II (Wege der Forschung,* Bd. CDXLV). Wissenschaftliche Buchgesellschaft Darmstadt, 1992.
Kelly, J. W. *The Faust Legend in Music.* Evanston, IL, 1960.

Kiesewetter, Carl. *Faust in der Geschichte und Tradition.* Second ed. Berlin, 1921.
Klett, Ada M. *Der Streit um Faust II seit 1900.* Jena, 1939.
McMillan, Douglas J. *Approaches to Teaching Goethe's Faust.* New York, 1987.
Palmer, P. M., and R. P. More. *The Sources of the Faust Tradition from Simon Magus to Lessing.* New York, 1936.
Pyritz, Hans, ed. *Goethe-Bibliographie* (continued by H. Nicolai and G. Burkhardt). Heidelberg, 1964.
Saine, Thomas P., ed. *Yearbook of the Goethe Society of North America.* Nine vols. to date. Columbia, SC, 1983– .
Schwerte, Hans. *Faust und das Faustische: Ein Kapitel deutscher Ideologie.* Stuttgart, 1962.
Wegner, Wolfgang. *Die Faustdarstellungen vom 16. Jahrhundert bis zur Gegenwart.* Amsterdam, 1962.

Books on Goethe's *Faust* in English

Atkins, Stuart. *Goethe's Faust: A Literary Analysis.* Cambridge, MA, 1958.
Bennett, Benjamin. *Goethe's Theory of Poetry: Faust and the Regeneration of Language.* Ithaca, NY, 1986.
Boyle, Nicholas. *Goethe's Faust, Part One.* Cambridge, 1987.
Brown, Jane K. *Goethe's Faust: The German Tragedy.* Ithaca, NY, 1986.
Brown, Jane K. *Faust: Theater of the World* (Twayne's Masterwork Studies). New York, 1992.
Brown, Jane K., Meredith Lee, and Thomas P. Saine, eds. *Interpreting Goethe's Faust Today.* Columbia, SC, 1994.
Cottrell, Alan P. *Goethe's Faust: Seven Essays.* Chapel Hill, NC, 1976.
Cottrell, Alan P. *Goethe's View of Evil and the Search for a New Image of Man in Our Time.* Edinburgh, Scotland, 1982.
Dieckmann, Liselotte. *Goethe's Faust: A Critical Reading* (Landmarks in Literature). Englewood Cliffs, NJ, 1972.
Durrani, Osman. *Faust and the Bible: A Study of Goethe's Use of Scriptural Allusions and Christian Religious Muyths in Faust I and II.* Bern and Frankfurt a. M., 1977.
Fairley, Barker. *Goethe's Faust: Six Essays.* Oxford, 1953; repr. 1965.
Gearey, John. *Goethe's Faust: The Making of Part I.* New Haven and London, 1981.
Gearey, John. *Goethe's Other Faust: The Drama, Part II.* Toronto and Buffalo, 1992.
Gillies, Alexander. *Goethe's Faust: An Interpretation.* Oxford, 1957.
Graham, Ilse. *Portrait of the Artist.* Berlin and New York, 1977.
Gray, Ronald. *Goethe the Alchemist.* Cambridge, 1952.
Haile, H. G. *Invitation to Goethe's Faust.* University, Alabama, 1978.
Jantz, Harold. *Goethe's Faust as a Renaissance Man.* Princeton, 1951.
Jantz, Harold. *The Mothers in Faust: The Myth of Time and Creativity.* Baltimore, 1969.
Jantz, Harold. *The Form of Faust: The Work of Art and Its Intrinsic Structures.* Baltimore, 1978.
Mason, Eudo. *Goethe's Faust: Its Genesis and Purport.* Berkeley, CA, 1967.
Pelikan, Jaroslav. *Faust the Theologian.* New Haven, 1995.
Salm, Peter. *The Poem as Plant: A Biological View of Goethe's Faust.* Cleveland, 1971.
Santayana, George. *Three Philosophical Poets: Lucretius, Dante and Goethe.* Cambridge, MA, 1910.
Vincent, Deirdre. *The Eternity of Being: On the Experience of Time in Goethe's Faust.* Bonn, 1987.
Wilkinson, E. M., and L. A. Willoughby. *Goethe: Poet and Thinker.* London, 1962.
Williams, John R. *Goethe's Faust.* London, 1987.